TRADE IN SERVICES

Global Regulation and the Impact on Key Service Sectors

Philip Raworth, B.A., LL.B., M.Phil., LL.M.
Professor Emeritus
University of Alberta
Barrister and Solicitor

OCEANA PUBLICATIONS, INC., Dobbs Ferry, New York

You may order this or any other Oceana publication by visiting Oceana's website at http://www.oceanalaw.com

Library of Congress Control Number: 2004109192

ISBN 0-379-21526-8

Manufactured in the United States of America on acid-free paper.

SUMMARY TABLE OF CONTENTS

TABLE OF CONTENTS

ABOUT THE AUTHOR

Philip Raworth, B.A. (Hons), M.Phil., LL.B., LL.M.
Professor of Law
Barrister and Solicitor

Philip Raworth first studied modern languages and linguistics at the University of Manchester in England. He speaks fluent English, French, German and Spanish and has a fair knowledge of Portuguese, Italian and Dutch. For several years, he taught German literature and linguistics at universities in England, Canada and Austria.

In 1974, Philip Raworth returned to university to study law and was admitted to the Bar of the Province of Alberta in Canada in 1978. The same year, he received the prestigious Duff-Rinfret Scholarship from the Canadian federal government in order to complete his LL.M.

Since 1979, Professor Raworth has taught law at the Universities of Ottawa and Alberta. From 1994 until 1999, he was Chairperson of the Department of Marketing, Economics and Law in the Faculty of Business at the University of Alberta. He has also practices law, both in Canada and Europe, in the areas of European Union and international commercial law. In September 2002, Professor Raworth retired from the University of Alberta as a Professor Emeritus. He now lives in Quebec and devotes his time to legal research.

Professor Raworth is the author of numerous articles and books on the European Union and international commercial law.

CHAPTER ONE
INTRODUCTION

I. SCOPE OF THE MONOGRAPH

In this monograph, we are concerned with the liberalization of trade in services at the international level. We look at the various barriers and measures that prohibit, restrict or make more costly the supply of services by a provider from one country to a recipient from another country, and we explain how the major international or regional agreements attempt to remove them. Ancillary aspects of trading services, such as intellectual property rights, liability and insurance of service providers, consumer protection, are beyond the scope of this monograph. The liberalization of financial, telecommunications and transportation services, as well as government procurement,[1] is discussed separately.

II. DEFINITION OF TRADE IN SERVICES

Trade in goods is a transparent and concrete transaction. An object is traded for its own sake and for its value alone. When goods are traded internationally, it is relatively easy, therefore, for countries to regulate their passage by means of tariffs and non-tariff restrictions. If necessary, they can even seize the goods in order to enforce their import or export regime.

The essence of a service transaction, on the other hand, is the conferral of an intangible benefit, such as the processing of data, travel, entertainment or the provision of insurance or legal advice. In its purest form, the provision of a service involves no object, and the transfer of money to pay for the service is unaccompanied by

1 I have used this term as it is the more common, but "public procurement" is perhaps the better term as it includes non-government entities in the public sector that may be obliged to procure in accordance with government procurement rules.

any corresponding transfer of merchandise. Such a service transaction is thus not susceptible of the same direct control as trade in goods. The country where the recipient of the service resides is forced instead to control the persons who provide or receive the service. Thus, the barriers to trade in services in its purest form are largely different in kind from those that exist for goods. They tend to be more recondite and difficult to eradicate.

Sometimes however, the intangible benefit of a service may be provided in connection with an object, in which case we may talk of "visible services."[2] The object itself is ancillary to the transaction, for it has little or no value by itself and the consideration is paid almost entirely for the service that it incorporates. Two examples are entertainment that is recorded on a videocassette or compact disk and professional advice that is contained within a report. To the extent that there is now an object whose passage can be controlled, the transaction could be regulated as trade in goods. This is effectively what happens where the value of the transaction can be attributed to the object, as in the case of videocassettes and compact disks. Thus, Article IV of the *General Agreement on Tariffs and Trade* (GATT)[3] regulates trade in cinematographic film, although this is, strictly speaking, a service transaction.[4] On the other hand, where it is not possible to attribute sufficient value to the object, as in the case of professional advice contained in a sheaf of papers, this approach is not feasible and the transaction is regulated as a service.

A third type of service transaction is where the intangible benefit is built into an object, as where a muffler is installed on an automobile, a key is duplicated or a power station is built. Here, the object transferred has an independent value, but the sum paid for it also includes the additional value of the service that went into its production or installation. As long as the object is traded across national borders, it is treated simply as trade in goods.[5] Where the object is not so traded, as in the case of a power station that is built in a foreign country, the transaction has to be treated as trade in services.

The types of services that are discussed above are called "commercial services" in order to distinguish them from "factor services," which involve the flow of money

---

2 Such services are sometimes called "tangible services." Indeed, the author has used the term himself in Keegan & Seringhaus, *Global Marketing Management* (Prentice Hall, Scarborough, 1996) at page 170. However, on reflection, this is surely a misnomer. The service component remains intangible even though it is delivered in connection with a tangible object. Thus, I now prefer the term "visible services."

3 GATT is now contained in Annex 1A of the *Marrakesh Agreement Establishing the World Trade Organization* (WTO Agreement) as GATT 1994. GATT 1994 includes the whole text of GATT 1947, including this Article, together with some additions. Annoyingly, the 1947 text is not always reproduced in collections of the agreements making up the WTO Agreement.

4 It is treated as a service transaction by the OECD *Code of Liberalization of Current Invisible Operations* (Invisibles Code)—*see* Annex A/H.

5 These types of services are subject to liberalization under Annex A/2 of the Invisibles Code, but the Code specifically states that this liberalization applies only if the importation of the goods concerned is liberalized by the importing Member.

from a foreign transaction or asset. The most common forms of factor services are dividends or profits from a foreign affiliate, interest from a foreign portfolio investment, rent from foreign property and royalties from a foreign licensee. Factor services are considered services for balance-of-payments accounting purposes. In fact, the epithet is totally misleading. In reality, they are capital flows unrelated to any underlying service activity. Thus, this monograph restricts itself to commercial services.

III. MODES OF SUPPLYING SERVICES ON THE INTERNATIONAL MARKET

Services may be traded internationally through any of the following four modes of supply:

List 1
Modes of Supplying Services on the International Market

1. The provider supplies the service from one country to a recipient in another country ("cross-border supply);[6]

2. The recipient travels to receive the service from the provider in the provider's country ("consumption abroad");

3. The provider supplies the service to the recipient from a permanent base in another country ("commercial presence");

4. The provider travels to supply the service to the recipient in another country and returns home ("presence of natural persons").

Modes 1, 2 and 4 are all normally referred to as "cross-border services"[7] or "cross-border transactions," but one must be careful not to confuse this term with that used for Mode 1.

In Mode 1, the provider supplies services from its home base to a recipient in another country. The country where the provider's base is located is the "home state" and the foreign country where the service is consumed is the "host state." Services may also be supplied under Mode 1 from a permanent base in a third country,[8] in which case this country would, for the sole purpose of this transaction, be considered the home state. In Mode 2, the service is supplied at the provider's home base

6 The terms in brackets are those used in the Schedules of Specific Commitments annexed to the *General Agreement on Trade in Services* (GATS), which forms Annex 1B of the WTO Agreement.

7 *See* Article 1213(2) of the *North American Free Trade Agreement* (NAFTA).

8 The wording of Article I:2(a) of GATS admits this possibility.

to a recipient from another country.[9] In this situation, no host country is directly involved in the transaction. In Modes 3 and 4, the service is provided in a foreign country through a permanent or temporary presence there, respectively, to a recipient from that country or a third country. Here, there is no home state directly involved, although the country where the permanent base is located may be considered as such.[10]

Some services can be supplied equally well through more than one mode of supply. A person wishing to hear a particular pianist can either go to a concert in another country or wait for the pianist to come and give a recital in his or her own country. In other cases, the mode of supply is largely predetermined by the nature of the service. Tourism services, for example, can only be provided to a recipient traveling to the destination country. On occasion, more than one mode of supply may be used to deliver a particular service. For example, a service may be supplied from a subsidiary in the recipient's country with some of the work being done on a cross-border basis by the parent company.

Let us look more closely at the various modes of supplying services on the international market.

A. CROSS-BORDER SUPPLY

Under this mode of supply, services are produced in one country and consumed in another. At one time, the only services that were traded in this way were visible services and traditional distance transactions such as international transportation. The advent of modern communications technology changed this situation. Radio, television, cinema, telephone and telex all increased the cross-border tradability of a number of services. For example, professional advice could be given over the telephone from one country to another, and entertainment taking place in one country could be viewed simultaneously in another.

More radical change, however, came with the advent of microelectronics-based technology, which has led to the emergence of a network-based cross-border trade in invisible services. By collapsing time and space at ever decreasing cost, technology has made it possible for many services that were hitherto based on face-to-face interaction to be produced in one country and consumed in another. An example is the use of automated teller machines in banking. This new technology has had a great impact on such information-intensive services as finance, consulting, engineering, education, professional services and tourism, in which sectors network-based trading has now reached considerable proportions.

9 This accords with the wording of Article 1213(2)(b) of NAFTA. Article I:2(b) of GATS, on the other hand, does not specify that the service must be supplied from the primary base. However, this must be so as otherwise the transaction falls under Mode 4.

10 *See infra* in the text.

B. CONSUMPTION ABROAD

Under this mode of supply, the recipient visits the provider's country to receive the service and then returns home. In many cases, this is simply the less common alternative to the provider coming to the recipient. It is, however, the only way of obtaining the service where the provider will or cannot move, as in the case of services connected with tourism or medical care. If you want to have dinner at Maxim's in Paris, you have no alternative but to go there. Wealthy Canadians who wish to receive medical treatment that they perceive as superior to that available in Canada traipse to the Mayo clinic in the United States.

C. COMMERCIAL PRESENCE

Under this mode of supply, the provider supplies the service from a permanent base in a foreign country to a recipient from that country or from a third country.

Many services still need a face-to-face interaction of provider and recipient, and it is not always possible to achieve this by one traveling to the other. The services offered by restaurants, hotels or education facilities, for example, as well as consumer services like key-cutting or muffler installation are normally supplied from a permanent location, which necessitates a commercial presence in the recipient's country. Increasingly, despite modern technological advances, other services, particularly professional services by lawyers and accountants, are being offered from permanent bases in the recipient's country rather than through cross-border transactions.

It is a moot point to what extent Mode 3 can be considered international trade in services. The United States, for instance, does not consider that service transactions carried out by foreign affiliates of US corporations constitute international trade. GATS, on the other hand, includes commercial presence among the modes of supplying services that it regulates.[11]

It seems clear that, where there is no transnational link in the provision of a service, the transaction cannot be considered to have an international character. Thus, where an individual or corporation permanently leaves the home country in order to set up an alternative establishment abroad, there is merely a change in the location of the home base. The services provided from it for the new home market are thus domestic in nature. Likewise, where a service is supplied in a country by the local franchisee of an individual or corporation, this is also a domestic operation. The only transnational link is the royalty payment, which is not a commercial service transaction.

On the other hand, it is a different matter where the foreign commercial presence is an affiliate of the provider in the form of a subsidiary or branch. Here, the transnational link is supplied by the organic relationship between the affiliate and the parent corporation. Moreover, to disregard services provided abroad in this way

11 Articles I:2(c) and XXVIII(c)(iii).

would exclude an increasingly important mode of supplying service on the international market. Thus, I have chose to follow the GATS approach in this monograph and include it.

D. PRESENCE OF NATURAL PERSONS

Under this mode of supply, the provider supplies the service to the recipient in the latter's country or a third country and then returns home. Professional and entertainment services are commonly provided through this mode. Typical examples are accountants who travel to audit a foreign company or entertainers who travel to another country to give a concert. Generally speaking, many of these services could be effected equally well by the recipient traveling to the provider, i.e. by Mode 2. However, in some instances this is not really feasible. It is much easier for an accountant to travel to where all the corporate books and documents are kept than have them sent to his or her home base. A surgeon is more likely to travel to perform an operation on a stricken patient in a foreign country than risk transporting the patient.

IV. CLASSIFICATION OF SERVICES AND SCOPE OF MONOGRAPH

The World Trade Organization (WTO) has a *Services Sectoral Classification List*, which was drawn up in May 1991 before the organization came into being. It provides a very good list of traded services, which illustrates the immense diversity and scope of the commercial services trade sector.

List 2
Traded Commercial Services

1. BUSINESS SERVICES

A. Professional Services

a. Legal Services

b. Accounting, auditing and bookkeeping services

c. Taxation Services

d. Architectural services

e. Engineering services

f. Integrated engineering services

g. Urban planning and landscape

h. Medical and dental services

i. Veterinary services

j. Services provided by midwives, nurses, physiotherapists and para-medical personnel

k. Other

B. Computer and Related Services

a. Consultancy services related to the installation of computer hardware

b. Software implementation services

c. Data processing services

d. Data base services

e. Other

C. Research and Development Services

a. R&D services on natural sciences

b. R&D services on social sciences and humanities

c. Interdisciplinary R&D services

D. Real Estate Services

a. Involving own or leased property

b. On a fee or contract basis

E. Rental/Leasing Services without Operators

a. Relating to ships

b. Relating to aircraft

c. Relating to other transport equipment

d. Relating to other machinery and equipment

e. Other

F. Other Business Services

a. Advertising services

b. Market research and public opinion polling services

c. Management consulting service

d. Services related to management consulting

e. Technical testing and analysis services

f. Services incidental to agriculture, hunting and forestry

g. Services incidental to fishing

h. Services incidental to mining

i. Services incidental to manufacturing

j. Services incidental to energy distribution

k. Placement and supply services of Personnel

l. Investigation and security

m. Related scientific and technical consulting services

n. Maintenance and repair of equipment (not including maritime vessels, aircraft or other transport equipment)

o. Building-cleaning services

p. Photographic services

q. Packaging services

r. Printing, publishing

s. Convention services

t. Other

2. COMMUNICATION SERVICES

A. Postal Services

B. Courier Services

C. Telecommunications Services

a. Voice telephone services

b. Packet-switched data transmission services

c. Circuit-switched data transmission services

d. Telex services

e. Telegraph services

f. Facsimile services

g. Private leased circuit services

h. Electronic mail

i. Voice mail

j. On-line information and data base retrieval

k. Electronic data interchange (EDI)

l. Enhanced/value-added facsimile services, incl. store and forward, store and retrieve

m. Code and protocol conversion

n. On-line information and/or data processing (incl. transaction processing)

o. Other

D. Audiovisual Services

a. Motion picture and video tape production and distribution services

b. Motion picture projection service

c. Radio and television services

d. Radio and television transmission services

e. Sound recording

f. Other

E. Other

3. CONSTRUCTION AND RELATED ENGINEERING SERVICES

A. General Construction Work for Buildings

B. General Construction Work for Civil Engineering

C. Installation and Assembly Work

D. Building Completion and Finishing Work

E. Other

4. DISTRIBUTION SERVICES

A. Commission Agents' Services

B. Wholesale Trade Services

C. Retailing Services

D. Franchising

E. Other

5. EDUCATIONAL SERVICES

A. Primary Education Services

B. Secondary Education Services

C. Higher Education Services

D. Adult Education

E. Other Education Services

6. ENVIRONMENTAL SERVICES

A. Sewage services

B. Refuse disposal services

C. Sanitation and similar services

D. Other

7. FINANCIAL SERVICES

A. All Insurance and Insurance-Related Services

a. Life, accident and health insurance services

b. Non-life insurance services

c. Reinsurance and retrocession

d. Services auxiliary to insurance (including broking and agency services)

B. Banking and Other Financial Services (excl. insurance)

a. Acceptance of deposits and other repayable funds from the public

b. Lending of all types, including consumer credit, mortgage credit, factoring and financing of commercial transaction

c. Financial leasing

d. All payment and money transmission services

e. Guarantees and commitments

f. Trading for own account or for account of customers, whether on an exchange, in an over-the-counter market or otherwise, the following:

- money market instruments (checks, bills, certificate of deposits, etc.)
- foreign exchange
- derivative products including, but not limited to futures and options
- exchange rate and interest rate instruments, including products such as swaps, forward rate agreements, etc.
- transferable securities
- other negotiable instruments and financial assets, incl. bullion

g. Participation in issues of all kinds of securities, including under-writing and placement as agent (whether publicly or privately) and provision of service related to such issues

h. Money broking

i. Asset management, such as cash or portfolio management, all forms of collective investment management, pension fund management, custodial depository and trust services

j. Settlement and clearing services for financial assets, including securities, derivative products, and other negotiable instruments

k. Advisory and other auxiliary financial services on all the activities listed in Article 1B of MTN.TNC/W/50, including credit reference and analysis, investment and portfolio research and advice, advice on acquisitions and on corporate restructuring and strategy

l. Provision and transfer of financial information, and financial data processing and related software by providers of other financial services

C. Other

8. HEALTH RELATED AND SOCIAL SERVICES (*other than those listed under 1.A.h-j.*)

A. Hospital Services

B. Other Human Health Services

C. Social Services

D. Other

9. TOURISM AND TRAVEL RELATED SERVICES

A. Hotels and Restaurants (including Catering)

B. Travel Agencies and Tour Operators Services

C. Tourist Guides Services

D. Other

10. RECREATIONAL, CULTURAL AND SPORTING SERVICES (*other than audiovisual services*)

A. Entertainment Services (including theatre, live bands and circus services)

B. News Agency Services

C. Libraries, Archives, Museums and Other Cultural Services

D. Sporting and Other Recreational Services

E. Other

11. TRANSPORT SERVICES

A. Maritime Transport Services

- a. Passenger transportation
- b. Freight transportation
- c. Rental of vessels with crew
- d. Maintenance and repair of vessels
- e. Pushing and towing services
- f. Supporting services for maritime transport

B. Internal Waterways Transport

- a. Passenger transportation
- b. Freight transportation
- c. Rental of vessels with crew
- d. Maintenance and repair of vessels
- e. Pushing and towing services
- f. Supporting services for internal waterway transport

C. Air Transport Services

- a. Passenger transportation
- b. Freight transportation
- c. Rental of aircraft with crew
- d. Maintenance and repair of aircraft
- e. Supporting services for air transport

D. Space Transport

E. Rail Transport Services

- a. Passenger transportation
- b. Freight transportation

c. Pushing and towing services

d. Maintenance and repair of rail transport equipment

e. Supporting services for rail transport services

F. Road Transport Services

a. Passenger transportation

b. Freight transportation

c. Rental of commercial vehicles with operator

d. Maintenance and repair of road transport equipment

e. Supporting services for road transport services

G. Pipeline Transport

a. Transportation of fuels

b. Transportation of other goods

H. Services Auxiliary to All Modes of Transport

a. Cargo-handling services

b. Storage and warehouse services

c. Freight transport agency services

d. Other

I. Other Transport Services

Most of these services are in principle subject to the general international rules on the provision of services. However, in certain sectors, notably financial services and telecommunications, there are specific sectoral rules that may apply in addition to the general rules or instead of them. Both are covered in this monograph.

V. INTERNATIONAL LEGAL INSTRUMENTS LIBERALIZING TRADE IN SERVICES

There are three categories of legal instruments regulating the global trade in services. The first comprises global agreements that are open to all nations. The most important of these is GATS, including its Third, Fourth and Fifth Protocols relating, respectively, to the movement of natural persons, basic telecommunications and financial services. Other important GATS-related documents discussed in this monograph are the *Guidelines for the Scheduling of Specific Commitments under the General Agreement on Trade in Services* (2001) (WTO Guidelines), the *Guidelines and Procedures for the Negotiations on Trade in Services* (2001), the *Modalities for the Treatment of Autonomous Liberalization* (2002) and the *Fifth Decision on Negotiations on Emergency Safeguard Measures* (2004). GATT, the *Understanding on Rules and Procedures Governing the Settlement of Disputes* (1994) (DSU), together with its *Rules of Conduct* (1996) (DSU

Rules of Conduct), and the *Agreement on Government Procurement* (1994) (GPA)[12] are also relevant for trade in services. The other major global instruments that affect trade in services are GATT, which has a limited but important application to trade in services, and the *Articles of the International Monetary Fund* (IMF Articles) dealing with exchange controls.

The second category of legal instruments consists of a number of instruments emanating from the Organization for Economic Cooperation and Development (OECD). The *Code of Liberalization of Current Invisible Operations* (1973) (Invisibles Code), the *Code of Liberalization of Capital Movements* (1982) (Capital Movements Code) and the *Declaration on International Investment and Multinational Enterprises* (1976), together with the *Third Revised OECD Decision on National Treatment* (1991), apply generally, albeit with varying scope, to trade in services. These sub-global agreements only bind the members of the OECD, which, for the most part, are developed nations. The Codes are binding, but the Declaration is more in the form of a gentlemen's agreement.

The third category comprises multilateral and bilateral economic integration agreements, of which there are literally hundreds in operation throughout the world today. I have restricted myself in this monograph to four representative multilateral agreements, one in North American (NAFTA), one in South America (Mercosur[13]), one in Europe (the European Union (EU)[14]) and one in Asia (the Association of East Asian Nations (ASEAN)). Certain other agreements modeled on these are also referred to. Because economic integration agreements are mostly between neighboring nations, they are often referred to as regional agreements.

VI. TERMINOLOGY

A. NATIONALS AND NATIONALITY

I have deliberately used the term "national" and "nationality" in preference to "citizen" and "citizenship" in this monograph. This is because, in some countries, foreign citizens who reside there permanently are assimilated to the status of nationals for the purposes of economic activity. This is the case, for example, in the three countries of NAFTA,[15] which fact is reflected in the Agreement.[16] European countries, by and large, are less generous in their treatment of foreign

12 The GPA is a plurilateral agreement, which means that WTO Members are not obliged to sign up to it. However, it is open to all Members and is thus to be considered a global instrument.

13 This is the normal acronym for the Common Market of the Southern Cone.

14 In the international instruments, the reference is to the European Community, which is the body responsible within the European Union for trade in services. The European Community is, however, part of the EU, and in this monograph I refer in most cases to the EU.

15 Canada, Mexico and the United States.

16 *See* Article 201 of NAFTA, where a "national" is defined as "a citizen or permanent resident of a Party." However, for the purpose of temporary entry, permanent residents are excluded.

permanent residents. As a result, rights under the *European Community Treaty* (EC Treaty) only apply to citizens of the Member States.[17]

Foreign-owned companies that are incorporated under local law are considered in most countries to be national companies although they may have to meet additional requirements. In the EU, for example, they must have their registered office, central administration or principal place of business within the Union.[18] Under NAFTA, they must be constituted or organized under the law of a Party or be a branch located in the territory of a Party, and they may also have to carry on business there.[19]

In this commentary, the term "national" is used to denote a company and a citizen of a state together with the legal and natural persons assimilated to that status. "Foreign" thus means a corporate entity or person that does not fit this definition. This may include the branch of a foreign-based company.

B. MARKET ACCESS

Market access with respect to international trade in services means the elimination of national measures that prevent or render unfeasible the supply of a service by a foreign provider.

C. NATIONAL TREATMENT

National treatment requires that foreign service providers be able to provide services in the host state[20] under conditions that are no less favorable than those which apply to national service providers. In other words, they must not suffer from any discrimination. This sounds quite straightforward, but the requirement can be interpreted in a narrow or broad way.

In its narrow sense, national treatment requires only that foreign service providers be subject to the same legal rules as nationals. In other words, it requires the abolition of measures that discriminate overtly against them on the basis of their citizenship or state of permanent residence. This is called discrimination in law. All that is required in the case of such discrimination in order to bring the offending measures within the national treatment principle is to change the law so that the rules are the same for both foreigners and nationals.

Identical legal treatment does not, however, guarantee complete equality of treatment for foreign providers, for many laws that apply to foreign and national providers alike discriminate in fact against the former. An example is the requirement that a bank have a minimum capital of its own before it can obtain a license to start

---

17 *See*, for example, Article 17.

18 ECT, Article 48.

19 NAFTA, Article 1213:2.

20 "Host state" denotes the foreign country where the service is consumed. Usually, but not always, this is the recipient's country. *See* the discussion *supra* in Chapter One, Section II.

operations. This is a reasonable requirement that invariably applies to domestic banks as well. However, whereas domestic banks have no problem with this requirement, it forces a foreign bank that already meets the own capital requirements of its home state[21] to duplicate its capital investment if it wishes to open a branch in the host state. The requirement that a service provider acquire host-state qualifications is another example of this discrimination in fact. A national provider will of necessity have such qualifications but for a foreign provider, particularly of cross-border services, it is a costly and time-consuming complication.

The elimination of discrimination in fact is more controversial than eliminating discrimination in law as it requires that foreigners not be subject to the non-discriminatory[22] rules that regulate the provision of services in a host country where these put them at a disadvantage vis-à-vis nationals. For this reason, national treatment often does not cover discrimination in fact. Even where it does, matters that have an important public interest dimension, such as licenses, authorizations, membership in professional and trade organizations, host-state qualifications, technical standards, prudential rules and linguistic competence, come under the rubric of domestic regulation. The only exception is in the EU, where they are subject to a modified national treatment obligation. It should also be noted that international agreements are construed strictly in favor of sovereign rights, which means that they must explicitly extend national treatment to cover discrimination in fact; otherwise, the narrower scope prevails.

National treatment does not require the elimination of disadvantages that are inherent in the foreign character of the transaction as these cannot be considered to constitute either form of discrimination. High taxes or low remuneration in the host country may discourage foreign providers, but there is no discrimination as long as they apply equally to nationals.

D. DOMESTIC REGULATION

Domestic regulation refers to that body of national rules that regulate on a non-discriminatory basis the provision of services in the host state. Some of these rules may discriminate in fact against foreign providers, in which case they come under the rubric of national treatment as long as it extends to discrimination in fact and the measures in question do not have an important public interest dimension.

E. MOST-FAVORED-NATION TREATMENT

The term "most-favored-nation (MFN) treatment" is somewhat misleading, as it gives the impression that a nation benefiting from this status is treated better than any other trading partner. This is not so. MFN treatment means that any trading

21 "Home state' is the country where the provider has its home base for the provision of the service in question—*see* the discussion *supra* in Chapter One, Section II.

22 The terms "discriminatory" and by extension "non-discriminatory" refer to measures that discriminate or not, as the case may be, on the basis of nationality.

advantages given to other trading partners must also be accorded to a nation with MFN status and that no trading disadvantages may be imposed on a nation with MFN status that are not imposed on other trading partners.

VII. MARKET ACCESS

A. THE BARRIERS TO MARKET ACCESS

Below is an illustrative list of national measures that can constitute market access barriers to the provision of services by a foreign provider by one or more modes of supply.

List 3
Market Access Barriers

CATEGORY 1 NATIONALITY REQUIREMENTS

a) prohibition or restrictions on the provision of a service by a foreign provider, usually via licenses, authorizations or mandatory membership in a professional or trade organization;

b) prohibition or restrictions on a recipient using the services of a foreign provider;

c) prohibition or restrictions on foreign capital investment in the host state, including mandatory local equity requirements;

d) prohibition or restrictions on foreign providers setting up a permanent establishment in the host state;

e) prohibition or restrictions on the movement and temporary presence of foreign providers in the host state;

f) prohibition or restrictions on foreign providers with respect to access to or use of networks necessary for the provision of a service (e.g. telecommunications, transport, distribution channels, stock markets, social security system, etc.);

CATEGORY 2 RESIDENCY REQUIREMENTS

g) requirement that a provider be a permanent resident of the host state or operate through a company incorporated there;

h) requirement that a provider have a period of residence in the host state prior to providing a service;

i) requirement that a provider of a service have a presence in the host state;

CATEGORY 3 OPERATIONAL BARRIERS

j) prohibition or restrictions (e.g. high tariffs) on the importation of inputs necessary to provide a service;

k) prohibition or restrictions on capital transfers in and out of the host state;

l) prohibition or restrictions on access to foreign exchange to pay for services or travel to receive them;

m) prohibition or restrictions on the provision of a service because of the existence of a public or private monopoly in the host state.

B. NATURE OF THE BARRIERS

Most of these market access barriers are self-explanatory, but in some cases precision is required. In the case of barrier (a), the restrictions are applied directly against the foreign provider, who is prohibited or restricted from offering the service. This is achieved mostly through withholding licenses or authorizations or prohibiting or restricting membership in professional organizations where membership is a pre-requisite for providing the service. In barrier (b), on the other hand, the barrier is more often indirect, taking the form of a legal requirement for the recipient to use a national provider. Two common examples are the mandatory use of national insurers to cover motor vehicle liability and national shipping companies to carry goods arriving from abroad by sea.

Barriers (c) and (d) relate to the same issue, namely the right of a provider to supply services from its own permanent commercial presence in the host country (Mode 3). This may be through a subsidiary, branch or some form of agency.[23] Where this involves removing restrictions on the foreign capital investment that is envisaged to set up the establishment, we are dealing with barrier (c). Where, on the other hand, it involves removing restrictions on foreigners setting up an establishment in the host state to provide a particular service, we are looking at barrier (d). The removal of barrier (d) is often referred to as "the right of establishment." However, normally it does not include a right of personal establishment, which is the right of natural persons to establish themselves physically in the host state and to operate the commercial presence in a self-employed capacity. Two exceptions are the EU and Mercosur.[24] The term therefore has a narrower meaning in the context of the international liberalization of trade in services than under EU law or in Mercosur.

Another point concerns the relationship between barriers (a) and (b) and barrier (g). The first two require the provider to be a national of the host state, which would permit services from abroad as long as they are provided by a national. Barrier (g), on the other hand, requires the provider to be based in the host state but entails no requirement of local nationality. Often, however, the barriers are cumulative, and the provider must be a resident national of the host state. Barrier (i) is distinguishable from (g) in that it requires only a presence in the host state, which

23 *See* the definition of "commercial presence" in Article XXVIII(d) of GATS.

24 Under the 2003 *Agreement on Residence*, Mercosur now provides for a right of personal establishment. For the right of personal establishment in the EU, see Chapter Four, Section II.B.2.

can be just a representative office. The provider need not reside there or operate through a branch or a locally-incorporated company.

Barrier (k) relates to transfers of capital into a host state in order to set up a permanent establishment or representative office as well as transfers of capital from the host state in the form of dividends (from subsidiaries) or profits (from branches). It also includes capital transfers that are an essential part of an underlying service transaction.

There is a close relationship between barriers (c) and (k) as both relate to restrictions on the flow of capital into a host state. However, the essence of barrier (c) is a restriction on foreigners investing in enterprises. Clearly, that will mean that a capital transfer that would otherwise have taken place does not happen, but that is not the purpose of the measure. Its aim is to prevent or limit foreign ownership of the host state's economy and has nothing to do with controlling currency flows. Indeed, it may well be limited to a certain sector of the economy, thus permitting investment in other areas as well as the capital transfers that go with it. It should also be noted that restrictions on capital transfers into a host country may also be imposed by the home country of the investor, whereas restrictions on foreign direct investment are imposed exclusively by the host country.

Exchange controls can take two forms.[25] Direct controls deny or limit access to currency exchange by such measures as prohibiting or limiting the purchase of foreign currency or its inflow into the host state, assigning access to foreign currency on a quota basis or requiring a license for the purchase or receipt of foreign currency. Indirect controls make it more costly or difficult to acquire foreign currency or transfer it to the host state without actually impeding the transaction. Examples are multiple exchange rates, interest-free deposits from purchasers of foreign currency and mandatory payment delays in settling accounts denominated in a foreign currency. Both types of controls are covered by provisions in agreements on exchange controls.

Barrier (f) refers to networks that are either operated or regulated by the state or a non-governmental agency that exercises delegated powers. Networks under strictly private control over which the state has neither a direct or indirect influence are not susceptible of international regulation. Where access or use is prohibited or restricted on grounds other than nationality, such as residence or qualifications, the issue comes under Category 2 or domestic regulation, respectively. Where access or use is available but under discriminatory conditions, the matter falls under national treatment.

The barriers in Category 1 are openly based on nationality or the state of permanent residence. Residency requirements (Category 2) are not discriminatory as they apply equally to nationals and non-nationals in the broad sense. Two of the operational barriers listed in Category 3, namely (j) and (m), are also usually imposed on a non-discriminatory basis. Exchange controls, on the other hand, would

25 *See* Article VIII:2 and 3 of the IMF Articles.

seem to be discriminatory by their very nature as they only affect foreign providers, but, as they are normally imposed on a general basis, they can be regarded as non-discriminatory. This distinction between discriminatory and non-discriminatory barriers is important where market access is achieved by way of a national treatment principle that covers only discrimination in law.[26]

C. CATEGORIZING NATIONAL MEASURES

Not all the measures listed above are absolute barriers to market entry by a foreign provider. For some providers and for some modes of entry, what is otherwise a market access barrier may only disadvantage the foreign provider. Restrictions that are not severe enough to deter market entry fall into the same category. Despite this fluidity between market access and national treatment, I have chosen to place national measures under one rubric or the other. Otherwise, the result is confusion. The choice of how to categorize a particular measure, however, is not always clear. GATS, for example, places quantitative restrictions under market access and residency requirements under national treatment, whereas I would categorize them in exactly the opposite way. It is necessary, therefore, to include some comments justifying my approach.

In general, the nationality requirements in Category 1 are, by their very nature, absolute barriers to the provision of a service in the host state by a foreign provider unless the restrictions are relatively minor. Mandatory local equity (barrier (c)) is not necessarily a market access barrier but may become so if, for example, it entails sharing the foreign provider's expertise or intellectual property rights. I have included all nationality requirements under market access.

The residency requirements in Category 2 are usually absolute barriers to market entry for the foreign provider of cross-border services. While foreign providers who are established in the host state will by this fact necessarily meet the requirements of permanent residence and local presence (barriers (g) and (i)), these same requirements may constitute a serious obstacle for the supplier of cross-border services. Barrier (g) is an absolute barrier in this latter situation, while barrier (i) prevents the supply of cross-border services where the scale or frequency of the activity does not warrant the expense of setting up a local presence in the host state. Similarly, the requirement of prior residency (barrier (h)) may not unduly hamper a foreign provider who is established in the host state but is usually an absolute barrier for providers of cross-border services. For me, residency requirements are primarily market access barriers.

Among the operational barriers in Category 3, the existence of monopolies (barrier (m)) is normally an absolute barrier to market entry. On other hand, the other three may only disadvantage the foreign provider. For example, tariffs on the importation of necessary inputs (barrier (j)) may increase the cost of providing a service without actually impeding it. Restrictions on importation, on the other hand,

26 The relationship between market access and national treatment is discussed *infra* in the text.

would prevent market entry. Exchange controls (barriers (k) and (l)) may similarly just add to the cost of providing the service, although they may be an absolute barrier if they effectively prevent the repatriation of profits from or transfers of necessary funds into the host state or prevent the recipient paying for the service in a convertible currency. Because of their obstructive potential, I have chosen to include all four measures as market access barriers.[27]

D. THE BARRIERS AND MARKET ENTRY MODES

Market access barriers do not affect in equal measure the four modes of supplying services internationally. The mode of supply that is the least affected by market access barriers is Mode 2 as no host state is directly involved in the transaction. The recipient's state may set up barriers against the provision and/or receipt of the service, such as nationality and residence requirements, but it will rarely be able to enforce them unless the service is intended to have legal effects in that state. For example, if a person travels abroad to obtain legal advice, it really matters little if the law of the recipient's state requires the lawyer to be a resident national unless, say, the advice is intended for use in a court of law there. Many barriers are in any case irrelevant to this mode of supply, namely certain nationality requirements (barriers (c), (d), (e) and (f)), prohibited or restricted access to necessary inputs (barrier (j)) and obstruction by host-state monopolies (barrier (m)). Barrier (l), on the other hand, will affect this mode of providing a service where they are prohibitive or restrictive enough to prevent the recipient traveling to receive the service from the provider or obtaining sufficient foreign currency to pay for it.

Mode 1 is more susceptible to market access barriers as a host state is now involved that can enforce its requirements through the presence of the recipient in the country. Nonetheless, if the recipient does not need to involve the state, it should again be possible to ignore the barriers in some situations. If, for example, the host state requires people to use a national provider for international telephone calls, the ways of modern telecommunications make it quite easy to circumvent this restriction. However, the caller will probably not be able to deduct the expenses from taxable income. As with Mode 2, many barriers are not relevant for Mode 1 although the latter mode may be affected by the existence of monopolies in the host state (barrier (m)). Restrictions and prohibitions on currency exchange (barriers (k) and (l)) remain a potent obstacle.

Generally speaking, nationality requirements (Category 1) do not affect the supply of services by Mode 3, as host states normally place foreign service providers established permanently in their countries on the same footing as national providers. Obvious exceptions are prohibitions or restrictions on foreign capital investment and on setting up a permanent establishment in the host state (barriers (c) and (d)). Where barrier (c) takes the form of mandatory local equity, this may be unaccept-

27 At least as far as limitations on inputs are concerned, GATS implicitly recognizes that they may constitute a market access barrier although it does not deal with them—*see* note 9 to Article XVI:1.

able to foreign providers where it involves sharing trade secrets or intellectual property rights. Mode 3 is also affected by prohibitions and restrictions on access to necessary inputs (barrier (j)) and monopolies (barrier (m)). Residency requirements (Category 2) are only a barrier if an excessive period of prior residence (barrier (h)) is required so that the foreign provider must wait so long that it becomes pointless to consider market entry. This is rarely the case. On the other hand, exchange controls are a significant barrier for this mode of supply where they involve measures prohibiting or severely restricting the capital transfers needed to set up an establishment in the host state or to repatriate revenue earned there (barrier (k)).

Mode 4 is the mode of supply that is the most vulnerable to market access barriers. It is not possible to circumvent them as in the case of Modes 1 and 2, and the foreign provider does not enjoy the benefits that normally flow from having a permanent base in the host state (Mode 3). All of the barriers are relevant with the exception of prohibitions and restrictions on foreign capital investment and setting up a permanent establishment in the host country (barriers (c) and (d)). Residency requirements (Category 2) and prohibitions or restrictions on the movement of natural persons into the host state (barrier (e)) are particularly obstructive.

VIII. NATIONAL TREATMENT

A. DISCRIMINATION IN LAW

The most common examples of discrimination in law are the following:

List 4
Examples of Discrimination in Law

CATEGORY 1 OPERATIONAL DISCRIMINATION

a) prohibitions or restrictions on the acquisition of real estate in the host state;

b) more costly or more difficult access to public or private networks;

c) more costly or more difficult access to professional or trade organizations;

d) more costly or more difficult procedures with respect to licenses and authorizations;

e) prohibition or restrictions on the distribution and marketing of the service, including advertising or other means of acquiring recipients;

f) more costly or more difficult conditions of operation, e.g. audit, record maintenance, fees;

g) discrimination against foreign providers by monopolies;

CATEGORY 2 FINANCIAL DISCRIMINATION

h) higher taxes on revenue, the service or a necessary input;

i) non-deductibility for tax purpose of the provider's expenses, *e.g.* advertising costs;

j) non-deductibility for tax purposes of the cost of the service to the recipient;

k) restricted or no access to tax credits, write-offs, duty-free imports etc;

l) restricted or no access to subsidies, loans and loan guarantees;

m) restricted or no access to insurance schemes, e.g. deposit insurance for banks;

n) higher charges for services, such as port charges, use of public networks, and financial securities and bonds;

o) higher capital requirements;[28]

CATEGORY 3 DISCRIMINATORY QUANTITATIVE RESTRICTIONS

p) restrictions on the number of service providers;

q) restrictions on the total value of service transactions or assets;

r) restrictions on the total number of service operations or the total quantity of service output;

s) restrictions on the total number of employees;

CATEGORY 4 DISCRIMINATORY PERFORMANCE REQUIREMENTS

t) export level requirements;

u) local content requirements;

v) local preference requirements;

w) mandatory technology transfer;

x) local training requirements;

y) minimum level of activity in the host state;

z) obligation to act as exclusive supplier to a specific market.

These measures are largely self-explanatory. However, it should be noted that restricting access to subsidies, loans and loan guarantees (measure (l)) to providers who are permanently established in the host state is not generally considered to violate the national treatment principle.[29]

---

28 This measure affects mainly financial services providers.

29 *See* NAFTA, Article 1108:7(b).

Operational and financial discrimination (Categories 1 and 2) are by their very nature discriminatory. On the other hand, quantitative restrictions (Category 3) and some performance requirements, in particular measures (u) and (v), may be imposed on a non-discriminatory basis, in which case they should be treated as domestic regulation unless they discriminate in fact against foreign providers.

Some of the measures listed above are capable of preventing market access altogether. This is true, in particular, of some performance requirements. While local content and preference requirements and even the obligation for local training (measures (u), (v) and (x)) should at most only inconvenience the foreign provider, the requirement of a minimum level of activity (measure (y)) may well deter foreign providers who cannot afford the investment that this level requires. Mandatory technology transfer (measure (w)) may be unacceptable, and the obligation to act as exclusive supplier to a specific market (measure (z)) may not be consistent with a provider's overall global strategy. Quantitative restrictions (Category 3) may similarly impede market entry where they severely limit activity. Nevertheless, these and all the other measures that are listed above by and large disadvantage foreign providers rather than exclude them from the market. This is why I place them under the rubric of national treatment.

As with market access barriers, measures that discriminate in law do not affect the modes of providing services in equal measure. Modes 1 and 2 are generally affected only by restrictions on advertising (measure (e)) and non-deductibility of the cost of the service by the recipient (measure (j)). The other measures do not apply or can be circumvented. In the case of Mode 4, however, most measures, except performance requirements (Category 4), may be relevant. There may be some operational discrimination (Category 1) against foreign providers established in the host country (Mode 3), but financial discrimination (Category 2) should be less of a problem. Quantitative restrictions (Category 3) may apply and it is with respect to Mode 3 that performance requirements (Category 4) are usually imposed.

B. DISCRIMINATION IN FACT

Measures that discriminate in fact against foreign providers but which have an important public interest dimension generally fall under the rubric of domestic regulation. Even those which remain to be dealt with as discrimination in fact will fall under domestic regulation where the national treatment provision does not cover this type of discrimination or where they do not in fact disadvantage the foreign provider.

Here is a list of the most common examples of measures that may constitute discrimination in fact:

List 5
Examples of Discrimination in Fact

a) requirement of a particular corporate form in the host state;

b) prohibition or restrictions on the use of home-state or host-state professional titles;

c) prohibition or restrictions on the use of home-state name;

d) prohibition or restrictions on the use of home-state nationals in senior and specialist positions;

e) requirement that the majority of a board of directors be citizens or permanent residents of the host state;

f) non-discriminatory performance requirements;

g) non-discriminatory quantitative restrictions.

One could argue that restrictions on the use of titles (measure (b)), home-state names (measure (c)) and home-state nationals (measure (d)) as well the requirement of citizenship or residence for the majority of directors (measure (e)) constitute discrimination in law as they are essentially directed at foreign providers. However, to the extent that they nevertheless also apply to national providers, they can be said to fall within discrimination in fact.

Under normal circumstances, neither measure (b) or (c) is likely to cause serious problems to the foreign provider. This is also true of the requirement of a particular corporate form (measure (a)) unless this causes a conflict with the corporate law of the home state. However, as they have the potential to disadvantage foreign providers, I have included them under discrimination in fact. As concerns prohibitions or restrictions on the use of home-state nationals (measure (d)), or intra-corporate transferees as they are often called, they put foreign providers at a potentially significant disadvantage by depriving them of people that they rely on to carry out their operations successfully. Although this type of restriction does not prevent a foreign provider from operating altogether, there can be circumstances, such as the setting up of a new establishment, where the presence of these intra-corporate transferees is important and an inability to rely on them significantly disadvantages the foreign provider. The requirement for a majority of the board to be citizens or residents may hamper the running of the enterprise.

The performance requirements that may on occasion be imposed on a non-discriminatory basis (measure (f)) are local content and local preference requirements. To the extent that these requirements require foreign providers to change their suppliers and so disrupt their normal mode of operations, they could put them at a disadvantage vis-à-vis national providers. Non-discriminatory quantitative restrictions (measure (g)) may disadvantage a foreign provider if the scope of activity that is permitted does not justify the investment involved in entering the market. Both these measures, however, are probably more likely to fall under domestic regulation.

None of the listed measures of discrimination in fact affect the supply of services by Mode 2, and only measures (a) and (g) may conceivably apply to Mode 1. All measures are susceptible of affecting Modes 3 and 4, but, with respect to Mode 3, it is reasonable that a provider established in a host state comply with the domestic rules on the supply of services. In this situation, they cannot really be considered to constitute discrimination in fact.

IX. MARKET ACCESS AND NATIONAL TREATMENT

There is a close relationship between market access and national treatment. Not only is this because many national measures can, depending on their effect on a particular mode of supply, fall under either rubric, but also because national treatment, by requiring foreign service providers to be treated in the same manner as national providers, can be used to secure a certain level of market access. The actual level depends on the scope of the national treatment requirement.

Traditionally, national treatment applies exclusively to provisions that openly discriminate on the basis of nationality. As such, it only requires the abolition of nationality requirements (Category 1[30]), as residency requirements (Category 2) have nothing to do with nationality, and the operational barriers listed in Category 3 are usually imposed on a non-discriminatory basis. Thus, these barriers are not caught by the traditional national treatment rule, which means that the rule has to be supplemented by additional provisions if they are to be removed and market access assured.

If national treatment extends to discrimination in fact, it would remove residency requirements, which clearly place foreign providers at a disadvantage. It is a moot point to what extent it would remove the operational barriers. It certainly would not deal with the problem of monopolies (barrier (m). However, many agreements have specific provisions on exchange restrictions (barrier (k) and (l)), importation of inputs (barrier (j) and monopolies.[31] A wide application of the national treatment principle that includes the removal of *all* national measures which disadvantage foreigners would thus appear capable of largely securing market access. However, it remains a questionable approach for two reasons.

In the first place, it is still the exception rather than the rule for national treatment to extend to discrimination in fact. Thus, by and large, national treatment does not provide an adequate means of securing market access.

---

30 The reference is to the illustrative list of market access barriers in List 3.

31 *E.g.* GATS, Articles VIII and XII. Barrier (j) is dealt with by GATT.

Secondly, using national treatment as a market access tool confuses two separate but equally important concepts. Market access concerns barriers that prohibit or seriously impede access to a particular market. National treatment concerns equality in the conditions under which a service is provided in the host state, not whether it can be supplied at all. It requires equality with respect to such issues as acquisition of land, access to subsidies, loan or loan guarantees, taxation and the overall conduct of business. In my view, the two concepts should be kept separate. GATS and the EU follow this approach, although the former has a rather idiosyncratic way of categorizing the various national measures. NAFTA, on the other hand, uses national treatment to liberalize trade in services on a general basis[32] but is obliged to supplement this approach with specific market access provisions as its national treatment principle does not extend to discrimination in fact. It is perhaps a testimony to the shortcomings of this approach that the recent *US-Chile Free Trade Agreement* (US-Chile Agreement), which is largely based on NAFTA, separates out market access from national treatment.[33]

X. DOMESTIC REGULATION

Domestic regulation includes all the non-discriminatory rules of the host state that regulate the provision of services within its borders to the extent that they do not fall within the rubric of discrimination in fact. The following matters come within domestic regulation:

List 6
Matters Falling within Domestic Regulation

a) licensing and authorization procedures;

b) requirement of membership in a host-state professional or trade organization;

c) requirement of host-state qualifications;

d) requirement to meet host-state technical standards;

e) prudential rules, including capital requirements;

f) requirement of competence in the host state language;

g) administration of domestic rules;

h) matters listed under discrimination in fact where the national treatment rule does not extend to discrimination in fact or where they do not in fact disadvantage the foreign provider.

---

32 Chapter 14 on financial services does distinguish between market access and national treatment.

33 US-Chile Agreement, Article 11.4.

Some of these measures are closely connected. The possession of host-state qualifications (measure (c)) can exist either as an independent pre-requisite for the provision of services in the host state or, very frequently, it is a necessary condition for obtaining membership in a professional organization, a license or an authorization (barriers (a) and (b)). Likewise, membership in a professional or trade organization may be an independent pre-requisite for providing services or it may be necessary for obtaining a license or an authorization. The administration of domestic rules (measure (g)) includes such matters as transparency, impartiality, timeliness and judicial review.

Measures (a) to (f) are capable of putting foreign providers of services at a serious disadvantage, but they come under domestic regulation because they are considered matters of public policy. Licensing and authorization procedures and mandatory membership requirements (measures (a) and (b)) are particularly problematic, especially where they require the foreign provider to possess host-state qualifications. In fact, in the case of cross-border services, they may prevent market access altogether. It is extremely onerous for a person to have to re-qualify in order to provide a service unless the time required is short or the scale of the activity is such that re-qualification is worth the time and effort.

The problem of technical standards (measure (d)) is perhaps less severe unless it requires a provider to change completely the way in which a service is supplied. The requirement of competence in the host language (measure (f)) constitutes an obstacle only for persons with poor linguistic abilities. Prudential rules (measure (e)), which affect financial service providers in particular, can also present significant obstacles to market access. The classic example is the requirement that branches of foreign banks meet the capital requirements of the host country in addition to those of the home country.

We have already discussed the problems posed by measures that may also constitute discrimination in fact (measure (h)). Generally speaking, they are less serious. In fact, non-discriminatory quantitative restrictions (measure (f) on List 5) could be seen to represent a policy decision by the host state to limit the scope of certain activities, in which case their elimination is a matter of domestic de-regulation rather than trade liberalization. The same is not true of the two performance requirements that may conceivably be imposed on a non-discriminatory basis (local content and local preference requirements), which have a definite protectionist quality even where they fall under domestic regulation. Indeed, to the extent that these performance requirements relate to the purchase of inputs for the provision of the service, they are prohibited by the *Agreement on Trade-Related Investment Measures* (TRIMS), which is part of Annex 1A to the WTO Agreement.[34]

34 Annex, point 1(a).

CHAPTER TWO

GLOBAL LIBERALIZATION OF TRADE IN SERVICES

I. GENERAL AGREEMENT ON TRADE IN SERVICES

A. INTRODUCTION

1. The Agreement

International trade in services was not regulated in a global and comprehensive manner until the advent of GATS. True, since 1973 there were multilateral rules for certain service sectors in the OECD Invisibles Code,[1] but the Code only applies to Members of the OECD and is limited in its coverage to certain, albeit important, sectors of the services industry. GATS is part of the WTO Agreement, which was adopted on April 15,1994 and entered into force on January 1,1995. It is found in Annex 1B of the WTO Agreement. GATS binds all Members of the WTO, which comprised 147 countries on April 23, 2004.

2. Application of GATS

GATS rules apply to all measures, which include any law, regulation, procedure, requirement or practice.[2] Theoretically, they bind all levels of government as well as non-governmental bodies that exercise delegated powers.[3] This last provision is essential for purposes of equity, as in some Members quasi-private bodies, such as professional associations, might exercise powers that in other Members are wielded directly by the state. As a general rule, however, GATS only requires

1 This Code is discussed in Chapter Three.

2 Article XXVIII(a).

3 Article I:3(a).

Members to take such reasonable measures as may be available to them to secure compliance with GATS rules by sub-central and non-governmental bodies.[4]

GATS provides for all services to be covered with very few exceptions.[5] Services supplied in the exercise of governmental authority are excluded.[6] By this is meant public services that are supplied by governments on a non-commercial and non-competitive basis.[7] In addition, the provisions on MFN treatment and the specific commitments on market access and national treatment do not apply to government procurement of services unless they are acquired with a view to commercial resale or to use in the supply of services for commercial sale.[8] However, government procurement in some service sectors is covered by the GPA, which is contained in Annex 4 of the WTO Agreement. The GPA is a plurilateral agreement, which means that Members of the WTO are not obliged to participate. Nevertheless, a number of significant world traders, such as the United States, Japan, Canada and the EU, are parties to the Agreement,[9] but they are not obliged to extend the benefits of the GPA to non-Parties. However, GATS provides for further negotiations on liberalizing the government procurement of services on a global basis.[10] These have taken place both within the Working Party on GATS Rules and the Committee on Government Procurement, but so far they have been without tangible results.

There are special rules contained in the GATS Annexes for financial services, telecommunications and air and maritime transport services. These supplement the general rules of the Agreement. They are discussed in Chapters Five, Six and Seven, respectively.

GATS applies to trade in services by any of the four modes of supplying services internationally to the extent that a Member's Schedule of Specific Commitments does not contain any limitations in this respect.[11] A commercial presence includes subsidiaries, branches and representative offices.[12]

---

4 *Ibid.*

5 Article I:3(b).

6 Article I:3(b).

7 Article I:3(c).

8 Article XIII:1. Access to the government procurement market is best seen as an issue of market access to a particular sector of the economy. Government procurement is discussed in Chapter Eight.

9 The Parties to the GPA are Canada, the European Communities (including its 25 member States: Austria, Belgium, Cyprus, Czech Republic, Denmark, Estonia, Finland, France, Germany, Greece, Hungary, Ireland, Italy, Latvia, Lithuania, Luxemburg, Malta, Netherlands, Poland, Portugal, Slovak Republic, Slovenia, Spain, Sweden, United Kingdom), Hong Kong China, Iceland, Israel, Japan, Korea, Liechtenstein, Netherlands with respect to Aruba, Norway, Singapore, Switzerland and the United States.

10 Article XIII:2.

11 Article I:2. These four modes are described in List 1.

12 Article XXVIII(d).

The GATS rules apply to the provision of services by means of cross-border supply or consumption abroad (Modes 1 and 2) as long as the service is provided, respectively, from the territory of one Member into the territory of another Member or in the territory of one Member to a service consumer of another Member.[13] In the case of natural persons, the service consumer must be a citizen or permanent resident of the other Member and actually live there.[14] However, permanent residents are only covered if the Member in which they reside has no citizens or accords substantially the same treatment to them as it does to its own citizens in respect of measures affecting trade in services. No Member is obliged to treat permanent residents of another Member more favorably than that other Member treats them. Where the consumer is a legal person, it must be constituted or otherwise organized under the law of the other Member and be engaged in substantive business operations in the territory of that Member or any other Member.[15]

With respect to the provision of services through commercial presence or the presence of natural persons (Modes 3 and 4), the service must be supplied in the territory of one Member by a service supplier of another Member.[16] Where the service supplier is a natural person, the same rule applies as for service consumers; he or she must be a citizen or permanent resident of the other Member.[17] If the supplier is a legal person, the rule differs according to the mode of supply. Where the service is supplied through Mode 4, the legal person on behalf of whom natural persons travel to provide the service must be constituted or otherwise organized under the law of the other Member and be engaged in substantive business operations in the territory of that Member or any other Member.[18] Where the service is supplied through Mode 3, the legal person constituting the commercial presence must be owned or controlled by citizens or permanent residents of the other Member or by legal persons constituted under the law of the other Member and engaged in substantive business operations in the territory of that Member or any other Member.[19] "Owned" means holding more than fifty percent of the equity interest,[20] and "controlled" means the power to name a majority of the directors or otherwise legally direct the presence's actions.[21]

---

13 Article I:2(a) and (b). *See also* the combined effect of Articles XVI:1 and XXVIII(f)(i).

14 *See* Article XXVIII(i), (j) and (k).

15 *See* Article XXVIII(i), (j) and (m)(i).

16 Article I:2(c) and (d). *See also* the combined effect of Articles XVI:1 and XXVIII(f)(ii).

17 *See* Article XXVIII(g), (j) and (k).

18 *See* Article XXVIII(g), (j) and (m)(i).

19 Article XXVIII(m)(ii).

20 Article XXVIII(n)(i).

21 Article XXVIII(n)(ii).

An interesting fact that emerges from the above rules is that where a service is provided by cross-border supply (Mode 1), there is no requirement that either the supplier or consumer be of a Member. However, this provision is subject to the GATS provision on denial of benefits.[22]

3. The GATS Approach

GATS defines what is meant by market access and national treatment, but apart from some specific, binding provisions, it leaves it up to the Members to negotiate commitments on these matters between themselves.[23] Members are free, subject to the need to reciprocate concessions from other Members, to identify which sectors and sub-sectors of their economies they wish to liberalize in the field of services. These are then listed in the national Schedules of Specific Commitments and are covered by the GATS provisions on market access and national treatment, albeit subject to any limitations and conditions that Members wish to retain or introduce.[24] Additional commitments may also be made on issues of domestic regulation. The national Schedules of Specific Commitments are an integral part of GATS and bind the Members.[25] Services that are the subject of a specific commitment are called "listed services."

While the GATS approach has the merit of separating out the concepts of market access and national treatment, it is not ideal. In the first place, it means that not all services benefit from the same treatment. On the one hand, there are the listed services for which specific commitments have been undertaken by the Members with respect to market access, national treatment and domestic regulation. Then, there are the other services, which are not the object of such commitments and only benefit from the provisions of GATS that have general application, such as those on MFN treatment and some aspects of domestic regulation.

The second problem is the "bottom-up" nature of the approach. Instead of liberalizing all services except those activities which it itself defines, GATS leaves it up to the Members to pick and choose the service sectors that they wish to liberalize. This cannot help but have a limiting effect on liberalization. Moreover, this choice is made during negotiations aimed at achieving mutual concessions, so that service sectors that are not important to a Member's negotiating partners may not be liberalized for this reason alone.

The Schedules of Specific Commitments under GATS are similar to the Schedules of tariff commitments attached to GATT. However, there is a crucial difference between the two. Whereas a GATT Schedule sets out new tariff bindings that represent uniquely concessions on the part of a Member, the GATS Schedules set out

---

22 This is discussed *infra* in the text.

23 Article XIX.

24 Articles XVI:1 and XVII:1.

25 Article XX:3.

not only commitments to liberalize but also, just as importantly, limitations on these commitments. The GATS Schedules are thus both liberalizing and restrictive so that their name is somewhat misleading. On the other hand, Members may not go beyond the limitations included in their Schedules so that at least they are a guarantee to economic operators in other Members that the conditions of entry into the market will not be changed to their disadvantage.

Specific commitments under GATS may be modified or withdrawn by a Member, but only after they have been in effect for at least three years.[26] Modification of commitments must not affect the application of the MFN principle.[27]

The modifying Member is required to notify the Council for Trade in Services no later than three months before the intended change is to be implemented.[28] Any Member whose benefits under GATS may be affected by the proposed change may request the modifying Member to enter into negotiations with a view to reaching agreement on a compensatory adjustment that maintains a general level of mutually advantageous commitments which is not less favorable to trade than the level existing prior to the negotiations.[29] This means that reduced liberalization in one services area is compensated by greater liberalization in another service sector. Any compensatory adjustment must be made on an MFN basis.[30]

If no agreement is reached before the end of the period provided for negotiations on compensation, the affected Member may refer the matter to arbitration.[31] No change may be made to a Schedule of Specific Commitment until the arbitration is completed.[32] The task of the arbitration is to establish what compensatory adjustments should be made, and the modifying Member has to comply with these findings before it can make the change to its specific commitments.[33] Otherwise, the affected Member may retaliate by withdrawing or modifying substantially equivalent benefits in conformity with the findings of the arbitration.[34] Such retaliation is not subject to the MFN rule as it is implemented solely against the modifying Member.

26 Article XXI:1(a).

27 They are subject to Article II:1.

28 Article XXI:1(b).

29 Article XXI:2(a).

30 Article XXI:2(b).

31 Article XXI:3(a).

32 This is implied by Article XXI:3(b).

33 Article XXI:4(a).

34 Article XXI:4(b).

4. The National Schedules

The national Schedules[35] all conform to a standard format that is based on the WTO Guidelines and which is intended to facilitate comparative analysis. The following information has to be inscribed in each column of the Schedule:

List 7
Columns of the Schedules of Specific Commitments

SECTOR OR SUBSECTOR COLUMN

This column contains a clear definition of the sector, sub-sector or activity that is the subject of the specific commitment.

MARKET ACCESS COLUMN

When a Member has undertaken a commitment in a sector or sub-sector, it must indicate for each mode of supply what limitations, if any, it maintains on market access. Limitations in this column typically concern quantitative restrictions,[36] requirement of a specific legal form of operation,[37] and mandatory local equity. A particular mode of supply may also be prohibited.

NATIONAL TREATMENT COLUMN

A Member wishing to limit national treatment in a service sector to which market access has been granted must indicate in this column the limitations for each mode of supply.

ADDITIONAL COMMITMENTS COLUMN

Entries in this column are not obligatory, but a Member may decide in a given sector to make additional commitments relating to measures of domestic regulation, such as qualifications, standards and licensing matters. This column must be used to indicate positive undertakings, not additional restrictions or limitations.

For each service sector or sub-sector that is opened up, the national Schedules thus indicate, with respect to each of the four modes of supply, any limitations on market access or national treatment that are to be maintained. An important point to note is that, at the beginning of most Schedules before the sections dealing with specific service areas, one finds the "horizontal" limitations that apply to all of the

35 The Schedule of the European Union (or the "European Communities" as it is referred to in the Schedule) binds all the Member States of the Union except the ten new States who joined on May 1, 2004.

36 The author doubts that these measures are really market access barriers. In this monograph, they are placed under the rubric of national treatment—*see* Chapter One, Section VIII.

37 *Ibid.*

service areas included in the Schedule. These often concern a particular mode of supply, notably Modes 3 and 4. Any evaluation of sector-specific commitments and limitations must therefore take the horizontal entries into account. Limitations that apply to a particular sector or sub-sector are listed subsequently in the section dealing with those specific services.

Where possible, the entries in national Schedules use the following uniform terminology:

- where there are no limitations on market access or national treatment in a given sector and mode of supply, the entry reads NONE. However, it should be noted that when the term NONE is used in the sector-specific part of the Schedule, it means only that there is no limitation specific to this sector or sub-sector; there may still be relevant horizontal limitations that apply.
- all entries in a Schedule bind the Member unless otherwise specified. In such a case, where a Member wishes to remain free in a given sector or mode of supply to introduce or maintain measures inconsistent with market access or national treatment, the Member enters in the appropriate space the term UNBOUND.
- in some situations, a particular mode of supply may not be technically possible or feasible. In such cases, the term UNBOUND is also used, preferably in conjunction with an explanatory footnote stating "UNBOUND due to lack of technical feasibility."

Nevertheless, in many cases there are textual descriptions of bound commitments that indicate limitations on market access or national treatment. Such entries, which vary in length considerably, do not use uniform terminology, but are based on one of two common approaches:

- the entry describes in the appropriate space the nature of the limitation, indicating the elements that make it inconsistent with Articles XVI and XVII of GATS, or
- the entry indicates a limited commitment by describing what the Member is offering rather than the limitations that it is maintaining. This approach is often used to indicate the market access opportunities attending the entry of certain categories of natural persons from other Members who supply services.

B. MARKET ACCESS

1. Market Access under GATS

Members are obliged to treat services and service suppliers from other Members in accordance with their specific commitments.[38] According to Article XVI:2, this means that, with respect to the services that are listed in a Member's Schedule of

38 Article XVI:1.

Specific Commitments, the Member must not maintain or adopt, either at national or regional level, quantitative restrictions,[39] prohibitions or restrictions on foreign capital investment, including mandatory local equity (barrier (c))[40] or the requirement of a particular corporate form.[41] Nationality requirements with respect to the provision and receipt of services (barriers (a) and (b)) are also covered as such requirements are considered by the WTO Guidelines to constitute a zero quota in violation of Article XVI:2(a).[42]

A footnote to Article XVI:1 adds two further obligations that flow from a specific commitment. [43] They relate to barrier (k). Where a market access commitment permits the cross-border supply of a service that is inextricably linked to a cross-border movement of capital, this capital movement must be allowed as well. Likewise, if a Member permits a service to be supplied through a commercial presence, it must allow any related transfers of capital into its territory.

Measures that prohibit or limit the importation of inputs needed for the supply of a listed service (barrier (j)), on the other hand, do not flow from a Member's specific commitments.[44] They relate to trade in goods and are regulated by GATT.[45]

Three points must be made about the list in Article XVI:2. In the first place, the obligations that it entails are not absolute. Members are free to impose terms, limitations and conditions in the second column of their Schedules on the market access obligations that flow from their specific commitments.[46] It is not clear, however, whether they may similarly restrict their capital transfer obligations. The wording of Articles XVI:1 and XX:1(a) is broad enough to permit limitations to be placed on these two obligations, but logic would suggest that this should not be possible. There is little point in making a commitment that is unrealizable due to currency controls. It could also be argued that these two obligations flow directly from GATS and not from a specific commitment by a Member, and as such cannot be limited. The issue is important as some developing countries, led by Brazil, have expressed concern that these two obligations require in effect a substantial liberalization of capital movements. This view is not shared by most developed countries, who view them more narrowly as relating to specific liberalizing measures.[47]

---

39 Article XVI:2(a)-(d).

40 Article XVI:2(f). The reference is to the illustrative list of market access barriers in List 3.

41 Article XVI:2(e).

42 Point 12.

43 Note 8 to Article XVI:1.

44 Note 9 to Article XVI:2(c).

45 *See* WTO Guidelines, Point 7. *See also infra* in the text.

46 Articles XVI:1 and XX:1(a).

47 *See* Report of the Meeting of February 26, 2003 of the Committee on Trade in Financial Services (Doc.S/FIN/M/39).

The second point is that, subject to any limitations in a national Schedule, the measures set out in Article XVI:2 must be eliminated whether or not they are applied on a discriminatory basis. In particular, this means that non-discriminatory quantitative restrictions must also be eliminated.

Finally, the list of market access barriers in Article XVI:2 that are to be abolished pursuant to a specific commitment is supposed to be exhaustive,[48] but it does not cover all the possible barriers. Some of these are covered by other provisions in GATS.

With respect to nationality requirements (Category 1), it should be noted that specific commitments on market access under GATS apply in principle to all four modes of supplying services.[49] Article XXVIII specifically states that this means the presence, including the commercial presence, of persons of a Member in another Member for the purpose of supplying services (Modes 3 and 4).[50] This would eliminate barriers ((d) and (e)). However, particular modes of supplying services, especially Modes 3 and 4, are often excluded or restricted in the Members' Schedules, either in the sector-specific section or, on a general basis, in the horizontal section at the beginning.

Despite the third paragraph of the Annex on Movement of Natural Persons Supplying Services under the Agreement, which encourages Members to negotiate specific commitments on the supply of listed services by Mode 4, little was originally achieved. Indeed, the ubiquity of barrier (e) led to a Decision being appended to the WTO Agreement calling for greater liberalization of the movement of natural persons to be negotiated within six months of the Agreement entering into force. As a result, a Third Protocol to GATS was concluded in 1995 that extends Members' specific commitments in this area.[51] These commitments do not prevent Members from regulating the entry and temporary residence of foreign service providers, including, it would seem, applying restrictions on the type of person who may enter the host country.[52] However national measures must not be applied in a manner that nullifies or impairs the benefits of a specific commitment. Visa requirements are not considered as falling into this category even where they are applied selectively.[53] Specific commitments on temporary entry and residence cover both the employed and the self-employed.

The issue of access to and use of public or private networks that are necessary for the provision of a service (barrier (f)) is not specifically addressed by GATS, except in the case of telecommunications networks where the Annex on

48 WTO Guidelines, Point 8.

49 Article XVI:1.

50 Article XXVIII(c)(iii). The right to establish a commercial presence does not entail a right of personal establishment—*see* the comments in Chapter One, Section VII.B.

51 It entered into force on January 30, 1996.

52 Annex on Movement of Natural Persons, Point 4.

53 Annex on Movement of Natural Persons, Note 13.

Telecommunications provides that access must be accorded for the supply of any listed service.[54] Access to and use of other networks is left to be covered by national treatment.

Among the operational barriers (Category 3), exchange controls on international transfers and payments for current transactions relating to specific commitments are prohibited by Article XI:1, except for balance-of-payment reasons. This deals with restrictions on payment for services and access to foreign currency for the purpose of traveling to receive a listed service (barrier (l)).[55]

Public and private monopolies (barrier (m)) are not referred to in Article XVI:2. Thus, Members are not required to abolish them, but they are under an obligation to ensure that any monopoly does not operate in a manner inconsistent with their specific commitments.[56] However, given that the existence of a monopoly necessarily prevents market entry, it is difficult to see how a monopoly could operate consistently with a commitment on market access. More comprehensible is the extension of the obligation to any services that a monopoly supplies outside the scope of its exclusive preserve.[57] Members must inform the Council for Trade in Services of any new grant of monopoly rights affecting the supply of services covered by its specific commitments.[58] The obligation also applies where a Member authorizes or establishes a small number of service providers and substantially prevents competition among them on its territory.[59]

Members may not limit the scope of their obligations under the provisions in Article XI on exchange controls or with respect to monopolies, as these obligations do not flow from their specific commitments but from GATS itself.

2. The GATS Approach to Market Access

The GATS approach to market access at least has the merit of distinguishing between market access and national treatment. However, it is open to considerable criticism.

In the first place, market access under GATS is quite restricted. It only applies to services that are listed in the national Schedules and, even here, the approach is unnecessarily exclusive. GATS determines in Article XVI:2 what a market access commitment entails, and Members are able only to limit it, not expand it. It is true that nothing prevents a Member assuming additional obligations that expand its market access commitments, but the fourth column is generally reserved for mat-

54 Annex, Point 5(a). The Annex on Telecommunications is discussed in Chapter Six.

55 Under the IMF Articles, however, no restrictions may be placed on access to foreign currency for the purpose of travel, even if the object of the journey is to receive an unlisted service.

56 Article VIII:1.

57 Article VIII:2.

58 Article VIII:4.

59 Article VIII:5.

ters of domestic regulation. A more radical approach, which is taken by the OECD Codes, would have been to prohibit any measure that acts as a barrier to the international supply of services, subject to any limitations that the Members wish to place in their Schedules. An alternative to these two extremes of exclusiveness and inclusiveness would have been to formulate Article XVI:2 as a list of minimum requirements rather than an exhaustive list, thereby leaving Members free to negotiate more extensive commitments as well as to limit their minimum obligations in their Schedules.

The GATS approach is also very idiosyncratic. It perversely considers residency requirements, which are not mentioned in Article XVI:2, to be a matter of national treatment or even domestic regulation when they do not disadvantage foreign providers in law or in fact.[60] This is plainly wrong. While it is true that residency requirements can on occasion just disadvantage the foreign provider, they are almost always a barrier to market entry in the case of cross-border services. Conversely, Article XVI:2 of GATS views discriminatory quantitative restrictions and the requirement of a particular corporate form as market access barriers whereas it is difficult to see that they do more than disadvantage foreign providers. It should also be recalled that, subject to any limitations in a national Schedule, the measures listed in Article XVI:2 must be eliminated whether or not they are applied on a discriminatory basis. Thus, GATS treats even non-discriminatory quantitative restrictions as market access barriers, which is highly questionable. Although such restrictions may on occasion discriminate in fact against foreign providers, they surely fall mostly within the rubric of domestic regulation. Preventing Members as a general rule from maintaining non-discriminatory quotas is to confuse trade liberalization with internal deregulation.[61]

Finally, GATS does not cover all the barriers to market access. It deals very inadequately with access to and use of networks (barrier (f)), which, in fact, it treats as a matter of national treatment. It contains no provisions on residency requirements (Category 2) or capital transfers out of the host country that are not inextricably linked to a service transaction, such as dividends and profits from affiliates (part of barrier (k)). However, here it could perhaps be argued that the flow of dividends and profits from foreign affiliates is a factor service and thus outside the scope of GATS, which is concerned with commercial services. It is also not clear under GATS whether the obligations with respect to capital movements linked to a service transaction or required for the establishment of a commercial presence are absolute or may be limited.

60 *See* WTO Guidelines, Point 14 and Point V of Attachment 1 of Annex 2.

61 *See* the discussion *supra* in Chapter One, Section VIII.B

3. Assessment of the National Schedules of Major Trading Partners of the United States[62]

Japan

Japan appears to impose the fewest formal restrictions on foreign service providers. However, discussions with industry representatives suggest that the national Schedule does not address all Japanese barriers to market entry. There is also little in the Schedule to facilitate supply of services through commercial presence (Mode 3).

European Union

Although EU-wide commitments generally appear to be among the most generous, they are subject to national measures by the Member States that are among the most restrictive.[63]

Canada

Canada-wide commitments are generous but are subject to provincial measures that may constitute significant barriers to market entry. However, Canada's commitments under NAFTA, which are more far-reaching than those under GATS, also bind the provinces.

Mexico

Mexico's commitments under GATS are very restricted. However, it is also subject to the NAFTA rules, which, despite some exemptions for Mexico, are significantly more extensive.

C. NATIONAL TREATMENT

1. National Treatment under GATS

The first section of Article XVII of GATS imposes a classic national treatment obligation by requiring that services and service providers from other Members receive treatment no less favorable than that which is accorded to national suppliers. Traditionally, this formulation only covers measures that discriminate in law.[64] The second section of Article XVII provides that Members can meet this requirement by either formally identical or formally different treatment. However, in both cases, the treatment must not favor national suppliers of services.[65] This is a somewhat unusual provision, and its purpose is obscure. It certainly does not permit a more lenient approach to national treatment; rather it would seem to aim at flexi-

62 These assessments are based on the executive summary of a December 1995 report issued by the US International Trade Commission entitled *General Agreement on Trade in Services: Examination of Major Trading Partners' Schedules of Commitments*.

63 Most of these national measures do not apply in the case of suppliers operating from a permanent base in a Member State of the European Union.

64 An illustrative list of such measures is found in List 4.

65 Article XVII:3.

bility, dispensing Members from changing rules that treat providers from other Members differently from national suppliers where this difference does not put the former at a disadvantage.

Controversy surrounds whether national treatment under GATS extends to discrimination in fact.[66] The third section of Article XVII provides that any treatment of service providers from other Members, whether formally identical or formally different, contravenes the national treatment rule if it modifies the conditions of competition in favor of national providers. McGovern takes the view that, despite the oblique wording, the national treatment obligation under GATS is still restricted to discrimination in law.[67] A little more clarity would have been welcome, but it is also possible, as Trebilcock and Howse intimate,[68] to interpret this provision as extending national treatment under GATS to cover discrimination in fact. This interpretation is supported by the WTO Guidelines,[69] but not all Members have followed this approach in their Schedules. Others have, however, listed limitations on measures that are capable of constituting discrimination in fact in the third column of their Schedules, which implies that they accept that Article XVII covers this type of discrimination.

Whatever the correct interpretation of Article XVII:3, the GATS national treatment rule does not extend to matters of public interest, such as licenses and host-state qualifications, that traditionally come within the rubric of domestic regulation.[70] Nor does it require Members to compensate for any inherent competitive disadvantages that result from the foreign character of a relevant service or service provider.[71]

GATS contains no exhaustive list of national measures that fall afoul of the national treatment principle. Instead, national treatment is said to cover "all measures affecting the supply of services."[72] Nevertheless, GATS contains some provisions that are intended to elucidate the scope of its national treatment rule, although they are not necessary, at times confusing and restricted to discrimination in law.

According to Article XXVIII, national treatment applies, *inter alia*, to the distribution and marketing of services, which covers measure (e) and possibly (j).[73] National measures on access to and use of network services in connection with the

66 List 5 contains an illustrative list of these measures.

67 E. McGovern, *International Trade Regulation*, (Globefield Press, Exeter, 1995) at para. 31.162.

68 M. Trebilcock and R. Howse, *The Regulation of International Trade* (Routledge, London 1995) at page 233.

69 Point 13.

70 *See* WTO Guidelines, Point 10.

71 Note 10 to Article XVII:1.

72 Article XVII:1.

73 Article XXVIII(b). The references are to the illustrative list of measures in List 4.

supply of a service (measure (b)) are singled out where these services are required by Members to be offered to the public generally.[74] There is nothing to suggest, however, that other networks are not equally covered by the national treatment rule. National measures concerning the payment and use of services are also specifically mentioned,[75] but it is difficult to see why. Exchange controls are more in the nature of a market access barrier (barrier (l)) and are covered in any case by Article XI of the Agreement. Non-discriminatory use of the services of providers from other Members is surely the very essence of national treatment and hardly needs to be singled out.

The WTO Guidelines provide that procedures with respect to licenses and authorizations contravene Article XVII if they are discriminatory in nature (measure (d)).[76] The same is presumably true of mandatory membership in professional or trade organizations (measure (c)). These points serve to illustrate the general principle of national treatment, but the same cannot be said of the position taken by the WTO Guidelines that residency requirements also come under the GATS provisions on national treatment.[77] They are surely market access barriers.

The obligation to apply the national treatment provisions of Article XVII is not absolute. In the first place, the obligation applies only to services on which a market access commitment has been given and are listed in a Member's Schedule.[78] Secondly, GATS permits Members to place conditions and qualifications in their Schedules on their national treatment obligation under Article XVII.[79]

A large number of discriminatory measures, both in law and in fact, are the subject of limitations in the Members' Schedules. They include restrictions on the acquisition of real estate (measure (a) on List 4), access to subsidies, loans or loan guarantees (measure (l) on List 4), differential tax treatment (measures (h) and (k) on List 4), licensing (measure (d) on List 4), use of the host-state language (measure (e) on List 5), access to insurance schemes (measure (m) on List 4), higher charges for public services (measure (n) on List 4), restrictions on the means of acquiring recipients (measure (e) on List 4), use of professional titles (measure (b) on List 5), the presence of home-state nationals in senior or board positions (measure (d) on List 5) and a few performance requirements (Category 4 on List 4 and measure (f) on List 5).

Some Members of the WTO also list nationality requirements in the national treatment column, which is regrettable as such annotations clearly belong in the market access column. Residence requirements, which in my view also constitute market access barriers rather than mere discrimination, are likewise invariably

74 Article XXVIII(c)(ii).

75 Article XXVIII(c)(i).

76 Point 10.

77 Point 14.

78 Article XVII:1.

79 Article XVII:1 and XX:1(b).

noted as exceptions to the national treatment obligation, but this is in accordance with the WTO Guidelines.[80] Conversely, limitations on the obligation to abolish quantitative restrictions are unfortunately found in the market access column of Members as they are considered by Article XVI:2 of GATS to constitute market access barriers.

Restrictions that are capable of falling under the rubric of both market access and national treatment should be placed only in the market access column of a Member's Schedule.[81] This is unfortunate as it can cause confusion. At the very least, it requires us to consult both the market access and national treatment columns of a Member's Schedule in order to establish exactly the scope of its national treatment obligation with respect to a particular listed service. However, under GATS, this is probably necessary anyway because of its idiosyncratic way of classifying market access and national treatment measures.

In addition to the general requirement of national treatment flowing from Article XVII, GATS contains a specific provision on one incidence of operational discrimination. Members must ensure that monopoly service providers do not operate in a manner inconsistent with their specific commitments on national treatment (measure (g) on List 4).[82] This obligation also applies where a Member authorizes or establishes a small number of service suppliers and substantially prevents competition between them on its territory.[83] It exists independently of a Member's specific commitments and cannot be limited in a Member's Schedule. It only applies, however, to listed services.

Non-discriminatory access to and use of public telecommunications transport networks and services are covered by the GATS Annex on telecommunications and discussed later in Chapter Six. Access to and use of other networks for the provision of listed services are covered by the general national treatment provision.

There is an exception to the national treatment rule in GATS that permits different treatment of providers from other Members where it is aimed at ensuring the equitable or effective imposition or collection of direct taxes in respect of services or service suppliers from other Members.[84] This exception covers such measures as those which:[85]

- apply to non-resident service providers in recognition of the fact that the tax obligation of non-residents is determined with respect to taxable items sourced or located in the Member's territory;

---

80 Point 14. I have not followed this approach in this monograph.

81 Article XX:2. *See also* WTO Guidelines, Point 18.

82 Article VIII:1.

83 Article VIII:5.

84 Article XIV(d).

85 Note 6 to Article XIV.

- apply to non-residents in order to ensure the imposition or collection of taxes in the Member's territory;
- apply to non-residents or residents in order to prevent the avoidance or evasion of taxes, including compliance measures;
- apply to consumers of services supplied in or from the territory of another Member in order to ensure the imposition or collection of taxes on such consumers derived from sources in the Member's territory;
- distinguish service providers subject to tax on worldwide taxable items from other service providers, in recognition of the difference in the nature of the tax base between them; and
- determine, allocate or apportion income, profit, gain, loss, deduction or credit of resident persons or branches, or between related persons or branches of the same person, in order to safeguard the Member's tax base.

2. The GATS Approach to National Treatment

In contrast to market access, the GATS approach to national treatment is inclusive and extends to all measures affecting the supply of services. It is unfortunate, however, that there is not more clarity as to whether or not its national treatment provisions extend to discrimination in fact. It should also be noted that national treatment in GATS is subject to two important limitations. It applies only to listed services and Members may place conditions and qualifications in their Schedules against the obligation.

The categorization by GATS of national measures that come within national treatment reflect the categorization for market access and is equally idiosyncratic. It is difficult to accept residency requirements as coming within the rubric of national treatment given that they are real barriers to the provision of cross-border services and in any case are imposed without regard for nationality. Conversely, discriminatory quantitative restrictions (except, of course, zero quotas) or the requirement of a particular corporate may disadvantage foreign providers but do not usually bar access to a market. However, GATS treats them as market access barriers with the result that limitations on the Members' commitments in this regard are found in the second column of their Schedules.

Whatever its shortcomings, however, the GATS national treatment provisions are certainly sufficient, because of their inclusive nature, to cover the measures of discrimination in law on List 4 and, depending on how it is interpreted, the measures of discrimination in fact on List 5.

D. DOMESTIC REGULATION

GATS permits the non-discriminatory domestic regulation of trade in services. This covers the measures set out in List 6, possibly excluding discrimination in fact (measure (h)[86]) if one interprets the GATS national treatment provision broadly. However, whatever the correct interpretation, the requirement of a particular corporate form (measure (a)[87]) and non-discriminatory quantitative restrictions (measure (g)), which are treated by GATS as market access barriers, must be eliminated.[88] By contrast, certain measures with respect to the domestic regulation of telecommunications are specifically permitted. These are discussed in Chapter Six.

GATS contains a number of rules dealing with domestic regulation. Some apply to all services, and certain stricter rules apply only to listed services.

In the first place, GATS requires, for all services, that Members publish promptly or otherwise make publicly available all relevant measures of general application pertaining to trade in services.[89] This includes international agreements to which a Member is a signatory. In addition, they are obliged to respond promptly to all requests from other Members for specific information on these measures.[90] Each Member must also inform the Council for Trade in Services, promptly or at least annually, of any new measures or changes to existing ones that significantly affect trade in listed services.[91] Alternatively, other Members may notify to the Council for Trade in Services any measure taken by a Member that, in their opinion, affects the operation of GATS.[92]

All measures of general application affecting trade in listed services must be administered in a reasonable, objective and impartial manner.[93] This includes processing applications for authorizations in a timely and transparent manner (measure (a)).[94] Members must maintain or institute procedures for the independent review of administrative decisions affecting trade in services to the extent that this is constitutionally possible.[95]

As regards requirements relating to qualifications, licenses and technical standards (measures (a), (c) and (d)), the Council for Trade in Services is charged with establishing rules to ensure that such requirements comply with the following principles:[96]

- they are based on objective and transparent criteria;

---

86 The reference is to the illustrative list of measures falling within domestic regulation in List 6.

87 The reference is to the illustrative list of measures constituting discrimination in fact in List 5.

88 GATS, Article XVI:2.

89 Article III:1.

90 Article III:4.

91 Article III:3.

92 Article III:5.

93 Article VI:1.

94 Article VI:3.

95 Article VI:2.

96 Article VI:4.

- they are not more burdensome than necessary; and
- in the case of licensing procedures, they are not in themselves a restriction on the supply of a service.

These principles probably also apply to mandatory membership in a professional or trade organization (measure (b)), in particular where membership is based on a license or the possession of host-state qualifications.

In the case of listed services, Members must ensure that their licensing and qualification requirements and technical standards adhere to the principles set out above even prior to the entry into force of any rules based upon them.[97] In addition, Members must provide for adequate procedures to verify the competence of foreign professionals offering listed services.[98] It should be noted that, where any of these requirements constitute a quantitative restriction in the sense of Article XVI:2, they constitute market access barrier (a) and must be eliminated.[99]

A Decision appended to the GATS[100] recommended that the Council for Trade in Services set up a Working Party to examine the domestic regulation of professional services. This was done, but a later Decision changed the scope and name of the Working Party. It is now called the Working Party on Domestic Regulation, but so far not much has been achieved except in the area of accounting, where the WTO has published *Guidelines for Mutual Recognition Agreements and Disciplines on Domestic Regulation*. The Guidelines stipulate *inter alia* that the terms for membership of professional organizations must be reasonable,[101] that account should be taken of home-state qualifications[102] and that host-state standards should serve legitimate objectives and take account of internationally-recognized standards.[103]

Members are free to agree among themselves on the mutual recognition of qualifications, work experience, licenses and certifications, but they must afford other interested Members the opportunity to negotiate their accession to any such agreement.[104] Members must not accord recognition in a manner that would constitute a means of discrimination between other Members in the application of its standards or criteria for the authorization, licensing or certification of service suppliers.[105]

---

97 Article VI:4.

98 Article VI:6.

99 WTO Guidelines, Point 10.

100 Decision on Professional Services.

101 Guidelines, Point 10.

102 Guidelines, Point 19.

103 Guidelines, Point 25.

104 Article VII:1, 2.

105 Article VII:3.

Members may also undertake additional commitments with respect to domestic regulation and note them in the fourth column of their Schedules.[106] Looking at the Schedules of the EU, the United States, Japan, Mexico and Canada, we can see that not many additional commitments have been made. There are a few commitments on transparency and reasonableness with respect to licenses, particularly in the financial services sector, and the right to use the home-state firm name. The United States has some commitments relating to the harmonization of state insurance regulations and the reform of the Glass-Steagall Act. There is nothing on technical standards and membership in professional organizations. The only reference to qualifications is the reduction by Japan of the qualifications needed to manage certain funds. Some additional commitments that are listed belong more appropriately elsewhere in the Schedules, such as the commitments on market access for foreign lawyers accorded by the EU, the United States, Japan and Canada, Portugal's additional commitment removing foreign investment restrictions or the commitments of Japan and Canada on reasonable and non-discriminatory access to various transport services. Members may not enter any restrictions on their obligations with respect to domestic regulation under GATS. The fourth column is only for additional commitments.

E. MOST-FAVORED-NATION TREATMENT

Article II:1 of GATS contains the traditional MFN principle. It requires Members of the WTO to treat services and service providers from one Member no less favorably than like services and service suppliers from any other country, whether it is a Member or not. Implicitly, this also means that any disadvantages imposed upon one Member must be extended to all Members. This MFN obligation, unlike market access and national treatment, applies to all measures relating to trade in services whether the services involved are the subject of a specific commitment or not.

The MFN obligation under GATS is a general obligation, but the Agreement singles out one instance. Members must ensure that their monopoly suppliers of services act in accordance with the MFN principle.[107]

A modified MFN rule applies to the mutual recognition of qualifications, work experience, licenses and certifications. Members are free to recognize them when they are obtained in particular countries without having to extend this benefit to all WTO Members.[108] However, they may not apply their standards or criteria for this recognition in a way that discriminates among Members.[109] Furthermore, they

106 Article XVIII.

107 Article VIII:1.

108 Article VII:1.

109 Article VII:3.

must afford adequate opportunity for other interested Members to participate in any such arrangements.[110]

The MFN obligation in GATS is subject to a number of exceptions. In the first place, Members may maintain existing measures that infringe the MFN principle as long as they appended a list of these exempted measures to the Article II Annex by the entry into force of GATS.[111] Among the major trading nations, only Japan has not established a list of MFN exemptions.[112] The list indicates the sectors or sub-sectors concerned, describes the measures and their inconsistency with Article II, names the country or countries to which they apply and states the intended duration of the exemptions and the conditions creating the need for them. Exemptions may relate to countries that are not Members of the WTO. They are not supposed to exceed a period of ten years[113] but many of them are of indefinite duration. The Council for Trade in Services has reviewed the lists of MFN exemptions pursuant to the Annex on Article II Exemptions[114] and approved on June 5, 2002 a document entitled *Procedures for the Certification of Terminations, Reductions and Rectifications of Article II (MFN) Exemptions*.[115] No actual changes were required to any of the lists.

A second exception concerns advantages that are given to adjacent countries, whether or not they are Members, to facilitate frontier trade between them in services that are both locally produced and consumed.[116] The MFN obligation is not to be construed as preventing such arrangements.

A third exception is in fact a general exemption from the provisions of GATS for economic integration agreements, but it has particular relevance for the MFN obligation. The whole purpose of these integration agreements is to liberalize trade between the member countries beyond the level that exists under the WTO rules. They must thus be allowed to accord each other treatment that is more favorable than that accorded to Members outside the agreement. Article V:1 of GATS permits this derogation from the MFN obligation as long as the agreement has substantial sectoral coverage and provides for the absence or elimination of substantially all discriminatory restrictions on trade in services between the member countries. The agreement must also not raise the overall level of barriers to trade

110 Article VII:2.

111 Article II:2.

112 Russia, of course, is not a Member of the WTO.

113 Annex on Article II Exemptions, Point 6.

114 Point 6.

115 Document number S/L/106.

116 Article II:3.

in services in respect of Members outside the agreement beyond the level applicable prior to the agreement.[117]

A fourth exception is similar to the third one but narrower in scope. GATS is not to be construed as preventing Members from establishing full integration of labor markets with other Members on a preferential basis.[118] Such agreements must, however, exempt citizens of the other contracting parties from all requirements concerning residency and work permits.

Finally, service providers from the other Members may be treated differently if the difference in treatment is the result of an agreement on the avoidance of double taxation.[119]

F. GENERAL EXCEPTIONS TO THE GATS RULES

1. Safeguard Exception

It was not possible to reach agreement on a safeguard mechanism during the Uruguay negotiations that led to the WTO Agreement. As a result, a temporary safeguard mechanism was inserted into GATS that was to operate during the three-year period that was set for completing negotiations on a definitive safeguard mechanism.[120] The temporary mechanism permits a Member to modify or withdraw a specific commitment once it has been in force for one year provided that the Member can show cause to the Council for Trade in Services why the modification or withdrawal cannot await agreement on a definitive safeguard mechanism. This implies, of course that the Council may refuse to accept the safeguard measure. It is not clear whether the compensation provisions of Article XXI apply in this situation.[121]

The definitive safeguard mechanism was supposed to be in place by January 1, 1998, but the negotiations that took place pursuant to Article X:1 did not yield any agreement. The negotiations are continuing within the Working Party on GATS Rules but still without coming up with an acceptable formula. The temporary mechanism remains in place and no definite time has been set for the completion of the negotiations.[122]

2. Balance-of-Payments Exception

This exception has already been mentioned in the context of market access. It allows Members who are faced with serious balance-of-payments and external fi-

117 Article V:4.

118 Article Vbis.

119 Article XIV(e).

120 Article X.

121 These provisions are discussed *supra* in the text. McGovern believes that the compensation provisions do apply—*see* McGovern, para. 31-151.

122 *Fifth Decision on Negotiations on Emergency Safeguard Measures*, March 15, 2004.

nancial difficulties or a threat thereof to apply restrictions on trade in listed services, either directly or by means of restrictions on payments or transfers related to such services.[123] A more flexible approach is suggested for developing countries, which takes into account, *inter alia,* their need to maintain a level of financial reserves adequate for the implementation of their plans for economic development.[124] Where exchange restrictions are used, they must be authorized by the IMF.[125]

Restrictions that are imposed for balance-of-payments reasons may not be used to protect a particular service sector[126] and are subject to the following conditions:[127]

- they must be applied on an MFN basis;
- they must be consistent with the rules of the IMF;
- they must avoid unnecessary damage to the commercial, economic and financial interests of any other Member;
- they must not exceed what is necessary to deal with the problem; and
- they must be temporary and be phased out progressively as the situation improves.

Any restrictions that are applied for balance-of-payment reasons must be promptly notified to the General Council.[128] The Member applying the measures must consult with the Committee on Balance-of-Payments Restrictions *inter alia* to assess their compliance with the conditions set out above and in particular their progressive phase-out.[129]

3. Economic Integration Exception

This exception permits Members to enter into economic integration agreements under which trade in services is liberalized between them to a greater degree than under GATS. Clearly, this is primarily an exception to the GATS MFN rule, but it may also entail the withdrawal or modification of specific commitments. Thus, this is a general exception. It is often referred to as the "regional" exception as most economic integration arrangements are regional by nature.

In order to qualify for this exception, economic integration agreements must comply with certain requirements. Firstly, they must have substantial sectoral coverage in terms of numbers of sectors, volume of trade affected and modes of

123 Article XII:1.

124 Article XII:1.

125 This is the import of Article XII:2(b). All Members of the WTO are also members of the IMF.

126 Article XII:3. However, developing Members may give priority to service areas that are more essential for their economic or development programs.

127 Article XII:2.

128 Article XII:4.

129 Article XII:5.

supply.[130] No mode of supply must be excluded. Secondly, the agreements must provide for the elimination of substantially all restrictions that infringe the national treatment rule, either upon their entry into force or within a reasonable time-frame.[131] In evaluating whether this second condition is met, consideration may be given to the relationship of the agreement to a wider process of economic integration or trade liberalization among the Members concerned.[132] Lastly, service suppliers from Members outside the agreement that are legal persons constituted under the laws of a Member who is a party to the agreement must be entitled to the treatment granted under the agreement provided that they engage in significant business operations in the territory of one or more of the parties.[133] A more flexible approach towards all three requirements is taken with respect to developing countries in accordance with their level of development.[134] For example, where an economic integration agreement involves only developing countries, more favorable treatment may be granted to legal persons owned or controlled by natural persons of the parties to the agreement.[135]

Economic integration agreements and any significant changes to them must be notified to the Council for Trade in Services, which may establish a working party to examine whether the agreement in consistent with the requirements set out above.[136] Based on the report of the working party, the Council may make recommendations to the parties to the agreement that it deems appropriate.[137] If practice under the GATT is any indication, it is likely that the Council will restrict itself to such recommendations and not refuse to apply the exception to a particular agreement.

An economic integration agreement must not result in the raising of the overall level of barriers to trade in services between the Members who are parties to the agreement and other Members compared to the level existing prior to the agreement.[138] If the agreement requires the parties to make any changes to their Schedules of Specific Commitments, these parties must provide at least ninety days advance notice of such changes.[139] The compensation and retaliation provisions of Article XXI apply to this situation.[140] However, a Member that is party to an

130 Article V:1(a) and note 1 to Article V.

131 Article V:1(b).

132 Article V:2.

133 Article V:6.

134 Article V:3(a).

135 Article V:3(b).

136 Article V:7(a).

137 Article V:7(a), (c).

138 Article V:4.

139 Article V:5.

140 These are discussed *supra* in the text.

agreement may not seek compensation for trade benefits that may accrue incidentally to any Member outside the agreement.[141]

4. General Exception

GATS permits certain general exceptions to the totality of its rules as long as the measures concerned are not applied in a manner that arbitrarily or unjustifiably infringes the MFN principle or constitutes a disguised restriction on trade in services.[142] The measures that are allowed are those that:

- are necessary to protect public morals or maintain public order, but only where there is a genuine and sufficiently serious threat to one of the fundamental interests of society;[143]
- are necessary to protect human, animal or plant life or health;[144]
- are necessary to secure compliance with laws and regulations consistent with GATS, in particular those relating to safety, the prevention of fraud, the effects of a default on service contracts and the protection of the privacy of individuals.[145]

Article XIV also contains two other exceptions with respect to taxation that relate, respectively, to the principles of national and MFN treatment.[146] They are discussed in those contexts.[147]

5. Security Exception

GATS also permits certain exceptions to the totality of its rules in the case of measures that are taken for reasons of national security.[148] The provision is modeled on the equivalent provision of GATT and excepts the following:

- the disclosure of information whose disclosure would be contrary to a Member's essential security interests;
- actions necessary for the protection of a Member's essential security interests relating to the supply of services for the purpose of provisioning a military establishment or taken in time of war or other international emergencies; and
- actions taken in pursuance of a Member's obligations under the United Nations Charter.

---

141 Article V:8.

142 Article XIV.

143 Article XIV(a) and note 5.

144 Article XIV(b).

145 Article XIV(c).

146 Article XIV(d), (e).

147 *See supra* in the text.

148 Article XIVbis(1).

Members must inform the Council for Trade in Services to the fullest extent possible of measures taken for national security reasons.[149]

6. Denial of Benefits

A Member may deny the benefits of GATS to a service that is supplied from or in the territory of a non-Member or where it is supplied by a legal person of a non-Member.[150] In the case of maritime transport services, benefits may be denied where the service is supplied by a vessel registered under the laws of a non-Member or where the person which operates and/or uses the vessel in whole or in part is a national of a non-Member.[151] Members to which a Member does not apply GATS are treated as non-Members for the purpose of the denial of benefits.

7. Confidential Information

No provision of the GATS obliges a Member to provide confidential information where this would impede law enforcement or otherwise be contrary to the public interest or where the provision of such information would prejudice legitimate commercial interests.[152]

G. DISPUTE SETTLEMENT

The dispute settlement provisions in GATS are somewhat cryptic,[153] and one has to rely on the DSU to understand properly how dispute settlement works under the Agreement. Members may have recourse to the DSU if a) they consider that any other Member has failed to carry out its obligations or specific commitments under the Agreement,[154] or if b) they consider that a benefit that they could reasonably have expected to accrue to them under a specific commitment of another Member is being nullified or impaired as a result of the application of a measure that does not conflict with GATS.[155]

The first step in the dispute settlement mechanism is consultations between the Members in dispute.[156] If a Member requests consultations, the Member requested shall, unless otherwise mutually agreed, reply within ten days and shall enter into consultations in good faith within thirty days of receipt of the request, with the aim of achieving a mutually satisfactory resolution of the matter. If the requested Member either does not respond or does not enter into consultations within the stipulated time periods, the requesting Member may proceed to ask for the estab-

149 Article XIVbis(2).

150 Article XXVII(a),(c).

151 Article XXVII(b).

152 Article IIIbis.

153 Article XXIII.

154 Article XXIII:1.

155 Article XXIII:3.

156 DSU, Article 4.

lishment of a panel. Also, if consultations fail to settle the dispute within sixty days after receipt of the request for consultations, the complaining party may request the establishment of a panel. If, during this sixty-day period, the parties agree that the consultations have failed, the complaining party may proceed to request a panel. Shorter timelines are specified in cases of urgency.

At any time in a dispute, any disputing party can request the use of good offices, conciliation or mediation as methods of dispute resolution.[157] They are undertaken voluntarily on the agreement of the disputing parties and may be started and terminated at any time. Once good office, conciliation or mediation procedures are terminated, a complaining party may then proceed with a request for the establishment of a panel. Also, if the disputing parties agree, these procedures may continue while the panel procedure is underway.

Where the complaining party requests a panel, the Dispute Settlement Body (DSB) must establish a panel by the DSB meeting following the first DSB meeting held to consider the panel request, unless the DSB decides by consensus not to establish a panel.[158] Thus, the establishment of a panel occurs in the vast majority of cases and it is important to note that the Member complained against cannot prevent it.

The function of panels is to assist the DSB in discharging its responsibilities.[159] Standard terms of reference are provided for panels unless the disputing parties otherwise agree on special terms of reference.[160] The standard terms call on the panel to examine the complaint in the light of the relevant provisions of GATS and to make such findings as will assist the DSB in making recommendations or giving rulings. Panels should consult regularly with the disputing parties.

The DSU attempts to ensure the objectivity and quality of the panels and their reports through criteria given for the composition of panels and the qualifications of panelists.[161] For example, although panelists may be government officials or non-governmental individuals, they must be well-qualified, have demonstrated some experience in international trade law or policy and they must serve in their individual capacities. In the case of GATS, panelists must have experience in issues related to GATS and/or trade in services.[162] Panels for disputes regarding sectoral matters must have the necessary expertise relevant to the specific services sector that the dispute concerns.[163] Citizens of Members whose governments are parties to the dispute may not serve on a panel concerned with that dispute unless

157 DSU, Article 5.

158 DSU, Article 6.

159 DSU, Article 11.

160 DSU, Article 7.

161 DSU, Article 8(1) to (4).

162 Decision on Certain Dispute Settlement Procedures for the General Agreement of Trade in Services, Point 3.

163 Decision on Certain Dispute Settlement Procedures, Point 4.

the disputing Members agree otherwise. The DSU Rules of Conduct require further as a governing principle that panelists be independent and impartial, avoid direct or indirect conflicts of interest and respect the confidentiality of proceedings of bodies pursuant to the dispute settlement mechanism.[164]

Normally, a panel is composed of three panelists, unless the disputants agree on a panel of five,[165] and the WTO Secretariat proposes nominations for the panelists to the disputing parties.[166] In the case of GATS, there is a special roster of panelists for which each Member suggests three individuals.[167] The disputing parties may not oppose the individuals proposed by the Secretariat unless there are compelling reasons for doing so. If there is no agreement on the panelists within twenty days of the establishment of the panel, at the request of either party, the Director-General appoints the panelists who he/she deems most appropriate no later than ten days after the request.[168]

Detailed rules are given for the panel process, including strict time limits for the conduct of the process.[169] The DSU requires that, as a general rule, the panel examination period, from the date of the composition of the panel and the agreement on its terms of reference to the date of issue of its final report to the disputing parties, not exceed six months. In urgent cases, the time limit is three months. If the panel considers that it cannot meet these deadlines, the time period from the establishment of the panel to the circulation of the panel report to the Members is extended to nine months.

Panels are required to follow the working procedures set out in Appendix 3 of the Understanding unless the panel decides otherwise after consulting the disputing parties. Panels can seek information and technical advice, expert opinions and written advisory opinions from expert review groups on factual issues concerning scientific or technical matters raised by a disputing party.[170] The DSU introduces an interim review phase in the panel process.[171] Following written submission and oral argument, the panel is required to issue the descriptive part of its draft report to the disputing parties, who are then given a period to time in which to submit their comments. Next, the panel is required to issue an interim report to them, containing both the descriptive aspects and the panel's findings and conclusions. A party may request that the panel review specific aspects of its interim report prior to circulation of its final report to the Members.

---

164 Point II.

165 DSU, Article 8(5).

166 DSU, Article 8(6).

167 Decision on Certain Dispute Settlement Procedures, Points 1 and 2.

168 DSU, Article 8(7).

169 DSU, Article 12.

170 DSU, Article 13. Appendix 4 to the DSU contains the rules and procedures for expert review groups.

171 DSU, Article 15.

The panel submits its findings in a final report to the DSB.[172] The panel report contains the findings of fact, the applicability of relevant provisions and the rationale for any findings and its recommendations. The final panel report is circulated to the Members and is then considered for adoption by the DSB after a twenty-day period has elapsed.

The DSU improves on the earlier GATT system for the adoption of panel reports. Previously, panel reports had to be adopted by the GATT Council by consensus before they were considered to have legal validity. Representatives of the disputing parties were entitled to participate in the process and so could block adoption of the report. By contrast, the DSU, although it permits the disputing parties to participate fully in the DSB process, requires that the final panel report be adopted by the DSB within sixty days of its circulation date unless a party to the dispute formally notifies the DSB of its decision to appeal or the DSB decides by consensus not to adopt the report. Thus, it is no longer possible for one of the disputants to block adoption of a panel report. However, if a party appeals, the panel report is not considered for adoption until the appeal process is terminated.

The DSU creates a new mechanism for the appeal of final panel reports to a standing Appellate Body.[173] The Appellate Body is composed of seven persons appointed by the DSB, three of whom will hear a particular appeal. The members of the Appellate Body must be persons of recognized authority with no government affiliation and possessing clear expertise in law and international trade in services. Only the parties to the dispute may appeal a panel report, and the appeal is limited to issues of law addressed in the panel report and legal interpretations given by the panel. Members of the Appellate Body must be representative of the WTO membership. The Appellate Body may uphold, modify or reverse the panel's legal findings and conclusions. As a general rule, the appellate procedure should be terminated within sixty days, and in no cases must it exceed ninety days. The report of the Appellate Body is circulated to Members and, within thirty days thereafter, it must be adopted by the DSB and unconditionally accepted by the disputing parties unless the DSB decides by consensus not to adopt the report.

As a general rule, the time period from the date the DSB establishes a panel to the date the DSB considers the panel or Appellate Body report for adoption must not exceed nine months when the panel report is not appealed or twelve months in the event the panel report is appealed.[174]

The aim of the GATS dispute settlement procedure differs depending on the reason for the dispute. Where the complaint concerns the failure by another Member to carry out its obligations or specific commitments under the Agreement, the panel or Appellate Body recommends to the defaulting Member the measures that

172 DSU, Article 16.

173 DSU, Article 17.

174 DSU, Article 20.

it should take in order to comply with its obligations or specific commitments.[175] Compensation is only utilized if immediate compliance is impracticable and then only on a temporary basis until compliance is achieved.[176] Where, however, the complaint concerns a measure by another Member that does not conflict with GATS but which is found by the DSB to be nullifying or impairing a benefit that the complaining Member could reasonably have expected to accrue to it under a specific commitment, there is no obligation to withdraw the measure.[177] Instead, the panel or Appellate Body recommends that the Members concerned enter into negotiations with the aim of agreeing upon a mutually satisfactory compensatory adjustment.[178] This adjustment may include the modification or withdrawal of the offending measure.

The DSB supervises the implementation of its recommendations by the Member concerned.[179] At a DSB meeting held within thirty days of the adoption of the panel or Appellate Body report, the Member must inform the DSB of its intentions concerning the report's recommendations. If a Member fails to comply, within a reasonable period of time as determined by the DSB, with a recommendation to enter into negotiations for compensation or if no agreement on compensation is reached within twenty days after the reasonable period of time has elapsed, any party having invoked the dispute settlement procedure may request authorization from the DSB to suspend the application of obligations and specific commitments under GATS to the Member concerned.[180] The DSB must authorize this suspension of obligations within thirty days after the reasonable period of time has elapsed unless it decides by consensus to reject the request for suspension. Arbitration is to be used when the Member concerned objects to the scope of the proposed suspension or argues that the principles and procedures have not been adhered to. The arbitration is carried out by the original panel if it can be reconstituted or, failing that, by an arbitrator selected by the Director-General.

Where a Member fails to follow, within a reasonable period of time as determined by the DSB, a recommendation to comply with its obligations or specific commitments under GATS, it must come to an agreement on compensation with the complaining Member. If no agreement is forthcoming within twenty days after the reasonable period of time has elapsed, the consequences are as outlined in the preceding paragraph.

As an alternative method of dispute settlement, the Understanding permits the disputing parties to utilize arbitration where they have agreed on this form of dispute

175 DSU, Article 19.

176 DSU, Article 22(1).

177 DSU, Article 26(1)(b).

178 GATS, Article XXIII:3; DSU, Article 26(1)(b).

179 DSU, Article 21.

180 DSU, Article 22(2).

resolution.[181] The disputing parties must agree on the arbitration procedure and agree to abide by the arbitral award. The provisions of the Understanding on supervision of the implementation of recommendations and rulings, on compensation and on the authorization of the suspension of concessions, apply *mutatis mutandis* to arbitral awards.

H. FURTHER NEGOTIATIONS ON LIBERALIZATION OF TRADE IN SERVICES

GATS obliges Members to enter into successive rounds of negotiations on specific commitments within five years of the date of entry into force of the WTO Agreement with a view to achieving a greater liberalization of trade in services.[182] Members are also required to enter into negotiations to establish disciplines governing domestic regulation,[183] the safeguard mechanism,[184] government procurement[185] and subsidies.[186]

Negotiations on specific commitments were initiated in January 2000, exactly five years after the entry into force of the WTO Agreement. They are conducted in Special Sessions of the Council for Trade in Services in accordance with the *Guidelines and Procedures for the Negotiations on Trade in Services*. The aim is to advance liberalization through transparent bilateral, plurilateral or multilateral negotiations. The main method of negotiation is the request-offer approach. Participants were supposed to submit initial requests for specific commitments by June 30, 2002 and initial offers by March 31, 2003.[187] As of July 2, 2004, forty-four offers had been received (counting the European Communities as one). This represents sixty-five Members who have submitted an offer, with the most recent being Brazil on June 28, 2004. Apart from least-developed country Members, some fifty-two Members have yet to submit an initial offer. The Special Session has expressed concern at this slow progress.

Progress has been equally slow in the other sets of negotiations, which take place primarily in the Working Party of GATS Rules and are supposed to be completed prior to the conclusion of the negotiations on specific commitments.

Commitments may, of course, be added to or improved autonomously at any time. A Member may seek credit for such autonomous liberalizing measures from its

181 DSU, Article 25.

182 Article XIX.

183 Article VI:4. *See* the comments *supra* in the text.

184 Article X:1. *See* the comments *supra* in the text.

185 Article XIII:2. *See* the comments *supra* in the text.

186 Article XV. These negotiations take place in the Working Party of GATS Rules.

187 Doha Declaration, Point 15.

trading partner through bilateral negotiations provided that the measure meets the following conditions:[188]

- it is subject to scheduling under Part III of GATS and/or affects the termination of an MFN exemption;
- it is compatible with the MFN principle;
- it is undertaken unilaterally by the liberalizing Member since previous negotiations pursuant to Article XIX:3 of GATS;
- it is applicable to any or all service areas.

The credit sought may take the form of a liberalizing measure undertaken by the trading partner, an agreement by the trading partner not to pursue a request addressed to the liberalizing Member or anything else that the two Members agree upon.[189]

II. GENERAL AGREEMENT ON TARIFFS AND TRADE

A. INTRODUCTION

1. The Agreement

GATT was an agreement signed by twenty-three countries in 1947 that came into force on January 1, 1948. For nearly fifty years, it was the sole global agreement that regulated international trade in goods. It was responsible for lowering tariffs from a historic high to an average of under 10%. It also prohibited a number of non-tariff barriers. In 1994, it was incorporated in an updated and amended form as "GATT 1994" into Annex 1A of the WTO Agreement. However, the original agreement still constitutes the major part of GATT 1994. GATT binds all the Members of the WTO, which comprised 147 countries on April 23, 2004.

2. Application of GATT

GATT covers border measures that affect trade in goods between Members of the WTO, as well as internal measures on taxes and charges, sale, offering for sale, purchase, transportation, distribution or use with respect to products imported from another Member. The origin of the goods is what is important. The nationality of the manufacturer is irrelevant.

GATT applies to the metropolitan customs territories of Members and such of their overseas territories that do not enjoy full autonomy in the conduct of their external commercial relations.[190] Territories that possess such autonomy must accede themselves to the WTO Agreement. The GATT rules bind central governments, and Members must also take such reasonable measures as may be

188 *Modalities for the Treatment of Autonomous Liberalization*, Chapter I:3.

189 Modalities, Chapter III:10.

190 This is the implication of Article XII:1 of the WTO Agreement. *See also* GATT, Article XXIV:1.

available to them to ensure observance of these rules by their sub-central governments and authorities.[191]

Given that it deals exclusively with trade in goods, GATT would seem to be irrelevant for this monograph. This is not so, however, as the Agreement affects trade in services in two ways. Firstly, its rules apply to the importation of inputs necessary for the provision of a service. Secondly, GATT applies to those visible service transactions that are regulated as trade in goods even though they are in essence services.[192] An example is cinematographic films. Strictly speaking, films constitute a service that is delivered by way of an object. If the performance that is captured on film were to take place on a stage, there would be no doubt that it is a service rather than a good that is being provided. The fact that the performance is encapsulated in an object that has itself little or no value should not change the essential nature of the transaction. Nevertheless, trade in cinematographic films is classified by national authorities as trade in goods and regulated expressly by GATT.[193]

The GATT rules with respect to internal measures do not apply to government procurement of goods unless they are acquired with a view to commercial resale or use in the production of goods for commercial sale.[194] However, government procurement of goods is covered by the GPA, to which a number of important trading nations are contracting parties.[195]

3. The GATT Approach

Under GATT, all products that are traded between Members are subject to its rules on non-tariff barriers, including internal measures. With respect to tariffs, however, Member negotiate between themselves on the basis of mutual concessions which goods they will place in their Schedule.[196] This is the bottom-down approach adopted also by GATS. However, there are two differences between the approaches of the two agreements. Firstly, the scope of products covered by the GATT Schedules is much broader than the services covered by those in GATS. Secondly, recent negotiations on tariffs have included an across-the-board reduction that applies to all products listed in the Members' Schedules, thus ensuring a broader liberalization.

Every three years Members may modify or withdraw a concession in their Schedule, but they must enter into negotiation with any Members who are significantly

191 Article XXIV:12.

192 *See* the discussion in Chapter One, Section II.

193 Article IV. However, the OECD classifies trade in films as a service transaction in Annex A/H of the Invisibles Code.

194 Article III:8(a).

195 *See* the remarks *supra* in the text.

196 Article XXVIIIbis.

affected in order to reach a mutually satisfactory agreement.[197] Failure to reach agreement exposes the modifying Member to retaliation.[198]

GATT deals separately with national treatment in Article III. The other provisions on non-tariff and tariff barriers are concerned with the entry of products onto the market of other Members. To this extent, we may say that GATT distinguishes between the two concepts.

B. MARKET ACCESS

GATT directly prohibits all quantitative restrictions on the importation of visible services (barriers (a) and (b)) and necessary inputs for the provision of services. (barrier (j)).[199] It also prohibits certain other non-tariff barriers that might restrict importation of these products, such as abuse of countervailing and anti-dumping duties,[200] abusive customs valuation[201] and excessive fees and formalities connected with importation.[202]

GATT, as we have seen, does not directly deal with the problem of high tariffs on visible services and inputs for services, which also have the potential, respectively, to restrict importation or render the provision of the service too expensive. Instead, as with specific commitments in GATS, reductions in tariffs are negotiated between Members. The tariff concessions resulting from these negotiations are incorporated into a Schedule for each Member, which must apply to the commerce of other Members treatment no less favorable than the tariff rates set out in its Schedule.[203] Members may modify or withdraw any tariff concessions every three years.[204] They must negotiate a mutually advantageous agreement with other interested Members, failing which these Members may withdraw substantially equivalent concessions initially negotiated with the modifying Member.[205]

C. NATIONAL TREATMENT

GATT prohibits the levying of discriminatory taxes or other charges against foreign products (measure (h))[206] and requires that they be accorded no less favorable treatment than domestic products in respect of all laws, regulations and requirements affecting their internal sale, offering for sale, purchase, transportation, dis-

197 Article XXVIII:1 and 2.

198 Article XXVIII:3.

199 Articles XI. A list of measures that constitute market access barriers is set out in List 3.

200 Article VI, supplemented by the *Agreement on Implementation of Article VI.*

201 Article VII, supplemented by the *Agreement on Implementation of Article VII.*

202 Article VIII.

203 Article II:1(a).

204 Article XVIII:1.

205 Article XXVIII:2,3.

206 Article III:2. A list of measures constituting discrimination in law is set out in List 4.

tribution or use (*inter alia* measures (b) and (e)).[207] National treatment here applies only to discrimination in law, but the scope of national treatment is broadened by the fact that the comparison is made between the foreign product and directly competitive or substitutable domestic products. Thus a lower tax on beer, which was mostly produced domestically, as against a higher tax on wine, which was mainly imported, was found to be discriminatory as wine and beer were considered directly competitive products. This approach is also applicable to visible services.

Screen quotas requiring the exhibition of films of national origin that are maintained in accordance with Article IV of GATT are exempt from the national treatment provision.[208] GATT requires that such quotas take the form of a specified minimum proportion of the total screen time actually utilized over a specified period of not less than a year.[209] This proportion is computed on the basis of screen time per theater per year or the equivalent thereof. In the EU, these quotas are applied on a European rather than a national basis.[210] The practical effect of these quotas is to reduce the exhibition of foreign films, which is equivalent to a quantitative restriction on them (measure (r)).

State enterprises or any enterprise that enjoys, formally or in effect, exclusive or special privileges must conform to the principle of national treatment in their purchases of visible services[211] (part of measure (g)), unless the visible services are for immediate or ultimate consumption in governmental use.[212]

D. DOMESTIC REGULATION

National treatment in GATT does not extend to discrimination in fact, and therefore the non-discriminatory domestic regulation of trade in goods is permitted. However, GATT requires that all laws, regulations and administrative decisions affecting the importation, sale, distribution and transport of visible services and inputs be published promptly and administered in a uniform, impartial and reasonable manner (measure (g)).[213] GATT also provides for the impartial review of administrative action regarding customs matters.[214]

---

207 Article III:4.

208 Article III:10.

209 Article IV(a). One could argue that these quotas are no longer justified. They were established in the immediate post-war years to deal with a scarcity of available outlets that no longer exists in a world of multiplex cinemas, multichannel television and video machines.

210 *See* Articles 5 and 6 of Council Directive 89/552 on the coordination of certain provisions laid down by law, regulation or administrative action in Member States concerning the pursuit of television broadcasting activities (OJ L298/89), as amended by Directive 97/36 (OJL202/97).

211 Article XVII:1(a).

212 Article XVII:2.

213 Article X:1, 3(a). A list of measures that come within domestic regulation is set out in List 6.

214 Article X:3(b), (c).

E. MOST-FAVORED-NATION TREATMENT

Article I:1 of GATT contains the traditional MFN principle. In the context of services, it requires Members of the WTO to grant to all other Members any advantage, favor, privilege or immunity that they grant to any other country with respect to the importation of visible services or necessary inputs for services. Certain historical preferences existing at the time the GATT was signed in 1947 are exempt from this MFN obligation,[215] but few of these are still relevant. More importantly, GATT permits Members to reserve a minimum proportion of screen time for films from particular foreign countries as long as this proportion does not exceed the level in effect on April 10, 1947.[216]

GATT contains a general exemption from its provisions for agreements setting up free trade areas or customs unions,[217] which has particular relevance for the MFN obligation. The whole purpose of these economic integration agreements is to liberalize trade between the member states beyond the level that exists under the WTO rules. They must thus be allowed to accord each other treatment that is more favorable than that accorded to their other trading partners. The GATT permits this derogation from the MFN obligation as long as the agreements provide for the elimination of substantially all discriminatory restrictions on trade in goods between the member countries and do not result in treatment of Members outside the agreement which is worse than that existing prior to the agreement.

The MFN rule has more relevance for visible services than necessary inputs. Unless an input is only available from a particular country, discrimination among the Members supplying this input is unimportant as long as it is available at a reasonable price to the service provider.

State enterprises or any enterprise that enjoys, formally or in effect, exclusive or special privileges must conform to the MFN principle in their purchases of visible services[218] (part of barrier (g)), unless the visible services are for immediate or ultimate consumption in governmental use.[219]

F. GENERAL EXCEPTIONS TO THE RULES

1. Safeguard Exception

The safeguard exception set out in Article XIX of GATT must be interpreted in accordance with the *Agreement on Safeguards* (Safeguards Agreement). Safeguard measures may be applied if a product is being imported into the territory of a Member in such increased quantities, absolute or relative to domestic production, such as to cause or threaten serious injury to domestic industry producing like or

215 Article I:2,3.

216 Article IV(c). Given the explosion since 1947 in the exportation of foreign films, this now represents a very small proportion of screen time.

217 Article XXIV. Nowadays, most customs unions take the form of a common market.

218 Article XVII:1(a).

219 Article XVII:2.

directly competitive products.[220] The measures may take the form of quantitative restrictions or a tariff surcharge and must be applied on an MFN basis.[221] They may last a maximum of eight years.[222] Compensation must be agreed with the exporting Members effected, failing which retaliation will be authorized.[223]

A provider of services who is unfortunate enough to have a necessary input fall victim to safeguard measures taken by the host country in which the service is to be supplied is unlikely to benefit either from the maximum duration of the measures or any compensatory adjustments.

2. Balance-of-Payments Exception

As in GATS, Members are permitted under GATT to take measures to safeguard their external financial position or balance-of-payments situation subject to the following conditions:[224]

- they must be applied on an MFN basis,[225] subject to some exceptions;[226]
- they must not exceed what is necessary to deal with the problem;[227]
- they must be temporary and phased out progressively as the situation improves;[228]
- they must avoid unnecessary damage to the commercial or economic interests of any other Member.[229]

Unlike GATS, GATT does not provide for the use of exchange restrictions, which it leaves exclusively up to the IMF.[230] Instead it provides for the imposition of quantitative restrictions, but these measures have a much more negative impact on trade than price-based measures such as tariff surcharges or import deposit requirements. As a result the 1994 *Understanding on the Balance-of-Payments Provisions of the General Agreement on Tariffs and Trade* (BoP Understanding), calls

220 GATT, Article XIX:1(a), Safeguards Agreement, Article 2(1).

221 GATT, Article XIX:1(a); Safeguards Agreement, Article 2(2).

222 Safeguards Agreement, Article 7(3).

223 GATT, Article XIX:3; Safeguards Agreement, Article 8.

224 Article XII:1.

225 Article XIII:1.

226 These are set out in Article XIV. For example, a temporary derogation from the MFN principle in the case of quotas is acceptable where it concerns a small part of a Member's external trade and where the benefits of the derogation outweigh any injury to other Members that it may cause.

227 Article XII:2(a).

228 Article XII:2(b).

229 Article XII:3(c).

230 Article XV:2.

for the use of such price-based measures in preference to quantitative restrictions unless the latter alone are capable of dealing with the problem.[231]

3. Economic Integration Exception

This exception permits Members to enter into economic integration agreements under which trade in goods is liberalized between them to a greater degree than under GATT. Clearly, this is primarily an exception to the GATT MFN rule, but it may also entail the withdrawal or modification of tariff concessions. Thus, it is a general exception. It is often referred to as the "regional" exception as most economic integration arrangements are regional by nature.

In order to qualify for this exception, economic integration agreements must provide for the elimination of duties and most other restrictions on substantially all trade in products between the member countries within a reasonable period.[232] An agreement must not have the effect of raising or making more restrictive the general incidence of the duties and regulations of commerce applicable in the member countries.[233] In theory, the WTO may refuse to apply the exception to an integration agreement that does comply with these requirements, but on the whole it has taken a rather lax approach. However, where rates of duty are raised inconsistently with the Schedules of Members parties to an agreement, compensatory adjustments must be negotiated or retaliation will be authorized.[234]

4. General Exception

GATT permits certain general exceptions to the totality of its rules as long as the measures concerned are not applied in a manner that arbitrarily or unjustifiably infringes the MFN principle or constitutes a disguised restriction on international trade in goods.[235] The provision is similar to the equivalent one in GATS, although there are some subtle differences in language.[236] The measures that may potentially affect trade in visible services and/or inputs are those that:

- are necessary to protect public morals;
- are necessary to protect human, animal or plant life or health;
- relate to the importation of gold or silver;
- are necessary to secure compliance with general laws, such those relating to customs enforcement, enforcement of monopolies, protection of intellectual property rights and the prevention of deceptive practices;
- relate to the products of prison labor.

---

231 BoP Understanding, Points 2 and 3.

232 Article XXIV;5(c) and 8.

233 Article XXIV:5(b), (c).

234 Article XXIV:6.

235 Article XX.

236 The GATS provision is discussed *supra* in the text.

5. Security Exception

This exception is the same of that in GATS, which is in fact modeled upon it.[237] However, there is no reporting requirement under GATT.

6. Non-Application of Agreement

Any Member may withhold or withdraw the application of any tariff concession in its Schedule where the Member with which the concession was initially negotiated has not become or has ceased to be a Member.[238] A Member does not apply the tariff concessions in its Schedule, or indeed the whole Agreement, to a Member if it or the other Member did not consent to such application at the time either became a Member unless they have entered into tariff negotiations with each other.[239]

G. DISPUTE SETTLEMENT

Members may have recourse to the dispute settlement procedure under GATT whenever they consider that a benefit accruing to them under the Agreement is being nullified or impaired as a result of:[240]

a) the failure by another Member to carry out its obligations under GATT;

b) the application of any measure by another Member even if it does not conflict with GATT; or

c) the existence of any other situation.

The procedure follows that laid out in the DSU, which is described above in the context of GATS.[241] However, in the case of (c), once the report of the panel or Appellate Body has been circulated, it is up to the WTO to decide what to do next.[242] It may make appropriate recommendations to the Members concerned or give a ruling.[243] It may even authorize retaliation by the complaining party where the circumstances are serious enough to justify such action, in which case the other Member is free to withdraw from GATT.

---

237 The GATS provision is discussed *supra* in the text.

238 Article XXVII.

239 Article XXXV:1

240 Article XXIII:1.

241 *See supra* in the text.

242 DSU, Article 26(2).

243 Article XXIII:2.

H. FURTHER NEGOTIATIONS ON LIBERALIZATION OF TRADE IN GOODS

Like GATS, GATT provides for Members to enter into negotiations from time to time in order to reduce tariffs and non-tariff barriers on trade in goods.[244] To this end, negotiations are presently underway under the auspices of the Doha Declaration (2001).[245] There is nothing to prevent Members from reducing or abolishing their tariffs unilaterally.

III. ARTICLES OF AGREEMENT OF THE INTERNATIONAL MONETARY FUND

A. INTRODUCTION

1. The Articles

Together with the GATT, the IMF was one of the foundation stones of the post-war organization of the world economy. Its role has changed somewhat over the years from an enforcer of fixed exchange rates to a lender of last resort for the restructuring of failing national economies. Its membership is global and exceeds even that of the WTO, notably by the inclusion of the Russian Federation, which is not yet a member of the WTO.

The IMF Articles were adopted at the United Nations Monetary and Financial Conference at Bretton Woods on July 22, 1944. They entered into force on December 27, 1945. They have been amended on a number of occasions, notably in 1976 to permit the use of floating exchange rates.[246] They bind all Members of the IMF, which comprised 184 countries at the end of 2003.

2. Application of the IMF Articles

The IMF rules apply to all measures that restrict the making of payments and transfers for current international transactions,[247] which include all service transactions.[248] They do not, however apply to transfers of capital,[249] such as foreign direct investment and transfers in the form of dividends or profits.[250] To the extent that travel is a service, the IMF rules probably apply to access to foreign currency for the purpose of traveling to receive or provide a service.

---

244 Article XXVIIIbis. This Article refers only to tariff negotiations, but non-tariff barriers have been included in the negotiations since the 1960's.

245 Point 16.

246 Article IV:2(b).

247 Article VIII:2, 3.

248 Article XXX(d)(1).

249 *See* Article XXX(d).

250 Article VI:3.

The IMF Articles are binding on the Members of the Fund without any precision as to which level of government. However, as exchange matters are invariably under the control of the central government, there is no problem with sub-central authorities. Overseas territories are represented by the country responsible for their monetary affairs.[251] The nationality of the persons involved in any particular current international transaction is irrelevant.

By their very nature, the IMF rules apply only to cross-border services.

The IMF rules are often incorporated into agreements affecting trade in services or, as in the case of GATT, apply instead of the provisions of the Agreement. An exception is GATS, which has its own provision on the introduction of exchange restrictions in the case of balance-of-payment problems, albeit with the condition that these restrictions be in accordance with the IMF Articles.[252]

3. The IMF Approach

The IMF Articles define themselves the obligations that Members assume on joining the Fund. Exemptions from certain rules may be granted by the IMF, but there is no question of Members picking and choosing the extent of their obligations.

The IMF Articles are only relevant to the issues of market access and MFN treatment, although they contain no explicit provisions on the latter.

B. MARKET ACCESS

The IMF prohibits the imposition of both direct and indirect exchange controls[253] on payments for services and probably access to foreign currency for the purpose of traveling to receive or provide a service (barrier (l)).[254] It also requires currency convertibility,[255] which is a prerequisite in a country for free access to foreign exchange. However, the IMF rules do not deal with capital transfers and thus do not eliminate barrier (k) and have no relevance for barrier (c). As a result, many agreements have specific provisions dealing with capital transfers.[256]

C. MOST-FAVORED-NATION TREATMENT

There is nothing in the IMF Articles that requires exchange restrictions to be applied on an MFN basis. However, in order to be effective, they have to be, and are always, applied in this way.

---

251 Article XXXI:2(g).

252 Articles XI:2 and XII:2(b).

253 *See* the discussion in Chapter One, Section VII.B. on the two types of exchange controls.

254 A list of market access barriers in found in List 3.

255 Article VIII:4.

256 *E.g.* GATS, note 8 to Article XVI; NAFTA, Article 1109:1.

D. GENERAL EXCEPTIONS TO THE RULES

There are two exceptions to the IMF rules that exist today. In the first place, a Member joining the IMF may maintain its existing restrictions on payments and transfers for current international transactions.[257] They must, however, remove them as soon as practicable. Secondly, and more importantly, the Fund may itself authorize Members of the IMF to apply exchange restrictions, normally in order to deal with balance-of-payments problems.[258] Formerly, the Fund was quite generous in according such authorizations, but it has become considerably more rigid in recent years. Indeed, the removal of existing exchange restrictions is often part of its conditions for restructuring loans.

E. ENFORCEMENT OF THE RULES

The IMF Articles do not provide for any dispute settlement procedure. Instead they provide for three stages of sanction for Members that flaunt the IMF rules. As a first step, a recalcitrant Member may be declared ineligible to use the general resources of the Fund.[259] If, after a reasonable period following such ineligibility, the Member persists in its failure to fulfill its obligations under the IMF Articles, its voting rights as a Member may be suspended.[260] Finally, if, after the expiry of a reasonable period following such suspension, the Member has not mended its ways, it may be required to withdraw from membership in the IMF.[261] It should, however, be noted that the second and third sanctions require quite large majorities in favor.

257 Article XIV:2.

258 Article VIII:2, 3.

259 Article XXVI:2(a).

260 Article XXVI:2(b).

261 Article XXVI:2(c).

CHAPTER THREE

LIBERALIZATION OF TRADE IN SERVICES UNDER THE OECD INSTRUMENTS

I. INTRODUCTION

A. THE ORGANIZATION FOR ECONOMIC COOPERATION AND DEVELOPMENT

The OECD was established in 1961 as a group of like-minded countries coming together to discuss, develop and refine economic and social policies. Its aims are to encourage economic growth and high employment with financial stability among its Members and contribute to the expansion of global trade. It is often considered a "rich man's club" as its Members are mainly the prosperous countries of Western Europe, Canada, the United States, Australia, New Zealand and Japan. Over the last few years, however, membership has expanded to less prosperous countries from Central Europe (Czech Republic, Hungary, Slovakia and Poland) as well as Mexico and South Korea. Turkey, another relatively poor country, was one of the original Members. Currently, there are thirty countries that are Members of the OECD.

B. THE INSTRUMENTS

The main OECD instruments that apply to trade in services on a general basis are the Invisibles Code (1973), the Capital Movements Code (1982) and the *Declaration on International Investment and Multinational Enterprises* (1976) (the Declaration). The two Codes are binding decisions of the OECD Council, but the Declaration is exhortatory in nature. However, the *Third Revised OECD Decision on National Treatment* (1991), which supplements the Declaration, is also in the form of a binding decision of the OECD Council. There is also the *OECD Arrangement on Officially-Supported Export Credits* (1978), which, though it cannot be said to regulate trade in services, affects it peripherally through its rules on credits for the export of services. All these instruments apply only to Members of the OECD, which comprised thirty countries as of August 1, 2004.

C. THE CODES

1. Application of the Codes

The Codes apply to "[a]ny law, decree, regulation, policy and practice taken by the authorities which may restrict the conclusion or execution of operations covered by the Codes. . . ."[1] Measures taken by self-regulatory authorities are treated as equivalent to measures taken by governments, and state enterprises are treated as if they were private enterprises.[2]

In principle, the Codes bind all levels of government in the Members but there are exceptions for the United States and Canada. The US exception is wider and simply exempts action by a State of the United States that comes within the jurisdiction of that State.[3] However, if another Member considers that its interests under the Codes are being prejudiced by such action and notifies the OECD, the US government undertakes to bring the provisions of the Code to the attention of the competent authorities of the State concerned together with an appropriate recommendation.[4] The Canadian exception takes the form of an undertaking by the government of Canada to carry out the provisions of the Codes to the fullest extent compatible with the constitutional system of Canada.[5]

Members are supposed to use their best efforts to ensure that the measures of liberalization required by the Codes are applied within their overseas territories as well.[6] They must also endeavor to apply them to all members of the IMF.[7]

The Capital Movements Code is the only multilateral agreement that requires the liberalization of all long and short-term capital movements.[8] They are listed in Annex A and include the removal of restrictions on inward direct investment and capital flows that are part of an underlying service transaction. The Code also grants a right to create, extend or acquire an enterprise, subsidiary or branch in another Member.[9] This is the so-called right of establishment.[10]

---

1 *OECD Codes of Liberalization of Capital Movements and of Current Invisible Operations: User's Guide* (2003) (User's Guide), p. 24.

2 User's Guide p. 23.

3 Codes, Annex C, Point 1.

4 Codes, Annex C, Point 2.

5 Codes, Annex D, Point 1.

6 Codes, Article 1(c).

7 Codes, Article 1(d)

8 Capital Movements Code, Articles 1(a) and 2(a).

9 Capital Movements Code, Annex A, List A/I.

10 *See* the comments in Chapter One, Section VII.B.

The importance of this Code for trade in services is twofold. Clearly the removal of restrictions on inward direct investment and other capital flows and the right of establishment remove major barriers ((c), (d) and part of barrier (k))[11] to the supply of services. Secondly, by removing exchange restrictions on the transfer of funds, the Code also liberalizes the underlying transaction, which may be a cross-border service. For example, permitting the flow of capital borrowed by a resident enterprise from a lender in another Member necessarily entails liberalization of the credit transaction itself.[12]

The Invisibles Code directly liberalizes a number of cross-border services, which are set out in Annex A.[13] The sectors involved are certain business services (repair, assembly, processing, finishing, construction), services connected with foreign trade (e.g. commission and brokerage, warehousing, transit), transport, insurance, banking and investment services, travel and tourism and films.[14] Travel includes travel to receive or provide a service.[15] Government procurement of these services is not excluded by the Code. The inclusion of films is interesting as, although trade in films is by its very nature a trade in services, it is normally treated as trade in goods.[16] The Invisibles Code also liberalizes capital flows in the form of dividends and profits (barrier (k)).[17]

The Codes apply to all cross-border transactions between different OECD countries that come within their scope.[18] Although the Codes distinguish between residents and non-residents of an OECD Member, the status of the persons involved in the transaction is essentially irrelevant. As long as the transaction is between two OECD Members, it is covered by the Codes. The Codes do not apply to purely domestic transactions between residents of the same country. Thus, they cover all modes of providing services except through commercial presence (Mode 3).

2. Approach of the Codes

The Codes set out the transactions that they cover, and these are listed in Annex A. They are not chosen freely by OECD Members, who may, however, lodge reservations relating to their obligations under the Codes.[19] These are listed in Annex B. They may be lodged when an item is added to Annex A, or when obligations

11 A list of market entry barriers is found in List 3.

12 Capital Movements Code, Annex A, List B/V/D/4. *See* too User's Guide, p.30.

13 Invisibles Code, Article 1(a) and 2(a).

14 *See* Invisibles Code, Annex A.

15 Invisibles Code, Annex A/G.

16 *See* the discussion in Chapter One, Section II.

17 Invisibles Code, Annex A/F. It may seem strange that the Invisibles Code cover these capital movements. The reason is that they are considered services for balance-of-payments purposes. *See* Chapter One, Section II.

18 Codes, Article 1(a).

19 Codes, Article 2(b).

relating to an item are extended or when obligations relating to an item begin to apply to a Member. In the case of capital movements, Annex A contains two lists, A and B. The general rule applies to items in List A, but reservations may be lodged at any time in respect of an item in List B. There are still reservations to the Capital Movements Code, but by and large capital controls have been abolished in OECD countries. More reservations still apply in the case of the Invisibles Code. The United States, for example, maintains reservations that reduce the scope of its obligations in maritime, inland waterway and road transport services.

The Codes do not distinguish between market access and national treatment. They are based instead on the uniform approach of removing restrictions to the conclusion or execution of the operations that they cover. Discrimination in law between residents and non-residents of an OECD Member, which is a breach of the national treatment principle, is considered to be such a restriction in the same way as market access barriers.[20] National measures that apply equally to residents and non-residents normally come under domestic regulation, but where they discriminate in fact against non-residents so as to put them at a serious disadvantage, they are treated as restrictions.[21] National measures that do not prevent operations but render them more costly are likewise considered to constitute restrictions.[22]

Liberalization under the Codes is based on four major principles: standstill, rollback, unilateralism and non-discrimination between OECD Members. Only the Capital Movements Code has an explicit standstill provision,[23] but the OECD has made it clear that this principle applies to both Codes.[24] Members may only maintain or introduce restrictions or extend existing restrictions by lodging reservations against their obligations under the Codes, and, with the exception of certain capital movements in List B to Annex A of the Capital Movements Code,[25] reservations may only be reduced or deleted, not added or extended. Reservations are considered temporary by nature and are subject to periodic peer review with a view to their withdrawal or modification (rollback).[26] Rollback occurs not as the result of negotiations for mutual concessions but as a unilateral act without the expectation of any concession in return from other OECD Members. Moreover, measures of liberalization must be applied in full to all OECD Members without discrimination regardless of

---

20 User's Guide, p. 25.

21 User's Guide, p. 48.

22 *Ibid.*

23 Capital Movements Code, Article 1(e).

24 User's Guide, p. 11.

25 *See* Capital Movements Code, Article 2(b)(iv). However, this exception is no longer important as capital controls have been completely abolished in practically all OECD countries.

26 Codes, Articles 2(b) and 12.

their reservations or any derogations which they may be invoking.[27] This principle of unilateralism is based on the idea that liberalization of capital movements or invisible operations is as much in a Member's own interest as it is an advantage for its trading partners.

3. The Codes and GATS

The importance of the Codes has certainly decreased since the advent of GATS, which to some extent supersedes the Invisibles Code and also prohibits restrictions on foreign direct investment and on capital transfers related to trade in services. Yet, the Codes retain certain advantages over GATS that justify their retention.

Unlike GATS, where Members of the WTO choose which service sectors they wish to liberalize (the "bottom-up" approach), the Codes themselves define the economic activities to which they apply (the "top-down" approach). This means that they have a potentially wider application. Let us examine two examples. Under GATS, capital transfers that are an essential part of an underlying service transaction are only liberalized if the particular service transaction is included in a Member's Schedule. Under the Capital Movements Code, all long and short-term capital transfers are liberalized, which in turn liberalizes any service transactions that underlie them. Secondly, although the coverage of the Invisibles Code is by no means as comprehensive as the Capital Movements Code, it does liberalize more or less completely the service sectors that it covers, which includes such major economic activities as banking, insurance, investment and transport services as well as travel and tourism. There is also no general exception for government procurement of services under the Invisibles Code. Of course, the obligations of Members under the Codes are subject to specific reservations, but the fact that they cannot pick and choose the activities that they wish to liberalize is an improvement on the GATS approach.

The Codes also take a broader approach than GATS to the national measures that must be prohibited in order to secure liberalization. GATS takes an exclusive approach that sets out an exhaustive list of market barriers that must be abolished but which leaves out certain barriers and also assumes that governments are incapable of devising new barriers that do not appear on the list The Codes, by contrast, prohibit inclusively any national measures that restrict the performance of the activities to which they apply. As in GATS, Members may limit their obligations by lodging reservations, but they do so on the basis of a much broader coverage.

27 Codes, Article 8.

Finally, the Codes provide for a right of establishment (barrier (d))[28] and the free flow of dividends and profits from the host country to the home country (part of barrier (k)).[29] GATS does not cover dividends and profits and, although in principle it provides for a right of establishment,[30] this is frequently curtailed in Members' Schedules.

D. THE DECLARATION

The Declaration applies to Argentina, Brazil and Chile in addition to the Members of the OECD. The adhering countries agree to endeavor to ensure that their territorial subdivisions apply the Declaration.[31] They also undertake to consider applying the Declaration to other than adhering countries.[32]

The Declaration has a more narrow scope than the Codes, for it concerns exclusively the application of the national treatment principle to the provision of services by commercial presence. It applies to and protects undertakings operating in the territory of an adhering country that are owned or controlled directly or indirectly by nationals of another adhering country.[33] The Declaration contains no definition of nationality, which term may or may not be restricted to citizens.

The Declaration does not affect the right of adhering countries to regulate the entry of foreign investment or the conditions of establishment of foreign enterprises (barriers (c) and (d)).[34]

Like the Codes, the Declaration is superseded to a large extent by GATS, except that the commitment under the Declaration cannot be limited in the same way as national treatment commitments under GATS. Exceptions are only permitted to maintain public order, protect essential security interests and fulfill commitments relating to international peace and security.

E. THE OECD ARRANGEMENT

Although it has no relevance for the liberalization of trade in services, which is at the heart of this monograph, mention should be made of the Arrangement that the OECD elaborated in 1978 to put an end to the feud between the Europeans (the French, in particular) and the United States over the use of government credits for the export of goods and/or services. The Arrangement has been updated various

---

28 Capital Movements Code, Annex A/I.

29 Invisibles Code, Annex A/F/1 and 2.

30 GATS, Article XXVIII(c)(iii).

31 Declaration, Article II:3.

32 Declaration, Article II:2.

33 Declaration, Article II:1.

34 Declaration, Article II:4.

times, and in 1998 it was substantially revised. It applies to Australia, Canada, the EU,[35] Japan, South Korea, New Zealand, Norway, Switzerland and the United States[36] and covers all official support by or on behalf of a government.[37] The three basic principles are that there must be a minimum down payment of 15%,[38] repayment must be made in five or ten years depending on the GNI of the recipient country,[39] and a minimum interest rate must be charged based on Commercial Interest Reference Rates (CIRRs).[40] Countries are divided into Categories I and II, and the repayment term of five years that applies to Category I countries may be extended to eight and a half years. CIRRs should, *inter alia*, represent final commercial lending interest rates in the domestic market of the currency concerned.

II. MARKET ACCESS

The Codes apply, subject to any reservations, to any measures "taken by the authorities which may restrict the conclusion or execution of operations covered by the Codes."[41] This formulation essentially covers all the market barriers to trade in those services covered by the Codes.[42] However, the Codes single out certain of these barriers.

The Capital Movements Code specifically provides for foreign direct investment and a right of establishment (barriers (c) and (d)).[43] With respect to foreign direct investment, this right obviously includes the ability to make the capital transfers necessary to set up in the host country, but an exception is made where the amount involved or other factors mean that the investment would have an exceptionally detrimental effect on the interests of the Member concerned. Establishment means the creation of an undertaking, subsidiary or branch or the purchase of an existing undertaking. It does not include a right of personal establishment, i.e. the right to settle or work in another OECD country.[44]

---

35 Among the ten states that joined the European Union on May 1, 2004, only the Czech Republic is a party to the Arrangement.

36 Arrangement, Point 3.

37 Arrangement, Point 5.

38 Arrangement, Point 9(a).

39 Arrangement, Point 10 and 11.

40 Arrangement, Point 18.

41 User's Guide, p. 24.

42 *See* List 3 for a list of such barriers.

43 Capital Movements Code, Annex A/I.

44 User's Guide, p. 62. *See* the discussion on barrier (d) in Chapter Two, Section VII.B.

The Invisibles Code liberalizes payment for the services that it covers,[45] capital outflows in the form of dividends or profits[46] and access to foreign currency in order to travel to receive a service.[47] This means that the two Codes, taken together, deal completely with currency barriers ((k) and (l)) within the scope of their application. With respect to banking and financial services, the Invisibles Code also provides for access to any private professional association, self-regulatory body, securities exchange or other body where membership is necessary to engage in these activities.[48] This provision, which deals with parts of barriers (a) and (f) may also apply to other service sectors covered by the Code.

The OECD User's Guide for the two Codes mentions two further market access barriers, namely nationality and residence requirements (Categories 1 and 2).[49] As the Guide points out, both defeat all possibility of the provision of cross-border services, although purely formal residency requirements, such as a mailing address, are acceptable. Monopolies (barrier (m)), on the other hand, are permitted.[50]

It is not easy to discern which measures the Codes categorize as market access barriers as they do not separate out the concepts of national treatment and market access. However, the comments in the User's Guide certainly indicate that it considers nationality and residency requirements to be barriers to market access. To this extent, therefore, the approach of the Codes in this matter is more akin to that taken in this monograph than in GATS.

As far as completeness is concerned, the OECD Codes effectively cover all market access barriers because of their inclusive approach, subject, of course, to any reservations taken by the Members.

III. NATIONAL TREATMENT

A. THE CODES

The Codes do not contain a specific national treatment provision. However, as mentioned earlier, discrimination in law against non-residents from other OECD countries is a restriction that must be abolished under the Codes, subject to any reservations.[51] Discrimination by monopolies is included.[52] The OECD User's

45 Invisibles Code, Articles 2(a) and 6.

46 Invisibles Code, Annex A/F/1 and 2.

47 Invisibles Code, Annex A/G.

48 Invisibles Code, Annex II to Annex A, Point 6.

49 User's Guide, p. 25.

50 User's Guide, p. 63.

51 Codes, Articles 1(a) and 2(a). *See also* User's Guide, p. 25.

52 User's Guide, pp. 23-24.

Guide singles out a number of such instances of discrimination, such as fiscal discrimination (measures (h), (i), (j) and (k)),[53] but any national measure that discriminates in this way against non-residents is considered to constitute a restriction that must be removed.

The Invisibles Code specifically curtails the exception to national treatment that is permitted under GATT for films.[54] While it accepts screen quotas requiring the exhibition of films of domestic origin during a specific minimum proportion of the total screen time actually utilized over a specific period of not less than one year, it introduces special, more favorable rules for certain types of foreign films. Original versions of feature films from other OECD Members that are in a language foreign to that of the importing Member must be a) excluded from the calculation of the screen quota for domestic films, or b) admitted for exhibition in specialized cinemas that are not subject to the screen quotas, or c) admitted for exhibition in regular cinemas under a global screen quota instead of a screen quota applying to individual cinemas.[55] Short information or documentary films produced in other OECD countries must gradually be excluded from the calculation of the screen quota for domestic films.[56] Any film produced under an international co-production arrangement must enjoy in all the OECD Members involved in the production the same treatment as domestically produced films.[57]

Generally speaking, measures that do not discriminate in law are considered to come under domestic regulation.[58] *A fortiori,* the same applies to any inherent competitive disadvantage arising from the cross-border nature of a transaction. However, where apparently neutral measures put non-residents at a definite disadvantage compared to residents, they become discriminatory in fact and must be removed. Thus, the requirement of incorporation, even where it applies equally to residents and non-residents, may require a non-resident who is already incorporated at home to set up a second incorporated entity in the host country. This is restrictive.[59] On the other hand, where incorporation is not permitted or is restricted to certain forms, the de facto discriminatory effect is less certain and the measure is acceptable.[60] Nationality or residency requirements for directors, managers or employees may have an inhibiting effect on setting up an establishment abroad (measures (d) and (e) on List 5), so they must be examined on a case-by-case basis

53 User's Guide, p. 24.

54 Invisibles Code, Annex V to Annex A. *See also* the discussion in Chapter Two, Section II.C.

55 Invisibles Code, Annex V to Annex A, Point 3.

56 Invisibles Code, Annex V to Annex A, Point 4.

57 Invisibles Code, Annex V to Annex A, Point 8.

58 User's Guide, p. 48.

59 User's Guide, p. 61.

60 *Ibid.* These measures appear as (a) in List 5 on measures that discriminate in fact.

to determine whether they fall within the liberalization obligations of Annex A/I of the Capital Movements Code.

National treatment under the Codes applies to all the services and capital movements that they cover. The Codes do not provide for any specific exceptions to national treatment, although Member may take reservations.

As with market access barriers, it is not easy to discern what measures the Codes characterize as coming under national treatment. It seems clear, however, that, unlike GATS, it does not categorize residency requirements in this way.[61]

Because of its inclusive approach, which regards all discriminatory measures as restrictions to be abolished, the Codes cover, subject to any reservations lodged by the Members, all the measures of discrimination in law set out in List 4 with the exception of access to subsidies (measure (l)), where discrimination is allowed.[62] However, systems of aid for the production of films for cinema exhibition may only be maintained as long as that they do not significantly distort international competition in export markets.[63] The measures on List 5 that constitute discrimination in fact and even the matters on List 6 that normally fall within domestic regulation are also covered to the extent that they put non-residents at a serious disadvantage.

B. THE DECLARATION

The Declaration exhorts the countries adhering to the Declaration, which are the OECD countries together with Argentina, Brazil and Chile, to accord national treatment to enterprises operating in their territory that are owned or controlled directly or indirectly by nationals of other adhering countries.[64] National treatment is described in the Declaration as "treatment . . . no less favorable than that accorded in like situations to domestic enterprises." There is nothing in this wording to suggest that the national treatment obligation extends to discrimination in fact. It does, however, cover all the measures of discrimination in law set out in List 4, but it is subject to the needs of adhering countries to maintain public order, protect their essential security interests and fulfill commitments relating to international peace and security.

The exceptions permitted by the Declaration have been abused by some adhering countries to introduce restrictions that have little to do with public order and security. A 1987 Recommendation of the OECD Council called upon the OECD countries to reconsider the totality of their exceptions to national treatment and to

61 User's Guide, p. 25.

62 User's Guide, p. 64.

63 Invisibles Code, Annex V to Annex A, Point 1.

64 Declaration, Para. II:1.

examine the possibility of removing or relaxing them.[65] It urged them to give priority attention to exceptions in areas where most OECD countries do not find it necessary to maintain restrictions and to exceptions within the services sector. Where these latter exceptions are based on prudential or consumer interests, they should be limited to those areas where such concerns predominate.

The rules on exceptions under the Declaration were further tightened up in 1991 by the *Third Revised OECD Decision on National Treatment* (Revised Decision). Members must now notify the OECD of all measures constituting exceptions to national treatment within sixty days of their adoption or modification.[66] These measures are examined by the Committee on International Investment and Multinational Enterprises at intervals of not more than three years with a view to the Committee making suitable proposals to Members to assist them in withdrawing their exceptions.[67]

IV. DOMESTIC REGULATION

The non-discriminatory domestic regulation of trade in services is permitted under the OECD Codes. Its scope covers any measures that do not discriminate on the basis of residency as long as they do not put non-residents at a serious disadvantage.[68] As a general principle, this includes such matters as licenses, authorizations, qualifications, membership in professional or trade bodies, standards, prudential rules and language competence (measures (a) to (f)[69]).

One matter of domestic regulation that is specifically permitted under the Codes are measures that are necessary to verify the authenticity of transactions or transfers and to prevent evasion of the Members' laws.[70] Members must, however, simplify these formalities as much as possible.

As domestic regulations lose their immunity from liberalization where they put residents from other Members at a serious disadvantage, the Codes require them to be included in the measures and amendments of measures that Members must regularly notify to the OECD.[71] These notifications are reviewed by the Committee on Capital Movements and Invisible Transactions (CMIT) to see whether they are

65 *Recommendation of the Council on Member Country Exceptions to National Treatment and National Treatment related Measures concerning Investment by established Foreign-controlled Enterprises (1987),* Point (a).

66 Revised Decision, Article 1(a).

67 Revised Decision, Articles 2(a) and (c) and 5(a)(i).

68 User's Guide, pp. 48-49.

69 The references are to the illustrative list of matters falling within domestic regulation in List 6.

70 Codes, Article 5.

71 Codes, Article 11(a).

having a *de facto* discriminatory effect, in which case the OECD will make suitable proposals to the Member concerned to remove the restriction.[72]

Alternatively, any Member who considers itself prejudiced by the domestic regulations in force in another Member because of their discriminatory effect may refer the matter to the OECD.[73] Once again, the OECD will make suitable suggestions for the removal or modification of the measure if it is having a restrictive effect.[74] An example where this procedure was used concerned the requirement of full retraining for non-resident professionals, which, though not discriminatory in law, is a huge disincentive to providing cross-border services.[75]

V. MOST-FAVORED-NATION TREATMENT

The Codes explicitly forbid Members to discriminate between other OECD Members when they authorize the conclusion and execution of operations that they have liberalized pursuant to the Codes.[76] Moreover, this MFN obligation must be observed even with respect to Members that have lodged reservations or invoked the derogation provisions of Article 7, as long as these other Members have complied with the procedures for notification and examination of their reservations and derogations.[77] Members must also endeavor to apply MFN treatment to all members of the IMF.[78]

The MFN obligation under the Codes is subject to two exceptions. The first, which is sanctioned by the Codes, permits Members that form part of a special customs or monetary system to liberalize capital movements and invisible transactions between themselves to a greater extent than between themselves and OECD Members outside the system.[79] An example is the European Economic and Monetary Union. Members may not use this exception to introduce new restrictions against OECD Members, and any restrictions against non-OECD countries outside the system must be maintained until these restrictions are removed against non-participating OECD Members.[80]

The second exception exists outside the Codes. It has arisen because some Members only allow residents of another OECD country to invest or establish themselves within their territory on terms similar to those applied to their own

72 Codes, Article 11(d).

73 Codes, Article 16(a).

74 Codes, Article 16(b).

75 User's Guide, p. 49.

76 Codes, Article 9.

77 Codes, Article 8.

78 Codes, Article 1(d).

79 Codes, Article 10.

80 User's Guide, p. 41.

residents by that other Member. This reciprocity approach is particularly prevalent in the financial services sector. The problem is that it leads to discrimination between OECD Members contrary to the MFN treatment required by the Capital Movements Code. As a result, a 1986 Decision of the OECD Council requires all measures and practices concerning reciprocity and/or involving an element of discrimination between OECD Members to be notified to the OECD and progressively abolished.[81] This must be done without extending the scope of restrictions on foreign direct investment or establishment.

The Declaration does not contain specific MFN provisions. However, the national treatment that it requires for enterprises owned or controlled by nationals of another adhering government does not permit any differentiation based on the country of which these persons are nationals.

VI. GENERAL EXCEPTIONS TO THE RULES OF THE CODES

Article 7 of the Codes provides for three possible derogations from the rules of the Codes for economic reasons. In the first place, a Member of the OECD need not take all the measures of liberalization required by Article 2(a) of the Codes if this is justified by its economic and financial situation.[82] The point of this derogation is not entirely clear as it has exactly the same effect as lodging reservations. Once surrendered, neither the reservation nor the derogation can be re-introduced. The only difference between them is that Members must justify invoking Article 7 whereas the making of reservations is freely exercisable.[83]

Once measures of liberalization have been undertaken pursuant to the Codes, a Member may withdraw them if they result in serious economic disturbance in the Member concerned.[84] A Member may suspend them if its overall balance of payments develops adversely at a rate and in circumstances, including the state of its monetary reserves, that it considers serious.[85] In this latter event, a Member must endeavor to ensure that its measures of liberalization are re-instated after eighteen months.[86] Where the Member considers that it will not be able to attain this objective, it must indicate its reasons in a report to the OECD.[87] If the OECD

81 *Decision of the Council regarding measures and practices concerning reciprocity and/or involving discrimination among investors originating in various OECD Member countries in the area of inward direct investment and establishment* (Decision), Point VIII:1 and 2. The Decision is found in Annex E to the Capital Movements Code.

82 Codes, Article 7(a).

83 *Cf.* Codes, Articles 2(b) and 13(b).

84 Codes, Article 7(b).

85 Codes, Article 7(c).

86 Codes, Article 7(d)(ii).

87 Codes, Article 15(b).

does not accept the validity of these reasons, the situation of the Member is examined at a special session of the OECD Council.[88]

All derogations under Article 7 must be applied in compliance with the MFN obligation and in such a way as to avoid unnecessary damage to the commercial or economic interests of other Members.[89]

Members making use of one of the derogations under Article 7 must notify the OECD and give reasons for its action.[90] The OECD through the CMIT considers the notifications and the reasons submitted in order to determine whether the Member is justified in invoking Article 7 and is applying the derogation in accordance with the conditions laid down in that Article.[91] If the OECD approves the derogation, it is reviewed automatically every six months or whenever a review is requested by another Member.[92] If the OECD disapproves the derogation or the manner in which it is being applied, it consults with the Member concerned with a view to restoring compliance with the Code.[93] If, after a reasonable period, the Member continues to invoke Article 7 without justification or applies a derogation that does not meet the conditions of Article 7, the situation of the Member is examined at a special session of the OECD Council.[94]

The other general exception is on the grounds of public order security.[95] The provisions of the Codes do not prevent a Member from taking action that it considers necessary for:

- the maintenance of public order or the protection of public health, morals and safety;
- the protection of its essential security interests; or
- the fulfillment of its obligations relating to international peace and security.

VII. ENFORCEMENT OF OECD OBLIGATIONS

The general philosophy of the OECD is that its Members undertake obligations that are in their interest as much as in that of their OECD trading partners. Thus, it relies on peer review and persuasion rather than an adversarial dispute settlement procedure in order to ensure that its rules are followed as completely as possible. We have already seen this approach in the way that derogations and discrimination in fact are handled. It is an approach that is taken as much by the binding Codes as

88 Codes, Article 15(e).
89 Codes, Article 7(e).
90 Codes, Article 13(a).
91 Codes, Article 13(b).
92 Codes, Article 13(c) and (d).
93 Codes, Article 13(f)(i).
94 Codes, Article 13(f)(ii).
95 Codes, Article 3.

the merely exhortatory Declaration with the result that both end up being essentially gentlemen's agreements.

If a Member considers that another Member has retained, introduced or reintroduced restrictions or exceptions to national treatment that are contrary to its obligations under the Codes or the Declaration, respectively, and if it considers itself to be prejudiced thereby, it may refer the matter to the OECD.[96] The Codes also expressly provide for a reference where a Member fails to respect the MFN principle. The matter is then examined by CMIT or the Committee on International Investment and Multinational Enterprises (CIME) and a report is made to the OECD Council, which consults with the Member concerned with a view to restoring compliance with the Code.[97]

The notification and examination procedure that exists for both the operations covered by the Codes and the national treatment obligation of the Declaration further helps to defuse potential disputes. Members are obliged to notify the OECD of all measures that have a bearing on the activities covered by the Codes and on national treatment, as well as any modifications of such measures.[98] The Organization, through CMIT and CIME, examines these notifications with a view to singling out any non-compliance with the Code or the Declaration. It then makes suitable proposals to assist Members in complying with their obligations.[99]

VIII. FURTHER LIBERALIZATION

Further liberalization under the OECD Codes and Declaration is achieved by peer pressure. Instead of negotiating mutual concessions among themselves, as is the approach in GATS, Members are encouraged to remove or reduce restrictions unilaterally. This process takes place by means of the periodic review by the OECD of reservations and exceptions to national treatment.[100] Prior to this review, Members must notify the OECD which reservations and exceptions they wish to retain and give their reasons for this.[101] The OECD, through CMIT and CIME, then examines the reservations and exceptions, together with the reasons given for their retention, and, where appropriate, makes proposals for their withdrawal.[102]

---

96 Codes, Article 17(a); Decision, Article 3(a).

97 Capital Movements Code, Article 20; Invisibles Code, Article 19; Decision, Article 5(a).

98 Codes, Article 11(1); Decision, Article 1.

99 Codes, Article 11(b); Decision, Article 2(c). The Codes do specifically refer to any such proposals, but this is effectively what happens.

100 Codes, Article 12(b); Decision, Article 2(a).

101 Codes, Article 12(a); Decision, Article 2(b).

102 Codes, Article 12(c); Decision, Article 2(c).

CHAPTER FOUR

REGIONAL LIBERALIZATION OF TRADE IN SERVICES

I. THE NORTH AMERICAN FREE TRADE AGREEMENT (1992) (AND THE CHILE AGREEMENTS)

A. INTRODUCTION

1. The Agreements

NAFTA grew out of the *US-Canada Free Trade Agreement* (US-Canada Agreement). This Agreement represented a major shift in Canadian policy towards the United States. Ever since the institution of the National Policy under the Conservative government of John A. MacDonald in 1879, Canada had followed a policy of high tariffs and imperial preference. Two previous attempts to negotiate a free trade agreement with the United States, in 1911 and 1948, foundered on opposition from those who believed that they would lead to union with the United States and the end of the association with Great Britain. As late as 1957, John Diefenbaker's Conservatives came to power on a policy of re-orienting Canadian trade away from the United States towards Britain.

Nevertheless, trade with the United States continued to expand at the expense of trade with Britain and Europe. Two other events were to push Canada finally to admit the inevitable. In 1965, the United States and Canada signed the *Autopact*, which brought about limited free trade in automobiles and parts. It was extremely successful from a Canadian perspective. Then, in 1973, Britain joined the European Community, thus effectively ending the *raison d'être* of imperial preference. Canada was on its own with its giant neighbor to the south. After a few years hesitation and a Royal Commission in 1986 on Canada's economic future, negotiations with the United States were opened in 1986 and a free trade agreement was signed on January 2, 1988.[1] It created the largest bilateral free trade area in the world.

No sooner had the US-Canada Agreement come into force than Mexico intimated its interest in a similar arrangement with the United States. Canada was at first very wary of this development[2] but joined in the tripartite negotiations in order not to be left out in the cold. The result was NAFTA, which was signed between Canada, Mexico and the United States on December 17, 1992 and came into effect on January 1, 1994. Almost immediately, Chile showed interest in joining the new grouping, but the US Senate refused to sanction negotiations to this end. Canada and Mexico, who were sympathetic to a country that had just thrown off an authoritarian regime, responded by negotiating separate free trade agreements with Chile, which entered into force on July 5, 1997 and August 1, 1999, respectively. The United States has now followed suit and the US-Chile Agreement came into force on January 1, 2004.

These three free trade agreements, taken together with NAFTA, do not have the effect of incorporating Chile completely into the NAFTA system as the four agreements are asymmetrical. The Canada-Chile and Mexico-Chile Agreements do not include financial services or government procurement, whereas NAFTA and the US-Chile Agreement do. Neither the Canada nor the US Agreements deal with standards with respect to services, whereas NAFTA and the Mexico Agreement do so in an albeit very limited way. Unlike the other three agreements, the US-Chile Agreement separates out the concepts of market access and national treatment. Despite these and other less significant differences, the bilateral agreements nevertheless largely follow the wording of NAFTA. Thus, the following discussion, which is limited to NAFTA, applies *mutatis mutandis* to the other agreements except where the contrary is stated. The equivalent provisions of the bilateral agreements are given in the footnotes.

2. Application of NAFTA

NAFTA applies to measures relating to the provision of cross-border services or services supplied from an establishment in a Party.[3] This includes any law, regulation, procedure, requirement or practice.[4] Its provisions bind all levels of government except where the Agreement provides otherwise.[5] Reference to a state

---

1 Ironically, it was concluded by a Conservative government and opposed by the Liberal opposition, which was a total reversal of their historical attitudes towards free trade with the United States.

2 The author shared this feeling. *See* P. Raworth, "A North American Common Market: A Canadian Perspective," in Fatemi (ed.) *International Trade and Finance. A North American Perspective* (Praeger, New York, 1988).

3 Articles 1101:1 and 1201:1. *See also* Articles G-01:1 and H-01:1 (Canada), 9-02:1 and 10-02:1 (Mexico) and 10.1:1 and 11.1:1 (USA).

4 Article 201:1. *See also* Articles B-01:1 (Canada), 2-01 (Mexico) and 2.1:1 (USA).

5 Article 105. *See also* Articles A-05 (Canada), 1-04 (Mexico) and 1.4 (USA).

or province includes local governments of that state or province[6] and, in the case of cross-border trade in services (Modes 1, 2 and 4), any non-governmental body in the exercise of any regulatory, administrative or other governmental authority delegated to it.[7] NAFTA extends to the metropolitan territories of the Parties as well as Puerto Rico in the case of the United States and the islands of Guadalupe and Revillagigedo in the case of Mexico.[8]

NAFTA applies in principle to all services except cross-border air services,[9] which means domestic and international air transportation services, whether scheduled or non-scheduled, and related support services. Aircraft repair and maintenance services performed on aircraft not in service and specialty air services[10] are covered by NAFTA. Special rules apply to financial services[11] and the government procurement of services,[12] while the telecommunications sector is subject both to the general rules on services and its own sectoral rules.[13] Public services such as law enforcement, correctional services, income security or insurance, social security or insurance, social welfare, public education, health and child care may be reserved to the state as long this is done on a non-discriminatory basis.[14] This corresponds to the exception in GATS for services supplied in the exercise of governmental authority.[15] Culture is excluded in the case of Canada for all modes of supply.[16]

NAFTA has explicit provisions on the provision of cross-border services (Modes 1, 2 and 4).[17] The provision of services through Mode 3, however, is covered only

6 Article 201:2. *See also* B-01:2 (Canada), 10-02:2 (Mexico) and 11.1:2 (USA). The US-Chile Agreement only has this provision with respect to cross-border services.

7 Article 1213:1. *See also* Articles H-12:1 (Canada), 10-02:2(b) (Mexico) and 11.1(2)(b) (USA).

8 Annex 201.1.

9 Article 1201:2(b). *See also* Articles H-01:2(b) (Canada), 10-02:3(b) (Mexico) and 11.1:4(b) (USA).

10 Specialty air services comprise such activities as aerial mapping, spraying, surveying, parachute jumping, heli-logging and flight training.

11 Articles 1101:3 and 1201:2(a) and Chapter 14. *See also* Articles 10.1:4 and 11.1:4(a) and Chapter 12 (USA). Neither the Canada-Chile nor Mexico-Chile Agreements apply to financial services.

12 Articles 1108:7(a) and 1201:2(c) and Chapter 10. *See also* Articles 10.7:5(a) and 11.1:4(c) and Chapter 9 (USA). Neither the Canada-Chile nor Mexico-Chile Agreements apply to government procurement.

13 Chapter 13. *See also* Chapters I (Canada), 12 (Mexico) and 13 (USA).

14 Articles 1101:4 and 1201:3(b). *See also* Articles G-01:4 and H-01:3(b) (Canada) and 9-02:4 and 10-02:4(b) (Mexico). With respect to the US-Chile Agreement, *see the following note.*

15 GATS, Article I:3(b). Article 11.1:6 (USA) is modeled on the GATS provision. The exception does not apply to services provided through a commercial presence in the US-Chile Agreement, but this may be an oversight.

16 Annex 2106. *See also* Annex 0-06 (Canada).

17 Article 1213:2. *See also* Articles H-12:2 (Canada), 10-01:1 (Mexico) and 11.12 (USA).

incidentally by Chapter 11[18] on investment and some general provisions of the Agreement.

The NAFTA rules apply to the provision of services by means of cross-border supply or consumption abroad (Modes 1 and 2) as long as the service is provided, respectively, from the territory of one Party into the territory of another Party or in the territory of one Party by a person of that Party to a person of another Party.[19] The situation where a person of one Party receives services in another Party from a person of a third Party is not covered. A person of a Party means a national or enterprise.[20] Nationals include citizens and permanent residents,[21] and an enterprise means an entity constituted or organized under the law of a Party or a branch located in the territory of a Party and, in each case, carrying on business there.[22]

With respect to the provision of services through the presence of natural persons (Mode 4), the service must be supplied in the territory of one Party by a national of another Party, as defined above.[23] There are no requirements with respect to the legal person on behalf of whom the service may be performed, as in GATS,[24] but, on the other hand, the provisions on temporary entry apply only to citizens of a Party.[25] Where services are supplied through Mode 3, the commercial presence must be owned or controlled directly or indirectly by an investor of another Party,[26] who may be a national, as defined above, or an enterprise of the other Party, as defined in Article 201:1.[27] NAFTA contains no definition of the terms "owned" and "controlled."

An interesting fact that emerges from the above rules is that where a service is provided by cross-border supply (Mode 1), there is no requirement that either the sup-

18 *See* Chapters G (Canada), 10 (Mexico) and 11 (USA). However, certain cross-border provisions in the US-Chile Agreement, including those on market access, apply to the supply of services through commercial presence—*see infra* in the text.

19 Article 1213:2(a) and (b). *See* also H-01:2(a) and (b) (Canada), 10-01:1(a) and (b) (Mexico) and 11.12(a) and (b) (USA).

20 Article 201:1. *See* also Articles B-01:1 (Canada), 2-01 (Mexico) and 2.1 (USA).

21 *Ibid.*

22 Article 1213:2. *See* also Articles H-01:2 (Canada), 10-01:1 (Mexico) and 11.12 (USA).

23 Article 1213:2(c). *See* also Articles H-01:2(c) (Canada), 10-01:1(c) (Mexico) and 11.12(c) (USA).

24 Article XXVIII(g), (j) and (m)(i).

25 This is the combined effect of Article 1603:1 and the definition of "business person" in Article 1608. *See* also Articles B-03:1 and B-08 (Canada), 13-01 and 13-04:1 (Mexico) and 14.3:1 and 14.9 (USA).

26 This is the combined effect of Article 1101:1(b) and the definition of an "investment of an investor of a Party" given in Article 1139. *See* also G-01:1(b) and G-40 (Canada), 9-02:1(b) and 9-01 (Mexico) and 10.1:1(b) and 10.27 (USA).

27 Unlike Article 1213:2, this definition does not require the enterprise to be carrying on business in the other Party. *See* also Articles B-01:1 (Canada), 2-01 (Mexico) and 2.1 (USA).

plier or consumer be of a Party. However, all these rules are subject to the provisions on the denial of benefits.[28]

3. The NAFTA Approach

NAFTA sets the scope of liberalization, not the Parties to the Agreement. All service sectors are covered except those which are specifically excluded by NAFTA. This is the so-called "top-down" approach as opposed to the "bottom-up" approach of GATS. However, as with the OECD Codes, which take the same approach as NAFTA, the Parties are allowed a range of reservations, which are set out in a number of Annexes in each Party's Schedule attached to the Agreement.

In the first place the Parties may choose to maintain certain existing non-conforming measures at all levels of government.[29] These reservations relate to their obligations under NAFTA with respect to national and MFN treatment, as well as to performance requirements and nationality or residency requirements for senior management and boards of directors in the case of commercial presence and to the need for a local presence for cross-border services. They are set out in Annex I. The Parties may also renew or amend non-conforming measures. Renewals must be done promptly and amendments may not decrease the conformity of the measure.

Secondly, reservations may be taken by the Parties with respect to specific sectors, subsectors or activities for which they may not only maintain existing but also adopt new or more restrictive measures that do not conform with the obligations mentioned in the preceding paragraph.[30] They are set out in Annex II.

Finally, a Party may reserve certain economic activities to itself and refuse to permit services related to them to be supplied through commercial presence by a provider from another Party.[31] These reservations are listed in Annex III. As yet, only Mexico has listed such reservations. They apply *inter alia* to the petroleum sector, electricity, satellite communications, telegraph and radio-telegraph services, postal services and the railways.

Once a Party has finalized its reservations, no further reservations may be added. A Party's obligations under NAFTA are only subject to modification or withdrawal by means of an exception to the rules or as a retaliatory act permitted under the Agreement.

---

28 *See infra* in the text.

29 Articles 1108:1 and 1206:1. *See also* Articles G-08:1 and H-06:1 (Canada), 9-09:1 and 1007:1 (Mexico) and 10.7:1 and 11.6:1 (USA).

30 Articles 1108:3 and 1206:3. *See also* Articles G-08:2 and H-06:2 (Canada), 9-09:2 and 1007:2 (Mexico) and 10.7:2 and 11.6:2 (USA).

31 Article 1101:2. *See also* Article 9-02:5 (Mexico). However, the Mexico-Chile Agreement provides that, if an investment in an activity appearing in Annex III is permitted, it is covered by the provisions of Chapter 9. Neither the Canada-Chile nor Mexico-Chile Agreements provide for such reservations.

NAFTA does not distinguish between market access and national treatment, except in the provisions on financial services.[32] Instead, it uses national treatment as the principal means for achieving market access as well as for securing equal treatment in the host NAFTA state for providers from other Parties. In the absence of any specific wording extending national treatment to discrimination in fact,[33] it is restricted under the Agreement to discrimination in law. Thus, it is unable to remove all the barriers to market entry. It needs to be supplemented by specific market access provisions in the Agreement. The United States seems to have realized that, in this respect, the NAFTA approach is inadequate as the US-Chile Agreement distinguishes between national treatment and market access. It reproduces the market access provisions of GATS, with the exception of the prohibition on limitations on foreign capital investment, and it does not permit any deviation from them.[34]

Another peculiarity about NAFTA is that it explicitly regulates only cross-border services. The provision of services through Mode 3 is covered only incidentally by Chapter 11[35] on investment and some general provisions of the Agreement. This is probably because the United States does not consider services supplied from a permanent foreign base (Mode 3) to constitute international trade in services.[36] However, as the subsequent discussions reveal, this approach causes problems. The United States now seems aware of them as, in the US-Chile Agreement, the provisions on market access and domestic regulation apply to all four modes of providing services.[37]

NAFTA does not impinge upon the Parties' rights and obligations towards each other under GATS,[38] but in case of conflict between the two, the NAFTA provision applies unless NAFTA provides otherwise in a specific case.[39] The preferential treatment accorded by the Parties to NAFTA to each other does not infringe the MFN principle of GATS as it comes within the economic integration exception.[40]

---

32 Article 1404.

33 *See* the discussion in Chapter One, Section VI.C.

34 Article 11.4 (USA).

35 *See* Chapters G (Canada), 10 (Mexico) and 11 (USA). However, certain cross-border provisions in the US-Chile Agreement, including those on market access, apply to the supply of services through commercial presence—*see infra* in the text.

36 *See* the discussion in Chapter One, Section III.C.

37 Article 11.1:3 (USA).

38 Article 103:1. *See also* Articles A-03:2 (Canada), 1-03:1 (Mexico) and 1.3 (USA).

39 Article 103:2. *See also* Articles A-03:2 (Canada) and 1-03:2 (Mexico). The US-Chile Agreement does not have this provision.

40 GATS, Article V. *See* the discussion in Chapter Two, Section I.F.3.

B. MARKET ACCESS

1. Cross-Border Services

Market access for the supply of services by providers from other Parties by way of Modes 1, 2 and 4 is handled on a general basis in NAFTA through the application of national treatment to such services.[41] The national treatment required is quite broad. The Parties must, of course, treat service providers from the other two Parties no less favorably than their own nationals,[42] but there are two additional rules. Firstly, national treatment under NAFTA means treatment no less favorable than that accorded by a state or province of a Party to service providers from other states or provinces in that Party.[43] Secondly, if a Party accords service providers from third countries treatment that is more favorable than its national treatment, it must extend this better treatment to its partners in NAFTA.[44]

Despite its somewhat broader scope, national treatment under NAFTA remains nevertheless limited to the prohibition of discrimination in law. This means that it only removes the market access barriers that are based on nationality, which, in the case of cross-border services, are barriers (a), (b), (e) and (f) in Category 1.[45] The residency requirements in Category 2 and the operational barriers in Category 3 are unlikely to be covered as they are almost invariably imposed on a non-discriminatory basis.

With respect to nationality requirements (Category 1), Article 1201:1 sets out a list of measures to which national treatment applies. These include measures respecting the delivery of a service (barrier (a) and its use (barrier (b).[46] It also singles out access to and use of distribution and transportation systems (part of barrier (f)),[47] while access to public telecommunications networks is guaranteed to all service suppliers from another Party in Chapter Thirteen on telecommunications

41 Article 1201:1(a) and (b). *See* also Articles H-02:1(a) and (b) (Canada) and 10-02:1(a) and (b) (Mexico). The US-Chile Agreement, on the other hand, has a general market access provision in Article 11.4. Chapter 14 of NAFTA on financial services also distinguishes between market access and national treatment.

42 Article 1202:1. *See* also Articles H-02:1 (Canada), 10-03:1 (Mexico) and 11.2:2 (USA).

43 Article 1202:2. *See* also Articles H-02:2 (Canada), 9.03:3 and 10.03:2 (Mexico) and 11.2:2 (USA). There is a certain irony here. In Canada, in some sectors, there are in fact more restrictions on inter-provincial trade than between Canada and its two NAFTA partners.

44 Article 1204. *See* also Articles H-04 (Canada) and 9-05 (Mexico). This is an odd provision. It must be rarity for a country to extend to third countries treatment more favorable than that which it accords its own nationals. In any case, the Parties to NAFTA would be entitled to this more favorable treatment by virtue of the MFN principle enshrined in Articles 1103 and 1203. The US-Chile Agreement sensibly omits this provision.

45 An illustrative list of market access barriers is given in List 3.

46 Article 1201:1(a) and (b). *See* also Articles H-01:1(a) and (b) (Canada), 10-02:1(a) and (b) (Mexico) and 11.1:1(a) and (b) (USA).

47 Article 1201:1(c). *See* also Articles H-01:1(c) (Canada), 10-02:1(c) (Mexico) and 11.1:1(c) (USA).

(part of barrier (f)).[48] The latter provisions are necessary as telecommunications networks are *sui generis* and need to be regulated by a separate chapter, but it is not clear why distribution and transportation are singled out among networks. However, it must be emphasized that the list in Article 1201:1 is merely illustrative. Access to or use of all networks is guaranteed on a general basis for providers of cross-border services from other Parties by virtue of the national treatment rule.

Article 1201:1 states that national treatment applies as well to the temporary residence in one Party of a service provider from another NAFTA Party (barrier (e)).[49] The detailed rules for persons wishing to supply services by Mode 4 are found in Chapter 16[50] and go some way to eliminating barrier (e). The Chapter applies to "business persons," which include providers of services but, in contrast to the other provisions on cross-border services in the Agreement, exclude persons who are not citizens of a Party.[51] On the other hand, the definition of business persons is broad enough to include both the self-employed and employees.

Service providers from one Party must first qualify for entry into the other Party under the normal immigration rules relating to public health and safety and national security.[52] There is no special treatment under NAFTA for service providers with respect to these basic criteria for entry. Subject to this limitation, however, the Parties must grant temporary entry to service providers from other Parties.[53] Temporary entry is defined as meaning entry into the territory of another NAFTA Party without the intent to establish permanent residence there.[54] It does not give the NAFTA provider any rights with respect to access to the employment market in that Party.[55] Clearly, the provider has the right to stay in the other NAFTA country in order to supply the service, but the maximum duration of this temporary res-

48 NAFTA, Article 1302:1. *See also* Articles I-02:1 (Canada), 12-03:2 (Mexico) and 13.2:1 (USA). Chapter 13 is discussed in Chapter Six.

49 Article 1201:1(d). *See also* Articles H-01:1(d) (Canada), 10-02:1(d) (Mexico) and 11.1:1(d) (USA).

50 *See also* Chapters K (Canada), 13 (Mexico) and 14 (USA).

51 *See* the definition of "business person" in Article 1608, which includes providers of services. *See also* Articles K-08 (Canada), 13-01 (Mexico) and 14.9 (USA). The Mexico-Chile Agreement expressly excludes permanent residents, but this is also clearly implicit in the other three agreements.

52 Article 1603:1 and Annex 1603:A(1) and D(1). Despite the lack of uniform wording, there would appear to be no substantive difference between these three provisions. *See also* Articles K-03:1 (Canada), 13-04:1 (Mexico) and 14.3:1 (USA) and Annexes K-03:A(1) and D(1) (Canada), 13-04:A(1) and D(1) (Mexico) and 14.3:A(1) and D(1) (USA).

53 Article 1603:1 and Annex 1603:A(1). *See also* Articles K-03:1 (Canada), 13-04:1 (Mexico) and 14.3:1 (USA) and Annexes K-03:A(1) (Canada), 13-04:A(1) (Mexico) and 14.3:A(1) (USA).

54 Article 1608. *See also* Articles K-08 (Canada), 13-01 (Mexico) and 14.9 (USA).

55 Article 1201:3(a). *See also* Articles H-01:3(a) (Canada), 10-02:4(a) (Mexico) and 11.1:5(a) (USA).

idence is not set down in the Agreement. It is, therefore, a matter to be regulated by national immigration law.

No employment authorization can be required of a service provider from another Party.[56] Nor may Parties impose prior approval procedures, petitions, labor certification tests or other similar procedures as a condition for temporary entry and residence.[57] Numerical restrictions are also prohibited. On the other hand, the Parties may require a service provider seeking temporary entry to obtain a visa or equivalent document.[58]

The actual procedure for obtaining temporary entry depends on the services to be provided. There are two categories of service providers. The first comprises those who are involved in the activities set out in Appendix 1603:A.1,[59] which, as far as services are concerned, means research and design, marketing, sales, distribution, after-sales service, professional services, financial services, public relations and advertising, tourism, translators and interpreters.[60] Professional services means business activities in a profession set out in Appendix 1603.D.1,[61] which lists, among other professionals, accountants, architects, computer systems analysts, economists, industrial designers, management consultants, dentists, occupational therapists, biochemists and geologists. The other category comprises all persons supplying other services.

The first category, provided they meet the normal immigration requirements, are entitled to temporary entry upon presentation of a) proof of citizenship of a Party, b) documentation proving that the business person will be engaged in providing a service that falls into the first category and describing the purpose of entry, and c) evidence demonstrating that the proposed service activity is international in scope and that the provider is not seeking to enter the local labor market.[62] This third requirement can be met by showing that the primary source of remuneration for the proposed service arises outside the host state and that the provider's principal place of business and the actual place of accrual of profits also remain

56 Annex 1603:A(1) and (3). Annex 1603:D(1), which covers professionals, does not have this provision, but each Party is obliged to provide confirming documentation, which amounts to the same thing. In any case, professionals are also covered by Annex A—*see infra* in the text. *See also* Annexes K-03:A(1) and (3) and D(1) (Canada), 13-04:A(1) and (3) and D(1) (Mexico) and 14.3:A(1) and D(1) (USA).

57 Annex 1603:A(4)(a) and D(2)(a). *See also* Annexes K-03:A(4)(a) and D(2)(a) (Canada), 13-04:A(4)(a) and D(2)(a) (Mexico) and 14.3:A(3)(a) and D(4)(a) (USA).

58 Annex 1603:A(5) and D(3). *See also* Annexes K-03:A(5) and D(3) (Canada), 13-04:A(5) and D(3) (Mexico) and Article 14.2:2 (USA).

59 Annex 1603:A(1). *See also* Annexes K-03:A(1) (Canada), 13-04:A(1) (Mexico) and 14.3:A(1) (USA).

60 *See also* Appendices K-03.A.1 (Canada), 13-04.A.1 (Mexico) and 14.3.A.1 (USA).

61 *See also* Appendices K-03.D.1 (Canada), 13-04.D.1 (Mexico) and 14.3.D.1 (USA).

62 Annex 1603:A(1). *See also* Annexes K-03:A(1) (Canada), 13-04:A(1) (Mexico) and 14.3:A(1) (USA).

predominantly outside that Party.[63] It is not entirely clear whether this third requirement applies to professionals. Annex D on professionals omits it[64] but Appendix 1603.A.1[65] lists these same professional services among those that are subject to Annex A, which has this requirement.[66]

Providers of services other than those listed in Appendix 1603.A.1 are subject to the regular immigration procedures.[67]

A Party may refuse to authorize a service provider from another Party where the temporary entry of that person would adversely affect the settlement of a labor dispute at the place of intended employment or the employment of any person involved in such a dispute.[68] The refusing Party must inform the service provider in writing of the reasons for the refusal and promptly notify the Party whose service provider has been refused entry.[69]

A common method of prohibiting or restricting the provision of a service by a foreign provider is through the requirement of citizenship or permanent residency for licenses and certifications (barrier (a)). Under NAFTA, the Parties were obliged, within two years of the entry into force of NAFTA, to eliminate such requirements for the licensing or certification of professional service providers from other Parties.[70] Failure to comply exposes a Party to retaliation. The other Parties may maintain similar requirements in the same sector or reinstate requirements that have been eliminated.[71] Not all the offending requirements have been removed, but NAFTA also provides also for ongoing consultations between the Parties with a view to eliminating any remaining requirements of this nature.[72]

As residency requirements (Category 2) are not covered by the national treatment provision of NAFTA, the Agreement deals specifically with these barriers. Article 1205 prohibits the requirement of a permanent residence or presence in the host

---

63 Annex 1603:A(2). *See also* Annexes K-03:A(2) (Canada), 13-04:A(2) (Mexico) and 14.3:A(2) (USA).

64 Annex 1603:D(1). *See also* Annexes K-03:D(1) (Canada), 13-04:D(1) (Mexico) and 14.3:D(1) (USA). However, the US-Chile Agreement also requires of professionals documentation attesting to the attainment of the minimum educational requirements or alternative credentials.

65 *See also* Appendices K-03.A.1 (Canada), 13-04.A.1 (Mexico) and 14.3.A.1 (USA).

66 Annex 1603:A(1). *See also* Annexes K-03:A(1) (Canada), 13-04:A(1) (Mexico) and 14.3:A(1) (USA).

67 Annex 1603:A(3). *See also* Annexes K-03:A(3) (Canada) and 13-04:A(3) (Mexico). The US-Chile Agreement has no equivalent provision, but the same rule must surely apply.

68 Article 1603:2. *See also* Articles K-03:2 (Canada), 13-04:2 (Mexico) and 14.3:2 (USA).

69 Article 1603:3. *See also* Articles K-03:3 (Canada), 13-04:3 (Mexico) and 14.3:3 (USA).

70 Article 1210:3. *See also* Articles H-10:3 (Canada) and 10-12:3 (Mexico). The US-Chile Agreement does not have this provision.

71 The Mexico-Chile Agreement only permits the maintenance of equivalent restrictions.

72 Article 1210:4. *See also* Articles H-10:4 (Canada), 10-12:4 (Mexico) and 11.10 (USA).

NAFTA state as a condition for the cross-border provision of services (barriers (g) and (i)).[73] The wording of the Article is wide enough, moreover, to extend the prohibition to the requirement of prior residence as well (barrier (h)).

NAFTA also has specific provisions dealing with the operational barriers to market entry (Category 3), which are similarly not eliminated by the national treatment approach. Prohibitions or restrictions on the importation of necessary inputs (barrier (j)) are disallowed under the provisions in the Agreement on the free movement of goods.[74] Exchange restrictions, whether imposed on payment for a service or on access to foreign currency for the purpose of traveling to receive a service (barrier (l)) as well as capital transfers arising from a cross-border financial transaction (part of barrier (k)) are implicitly prohibited in that they are only permitted as a balance-of-payments exception.[75] In the rare event that exchange controls were aimed specifically against providers from other NAFTA Parties, they would contravene the national treatment provision of NAFTA and, with respect to controls on payment for services, the illustrative list in Article 1201:1(b), which refers to the sale and purchase of services.[76]

Monopolies (barrier (m)) are permitted[77] but a Party must ensure that they act in a manner that is consistent with a Party's obligations under NAFTA when exercising delegated authority in connection with the monopoly service, such as the power to issue licenses and approve commercial transactions.[78] Parties must also ensure that, except to comply with their terms of reference, monopolies act solely in accordance with commercial considerations in their purchases or sales of the monopoly goods or services.[79] State enterprises are also permitted,[80] but the rules on their conduct apply under NAFTA only to financial services and the provision of services through commercial presence and are mentioned in those contexts.[81]

73 *See also* Articles H-05 (Canada), 10-05 (Mexico) and 11.5 (USA).

74 Chapter 3. *See also* Chapters C (Canada), 3 (Mexico) and 3 (USA).

75 *See infra* in the text.

76 *See also* Articles H-01:1(b) (Canada), 10-02:1(b) (Mexico) and 11.1:1(b) (USA).

77 Article 1502:1. *See also* Articles J-02:1 (Canada), 14-03:2 (Mexico) and 16.3:1 (USA).

78 Articles 1502:3(a). *See also* Articles J-02:3(a) (Canada), 14.03:4(a) (Mexico) and 16.3:3(a) (USA).

79 Article 1502:3(b). *See also* Articles J-02:3(b) (Canada), 14-03:4(b) (Mexico) and 16.3:3(b) (USA).

80 Article 1503:1. *See also* Articles J-03:1 (Canada), 14.04:1 (Mexico) and 16.4:1 (USA).

81 Article 1503:2 and 3. *See also* Articles J-03:2 and 3 (Canada), 14-04:2 and 3 (Mexico) and 16.4:2 and 3 (USA). However, under the US-Chile Agreement, the obligation with respect to the exercise of delegated power also applies to state enterprises.

2. Services Supplied from a Commercial Presence

Market access for suppliers of services by means of a commercial presence in the host NAFTA state (Mode 3) is provided incidentally by Chapter 11[82] on investment and certain other provisions of the Treaty.

The general requirement of national treatment for investors from another NAFTA Party applies to service providers from one Party who are supplying services from a commercial presence in another Party.[83] The two additional national treatment rules that apply to cross-border services also apply here. Thus, the service providers from another Party must receive treatment no less favorable than that accorded by a state or province of a Party to service providers and their services from other states or provinces in that Party.[84] Also, if a Party accords services providers from third countries treatment that is more favorable than its national treatment, it must extend this better treatment to service providers from its partners in NAFTA.[85]

As with cross-border services, national treatment for providers of services from a commercial presence in a host NAFTA state remains limited to the prohibition of discrimination in law. This means that it only covers the market access barriers that are based on nationality, which, in the case of services provided through Mode 3, are barriers (a), (b), (c), (d) and (f). With respect to the setting up of a permanent establishment (barrier (d)), this establishment may be a subsidiary, joint venture, partnership or branch.[86] However, as the right of establishment under NAFTA does not connote a right to personal establishment, it is difficult to see how an establishment could take the form of a sole proprietorship. National treatment eliminates restrictions on capital investment by providers from another Party (barrier (c)), but, for greater certainty, NAFTA specifically prohibits the requirement of mandatory local equity.[87] Part of barrier (f) is dealt with explicitly in Chapter 13, which provides for access to and use of public telecommunications networks by service providers from other Parties.[88]

Unlike Chapter 12 on cross-border services, Chapter 11 contains no provision for the Parties to eliminate citizenship requirements for licenses and certifications for professional service providers (barrier (a)). This is unfortunate, as such require-

---

82 *See* also Chapters G (Canada), 9 (Mexico) and 10 (USA). However, in the US-Chile Agreement, the provisions on market access and domestic regulation with respect to cross-border services also apply to services supplied through a commercial presence—*see* Article 11.4.

83 Articles 1101:1 and 1102:1 and 2. *See* also Articles G-01:1 and G-02: 1 and 2 (Canada), 9-02:1 and 9-03:1 and 2 (Mexico) and 10.1:1 and 10.2:1 and 2 (USA).

84 Article 1102:3. *See* also Articles G-02:3 (Canada), 9-03:3 (Mexico) and 10.2:3 (USA).

85 Article 1104: *See* also Articles G-04 (Canada) and 9-05 (Mexico). The US-Chile Agreement does not have this odd provision. *See* also note 440.

86 Article 1139. *See* also Articles G-39 (Canada), 9-01 (Mexico) and 10.27 (USA).

87 Article 1102:4(a). *See* also Articles G-02:4(a) (Canada) and 9-03:4(a) (Mexico). The US-Chile Agreement does not include this provision.

88 NAFTA. Article 1302:1. *See* also Articles I-02:1 (Canada), 12-03:2 (Mexico) and 13.2:1 (USA). Chapter 13 is discussed in Chapter Six.

ments are as much a barrier for service providers established in a host state as for providers of cross-border services.

Residency requirements (Category 3) are not covered by the national treatment rule in Chapter 11 of NAFTA as they are not based on discrimination in law. Indeed, Article 1111:1 explicitly permits them.[89] However, except for the requirement of prior residence, they are not an issue for providers of services from a commercial presence.

The operational barriers to the provision of services through Mode 3 (Category 3) are, on the other hand, covered by specific provisions in the Agreement. Prohibitions or restrictions on the importation of inputs that are necessary to provide a service (barrier (j)) are covered, as in the case of cross-border services, by the provisions in NAFTA on free movement of goods.[90] Exchange controls on capital transfers in and out of the host country in the form of investment, dividends and profits as well as transfers related to a particular service transaction (barrier (k)), are expressly prohibited.[91] However, a Party may prevent a transfer through the equitable, non-discriminatory and honest application of its laws relating *inter alia* to bankruptcy and insolvency, dealing in securities, criminal or penal offenses and the satisfaction of judgments in adjudicatory proceedings.[92] Exchange controls on payment for services or travel to receive them (barrier (l)) are not relevant for services provided from a commercial presence.

Monopolies and state enterprises (barrier (m)) are permitted,[93] but they must both act in manner that is consistent with a Party's obligations under NAFTA when exercising delegated authority in connection with the monopoly service, such as the power to issue licenses and approve commercial transactions.[94] As in the case of cross-border services, Parties must ensure that, except to comply with their terms of reference, monopolies act solely in accordance with commercial considerations in their purchases or sales of the monopoly goods or services.[95] There is no equivalent provision for state enterprises.

3. The NAFTA Approach to Market Access

The way NAFTA characterizes national measures as market access barriers or matters of national treatment is not easy to fathom as it does not explicitly separate out these two concepts. However, it seems implicitly to take an approach that ac-

89 See also Articles G-01:1 (Canada), 9-12:1 (Mexico) and 10.10:1 (USA).

90 Chapter 3. *See* also Chapters C (Canada), 3 (Mexico) and 3 (USA).

91 Article 1109:1. *See* also Articles G-09:1 (Canada), 9-10:1 (Mexico) and 10.8:1 (USA).

92 Article 1109:4. *See* also Articles G-09:4 (Canada), 9-10:4 (Mexico) and 10.8:5 (USA).

93 Articles 1502:1 and 1503:1. *See* also Articles J-02:1 and J-03:1 (Canada), 14-03:2 and 14-04:1 (Mexico) and 16.3:1 and 16.4:1 (USA).

94 Articles 1502:3(a) and 1503:2. *See* also Articles J-02:3(a) and J-03:2 (Canada), 14-03:4(a) and 14.4:2 (Mexico) and 16.3:3(a) and 16.4:2 (USA).

95 Article 1502:3(b). *See* also Articles J-02:3(b) (Canada), 14-03:4(b) (Mexico) and 16.3:3(b) (USA).

cords with that taken in this monograph rather than the approach taken by GATS.[96] For example, the fact that, despite its provisions on national treatment, NAFTA has a specific provision prohibiting residency requirements for cross-border service providers indicates that it does not consider them as falling within the ambit of national treatment. Conversely, the absence of any specific provisions on discriminatory quantitative restrictions indicates that this matter is considered to come within the ambit of national treatment.

The two peculiarities with the NAFTA approach to market access are its use of national treatment to achieve this and its exclusion of the supply of services through commercial presence as an independent issue to be addressed by the Agreement. Both can cause problems. However, despite them, NAFTA deals more or less comprehensively with the issue of market access. This is due in part to the fact that it takes an inclusive approach. It does not set down an exhaustive list of market access barriers, like GATS, but obliges the Parties to remove all discrimination in law against services providers from other Parties, albeit subject to reservations that they are allowed to make.[97]

In the case of cross-border services, most of the barriers to market access are covered, although more explicitness in the case of exchange controls (barrier (k)) would have been welcome. The only significant problem is the requirement that persons wishing temporary entry in connection with the supply of services by Mode 4 be a citizen of a Party. There is no doubt some reason for this requirement, but it is quite restrictive.

With respect to services supplied through a commercial presence, a combination of the provisions on investment and some general provisions in the Agreement provide a significant degree of market access. Indeed, the issue of exchange controls (barrier (l)) is covered more explicitly than for cross-border services. There are, however, problems. The requirement of prior residency (barrier (h)) is tolerated, and there is no obligation to eliminate nationality requirements for licenses and certifications for professional service providers (barrier (a)). Both requirements can constitute as potent an obstacle to the provision of services through Mode 3 as to the provision of cross-border services.

C. NATIONAL TREATMENT

1. Introduction

The national treatment provisions of NAFTA, which are discussed above, serve also to require that service providers from another NAFTA Party be able to supply

96 By contrast, the US-Chile Agreement is more akin to GATS in its approach, as it regards quantitative restrictions and corporate form requirements as coming under market access—*see* Article 11.4.

97 It is noteworthy that even the market access provision in Article 11.4 of the US-Chile Agreement, which is modeled on GATS, does not purport to be exhaustive. The difference in wording from Article XVI:1 of GATS is subtle but crucial.

services under the Agreement on the same legal footing as domestic providers. They do not cover discrimination in fact.

2. Cross-Border Services

The general requirement of national treatment for providers of cross-border services should be sufficient to cover all the measures of discrimination in law that appear on List 4 to the extent that they are relevant to the supply of services by Modes 1, 2 and 4. This would normally exclude measures (a), (i), (k), (l), (m), (o) and Category 4,[98] which are more likely to apply only to the provision of services through Mode 3.

Article 1201:1 of NAFTA singles out in an illustrative list certain operational measures to which national treatment applies. These are discrimination with respect to the distribution and marketing of a service, which includes restrictions on advertising and other means of acquiring recipients (measure (e)),[99] and discriminatory bonds or other forms of financial security required as a condition for the provision of a service (measure (n)).[100] Distribution and transportation networks are also singled out,[101] and there are detailed provisions on telecommunications networks (part of measure (b)) that are discussed later. However, discrimination concerning access to or use of all networks is prohibited by the general provision on national treatment.

NAFTA also deals specifically with monopolies (measure (g)).They are required to provide non-discriminatory treatment to service providers of other Parties in their purchases and sales of monopoly goods or services and where they exercise any regulatory, administrative or other governmental authority over such matters as licenses and fees.[102] The same obligations do not apply to state enterprises.[103]

National treatment also applies, albeit subject to any contrary provisions in a tax convention, to income tax relating to the purchase or consumption of a particular service.[104] This deals to some extent with financial measures (h) and (j).

Non-discriminatory quantitative restrictions are not covered by the national treatment provision in the Agreement. This is not a major problem as they normally fall under the rubric of domestic regulation. However, they are capable of putting

98 An illustrative list of measures constituting discrimination in law is found in List 4.

99 Article 1201:1(a). *See also* Articles H-01:1(a) (Canada), 10-02:1(a) (Mexico) and 11.1:1(a) (USA).

100 Article 1201:1(e). *See also* Articles H-01:1(e) (Canada), 10-02:1(e) (Mexico) and 11.1:1(e) (USA).

101 Article 1201:1(c). *See also* Articles H-01:1(c) (Canada), 10-02:1(c) (Mexico) and 11.1:1(c) (USA).

102 Article 1502:3(a) and (c). *See also* Articles J-02:3(a) and (c) (Canada), 14-03:4(a) and (c) (Mexico) and 16.3:3)a) and (c) (USA).

103 Article 1503:3. *See also* Articles J-03:3 (Canada), 14-04:3 (Mexico) and 16.4:3 (USA).

104 Article 2103:4(a). *See also* Articles O-03:4(a) (Canada) and 23.3:4(a). The Mexico-Chile Agreement does not have this provision.

a foreign provider of cross-border services at a disadvantage, in which case they constitute discrimination in fact (measure (g)).[105] NAFTA requires the Parties to list any non-discriminatory quantitative restrictions in Annex V and to negotiate with each other periodically to eliminate them.[106]

3. Services Supplied From a Commercial Presence

The general requirement of national treatment for investors of another NAFTA Party and their investments applies to service providers from one Party who are supplying services from a commercial presence in another Party. It should be sufficient to cover all the measures of discrimination in law on List 4, all of which are relevant to the provision of services by Mode 3. This includes operational discrimination (Category 1), financial discrimination (Category 2), discriminatory quantitative restrictions (Category 3) and discriminatory performance requirements (Category 4). One instance of financial discrimination, however, is permitted. The national treatment provision of Chapter 11 does not apply to subsidies or grants by a Party or a state enterprise, including government-supported loans, guarantees and insurance.[107]

Certain instances of discrimination are singled out for prohibition. As far as operational discrimination is concerned, monopolies and state enterprises must provide non-discriminatory treatment to providers of services from another Party in their purchases and sales of monopoly goods or services (part of measure (g)) and where they exercise any regulatory, administrative or other governmental authority over such matters as licenses and fees.[108]

Chapter 11 singles out certain performance requirements.[109] These are export level requirements (measure (t)), local content requirements (measure (u)), local preference requirements (measure (v)), mandatory technology transfers (measure (w)) and exclusive supply obligations (measure (a)). All of these measures are prohibited whether or not they discriminate in law. Thus, they are not permitted if they discriminate only in fact or even if they do not disadvantage foreign providers at all and fall under the rubric of domestic regulation. The prohibition extends to service providers from non-Parties. It does not cover local training and minimum activity requirements (measures (x) and (y)), which, however fall afoul of the general national treatment provision if they discriminate in law.

---

105 An illustrative list of measures constituting discrimination in fact is found in List 5.

106 Article 1207. *See also* Articles H-07 (Canada) and 10-08 (Mexico). Quantitative restrictions are treated as market access barriers in the US-Chile Agreement—*see* Article 11.4.

107 Article 1108:7(b). *See also* Articles G-08:7(b) (Canada), 9-09:7(b) (Mexico) and 10.7:5(b) (USA).

108 Article 1502:3(a) and (c) and 1503:2 and 3. *See also* Articles J-02:3(a) and (c) and J-03:2 and 3 (Canada), 14-03:4(a) and (c) and 14-04:2 and 3 (Mexico) and 16.3:3(a) and (c) and 16.4: 2 and 3 (USA).

109 Article 1106:1. *See also* Articles G-06:1 (Canada), 9-07:1 (Mexico) and 10.5:1 (USA).

Parties are not allowed to condition the receipt of any advantage (e.g. subsidy, grant, contract etc) on a provider meeting certain export or foreign exchange levels or complying with local preference or content requirements.[110] They may, however, condition it on compliance with a requirement to locate production, provide a service, train or employ workers, construct or expand particular facilities or carry on research and development in the host state.[111]

Chapter 11 contains two other provisions relating to discrimination in fact. It prohibits Parties from requiring that a majority on boards of directors be citizens[112] or residents of the host state (measure (e)) if this requirement materially impairs the ability of the provider from another Party to exercise control over its enterprise.[113] It also prohibits outright any requirement that senior management positions be held by its nationals (measure (d)),[114] but this prohibition does not require Parties to allow persons from other NAFTA Parties to reside and work permanently in the host state as these intra-company transferees are subject to the rules on temporary entry.[115] They must be citizens of a Party[116] and be rendering services in a capacity that is managerial, executive or involves specialized knowledge.[117] They must meet existing immigration rules relating to public health and safety and national security and may be required to obtain a visa or equivalent document.[118] A Party may further require the employee to have been continuously employed for one year within the three-year period immediately preceding the date of application for temporary entry.[119] As long as a company transferee meets all these conditions, he or she must be admitted and provided with confirming documentation. No labor certification tests or equivalent procedures may be required as a condition for

110 Article 1106:3. *See also* Articles G-06:3 (Canada), 9-07:3 (Mexico) and 10.5:2 (USA).

111 Article 1106:4. *See also* Articles G-06:4 (Canada), 9-07:4 (Mexico) and 10.5:3(a) (USA).

112 The provision somewhat oddly refers to a requirement that the directors be "of a particular nationality." It would be extremely unusual for a country to require directors of its companies to be foreign nationals, and so we may assume that the requirement refers to nationality of the host state.

113 Article 1107:2. *See also* Articles G-07:2 (Canada), 9-08:2 (Mexico) and 10.6:2 (USA).

114 Article 1107:1. *See also* Articles G-07:1 (Canada), 9-08:1 (Mexico) and 10.6:1 (USA). The comments in note 119 apply here as well.

115 Annex 1603:C. *See also* Annexes K-03:C (Canada), 13-04:C (Mexico) and 14.3:C (USA).

116 *See* the definition of "business person" in Article 1608, which includes corporate transferees. *See also* Articles K-08 (Canada), 13-01 (Mexico) and 14.9 (USA). The Mexico-Chile Agreement expressly excludes permanent residents, but this is also clearly implicit in the other three agreements.

117 Annex 1603:C(1). *See also* Annexes K-03:C(1) (Canada), 13-04:C(1) (Mexico) and 14.3:C(1) (USA).

118 Annex 1603:C(1) and (3). *See also* Annexes K-03:C(1) and (3) (Canada), 13-04:C(1) and (3) (Mexico) and Article 14.2 and Annex 14.3:C(1) (USA).

119 Annex 1603:C(1). *See also* Annexes K-03:C(1) (Canada), 13-04:C(1) (Mexico) and 14.3:C(1) (USA).

temporary entry and no numerical restrictions may be imposed.[120] The length of time that an intra-company transferee may remain in the host state is up to the domestic law of that Party.

Unlike Chapter 12, Chapter 11 does not contain provisions on the elimination of non-discriminatory quantitative restrictions.

4. The NAFTA Approach to National Treatment

As NAFTA does not distinguish between national treatment and market access, it is difficult to discern exactly which measures it assigns to national treatment. However, as pointed out previously, residency requirements do not come within this rubric. Conversely, by not explicitly mentioning discriminatory quantitative restrictions, the Agreement implies that these measures do fall under national treatment. In both cases, this is a better approach than that adopted by GATS.[121]

National treatment under NAFTA is restricted to discrimination in law, although there are provisions prohibiting some measures that constitute discrimination in fact. Unfortunately, the obligation to eliminate non-discriminatory quantitative restrictions only applies to cross-border services, although they can also hamper the provision of services from a commercial presence.

D. DOMESTIC REGULATION

The non-discriminatory domestic regulation of trade in services is permitted under NAFTA as under other agreements. This covers the measures set out in List 6, including discrimination in fact (measure (h))[122] to the extent that it is not expressly prohibited by the Agreement. This is the case with respect to providers of services from a commercial presence regarding some restrictions on the use of home-state nationals (measure (d))[123] and non-discriminatory performance requirements (measure (f)).[124] Non-discriminatory quantitative restrictions (measure (g)), on the other hand, are permitted, but, with respect to cross-border services, they must be set out in the Parties' Schedules to Annex V and are subject to negotiations to remove them.[125] The Parties may also prescribe special formalities for providers who wish to set up an establishment in another Party.[126] Such

---

120 Annex 1603:C(2). *See also* Annexes K-03:C(2) (Canada), 13-04:C(2) (Mexico) and 14.3:C(2) (USA).

121 *See* the discussion in Chapter Two, Sections I.B.2 and I.C.2.

122 The references are to List 5, which contains an illustrative list of measures constituting discrimination in fact.

123 Article 1107:1. *See also* Articles G-07:1 (Canada), 9-08:1 (Mexico) and 10.6:1 (USA).

124 Article 1106. *See also* Articles G-06 (Canada), 9-07 (Mexico) and 10.4 (USA).

125 Article 1207. *See also* H-07 (Canada) and 10-08 (Mexico). Under Article 11.4 of the US-Chile Agreement, all quantitative restrictions on the provision of cross-border services are considered market access barriers and must be eliminated.

126 Article 1111:1. *See also* Articles G-11:1 (Canada), 9-12:1 (Mexico) and 10.10:1 (USA).

formalities may include a requirement to incorporate under the laws of the host Party, which excludes the use of a branch (measure (a)).

Apart from its provisions on telecommunications, which are discussed in Chapter Six, NAFTA contains some rules on domestic regulation. In the first place, it requires the Parties to publish promptly or otherwise make available all relevant measures of general application pertaining to trade in services.[127] The wording of the provision is broad enough to cover all modes of supplying services. If possible, they should publish them in advance of their adoption.[128] Parties must also notify other Parties of proposed or actual measures[129] and respond promptly to their requests for information.[130]

With respect to cross-border services alone, the Parties must publish explanatory material in a consolidated document regarding the requirements for the temporary entry of service providers in connection with the supply of services through Mode 4.[131] They must also provide them with such materials as will enable them to become acquainted with the measures relating to temporary entry.[132]

All measures of domestic regulation affecting trade in services must be administered in a consistent, impartial and reasonable manner, which includes affording affected persons an opportunity to present their case prior to any final administrative action as long as time, the nature of the proceeding and the public interest permit this.[133] The Parties must maintain or establish institute tribunals or procedures for prompt review and, where warranted, correction of final administrative decisions affecting trade in services.[134] Persons must have a reasonable opportunity to defend themselves.[135]

Only providers of cross-border professional services benefit from the stipulation that applications for licenses or certifications must be dealt with in a timely and transparent manner.[136] This seems unnecessarily restrictive, and it is noteworthy that, in the US-Chile Agreement, this stipulation applies generally to cross-border

127 Article 1802:1. *See also* Articles L-02:1 (Canada), 16-03:1 (Mexico) and 20.2:1 (USA).

128 Article 1802:2. *See also* Articles L-02:2 (Canada), 16-03:2 (Mexico) and 20.2:2 (USA).

129 Article 1803:1. *See also* Articles L-03:1 (Canada), 16-04:1 (Mexico) and 20.3:1 (USA).

130 Article 1803:2. *See also* Articles L-03:2 (Canada), 16-04:2 (Mexico) and 20.3:2 (USA).

131 Article 1604:1(b). *See also* Articles K-04:1(b) (Canada), 13-05:1(b) (Mexico) and 14.4:1(b) (USA).

132 Article 1604:1(a). *See also* Articles K-04:1(a) (Canada), 13-05:1(a) (Mexico) and 14.4:1(a) (USA).

133 Article 1804. *See also* Articles K-04 (Canada), 16-05 (Mexico) and 20.4 (USA).

134 Article 1805:1. *See also* Articles L-05:1 (Canada), 16-06:1 (Mexico) and 20.5:1 (USA).

135 Article 1805:2(a). *See also* Articles L-05:2(a) (Canada), 16-06:2(a) (Mexico) and 20.5:2(a) (USA).

136 Annex 1210.5:A(1). *See also* Annexes H-10.5:A(1) (Canada) and 10.12:A(2) (Mexico).

services.[137] Professional services in this context mean services, the provision of which require specialized post-secondary education or equivalent training or experience and for which the right to practice is regulated by a Party.[138]

The Parties must endeavor to ensure that measures relating to the licensing or certification of providers of cross-border services from other Parties meet the following criteria:[139]

a) they are based on objective and transparent criteria;

b) they are not more burdensome than necessary, and

c) they do not constitute a disguised restriction on cross-border services.

This provision is somewhat narrow as it does not include qualifications or membership in professional or trade organizations, although these matters may be covered where they are prerequisites for obtaining a license or certification. NAFTA encourages the temporary licensing of professional service providers and civil engineers.[140] A whole chapter is devoted to technical standards, but it only applies to land transportation and telecommunications services.[141] It is best discussed in the context of those service areas.

Where a Party recognizes education, experience, licenses or certifications obtained in another Party or in a non-Party, it is not obliged, despite the MFN rule set out in Article 1203,[142] to extend this recognition to another Party.[143] However, it must give this Party the opportunity to demonstrate that recognition is appropriate.[144]

Additional commitments in the area of domestic regulation as it affects cross-border services, in particular with respect to non-discriminatory quotas, licensing and performance requirements, may be undertaken and listed in a Party's Schedule to Annex VI. It should be noted, however, that non-discriminatory performance re-

---

137 Article 11.8:1.

138 Article 1213:2. *See* also Articles H-13:2 (Canada), 10.01:1 (Mexico) and 11.12:2 (USA).

139 Article 1210:1. *See* also H-10:1 (Canada), 10.12:1 (Mexico) and 11.8:2 (USA). The US-Chile Agreement is more comprehensive and covers qualifications and standards as well.

140 Annex 1210.5:A(5) and C. *See* also Annexes H-10.5:A(5) and C (Canada), 10-12:A(6) (Mexico) and 11.9:A(4) and C (USA). The Mexico-Chile Agreement does not mention the temporary licensing of civil engineers.

141 Article 915:1 *See* also Article 8-01:1 (Mexico), where it is restricted to computer-related services. In the US-Chile Agreement it is restricted to goods, and there is no equivalent chapter in the Canada-Chile Agreement.

142 *See* also Articles H-03 (Canada), 10-04 (Mexico) and 11.3 (USA).

143 Article 1210:2(a). *See* also Articles H-10:2(a) (Canada), 10-12:2(a) (Mexico) and 11.9:2 (USA). The US-Chile Agreement reproduces the GATS requirement that the manner of recognition not constitute a means of discrimination between countries in the application of its standards or criteria or a disguised restriction on trade in services—see Article 11.9:4.

144 Article 1210:2(b). *See* also Articles H-10:2(b) (Canada), 10-12:2(b) (Mexico) and 11.9(3) (USA).

quirements must be abolished under Chapter 11 with respect to providers of services from a commercial presence.[145]

NAFTA's treatment of domestic regulation is somewhat timid. It is also unfortunate that, because the Agreement does not explicitly cover providers of services through a commercial presence, the measures relating to licensing and certification do not apply to them. After all, they are as much affected by these procedures as providers of cross-border services.

E. MOST-FAVORED-NATION TREATMENT

A Party to NAFTA must treat service providers from another Party, regardless of the mode of supply, no less favorably than service providers from any other country, whether it is a Party or non-Party.[146] In the case of commercial presence, this obligation extends to the establishment, acquisition, expansion, management, conduct and operation of the presence. Where national treatment provides better treatment than MFN treatment, then service providers from another Party must receive the former.[147] In other words, a Party cannot escape its obligation to provide national treatment to other Parties by hiding behind the MFN principle. However, the provision is rather pointless, as the Parties would be entitled to this treatment anyway under the national treatment provisions of NAFTA. The Chile-US Agreement sensibly omits it.

Monopolies and, in the case of services supplied from a commercial presence, state enterprises must provide the MFN treatment described above to providers of services from other Parties in their purchases and sales of the monopoly goods or services and also where they exercise regulatory authority over such matters as licenses and fees.[148]

The MFN rule does not apply to treatment accorded by a Party pursuant to agreements or with respect to sectors that are set out in its Schedule to Annex IV.[149] It also does not apply to an advantage accorded by a Party to another Party or non-Party pursuant to a tax convention.[150]

---

145 *See supra* in the text.

146 Articles 1103 and 1203. *See also* G-03 and H-03 (Canada), 9-04 and 10-04 (Mexico) and 10.3 and 11.3 (USA). The bilateral agreements only refer to equal treatment with non-Parties as there are only two Parties to the agreements.

147 Articles 1104 and 1204. *See also* G-04 and H-04 (Canada), 9-05 and 10-05 (Mexico), and 10.4 and 11.3 (USA).

148 Article 1502:3(a) and (c), 1503: 2 and 3 and 1505. *See also* Articles J-02:3(a) and (c), J-03: 2 and 3 and J-04 (Canada), 14-03:3(a) and (c), 14-04: 2 and 3 and 14-01 (Mexico) and 16.3:3(a) and (c), 16.4: 2 and 3 and 16.9 (USA).

149 Article 1108:6. *See also* Articles G-08:6 (Canada) and 9-09:5 (Mexico). The US-Chile Agreement does not provide for this exception.

150 Article 2103:4(c). *See also* Articles O-03:4(c) (Canada) and 23.3:4(c) (USA). There is no equivalent provision in the Mexico-Chile Agreement.

A modified MFN rule applies to the mutual recognition of qualifications, experience, licenses and certifications in the case of the providers of cross-border services. Parties are free to recognize them when they are obtained in a particular country, whether a Party or a non-Party, without having to extend this benefit to the other Parties.[151] However, they must afford adequate opportunity for other interested Parties to participate in any such arrangements.

F. GENERAL EXCEPTIONS TO THE RULES

1. Safeguard Exception

In NAFTA, this exception applies only to trade in goods.[152]

2. Balance-of-Payments Exception

Parties are allowed to introduce exchange controls on capital transfers (barrier (k))[153] and access to foreign currency for purpose of purchasing the services of a provider from another Party or for that of traveling to receive them (barrier (l)) only if they are experiencing serious balance-of-payments difficulties or the threat thereof.[154] A Party may adopt or maintain controls that give a priority to services that are essential to its economic program, but they may not protect a specific sector unless this is done consistently with the economic adjustment measures required by the IMF and with Article VIII:3 of the IMF Articles.[155]

As soon as practicable after imposing controls for balance-of-payments reasons, a Party must submit any current account exchange restrictions (barrier (l)) to the IMF for review and approval under Article VIII of the IMF Articles.[156] It must also enter into consultations with the IMF on the economic adjustment measures needed to deal with the fundamental underlying structural problems that are causing the difficulties and apply them.

---

151 Article 1210:2. *See also* Articles H-10:2 (Canada), 10-12:2 (Mexico) and 11.9(2) and (3) (USA). However, the US-Chile Agreement reproduces in Article 11.9(4) the GATS requirement that recognition not be accorded in such a way as to constitute a means of discrimination between countries in the application of its standards or criteria for recognition.

152 Articles 802 and 803. *See also* Articles F-01 and F-02 (Canada), 6-02 and 6-03 (Mexico) and 8.1 (USA).

153 The reference is to the illustrative list of market access barriers in List 3.

154 Article 2104:1. *See also* Articles O-04:1 (Canada) and 19-06:1 (Mexico). Balance-of-payment restrictions may only be imposed on goods under the US-Chile Agreement.

155 Article 2104:4. *See also* Articles O-04:4 (Canada) and 19-06:4 (Mexico). Article VIII:3 of the IMF Articles prohibits the use of discriminatory currency arrangements or multiple currency practices.

156 Article 2104:2. *See also* Articles O-04:2 (Canada) and 19-06:2 (Mexico).

Any exchange controls that are imposed must meet the following conditions:[157]

- they must avoid unnecessary damage to the commercial, economic or financial interests of another Party;
- they must not be more burdensome than necessary to deal with the difficulties or threat thereof;
- they must be temporary and be phased out progressively as the situation improves;
- they must be consistent with any economic adjustment measures required by the IMF;
- they must be applied on a national treatment or MFN basis, whichever offers the best treatment;
- they must, in the case of controls on payments for current international transactions (barrier (l)), be consistent with Article VIII:3 of the IMF Articles on the avoidance of discriminatory currency practices;
- they must, in the case of controls on international capital transactions (barrier (k)), be consistent with Article VI of the IMF Articles[158] and be imposed only in conjunction with controls on current international transactions;
- they must, in the case of controls on capital transfers, not substantially impede transfers from being made in freely usable currencies at a market rate of exchange; and
- they must not take the form of quotas, licenses or similar measures.

3. General Exception

NAFTA permits the adoption or enforcement by any Party of measures necessary to secure compliance with its laws and regulations as long as they are not inconsistent with the Agreement and are not applied in a manner that arbitrarily or unjustifiably infringes the MFN principle or constitutes a disguised restriction on trade in services.[159] The exact scope of this exception is not really clear. It is explicitly said to cover measures relating to health and safety and consumer protection, but there is no mention of public order or morals. The US-Chile and Mexico-Chile Agreements incorporate Article XIV of GATS, which is a clearer provision.[160] In none of the Agreements does the exception apply to services provided from a commercial presence.

---

157 Article 2104:3 and 5. *See also* Articles O-04:3 and 5 (Canada) and 19-06:3 and 5 (Mexico).

158 This Article requires *inter alia* that such controls not be exercised in a manner that restricts payments for current transactions.

159 Article 2101:2. *See also* Article O-01:2 (Canada).

160 Articles 19-02:2 (Mexico) and 23.1:2 (USA). *See* the discussion on the GATS provision in Chapter Two, Section I.F.4.

4. Security Exception

NAFTA also permits certain exceptions to the totality of its rules in the case of measures that are taken for reasons of national security.[161] The provision is similar to that found in GATS and excepts the following with respect to services:

- the disclosure of information whose disclosure would be contrary to a Member's essential security interests;
- traffic and transactions in services undertaken directly or indirectly for the purpose of supplying a military or other security establishment;
- measures taken in time of war or other international emergency;
- measures relating to the implementation of non-proliferation policies or agreements; and
- actions taken in pursuance of a Member's obligations under the United Nations Charter.

5. Denial of Benefits

A Party may deny the benefits of Chapters 11 and 12 of NAFTA to a provider of services from a commercial presence or of cross-border services where the enterprise involved in providing the services is owned or controlled, respectively, by investors or nationals of a non-Party, if:[162]

- the denying Party does not maintain diplomatic relations with the non-Party; or
- the denying Party adopts or maintains measures with respect to the non-Party that prohibit transactions with the enterprise or that would be violated or circumvented if benefits under these Chapters were accorded to the enterprise; or
- subject to prior notification and consultation, the enterprise has no substantial business activities in the territory of the Party under whose law it is constituted or organized or, in the case of cross-border services, in the territory of any Party.

6. Taxation

Nothing in NAFTA may affect the rights and obligations of any Party under a tax convention, the provisions of which take precedence over those of NAFTA.[163] In addition, the provisions on national and most-favored nation treatment of service providers from other Parties do not apply to a non-conforming provision of

---

161 Article 2102. *See also* Articles 0-02 (Canada), 19-03 (Mexico) and 23.2 (USA).

162 Articles 1113 and 1211. *See also* Articles G-13 and H-11 (Canada), 9-14 and 10-13 (Mexico) and 10.11 and 11.11 (USA). Under the Mexico-Chile Agreement, benefits may only be denied to a provider of cross-border services if the enterprise involved in providing them is owned and controlled by person of a non-Party and the enterprise does not carry on substantial business activities in the Party where it is located.

163 Article 2103:2. *See also* Articles O-03:2 (Canada), 19-05:2 (Mexico) and 23.3:2 (USA).

any existing taxation measure.[164] Such measures may be renewed promptly or amended to the extent that the amendment does not decrease their conformity.[165] The exception also apples to new taxation measures adopted by the Parties that are aimed at ensuring the equitable and effective imposition or collection of taxes as long as the measures do not discriminate between services of the Parties or arbitrarily nullify or impair benefits accruing under the Agreement.[166]

7. Confidentiality Exception

No provisions of NAFTA may be construed to require a Party to disclose information where this would impede law enforcement or infringe the laws protecting personal privacy.[167]

G. DISPUTE SETTLEMENT

1. Dispute Settlement Between the Parties

NAFTA has a quite elaborate dispute settlement procedure that Parties may invoke when they consider that an actual or proposed measure of another Party breaches the Agreement or where it nullifies or impairs any benefit that they could reasonably have expected to accrue to them under Chapter 12 on the cross-border trade in services.[168] The procedure can only be used in the case of refusals to grant temporary entry under Chapter 16 if the matter involves a pattern of practice and the business person has exhausted the available administrative remedies.[169]

As a first step, a Party requests in writing consultations with the other Party, during which the Parties are obliged to make every effort to arrive at a mutually satisfactory resolution of the dispute that does not adversely affect the interests under NAFTA of the third Party.[170] If the Parties fail to resolve the matter within thirty days of a request for consultations or any other period on which they agree, either Party may request in writing a meeting of the Commission.[171] It states in the request the measure at issue and the provisions of NAFTA that it considers relevant.[172] Unless it decides otherwise, the Commission convenes within ten days

164 Articles 2104:4(d). *See also* Articles O-03:4(d) (Canada) and 23.3:4(d) (USA). There is no equivalent provision in the Mexico-Chile Agreement.

165 Articles 2104:4(e), (f). *See also* Articles O-03:4(e), (f) (Canada) and 23.3:4(e), (f) (USA). There is no equivalent provision in the Mexico-Chile Agreement.

166 Articles 2104:4(g). *See also* Articles O-03:4(g) (Canada) and 23.3:4(g) (USA). There is no equivalent provision in the Mexico-Chile Agreement.

167 Article 2105. *See also* Articles O-05 (Canada), 19-04 (Mexico) and 23.5 (USA).

168 Article 2004. *See also* Articles N-04 (Canada), 18-02 (Mexico) and 22.2 (USA).

169 Article 1606:1. *See also* Articles K-06 (Canada), 13-07 (Mexico) and 14.6 (USA).

170 Article 2006:1 and 5. *See also* Articles N-06:1 and 5 (Canada), 18-04:1 and 5 (Mexico) and 22.4:1 and 5 (USA).

171 Article 2007:1. *See also* Articles N-07:1 (Canada), 18-05:1 (Mexico) and 22.5:1 (USA).

172 Article 2007:3. *See also* Articles N-07:3 (Canada), 18-05:3 (Mexico) and 22.5:3 (USA).

and endeavors to resolve the dispute promptly.[173] If it fails to do so within thirty days or such other period as the Parties agree, either Party may request the Commission in writing to establish an arbitral panel.[174] The panel must be established on delivery of the request. The third Party is entitled to be joined as a complaining Party if it considers that it has a substantial interest in the matter.[175] It must deliver notice of this intention to the disputing Parties and the Commission Secretariat no later than seven days after the date of delivery of the request for the establishment of the panel.

The panel comprises five members.[176] The disputing Parties have fifteen days from delivery of the request for the establishment of the panel to agree on the Chair of the panel, failing which a disputing Party chosen by lot selects as Chair an individual who is not a citizen of that Party. Within fifteen days of the selection of the Chair, each disputing Party selects two panelists who are citizens of the other disputing Party, failing which such panelists are chosen by lot from the roster of panelists. The roster contains thirty individuals who are appointed by consensus of the Parties for unrenewable terms of three years.[177] They must have expertise in law, international trade, other matters covered by NAFTA or the resolution of international trade disputes. They must be independent of and not take instructions from any Party. If a disputing Party selects as panelist an individual who is not on the roster, the other disputing Party may exercise a peremptory challenge against this individual within fifteen days after he or she has been proposed.[178] The same rules apply *mutatis mutandis* where the dispute involves all three NAFTA Parties.[179]

Unless the disputing Parties agree otherwise, the terms of reference of the panel are to examine the matter in the light of the relevant provisions of the Agreement and to make findings, determinations and recommendations.[180] If a Party wishes to argue nullification or impairment of benefits, the terms of reference must so indicate.[181] Within ninety days after the last panelist is selected, the panel presents its initial report to the Parties, on which they may submit written comments within fourteen days.[182] The final report is presented to the disputing Parties within thirty

173 Article 2007:4. *See also* Articles N-07:4 (Canada), 18-05:4 (Mexico) and 22.5:4 (USA).

174 Article 2008:1 and 2. *See also* Articles N-08: 1 and 2 (Canada), 18-06:1 and 2 (Mexico) and 22.6:1 (USA).

175 Article 2008:3. For obvious reasons, this provisions does not exist in the other agreements.

176 Article 2011:1. *See also* Articles N-11:1 (Canada), 18-09:1 to 4 (Mexico) and 22.9:1 (USA).

177 Article 2009. *See also* Articles N-09 (Canada), 18-07 (Mexico) and 22.7 (USA).

178 Article 2011:3. *See also* Articles N-11:2 (Canada), 18-09:5 (Mexico) and 22.9:2 (USA).

179 Article 2011:2. For obvious reasons, this provision does not exist in the other agreements.

180 Article 2012:3. *See also* Articles N-12:3 (Canada), 18-10:3 (Mexico) and 22.10:4 (USA).

181 Article 2012:4. *See also* Articles N-12:4 (Canada), 18-10:4 (Mexico) and 22.10:5 (USA).

182 Article 2016:2 and 4. *See also* Articles N-15:2 and 4 (Canada), 18.13:2 and 4 (Mexico) and 22.12:3 and 5 (USA).

days of the presentation of the initial report unless the Parties agree otherwise.[183] It is then transmitted within a reasonable time to the Commission together with any written views that a disputing Party desires to be appended. The final report is published fifteen days after it is transmitted to the Commission.

On receipt of the final report, the disputing Parties are summoned to agree on a resolution of the dispute.[184] Wherever possible, this should involve the non-implementation or removal of a measure that infringes NAFTA or which causes nullification or impairment of benefits or, failing such a resolution, compensation. If the Parties fail to reach an agreement on these terms within thirty days of receiving the final report, the complaining Party may suspend the application to the other Party of benefits of equivalent effect until such time as agreement is reached on a resolution of the dispute.[185] Benefits should first be suspended in the same sector or sectors affected by the measure unless the complaining Party considers that this is not practicable or effective.[186] On the written request of the other Party, the Commission must establish a panel to determine whether the level of benefits suspended by the complaining Party is manifestly excessive.[187] The panel presents its determination within sixty days after the last panelist is selected or such other period as the disputing Parties agree.

Disputes with regard to matters that are regulated by both GATS and NAFTA may be settled in either forum at the discretion of the complaining Party.[188] However, before a Party initiates a dispute settlement proceeding under GATS, it must notify the third Party of its intention.[189] If the third Party is also affected by the dispute and wishes to have recourse to the dispute settlement procedure under NAFTA, it must inform the notifying Party and the Parties must consult with a view to agreeing on a single forum. If the Parties cannot agree, the dispute is normally settled under the NAFTA procedure. Once dispute settlement procedures have been initiated under NAFTA or GATS, the choice of forum is definitive.[190]

2. Submission by Providers of Claims to Arbitration

Providers from a NAFTA Party who are providing services in another NAFTA Party by commercial presence (Mode 3) have, as we have seen, incidental rights

183 Article 2017. *See also* Articles N-16 (Canada), 18.14 (Mexico) and 22.13 (USA).

184 Article 2018. *See also* Articles N-17 (Canada), 18.15 (Mexico) and 22.14 (USA).

185 Article 2019:1. *See also* Articles N-18:1 (Canada), 18-16 1 and 2 (Mexico) and 22.15:1 and 2 (USA).

186 Article 2019:2. *See also* Articles N-18:2 (Canada) and 18-16:3 (Mexico). The US-Chile Agreement does not have an equivalent provision.

187 Article 2019:3. *See also* Articles N-18.3 (Canada), 18-16:4 (Mexico) and 22.15:3 (USA).

188 Article 2005:1. *See also* Articles N-05:1 (Canada), 18-03:1 (Mexico) and 22.3:1 (USA). NAFTA refers to GATT as GATS did not exist when it was signed. However, it also refers to agreements negotiated thereunder, which includes GATS. The other three agreements refer simply to the WTO Agreement, of which GATS is a part.

189 Article 2005:2. For obvious reasons, the other three agreements do not have this provision.

190 Article 2005:6. *See also* Articles N-05:4 (Canada), 18-03:2 (Mexico) and 22.3:2 (USA).

under Chapter 11 on investment as well as protection against monopolies and state enterprises where they act inconsistently with a Party's obligations under Chapter 11 with respect to their delegated powers. Where these rights or obligations are breached, the investor/provider itself may submit a claim to arbitration, without prejudice to the rights of any Party under the NAFTA dispute settlement procedure, as long as the investor/provider has incurred loss or damage by reason of the breach.[191] The claim must be made before three years have elapsed since the investor/provider became aware, or should have become aware, of the alleged breach and the loss or damage.[192]

The disputing parties should first attempt to settle the claim through consultations or negotiation.[193] Where an investor/provider intends to submit the claim to arbitration, it must notify the Party concerned in writing at least ninety days before the claim is submitted.[194] The notice must specify the provisions of Chapter 11 alleged to have been breached, the issues and factual basis for the claim and the relief sought and the approximate amount of damages claimed. A disputing investor/provider may submit the claim to arbitration provided that six months have lapsed since the events giving rise to the claim.[195] It may be submitted under the 1965 *Convention on the Settlement of Investment Disputes between States and Nationals of Other States* (ICSID Convention), provided that both the disputing Party and the Party of the disputing investor/provider are parties to the Convention, the Additional Facility Rules of ICSID, provided that either the disputing Party or the Party of disputing investor, but not both, is a party to the ICSID Convention, or the Arbitration Rule of the United Nations Commission on International Trade Law (UNCITRAL Rules).[196] A claim is submitted for arbitration when the request for arbitration has been received by the Secretary-General of ICSID or the notice of arbitration given under the UNCITRAL Rules is received by the disputing Party.[197]

Unless the disputing parties agree otherwise, the Arbitration Tribunal consists of three arbitrators, one appointed by each of the disputing parties and the third, who is the presiding arbitrator, appointed by agreement of the parties.[198] If the Tribunal is not constituted within ninety days from the date of submission of the claim, the Secretary-General of ICSID appoints, at his or her discretion, the arbitrator or ar-

---

191 Article 1115 and 1116:1. *See* also Articles G-16 and G.17:1 (Canada), 9-16 and 9-17:1 (Mexico) and 10.15:1 (USA).

192 Article 1116:2. *See* also Articles G-17:2 (Canada), 9-17:2 (Mexico) and 10.17:1 (USA).

193 Article 1118. *See* also Articles G-19 (Canada), 9-19 (Mexico) and 10.14 (USA).

194 Article 1119. *See* also Articles G-20 (Canada), 9-20 (Mexico) and 10.15:1 to 4 (USA).

195 Article 1120:1 *See* also Articles G-2:1 (Canada), 9-21:1 (Mexico) and 10.15:5 (USA).

196 The arbitration rules of the United Nations Commission on International Trade Law were approved by the UN General Assembly on December 15, 1976.

197 Article 1137:1. *See* also Articles G-38:1 (Canada), 9-38:1 (Mexico) and 10.15:6 (USA).

198 Article 1123. *See* also Articles G-24 (Canada), 9-24 (Mexico) and 10.18:1 (USA).

bitrators not yet appointed.[199] However, the Secretary-General must appoint the presiding arbitrator from a roster of presiding arbitrators or, if no such arbitrator is available, from the ICSID panel of arbitrators.[200] The presiding arbitrator may not be a national of the disputing Party or the Party of the disputing investor/provider.

The Tribunal decides the issues in dispute in accordance with the applicable rules of international law with respect to governing law.[201] When it makes its final award, the Parties must provide for the enforcement in their territories of any damages awarded.[202]

H. FURTHER NEGOTIATIONS ON LIBERALIZATION OF TRADE IN SERVICES UNDER NAFTA

Apart from the obligation to negotiate at least every two years the liberalization of non-discriminatory quantitative restrictions with respect to cross-border services,[203] the Parties are under no formal requirement to negotiate further liberalization of services under NAFTA. However, the Free Trade Commission that is set up under the Agreement, has a mandate to oversee the further elaboration of NAFTA, which obviously includes such further liberalization.[204]

II. THE EUROPEAN UNION (AND THE EUROPEAN AGREEMENTS)

A. INTRODUCTION

1. The Treaties

The European Community Treaty

The EU is based on three major treaties: the EC Treaty (1957), the *European Atomic Energy Community Treaty* (EAECT (1957) and the *Treaty on European Union* (TEU) (1992), as amended by the *Single European Act* (1986), the *Treaty of Amsterdam* (1997) and the *Treaty of Nice* (2001). The provisions on trade in services between the Member States of the Union are found exclusively in the EC Treaty. It is, therefore, this Treaty with which we are concerned in this monograph.

The EC Treaty started life as the *Treaty establishing the European Economic Community* (EECT), which was signed in Rome on March 25, 1957 by Belgium,

---

199 Article 1124:2. *See also* Articles G-25:2 (Canada), 9-25:2 (Mexico) and 10.18:3 (USA).

200 Article 1124:3. *See also* Articles G-25:3 (Canada) and 9-25:3 (Mexico). The US-Chile Agreement does not contain this provision.

201 Article 1131:1. *See also* Articles G-32:1 (Canada), 9-32:1 (Mexico) and 10.21:1 (USA).

202 Article 1136:4. *See also* Articles G-37:4 (Canada), 9-37:4 (Mexico) and 10.25:7 (USA).

203 Article 1207:4. *See also* Articles H-07:4 (Canada) and 10-08:4 (Mexico). The US-Chile Agreement treats non-discriminatory quantitative restrictions as market access barriers.

204 Article 2001:2(b). *See also* Articles N-01:2(b) (Canada) and 21.1:2(b) (USA). The Mexico-Chile Agreement does not have this provision.

France, Germany, Italy, Luxembourg and the Netherlands. It came into effect on January 1, 1958. The Treaty established a common market for the Member States, which was supplemented by two sectoral agreements, the EAECT and the now defunct *Treaty establishing the European Coal and Steel Community* (ECSC Treaty). The EECT obviously dominated the other two sectoral common markets and, in 1992, the TEU changed its name to the European Community (EC or "Community") and the EECT became the EC Treaty. The TEU established the EU in November 1993 with a rather awkward three-pillared structure comprising the EC supplemented by the Common Foreign and Security Policy and Police and Judicial Cooperation in Criminal Matters.[205] It also provided for Economic and Monetary Union, the final stage of which, including the introduction of the Euro, was accomplished on January 1, 1999. The ECSC Treaty expired on July 24th, 2002 and the coal and steel sector was incorporated into the EC.

Denmark, Ireland and the United Kingdom joined the EEC on January 1, 1973. They were followed by Greece on January 1, 1981, Spain and Portugal on January 1, 1986, Austria, Finland and Sweden on January 1, 1995 and Cyprus, the Czech Republic, Estonia, Hungary, Latvia, Lithuania, Malta, Poland, Slovakia and Slovenia on May 1, 2004.

Nomenclature is very confusing in the EU. Although the EC is part of the Union, the terms "Community" and "Community law" are nevertheless used to distinguish it from the other two pillars of the Union. However, as Community law is as much EU law as any instruments emanating from the other two pillars of the Union, I prefer to use the term EU law. In any case, under the new European Constitution, the term "EU" will completely supplant the term "Community."[206]

The Agreement on the European Economic Area

The Agreement on the European Economic Area (AEEA) was signed in 1992 and came into effect on January 1, 1994. The original signatories were the twelve Member States of the EU at the time and the states making up the European Free Trade Association (EFTA),[207] namely Austria, Finland, Iceland, Liechtenstein, Norway, Sweden and Switzerland. Austria, Finland and Sweden joined the EU in 1995, and the Swiss rejected adhesion to the AEEA in a national referendum. The AEEA, therefore, applies only to Iceland, Liechtenstein and Norway, and its effect is to extend to these three EFTA countries the EU rules on trade in services. It also incorporates the secondary legislation of the EU[208] and the jurisprudence of the

205 The original name—Cooperation in Justice and Home Affairs—was changed by the Treaty of Amsterdam.

206 However, given the French rejection of the Constitution, it is unlikely that it will enter into force.

207 EFTA was set up in 1960 at British urging as a rival to the newly-created European Economic Community. Portugal was also among its original members but left in 1986 to join the European Communities, as the European Union was then called.

208 *Articles 7, 31(2), 36(2) and 47(2). See also Annexes IV to XIII.*

Court of Justice.[209] In 1999, the Swiss Confederation signed a separate agreement with the EU dealing *inter alia* with the free movement of services,[210] thereby putting it vis-à-vis the EU in more or less the same position as the other EFTA states.

The AEEA reproduces almost word for word the provisions of the EC Treaty on establishment and services. Thus, the ensuing discussion of the EC Treaty applies *mutatis mutandis* to the AEAA, and the equivalent provisions of this Agreement are given in the footnotes in italic script.

The Vaduz Convention

The original EFTA Agreement did not include any provisions on the free movement of services. The effect of the AEEA was to remove the restrictions on trade in services between Iceland, Liechtenstein and Norway. These restrictions continued to exist, however, between these three EFTA states and Switzerland. Once Switzerland signed the agreement providing for the free movement of services between the Confederation and the EC, this situation became untenable. Consequently, the original treaty establishing EFTA was updated to include provisions on the free movement of services. The Vaduz Convention, which was signed on June 21, 2001 and came into effect on June 1, 2002, establishes more or less the same regime for trade in services between the EFTA countries as exists within the EU. There are, however, differences, and thus it is not possible to give references to the Vaduz Convention in the footnotes.

2. Application of the EC Treaty

EU law is more akin to federal law than international law.[211] The Treaty provisions on services are to a great extent directly applicable in the Member States, as are regulations adopted by the Council, the European Parliament or the Commission.[212] Direct applicability means that the EU provision takes effect within the legal orders of the Member States without the need for national implementation. It also means that, where a provision establishes rights for persons that are clear, precise and unconditional and which do not accord the Member States any discretion in their application, these rights must be enforced by national courts at the suit of the person concerned.[213] This is the doctrine of direct effect.[214] Directives adopted by the EU institutions have to be transposed into national law, but, as they are very

209 *Article 6.*

210 It is the 1999 *Agreement between the European Community and its Member States and the Swiss Confederation on the Free Movement of Persons*, OJ L114/02.

211 On the legal order of the EU, *see* P. Raworth, *Introduction to the Legal System of the European Union* (Oceana Publications, New York, 2001), Chapter VII.

212 *See* Articles 249; *7(a). See also Reyners* v. *The Belgian State*, 2/74, [1974] 2 CMLR 305; *van Binsbergen* v. *Bestuur van de Bedrijfsvereniging voor de Metaalnijverheid*, 33/74, [1974] 1 CMLR.

213 *See van Duyn* v. *Home Office*, 41/74, [1974] ECR 1337.

214 The concepts of direct applicability and direct effect are sometimes confused, but they are quite separate. *See* Raworth at pp. 114-116.

detailed, this is really just a formality. Moreover, the provisions of a directive are also directly effective where they meet the test set out above and if the time for their transposition has passed or they have been improperly transposed.[215] Directly applicable EU law and national laws transposing EU directives take precedence over national law[216] and bind all levels of government in the Member States as well as non-governmental bodies exercising delegated powers.[217] EU law deals with all aspects of trade in services.

EU law applies to the metropolitan territory of the twenty-five Member States of the EU. It does not apply to the Faeroe Islands, the Sovereign Base Areas of the United Kingdom in Cyprus or the Channel Islands. Gibraltar is excluded from the customs territory of the EU and from certain legislation. Since 1993, EU law does not apply to Andorra. Special rules exist for the non-European territories of the Member States over which they exercise sovereignty and which are listed in Annex II.

The EC Treaty covers all services, which specifically include activities of an industrial and commercial character as well the activities of craftsmen and the professions.[218] Two sectors are singled out for special treatment. Transport services are covered by separate provisions,[219] which originally did not apply to air and sea transport.[220] The Council was given the power to extend their application,[221] which it has now done.[222] The opening up of the market in banking and insurance was to be effected in step with the liberalization of capital movements,[223] which has now happened.[224] Unusually, the government procurement sector is subject to the general rules of the EC Treaty although a number of directives exist that deal with the special problems that arise in this sector.[225]

215 *See van Duyn.*

216 *See* the decision of the Court of Justice of the Communities in *Costa* v. *Enel*, 6/64, [1964] ECR 585; *Internationale Handelsgesellschaft m.b.H* v. *Einfuhr- und Vorratsstelle für Getreide und Futtermittel*, 11/70, [1970] ECR 1125; *Amministrazione delle Finanze dello Stato* v. *Simmenthal SpA*, 106/77, [1978] ECR 629. *See also* P. Raworth at pp.116-118.

217 This is how the Court of Justice has interpreted Article 10 of the ect (*Article 3 of the* AEEA)—*see Fratelli Constanzo v. Commune di Milano*, 103/88, [1989] E.C.R. 1839 at 1871.

218 Articles 50; *37*.

219 Articles 51(1); *38*. The transport provisions are found in Articles 70-80 (*47-52*).

220 Article 80(1); *47(1)*.

221 Article 80(2). This provision is not found in the AEEA, but the EC transport rules apply by virtue of *Article 47(2)* of the Agreement. They are found in *Annex XIII* to the AEEA.

222 The Community's transport legislation is discussed in Chapter Seven.

223 Article 51(2). This provision does not exist in the AEEA as capital movements had been liberalized when it was signed—*see* Articles 40 and 41.

224 Articles 56; *40* and *41*.

225 Government procurement in the Community is discussed in Chapter Eight.

There are, however, some limitations on the freedom to provide services under the EC Treaty. Certain postal services, for example, may be reserved to the public or private body entrusted with ensuring universal postal service in a Member State to the extent that this is necessary to effect this service.[226] There is not, however, in the EC Treaty a general exception for public services along the lines of GATS.[227] Instead, there is a general exception for activities connected with the exercise of official authority.[228]

The scope of this exception is not entirely clear. The EC Treaty permits its use even where the activity in question has only an occasional connection with the exercise of official authority. This formulation raises two questions, namely whether an activity in its entirety may be barred to non-nationals[229] where its pursuit involves an *optional* connection with official authority, and secondly, whether mere contact with a person exercising official authority is sufficient to establish the necessary connection.

Both these questions were raised in *Reyners,*[230] a case that concerned a Dutchman who was denied access to the Belgian legal profession, *inter alia* on the basis of this exception. All the Member States that made submissions to the Court of Justice of the European Communities[231] agreed that the use of the exception was only justified if the activities of a lawyer in Belgium *necessarily* involved a connection with the exercise of official authority. The Irish, British and Dutch governments also took the view that there was no such necessary connection at issue, but Belgium, supported by Germany, maintained that it was provided by the lawyer's inevitable contact with the judicial process.

In its judgment, the Court of Justice strongly supported the unanimous opinion of the Member States making submissions that exclusion of non-nationals from an entire activity is only warranted where a connection with the exercise of official authority is an integral part of that activity. Referring specifically to the legal profession, the Court asserted that the connection must be "linked with that profession in such a way that freedom of establishment [or the provision of services on a cross-border basis] would result in imposing on the Member State concerned the obligation to allow the exercise, even occasionally, by non-nationals of functions

226 Directive 97/67 (OJ L15/98), Article 7.

227 The provision in question is GATS, Article I:3(b).

228 Articles 45 and 55; *32* and *39*.

229 "Non-nationals" means nationals from other Member States as opposed to third-country nationals, who are from non Members.

230 *Reyners.*

231 This is the Court that rules on the interpretation and application of the ECT and Community secondary legislation. Henceforth, the court is referred to as the "Court of Justice".

appertaining to official authority."[232] The Court then went on to reject the Belgian and German contention that mere contact with the judicial process, which it accepted as an integral part of the legal profession in Belgium, constituted the requisite connection.[233]

Reyners thus answers the two questions raised by the wording of Article 45[234] in the negative. It makes it very clear that an entire services area is not to be judged by the nature of certain optional activities within it, and that a connection with official authority requires that a non-national actually exercise the authority him or herself.

This still leaves unanswered the question of the definition of "official authority." *Reyners* tells us only that judicial power comes within the concept but that the normal duties of a lawyer do not. This is unfortunate as both the Commission and the Advocate-General gave the Court ample opportunity to pronounce more broadly on the issue by setting forth their own definitions. The Commission suggested that it referred to "prerogatives outside the general law,"[235] while the Advocate-General invoked in grand Hegelian manner "the sovereignty and majesty of the state."[236] The prerogatives that exist outside the general law are the executive, legislative and judicial powers of the state to affect the rights of citizens, and this is surely what is meant by "official authority."

Using this definition, the activities of notaries public and process servers when they act as an arm of the executive are among the activities barred to non-nationals. On the other hand, chartered accountants do not fit the definition as their reports remain private documents even if they are prepared pursuant to a statutory obligation. In *Haug,*[237] the Comptroller of the British Patent Office rejected the use of the exception in the case of patent agents, pointing out that "any official authority in relation to patents is exercised by the Courts and various government departments."[238] The criterion common to all these examples is whether or not the activity involves an executive, legislative or judicial act. Where it does, the exception applies; otherwise it does not.

---

232 *Reyners* at 309.

233 *Ibid.* The Court said the following: "Professional activities involving contacts, even regular and organic, with the courts, including even compulsory cooperation in their functioning, do not constitute, as such, connection with the exercise of official authority."

234 *Article 32.*

235 *Reyners* at 640.

236 *Reyners* at 318.

237 *Haug* v. *Registrar of Patent Agents*, [1976] 1 CMLR 491.

238 *Haug* at 493.

The second paragraph of Article 45 gives the Council an ill-defined authority to extend the use of the exception.[239] It would seem that this provision is intended to complement the strict limits placed upon the use of the exception in the first paragraph of Article 45 by permitting the Council to declare that certain activities shall be deemed as a matter of law to be connected with the exercise of official authority. This is what the Council did on the one occasion it used its authority under this provision.[240]

The EU rules on services cover all four modes of supplying them. Article 49[241] gives a right to provide cross-border services from an establishment in a Member State to a recipient in any other Member State. This includes supply by the presence of natural persons (Mode 4).[242] Article 43[243] gives a right to set up and operate a commercial presence in any other Member State, from which, of course, services can be provided.

The above rights apply to nationals as well as to companies or firms that are formed under the law of a Member State and which also have their registered office, central administration or principal place of business somewhere in the EU.[244] Companies or firms may be constituted under civil or commercial law and include cooperative societies and other legal persons governed by public or private law, save for those which are non-profit-making.[245] The term "nationals" is restricted to citizens. Under Article 17 of the EC Treaty,[246] it is EU citizens that enjoy the rights conferred by the Treaty, and, in order to be an EU citizen, one must be a citizen of a Member State.[247] Moreover, the Council is given the power to extend the provisions on cross-border services to third-country nationals,[248] which clearly implies that they are not already covered by them. This has not been done, and so third-country nationals will have to rely on GATS or the OECD Codes if they wish to provide services within the EU. There is no citizenship requirement, however, for recipients of services provided under the EC Treaty.

---

239 There is no equivalent provision in the AEEA. However, any secondary legislation enacted by the Council pursuant to this paragraph would be binding on EFTA states by virtue of *Article 7* of the Agreement.

240 Directive 68/363, OJ L297/68. However, this Directive is no longer in force.

241 *Article 36.*

242 Article 50, 3rd para; *37, 3rd para.*

243 *Article 31.*

244 Articles 43, 48, 49 and *55; 31, 34, 36 and 39.*

245 Articles 48, 2nd. para; *34, 2nd para.*

246 There is no equivalent provision in the AEEA, but citizenship of an EFTA or EU Member State is certainly required.

247 *See* the comments on this narrow definition in L.W. Gormley, *Introduction to the Law of the European Communities* (3rd edition, London, Kluwer Law International, 1998) at p. 175.

248 Article 49, 2nd para. There is no equivalent provision in the AEEA.

3. Approach of the EC Treaty

Like NAFTA and the OECD Codes, the EC Treaty takes a top-down approach. It includes all services except those that it specifically excludes, which are activities connected, even occasionally, with the exercise of official authority. Some other services, such as postal services, may be reserved under EU law. The Member States are not allowed to enter any reservations with respect to their obligations under the Treaty.[249]

I prefer to see market access as treated separately from national treatment in the EC Treaty, as the Treaty distinguishes in the operative provisions on personal mobility between removing restrictions on the free movement of workers, freedom of establishment and freedom to provide services, on the one hand, and the removal of discrimination based on nationality, on the other. The former, which is market access, is found respectively in Articles 39(1), the first paragraph of Article 43 and Article 49,[250] whereas the latter, which is national treatment, is found respectively in Article 39(2), the second paragraph of Article 43 and the third paragraph of Article 50.[251] There is also a general provision on national treatment in Article 12.[252] Unfortunately, the Court of Justice has muddied the waters somewhat by its view that Articles 39 to 55 on personal mobility implement the national treatment provision in Article 12 of the Treaty.[253] However, there is nothing in the Court's judgments on this point to suggest that this is the only function of these Articles.

Like NAFTA, the EC Treaty separates out cross-border services (Modes 1, 2 and 4), which are covered by Articles 49 to 55,[254] and services provided from a commercial presence (Mode 3), which are covered implicitly by Articles 43 to 48 on establishment.[255] Article 39[256] covers the free movement of workers and may apply to employees who are posted abroad temporarily to provide services in another Member State on behalf of their employer.[257] Despite this separation, however, both the Court of Justice and the Council have endeavored to create an integrated scheme out of these various Articles. The Court has stressed on numer-

249 The is implied by Articles 10 and 299 *Articles 3 and 126*).

250 *Articles 28(1), 31(1), 1st para and 36.*

251 *Articles 28(2), 31(1), 2nd para. and 37, 3rd para.*

252 *Article 4.*

253 *See* e.g. *Gaetano Donà* v. *Mario Mantero*, 13/76, [1976] 2 CMLR at 586.

254 *Articles 36 to 39.*

255 *Articles 31 to 35.*

256 *Article 28.*

257 I believe that it does, but in any case Directive 96/71 concerning the posting of workers in the framework of the provision of services (OJ L18/97) makes clear that such employees are indeed covered by the EC Treaty rules, even if not by Article 39.

ous occasions that they are based on identical principles,[258] and the Council has taken a similarly integrative approach in its legislation.[259] This approach is facilitated by the fact that the provisions in Articles 45 to 48 on official authority, the public policy exception, qualifications, access to self-employed activities and the definition of companies and firms are said to apply as well to cross-border services.[260]

Originally, the liberalization of trade in services in the Community was not achieved by operation of the EC Treaty but by a series of Council directives and regulations. Many liberalized specific activities, while others set out the rights of movement and residence. However, at the expiry of the transitional period on January 1, 1970, the Court of Justice decided, in two landmark cases,[261] that the provisions on establishment and services in the EC Treaty had become directly applicable, which meant that they had legal effect in the Member States without the need for national implementing legislation. The Court declared that the secondary legislation authorized by the EC Treaty had never been envisaged as an indispensable means of implementing these particular Treaty provisions.

The initial reaction of the Community institutions to the Court's ruling was to stop adopting secondary legislation in implementation of the EC Treaty's provisions on establishment and services. This approach was too radical, however, as the European Parliament and the Council somewhat belatedly recognized in their joint Directive 99/42.[262] They reiterate the Court's ruling that the liberalization of trade in services within the EU is now achieved directly by the Treaty and accept that this makes a number of directives in the area redundant.[263] Nonetheless, they point out that "certain of the directives' provisions designed to facilitate the effective exercise of the right of establishment and freedom to provide services should be retained, particularly where they usefully prescribe how obligations under the Treaty are to be discharged."[264] The Directive repeals a number of directives but leaves in place those that it considers still useful. Apart from important legislation in certain sectors such as financial services and telecommunications, there is still secondary legislation dealing with traders in and distributors of toxic products, lawyers, health care professionals, pharmacists and architects. Many of the provi-

---

258 *See Walrave and Koch* v. *Association Union Cycliste Internationale,* 36/74, [1975] 1 CMLR at 332 and *The State* v. *Jean Noël Royer,* 48/75, [1976] 2 CMLR at 636.

259 *See infra* in the text.

260 Articles 55; *39.*

261 *Reyners* and *van Binsbergen.*

262 EP/Council Directive 99/42 establishing a mechanism for the recognition of qualifications in respect of the professional activities covered by the Directives on liberalization and transitional measures and supplementing the general system for the recognition of qualifications (OJ L201/99).

263 Preamble, 1st recital. Somewhat perversely, the wording refers only to national treatment whereas it is also the market access provisions that are directly applicable.

264 Preamble, 2nd recital.

sions of these directives deal with the problems posed by domestic regulation. There are also directives dealing with freedom of movement and residence.

The relationship between the EC Treaty and GATS is straightforward. The EC Treaty regulates trade in services between the Member States of the EU to the exclusion of GATS. GATS regulates the trade in services of the EU as a whole with non-Member States that are Members of the WTO. With the exception of cultural and audiovisual services, educational services and social and human health services, where jurisdiction is shared with the Member States, the EU has exclusive authority over trade in services between Member States and non-Member States.[265] The preferential treatment accorded by the Member States of the EU to each other does not infringe the MFN principle of GATS as it comes within the economic integration exception.[266]

B. MARKET ACCESS

1. Introduction

Although the EC Treaty separates out cross-border services from services supplied from a commercial presence, it nevertheless presents an integrated system of rules that apply to both types of services. We shall, therefore, discuss them together.

2. Market Access under the EC Treaty

The EC Treaty requires with respect to EU citizens the removal of all restrictions on the freedom to supply services within the EU by any mode, including restrictions on the employment of natural persons to supply services through Mode 4.[267] This covers in principle all the categories of market entry barriers on List 3, although the operational barriers (Category 3) are also the subject of specific provisions.

Prohibitions and restrictions on the importation of visible services and inputs that are needed to provide a service (barrier (j)) are forbidden by the provisions abolishing tariffs and quantitative restrictions on all goods that are traded between the Member States.[268] All restrictions on the movement of capital and on payments between Member States (and between Member States and third countries) (barriers (k) and (l)) are prohibited by Article 56.[269] Currency restrictions imposed for balance-of-payments reasons are only permitted for Member States outside the

265 Article 133. There is no common commercial policy under the AEEA.

266 GATS, Article V. *See* the discussion in Chapter Two, Section I.F.3.

267 Articles 39(1), 43, 1st para and 49, 1st para.; *28(1), 31(1) 1st para and 36(1).*

268 Articles 25 and 28: *10 and 11.*

269 *Articles 40 and 41.*

Eurozone.[270] Public and private monopolies (barrier (m)) are not prohibited by the EC Treaty. However, public monopolies must act in a manner that is consistent with a Member State's market access obligations.[271] This obligation applies also to undertakings that, while not controlled by the state, have nevertheless been granted special or exclusive rights by Member States. Private monopolies must act in accordance with the EC's anti-trust rules.

Other provisions in the EC Treaty clarify the scope of particular market access commitments. Thus, Article 294 expressly prohibits restrictions on non-national shareholdings in the host Member State (barrier (c)).[272] The right of establishment is defined in Article 43 as the right not only to set up agencies, branches and subsidiaries (barrier (d)) but also the right to take up residence and operate these establishments.[273] This right of personal establishment is a hallmark of the EC Treaty that distinguishes it from other agreements, such as GATS and NAFTA. There is also an express provision giving persons the right to pursue their activities temporarily in another Member State in order to provide a service through the presence of natural persons (barrier (e)).[274]

The prohibition on quantitative restrictions on the importation and exportation of goods between Member States, as well as all measures having equivalent effect, applies, according the jurisprudence of the Court of Justice, *mutatis mutandis* to trade in services as well.[275] This covers barriers (a) and (b).

Because of the comprehensive scope and direct application of the EC Treaty provisions on market access for the provision of services, the secondary legislation is no longer very important from this perspective. The only market access provision in the directives on specific activities that is still relevant concerns access to social security systems by health care professionals (part of barrier (f)). In Europe, most medical services are covered by national social security systems. Private health care exists in some EU countries, but a provider of cross-border services who does not have access to the social security system is reduced to serving the private market, which is small or may not even exist. This constitutes, therefore, a potent barrier to market access. Accordingly, the health care directives all provide that a supplier of health care services must have access to the social security scheme of

---

270 Articles 119(4) and 120(4). The Eurozone consists of those Member States that have entered the third stage of Economic and Monetary Union and adopted the Euro as their common currency. Denmark, Sweden and the United Kingdom are not members of the Eurozone. There is no balance-of-payments exception in the AEEA.

271 Articles 86(1); *59(1).*

272 *Article 124.*

273 *Article 31.*

274 Articles 50, 3rd para; *37, 3rd para.*

275 *See Commission v. The Netherlands*, C-353/89, [1991] ECR at I-4097.

the host state.[276] However, the provider must inform the competent authorities of the host state before the services are provided or, in urgent cases, as soon as possible afterwards. Member States may apply to non-nationals any non-discriminatory requirement for special training as a prerequisite for access to the national social security scheme as long as the period does not exceed six months.[277]

The modalities of the general right under the EC Treaty to move and reside freely within the territory of the Member States,[278] which is obviously very relevant for providers of services, is regulated in detail by Directive 04/38.[279] This Directive requires Member States to grant Union citizens who wish to provide services by Modes 3 or 4 leave to enter their territories with a valid identity card or passport.[280] In fact, under the Schengen Agreement abolishing border controls, not even this trifling formality is observed except in extraordinary circumstances. The United Kingdom and Ireland, however, are not parties to Schengen and exercise border controls on a regular basis.

Once in another Member State, a Union citizen may remain there for three months without any conditions or formalities[281] except possibly the requirement of reporting his or her presence.[282] This time period may well be sufficient for the provision of a service by presence of natural persons. If not, or if the services are to be supplied from a commercial presence, the provider comes under the rules on a right of residence for more than three months.

Such a right must be granted to all Union citizens who are working in an employed or self-employed capacity in the host Member State or who are enrolled in a private or public educational establishment.[283] Students, who can be regarded as the recipients of a service, must prove, however, that they have sufficient resources not to become a burden on the social assistance system of the host state and that they have comprehensive health insurance cover. If a non-national stays for over three months in another Member State, he or she may have to register with the relevant authorities.[284] The registration certificate must be issued on presentation of a valid identity card or passport together with confirmation of em-

---

276 *See, e.g.* Directives 93/16 (doctors) (OJ L165/93), Article 18 and 78/686 (dentists), (OJ L233/78), Article 16.

277 *See*, e.g. Directives 93/16 (doctors), Article 21 and 78/686 (dentists), Article 20.

278 Article 18(1). The AEEA has no equivalent provision, but Directive 04/38 applies by virtue of *Article 7* of the Agreement.

279 EP/Council Directive 04/38 on the right of citizens of the Union and their family members to move and reside freely within the territory of the Member States amending Regulation 1612/68 and repealing Directives 64/221, 68/360, 72/194, 73/148, 75/34, 75/35, 90/364, 90/365 and 93/96 (OJ L158/04).

280 Article 5(1).

281 Article 6(1).

282 Article 5(5).

283 Article 7(1)(a) and (c).

284 Article 8(1).

ployment or proof of self-employment.[285] Students must show proof of enrollment and health insurance and make a declaration that they have sufficient resources. Member States may only verify this information where there is a reasonable doubt as to whether the service provider or student satisfies the conditions for residence. As for health insurance, most Union citizens will have coverage from their home country that is valid in the host Member State under EU law.

Member States may require providers of services to prove their qualifications.[286] In the case of health care professionals, a host Member State may require a person who is providing services in its territory through presence of natural persons to supply one or more of the following documents:[287]

- a declaration concerning the provision of these services;
- a certificate stating that the person concerned is lawfully pursuing the activities in question in the Member State where he is established;
- a certificate that the person concerned holds one or other of the diplomas, certificates or other evidence of formal qualification appropriate for the provision of the services in question.

Union citizens providing services by means of a commercial presence in another Member State and who have resided there legally for a continuous period of five years obtain a right of permanent residence.[288]

Entry and residence in another Member State are subject under the EC Treaty to restrictions imposed by the host state on grounds of public policy, public security or public health.[289] The use of this exception is also governed by Directive 04/38. Any such measures must be proportionate and based exclusively on the personal conduct of the individual concerned.[290] A previous criminal conviction does not automatically justify taking such measures. Rather, the personal conduct of the individual must represent a genuine, present and sufficiently serious threat affecting one of the fundamental interests of society. Restrictions must not serve economic ends.[291] Expulsion of EU citizens with a right of permanent residence is only permitted on serious grounds of public policy or security[292] and, in the case of EU citizens who have resided in the Member State for the previous ten years, on

285 Article 8(3).

286 *See* Directive 77/249 (lawyers) (OJ L78/77), Article 7(1); Directive 99/42 establishing a mechanism for the recognition of qualifications in respect of the professional activities covered by the Directives on liberalization and transitional measures and supplementing the general system for the recognition of qualifications (OJ L201/99), Article 8.

287 *See* Directive 93/16 (doctors), Article 17(3).

288 Article 16(1).

289 Articles 46(1); *33.*

290 Article 27(2).

291 Article 27(1).

292 Article 28(2).

imperative grounds of public security.[293] The only diseases justifying measures restricting freedom of movement are the diseases with epidemic potential as defined by the World Health Organization and other infectious diseases or contagious parasitic diseases that are the subject of protective provisions applying to nationals of the host Member State.[294] Diseases occurring after three months from the date of arrival of the EU citizen in the host Member States cannot be a ground for expulsion.[295]

3. The EC Treaty Approach to Market Access

The EC Treaty distinguishes between the removal of restriction on the provision of services, which is market access, and the right to provide them on the same terms as nationals, which is national treatment. However, as it does not go further in separating out the concepts of market access and national treatment, it is not possible to discern which measures it categorizes as market access barriers. However, its inclusive approach of requiring the abolition of all restrictions on the provision of services certainly covers all the barriers that are listed on List 3. Indeed, it goes beyond other agreements by granting a right of personal establishment, which is exercised subject to the conditions and according to the procedures set out in Directive 04/38.

C. NATIONAL TREATMENT

1. Introduction

Article 12 of the EC Treaty contains a general prohibition against discrimination on grounds of nationality.[296] An earlier view, which was advanced by national courts,[297] the Commission[298] and some scholars,[299] was that this Article was the basis for national treatment in all matters covered by the EC Treaty, including the provisions of services. However, the Court of Justice, with a few exceptions,[300] has ruled that Article 12 is implemented with respect to the provision of services

---

293 Article 28(3)(a).

294 Article 29(1).

295 Article 29(2).

296 *Article 4.*

297 *See* the wording of the reference from the national court in *Patrick Christopher Kenny* v. *Insurance Officer*, 1/78, [1978] 3 C.M.L.R. 651.

298 The Commission advanced Article 12 (then Article 7) as the basis for a non-national family's claim to a fare reduction card in *Fiorini v. Société Nationale des Chemins de Fer*, 32/75, 1 CMLR 573.

299 *See e.g.* the 1980 edition of D. Wyatt and A. Dashwood, *The Substantive Law of the EEC* (Sweet and Maxwell, London) at p. 190.

300 In *Roland Rutili v. Minister of the Interior*, 36/75, 1 CMLR 140, the Court ruled that a partial restriction on the residence of an Italian worker in France did not come within the public policy exception in Article 39(3) and hence contravened the national treatment provision of Article 12.

by the personal mobility provisions of the EC Treaty and the secondary legislation of the EU that is based on them.[301]

The Court's view is not without its problems. As regards employed persons who are providing services in another Member State for their employer by Mode 4 and self-employed persons supplying services through a commercial presence, this view makes sense as both Article 39(2) and the second paragraph of Article 43 contain a general national treatment provision relating to these persons.[302] On the other hand, as regards cross-border services, the national treatment provision in the third paragraph of Article 50[303] relates only to persons supplying services in another Member State by a temporary presence. The Court, however, ignores these difference and interprets the rights set out in Articles 39 to 55 as an integrated scheme of rules.[304] In the final analysis, therefore, national treatment under the EC Treaty applies in the same manner to all providers of services, regardless of the mode of supply, despite the Court's refusal to base it on a common provision, *viz.* Article 12.[305]

2. The Prohibition of Discrimination

The Treaty provisions on national treatment in the area of personal mobility refer to the abolition of any discrimination based on nationality[306] or to the provision of services under the same conditions as nationals of the host state.[307] Neither formula clearly prohibits discrimination in fact. However, the Council and the Court have interpreted both as applying to discrimination in fact as well as in law. In Title III of the General Programs on establishment and the provision of cross-border services, the Council accepted that national treatment requires the elimination of all national rules "where, *although applicable irrespective of nationality*, their effect is exclusively or primarily, to hinder the taking up or pursuit of an . . . activity by foreign [i.e. non-] nationals."[308] In the Preamble to Regulation 1612/68,[309] the Council states plainly that national treatment under the EC Treaty "requires equality of treatment in fact and in law."[310] The Court has been equally forthright, stating clearly that national treatment under the EC Treaty forbids "not only overt

301 *See Gaetano Donà* at 586. *See* too *Walrave and Koch* at 332 and *Kenny* at 666. *See also* Gormley at pp. 163-164.

302 *Articles 28(2) and 31(1), 2nd para.*

303 *Article 37, 3rd para.*

304 *See Walrave and Koch* at 332 and *Royer* at 619.

305 *Article 4.*

306 Articles 39(2); *28(2).*

307 Articles 43, 2nd para and Article 50, 3rd para; *31(1), 2nd para and 37, 3rd para.*

308 General Program on establishment, Title III.B. Similar wording was used in Title III.A, paragraph 4 of the General Program on cross-border services. Both programs have now been implemented and are no longer in effect.

309 Council Regulation 1612/68 on freedom of movement for workers within the Community (OJ L257/68).

310 5th recital.

discrimination by reason of nationality, but also all covert forms of discrimination which, by the application of other criteria of differentiation, *lead in fact to the same result.*"[311]

Thus, national treatment under the EC Treaty prohibits discrimination both in law and in fact and covers all the measures set out in Lists 4 and 5. Of course, for a measure to constitute discrimination in fact, it must put the non-national at a disadvantage; otherwise it falls under domestic regulation (measure (h)[312]).

A few specific discriminatory measures are dealt with specifically under EU law. A non-national who is established in another Member State has the right to acquire and use land and buildings there (measure (a) on List 4).[313] Non-national providers established in another Member State must have equal access to state aids (measure (l) on List 4).[314] The right to use home-state and host state professional titles (measure (b) on List 5) is granted on a general basis by Directives 89/48[315] and 92/51,[316] and specifically for certain professions such as lawyers,[317] health-care professionals[318] and pharmacists.[319] The right to use host-state professional titles is sometimes subject to meeting certain conditions, such as admission to the profession in the case of lawyers.

A special word is necessary about public monopolies (measure (g) on List 4). State monopolies are permitted, but Article 31(1) of the EC Treaty[320] requires Member States to ensure that those engaged in the purchase and sale of *goods* do not discriminate against goods from other Member States. Oddly, there is no similar requirement in the case of services. Hence in *Sacchi,*[321] a state television monopoly involved in the purchase of television programs was not found to be subject to the rule.

---

311 *Giovanni Maria Sotgiu* v. *Deutsche Bundespost*, 152/73, [1974] CMLR at 164.

312 An illustrative list of measures that fall under domestic regulation is found in List 6.

313 Article 44(2)(e). There is no equivalent provision in the AEEA, but this right probably flows in any case from the general right to equality of treatment.

314 *See* Article 44(2)(h). There is no equivalent provision in the AEEA.

315 Council Directive 89/48 on a general system for the recognition of higher-education diplomas awarded on completion of professional education and training of at least three years' duration (OJ L19/89), Articles 7(1) and (2).

316 Council Directive 92/51 on a second general system for the recognition of professional education and training to supplement Directive 89/48 (OJ L209/92), Article 11(1) and (2).

317 Directives 77/249 (OJ L78/77), Article 3 and 98/5 (OJ L77/98), Articles 2, 4 and 10(2).

318 *See* e.g. Directive 93/16 (doctors), Articles 10(1) and 19.

319 Directive 84/433 (OJ L253/85), Articles 7(1) and 14.

320 *Article 16(1).*

321 *The State* v. *Sacchi*, 155/73, [1974] 2CMLR 177.

The rule is stricter for public undertakings,[322] which are common in Europe where, despite privatization, the state is still often involved in a wide range of commercial activities. Member States are prohibited from enacting or maintaining in force any measure relating to the operation of public undertakings that conflicts with the rules of the EC Treaty, which includes the national treatment principle.[323] Greece, for example, was not allowed to direct public undertakings to take out insurance only from national companies.[324] This prohibition applies also to undertakings that, while not controlled by the state, have nevertheless been granted special or exclusive rights by Member States.

National treatment under the EC Treaty does not cover disparities in the legislation of the different Member States as long as the legislation is based on objective criteria and is without regard to nationality.[325] Neither does national treatment cover differences between Member States arising from natural phenomena.[326] These limitation are narrower than GATS, where national treatment does not extend to any inherent competitive disadvantages that result from the foreign character of a relevant service or service provider.[327]

The only possible exception that is permitted to the national treatment rule of the EC Treaty concerns state aids to domestic undertakings, including providers of services. These subsidies are not prohibited as such, but where they distort or threaten to distort competition between national and non-nationals, they are prohibited in so far as they affect the cross-border trade in services.[328] Non-nationals who are established in a host Member State must have equal access to such subsidies as part of their right to equal treatment.

3. The Extended Scope of National Treatment under the EC Treaty

EU law makes it possible for providers of services from one Member State to reside for extended periods and even permanently in another Member State. As a result, the EC has evolved a concept of national treatment that gives a correspondingly broader array of rights to non-nationals that go beyond mere equality with respect to the provision of services. Essentially, any measure or situation that affects the life of a non-national in a host Member State in a negative way must be dealt with. This gives national treatment an almost limitless scope within the EC, but we shall look here at only three examples, which are specifically dealt with by the Treaty and the secondary legislation.

---

322 Public undertakings were defined in Article 2 of Commission Regulation 80/723 (OJ L195/80) as "any undertaking over which the public authorities may exercise directly or indirectly a dominant influence."

323 Articles 86(1); *59(1).*

324 *Commission* v. *Greece,* 226/87, [1988] ECR 3611.

325 *See Ministère public* v. *Lambert*, 308/86, [1988] ECR at 4392. *See also* Gormley at p. 171.

326 *See Procureur du Roi* v. *Debauve et al*, 52/79, [1980] 833 at 858.

327 Note 10 to GATS Article XVII:1.

328 Articles 87(1); *61(1).*

The conditions of life in the host state do not just relate to conditions of employment, which are the sole concern of the national treatment provisions in the Treaty Articles on personal mobility.[329] Thus, in Regulation 1612/68, which implements Article 39(2),[330] the Council extends the rights of workers to social and tax advantages, access to vocational training, access to management posts of trade unions and housing.[331] Children of non-national workers must be admitted to the host state's general educational, apprenticeship and vocational training courses under the same conditions as nationals.[332] The Court of Justice not only endorsed these provisions, which go well beyond Article 39(2), but has interpreted them even more widely than their wording would seem to permit. In *Michel S,* for example, it held that a Belgian means-tested grant to handicapped persons was payable to the son of an Italian worker under Article 12 of Regulation 1612/68, which guarantees access to education for the children of non-nationals. It argued disingenuously that the fact that such a benefit was not included did not mean that the Council had intended to exclude it and rejected any suggestion that it had nothing to do with education![333] Perhaps even more importantly, the Court sees the rights enshrined in Regulation 1612/68 as flowing directly from the national treatment provisions of the EC Treaty which means that they also accrue to self-employed persons residing in another Member State.[334]

Europeans are covered by generous social security systems with respect to such matters as benefits for sickness, invalidity, maternity, death, accidents at work and unemployment. However, most of these national schemes based access to benefits and in some cases their amount on the period of time that the person has been covered by the scheme. Some schemes only paid to persons who were resident in the country and, in the case of health insurance, only if the treatment was received at home. The drafters of the EC Treaty were aware of these problems, and Article 42[335] empowers the Council to make specific arrangements in the field of social security for migrant workers. The first concerns aggregation of all periods spent under the social security schemes of the Member States for the purposes of acquiring and calculating benefits. The second concerns the payment of benefits to persons resident in other Member States.

---

329 Articles 39(2), 43, 2nd para. and 50, 3rd para; *28(2), 31(1), 2nd para and 37, 3rd para.* This is another reason to reprove the Court's decision that Article 12, which has a broad scope, is implemented in the area of personal mobility by these Articles.

330 *Article 28(2).*

331 Articles 7 to 9.

332 Article 12.

333 *Michel S* v. *Fonds National de Reclassement Social des Handicapés*, 76/72, [1973] ECR at 464.

334 *Fracas* v. *The Belgian State*, 7/75, [1975] 2 CMLR at 450.

335 *Article 42*. This Article applies to both employees and the self-employed.

Article 42 was implemented by Regulation 1408/71,[336] but, as with Regulation 1612/68, it goes beyond the scope of the empowering Article to deal comprehensively with all the social security problems associated with personal mobility rights. Thus, in addition to aggregation and portability, it provides for a non-discriminatory calculation of the amount of benefits together with the removal of discriminatory prerequisites and deals with the problem of overlapping benefits. It also sets up a scheme under which EU citizens may receive medical treatment anywhere in the EU and be reimbursed by their home state for eligible expenses. An amendment in 1981 made the Regulation applicable to both employees and the self-employed.

Finally, the inability to be accompanied by one's family to a host state or the inability of the spouse to pursue his or her activities also acts as a real disincentive where the provider's stay another Member State is intended to be long or permanent. Thus, Directive 04/38 provides that the non-national spouse and dependant children of an EU citizen, as well as the direct ascendants of either the citizen or the spouse, have a right to enter and reside in the Member State with the EU citizen who is providing the services in an employed or self-employed capacity.[337] The right of residence is co-extensive with that of the EU citizen. It survives the death or departure of the citizen or a divorce from him or her.[338] Non-national family members have a right to take up employment or self-employment in the host Member State and benefit from national treatment.[339]

4. The EC Treaty Approach to National Treatment

The EC Treaty categorizes as coming under the rubric of national treatment all measures that place non-nationals at a legal or factual disadvantage vis-à-vis nationals of the host Member State in all aspects of their life in the other state. It is a much broader concept of national treatment than in other agreements, and it not only covers but goes beyond the examples of discrimination in law and fact that appear on Lists 4 and 5.

D. DOMESTIC REGULATION

1. The General Approach

The EC Treaty treats the non-discriminatory domestic regulation of trade in services as a separate issue from national treatment and market access. Instead of dealing with it directly, it leaves it up to the Council to issue directives for the coordination of national rules concerning the taking-up and pursuit of service

336 OJ L149/71.

337 Articles 5(1), 7(1)(d) and (2) and 16(1) and (2).

338 Articles 12(1) and 13(1).

339 Articles 23 and 24(1).

activities and, in particular, for the mutual recognition of formal qualifications.[340] However, the Court of Justice insisted early on in *Wilhelm* that this approach only applies where "the [domestic rules] affect all persons coming within their application according to objective criteria and without regard to nationality."[341] The implication of this ruling is that, where objective criteria are lacking, domestic regulation constitutes discrimination in fact if it disadvantages non-nationals and hence falls afoul of the requirement of national treatment.

Originally, the Court left the Member States a large measure of discretion in deciding whether these criteria existed. This changed with the Court's ruling in *Thieffry*, where it rejected a French decision prohibiting a Belgian lawyer from practicing in France on the basis that, having accepted the adequacy of the Belgian's legal qualifications, it had no objective criteria for its decision.[342] A little later, the Court developed the concept of proportionality, under which a national rule becomes discriminatory if it represents a disproportionate interference with personal mobility. In *Coenen*, the Court held that the requirement of a presence in the host-state for providers of cross-border insurance services falls into this category unless the Member State in question does not have less stringent measures at its disposal to achieve its legitimate ends.[343] In *van Wesemael*, the Court further developed this concept to prohibit national rules that serve an objective purpose that is already adequately safeguarded. It ruled that a Member State could not require a non-national provider of employment services to obtain a license where its activities were already subject in its home state "to proper supervision covering all employment agent activity. . . ."[344] Finally, the Court also narrowed the scope of the objective criteria, requiring in a 1989 case that the national measure be justified "by overriding reasons relating to the public interest."[345]

As a result of the Court's jurisprudence, we can say that, under EC law, the non-discriminatory domestic regulation of the provision of services in the Member States constitutes discrimination in fact that must be abolished where it:

a) disadvantages the non-national provider, and

b) is not justified by overriding reasons relating to the public interest, or

---

340 Article 47(1) and (2); The AEEA does not have an equivalent provision, but the secondary legislation of the EC on domestic regulation applies by virtue of *Article 7* of the Agreement.

341 *Wilhelm and others* v. *Bundeskartellamt*, 14/68, [1969] CMLR at 121.

342 *Thieffry* v. *Conseil de l'Ordre des Avocats à la Cour de Paris,* 71/76, [1972] 2 CMLR at 405.

343 *Robert Gerardus Coenen and others v. Sociaal-Economische Raad*, 39/75, [1976] 1 CMLR at 39. It is now recognized that the requirement of residence is never acceptable under Community law—see Directive 77/249, Preamble, 1st recital.

344 *Ministère Public et Chambre Syndicale des Agents Artistiques et Impresarii de Belgique A.s.b.l.* v. *Willy van Wesemael and Jean Poupaert*, 110/78, [1978] 3 C.M.L.R. at 111-112.

345 *Commission* v. *The Netherlands*, C-353/89, 1 ECR at 4093-4094.

c) is disproportionate either in the sense that less stringent measures are available or that the public interest is already adequately safeguarded by the applicable rules of another Member State.[346]

We shall now look at how this general rule has been applied to the specific issues of domestic regulation that appear in List 6. In doing so, it will become clear that the EC, unlike most other international agreements covering trade in services, deals effectively and comprehensively with them.[347]

2. Licenses and Authorizations

Licenses and authorizations may be required of non-national providers supplying services through a commercial presence (measure (a)). With respect to providers of cross-border services, they may only be required where they serve to protect a public interest that is not already adequately safeguarded by the supervision exercised by the provider's home state. An example of where the requirement of a license was upheld by the Court is the *Webb* case.[348] Here, the conditions that had to be met by the British employment agency wishing to provide its services in the Netherlands were inspired by the Dutch government's concern for good industrial relations and respect for the interests of the workforce. These were not the criteria that governed the granting of the license in the United Kingdom, and consequently the Dutch license requirement did not represent an unnecessary duplication. As the Court put it: "[I]n view of the differences between one Member State and another . . . and the diversity of the criteria which may be applied with regard to the pursuit of activities of that nature . . . the Member State in which the services are to be supplied has unquestionably the right to require possession of a license. . . ."[349]

Where the granting of licenses or authorization is conditional on the possession of certain formal qualifications, the EC law on mutual recognition applies. This is discussed below.

346 The proposed EP/Council Directive on services in the internal market (COM(2004) 2 final/3) would go further and introduce the home state principle, under which a service provider would be bound solely by the law of the home Member State. The host Member State would not be able to restrict the providers of services from other Member States in any way. This proposal has provoked howls of protest from France and some other Member States on the left of the political spectrum, who see it as an example of "Anglo-Saxon liberalism." Anxious to avoid rocking the boat before the referendum in France on the European Constitution, the President of the Commission has ordered the proposal to be re-drafted. The originator of the proposal, the Dutchman Frits Bolkestein, has made some choice comments on the French political establishment.

347 The signatories of the EEA are bound by the Court's jurisprudence by virtue of *Article 6* of the Agreement and the secondary legislation of the EC by virtue of *Article 7*.

348 *Criminal Proceedings Against Alfred John Webb*, 279/80, [1981] ECR 3305.

349 *Webb* at 3325.

3. Membership in Professional or Trade Organizations

Originally, there was no general dispensation from national rules requiring membership in a professional or trade organization as a prerequisite to the provision of services (measure (b)). However, the liberalizing directives that were adopted in order to facilitate the provision of services through a commercial presence and on a cross-border basis often gave a right to membership in the former case and an exemption from or automatic membership in the latter. It is now recognized that the EC Treaty requires that providers of cross-border services be exonerated from membership[350] and that those supplying services through a commercial presence be awarded membership automatically.[351]

4. Host-State Qualifications

The Court of Justice has always accepted that the possession of host-state qualifications (measure (c)) is a legitimate requirement that serves the public interest in the quality of the service being rendered[352] while insisting that qualifications obtained in another Member State that are recognized as being of equal worth must be accepted in their stead.[353]

Originally, there was no obligation on Member States to evaluate qualifications obtained elsewhere in the EU, but this has changed. The general rule on formal qualifications as it now stands permits Member States to lay down a level of qualification where the EU has not set harmonized minimum standards but obliges them to take account of qualifications acquired in another Member State and to afford them recognition where they correspond to the level of qualification that the Member State in question requires.[354] This general rule of mutual recognition, which flows from the Treaty, has not, however, rendered nugatory the Council's power under Article 47(1) to issue directives for the mutual recognition of formal qualifications, for there are a number of problems that it does not solve.

In the first place, the rule accords considerable discretion to the host state. Thus, in order to establish a more objective procedure, the Council has enacted two directives requiring the mutual recognition of post-secondary diplomas that are a prerequisite in the host state for the pursuit of an activity. Directive 89/48 applies to diplomas or other evidence of formal qualifications that:[355]

- are awarded by a Member State,
- show that the holder has successfully completed a post-secondary course of at least three years' duration at a university or equivalent institution and, where

350 *See* Directive 93/16 (doctors), Preamble, 12th recital.

351 *See* Directive 93/16 (doctors), Preamble, 2nd recital.

352 *Ministère Public* v. *Vincent Auer*, 136/78, [1979] 2 CMLR 373.

353 *Thieffry*.

354 *See* Directive 89/48, Preamble, 5th recital.

355 Article 1(a).

appropriate, has successfully completed the professional training required in addition to the post-secondary course, and

- show that the holder has the professional qualifications for the pursuit of the activity in the host state.

Directive 92/51, which is cast in similar terms, applies to post-secondary courses of at least one year's duration.[356] These two directives are complemented by Directive 99/42, which applies to an array of other activities.[357]

Secondly, the general rule cannot be used where an activity is regulated[358] in the host state but not in the home state, for here the provider will usually not have formal qualifications that correspond to those required in the host state. This situation is covered by the mutual recognition directives. Directive 89/48 stipulates that a host state cannot refuse to authorize a national of another Member State to pursue an activity on the ground of inadequate qualifications if the applicant has pursued the activity full-time for two years during the previous ten years in another Member State where the activity is not regulated as long as the applicant possesses evidence of formal qualifications that:[359]

- are awarded by a Member State,
- show that the holder has successfully completed a post-secondary course of at least three years' duration at a university or equivalent institution and, where appropriate, has successfully completed the professional training required in addition to the post-secondary course, and
- have prepared the holder for the pursuit of the activity.

Directive 92/51 contains a similar provision *mutatis mutandis*.[360] Directive 99/42 provides for varying periods of work experience to compensate for formal evidence of general, commercial or professional knowledge.[361]

The third problem is that the general rule provides no mechanism for dealing with the situation where the formal qualifications of the non-national provider are inferior to those required by the host state. Such a mechanism is included in the mutual recognition directives. Under Article 4 of Directive 89/48, a host state may require a provider to produce evidence of professional experience where the duration of his or her education and training is at least one year less than that required in the host state, which experience cannot, however, be required to exceed four years. Where the problem is that the matters covered by the education and training received differ substantially from those covered by the diploma required in the

356 Article 1(a).

357 Article 3(1).

358 By "regulated" is meant an activity for which a diploma or other evidence of formal qualifications is a prerequisite for exercising the activity.

359 Article 3.

360 Article 3.

361 Article 4.

host state, the latter may require the provider to complete an adaptation period (pursuit of the regulated profession under the responsibility of a qualified member of the profession) not exceeding four years or to take an aptitude test (a test of the professional knowledge of the provider). As a general principle, the provider must be given the right to choose between these two methods.[362] Where the host state intends to require an adaptation period or an aptitude test, it must first examine whether the knowledge acquired by the provider in the course of his or her professional experience is such that it fully or partly covers the substantial difference. Directive 92/51 contains similar provisions.[363] Under Article 3(1) of Directive 99/42, there is only the option of requiring an adaptation period or aptitude test where there is a substantial difference between the qualifications required by the host state and those held by the provider.

Finally, it should be noted that neither the general rule nor the mutual recognition directives apply to the health-care and pharmaceutical professions, for in these areas the Treaty stipulates that mutual recognition of qualifications is dependent upon the prior establishment of common minimum standards of education.[364] There are now directives establishing minimum standards for obtaining diplomas in nursing,[365] dentistry,[366] veterinary medicine,[367] midwifery,[368] pharmacy,[369] and medicine.[370] Mutual recognition of qualifications in these fields is accorded to diplomas that meet these minimum standards.[371] The same approach is used for architects.[372] In the case of lawyers, on the other hand, mutual recognition is accorded pursuant to Directive 89/48.[373]

5. Host-State Technical Standards

The EC rule on the mutual recognition of standards in the area of services is identical to that appertaining to goods, as laid down by the Court of Justice. It also reflects the general approach to domestic regulation. The Court accepts that Member States may set their own standards in the absence of common EU standards (measure (d)), but these norms must serve an overriding reason

---

362 Article 4(1)(b).

363 Article 4.

364 Article 47(3). There is no equivalent provision in the AEEA, but EC secondary legislation on the topic binds the EFTA States by virtue of *Article 7* of the Agreement.

365 Directive 77/453, OJ L176/77.

366 Directive 78/687, OJ L223/78.

367 Directive 78/1027, OJ L362/78.

368 Directive 80/155, OJ L33/80.

369 Directive 85/432, OJ L253/85.

370 Directive 93/16.

371 *See* Directive 93/16 (doctors), Articles 2, 4 and 6.

372 Directive 85/384, OJ L223/85, Article 1.

373 Directive 98/5, Preamble, 2nd recital.

relating to the public interest and not duplicate controls existing in another Member State.[374]

6. Prudential Rules

Prudential rules (measure (e)) apply to the financial services sector and are discussed in Chapter Three.

7. Requirement of Competence in the Host-State Language

The requirement of competence in the host-state language (measure (f)) is tolerated as long as it is manifestly needed in order to provide the particular service in question.[375]

8. Administration of Domestic Rules

Apart from Article 44(2)(c),[376] which calls for the abolition of administrative procedures and practices that are an obstacle to the provision of services through a commercial presence, the EC Treaty is silent on the administration of domestic rules (measure (g)). However, there are provisions in the secondary legislation that in all probability have general application by virtue of Article 10 of the Treaty, which requires Member States to facilitate the achievement of the EU's tasks.[377]

The mutual recognition directives and the specific directives on mutual recognition in the health-care area all provide for a timely and transparent treatment of an application for an authorization to provide services in another Member State.[378] The former also require the availability of judicial review of any decision by the host state authorities.

Where a Member State requires proof of good character or proof that a person has not been declared bankrupt, it must accept appropriate documentation from the home state of the provider.[379] If such documentation is not available, it must accept a declaration on oath or solemn declaration by the provider.[380] Similarly, certificates of physical or mental health must be accepted from the

---

374 *Rewe-Zentral AG* v. *Bundesmonopolverwaltung für Branntwein,* 120/78, [1979] ECR 649.

375 *See* Directives 93/16 (doctors), Article 20(3) and 78/686 (dentists), Article18(3). *See also* Regulation 1612/68 (OJ L257/68), Article 3(1).

376 There is no equivalent provision in the AEEA.

377 *Article 3.*

378 *See* Directives 89/48, Article 8(2), 92/51, Article 12(2), 99/42, Article 3(2), 85/433 (pharmacists), Article 12(1), 93/16 (doctors), Article 15(1) and 98/5 (lawyers), Article 9.

379 *See* Directives 89/48, Article 6(1), 92/51, Article 10(1), 99/42, Article 9(1), 85/433 (pharmacists), Article 8(1) and 93/16 (doctors), Article 11(1).

380 *See* Directives 89/48, Article 6(1), 92/51, Article 10(1) and 99/42, Article 9(3). This possibility is not present in the health-care directive.

home state.[381] Providers must be able to prove financial standing by presenting certificates issued by a bank in the home state.[382] Where a provider is required to give proof of insurance coverage against professional liability, certificates issued by an insurance company in another Member State must be accepted.[383] If a non-national provider is unable to take the oath that is required in the host state as a prerequisite for supplying a service,[384] an alternative oath must be available.[385]

9. Discrimination in Fact

Where they do not disadvantage non-national providers of services vis-à-vis domestic providers or, if they do, where they are justified by an overriding public interest and are proportionate to the interest to be protected, the measures of discrimination in fact on List 5 come under the rubric of domestic regulation (measure (h)). This may often be the case, in particular, with the requirement of a particular corporate form (measure (a)) and non-discriminatory performance requirements and quantitative restrictions (measures (f) and (g)).

E. MOST-FAVORED-NATION TREATMENT

The EC Treaty does not contain an explicit provision requiring equal treatment of the Member States. However, when Article 17(2)[386] states that citizens of the EU shall enjoy the rights conferred by the Treaty, it is implicit that this means all citizens without distinction of Member State. Moreover, the prohibition in Article 12[387] on "any discrimination on grounds of nationality" also implicitly includes discrimination as between other Member States. The position of the EC Treaty is therefore clear, and Article 39, which implements Article 12 with respect to the free movement for workers, explicitly prohibits "any discrimination based on nationality *between* workers of the Member States."[388] On the other hand Articles 43 and 50,[389] which implement Article 12 with respect to establishment and the cross-border provision of services, respectively, are more narrowly centered on national treatment. However, this is unlikely to mean that the MFN principle does not apply to the provision of services. In the first place, the Court takes an integrative approach to both the Treaty as a whole and, in particular, the provisions on

381 *See* Directives 89/48, Article 6(2), 92/51, Article 10(2), 99/42, Article 9(2), 85/433 (pharmacists), Article 10 and 93/16 (doctors), Article 13.

382 *See* Directives 89/48, Article 6(5), 92/51, Article 10(6) and 99/42, Article 9(5).

383 *See* Directives 89/48, Article 6(6), 92/51, Article 10(6), 99/42, Article 9(5), 85/433 (pharmacists), Article 13 and 93/16 (doctors), Article 16.

384 An example would be the oath of loyalty to the Crown that is required of lawyers in the United Kingdom.

385 *See* Directives 89/48, Article 6(4), 92/51, Article 10(4), 85/433 (pharmacists), Article 13 and 93/16 (doctors), Article 16.

386 There is no equivalent Article in the AEEA.

387 *Article 4.*

388 Articles 39(2); *28(2).*

389 *Articles 31(1) and 37.*

personal mobility. Secondly, providers from other Member States can always have recourse to Article 17(2), which has independent force.

F. THE GENERAL EXCEPTIONS TO THE RULES

1. Introduction

The approach to general exceptions in the EC Treaty is much more restrictive than in other treaties. This is due to the essential difference between entities like the WTO and even NAFTA, which are international organizations, and the EU, which is a confederal association of states.[390] EU law is quasi-federal and, as such, must, to the largest possible extent, apply uniformly throughout the EU. Thus, neither the safeguard exception nor the denial of benefits are permitted,[391] and the other exceptions are more circumscribed, including the security exception. All the exceptions are strictly construed *against* national sovereignty,[392] which is exactly opposite to the approach taken by international law.

2. Balance-of-Payments Exception

The Member States that have entered the third stage of Economic and Monetary Union within the EC have adopted the Euro as their common currency and transferred their control over monetary policy to the EU and, more specifically, the European Central Bank. For these Member States, therefore, the balance-of-payments exception no longer exists under the EC Treaty.[393]

Those Member States that have not entered the third stage of Economic and Monetary Union, namely, Denmark, Sweden and the United Kingdom, may still make use of this exception against other Member States where they are in difficulties or are seriously threatened by difficulties as regards their balance-of-payments.[394] As a first step, they may take measures that are in accordance with the provisions of the Treaty. The Commission then investigates the position of the Member State in question and any action that it has taken, and it recommends what measures the Member State should take. If the action taken by the Member State and the measures suggested by the Commission prove inadequate to deal with the problem, the Commission recommends that the Council grant mutual assistance to the

390 No-one really agrees on the nature of the EU, but it is certainly no longer an international organization but probably not yet a confederation. For an in-depth discussion of the nature of the EU and the various views upon it, *see* P. Raworth, "Too Little, Too Late? Maastricht and the Goal of a European Federation," in *Archiv des Völkerrechts*, Vol. 2, Bk. 1, pp. 24-53.

391 The AEEA contains a safeguard exception in *Articles 112-114*.

392 *See van Duyn* at 1350; *Commission* v. *Italy*, 7/68, [1968] ECR at 430.

393 Articles 119(4) and 120(4). There are no equivalent provisions in the AEEA, as the EFTA states are not in the Economic and Monetary Union. However, there is no balance-of-payments exception in the AEEA.

394 Article 119(1), 1st para.

Member State in difficulties.[395] If mutual assistance is not granted by the Council or if it proves insufficient to deal with the problem, the Commission authorizes the Member State to take protective measures in accordance with the conditions and details that it lays down.[396] Such authorization may be revoked or modified by the Council.[397]

In the event of a sudden balance-of-payments crisis and where a decision to grant mutual assistance is not taken immediately, the Member State may take the necessary protective measures unilaterally.[398] They must cause the least possible disturbance to the functioning of the common market and not be more restrictive than is necessary to remedy the problem. The Commission and the other Member States must be informed of the measures no later than when they enter into force.[399] The Council may amend, suspend or revoke these protective measures.[400]

3. General Exception

There exists a general exception for trade in goods, which permits prohibitions and restrictions on the importation and exportation of goods as between Member States that are justified on grounds of public morality, public policy or public security, the protection of health and life of humans, animals and plants, the protection of national cultural treasures and the protection of industrial and commercial property.[401] Somewhat illogically, the same exception does not exist in the EC Treaty for trade in services, and it would seem opportune to have recourse to the Court's assimilation approach[402] and extend the general exception for goods to services. It is not certain, however, that the Court is prepared to go this far.[403]

4. Security Exception

The EC Treaty contains a double-headed security exception in so far as it applies to services. Firstly, no provisions of the Treaty oblige Member States to supply information that may compromise the essential interests of their security.[404] Secondly, Member States may take whatever measures are necessary to deal with serious internal disturbances as well as in the event of war, threat of war and in order to carry out any obligations they have assumed for the purpose of maintaining

395 Article 119(1), 2nd para.

396 Article 119(3), 1st para.

397 Article 119(3), 2nd para.

398 Article 120(1).

399 Article 120(2).

400 Article 120(3).

401 Articles 36; *13.*

402 *See Commission* v. *The Netherlands*, C-353/89, 1 ECR at 4093-4094.

403 *See* Gormley at pp. 756-757.

404 Articles 296(1)(a); *123(a).*

peace and international security.[405] However, a Member State wishing to take such measures must consult with the other Member States with a view to taking common action to prevent the functioning of the common market being affected by the measures.[406]

If any measures taken pursuant to the security exception have the effect of distorting the conditions of competition in the common market, the Commission and the Member State concerned must examine together how the measures can be adjusted to prevent this.[407] In addition, the Commission or any Member State may have direct recourse to the Court of Justice if it considers that a Member State is making improper use of either head of the security exception.[408]

G. ENFORCEMENT OF EUROPEAN UNION LAW

1. Introduction

The traditional dispute settlement procedure in international agreements consists of consultations, panel reports and retaliation in the absence of a mutually satisfactory resolution of the dispute. Such a mechanism is totally unsuited to a system of law like that of the EU, which creates personal rights and which, by reason of its quasi-federal nature, must be applied uniformly.[409] Thus, EU law is enforced by the national courts and the Court of Justice. The national courts interpret and apply EU law as part of their everyday interpretation and application of national law, of which the former is an integral part. This includes enforcing personal rights accorded by EU law. The Court of Justice, as the final arbiter with respect to the interpretation and application of EU law,[410] guides the national courts and deals with problems with or between the Member States.

2. Enforcement by the National Courts

The role of the national courts in the enforcement of EU law is primordial as most cases concerning its everyday interpretation and application come before them as an intrinsic element of their enforcement of national law. However, left to their own devices, it is very likely that differences would emerge between them with the result that EU law would not be applied uniformly throughout the EC. There is

---

405 Articles 297; *123(c)*

406 Article 297. There is no equivalent provision in the AEEA.

407 Article 298, 1st para. There is no equivalent provision in the AEEA.

408 Article 298, 2nd para. There is no equivalent provision in the AEEA.

409 The dispute settlement procedure in the AEEA is a hybrid. It provides for a reference to the Court of Justice of the EU in certain circumstances, but otherwise relies on dispute settlement by the EEA Joint Committee with retaliation by the aggrieved party as a final resort—*Article 111.*

410 Article 220, 1st para.

thus a need for a supreme court to make sure that uniformity is maintained in accordance with its rulings. This is the role of the Court of Justice.[411]

The Court operates not by way of an appeal from the parties before the national court but by a reference from the national court itself before which the issue involving EU law has been raised.[412] The outcome is, however, essentially the same, as the Court of Justice gives a decision that binds the court making the reference.[413] Furthermore, the case law of the Court of Justice is also generally accepted as binding on national courts in the same way as precedents set by the US Supreme Court are binding on inferior courts.[414] National courts must follow this case law even if it means disregarding national laws that are incompatible with it.[415] On the other hand, they may not impugn the validity of a EU measure. This may only be done by the Court of Justice in actions brought by a Member State, the European Parliament, the Council or the Commission on grounds of lack of competence, infringement of an essential procedural requirement, infringement of the EC Treaty or misuse of powers.[416] If the action is well-founded, the Court declares the act concerned to be void.[417] The only recourse of national courts in this situation is to refer the matter to the Court of Justice.[418] Otherwise, they are obliged to apply the measure.

Any national court may refer a matter to the Court of Justice if it involves a question of interpretation or validity of EU law on which it considers that a ruling is necessary to enable it to give judgment.[419] However, courts against whose decisions there is no judicial remedy under national law are obliged to refer under these circumstances.[420] There are two major problems with this procedure.

In the first place, it is not entirely clear which national courts are obliged to refer. The abstract view is that the obligation apples only to the highest court in the land, but it would seem more sensible to make it the highest court in a particular case. Not all matters are susceptible of being heard by the former. Even the second view is not without its problems, as it may not be clear during the proceedings before a lower court whether any appeal from it would be granted, in which case that lower court itself becomes the court of last instance.

---

411 *See* the comments of the Court of Justice in *Rheinmühlen-Düsseldorf* v. *Einfuhr- und Vorratsstelle für Getreide und Futtermittel*, 166/73, [1974] ECR at 38.

412 Article 234.

413 *See Milch-Fett und Eierkontor GmbH* v. *Hauptzollamt Saarbrücken*, 29/68, [1969] ECR at 180.

414 *See Brasserie du Pêcheur et al* v. *Germany et al*, C-46/93 and 48/93, [1996] ECR at I-1145.

415 *See Simmenthal SpA* v. *Commission*, 92/78, [1979] ECR at 777.

416 Article 230, 2nd para.

417 Article 231, 1st para.

418 *See Foto-Frost* v. *Hauptzollamt Lübeck-Ost*, 314/85, [1987] ECR at 4232.

419 Article 234, 1st and 2nd paras.

420 Article 234, 3rd para.

Secondly, national courts can avoid referring a matter to the Court by alleging that the issue has already been adjudicated satisfactorily by the Court (*acte éclairé*) or that the answer is self-evident *(acte clair).* In the *CILFIT* case[421] the Court sought to circumscribe the use of these devices, particularly the *acte clair*, which is more open to abuse. In order to evoke this principle, a national court must be "convinced that the matter is equally obvious to the courts of the other Member States and to the Court of Justice."[422] Fortunately, the national courts have in large measure cooperated with the Court of Justice.

3. Enforcement by the Court of Justice

Apart from the crucial role of its preliminary rulings on references from national courts, the Court of Justice also handles infringements of their Treaty obligations by Member States and disputes between them on the interpretation of the EC Treaty. No matter relating to the interpretation or application of the Treaty may be submitted by the Member States to any other body.[423] Once again, the paramount concern is uniformity, particularly with respect to the proper and timely transposition of EU directives.

At the suit of the Commission or a Member State, the Court can rule that a Member State has failed to fulfill an obligation under the Treaty.[424] The Member State is obliged to take the necessary measures to comply with the Court's judgment. Otherwise, the Court, at the specification of the Commission, may impose a lump sum or penalty payment on it.[425]

The procedure differs depending who brings the action. The Commission may bring an action after first giving the Member State concerned the opportunity to comply with its opinion on the matter.[426] Member States must first bring the matter before the Commission for it to deliver an opinion to the offending Member State.[427] It is only if the Commission does not do this within three months that they can bring the matter themselves before the Court. In the case of abuse by Member States of the security exception, both the Commission and the Member States can bring the matter directly before the Court.[428]

---

421 *Srl CILFIT et al* v. *Ministry of Health*, 283/81, [1982] ECR at 3415.

422 *Ibid.* at 3430.

423 Article 292.

424 Article 228(1).

425 Article 228(2), 1st para.

426 Article 226.

427 Article 227.

428 Article 298, 2nd para.

Member States may submit any dispute between them regarding the EC Treaty to the Court of Justice.[429] Under no circumstances may Member States rely on their own interpretation of the Treaty.

H. FURTHER DEVELOPMENT OF EUROPEAN UNION LAW

After a brisk start, liberalization in the EC became bogged down in the 1970's. By the time Jacques Delors took over the presidency of the Commission, the construction of the internal market, which includes the liberalization of trade in services, was far from complete. Delors and the senior British Commissioner, Lord Cockfield, put together a blueprint for completing the internal market by December 31, 1992.[430] The blueprint was accepted by the leaders of the Member States in June 1985 and, despite much skepticism, was substantially implemented. Since then, further progress has been made, and it can be said that there is more or less complete freedom to provide services in the EU by all four modes.

EU law is, however, dynamic, and there are constant refinements to deal with new problems and older problems that have previously proved intractable. Two recent directives in the investment services sector illustrate this. Directive 04/39[431] updates and expands an earlier investment services directive in order to deal with new issues that have arisen, while Directive 04/25[432] finally harmonizes rules on takeover bids after many years of discussion and disagreement.

III. MERCOSUR: MONTEVIDEO PROTOCOL ON TRADE IN SERVICES

A. INTRODUCTION

1. The Agreement and Protocol

The first attempt at economic integration in South America was the Latin American Free Trade Agreement, which was signed at Montevideo in 1960. It was not successful and was replaced in 1980 by the Latin American Integration Association. This arrangement fared no better than its predecessor, and since then, economic integration in South American has proceeded on a more narrow, regional basis. Already since 1969, there has been the Andean Pact, which groups Bolivia, Columbia, Ecuador, Peru and Venezuela. On March 26, 1991, the Treaty of Asunción was signed, which established the Southern Cone Common Market between Argentina, Brazil, Paraguay and Uruguay. Mercosur (Mercosul in Portuguese), as this arrangement is called, came into being on November 29, 1991. Chile and Bolivia became associated states in 1996, and Peru is now showing the same interest.

---

429 Article 239.

430 This was the famous White Paper entitled *Completing the Internal Market* (COM (85) 310 final).

431 OJ L145/04.

432 OJ L142/04.

The Treaty of Asunción provides for the free movement of services but contains no operative provisions. These are found in the Montevideo Protocol, which was signed on December 15, 1997. The Montevideo Protocol follows a GATS-plus approach. Liberalization of trade in services is to be achieved by improving, as between the Member States, on the specific commitments that they have already assumed under GATS. Beyond this, the GATS rules discussed earlier are largely reproduced by the Protocol. The discussion that follows may thus seem at times repetitive, but this is better than requiring readers constantly to refer back to the GATS Section.

2. Application of the Protocol

The Montevideo Protocol applies to all laws, regulations, rules, procedures, decisions and administrative actions that affect trade in services.[433] It applies to all levels of government and non-governmental institutions that exercise delegated powers. This last provision is essential for purposes of equity, as in some Member States quasi-private bodies might exercise powers that in other Member States are wielded directly by the state. Member States must take the necessary measures that are within their power to ensure that their sub-central and non-governmental bodies comply with the Protocol.[434] This provision would appear stricter than the equivalent one in GATS, which only requires Members to take such reasonable measures as may be available to them.[435] However, the practical result is likely the same.

The Protocol provides for all services to be covered with very few exceptions. Services supplied in the exercise of governmental authority are excluded.[436] By this is meant public services that are supplied by governments on a non-commercial and non-competitive basis.[437] This includes the activities of central banks, activities forming part of a statutory system of social security or public retirement plans and other activities conducted by a public entity involving directly or indirectly government funds.[438]

Scheduled and non-scheduled air transport services and auxiliary air traffic services are not excluded *per se*, but the application of the Protocol is subject to some limitations, which are set out in the Annex on Air Transport Services.[439]

The provisions in the Protocol on MFN treatment and the specific commitments on market access and national treatment undertaken pursuant to it do not apply to

---

433 Articles II:1 and XVIII:1(a).

434 Article II:3(a).

435 Article I:3(a).

436 Article II:3(b).

437 Article II:3(c).

438 Annex on Financial Services, Point 1(b).

439 Point 6 of the Annex calls for it to be revised within three years of the entry into force of the Protocol, but this has not happened.

government procurement of services unless they are acquired with a view to commercial resale or to use in the supply of services for commercial sale.[440] The Member States are supposed to agree on common disciplines in the matter of government procurement, but this has not yet happened. Government procurement in some service sectors is covered by the GPA, which is contained in Annex 4 of the WTO Agreement, but none of the Member States are parties to the Agreement.

There are special rules under the Protocol for certain sectors of the economy, i.e. financial services and land, water and air transport services. These are discussed in Chapters 5 and 7, respectively.

The Protocol applies to trade in services by any of the four modes of supplying services internationally to the extent that a Member State's Schedule of Specific Commitments does not contain any limitations in this respect.[441] A commercial presence includes subsidiaries, branches and representative offices.[442]

The rules set out in the Protocol apply to the provision of services by means of cross-border supply or consumption abroad (Modes 1 and 2) as long as the service is provided, respectively, from the territory of one Member State into the territory of another Member State or in the territory of one Member State to a service consumer of another Member State.[443] In the case of natural persons, a service consumer must be a citizen or permanent resident of the other Member State and actually live there.[444] Where the consumer is a legal person, it must be constituted or otherwise organized under the law of the other Member State, have its head office in that State and carry on or intend to carry on substantive business operations in the territory of that Member State or any other Member State.[445]

With respect to the provision of services through commercial presence or the presence of natural persons (Modes 3 and 4), the service must be provided in the territory of one Member State from a permanent or temporary base there, respectively, by a service provider of another Member State.[446] Where the service provider is a natural person, he or she must be a citizen or permanent resident of the other Member State and actually live there.[447] If the provider is a legal person, it must be constituted or otherwise organized under the law of the other Member State, have its head office in that State and carry on or intend to carry on substan-

440 Article XV:1. Access to the government procurement market is best seen as an issue of market access to a particular sector of the economy. Government procurement is discussed in Chapter Eight.

441 Article II:2. These four modes are described in List 1.

442 Article XVIII:1(c).

443 Article II:2(a) and (b).

444 *See* Article XVIII:1(g), (h) and (i).

445 *See* Article XVIII:1 (h) and (k).

446 Article II:2(c) and (d).

447 *See* Article XVIII:1(f), (h) and (i).

tive business operations in the territory of that Member State or any other Member State.[448]

An interesting fact that emerges from the above rules is that where a service is provided by cross-border supply (Mode 1), there is no requirement that either the supplier or consumer be of a Member State. However, this provision is subject to the provision in the Protocol on denial of benefits.[449]

3. Approach of the Protocol

Like GATS, the Protocol defines what is meant by market access and national treatment[450] but, apart from some specific provisions, leaves it up to the Member States to negotiate commitments on these matters between themselves. Member States are free, albeit on a mutually advantageous basis that secures an overall balance between them, to identify which additional sectors and sub-sectors of their economies they wish to liberalize in the field of services.[451] These commitments are then listed in the Member States' Schedules of Specific Commitments,[452] which are an integral part of the ASEAN Agreement.[453] The commitments are covered by the provisions in the Protocol on market access and national treatment, subject to any limitations and conditions that Member States wish to retain or introduce. The Member States may also abolish restrictions that still apply to services already listed under GATS and make additional commitments on issues of domestic regulation. Service sectors, sub-sectors, activities or measures that are not specified in a Schedule of Specific Commitments do not benefit from extended liberalization.[454]

The aim of the Protocol is to liberalize service areas that are not already liberalized by the Member States under GATS and to reduce restrictions in areas that are already liberalized.[455] However, the process of liberalization must respect the right of each Member State to introduce new restrictions in order to achieve national policy objectives as long as these restrictions do not annul or impair the State's obligations under the Protocol, in particular its specific commitments.[456] Moreover, if a Member State introduces new restrictions on market access or national treatment for foreigners with respect to the supply of a service that is not the subject of a specific commitment, it must exempt services and service pro-

448 *See* Article XVIII:1 (h) and (k).

449 This is discussed in Chapter Four, Section III.F.2.

450 *See* Articles IV and V.

451 Article XIX:1.

452 Article VII:1.

453 Article VIII.

454 Article VII:2(b).

455 Article XIX:1.

456 Article XIX:4.

viders of the other Member States from these restrictions if the service is listed in *all* their Schedules.[457]

Like GATS, the approach of the Protocol has the merit of separating out the concepts of market access and national treatment. At the same time, it has the same disadvantage of not treating all services in the same manner. On the one hand, there are the listed services to which the specific commitments on market access and national treatment apply. Then, there are the other services, which are not the object of such commitments and only benefit from the provisions of the Protocol that have general application, such as those on MFN treatment, domestic regulation, transparency and anti-competitive practices.

The Protocol takes the same "bottom-up" approach as GATS, but, at the same time, it sets down a deadline of ten years for completing its Program of Liberalization of trade in services.[458] Moreover, negotiations to complete this task are to take place annually, and four rounds of negotiations have already been completed in six years. While not forgetting the additional protocols on financial services, movement of natural persons and telecommunications, which are major achievements, GATS is still struggling with the first round of new negotiations. The more coercive approach of the Protocol limits the ability of Member States to pick and choose at will which services they liberalize and reduces the danger that less important service sectors will be left aside. The new obligation to follow suit where the other three Member States take on a new market access commitment for a particular mode of supply[459] will also promote wider liberalization.

As with the Schedules of Specific Commitments under GATS, the national Schedules annexed to the Protocol not only contain commitments to liberalization but also limitations and conditions on this liberalization. However, Member States may not go beyond the restrictions included in their Schedules so that at least they are a guarantee to economic operators in the other Member States that the conditions of entry into the market will not be changed to their disadvantage.

Member States may modify or withdraw specific commitments included in their Schedules at any time during period of implementing the Program of Liberalization.[460] Any such measure must respect the principle of non-retroactivity in order to preserve acquired rights. Member States may only avail themselves of this right in exceptional circumstances, and they must notify the Common Market Group and explain to it the facts, reasons and justifications for their action. In addition, a modifying Member State must consult with the Common Market Group and any affected Member State with a view to reaching a consensual agreement on the specific measure to be applied and the time period in which it will be in force.

---

457 Decision 11/01 of the Common Market Council, Article 1.

458 Article XIX:1.

459 Decision 11/01 of the Common Market Council, Article 2, last para.

460 Article XX.

The national Schedules annexed to the Montevideo Protocol are identical in form to those appended to GATS. For each service sector or sub-sector that is opened up, the national Schedules indicate, with respect to each of the four modes of supply, any limitations on market access or national treatment that are to be maintained. These are found in columns two and three, respectively. Like GATS, the Protocol requires limitations that apply both to market access and national treatment to be recorded in column two.[461] However, the Member States do not always follow this requirement and place the limitations in both columns two and three. Another important point to note is that, at the beginning of the Schedules before the sections setting out limitations with respect to specific service areas, one finds horizontal limitations that apply to all of the service areas included in the Schedule. Any evaluation of sector-specific commitments must take these horizontal entries into account. Additional commitments relating to measures of domestic regulation, such as qualifications, standards and licensing matters, are listed in the fourth column of the Schedules. This column must be used to indicate positive undertakings, not additional restrictions or limitations.

More details on the format of the national Schedules can be found in Chapter Two, Section I.A.4.

The Protocol is silent on its relationship to GATS. Presumably, however, it does not impinge upon the Member States' rights and obligations towards each other under GATS, although, in case of conflict between the two, the Protocol clearly prevails. The preferential treatment accorded by the Member States to each other does not infringe the MFN principle of GATS as it comes within the economic integration exception.[462]

B. MARKET ACCESS

1. Market Access under the Protocol

Member States are obliged to treat services and service suppliers from other Member States in accordance with their specific commitments.[463] According to Article IV:2, this means that, with respect to the services that are listed in a Member State's Schedule of Specific Commitments, the Member State must not maintain or adopt, either at national or regional level, quantitative restrictions,[464] prohibitions or restrictions on foreign capital investment, including mandatory local equity (barrier (c))[465] or the requirement of a particular corporate form.[466] Nationality requirements with respect to the provision and receipt of services (barriers (a)

461 Article VII:3.

462 GATS, Article V. *See* the discussion in Chapter Two, Section I.F.3.

463 Article IV:1.

464 Article IV:2(a)-(d).

465 Article IV:2(f). The reference is to the illustrative list of market access barriers in List 3.

466 Article IV:2(e).

and (b)) are also covered as such requirements are normally considered to constitute a zero quota in violation of Article IV:2(a).[467]

Article IV:1 adds two further obligations that flow from a specific commitment.[468] They relate to barrier (k). Where a market access commitment permits the cross-border supply of a service that is inextricably linked to a cross-border movement of capital, this capital movement must be allowed as well. Likewise, if a Member State permits a service to be supplied through a commercial presence, it must allow any related transfers of capital into its territory.

Measures that prohibit or limit the importation of inputs needed for the supply of a listed service (barrier (j)), on the other hand, do not flow from a Member's specific commitments.[469] They relate to trade in goods and are regulated either by GATT or the appropriate provisions in the Treaty of Asunción.[470]

Three points must be made about the list in Article IV:2. In the first place, the obligations that it entails are not absolute. Member States are free to impose terms, limitations and conditions in their Schedules on the market access obligations that flow from their specific commitments.[471] Unlike GATS, the Protocol makes it clear that this includes the obligations relating to capital transfers,[472] although logically it would appear pointless to make a specific commitment that is unrealizable because of exchange controls.

The second point is that, subject to any limitations in a national Schedule, the measures set out in Article IV:2 must be eliminated whether or not they are applied on a discriminatory basis. In particular, this means that non-discriminatory quantitative restrictions must be eliminated.

Finally, the list of market access barriers in Article IV:2 that are to be abolished pursuant to a specific commitment is probably exhaustive.[473] It does not cover all the possible barriers, but some of these are covered by other provisions in the Protocol.

With respect to nationality requirements (Category 1), it should be noted that specific commitments on market access under the Protocol apply in principle to all

---

467 *See* WTO Guidelines, Point 12.

468 The inclusion of these two obligations is a little surprising as developing countries, among them Brazil, have expressed concern about their scope—*see* the discussion in Chapter Two, Section I.B.1.

469 Note 9 to Article XVI:2(c).

470 Annex I, Article 1. *See also* WTO Guidelines, Point 7.

471 Article VII:1.

472 Article VII:2(b).

473 It is modeled on Article XVI:2 of GATS, which, according to Point 8 of the WTO Guidelines, is supposed to be exhaustive.

four modes of supplying services,[474] and the Protocol specifically states that this includes the presence, including the commercial presence, of persons of a Member State in another Member State for the purpose of providing services (Modes 3 and 4).[475] This would eliminate barriers ((d) and (e)). However, particular modes of supplying services, especially Mode 4, are often excluded, either in the sector-specific section of a Schedule or, on a general basis, in the horizontal section at the beginning.

The Annex on the Movement of Natural Persons Supplying Services encourages the Member States to negotiate specific commitments on the supply of services by Mode 4.[476] Such commitments do not prevent a Member State from regulating the entry and temporary residence of natural persons in its territory, provided that the measures do not nullify or impair the benefits accruing from a specific commitment.[477] The national measures may include a visa requirement.

In December 2003, the Member States signed an Agreement to create a "Visa Mercosur."[478] This visa is available to directors, executives, managers, scientists, researchers, professors, artists, sports people, journalists, highly qualified or specialized technicians and graduate professionals and permits them to provide services on a temporary basis in another Member State for period of up to four years.[479] Although this is not explicitly stated in the Agreement, it is implicit that the host Member State is only obliged to permit the provision of listed services. The granting of the visa may not be made subject to an economic means test or any prior labor authorization.[480] It permits multiple entries and exits.[481] The visa can be obtained from the nearest consulate of the host Member State in the home Member State on presentation of a passport, a birth certificate, the contract showing the nature and duration of the services to be provided, a clean police record, a health certificate and a curriculum vitae.[482] Persons wishing to enter another Member State with a Visa Mercosur must meet all the regular immigration requirements.[483] Artists, sports people, professors, scientists, journalists and specialized professionals and technicians are exempt from the requirement of a visa altogether under a separate agreement if they intend to remain in the host Member

474 Article IV:1.

475 Article II:1(iv). The right under the Protocol to establish a commercial presence does not entail a right of personal establishment—*see* the comments in Chapter One, Section VII.B.

476 Point 3.

477 Point 4.

478 The Agreement is annexed to Decision 16/03 of the Common Market Council.

479 Articles 1 and 2:1.

480 Article 2:3.

481 Article 2:4.

482 Articles 3 and 5.

483 Article 7:1.

State for no longer than 180 days.[484] Both agreements only apply to citizens of a Member State.

Citizens of a Member State who wish to set up a permanent commercial presence in another Member State in order to provide listed services by Mode 3 may now do so under the Agreement on Residence, which was signed on December 6, 2003. They first obtain a temporary residence for two years upon presentation of their passport or identity card, a birth certificate, proof of no criminal record over the last five years and a health certificate.[485] Once in the host Member State, they have a right to work in a self-employed capacity and may transfer profits home from the host Member State (part of barrier (k)).[486] After two years, they must apply for permanent residence, which they may acquire if they can show proof of adequate means of subsistence and no criminal record in the host Member State.[487]

Among the operational barriers (Category 3), barrier (j) is handled by the Treaty of Asunción. The Protocol contains no provisions on exchange controls, but the Member States are bound by the Articles of the IMF, which prohibit restrictions on the making of payments and transfers for current international transactions.[488] This would include restrictions on access to foreign currency to pay for services and for the purpose of traveling to receive a service (barrier (l)).

Public and private monopolies (barrier (m)) are permitted, but they are subject to the Protocol on the Defense of Competition.[489] Article IV of this Protocol prohibits acts that limit, restrict or distort competition or market access within Mercosur or which constitute abuse of a dominant position to the extent that they affect trade between the Member States. The rules of the Protocol may not, however, prevent state monopolies from carrying out their legal duties.[490]

Member States may not limit the scope of their obligations under the Treaty of Asunción, the agreements on temporary and permanent residence, the IMF Articles on exchange controls or the provisions on monopolies in the Competition Protocol, as these obligations exist independently of their specific commitments.

---

484 Articles 1, 2:1 and 6 of the *Agreement on Exemption from Visas*, which is annexed to Decision 48/00 of the Common Market Council.

485 Article 4.

486 Articles 8:2 and 9:5.

487 Article 5.

488 Article VIII:2 and 3. Historically, however, these countries have often been allowed to impose such restrictions.

489 Article XII. The Protocol is annexed to Decision 18/96 of the Common Market Council. It entered into force on September 8, 2000.

490 Article II.

2. Approach of the Protocol to Market Access

The approach of the Protocol to market access barriers mirrors that of GATS with only a few differences and so the discussion in Chapter Two, Section I.B.2 largely applies.

One minor difference between GATS and the Protocol is that the latter makes it clear that Member States may impose restrictions in their Schedules on their obligations to permit capital transfers that are linked to the supply of a cross-border service or which are required to establish a commercial presence.

As far as the categorization of barriers is concerned, the Protocol appears to follow the GATS approach, but the Schedules of the Member States are even more idiosyncratic than GATS. Residence requirements are treated both as market access barriers and as a matter of national treatment. Even nationality requirements are sometimes treated as a matter of national treatment. Restrictions on the use of senior personnel from the home Member State come variously under market access and national treatment. According to the Argentinian Schedule, the requirement for host-state qualifications, which is normally considered a matter of domestic regulation, may constitute a market access barrier.

More important, perhaps, is the difference in coverage. The Agreement on the Visa Mercosur provides for an independent and detailed right to provide listed services by a temporary presence in the host state (barrier (e)), whereas in GATS such a right has to be gleaned from a Member's specific commitments. The Agreement on Residence not only provides a similarly independent right to set up a permanent establishment in the host Member State (barrier (d)) but also a right of personal establishment. Only the EU bestows a similar right. However, both agreements are limited to citizens of the Member States, which is restrictive, and the Visa Mercosur is only available for a set group of persons.

The Agreement on Residence also provides for the right to make capital transfers out of the host Member State (part barrier (k)), which is absent from GATS. On the other hand, the Protocol has no provisions on exchange controls for the purchase of services or travel to receive them (barrier (l)), so it is necessary to rely on the Member States' obligations under the IMF Articles. Like GATS, the Protocol treats the issue of access to and use of networks (barrier (f)) as a matter falling under national treatment. It has no provisions on telecommunications networks and services.

C. NATIONAL TREATMENT

1. National Treatment under the Protocol

The first section of Article V of the Protocol imposes a classic national treatment obligation by requiring that services and service providers from other Member States receive treatment no less favorable than that which is accorded to national suppliers. Traditionally, this formulation only covers measures that discriminate in law.[491] The third section of Article V provides that Member States can meet this requirement by either formally identical or formally different treatment. However, in both cases, the treatment must not favor national suppliers of services.[492] This is a somewhat unusual provision, and its purpose is obscure. It certainly does not permit a more lenient approach to national treatment; rather it would seem to aim at flexibility, dispensing Member States from changing rules that treat providers from other Member States differently from national suppliers where this difference does not put the former at a disadvantage.

As we have seen, controversy surrounds whether national treatment under GATS extends to discrimination in fact. The fourth section of Article V of the Protocol contains the same wording as Article XVII:3 of GATS, and the same considerations must apply to it.[493] However, with the exception of Paraguay, which lists restrictions on the use of senior corporate personnel (measure (d))[494] in its national treatment column,[495] none of the Member States have listed examples of discrimination in fact in their Schedules.

Whatever the correct interpretation of Article V:4, the national treatment rule in the Protocol does not extend to any inherent competitive disadvantages that result from the foreign character of a relevant service or service provider.[496] Nor is it probable that it extends to matters of public interest, such as licenses and host-state qualifications, which traditionally come within the rubric of domestic regulation.[497]

The Protocol contains no exhaustive list of national measures that fall afoul of the national treatment principle. Instead, national treatment is said to cover "all measures affecting the provision of services."[498] Nevertheless, the Protocol contains some provisions that are intended to elucidate the scope of its national treatment rule, although they are not necessary, rather confusing and restricted to discrimination in law.

National measures on access to and use of network services in connection with the supply of a service (measure (b)) are singled out where these services are required by Member States to be offered to the public generally.[499] There is nothing to suggest, however, that other networks are not equally covered by the national treatment rule. National measures concerning the supply, use and payment of services

491 An illustrative list of such measures is found in List 4.

492 Article V:4.

493 *See* the discussion in Chapter 2, Section I.C.1.

494 List 5 contains an illustrative list of these measures.

495 Argentina also lists restrictions on the use of senior corporate personnel in its Schedule, but in the market access column!

496 Article V:2.

497 *See* WTO Guidelines, Point 10.

498 Article V:1.

499 Article II:1(iii).

are also specifically mentioned.[500] It is difficult to see why. Payment involves mainly exchange controls, which are more in the nature of a market access barrier (barrier (l)), and the non-discriminatory supply and use of the services of providers from other Member States are surely the very essence of national treatment and hardly need to be singled out.

The WTO Guidelines provide that procedures with respect to licenses and authorizations contravene Article XVII if they are discriminatory in nature (measure (d)).[501] The same is presumably true of mandatory membership in professional or trade organizations (measure (c)). Both these points probably apply to the Protocol, which is cast in practically identical language to the GATS provisions. This is unfortunately also the case with the position taken by the WTO Guidelines that residency requirements come under national treatment.[502] They are surely market access barriers.

The obligation to apply the national treatment provisions of Article V is not absolute. In the first place, the obligation applies only to services on which a market access commitment has been given and are listed in a Member State's Schedule.[503] Secondly, the Protocol permits Member States to place terms, limitations and conditions in their Schedules on their national treatment obligation.[504]

Most of the limitations in the Schedules of the Member States have to do with the requirement of residence. Uruguay even includes nationality requirements in its national treatment column, which is regrettable as such annotations clearly belong in the market access column. Argentina has restrictions on its specific commitments as to the acquisition of land (measure (a) on List 4), but perversely they are listed in the market access column..

Restrictions that are capable of falling under the rubric of both market access and national treatment should be placed only in the market access column of a Member State's Schedule.[505] This is unfortunate as it can cause confusion. At the very least, it requires us to consult both the market access and national treatment columns of a Member State's Schedule in order to establish exactly the scope of its national treatment obligation with respect to a particular listed service. However, this is probably necessary anyway because of the idiosyncratic way in Mercosur of classifying market access and national treatment measures.

Unlike GATS, the Protocol has no provisions on monopolies (measure (g)) or non-discriminatory access to and use of telecommunications networks and service

500 Article II:1(i) and (ii).

501 Point 10.

502 Point 14.

503 Article VII:2(a).

504 Article VII:2(b).

505 Article VII:3.

(part of measure (b)), although both matters are covered on a general basis by the Protocol's national treatment rule.

The Agreement on Residence has far-reaching provisions with respect to national treatment of providers from a Member State who are established in another Member State and providing services there from a commercial presence (Mode 3). They resemble those existing under EU Law. The provider enjoys the same economic, cultural, social and civil rights and liabilities as nationals,[506] as do members of his or her family.[507] This includes equality with respect to labor laws, in particular those dealing with salary, working conditions and social security.[508]

There is an exception to the national treatment rule in the Protocol that permits different treatment of providers from other Member States where it is aimed at ensuring the equitable or effective imposition or collection of direct taxes in respect of services or service suppliers from other Member States.[509] This exception is similar to that in GATS, which covers such measures as those which:[510]

- apply to non-resident service providers in recognition of the fact that the tax obligation of non-residents is determined with respect to taxable items sourced or located in the Member State's territory;
- apply to non-residents in order to ensure the imposition or collection of taxes in the Member State's territory;
- apply to non-residents or residents in order to prevent the avoidance or evasion of taxes, including compliance measures;
- apply to consumers of services supplied in or from the territory of another Member State in order to ensure the imposition or collection of taxes on such consumers derived from sources in the Member State's territory;
- distinguish service providers subject to tax on worldwide taxable items from other service providers, in recognition of the difference in the nature of the tax base between them; and
- determine, allocate or apportion income, profit, gain, loss, deduction or credit of resident persons or branches, or between related persons or branches of the same person, in order to safeguard the Member State's tax base.

2. Approach of the Protocol to National Treatment

The approach of the Protocol to national treatment mirrors that of GATS with one major difference. Thus, rather than repeat verbatim what was said about the GATS approach, readers are directed to the discussion in Chapter Two, Section I.C.2.

---

506 Article 9:1.

507 Article 9:2.

508 Article 9:5.

509 Article XIII(d).

510 GATS, Note 6 to Article XIV.

The major difference concerns the extent of national treatment accorded to providers who are established in another Member State. It goes beyond the removal of discriminatory measures with respect to the operation of the commercial presence and accords equal rights in society to the provider. Here, the Protocol is much in advance of GATS and nearer to the EU.

D. DOMESTIC REGULATION

The approach of the Protocol with respect to domestic regulation is similar to that of GATS. It permits the non-discriminatory domestic regulation of trade in services, such as the measures set out in List 6. Discrimination in fact (measure (h)) may be covered by the national treatment provision of the Protocol and be excluded. However, most Member States do not follow this approach in practice. Whatever the case may be, the requirement of a particular corporate form (measure (a)) and non-discriminatory quantitative restrictions (measure (g)) are treated by the Protocol as market access barriers and must be eliminated.[511]

The Protocol contains a number of rules dealing with domestic regulation. Unlike GATS, it applies these rules to all services, whether they are listed or not.

In the first place, the Protocol requires that Member States publish promptly or otherwise put at the disposition of the public all relevant measures of general application pertaining to trade in services.[512] This includes international agreements to which a Member State is a signatory. In addition, they are obliged to respond promptly to all requests from other Member States for specific information on these measures.[513] Each Member State must also inform the Trade Commission of Mercosur, promptly or at least annually, of any new measures or changes to existing ones that affect significantly trade in services.[514] Alternatively, other Member States may notify to the Trade Commission any measure taken by a Member State that, in their opinion, affects the operation of the Protocol.[515] All measures of general application affecting trade in services must be administered in a reasonable, objective and impartial manner.[516] This includes processing applications for licenses, registrations or any other type of authorization in a timely and transparent manner (measure (a)).[517] Member States must maintain or institute procedures for the independent review of administrative decisions affecting trade in services to the extent that this is constitutionally possible.[518]

511 Article IV:2.

512 Article VIII:1.

513 Article VIII:4.

514 Article VIII:3.

515 Article VIII:5.

516 Article X:1.

517 Article X:3.

518 Article X:2.

As regards requirements relating to qualifications, licenses and technical standards (measures (a), (c) and (d)), the Member States must ensure that such requirements comply with the following principles:[519]

- they are based on objective and transparent criteria;
- they are not more burdensome than necessary; and
- in the case of licensing procedures, they are not in themselves a restriction on the supply of a service.

These principles probably also apply to mandatory membership in a professional or trade organization (measure (b)), in particular where membership is based on a license or the possession of host-state qualifications. Member States may establish adequate procedures to verify the competence of professionals from other Member States.[520] It should be noted that, where any of these requirements constitute a quantitative restriction in the sense of Article IV:2, they constitute market access barrier (a) and must be eliminated.[521]

Member States are free to agree among themselves or with a non-Member State on the mutual recognition of qualifications, work experience, licenses and certifications, but they must afford any interested Member State the opportunity to negotiate an agreement or arrangement of comparable effect with them.[522] At the same time, the Member States are committed to encouraging the competent bodies in their territories to work together in order to develop mutually acceptable standards and criteria for the exercise of activities and professions in the services sector, and to make recommendations to the Common Market Group on mutual recognition.[523] So far, mutual recognition has been accorded only to graduate and post-graduate degrees and for the sole purpose of teaching or undertaking research at a university in another Member State.[524] The arrangement has been extended to Bolivia and Chile.[525]

Member States may also undertake additional commitments with respect to domestic regulation and note them in the fourth column of their Schedules.[526] There are few such commitments. Paraguay has some commitments on professional qualifications and on the publication of general conditions for interconnection to the public telecommunications networks. Otherwise, the few other commitments are out of place as they deal with market access. Brazil has commitments on the use of the public telecommunications network and on commercial presence for the

---

519 Article X:4.

520 Article X:5.

521 *See* WTO Guidelines, Point 10.

522 Article XI:1.

523 Article XI:2.

524 Decision 4/99 of the Common Market Council.

525 Decision 5/99 of the Common Market Council.

526 Article VI.

provision of reinsurance, retrocession and credit and factoring services. Paraguay has a commitment on interconnection to the public telecommunications network and on the removal of the state monopoly in telephone, telex, telegraph and fax services. Member States are not supposed to enter any restrictions on their obligations with respect to domestic regulation, although Uruguay has done so for financial services.

E. MOST-FAVORED-NATION TREATMENT

Article III:1 of the Protocol contains the traditional MFN principle. It requires Member States to treat services and service providers from one Member State no less favorably than like services and service suppliers from any other Member State or non-Member State. Implicitly, this also means that any disadvantages imposed upon one Member State must be extended to all Member States. This MFN obligation, unlike market access and national treatment, applies to all measures relating to trade in services whether the services involved are the subject of a specific commitment or not. It is a general obligation.

A modified MFN rule applies to the mutual recognition of qualifications, work experience, licenses and certifications. Member States are free to recognize them when they are obtained in particular countries without having to extend this benefit to all Member States.[527] However, Member States must afford adequate opportunity for other interested Member States to negotiate comparable arrangements.

An exception to the MFN obligation in the Protocol concerns advantages that are given to adjacent countries, whether or not they are Member States, to facilitate frontier trade between them in services that are both locally produced and consumed.[528] The MFN obligation is not to be construed as preventing such arrangements.

There is also an exception that allows service providers from the other Member States to be treated differently if the difference in treatment is the result of an agreement on the avoidance of double taxation.[529]

Unlike GATS, the Protocol does not give Member States a general right to maintain any existing measures that infringe the MFN principle as long as they list them in an Annex on MFN exemptions.

F. GENERAL EXCEPTIONS TO THE RULES

Neither the Protocol nor the Treaty of Asunción provide for a safeguard or balance-of-payments exception. The general exception, security exception and provision on confidential information are identical to the provisions in GATS, and the reader is referred to the discussion of these exceptions in Part Two, Section II.F.

527 Article XI:1.

528 Article III:2.

529 Article XIII(e).

The Protocol does not, of course, contain a regional economic integration exception. Instead it benefits from this exception. On the other hand, it has its own denial of benefits exception. A Member State may deny the benefits of the Protocol to a service provider from another Member State where the service is being provided by a natural or legal person who is from a non-Member State.[530] This provision operates regardless of whether the service is supplied by the provider or another person on his or her behalf, but it does not apply to third-country citizens who are permanent residents of a Member State. Denial of benefits is subject to prior notification and consultation with the Member State of the provider.

G. DISPUTE SETTLEMENT

1. Introduction

Disputes between Member States with respect to the application, interpretation or breach of the commitment undertaken pursuant to the Montevideo Protocol are resolved in conformity with the dispute settlement procedures in force in Mercosur.[531] These are found in the 2001 Protocol of Olivos and its Rules of Procedure (Olivos).[532] There is also provision for natural and legal persons to enforce their rights under the Montevideo Protocol.

2. Dispute between Member States

First of all, the Member States involved in a dispute must attempt to resolve the matter by direct negotiations.[533] Unless the Member States agree otherwise, these negotiations must not exceed a period of fifteen days from their initiation.[534] If the negotiations do not result in a resolution of the dispute, any Member State may immediately initiate the arbitration procedure[535] or, by common accord, the disputing Member States may submit the dispute to the Common Market Group.[536] In the latter case, the Common Market Group examines the matter, hears the disputing Member States and, if it considers necessary, consults experts.[537] The Common Market Group then issues detailed recommendations for a resolution of the dispute,[538] which must happen within thirty days of the date of the meeting at which the dispute was submitted to the Group.[539]

530 Article XVII.

531 Article XXIV.

532 They are annexed to Decision 37/03 of the Common Market Council.

533 Olivos, Article 4.

534 Olivos, Article 5:1.

535 Olivos, Article 6:1.

536 Olivos, Article 6:2.

537 Olivos, Article 6:2(i).

538 Olivos, Article 7:1.

539 Olivos, Article 8.

Where a dispute is not resolved by direct negotiations or by the intervention of the Common Market Group, as the case may be, any Member State involved in the dispute may have recourse to the arbitration procedure.[540] The arbitration proceedings take place before an ad hoc tribunal composed of three arbitrators.[541] Each disputing Member State names an arbitrator within fifteen days from the date on which the Administrative Secretariat of Mercosur notifies them of the initiation of the arbitration procedure.[542] Failing this, an arbitrator is chosen by lot from among the arbitrators on the Member State's list.[543] The third arbitrator, who chairs the tribunal, is either chosen by common accord of the Member States concerned or by lot where such accord is not possible.[544] The chairperson may not be a national of the disputing Member States.

The tribunal may order provisional measures where there exists well-founded grounds for believing that the maintenance of the status quo will cause serious and irreparable damage to one of the disputing Member States.[545] The final decision of the tribunal must be made within sixty days from the date on which the Administrative Secretariat of Mercosur gave notice of the acceptance by the chairperson of his or her appointment.[546] This period may be extended by the tribunal for thirty days.

Any disputing Member State may appeal for a review of the arbitral award to the Permanent Review Tribunal within fifteen days of being notified of the award.[547] The review is restricted to questions of law and judicial interpretation.[548] The Review Tribunal is composed of five judges. Each of the four Member States appoints a judge for a two-year term that can be renewed once.[549] The fifth judge is appointed by common accord of the Member States for a three-year period that can only be renewed with the agreement of all Member States.[550] Where the Member States are unable to agree upon the fifth judge, he or she is appointed by lot. Where the dispute involves two Member States, the Review Tribunal consists of three judges, two of which must be nationals of the disputing Member States and the third, who presides over the proceedings, must not.[551] Where more than two

540 Olivos, Article 9:1.

541 Olivos, Article 10:1. Strangely, there is no provision for constituting the tribunal where more than two Member States are involved.

542 Olivos, Article 10:2(i).

543 Olivos, Article 10:2(ii).

544 Olivos, Article 10(3).

545 Olivos, Article 15:1.

546 Olivos, Article 16.

547 Olivos, Article 17:1.

548 Olivos, Article 17:2.

549 Olivos, Article 18:1 and 2.

550 Olivos, Article 18:3.

551 Olivos, Article 20:1.

Member States are involved, the Tribunal consists of five judges.[552] The Review Tribunal may confirm, modify or revoke the decision of the ad hoc tribunal, and its decision replaces the former.[553] As an alternative procedure, disputing Member States may agree to submit a dispute directly to the Review Tribunal.[554]

Decisions of an ad hoc tribunal that are not appealed and all decisions of the Permanent Review Tribunal are binding on the parties to the dispute.[555] Member States must comply with a decision within the period of time set down in the decision or, if no time period is set down, within thirty days.[556] Failing this, the other Member State or States may bring the matter back before the ad hoc tribunal or Review Tribunal, as the case may be.[557] They also have one year from when a decision should have been complied with to take retaliatory action in the form of a suspension of concessions and other obligations under the Protocol, where possible with respect to the same services sector.[558] The Member State against which retaliatory action is taken may bring the matter before the ad hoc tribunal or Review Tribunal, as the case may be, if it considers that this action is unwarranted or excessive.[559] The resulting decision is binding on the Member State taking retaliatory action.[560]

Where a dispute involves obligations under both the Montevideo Protocol and GATS, the complaining Member State may elect one or the other forum for a resolution of the dispute.[561] The choice is binding on all Member States involved in the dispute and irreversible.

3. Claims of Natural and Legal Persons

Natural and legal persons may submit claims that they are affected by measures taken by a Member States in violation of the Montevideo Protocol, including specific commitments in a Member State's Schedule, to their National Section of the Common Market Group.[562] If the National Section accepts the validity of the claim and as long as no dispute on the same matter is in progress between the Member States concerned, the National Section undertakes consultations with the National Section of the offending Member State.[563] If these consultations do not

---

552 Olivos, Article 20:2.

553 Olivos, Article 22.

554 Olivos, Article 23.

555 Olivos, Article 26.

556 Olivos, Article 29:1.

557 Olivos, Article 30:1.

558 Olivos, Article 31:1 and 2.

559 Olivos, Article 32:1 and 2.

560 Olivos, Article 32:3.

561 Olivos, Article 1:2.

562 Olivos, Articles 39 and 40.

563 Olivos, Article 41:1.

resolve the matter within fifteen days, the National Section submits the claim to the Common Market Group without further ado.[564]

Unless the Common Market Group rejects the claim by consensus, it convenes a group of experts, which must issue a report within thirty days of being appointed.[565] The group hears both the person and the Member States involved and then submits its report to the Common Market Group.[566] If the report rejects the validity of the claim, the Common Market Group terminates the proceeding.[567] Otherwise, any other Member State may request the offending Member State to take corrective measures or eliminate the measures in question.[568] If this is not done within fifteen days, the requesting Member State may invoke the arbitration procedure described previously.

H. FURTHER NEGOTIATIONS ON LIBERALIZATION OF TRADE IN SERVICES

The Protocol sets ten years (i.e. until 2008) for realizing its Program of Liberalization of trade in services.[569] To this end, the Member States are supposed to enter into successive rounds of negotiations every year. So far, there have been five rounds of negotiations, two ending in 2000, a third in 2001, a fourth in December 2003 and a fifth in December 2004.[570] As from the fourth round of negotiations, where three Member States take on a commitment to liberalize a service sector or sub-sector for a particular mode of supply, the fourth Member State is obliged to follow suit.[571]

IV. ASSOCIATION OF SOUTH EAST ASIAN NATIONS: THE FRAMEWORK AGREEMENT ON SERVICES

A. INTRODUCTION

1. The Agreement

The Association of South East Asia Nations (ASEAN) was set up in 1967 by Indonesia, Malaysia, Philippines, Singapore and Thailand. Brunei joined in 1984, Vietnam in 1995, Laos and Myanmar in 1997 and Cambodia in 1999. In 1992, at the ASEAN Summit in Singapore, the Member States of ASEAN at the time signed the *Framework Agreement on Enhancing ASEAN Economic Cooperation*,

564 Olivos, Article 41:1 and 2.

565 Olivos, Article 42:1 and 2.

566 Olivos, Articles 42:3 and 44:1.

567 Olivos, Article 44:1(ii).

568 Olivos, Article 44:1(i).

569 Article XIX:1.

570 *See* Decision 29/04 of the Common Market Council. The list of specific commitments for the fifth round includes all the commitments of previous rounds.

571 Decision 11/01, Article 2, last para.

which aimed at the completion of an ASEAN Free Trade Area (AFTA) within fifteen years.[572] AFTA only covers trade in goods but the Framework Agreement provides for further intra-AFTA Agreements.[573] On December 15, 1995, the Member States signed the *Framework Agreement on Services* (The Agreement).

Like the Montevideo Protocol, the Agreement follows a GATS-plus approach. Liberalization of trade in services is to be achieved by improving, as between the Member States, on the specific commitments that some of them have already assumed under GATS. Beyond this, the GATS rules discussed earlier largely apply. Unlike the Protocol, however, the Agreement incorporates these rules by reference instead of reproducing them.[574] Although the practical result is more or less the same, it is more appropriate in the case of the Agreement to refer frequently to GATS rules.

It should be noted that neither Vietnam or Laos are Members of the WTO and hence have not made any specific commitments under GATS. Their obligations to the other ASEAN Member States are thus delimited exclusively by the commitments which they assume under the Agreement. On the other hand, the other Member States of ASEAN, which have made specific commitments under GATS, must apply them to Vietnam and Laos.[575]

2. Application of the Agreement

The rules of the Agreement apply to all measures, which include any law, regulation, procedure, requirement or practice.[576] Theoretically, they bind all levels of government as well as non-governmental bodies that exercise delegated powers.[577] This last provision is essential for purposes of equity, as in some Member States quasi-private bodies, such as professional associations, exercise powers that in other Member States are wielded directly by the state. As a general rule, however, the Agreement only requires Member States to take such reasonable measures as may be available to them to secure compliance with its rules by sub-central and non-governmental bodies.[578]

The Agreement requires the liberalization of trade in services in a substantial number of sectors with the ultimate goal of free trade area in services.[579] Services supplied in the exercise of governmental authority, however, are excluded by vir-

---

572 Framework Agreement on Economic Cooperation Article 2.A.1.

573 Framework Agreement on Economic Cooperation, Article 1:3.

574 Article XIV:1.

575 *See* the *Protocol to Implement the Third Package of Commitments under the ASEAN Framework Agreement on Services,* Point 1.

576 GATS, Article XXVIII(a). All GATS Articles that apply under the Agreement are incorporated by virtue of Article XIV:1 of the Agreement.

577 GATS, Article I:3(a).

578 *Ibid.*

579 Articles I(b) and (c) and III.

tue of GATS.[580] By this is meant public services that are supplied by governments on a non-commercial and non-competitive basis.[581] On the other hand, it is not clear whether the GATS exclusion of air traffic rights and services directly related to the exercise of such rights[582] also applies in the case of the Agreement. This would appear to be the case as the specific commitments of the Member States with respect to air transport are limited to those services not excluded by GATS, such as the sales and marketing of air transport services, aircraft repair and maintenance and computer reservation services.[583]

The provisions on MFN treatment incorporated from GATS and the specific commitments on market access and national treatment undertaken pursuant to the Agreement do not apply to the government procurement of services unless these are acquired with a view to commercial resale or to use in the supply of services for commercial sale.[584] Government procurement in some service sectors is covered by the GPA, which is contained in Annex 4 of the WTO Agreement, but only Singapore among the Member States is a signatory to this plurilateral agreement. It is not obliged to extend the benefits of the GPA to the other Member States that are not signatories.

The special rules in the GATS Annexes for certain sectors of the economy, i.e. financial services, telecommunications and air maritime transport services, are similarly incorporated by reference into the Agreement as they are an integral part of GATS.[585] There is also a separate *e-ASEAN Framework Agreement*, which commits the Member States to accelerating their commitments with respect to information and communications-related services.[586] This Framework Agreement is discussed briefly in Chapter Six.

The Agreement applies to trade in services by any of the four modes of supplying services internationally to the extent that a Member State's Schedule of Specific Commitments does not contain any limitations in this respect.[587] A commercial presence includes subsidiaries, branches and representative offices.[588]

The Agreement applies to the provision of services by means of cross-border supply or consumption abroad (Modes 1 and 2) as long as the service is provided, respectively, from the territory of one Member State into the territory of another

580 GATS Article I:3(b).

581 GATS Article I:3(c).

582 GATS Annex on Air Transport Services, Point 2. "Air traffic rights" are defined in Point 6(d) of the Annex as the right of scheduled and non-scheduled air transport carriers to carry passengers, cargo and mail either within a country or internationally.

583 *See* GATS Annex on Air Transport Services, Point 3.

584 GATS Article XIII:1.

585 GATS, Article XXIX.

586 e-ASEAN Framework Agreement, Article 6:1.

587 GATS Article I:2. These four modes are described in List 1.

588 GATS Article XXVIII(d).

Member State or in the territory of one Member State to a service consumer of another Member State.[589] In the case of natural persons, the service consumer must be a citizen or permanent resident of the other Member State and actually live there.[590] However, permanent residents are only covered if the Member State in which they reside accords substantially the same treatment to them as it does to its own citizens in respect of measures affecting trade in services. No Member State is obliged to treat permanent residents of another Member State more favorably than that other Member State treats them. Where the consumer is a legal person, it must be constituted or otherwise organized under the law of the other Member State and be engaged in substantive business operations in the territory of that Member State or any other Member State.[591]

With respect to the provision of services through commercial presence or the presence of natural persons (Modes 3 and 4), the service must be supplied in the territory of one Member State by a service supplier of another Member State.[592] Where the service supplier is a natural person, the same rule applies as for service consumers; he or she must be a citizen or permanent resident of the other Member State.[593] If the supplier is a legal person, the rule differs according to the mode of supply. Where the service is supplied through Mode 4, the legal person on behalf of whom natural persons travel to provide the service must be constituted or otherwise organized under the law of the other Member State and be engaged in substantive business operations in the territory of that Member State or any other Member State.[594] Where the service is supplied through Mode 3, the legal person constituting the commercial presence must be owned or controlled by citizens or permanent residents of the other Member State or by legal persons constituted under the law of the other Member State and engaged in substantive business operations in the territory of that Member State or any other Member State.[595] "Owned" means holding more than fifty percent of the equity interest,[596] and "controlled" means the power to name a majority of the directors or otherwise legally direct the presence's actions.[597]

An interesting fact that emerges from the above rules is that where a service is provided by cross-border supply (Mode 1), there is no requirement that either the

---

589 GATS Article I:2(a) and (b). *See also* the combined effect of Articles XVI:1 and XXVIII(f)(i).

590 *See* GATS Article XXVIII(i), (j) and (k).

591 *See* GATS Article XXVIII(i), (j) and (m)(i).

592 GATS Article I:2(c) and (d). *See also* the combined effect of Articles XVI:1 and XXVIII(f)(ii).

593 *See* GATS Article XXVIII(g), (j) and (k).

594 *See* GATS Article XXVIII(g), (j) and (m)(i).

595 GATS Article XXVIII(m)(ii).

596 GATS Article XXVIII(n)(i).

597 GATS Article XXVIII(n)(ii).

supplier or consumer be of a Member State. However, this provision is subject to the provision in the Agreement on denial of benefits.[598]

3. Approach of the Agreement

The Agreement incorporates the GATS definitions of what is meant by market access and national treatment and then, subject to certain specific provisions, leaves it up to the Member States to negotiate commitments on these matters between themselves.[599] Member States are free, albeit on a mutually beneficial basis,[600] to identify which sectors and sub-sectors of their economies they wish to liberalize in the field of services. These commitments are then listed in the Member States' Schedules of Specific Commitments,[601] which are an integral part of the Agreement.[602] The commitments are covered by the incorporated provisions of GATS on market access and national treatment, subject to any limitations and conditions that Member States wish to retain or introduce. The Member States may also abolish restrictions that still apply to services already listed under GATS and make additional commitments on issues of domestic regulation.

Unlike the other agreements, the Agreement authorizes, as from January 1, 2005, two or more Member States to go it alone. They may agree among themselves on the additional liberalization of certain service sectors or sub-sectors without being obliged to extend this liberalization to the other non-participating Member States.[603] However, any Member State may in due course become a party to such an agreement upon making offers at similar or acceptable levels to the participating Member States.[604]

The aim of the Agreement is to liberalize service areas that are not already liberalized by the Member States under GATS and to reduce restrictions in areas that are already liberalized.[605] New or more discriminatory measures or market access limitations are not permitted.[606] Service sectors and sub-sectors, activities or measures that are not specified in a Schedule of Specific Commitments do not benefit from extended liberalization.[607] In the case of Vietnam and Laos, it should be remembered that their commitments under the Agreement are stand-alone commitments as they are not parties to GATS.

598 This is discussed in Chapter Four, Section IV.F.

599 Article IV:1.

600 *See* Framework Agreement on Economic Cooperation, Article 1:2.

601 Article IV:2.

602 Article VIII.

603 Article IVbis:1, inserted by the 2003 *Protocol to Amend the ASEAN Framework Agreement on Services*, Article 1.

604 Article IVbis:3.

605 Article 1(c). The Agreement is not as clear as the Montevideo Protocol, but this is surely what is meant by expanding the "depth and scope" of the liberalization under GATS.

606 Article III(b).

607 Article VII:2(b).

The Agreement incorporates the GATS approach, which has the merit of separating out the concepts of market access and national treatment. At the same time, it has the disadvantage of not treating all services in the same manner. On the one hand, there are the listed services to which the specific commitments on market access, national treatment and domestic regulation apply. Then, there are the other services, which are not the object of such commitments and only benefit from the incorporated provisions of GATS that have general application, such as those on MFN treatment and some aspects of domestic regulation.

The Agreement takes the same "bottom-up" approach as GATS, but, at the same time, it sets a definite goal of liberalizing trade in a substantial number of service sectors within a reasonable time-frame.[608] The Protocol on the fourth package of commitments goes further and calls for a free flow of services by 2020 or earlier. Three rounds of negotiations have already been completed in nine years and extended commitments undertaken with respect to air transport services, business services, construction, financial services, maritime transport, telecommunications and tourism. While not forgetting the additional protocols on financial services, movement of natural persons and telecommunications, which are major achievements, GATS is still struggling with its first round of new negotiations. The more aggressive approach of the Agreement limits the ability of Member States to pick and choose at will which services they liberalize and reduces the danger that less important service sectors will be left aside.

As with the Schedules of Specific Commitments under GATS, the national Schedules that arise from negotiations under the Agreement not only contain commitments to liberalization but also limitations and conditions on this liberalization. However, Member States may not go beyond the restrictions included in their Schedules so that at least they are a guarantee to economic operators in the other Member States that the conditions of entry into the market will not be changed to their disadvantage.

Specific commitments undertaken pursuant to the Agreement may be modified or withdrawn by a Member State, but only after they have been in effect for at least three years.[609] Modification of commitments must not affect the application of the MFN principle.[610]

The modifying Member State is required to notify the Member States and the ASEAN Secretariat no later than three months before the intended change is to be implemented.[611] It must also enter into negotiations with any affected Member State to agree on a necessary compensatory adjustment.[612] Member States must ensure that they maintain a general level of mutually advantageous commitments

608 Article III(a).

609 Article X:1.

610 They are subject to GATS Article II:1.

611 Article X:1(a).

612 Article X:1(b).

that is not less favorable to trade than the level existing prior to the negotiations.[613] This means that reduced liberalization in one services area is compensated by greater liberalization in another service sector. Any compensatory adjustment must be made on an MFN basis.[614]

No time limit is set for concluding the negotiations on compensatory adjustment and no mechanism exists for dealing with a failure to reach agreement. The GATS provisions on arbitration in this situation do not apply here as the Agreement has its own specific provisions. The Senior Economic Officials Meeting (SEOM) may, with the endorsement of the ASEAN Economic Ministers (AEM) draw up additional procedures,[615] but so far none exist. Presumably, however, a Member State that is adversely affected by the changes may have recourse to the ASEAN dispute settlement mechanism.

The national Schedules that arise pursuant to the Agreement and which form an integral part of it[616] are identical in form to those appended to GATS. For each service sector or sub-sector that is opened up, the national Schedules indicate, with respect to each of the four modes of supply, any limitations on market access or national treatment that are to be maintained. These are found in columns two and three, respectively. Limitations that apply both to market access and national treatment are to be recorded in column two.[617] Another important point to note is that, at the beginning of the Schedules before the sections setting out limitations with respect to specific service areas, one finds horizontal limitations that apply to all of the service areas included in the Schedule. Any evaluation of sector-specific commitments must take these horizontal entries into account. Additional commitments relating to measures of domestic regulation, such as qualifications, standards and licensing matters, are listed in the fourth column of the Schedules. This column must be used to indicate positive undertakings, not additional restrictions or limitations.

More details on the format of the national Schedules can be found in Chapter Two, Section I.A.4.

The Agreement does not impinge upon the Member States' rights and obligations towards each other under GATS,[618] but in case of conflict between the two, the Agreement clearly prevails.[619] The preferential treatment accorded by the Member

613 Article XXI:2(a).

614 Article XXI:2(b).

615 Article X:4.

616 Article VIII.

617 GATS XX:2.

618 Article IX:1.

619 Article XIV:1.

States to each other does not infringe the MFN principle of GATS as it comes within the economic integration exception.[620]

B. MARKET ACCESS

1. Market Access under the Agreement

Member States are obliged to treat services and service suppliers from other Member States in accordance with their specific commitments.[621] According to the definition of market access incorporated from GATS, this means that, with respect to the services that are listed in a Member State's Schedule of Specific Commitments, the Member State must not maintain or adopt, either at national or regional level, quantitative restrictions,[622] prohibitions or restrictions on foreign capital investment, including mandatory local equity (barrier (c))[623] or the requirement of a particular corporate form.[624] Nationality requirements with respect to the provision and receipt of services (barriers (a) and (b)) are also covered as such requirements are considered by the WTO Guidelines to constitute a zero quota in violation of Article XVI:2(a) of GATS.[625]

Two further obligations flow from a specific commitment relating to barrier (k).[626] Where a market access commitment permits the cross-border supply of a service that is inextricably linked to a cross-border movement of capital, this capital movement must be allowed as well. Likewise, if a Member State permits a service to be supplied through a commercial presence, it must allow any related transfers of capital into its territory.

Measures that prohibit or limit the importation of inputs needed for the supply of a listed service (barrier (j)), on the other hand, do not flow from a Member State's specific commitments.[627] They relate to trade in goods and are regulated either by GATT or the Common Effective Preferential Tariff set up pursuant to AFTA.[628]

Three points must be made about the definition of market access barriers that the Agreement imports from GATS. In the first place, the obligations that it entails are not absolute. Member States are free to impose terms, limitations and conditions in the second column of their Schedules on the market access obligations that flow

620 GATS, Article V. *See* the discussion in Chapter Two, Section I.F.3.

621 Article IV:1.

622 GATS Article XVI:2(a)-(d).

623 GATS Article XVI:2(f). The reference is to the illustrative list of market access barriers in List 3.

624 GATS Article XVI:2(e).

625 Point 12.

626 Note 8 to GATS Article XVI:1.

627 Note 9 to GATS Article XVI:2(c).

628 *See* WTO Guidelines, Point 7. *See also* the discussion in Chapter Two, Section II.B.

from their specific commitments.[629] It is not clear, however, whether they may similarly restrict their capital transfer obligations. The wording of Articles XVI:1 and XX:1(a) of GATS, which are incorporated into the Agreement, is broad enough to permit limitations to be placed on these two obligations, but logic would suggest that this should not be possible. There is little point in making a commitment that is unrealizable due to currency controls. It could also be argued that these two obligations flow directly from the provision incorporated from GATS and not from a specific commitment by a Member State pursuant to the Agreement, and as such cannot be limited. The issue is important as some developing countries, supported by the ASEAN countries, have expressed concern that these two obligations require in effect a substantial liberalization of capital movements. This view is not shared by most developed countries, who view them more narrowly as relating to specific liberalizing measures.[630]

The second point is that, subject to any limitations in a national Schedule, the measures that are defined in GATS as market access barriers must be eliminated whether or not they are applied on a discriminatory basis. In particular, this means that non-discriminatory quantitative restrictions must also be eliminated.

Finally, the list of market access barriers that are to be abolished pursuant to a specific commitment under the Agreement is supposed to be exhaustive,[631] but it does not cover all the possible barriers. Some of these are covered by other provisions imported from GATS.

With respect to nationality requirements (Category 1), it should be noted that specific commitments on market access under the Agreement apply in principle to all four modes of supplying services.[632] GATS specifically states that this means the presence, including the commercial presence, of persons of a Member State in another Member State for the purpose of supplying services (Modes 3 and 4).[633] This would eliminate barriers ((d) and (e)). However, particular modes of supplying services, especially Modes 3 and 4, are often excluded or restricted in the Member States' Schedules, either in the sector-specific section or, on a general basis, in the horizontal section at the beginning. Few extended commitments have been undertaken in this area under the Agreement, and nothing prevents Member States from regulating the entry and temporary residence of service providers from other Member States, including, it would seem, applying restrictions on the type of per-

629 GATS Articles XVI:1 and XX:1(a).

630 *See* Report of the Meeting of February 26, 2003 of the Committee on Trade in Financial Services (Doc.S/FIN/M/39).

631 WTO Guidelines, Point 8.

632 GATS Article XVI:1.

633 GATS Article XXVIII(c)(iii). The right to establish a commercial presence does not entail a right of personal establishment—*see* the comments in Chapter One, Section VII.B.

son who may enter the host country.[634] However national measures must not be applied in a manner that nullifies or impairs the benefits of a specific commitment. Visa requirements are not considered as falling into this category even where they are applied selectively.[635] Specific commitments on temporary entry and residence cover both the employed and the self-employed.

Among the operational barriers (Category 3), exchange controls on international transfers and payments for current transactions relating to specific commitments are prohibited, except for balance-of-payment reasons.[636] This deals with restrictions on payment for services and access to foreign currency for the purpose of traveling to receive a listed service (barrier (l)).[637]

Member States are not required to abolish public or private monopolies (barrier (m)), but they are under an obligation to ensure that any monopoly does not operate in a manner inconsistent with their specific commitments.[638] However, given that the existence of a monopoly necessarily prevents market entry, it is difficult to see how a monopoly could operate consistently with a commitment on market access. More comprehensible is the extension of the obligation to any services that a monopoly supplies outside the scope of its exclusive preserve.[639] Under GATS, Members must inform the Council for Trade in Services of any new grant of monopoly rights affecting the supply of services covered by their specific commitments.[640] However, the 1998 ASEAN *Protocol on Notification Procedures* (Protocol on Notifications), which would seem to supplant the notification provisions of GATS, only requires Member States to notify SEOM and the ASEAN Secretariat[641] in this situation where the grant nullifies or impairs benefits accruing to another Member State under the Agreement or may impede the attainment of its objective to liberalize trade in services.[642]

As regards access to and use of public or private networks that are necessary for the provision of a service (barrier (f)), this issue is left by ASEAN to be covered by national treatment except in the case of telecommunications networks. The ASEAN rules on the latter are imported from GATS and discussed in Chapter Six.

---

634 GATS Annex on Movement of Natural Persons, Point 4.

635 GATS Annex on Movement of Natural Persons, Note 13.

636 GATS Article XI:1.

637 Under the IMF Articles, however, to which all the Member States subscribe, no restrictions may be placed on access to foreign currency for the purpose of travel, even if the object of the journey is to receive an unlisted service. However, the IMF permits some derogations for balance-of-payments reasons.

638 GATS Article VIII:1.

639 GATS Article VIII:2.

640 GATS Article VIII:4. In the ASEAN Agreement, SEOM carries out the functions of the General Council for Trade in Services under GATS. It is assisted by the ASEAN Secretariat, to which notifications are made.

641 Protocol on Notifications, Article 3.

642 Protocol on Notifications, Article 1(2).

Member States may not limit the scope of their obligations with respect to exchange controls or monopolies, as these obligations do not flow from their specific commitments under the Agreement but from the provisions that it imports directly from GATS.

2. The Approach of the Agreement to Market Access

The Agreement follows the GATS approach to market access, and thus the discussion in Chapter Two, Section I.B.2 applies to it as well.

C. NATIONAL TREATMENT

1. National Treatment under the Agreement

The definition of national treatment in Article XVII of GATS is incorporated into the Agreement. The first section of this Article imposes a classic national treatment obligation by requiring that services and service providers from other Member States receive treatment no less favorable than that which is accorded to national suppliers. Traditionally, this formulation only covers measures that discriminate in law.[643] The second section of Article XVII provides that Member States can meet this requirement by either formally identical or formally different treatment. However, in both cases, the treatment must not favor national suppliers of services.[644] This is a somewhat unusual provision, and its purpose is obscure. It certainly does not permit a more lenient approach to national treatment; rather it would seem to aim at flexibility, dispensing Member States from changing rules that treat providers from other Member States differently from national suppliers where this difference does not put the former at a disadvantage.

As we have seen, controversy surrounds whether national treatment under GATS extends to measures that discriminate in fact.[645] As the Agreement incorporates the relevant provision of GATS, the same considerations apply to it. However, whatever the correct interpretation of Article XVII:3, the GATS national treatment rule does not extend to matters of public interest, such as licenses and host-state qualifications, that traditionally come within the rubric of domestic regulation.[646] Nor does it require Member States to compensate for any inherent competitive disadvantages that result from the foreign character of a relevant service or service provider.[647]

GATS contains no exhaustive list of national measures that fall afoul of its national treatment principle. Instead, national treatment is said to cover "all mea-

---

643 An illustrative list of such measures is found in List 4.

644 GATS Article XVII:3.

645 *See* the discussion in Chapter Two, Section I.C.1.

646 *See* WTO Guidelines, Point 10.

647 Note 10 to GATS Article XVII:1.

sures affecting the supply of services."[648] Although the Agreement imports those provisions from GATS that are intended to elucidate the scope of its national treatment rule, they are not, as we have seen, particularly helpful.[649]

The obligation to apply the GATS national treatment rule is not absolute. In the first place, the obligation applies only to services on which a market access commitment has been given pursuant to the Agreement and are listed in a Member State's Schedule.[650] Secondly, Member States are permitted to place conditions and qualifications in their Schedules on their national treatment obligation.[651]

Restrictions that are capable of falling under the rubric of both market access and national treatment should be placed only in the market access column of a Member State's Schedule.[652] This is unfortunate as it can cause confusion. At the very least, it requires us to consult both the market access and national treatment columns of a Member State's Schedule in order to establish exactly the scope of its national treatment obligation with respect to a particular listed service. However, under the Agreement, this is probably necessary as it adopts GATS idiosyncratic way of classifying market access and national treatment measures.

In addition to the general requirement of national treatment flowing from Article XVII, GATS contains a specific provision on one incidence of operational discrimination. Members must ensure that monopoly service providers do not operate in a manner inconsistent with their specific commitments on national treatment (measure (g) on List 4).[653] This obligation also applies where a Member authorizes or establishes a small number of service suppliers and substantially prevents competition between them on its territory.[654] It exists independently of a Member's specific commitments and cannot be limited in a Member's Schedule. It only applies, however, to listed services.

Non-discriminatory access to and use of public telecommunications transport networks and services are covered by the GATS Annex on telecommunications and discussed later in Chapter Six. Access to and use of other networks (measure (b)) are covered by the general national treatment provision.

There is an exception to the national treatment rule in GATS that permits different treatment of providers from other Member States where it is aimed at ensuring the equitable or effective imposition or collection of direct taxes in respect of services

---

648 GATS Article XVII:1.

649 *See* the discussion in Chapter Two, Section I.C.1.

650 GATS Article XVII:1.

651 GATS Article XVII:1 and XX:1(b).

652 GATS Article XX:2. *See also* WTO Guidelines, Point 18.

653 Article VIII:1.

654 Article VIII:5.

or service suppliers from other Member States.[655] This exception covers such measures as those which:[656]

- apply to non-resident service providers in recognition of the fact that the tax obligation of non-residents is determined with respect to taxable items sourced or located in the Member State's territory;
- apply to non-residents in order to ensure the imposition or collection of taxes in the Member State's territory;
- apply to non-residents or residents in order to prevent the avoidance or evasion of taxes, including compliance measures;
- apply to consumers of services supplied in or from the territory of another Member State in order to ensure the imposition or collection of taxes on such consumers derived from sources in the Member State's territory;
- distinguish service providers subject to tax on worldwide taxable items from other service providers, in recognition of the difference in the nature of the tax base between them; and
- determine, allocate or apportion income, profit, gain, loss, deduction or credit of resident persons or branches, or between related persons or branches of the same person, in order to safeguard the Member State's tax base.

2. The Approach of the Agreement to National Treatment

The Agreement follows the GATS approach to national treatment, and thus the discussion in Chapter Two, Section I.C.2 applies to it as well.

D. DOMESTIC REGULATION

The Agreement imports some of the GATS provisions on domestic regulation but not all. It also supplements them with its own provisions.

The Agreement permits the non-discriminatory domestic regulation of trade in services. This covers the measures set out in List 6, possibly excluding discrimination in fact (measure (h)[657]) if one interprets the imported GATS national treatment provision broadly. However, whatever the correct interpretation, the requirement of a particular corporate form (measure (a)[658]) and non-discriminatory quantitative restrictions (measure (g)), which are treated by GATS as market access barriers, must be eliminated.[659] By contrast, certain measures with respect to

655 GATS Article XIV(d).

656 Note 6 to GATS Article XIV.

657 The reference is to the illustrative list of measures falling within domestic regulation in List 6.

658 The reference is to the illustrative list of measures constituting discrimination in fact in List 5.

659 GATS, Article XVI:2.

the domestic regulation of telecommunications are specifically permitted. These are discussed in Chapter Six.

The Agreement contains a number of rules dealing with domestic regulation. Some are imported from GATS, others flow directly from the Agreement. Some rules only apply to listed services.

In the first place, Member States must, for all services, publish promptly or otherwise make publicly available all relevant measures of general application pertaining to trade in services.[660] This includes international agreements to which a Member State is a signatory. These agreements must be consistent with the principles, objectives and terms of the Agreement.[661] Member States were also obliged, upon the signing of the Agreement, to notify the ASEAN Secretariat of any agreements affecting trade in services to which they were signatories.[662]

Member States are obliged to respond promptly to all requests from other Member States for specific information on measures affecting trade in services.[663] Under GATS, Members must also inform the Council for Trade in Services of any new measures or changes to existing ones that significantly affect trade in listed services.[664] However, the ASEAN Protocol on Notifications only requires Member States to notify SEOM and the ASEAN Secretariat where the measure may nullify or impair any benefit to another Member State under the Agreement or impede its objective of liberalizing trade in services.[665] The Protocol does not, like GATS, provide for other Member States to notify these bodies of any measure taken by another Member State.

All measures of general application affecting trade in listed services must be administered in a reasonable, objective and impartial manner.[666] This includes processing applications for authorizations in a timely and transparent manner (measure (a)).[667] Members must maintain or institute procedures for the independent review of administrative decisions affecting trade in services to the extent that this is constitutionally possible.[668]

As regards requirements relating to qualifications (measure (c)) and standards (measure (d)), the Member States have chosen the road of mutual recognition agreements rather than, like GATS, the application of common principles. These agreements are intended to have general application and are not just restricted to

---

660 GATS Article III:1.

661 Article IX:2.

662 Article IX:3.

663 GATS Article III:4.

664 GATS Article III:3. *See* note 705.

665 Protocol on Notifications, Article 1(2).

666 GATS Article VI:1.

667 GATS Article VI:3.

668 GATS Article VI:2.

persons supplying listed services. An agreement has been reached on the qualifications of professional services providers, and negotiations are currently underway in the areas of engineering, architecture, accountancy, surveying and tourism. Mutual recognition in these areas will also have a liberalizing effect on the requirements of licenses and mandatory membership in professional or trade organizations (measures (a) and (b)). The mutual recognition agreements on standards, however, are, at present, more relevant for trade in goods than services. It should be noted that where any of these requirements constitute a quantitative restriction in the sense of Article XVI:2 of GATS, they constitute market access barrier (a) and must be eliminated.[669]

The Member States may enter into agreements or arrangements to recognize the education or experience obtained, requirements met or licenses or certifications granted in another Member State, but they are not obliged to do so.[670] Other Member States wishing to join such agreements or arrangements should be given the equal opportunity to do so at any time.[671]

Member States may also undertake additional commitments with respect to domestic regulation and note them in the fourth column of their Schedules.[672] They may not enter any restrictions on their obligations with respect to domestic regulation. The fourth column is only for additional commitments.

E. MOST-FAVORED-NATION TREATMENT

The Agreement imports Article II:1 of GATS, which contains the traditional MFN principle. It requires Member States to treat services and service providers from one Member State no less favorably than like services and service suppliers from any other country, whether it is a Member State or not. Implicitly, this also means that any disadvantages imposed upon one Member State must be extended to all Member States. This MFN obligation, unlike market access and national treatment, applies to all measures relating to trade in services whether the services involved are the subject of a specific commitment under the Agreement or not.

The MFN is a general obligation under the Agreement, but certain specific instances are singled out. Those Member States that belong to the WTO must extend their specific commitments under GATS to all Member States even if, as in the case of Vietnam and Laos, they are not yet Members of the WTO.[673] All Member States must ensure that their monopoly suppliers of services act in accordance

669 WTO Guidelines, Point 10.

670 Article V:1 and 2.

671 Note 1 to Article V:2.

672 GATS Article XVIII.

673 *See* the *Protocol to Implement the Third Package of Commitments under the ASEAN Framework Agreement on Services,* Point 1.

with the MFN principle.[674] Finally, where a compensatory adjustment is made pursuant to a modification by a Member State of its Schedule of Specific Commitments, this must be done on an MFN basis.[675]

A modified MFN rule applies to agreements on mutual recognition and enhanced liberalization between a limited number of Member States. Member States are free to recognize education or experience obtained, requirements met or licenses or certifications granted in a certain Member State without having to extend this benefit to the other Member States.[676] However, they must afford equal opportunity for other interested Member States to join any such agreements or arrangements.[677] Likewise, certain Member States may, as from January 1, 2005, agree to liberalize trade in services between themselves on a preferential basis.[678] Any extension of this greater liberalization to the other Member States is voluntary. However, Member States that are not a party to a preferential agreement must be allowed to become a party upon making offers at similar or acceptable levels to the participating Member States.[679]

The MFN obligation is subject to a number of exceptions. In the first place, Member States may maintain existing measures that infringe the MFN principle as long as they entered these exempted measures in the MFN Exemptions List by the entry into force of the Agreement.[680] Among the exempted measures that must be listed are international agreements to which the Member States are signatories.[681] The List indicates the sectors or sub-sectors concerned, describes the measures and their inconsistency with Article II of GATS, names the country or countries to which they apply and states the intended duration of the exemptions and the conditions creating the need for them. Exemptions may relate to countries that are not Member States. They are not supposed to exceed a period of ten years.[682] GATS provides for the Council for Trade in Services to review the MFN exemptions periodically,[683] a task that presumably falls to SEOM under the Agreement.[684] So far there has been no review.

A second exception concerns advantages that are given to adjacent countries, whether or not they are Member States, to facilitate frontier trade between them in

674 GATS Article VIII:1.

675 Article X:3.

676 Note 1 to Article V:1.

677 *Ibid.*

678 Article IVbis:1.

679 Article IVbis:3.

680 GATS Article II:2; Note 2 to Article IX:1 of the Agreement.

681 Note 2 to Article IX:1.

682 GATS Annex on Article II Exemptions, Point 6.

683 GATS Annex on Article II Exemptions, Point 3.

684 *See* ArticleXI:1.

services that are both locally produced and consumed.[685] The MFN obligation is not to be construed as preventing such arrangements.

A third exception is that the Agreement is not to be construed as preventing Member States from establishing full integration of labor markets with other Member States on a preferential basis.[686] Such agreements must, however, exempt citizens of the other participating Member States from all requirements concerning residency and work permits.

Finally, service providers from the other Member States may be treated differently if the difference in treatment is the result of an agreement on the avoidance of double taxation.[687]

F. GENERAL EXCEPTIONS TO THE RULES

The Agreement incorporates the GATS rules with respect to the safeguard exception, balance-of-payments exception, general exception, security exception and confidential information.[688] The reader is thus directed to the discussion of these exceptions in Chapter Two, Section I.F.

The Agreement does not, of course, contain a regional economic integration exception. Instead it benefits from this exception. On the other hand, it has its own denial of benefits exception.[689] A Member State may deny the benefits of the Agreement to a service provider who is a natural person of a non-Member State or a legal person owned or controlled by persons of a non-Member State that is constituted under the laws of a Member State but which does not engage in substantive business operations in the territory of a Member State. "Owned" means holding more than fifty percent of the equity interest,[690] and "controlled" means the power to name a majority of the directors or otherwise legally direct the presence's actions.[691]

G. DISPUTE SETTLEMENT

As no specific dispute settlement mechanism has been established for the purposes of the Agreement, the ASEAN *Protocol on Dispute Settlement Mechanism* applies to disputes arising under the Agreement.[692] However, Member States are

685 GATS Article II:3.

686 GATS Article Vbis.

687 GATS Article XIV(e).

688 By way of Article XIV:1.

689 Article VI.

690 GATS Article XXVIII(n)(i).

691 GATS Article XXVIII(n)(ii).

692 Article VII.

free to seek recourse to other fora for the settlement of a dispute, such as GATS, at any stage before SEOM makes a ruling on the panel report.[693]

It should also be noted that, in order to prevent disputes arising in the first place, the Protocol on Notifications requires Member States to notify SEOM and the ASEAN Secretariat of measures that may nullify or impair a benefit to another Member State or may impede the attainment of any objective of the Agreement.[694] This must be done at least sixty days before such measures take effect, and the Member State taking the action must provide adequate opportunity for prior discussions with Member States concerned.[695]

Independently of the notification procedure described above, if a Member State considers that any benefit accruing to it under the Agreement is being nullified or impaired or that the attainment of any objective of the Agreement is being impeded as a result of the failure of another Member State to carry out its obligations under the Agreement, it may request consultations with that other Member State.[696] The latter Member State must reply to the request within ten days of its receipt and must enter into consultations within thirty days.[697] At any time, the parties in dispute may agree to good offices, conciliation or mediation.[698] These procedures may continue while the dispute proceeds if the parties so agree.[699]

If consultations fail to settle the dispute within sixty days after receipt of the request for them and any good offices, conciliation or mediation procedures that are underway are terminated, the matter is referred to SEOM.[700] SEOM either establishes a panel within thirty days from the referral or tries to deal with the dispute itself in the hope of achieving an amicable settlement.[701] In the latter scenario, SEOM is still obliged to establish a panel within thirty days if there is no amicable settlement.

SEOM determines the size, composition and terms of reference of the panel,[702] the function of which is to make an objective assessment of the dispute and adopt such other findings as will assist SEOM in making its ruling.[703] The panel submits its report to SEOM within sixty days of its formation, with the possibility of an ex-

693 Protocol on Dispute Settlement, Article 1:3.

694 Protocol on Notifications, Article 1:2(a) and (b).

695 Protocol on Notifications, Article 2.

696 Protocol on Dispute Settlement, Article 2:2.

697 Protocol on Dispute Settlement, Article 2:3.

698 Protocol on Dispute Settlement, Article 3:1.

699 Protocol on Dispute Settlement, Article 3:2.

700 Protocol on Dispute Settlement, Articles 3:1 and 4:1.

701 Protocol on Dispute Settlement, Article 4:4.

702 Protocol on Dispute Settlement, Article 5:3.

703 Protocol on Dispute Settlement, Article 5:1.

tension for an additional ten days.[704] SEOM considers the report of the panel and makes a ruling on the dispute within thirty says of receiving the report, again with the possibility of an extension for an additional ten days.[705] The parties may appeal the ruling to the ASEAN Economic Ministers (AEM) within thirty days.[706] AEM makes a decision on the appeal within another thirty days, with the possibility of an extension for an additional ten days.[707] The decision of AEM is final and binding on the parties to the dispute.

A Member State must comply with the ruling of the SEOM or AEM within a reasonable period of time.[708] The reasonable period of time is that period mutually agreed by the parties to the dispute but it may under no circumstances exceed thirty days from the relevant decision. If the Member State concerned fails to comply within the reasonable period of time, it must, if requested, enter into negotiations with the other Member State with a view to developing mutually acceptable compensation.[709] If no satisfactory compensation has been agreed within twenty days after the expiry of the reasonable period of time, the other Member State may request authorization from AEM to suspend the application to the Member State concerned of concessions or other obligations under the Agreement. Neither compensation nor retaliation are preferred to full implementation of the final ruling to bring a measure into conformity with the Agreement.[710]

The total period for the disposal of a dispute may not exceed 290 days.[711]

H. FURTHER NEGOTIATIONS ON LIBERALIZATION ON TRADE IN SERVICES

The Member States are obliged to enter into successive negotiations in order to achieve free trade in services by 2020 or earlier.[712] So far, apart from the Protocol to implement the initial package of specific commitment that was agreed in 1997, there have been three further rounds of negotiations. These ended, respectively, with the Protocols of 1998, 2001 and 2004. The fourth Protocol marks significant liberalization of the air and maritime transport, business services, construction, financial services, telecommunications and tourism sectors.

704 Protocol on Dispute Settlement, Article 6:2.

705 Protocol on Dispute Settlement, Article 7.

706 Protocol on Dispute Settlement, Article 8:1.

707 Protocol on Dispute Settlement, Article 8:2.

708 Protocol on Dispute Settlement, Article 8:3.

709 Protocol on Dispute Settlement, Article 9:1.

710 Protocol on Dispute Settlement, Article 9:2.

711 Protocol on Dispute Settlement, Article 10.

712 Article IV:1 and the *Protocol to Implement the Fourth Package of Commitments under the ASEAN Framework Agreement on Services*.

CHAPTER FIVE

LIBERALIZATION OF TRADE IN FINANCIAL SERVICES

I. GENERAL AGREEMENT ON TRADE IN SERVICES

A. THE INSTRUMENTS

There are six instruments that, together, regulate trade in financial services under GATS. The basic framework remains GATS itself, but it is supplemented by the two Annexes on Financial Services, the Decision on Financial Services, the Understanding on Commitments in Financial Services and the Fifth Protocol to GATS.[1] The first five instruments all date from 1994, while the Fifth Protocol was signed in November 14, 1997 and went into effect on March 1, 1999.

GATS has already been examined in Chapter Two. The first Annex clarifies the application of certain GATS rules to financial services and defines the scope of financial services. The second Annex and the Decision set out transitional rules with respect to specific commitments and MFN exemptions. The Fifth Protocol contains as appendices new schedules of commitments on financial services, which replace those originally negotiated under GATS. All four documents have the same binding quality as GATS itself. However, the Fifth Protocol has not been accepted by all WTO Members.[2]

---

1 The Fifth Protocol replaces the Second Protocol, which has now lapsed and is of no legal effect.

2 Those who had accepted it as of November 2003 are: Australia, Bahrain, Bulgaria, Canada, Chile, Colombia, Costa Rica, Cyprus, Czech Republic, Dominican Republic, Ecuador, El Salvador, Egypt, the European Union on behalf of fifteen of its Member States (Austria, Belgium, Denmark, Finland, France, Germany, Greece, Ireland, Italy, Luxembourg, Netherlands, Portu-

The Understanding was negotiated at the same time as GATS between most of the OECD countries,[3] but its legal status is not clear. At a meeting of the Committee on Trade in Financial Services on February 26, 2003, the representative from Hong Kong asked the WTO Secretariat to clarify the legal status of the Understanding. The Secretariat could only reply, rather unhelpfully, that the Understanding constitutes an alternative formula for negotiating specific commitments,[4] which suggests that it is probably not binding. This is supported by the Understanding itself, which seems to indicate that the specific commitments assumed pursuant to it must be inscribed in a Member's Schedule in order to have legal effect.[5] This is certainly the view of Trebilcock and Howse.[6]

B. SECOND ANNEX, THE DECISION AND THE FIFTH PROTOCOL

The United States was not satisfied with the initial commitments on financial services, and it announced that it was going to apply a general MFN exemption with respect to its own commitments, which it would only apply on the basis of reciprocity. However, pursuant to the Decision on Financial Services, the United States agreed to suspend the application of its MFN exemption for six months after the entry into force of the WTO Agreement in order to allow Members a period of time in which to improve on their specific commitments on financial services.[7] During this time, Members were free to list new MFN exemptions, in derogation from the Annex on Article II Exemptions,[8] and to improve, modify or withdraw their specific commitments on financial services.[9]

The Second Protocol containing new commitments on financial services was adopted on July 21, 1995, but the United States was not impressed. Another round of negotiations ended in the conclusion of the Fifth Protocol. The United States now agreed to drop its general MFN exemption.

C. ANNEX ON FINANCIAL SERVICES

The main Annex on Financial Services defines the application of GATS to financial services. The GATS rules, as clarified by the Annex, apply to all the modes of

---

gal, Spain, Sweden and the United Kingdom), Ghana, Honduras, Hong Kong (China), Hungary, Iceland, India, Indonesia, Israel, Japan, Kenya, South Korea, Kuwait, Macau (China), Malaysia, Malta, Mauritius, Nicaragua, Nigeria, New Zealand, Norway, Pakistan, Peru, Poland, Romania, Senegal, Singapore, Slovakia, Slovenia, South Africa, Sri Lanka, Switzerland, Thailand, Tunisia, Turkey, United States, Uruguay and Venezuela.

3 Mexico, for instance, does not subscribe to the Understanding.

4 Doc. S/FIN/M/39 at paras. 24-25.

5 Understanding, Preamble, 2nd para.

6 M.J. Trebilcock and R. Howse at page 242.

7 Para. 1. The Decision does not specifically name the United States.

8 Point 2 of the Annex requires these exemptions to be listed before the entry into force of the WTO Agreement.

9 Second Annex, Points 1 and 2 and Decision, para. 1.

supply and all measures affecting the supply of financial services,[10] which are described in a very broad way as including all insurance and insurance-related services and all banking and other financial services.[11] These services include the following:

- direct insurance (including co-insurance):

  (A) life;

  (B) non-life;

- reinsurance and retrocession;
- insurance intermediation, such as brokerage and agency;
- services auxiliary to insurance, such as consultancy, actuarial, risk assessment and claim settlement services;
- acceptance of deposits and other repayable funds from the public;
- lending of all types, including consumer credit, mortgage credit, factoring and financing of commercial transaction;
- financial leasing;
- all payment and money transmission services, including credit, charge and debit cards, travelers checks and bankers drafts;
- guarantees and commitments;
- trading for own account or for account of customers, whether on an exchange, in an over-the-counter market or otherwise, the following:

  (A) money market instruments (including checks, bills, certificates of deposits);

  (B) foreign exchange;

  (C) derivative products including, but not limited to, futures and options;

  (D) exchange rate and interest rate instruments, including products such as swaps, forward rate agreements;

  (E) transferable securities;

  (F) other negotiable instruments and financial assets, including bullion;

- participation in issues of all kinds of securities, including underwriting and placement as agent (whether publicly or privately) and provision of services related to such issues;
- money broking;

---

10 Annex, Point 1(a).

11 Annex, Point 5(a).

- asset management, such as cash or portfolio management, all forms of collective investment management, pension fund management, custodial, depository and trust services;
- settlement and clearing services for financial assets, including securities, derivative products, and other negotiable instruments;
- provision and transfer of financial information, and financial data processing and related software by suppliers of other financial services;
- advisory, intermediation and other auxiliary financial services on all the activities listed in subparagraphs (v) through (xv), including credit reference and analysis, investment and portfolio research and advice, advice on acquisitions and on corporate restructuring and strategy.

Financial services must be supplied by a natural or legal person of a Member but the supplier may not be a public entity.[12] Public entities are defined as a government, central bank, monetary authority or an entity owned or controlled by a Member that is principally engaged in carrying out governmental functions or activities for governmental purposes.[13] Private entities that perform functions normally performed by a central bank or monetary authority are also considered public entities when they exercise these functions. [14]

Financial services supplied in the exercise of governmental authority are excluded from liberalization by virtue of Article 1:3(b) of GATS. Such services are defined by the Annex as meaning the activities of a central bank, monetary authority or any other public entity in pursuit of monetary or exchange rate policies, activities forming part of a statutory system of social security or public retirement plans and other activities conducted by a public entity involving directly or indirectly government funds.[15] However, if a Member allows any of these last two sets of activities to be conducted by its financial service suppliers in competition with a public entity or a financial service supplier, such activities are not excluded from liberalization.[16]

The Annex adds prudential supervision to the measures that are permitted under GATS as domestic regulation (measure (e)[17]).[18] The measures included by the Annex under prudential supervision are those for the protection of investors, depositors, policy holders or persons to whom a fiduciary duty is owed by a financial service supplier, as well as those needed to ensure the integrity and stability of the financial system. If a prudential measure does constitute discrimination in fact, it

12 Annex, Point 5(b).

13 Annex, Point 5(c)(i).

14 Annex, Point 5(c)(ii).

15 Annex, Point 1(b) and (d).

16 Annex, Point 1(c).

17 The reference is to the illustrative list of measures falling under domestic regulation in List 6.

18 Annex, Point 2(a).

is nevertheless permitted but must not be used as a means of avoiding a Member's commitments or obligations under GATS.

The GATS provisions on mutual recognition are extended by the Annex to prudential supervision, albeit in a rather opaque fashion. A Member may recognize the prudential measures of any other country, whether a Member or not, by means of harmonization, an agreement or arrangement or unilaterally.[19] The Member must afford adequate opportunity for other interested Members to participate in any agreement or arrangement or to negotiate a comparable one under circumstances where there would be equivalent regulation, supervision, implementation of such regulation and, if appropriate, procedures concerning the sharing of information between the parties to the agreement or arrangement.[20] Where recognition is accorded unilaterally, other Members must be given the possibility of demonstrating that this equivalency exists. If they do so, presumably recognition must then be accorded to them, but this is not explicitly stated in the Annex. There is no similar provision where recognition is based on harmonization, but the sense of the Annex is surely that recognition should also be extended in this situation to other Members that demonstrate equivalency.

The Annex supplements the confidentiality provisions of GATS by dispensing Members from any requirement to disclose information relating to the affairs and accounts of individual customers or any confidential or proprietary information in the possession of public entities.[21]

Finally, the Annex requires that panels that are set up to deal with disputes on prudential issues and other financial matters have the necessary expertise relevant to the specific financial service under dispute.[22]

D. UNDERSTANDING ON COMMITMENTS IN FINANCIAL SERVICES

1. General Comments

The Understanding provides an alternative approach to scheduling specific commitments under GATS in the area of financial services.[23] Instead of negotiating their commitments on an ad hoc basis with other Members, Members who subscribe to the Agreement agree to negotiate on the basis of a pre-defined series of commitments that are set out in the Understanding. The aim is a higher degree of liberalization, although Members are not obliged to follow the Understanding in its entirety. It is specifically stated that the Understanding creates no presumption as to the degree of liberalization to which a subscribing Member is committed.[24] Members are thus allowed to place conditions, limitations and qualifications on

19 Annex, Point 3(a).

20 Annex, Point 3(b).

21 Annex, Point 2(b).

22 Annex, Point 4.

23 Understanding, Preamble, Point 1.

24 Understanding, Preamble (iv).

the commitments set out in the Understanding, and in practice they subject them to both sector-specific and horizontal restrictions in their Schedules. However, unlike GATS, the Understanding has standstill provisions; these restrictions must be limited to *existing* non-conforming measures.[25]

The Understanding relates exclusively to the way in which specific commitments are negotiated and in no way supplants GATS.[26] All the provisions of the Agreement still apply to financial services, including the definition of market access and national treatment in Part III. In particular, the GATS MFN rule applies so that any commitments resulting from an application of the Understanding must be extended to all WTO Members.[27] However, on two occasions, the Understanding does modify the GATS rules in favor of a greater degree of liberalization. GATS excludes government procurement from the market access, national treatment and MFN obligations of Members,[28] but the Understanding requires subscribing Members to accord MFN and national treatment to financial service providers from other Members as regards the purchase or acquisition of financial services by their public entities.[29] The GATS tolerates monopolies,[30] whereas the Understanding requires Members to list existing monopoly rights in their Schedule and to endeavor to eliminate or reduce them.[31]

The Understanding raises a number of issues. In the first place, there is the question whether a subscribing Member is obliged to apply the Understanding exclusively. Trebilcock and Howse suggest this is the case[32] whereas McGovern is more ambivalent.[33] The Understanding itself states that it does not prejudice the right of any subscribing Member to schedule its specific commitments in accordance with the GATS approach,[34] which seems to indicate that Members do not have to apply it exclusively. In practice, this is how the subscribing Members have interpreted it. Thus, the EU, with the exception of Sweden, uses the GATS approach for scheduling its commitments on financial services with respect to their supply by presence of natural persons (Mode 4).[35]

The Understanding would not appear to be a legally binding instrument, which leads Trebilcock and Howse to take the view that any commitments arising from

---

25 Understanding, Point A.

26 Understanding, Preamble (i).

27 Understanding, Preamble (iii).

28 GATS, Article XIII:1.

29 Understanding, Point B.2.

30 GATS, Article VIII.

31 Understanding, Point B.1.

32 Trebilcock and Howse at p. 242.

33 E. McGovern at para. 31.3221.

34 Understanding, Preamble (ii).

35 In fact, their so-called Mode 4 commitments have nothing to do with this mode of supply. They are restricted to intra-corporate transferees, which relate to Mode 3, and persons prospecting for clients.

its application must be inscribed in a Member's Schedule in order to have legal force.[36] The approach taken by the subscribing Members, however, is to incorporate the commitments set out in the Understanding into their Schedules by reference. The normal formula is to state that commitments on financial services are undertaken by the Member in accordance with the provisions of the Understanding. This is surely sufficient, although the Japanese approach of expressly making the Understanding an integral part of its Schedule has the merit of greater legal certainty. It should be noted that once a Member incorporates the Understanding, it is obliged, subject to any restrictions it sets, to endeavor to eliminate or reduce monopoly rights even it omits, as is often the case, to list such monopoly rights in its Schedule.

The format of the Understanding divides obligations into market access and national treatment commitments. This is somewhat misleading. The market access part also includes national treatment matters and even domestic regulation, while the national treatment part includes a measure that could come under market access. It is wise, therefore, not to rely too heavily on this division.

A final issue concerns whether the commitments set out in the Understanding are exhaustive, or whether subscribing Members are free to undertake additional market access and national treatment obligations. There is nothing in the Understanding to prevent this, and the fact that the EU, Japan and Canada all expressly provide in their Schedules that their commitments are limited in certain cases to those listed in the Understanding would indicate that such limitation is not automatic.

2. The Commitments

The Understanding requires market access and national treatment to be afforded for the supply of the following financial services through cross-border supply (Mode 1):[37]

- insurance relating to maritime and commercial aviation and space launching, where the insurance covers the goods being transported, the vehicle transporting the goods or any liability arising therefrom;
- insurance of goods in international transit;
- reinsurance and retrocession;
- auxiliary insurance services, such as consulting, actuarial, risk assessment and claim settlement services;
- provision and transfer of financial information and financial date processing;
- advisory and other auxiliary financial services, excluding intermediation but including credit reference and analysis, investment and portfolio research and advice on acquisitions and on corporate restructuring and strategy.

36 Trebilcock and Howse at p.242.

37 Understanding, Point B.3.

The supply of these services may be as a principal, through an intermediary or as an intermediary. The United States excludes the last two types of financial services in the list above.

The Understanding further requires subscribing Members to permit their residents to purchase in the territory of any other Member (Mode 2—consumption abroad) the following financial services:

- insurance relating to maritime and commercial aviation and space launching, where the insurance covers the goods being transported, the vehicle transporting the goods or any liability arising therefrom;
- insurance of goods in international transit;
- reinsurance and retrocession;
- auxiliary insurance services, such as consulting, actuarial, risk assessment and claim settlement services;
- acceptance of deposits and other repayable funds from the public;
- lending of all types, including consumer credit, mortgage credit, factoring and financing of commercial transaction;
- financial leasing;
- all payment and money transmission services, including credit, charge and debit cards, travelers checks and bankers drafts;
- guarantees and commitments;
- trading for own account or for account of customers, whether on an exchange, in an over-the-counter market or otherwise, the following:

  (A) money market instruments (including checks, bills, certificates of deposits);

  (B) foreign exchange;

  (C) derivative products including, but not limited to, futures and options;

  (D) exchange rate and interest rate instruments, including products such as swaps, forward rate agreements;

  (E) transferable securities;

  (F) other negotiable instruments and financial assets, including bullion;
- participation in issues of all kinds of securities, including underwriting and placement as agent (whether publicly or privately) and provision of services related to such issues;
- money broking;
- asset management, such as cash or portfolio management, all forms of collective investment management, pension fund management, custodial, depository and trust services;

- settlement and clearing services for financial assets, including securities, derivative products, and other negotiable instruments;
- provision and transfer of financial information, and financial data processing and related software by suppliers of other financial services;
- advisory, intermediation and other auxiliary financial services on all the activities listed in subparagraphs (v) through (xv), including credit reference and analysis, investment and portfolio research and advice, advice on acquisitions and on corporate restructuring and strategy.

The United States excludes all but the first four types of financial services in the list above. Some Members, such as Canada and the United States, state that their commitments do not extend to allowing financial service suppliers from other Members to solicit for business on their territories.

The Understanding requires subscribing Members to grant financial service suppliers from other Members the right to establish or expand a commercial presence within their territory (Mode 3), including through the acquisition of existing enterprises (barrier (d)[38]).[39] This does not include a right to personal establishment, but Members must permit intra-corporate transfers in the case of the following persons:[40]

- senior management personnel possessing essential proprietary information;
- specialists in the operation of the establishment; and
- subject to the availability of qualified personnel in the host Member, specialists in computer services, telecommunications services and accounts as well as actuarial and legal specialists.

Intra-corporate transfers are sometimes erroneously associated with the supply of services by the presence of natural persons (Mode 4). In fact, they relate to supply through a commercial presence (Mode 3) and are an example of discrimination in fact (measure (d)[41]) where they are not permitted.

The Understanding permits Members to impose terms, conditions and procedures for authorization on the establishment of a commercial presence in a host Member as long they do not circumvent the Member's obligation to permit such a presence.[42] The EU and Japan, for example, require a particular corporate form, which can constitute discrimination in fact (measure (a)).

The Understanding requires subscribing Members to permit financial service providers from other Members established on their territory to offer new financial

---

38 List 3 contains an illustrative list of market access barriers.

39 Understanding, Point B 5.

40 Understanding, Point B.9.

41 List 5 contains an illustrative list of measures constituting discrimination in fact.

42 Understanding, Point B.6.

services,[43] which are defined as services that are not supplied in the territory of the host state but which are supplied in the territory of another Member.[44] However, in a number of Members, the admission to market of a new financial service is subject to the existence of and consistency with a regulatory framework for prudential supervision.

Transfers of information and the processing of financial information as well as the transfer of equipment must be allowed under the Understanding where they are necessary for the conduct of the ordinary business of a financial service supplier.[45] This covers market access barriers (f) and (j). Members retain the right to protect personal data, personal privacy and the confidentiality of individual records as long as such right is not used to circumvent the GATS rules.

The Understanding requires subscribing Members to endeavor to remove or limit the discriminatory effects on financial service providers from other Members of certain non-discriminatory measures.[46] These measures, which are essentially prudential in nature, come under domestic regulation because of their public policy aspect, but they have the potential to discriminate in fact against foreign providers. They fall into four categories:

a) measures that prevent financial service providers from offering in the host state, in the form determined by that Member, all the financial services permitted by the host state;

b) measures that limit the expansion of the activities of financial service providers into all parts of the territory of a Member;

c) measures that apply jointly to banking and investment services and the foreign financial service provider concentrates its activities in the provision of investment services;

d) measures that, although non-discriminatory, nevertheless adversely affect the ability of foreign financial providers to operate, compete or enter the host state market.

Measures (a) refer to restrictions, such as those prescribed by the U.S. *Glass-Steagall Act*, on one entity carrying out simultaneously banking, investment and insurance services. Glass-Steagall has now been repealed by the *Gramm-Leach Billey Act*, but insurance activities must still be carried on separately.

An example of measures (b) is the interdiction on inter-state banking that used to operate in the United States. Such measures should be distinguished from non-discriminatory quantitative restrictions, which, under Article XVI:2 of GATS, are categorized as market access barriers and must be eliminated. In the case of quo-

43 Understanding, Point B.7.

44 Understanding, Point D.3.

45 Understanding, Point B.8.

46 Understanding, Point B.10.

tas, the extent of the growth of the business is absolutely circumscribed; in the case of geographical limits, the business may grow freely but may not expand to other parts of the Member's territory. However, if the parts of the national territory concerned constitute separate markets, these limits are akin to a market barrier (a). However, as they are non-discriminatory and can be justified to some extent on prudential grounds, they fall under domestic regulation. Since the legalization of inter-state banking in the United States,[47] however, such measures are no longer such an important issue.

With respect to measures (c), some countries require investment activities to be carried on by credit institutions, and the prudential rules are based on this coalescence. Such a system creates problems for foreign institutions that specialize in investment activities alone. An example of measures (d) are capital requirements that force a foreign bank that has already met the capital requirement of its home Member to duplicate the process when it establishes itself in a host Member.

The removal or limitation of the discriminatory effects on foreign financial service providers of the measures described above must not unfairly discriminate against domestic financial service providers. With respect to measures (a) and (b), subscribing Members are subject to an exhortatory standstill provision in that they must endeavor not to limit or restrict the present degree of market access or the benefits already enjoyed by the financial service suppliers of other Members.[48]

The national treatment provision of GATS is not circumscribed like the market access provision in Article XVII. Thus, it has general application. Nevertheless, the Understanding singles out three particular examples of discrimination in law concerning the provision of financial services that are covered by national treatment.[49] These are access to payment and clearing systems (measure (b)),[50] access to official funding and refinancing facilities (measures (k) and (l)) and membership in or access to any self-regulatory body, securities or futures exchange or market, clearing agency or any other organization where this is required for the provision of financial services on an equal basis with domestic providers (measures (b) and (c)). The last example, which applies only to foreign financial service providers established in the host state, can also constitute a market access barrier (barriers (a) and (f)).

Some subscribing Members, such as Canada and Sweden, claim in the headnotes to the section on financial services in their Schedules to schedule their commitments with respect to the supply of services through the presence of natural persons (Mode 4) in accordance with the Understanding. In fact, the Understanding has no commitments with respect to this mode of supply. The provision dealing

47 *Interstate Banking and Branch Banking Efficiency Act, 1997.*

48 Understanding, Point B.11.

49 Understanding, Points C.1 and 2.

50 The references are to List 4, which sets out an illustrative list of measures constitution discrimination in law.

with temporary entry relates exclusively to the intra-corporate transfer of personnel within the context of a commercial presence,[51] which is Mode 3, not Mode 4.

II. NORTH AMERICAN FREE TRADE AGREEMENT (AND THE US-CHILE AGREEMENT)

A. INTRODUCTION

1. Chapter Fourteen

Financial services are covered by NAFTA and the US-Chile Free Trade Agreement. The provisions of the two agreements are very similar, and references in the footnotes are to both. Neither the Canada-Chile nor the Mexico-Chile Agreements apply to financial services.[52]

Unlike GATS where financial services are liberalized under the main provisions of the Agreement, albeit clarified and modified by various other instruments, NAFTA regulates trade in financial services separately in Chapter 14.[53] Nevertheless, Chapter 14 does incorporate certain provisions from Chapter 12 on cross-border services and Chapter 11 on investment.[54]

Uncertainty surrounds the status of the provision in Article 1106 on performance requirements. Article 1101:3 states that Chapter 11 on investment does not apply to *measures that are covered by Chapter 14*.[55] Taking into consideration both the provisions of Chapter 14 and the provisions of Chapter 11 that it incorporates, this leaves performance requirements that are not covered. One could argue that, consequently, they are regulated by Article 1106 even in the case of financial services. Article 1410:2, which states that it does not affect a Party's obligations under Article 1106, seems to confirm this view. On the other hand, if matters not covered by Chapter 14 are regulated by default by Chapter 11, what is the point of incorporating a number of specific Articles from Chapter 11 into Chapter 14? It is also significant that the US-Chile Agreement, which contains the same provision as Article 1101:3,[56] nevertheless states clearly that no provisions from the chapters on investment and cross-border services, other than those expressly incorporated, apply to financial services.[57] This is the approach taken in this monograph with respect to NAFTA with the proviso that there is a counter-argument that perhaps merits readers perusing the previous discussion of performance requirements.[58]

---

51 Understanding, Point B.9.

52 Articles G-01:2 and H-01:2(a) (Canada) and 9-02:2 and 10-02:3(a) (Mexico).

53 Chapter 12 (USA).

54 Article 1401:2. *See also* Article 12.1:2 (USA).

55 Article 10.1:4 (USA).

56 Article 10.1:4 (USA).

57 Article 12.1:2.

58 *See* Chapter Four, Sections I.C.3.

Both Agreements, on the other hand, are clear that financial services are subject to their provisions outside of the chapters on investment and cross-border services, namely those on the importation of inputs, government procurement, telecommunications, monopolies, temporary entry and most of the general exceptions. The regular dispute settlement procedures also apply, with some limitation as well as additions, to disputes relating to financial services.

2. Application of Chapter Fourteen

The rules set out in Chapter 14 apply to measures relating to the provision of financial services, which include any law, regulation, procedure, requirement or practice.[59] The Chapter binds all levels of government without exception.[60] Reference to a state or province includes local governments of that state or province.[61] NAFTA extends to the metropolitan territories of the Parties as well as Puerto Rico in the case of the United States and the islands of Guadalupe and Revillagigedo in the case of Mexico.[62]

The financial services covered by Chapter 14 are defined very broadly as "a service of a financial nature, including insurance, and a service incidental or auxiliary to a service of a financial nature.[63] The US-Chile Agreement uses more or less the same definition but also includes the illustrative list of financial services from the GATS Annex on Financial Services.[64] It would seem safe to assume that this list is also applicable to Chapter 14 of NAFTA.

No financial services are explicitly excluded by Chapter 14, but the Parties, or their public entities, may reserve to themselves the conduct or provision of activities or services that form part of a public retirement plan or statutory system of social security, or which are undertaken for the account or with the guarantee or using the financial resources of a Party or its public entities.[65] A public entity is defined as a central bank or monetary authority or any financial institution that is owned or controlled by a Party.[66] This exception corresponds to the exception in GATS for services supplied in the exercise of governmental authority.[67] Govern-

59 Article 201:1. *See also* Article 2.1:1 (USA).

60 Article 105. *See also* Article 1.4 (USA). The wording of the provision provides for exceptions to this rule, but there are none in Chapter 14.

61 Article 201:2. The US-Chile Agreement does not contain this provision.

62 Annex 201.1.

63 Article 1416.

64 Article 12.19. This list is reproduced in Section I.A.3 of this Chapter.

65 Article 1401:3. *See* Article 12.1:3 (USA). The US-Chile Agreement provides that the Chapter applies where a Party allows any of these activities or services to be conducted or provided by its financial institutions in competition with a public entity or a financial institution.

66 Article 1416. *See also* Article 12.19 (USA).

67 GATS, Article I:3(b).

ment procurement of services is covered by Chapter 10,[68] but it should be noted that both Mexico and Canada exclude financial services pursuant to Article 1001:1(b).[69]

The NAFTA rules on financial services apply to the cross-border trade in services (Modes 1, 2 and 4) and to services supplied from a financial institution established in another Party (Mode 3).[70]

The provision of services by means of cross-border supply or consumption abroad (Modes 1 and 2) must take place, respectively, from the territory of one Party into the territory of another Party or in the territory of one Party by a person of that Party to a person of another Party.[71] The situation where a person of one Party receives services in another Party from a person of a third Party is not covered. A person of a Party means a national or enterprise, but this does not include the branch of an enterprise of a non-Party.[72] Nationals include citizens and permanent residents.[73] An enterprise is defined as an entity that is constituted or organized under the law of a Party.[74]

With respect to the provision of services through the presence of natural persons (Mode 4), the service must be supplied in the territory of one Party by a national of another Party, as defined above.[75] However, the provisions on temporary entry apply only to citizens of a Party.[76]

Where services are supplied through Mode 3, the commercial presence must be owned or controlled directly or indirectly by an investor of another Party,[77] who may be a national, as defined above, or an enterprise of the other Party, as defined in Article 201:1. Chapter 14 contains no definition of the terms "owned" and "controlled."

An interesting fact that emerges from the above rules is that where a service is provided by cross-border supply (Mode 1), there is no requirement that either the supplier or consumer be of a Party. However, all these rules are subject to the provisions on the denial of benefits.

---

68 Chapter 9 (USA).

69 Under the US-Chile Agreement, financial services are excluded by Chile.

70 Article 1401:1. *See also* Article 12.1:1.

71 Article 1416. *See also* Article 12.19 (USA).

72 Articles 201:1 and 1416. *See also* Articles 2.1 and 12.19 (USA).

73 *Ibid.*

74 Article 201:1 *See also* Article 2.1 (USA).

75 Article 1416. *See also* Article 12.19 (USA).

76 This is the combined effect of Article 1603:1 and the definition of "business person" in Article 1608. *See also* Articles 14.3:1 and 14.9 (USA).

77 This is the combined effect of Article 1416 and the definition of an "investment of an investor of a Party" given in Article 1139, which is incorporated into Chapter 14. *See also* Articles 12.19 and 10.27 (USA).

3. The Approach of Chapter 14

Chapter 14 sets the scope of liberalization, not the Parties to the Agreement. All financial services are covered except in the case of government procurement and certain financial services and activities that may be reserved. This is the so-called "top-down" approach as opposed to the "bottom-up" approach of GATS. However, as with the OECD Codes, which take the same approach, the Parties are allowed a range of reservations, which are set out in each Party's Schedule in Annex VII to the Agreement.

In the first place the Parties may choose to maintain certain existing non-conforming measures at all levels of government.[78] These reservations relate essentially to the Parties' obligations with respect to market access and national and MFN treatment. For example, Canada continues to restrict in certain circumstances the purchase of reinsurance services by a Canadian insurer from a non-resident insurer to no more than twenty-five percent of the risks undertaken by the insurer purchasing the reinsurance. Mexico uses its reservations to phase in its obligations by an expanding set of limits on the aggregate market share of foreign financial institutions and on the individual market share of any individual foreign financial institution. The Parties may also renew or amend these non-conforming measures. Renewals must be done promptly and amendments may not decrease the conformity of the measure. The reservations are set out in Section A of a Party's Schedule to Annex VII. Each reservation contains the following elements:

- reference to the sector or sub-sector in which the reservation is taken;
- industry classification of the activity covered by the reservation;
- specification of the obligation for which the reservation is taken;
- level of government maintaining the measure for which the reservation is taken;
- measures that are involved by the reservation;
- description of the non-conforming measures;
- any commitment for the liberalization of the measures after the date of entry into force of NAFTA.

Secondly, reservations may taken by the Parties with respect to new non-conforming measures that a Party may subsequently adopt.[79] These are set out in Section B of a Party's Schedule to Annex VII. For example, Canada reserves the right to adopt any measure relating to cross-border trade in securities that derogates from its market access or MFN obligations. Mexico includes a safeguard mechanism that can be used to freeze the aggregate market share of foreign financial institutions.

78 Article 1409:1 *See also* Article 12.9:1 (USA).

79 Article 1409:2. *See also* Article 12.9:2 (USA).

Reservations that are lodged by the Parties pursuant to Chapters 11 and 12 with respect to a Party's national and MFN treatment obligations under these Chapters are deemed to be constitute a reservation to the same obligations under Chapter 14 to the extent that the measure set out in the reservation is covered by Chapter 14.

By contrast to its reservations, a Party to NAFTA may undertake certain specific additional commitments with respect to financial services, which it lists in Section C of its Schedule to Annex VII. For example, Mexico may approve the affiliation of a commercial bank or securities firm with a commercial or industrial corporation that is established in Mexico.

Chapter 14 covers both cross-border services and services provided from a commercial presence. It also separates out, albeit without being explicit and in rather muddled fashion, market access from national treatment.[80] There are separate Articles on market access for the two major ways of providing services, but the other provisions apply, where applicable, to both.

B. MARKET ACCESS

1. Services Supplied from a Commercial Presence

Article 1403 is the main Article on market access for financial services supplied from a commercial presence, but only its provision on the right of establishment sets out a binding commitment. The other rights are only recognized in principle.

The right to establish a financial institution in another Party, which removes barrier (d),[81] applies in principle to any type of commercial entity, including a branch.[82] However, it is limited to financial services providers that do not already own or control a financial institution in the host Party, and this Party may require the provider to incorporate the financial institution under its law, which precludes the commercial presence taking the form of a branch. The right of establishment does not extend to a right of personal establishment, but there are provisions on intra-corporate transferees that discussed under the rubric of national treatment.

The Parties recognize the principle in Article 1403 that providers of financial services from other Parties established on their territory should be able to provide a range of financial services,[83] which relates to barriers (a) and (b). This principle is subject to any requirements by the host Party that different types of financial services be supplied by separate financial institutions. This provision was needed because of the *Glass-Steagall Act* in the United States, which required banking, insurance and investment services to be provided by separate institutions. This

---

80 Article 12.4 of the US-Chile Agreement is clearer. It is entitled "Market Access" and reproduces, *mutatis mutandis* Article XVI:2 of GATS.

81 Article 1403:4. *See also* Article 12.4(a) (USA). The reference is to the illustrative list of market access barriers in List 3.

82 This is the combined effect of Articles 201 and 1416. *See also* Articles 2.1 and 12.19 (USA).

83 Article 1403:2(a). There is no equivalent provision in the US-Chile Agreement.

Act has now been repealed by the *Gramm-Leach Billey Act*, but insurance activities must still be carried on separately. The principle is also recognized that these providers should not be subject to any restrictions that exist in a Party on foreign ownership of financial institutions. This relates to barrier (c), but it does not prevent the Parties from limiting in a non-discriminatory way the share that any one person may hold in a financial institution.

Article 1403 recognizes two other principles with respect to providers of financial services from a Party that are established in another Party, but neither have been considered market access barriers in this monograph. However, as they are covered by Article 1403, they are discussed here.

The first of these principles is that these providers should be able to establish a financial institution in another Party in the legal form that they wish,[84] except in the case of the provision of a new financial service.[85] The requirement of a particular corporate form has been categorized in this monograph as an example of discrimination in fact[86] as it is invariably imposed on a non-discriminatory basis and, at most, disadvantages the provider. However, NAFTA is here taking the same approach as GATS, which also regards this requirement as a market access barrier.[87]

The second principle is the right to expand geographically in a Party's territory. Geographical restrictions, such as the prohibition on inter-state banking in the United States, that bar access to certain parts of a national territory that represent independent markets are indeed akin to market barrier (a). However, as they are normally imposed on a non-discriminatory basis and have some prudential justification, they surely fall more properly under domestic regulation. In fact, this is now rather a dead issue, as inter-state banking has been permitted in the United States since the passing in 1997 of the *Interstate Banking and Branch Banking Efficiency Act*. As a result, Article 1702:2 of the US-Canada Agreement, which is incorporated into Chapter 14[88] and guarantees Canadian banks the inter-state banking rights they enjoyed prior to the Free Trade Agreement, is also obsolete.

The change of the law in the United States on inter-state banking is supposed to lead to a review of the market access principles set out in Article 1403, with a view to adopting arrangements that will permit providers of financial services

84 Article 1403:1. *See also* Article 12.4(b) (USA). Trebilcock and Howse, at page 240, interpret Article 1403:1 as meaning that the right of establishment itself is only recognized as a principle. However, this interpretation conflicts with Article 1403:4.

85 Article 1407:1. *See also* Article 12.6:2 (USA).

86 Measure (a) on the list of examples of discrimination in fact in List 5.

87 *See* GATS Article XVI:2(e).

88 Article 1401:4. There is no equivalent provision in the US-Chile Agreement.

from other Parties to choose the corporate form of their establishment.[89] This review will not include the market access limitations specified in Section B of Mexico's Schedule to Annex VII.[90]

Another issue for providers established in another Party are exchange controls on capital transfers in and out of the host country in the form of investment, dividends and profits as well as transfers related to a particular service transaction (barrier (k)). These are expressly prohibited by Article 1109, which is incorporated into Chapter 14.[91] However, a Party may prevent or limit transfers through the equitable, non-discriminatory and honest application of its laws relating to maintaining the safety, soundness, integrity and financial responsibility of financial institutions.[92] Exchange controls on payment for services or travel to receive them (barrier (l)) are not relevant for services provided from a commercial presence.

2. Cross-Border Services

Article 1404 is the main Article on market access for cross-border financial services, but, although it establishes rights rather than principles, it is somewhat restrictive. It grants a right to all persons located on a Party's territory and its nationals wherever located to receive cross-border services, which removes barrier (b) and by extension (a), but excludes services that are supplied by Mode 4 (presence of natural persons).[93] However, all three modes of providing cross-border services are covered by the standstill provision in the Article that prohibits the Parties from adopting, except by way of reservations in Section B of their Schedule to Annex VII, any measure that restricts trade in cross-border services below the level permitted by a Party on the day of entry into force of NAFTA.[94] In addition, the Parties were bound to consult no later than January 1, 2000 on the further liberalization of cross-border trade in financial services.[95] In particular, the Parties were to consider the possibility of allowing a wider range of insurance services and to determine whether the limitations on cross-border insurance services set out in Section A of Mexico's Schedule to Annex VII should be maintained, modified or eliminated.[96]

89 Article 1403:3. There is no equivalent provision in the US-Chile Agreement.

90 Annex 1403.3. There is no equivalent provision in the US-Chile Agreement.

91 Articles 1109:1 and 1401:2. *See also* Articles 10.8:1 and 12.1:2(USA).

92 Article 1410:4. *See also* Article12.10:3 (USA).

93 Article 1404:2. *See also* Article 12.5:2 (USA).

94 Article 1404:1. The US-Chile Agreement does not have an equivalent provision.

95 Article 1404:4 and Annex 1404.4. There are no equivalent provisions in the US-Chile Agreement.

96 Annex 1404.4

The detailed rules for persons wishing to supply financial services by Mode 4, where they have a right to do, are found in Chapter 16[97] and go some way to eliminating barrier (e). The Chapter applies to business persons, which include financial services personnel, defined as insurers, bankers or investment brokers, who are engaged in commercial transactions for a financial institution located in another Party.[98] However, in contrast to the provisions on cross-border financial services in Chapter 14, Chapter 16 excludes persons who are not citizens of a Party.[99] On the other hand, the definition of business persons is broad enough to include both the self-employed and employees.

Financial services providers from one Party must first qualify for entry into the other Party under the normal immigration rules relating to public health and safety and national security.[100] There is no special treatment under NAFTA for financial services providers with respect to these basic criteria for entry. Subject to this limitation, however, the Parties must grant temporary entry to financial services providers from other Parties.[101] Temporary entry is defined as meaning entry into the territory of another Party without the intent to establish permanent residence there.[102] Clearly, the provider has the right to stay in the other Party in order to supply the financial service, but the maximum duration of this temporary residence is not set down in the Agreement. It is, therefore, a matter to be regulated by national immigration law.

Thus, provided they meet the normal immigration requirements, financial services providers are entitled to temporary entry into another Party upon presentation of a) proof of citizenship of a Party, b) documentation proving that the business person will be engaged in providing a financial service and describing the purpose of entry, and c) evidence demonstrating that the proposed financial service activity is international in scope and that the provider is not seeking to enter the local labor market.[103] This third requirement can be met by showing that the primary source of remuneration for the proposed service arises outside the host state and that the provider's principal place of business and the actual place of accrual of profits also remain predominantly outside that Party.[104]

97 Chapter 14 (USA).

98 *See* the combined effect of Articles 1603:1, 1608, Annex 1603:A.1 and Appendix 1603:A.1. *See also* Articles 14.3:1, 14.9, Annex 14.3:A.1 and Appendix 14.3:A.1.

99 *See* the definition of "business person" in Article 1608. *See also* Article 14.9 (USA).

100 Article 1603:1 and Annex 1603:A.1. *See also* Article 14.3:1 and Annex 14.3:A.1 (USA).

101 *Ibid.*

102 Article 1608. *See also* Article 14.9 (USA).

103 Annex 1603:A.1. *See also* Annex 14.3:A.1 (USA).

104 Annex 1603:A.2. *See also* Annex 14.3:A.2 (USA).

No employment authorization can be required of a financial services provider from another Party.[105] Nor may Parties impose prior approval procedures, petitions, labor certification tests or other similar procedures as a condition for temporary entry and residence.[106] Numerical restrictions are also prohibited. On the other hand, the Parties may require a financial services provider seeking temporary entry to obtain a visa or equivalent document.[107]

A Party may refuse to authorize a financial services provider from another Party where the temporary entry of that person would adversely affect the settlement of a labor dispute at the place of intended employment or the employment of any person involved in such a dispute.[108] The refusing Party must inform the financial services provider in writing of the reasons for the refusal and promptly notify the Party whose financial services provider has been refused entry.[109]

Certain exchange restrictions can obstruct market access for cross-border services. Thus, controls imposed on payment for a service or on access to foreign currency for the purpose of traveling to receive a service (barrier (l)) as well as capital transfers arising from a cross-border financial transaction (part of barrier (k)) are implicitly prohibited by NAFTA in that they are only permitted as a balance-of-payments exception.[110]

3. Provisions Applicable to All Modes of Providing Services

The provisions in NAFTA on access to telecommunications networks (part of barrier (f)), the importation of necessary inputs (barrier (j)) and monopolies (barrier (m)) apply to the supply of financial services.[111] They are complemented by certain provisions that apply specifically to financial services.

Monopolies and state enterprises (barrier (m)) are permitted under NAFTA,[112] but they must both act in manner that is consistent with a Party's obligations under Chapter 14 when exercising delegated authority in connection with the monopoly service, such as the power to issue licenses and approve commercial transactions.[113] Parties must also ensure that, except to comply with their terms of reference, monopolies act solely in accordance with commercial considerations in their

---

105 Annex 1603:A.1 and 3. *See also* Annex 14.3:A.1 (USA).

106 Annex 1603:A.4(a). *See also* Annex 14.3:A.3(a) (USA).

107 Annex 1603:A.5. *See also* Article 14.2:2 (USA).

108 Article 1603:2. *See also* Article 14.3:2 (USA).

109 Article 1603:3. *See also* Article 14.3:3 (USA).

110 Article 2104:1, 2, 3 and 6. The balance-of-payments provision of the US-Chile Agreement only applies to trade in goods—*see* Article 23.4 (USA).

111 *See* the discussion in Chapter Four, Section I.B.1 and 2.

112 Articles 1502:1 and 1503:1. *See also* Articles 16.3:1 and 16.4:1 (USA).

113 Articles 1502:3(a) and 1503:2. *See also* Articles 16.3:3(a) and 16.4:2 (USA).

purchases or sales of the monopoly goods or services.[114] There is no equivalent provision for state enterprises.

Access to telecommunications networks includes, in the case of financial services providers, the right to transfer information into or out of a host Party's territory for data processing where this is required in the ordinary course of providing a financial service.[115] The free flow of data is not subject to any obligations with respect to the protection of personal privacy or commercial confidentiality, which is somewhat unusual.[116]

The Parties must allow financial services providers of another Party to provide new financial services, subject to a refusal for prudential reasons.[117] These are defined as a financial service that is not provided in the host Party's territory but which is provided within the territory of another Party.[118] This includes any new form of delivery of a financial service or the sale of a financial product that is not sold in the host Party's territory. However, this right is limited to new services of a type similar to those services that the host Party permits its own financial services providers, in like circumstances, to provide under its domestic law. The US-Chile Agreement is even more restrictive. The new financial service must be one that the host Party would permit its own financial services providers to supply, and its introduction must not require the host Party to adopt a new law or modify an existing one.[119]

Where a Party requires as a prerequisite for providing a service that a financial services provider of another Party join or have access to a self-regulatory organization, such as a securities or futures exchange, that exercises regulatory authority over financial services providers, this requirement may not infringe the market access obligations set out in Chapter 14.[120] This provision relates to barrier (a).

A final market access provision is incorporated from the US-Canada Agreement.[121] It preserves the right of Canadian banks to deal in US and Canadian government securities that existed prior to the Agreement.[122]

---

114 Article 1502:3(b). *See also* Article 16.3:3(b) (USA).

115 Article 1407:2. There is no equivalent provision in the US-Chile Agreement.

116 *See* Trebilcock and Howse at p. 240.

117 Article 1407:1. *See also* Article 12.6:1 and 2 (USA).

118 Article 1416. This definition does not appear in the US-Chile Agreement.

119 Article 12.6:1 (USA).

120 Article 1402. The equivalent Article in the US-Chile Agreement (12.12) applies only to national and MFN treatment.

121 Article 1401.4.

122 US-Canada Agreement, Article 1702:2.

C. NATIONAL TREATMENT

The national treatment provision in Chapter 14 applies to both cross-border services and services provided from an establishment in another Party.[123] It does not apply to the granting by a Party to a financial services provider of an exclusive right to provide a service forming part of a public retirement plan or statutory system of social security.[124]

The provision is couched in the same terms as the equivalent provisions in Chapters 11 and 12 and requires treatment no less favorable than that accorded, in like circumstances, to domestic providers of financial services. However, Chapter 14 has an additional provision that raises an interesting question. Article 1405:5 requires that a Party's national treatment of financial services providers from other Parties must afford them *equal competitive opportunities.* This is defined as meaning that a Party's national treatment must not disadvantage them in their ability to provide financial services as compared with the ability of the host Party's own providers to supply such services in like circumstances.[125] As Trebilcock and Howse point out,[126] this raises the distinct possibility that national treatment for financial services providers under Chapter 14 extends to discrimination in fact. This additional provision is not found in the US-Chile Agreement.

Certain specific incidences of discrimination, both in law and fact, are singled out.[127] Financial services providers from other Parties must be accorded membership in or access to self-regulatory bodies on a non-discriminatory basis (measure (c) on List 4).[128] The provisions on non-discriminatory access to telecommunications networks apply to financial services (part of barrier (b) on List 4).[129] Monopolies and state enterprises must provide non-discriminatory treatment to providers of financial services from another Party in their purchases and sales of monopoly goods or services (part of measure (g) on List 4),[130] but, in the case of state enterprises, this obligation only covers established service providers. By contrast, state enterprises are under the same obligation of national treatment as monopolies where they, like monopolies, exercise any regulatory, administrative or other governmental authority over such matters as licenses and fees.[131]

Chapter 14 allows Parties to require that a simple majority on the boards of directors of financial institutions established in a host Party be citizens or residents of

---

123 Article 1405:1 to 3. *See also* Article 12.2:1 to 3 (USA).

124 Article 1410:3. This exception does not exist in the US-Chile Agreement.

125 Article 1405:6.

126 Trebilcock and Howse at p. 240.

127 List 4 contains an illustrative list of measures constituting discrimination in law, and List 5 does the same for discrimination in fact.

128 Article 1402. *See also* Article 12.12 (USA).

129 *See* the discussion in Chapter Four, Section I.C.2 and 3.

130 Article 1502:3(c) and 1503:3. *See also* Articles 16.3:3(c) and 16.4:3 (USA).

131 Article 1502:3(a) and 1503:2. *See also* Articles 16.3:3(a) and 16.4: 2 (USA).

the host Party or a combination thereof,[132] thus permitting measure (e) on List 5. However, it prohibits any requirement that senior management or other essential positions be held by nationals of the host Party (measure (d)).[133] This prohibition does not require Parties to allow persons from other NAFTA Parties to reside and work permanently in the host state as these intra-company transferees are subject to the rules on temporary entry.[134] They must be citizens of a Party[135] and be rendering services in a capacity that is managerial, executive or involves specialized knowledge.[136] They must meet existing immigration rules relating to public health and safety and national security and may be required to obtain a visa or equivalent document.[137] A Party may further require the employee to have been continuously employed for one year within the three-year period immediately preceding the date of application for temporary entry.[138] As long as a company transferee meets all these conditions, he or she must be admitted and provided with confirming documentation. No labor certification tests or equivalent procedures may be required as a condition for temporary entry and no numerical restrictions may be imposed.[139] The length of time that an intra-company transferee may remain in the host state is up to the domestic law of that Party.

It is not clear whether the provisions in Article 1106 on performance requirements, which, depending on their nature, may constitute discrimination in law (measures (t) to (z) on List 4) or in fact (measure (f) on List 5), apply to the financial commercial establishments. If so, the reader is directed to the discussion of these requirements in Chapter Four, Section I.C.3.

With respect to the provision of financial services by consumption abroad (Mode 2) or cross-border supply (Mode 1), the Parties are under no obligation to permit providers of such services from another Party to solicit business in their territory.[140] For these modes, therefore, measure (e) on List 4 is permitted.

D. DOMESTIC REGULATION

The non-discriminatory domestic regulation of trade in financial services is permitted under NAFTA as for trade in services generally. It is quite possible,

---

132 Article 1408:2. *See also* Article 12.8:2 (USA).

133 Article 1408:1. *See also* Article 12.8:1 (USA). The provision somewhat oddly refers to a requirement that the persons concerned be "of a particular nationality." It would be extremely unusual for a country to require the senior managers of its companies to be foreign nationals, and so we may assume that the requirement refers to nationality of the host state.

134 Annex 1603:C. *See also* Annex 14.3:C (USA).

135 *See* the definition of "business person" in Article 1608, which includes corporate transferees. *See also* Article 14.9 (USA).

136 Annex 1603:C(1). *See also* Annex 14.3:C(1) (USA).

137 Annex 1603:C(1) and (3). *See also* Article 14.2 and Annex 14.3:C(1) (USA).

138 Annex 1603:C(1). *See also* Annex 14.3:C(1) (USA).

139 Annex 1603:C(2). *See also* Annex 14.3:C(2) (USA).

140 Article 1404:2. *See also* Article 12.5:2 (USA).

however, that its scope is more limited as national treatment with respect to the provision of financial services may extend to discrimination in fact (measure (h)[141]). Whatever the case may be, nationality requirements for senior and specialist personnel in financial institutions established in another Party (measure (d)[142]) are specifically prohibited,[143] as may be non-discriminatory performance requirements (measure (f)).[144] On the other hand, the requirement that a simple majority on the boards of directors of financial institutions established in a host Party be citizens or residents of the host Party or a combination thereof (measure (e)) is a permitted measure of domestic regulation.[145]

Certain other measures of domestic regulation are specifically permitted. The most important of these in the area of financial services are prudential measures. Thus, the Parties are free to adopt or maintain measures that are necessary for:

- the protection of investors, depositors, participants in financial markets, policy-holders, policy-claimants or persons to whom a fiduciary duty is owed by a financial service supplier;
- the maintenance of the safety, soundness, integrity and financial responsibility of financial service suppliers;
- ensuring the integrity and stability of a Party's financial system.[146]

Without prejudice to these measures of prudential regulation, a Party may also require the registration of cross-border financial services providers from other Parties and of financial instruments.[147] With respect to the provision of new financial services, a Party may determine the institutional and legal form through which the service may be provided and may require authorization for its provision.[148]

Parties may prescribe special formalities for providers who wish to set up a financial establishment in another Party.[149] Such formalities may include a requirement to incorporate under the laws of the host Party, which excludes the use of a branch,

---

141 The reference is to List 6, which contains an illustrative list of measures falling within domestic regulation.

142 The references are to List 5, which contains an illustrative list of measures constituting discrimination in fact.

143 Article 1408:1. *See also* Article 12.8:1 (USA). Under Article 12.4 of the US-Chile Agreement, non-discriminatory quantitative restrictions (measure (g) on List 5) are treated as market access barriers and must also be eliminated.

144 *See* the discussion *supra* in the text.

145 Article 1408:2. *See also* Article 12.8:2 (USA).

146 Article 1410:1. *See also* Article 12.10:1. The US-Chile Agreement does not include the third rationale.

147 Article 1404:3. *See also* Article 12.5:3 (USA).

148 Article 1407:1. *See also* Article 12.6:2 (USA).

149 Articles 1111:1, 1401:2 and 1403:4. *See also* Articles 10.10:1 and 12.1:2 (USA).

and even the requirement of residency. Other terms and conditions may be imposed as long as they are non-discriminatory.[150]

With respect to access to and use of public telecommunications transport networks and services, the Parties may take such measures as are necessary to ensure the security and confidentiality of messages or to protect the privacy of subscribers to these networks and services.[151] They may also impose conditions that are necessary to safeguard the public service responsibilities of the providers of these networks and services or to protect the technical integrity of public networks and services.[152] These conditions may include:[153]

- restrictions on resale or shared use of public telecommunications services;
- requirement to use specified technical interfaces for interconnection to public networks and services;
- certain restrictions on the interconnection of private leased or owned circuits;
- a licensing, permit, registration or notification procedure, which must, however, be transparent and expeditious.

Non-discriminatory measures of general application taken by any public entity in pursuit of monetary and related credit policies or exchange rate policies are also permitted.[154]

Both the general Agreement and Chapter 14 contain some rules on domestic regulation.

In the first place, the Parties are required to publish promptly or otherwise make available all relevant measures of general application pertaining to trade in financial services.[155] They must notify other Parties of proposed or actual measures[156] and respond promptly to their requests for information.[157]

In addition, the Parties must, to the extent that it is practicable, provide in advance to all interested persons any measure of domestic regulation of financial services so as to allow them an opportunity to comment on the measure.[158] Each Party's regulatory authorities must also make available to interested persons their requirements for completing applications relating to the provision of finan-

150 Article 1403:4(b).

151 Article 1302:5. *See also* Article 13.2:4 (USA).

152 Article 1302:6. *See also* Article 13.2:5 (USA).

153 Article 1302:7. *See also* Article 13.2:6 (USA).

154 Article 1410:2. *See also* Article 12.10:2 (USA).

155 Article 1802:1. *See also* Article 20.2:1 (USA).

156 Article 1803:1. *See also* Article 20.3:1 (USA).

157 Article 1803:2. *See also* Article 20.3:2 (USA).

158 Article 1411:1. *See also* Article 12.11:2 (USA).

cial services.[159] Within 180 days of the entry into force of NAFTA, the Parties were obliged to set up one or more inquiry points to respond in writing to all reasonable inquiries from interested persons regarding measures of general application affecting the provision of financial services.[160]

With respect to cross-border financial services, the Parties must publish explanatory material in a consolidated document regarding the requirements for the temporary entry of financial services providers in connection with the supply of financial services through Mode 4.[161] They must also provide them with such materials as will enable them to become acquainted with the measures relating to temporary entry.[162]

All measures of domestic regulation affecting trade in financial services must be administered in a consistent, impartial and reasonable manner, which includes affording affected persons an opportunity to present their case prior to any final administrative action as long as time, the nature of the proceeding and the public interest permit this.[163] The Parties must maintain or establish tribunals or procedures for prompt review and, where warranted, correction of final administrative decisions affecting trade in financial services.[164] Persons must have a reasonable opportunity to defend themselves.[165]

On the request of any applicant for the provision of financial services, a Party's regulatory authority must inform the applicant of the status of the application.[166] If such authority requires additional information, it must notify the applicant accordingly without delay. It must make a decision on the application within 120 days and must promptly notify the applicant.[167] Where it is not practicable for the decision to be made within 120 days, the applicant must be notified and the decision made within a reasonable time. Where an authorization is required for the provision of a new financial service, a decision must be made within a reasonable time and the authorization may only be refused for prudential reasons.[168]

Chapter 14 contains no provisions on the licensing and certification of providers of financial services, but it does require that any domestic rules on membership in self-regulatory bodies (measure (b) on List 6) not contravene a Party's obligations

---

159 Article 1411:2. *See also* Article 12.11:3 (USA).

160 Article 1411:6. *See also* Article 12.11:6 (USA).

161 Article 1604:1(b). *See also* Article 14.4:1(b) (USA).

162 Article 1604:1(a). *See also* Article 14.4:1(a) (USA).

163 Article 1804. *See also* Article 20.4 (USA).

164 Article 1805:1. *See also* Article 20.5:1 (USA).

165 Article 1805:2(a). *See also* Article 20.5:(2(a) (USA).

166 Article 1411:3. *See also* Article 12.11:4 (USA).

167 Article 1411:4. *See also* Article 12.11:5 (USA).

168 Article 1407:1. *See also* Article 12.6:2 (USA).

under the Chapter.[169] There is no provision for additional commitments regarding the domestic regulation of financial services.

Chapter 14 contains a somewhat opaque mutual recognition provision. A Party may recognize the prudential measures of another Party or of a non-Party unilaterally or by means of harmonization or an agreement or arrangement.[170] This Party must afford adequate opportunity for other interested Parties to demonstrate equivalency in their prudential rules and, if appropriate, in the procedures concerning the sharing of information between the Parties.[171] If equivalency is shown by an interested Party, it must be afforded adequate opportunity to participate in any agreement or arrangement or to negotiate a comparable one.[172] There is no similar provision where recognition is based on harmonization or accorded unilaterally, but the sense of the provision is surely that recognition should also be extended in these situations to other Parties.

E. MOST-FAVORED NATION TREATMENT

A Party to NAFTA must treat financial services providers from another Party, regardless of the mode of supply, no less favorably than financial services providers from any other country, whether it is a Party or not.[173] This MFN principle specifically applies to self-regulatory bodies.[174] In addition, monopolies and state enterprises must provide MFN treatment to financial services providers of other Parties where they exercise regulatory authority over such matters as licenses and fees.[175] Monopolies and, in the case of financial services supplied from a commercial presence, state enterprises must also apply the MFN principle to their purchases and sales of goods or services.[176]

The MFN principle does not apply to any advantage accorded by a Party to another Party or non-Party pursuant to a tax convention.[177] A modified MFN rule applies to the recognition of the prudential measures of another Party or non-Party.[178] Parties are not obliged to extend this recognition to the other Parties, but they must afford them an adequate opportunity to demonstrate equivalency in their prudential measures and to participate in any agreement or arrangement.

169 Article 1402. *See also* Article 12.12 (USA).

170 Article 1406:2. *See also* Article 12.3:2 (USA).

171 Article 1406:3. *See also* Article 12.3:3 (USA).

172 Article 1406:4. *See also* Article 12.3:4 (USA).

173 Article 1406:1. *See also* Article 12.3:1 (USA).

174 Article 1402. *See also* Article 12.12 (USA).

175 Articles 1502:3(a) and 1503:2. *See also* Articles 16.3:3(a) and 16.4:2 (USA).

176 Articles 1502:3(c) and 1503:3. *See also* Articles 16.3:3(c) and 16.4:3 (USA).

177 Article 2103:4(c). *See also* Article 23.3:4(c) (USA).

178 Article 1406:2-4. *See also* Article 12.3:2-4 (USA).

F. GENERAL EXCEPTIONS TO THE RULES

1. Safeguard Exception

In NAFTA, this exception applies only to trade in goods.[179]

2. Balance-of-Payments Exception

Parties are allowed to introduce exchange controls on capital transfers (barrier (k))[180] and access to foreign currency for purpose of purchasing the financial services of a provider from another Party or for that of traveling to receive them (barrier (l)) only if they are experiencing serious balance-of-payments difficulties or the threat thereof.[181] A Party may adopt or maintain controls that give a priority to services that are essential to its economic program, but they may not protect a specific financial services sector unless this is done consistently with the economic adjustment measures required by the IMF and with Article VIII:3 of the IMF Articles.[182]

As soon as practicable after imposing controls for balance-of-payments reasons, a Party must submit any current account exchange restrictions (barrier (l)) to the IMF for review and approval under Article VIII of the IMF Articles.[183] It must also enter into consultations with the IMF on the economic adjustment measures needed to deal with the fundamental underlying structural problems that are causing the difficulties and apply them.

Any exchange controls that are imposed on the cross-border trade in financial services must meet the following conditions:[184]

- they must avoid unnecessary damage to the commercial, economic or financial interests of another Party;
- they must not be more burdensome than necessary to deal with the difficulties or threat thereof;
- they must be temporary and be phased out progressively as the situation improves;
- they must be consistent with any economic adjustment measures required by the IMF; and
- they must be applied on a national treatment or MFN basis, whichever offers the best treatment.

---

179 Articles 802 and 803. *See also* Article 8.1 (USA).

180 The reference is to the illustrative list of market access barriers in List 3.

181 Article 2104:1. Balance-of-payment restrictions may only be imposed on goods under the US-Chile Agreement.

182 Article 2104:4. Article VIII:3 of the IMF Articles prohibits the use of discriminatory currency arrangements or multiple currency practices.

183 Article 2104:2.

184 Article 2104:3.

A Party may not impose more than one measure on any transfer involving a cross-border financial service unless this is done consistently with the economic adjustment measures required by the IMF and with Article VIII:3 of the IMF Articles.[185] In addition an imposing Party must notify and consult with the other Parties to assess its balance-of-payments situation and the measures that it has adopted.[186] During such consultations, the Parties must consider whether the measures adopted by the imposing Party meet the conditions outlined above, in particular with respect to their temporary nature.[187] They must base their conclusions on the assessment by the IMF of the balance-of-payments situation of the imposing Party.[188]

3. General Exceptions

No general exceptions are permitted with respect to financial services.[189]

4. Security Exception

The NAFTA security exception applies. This permits certain exceptions to the totality of the rules of the Agreement, including Chapter 14, in the case of measures that are taken for reasons of national security.[190] The provision is similar to that found in GATS and excepts the following with respect to financial services:

- the disclosure of information whose disclosure would be contrary to a Member's essential security interests;
- traffic and transactions in services undertaken directly or indirectly for the purpose of supplying a military or other security establishment;
- measures taken in time of war or other international emergency;
- measures relating to the implementation of non-proliferation policies or agreements; and
- actions taken in pursuance of a Member's obligations under the United Nations Charter.

5. Denial of Benefits

The denial of benefits provisions of Chapters 11 and 12 are incorporated into Chapter 14.[191] A Party may deny the benefits of Chapter 14 to a provider of

185 Article 2104:6(a).

186 Article 2104:6(b).

187 Article 2104:7(a).

188 Article 2104:7(b).

189 Article 2101. *See also* Article 23.01 (USA).

190 Article 2102. *See also* Article 23.2 (USA).

191 Article 1401:2. *See also* Article 12.1:2 (USA).

financial services from a commercial presence or on a cross-border basis where the enterprise involved in providing the services is owned or controlled, respectively, by investors or nationals of a non-Party, if:[192]

- the denying Party does not maintain diplomatic relations with the non-Party; or
- the denying Party adopts or maintains measures with respect to the non-Party that prohibit transactions with the enterprise or that would be violated or circumvented if benefits under Chapter 14 were accorded to the enterprise; or
- subject to prior notification and consultation, the enterprise has no substantial business activities in the territory of the Party under whose law it is constituted or organized or, in the case of cross-border services, in the territory of any Party.

6. Taxation

Nothing in NAFTA may affect the rights and obligations of any Party under a tax convention, the provisions of which take precedence over those of NAFTA.[193] In addition, the provisions on national and most-favored nation treatment of financial services providers from other Parties do not apply to a non-conforming provision of any existing taxation measure.[194] Such measures may be renewed promptly or amended to the extent that the amendment does not decrease their conformity.[195] The exception also apples to new taxation measures adopted by the Parties that are aimed at ensuring the equitable and effective imposition or collection of taxes as long as the measures do not discriminate between services of the Parties or arbitrarily nullify or impair benefits accruing under Chapter 14 of the Agreement.[196]

7. Confidentiality Information

Chapter 14 does not require a Party to disclose information that is related to the financial affairs and accounts of individual customers of financial institutions or cross-border financial services providers, or which would impede law enforcement or otherwise be contrary to the public interest or prejudice the legitimate commercial interests of particular enterprises.[197]

---

192 Articles 1113 and 1211. *See also* Articles 10.11 and 11.11 (USA).

193 Article 2103:2. *See also* Article 23.3:2 (USA).

194 Articles 2104:4(d). *See also* Article 23.3:4(d) (USA).

195 Articles 2104:4(e), (f). *See also* Article 23.3:4(e), (f) (USA).

196 Articles 2104:4(g). *See also* Article 23.3:4(g) (USA).

197 Article 1411:5. *See also* Article 12.7 (USA).

G. DISPUTE SETTLEMENT

1. Dispute Settlement Between the Parties

The regular NAFTA dispute settlement procedure, which is described in Chapter Four, Section G.1, applies to disputes involving Chapter 14.[198] However, the Parties must maintain a roster of up to fifteen individuals to serve specifically as financial services panelists.[199] The members of this roster must:[200]

- have expertise or experience in financial services law or practice;
- be chosen strictly on the basis of objectivity, reliability and sound judgment;
- be independent of the Parties; and
- comply with a code of conduct.

Where a Party claims that a dispute arises under Chapter 14, the normal panel selection procedure applies except that, if the disputing Parties so agree, the panel must be composed exclusively of panelists meeting the qualifications set out above.[201] Where there is no agreement, each disputing Party may select panelists that meet these qualifications or those that apply as a general rule to panelists as set out in Article 2010:1.[202] If the Party complained against invokes prudential reasons pursuant to Article 1410:1, the chair of the panel must meet the above qualifications.[203]

Where the panel finds a measure to be inconsistent with a Party's obligations under the Agreement, including Chapter 14, the following methods of retaliation are permitted:[204]

- where the measure affects only the financial services sector, the complaining Party may suspend benefits only in this sector;
- where the measure affects the financial services sector and any other sector, the complaining Party may suspend benefits in the financial services sector to the extent that the measure affects this sector;
- where the measure does not affect the financial services sector, the complaining Party may not suspend benefits in this sector.

Independently of the dispute settlement procedure, a Party may request consultations with another Party regarding any matter that affects trade in financial ser-

198 Article 1414:1. *See also* Article 12.17:1 (USA).

199 Article 1414:2. *See also* Article 12.17:3 (USA).

200 Article 1414:3. *See also* Article 12.17:4 (USA).

201 Article 1414:4(a). *See also* Article 12.17:5(a) (USA).

202 Article 1414:4(b)(i). *See also* Article 12.17:5(b)(i) (USA).

203 Article 1414:4(b)(ii). *See also* Article 12.17:5(b)(ii) (USA).

204 Article 1414:6. *See also* Article 12.17:6 (USA).

vices.[205] The other Party must give sympathetic consideration to the request for consultations, and the consulting Parties must report the results of their consultations to the Financial Services Committee. Where the matter involves domestic regulation, a Party may request that the regulatory authorities of the other Party participate in the consultations.[206]

2. Submission by Providers of Claims to Arbitration

Providers of financial services from a commercial presence have the same right as providers of other services to submit a claim to arbitration, but only for breaches by the host Party of its obligations with respect to transfers of capital (Article 1109), special formalities in connection with establishment (Article 1111) and denials of benefits (Article 1113).[207] The procedure is that described in Chapter Four, Section G.2 except that where the host Party invokes prudential reasons pursuant to Article 1410, the Tribunal shall, on the request of the host Party, refer the matter in writing to the Financial Services Committee for a decision.[208] The Committee decides whether and to what extent prudential reasons are a valid defense to the claim of the financial services provider.[209] Its decision is binding on the Tribunal.

If the Committee has not decided the issue within sixty days of the receipt of the referral, the host Party or the Party of the disputing provider may request the establishment of an arbitral panel.[210] The panel is constituted in the manner outlined above for disputes involving financial services. The panel's report is binding on the Tribunal. Where no request for the establishment of a panel has been made within ten days of the expiry of the sixty-day period for the Committee to decide the issue, the Tribunal is free to decide the matter.[211]

H. FURTHER NEGOTIATIONS

The Parties were under an obligation to consult, no later than January 1, 2000, on further liberalization of the cross-border trade in financial services, in particular with respect to insurance services.[212] So far, no further liberalization has been agreed.

---

205 Article 1413:1. *See also* Article 12.16:1 (USA).

206 Article 1413:3. There is no equivalent provision in the US-Chile Agreement.

207 Article 1401:2. *See also* Article 12.1:2 (USA).

208 Article 1415:1. *See also* Article 12.18:1 (USA).

209 Article 1415:2. *See also* Article 12.18:2 (USA).

210 Article 1415:3. *See also* Article 12.18:3 (USA).

211 Article 1415:4. *See also* Article 12.18:4 (USA).

212 Article 1404:4. There is no equivalent provision in the US-Chile Agreement.

III. THE EUROPEAN UNION (AND THE EEA AGREEMENT)

A. INTRODUCTION

The EU has secondary legislation based on the EC Treaty that sets up liberalized regimes for banking, insurance and investment services in the EU. These regimes provide for complete freedom to provide services throughout the EU on a cross-border basis (Modes 1, 2 and 4) as well as from a permanent establishment in another Member State (Mode 3). Although the regimes are essentially similar for all three branches of the financial services sector, there are enough differences in detail between them to warrant discussing each separately.

In addition to the directives that set up these liberalized regimes, there are a number of other directives dealing with prudential and other matters pertaining to the supply of financial services. As the focus of this monograph is the liberalization of services, however, these other directives are not discussed.

The secondary legislation of the EU on financial services applies to the Contracting Parties to the EEA Agreement (Iceland, Liechtenstein and Norway).[213]

B. THE BANKING REGIME OF THE EUROPEAN UNION

EP/Council Directive 2000/12 relating to the taking up and pursuit of the business of credit institutions, OJ L126/2000[214]

1. Introduction

Overview

Directive 00/12 (the Directive) codifies and combines into a single text a number of earlier directives[215] relating to the freedom to pursue the business of a credit institution and the rules pertaining to the prudential supervision of such institutions.

213 *See* EEA Agreement, Articles 7 and 36(2) and Annex IX.

214 As amended by Directives 00/28 (OJ L275/00), 02/87 (OJ L35/03) and 04/39 (OJ L145/04).

215 These are: Council Directive 73/183 on the abolition of restrictions on freedom of establishment and freedom to provide services in respect of self-employed activities of banks and other financial institutions (OJ L194/73), Council Directive 77/780 on the coordination of laws, regulations and administrative provisions relating to the taking up and pursuit of the business of credit institutions ("First Banking Directive") (OJ L322/77), Council Directive 89/299 on the own funds of credit institutions (OJ L124/89), Council Directive 89/646 on the coordination of laws, regulations and administrative provisions relating to the taking up and pursuit of the business of credit institutions ("Second Banking Directive") (OJ L386/89), Council Directive 89/647 on a solvency ratio for credit institutions (OJ L386/89), Council Directive 92/30 on the supervision of credit institutions on a consolidated basis (OJ L110/92), and Council Directive 92/121 on the monitoring and control of large exposures of credit institutions (OJ L29/93). All these directives and their amendments are repealed by Directive 00/12.

The EU[216] banking regime resides on the principles of mutual recognition, one-state prudential supervision, cooperation between the competent authorities[217] of the Member States and a common approach to third countries.[218] Credit institutions authorized in a Member State can obtain a single license that enables them to pursue their primary activities throughout the EU, either through a branch or by way of provision of services, on the basis of this one authorization. The Member State that authorizes a credit institution is called the "home Member State"[219] and is responsible for the prudential supervision of all its activities within the EU. However, host Member States, which is where a credit institution authorized elsewhere in the EU has a branch or provides services,[220] have responsibility at present for supervising the liquidity of branches and for measures resulting from the implementation of their monetary policies where they still retain control over them.[221] They may also enforce those of their own laws that exist to protect the general good.[222]

Scope

The EU banking regime applies to all credit institutions with the exception of the central banks of Member States, post office giro institutions and certain credit institutions peculiar to particular Member States.[223] A credit institution is defined as an undertaking whose business is to receive deposits or other repayable funds from the public and to grant credits for its own account or an electronic money institution within the meaning of Directive 00/46.[224]

The activities of credit institutions that are covered by the Directive are the following:[225]

1) Acceptance of deposits and other repayable funds;

---

216 Directive 00/12 is enacted pursuant to the European Community Treaty and references in it are to the "Community" rather than the EU. However, the Community is part of the EU and it seems simpler to refer to it as such. Under the proposed European Constitution, the term "EU" would have supplanted completely the term "Community" or "EC."

217 "Competent authorities" means the national authorities that are empowered by law or regulation to supervise credit institutions (Article 1(4)). In the text, I have normally referred simply to the "Member States" when their competent authorities are meant.

218 A "third country" is a country that is not a Member State of the EU.

219 Article 1(6).

220 Article 1(7).

221 Article 27. In the cases of Austria, Belgium, Finland, France, Germany, Greece, Ireland, Italy, Luxembourg, Netherlands, Portugal and Spain, monetary policy is decided at EU level.

222 Preamble, 17th recital.

223 Article 2(1) and (2).

224 Article 1(1)(a) and (b). Under Article 1(3)(a) of EP/Council Directive 00/46 on the taking up, pursuit of and prudential supervision of the business of electronic money institutions (OJ L275/00), an "electronic money institution" is defined as an undertaking or any other legal person that issues means of payment in the form of electronic money.

225 Annex I.

2) Lending;

3) Financial leasing;

4) Money transmission services;

5) Issuing and administering means of payment (e.g. credit cards, travelers' checks and bankers' drafts);

6) Guarantees and commitments;

7) Trading for own account or for account of customers in

a) money market instruments,

b) foreign exchange,

c) financial futures and options,

d) exchange and interest rate instruments, and

e) transferable securities;

8) Participation in securities issues and the provision of services related to such issues;

9) Advice to undertakings on capital structure, industrial strategy and related questions and advice as well as services relating to mergers and the purchase of undertakings;

10) Money broking;

11) Portfolio management and advice;

12) Safekeeping and administration of securities;

13) Credit reference services;

14) Safe custody services.

Financial institutions other than credit institutions are covered by the rules of free movement subject to certain conditions.[226] Financial institutions are defined as undertakings whose principal activity is to carry on all the banking activities covered by the Directive with the exception of the right to accept deposits and other repayable funds from the public.[227] This latter activity may only be carried on by credit institutions.[228]

All credit institutions, post office giro institutions and certain credit institutions peculiar to particular Member States as well as financial institutions, but excluding the central banks of Member States, are subject to the rules on consolidated su-

226 Article 19, 1st para. These conditions are discussed *infra* in the text.

227 Article 1(5).

228 Article 3.

pervision.[229] These rules also apply to financial holding companies[230] and mixed-activity holding companies.[231]

National Law

The EU banking regime does not entirely replace the national systems. National law may still apply but subject to the EU rules on authorization, prudential supervision and freedom of movement. The Directive specifically allows home Member States to establish stricter national rules with respect to initial capital, qualified holdings,[232] professional secrecy and non-financial holdings,[233] and on occasion it leaves the Member States some measure of discretion in the implementation of its rules.

2. Authorization of Credit Institutions

General Provisions

Credit institutions must obtain an authorization before commencing their activities from their home Member State.[234] In the case of a legal person, this is where the credit institution has its registered office or, if it has no registered office under its national law, its head office.[235] In the case of credit institutions that are not legal persons, the home Member State is where they have their head office.[236]

The authorization provisions of the Directive also apply to the authorization of the branches of credit institutions whose head offices are outside the EU[237] as well the direct or indirect subsidiaries of parent undertakings from third countries.[238] In both cases, the Commission must be informed. Where the credit institution being authorized is a subsidiary of a credit institution or financial or mixed-activity

---

229 Article 2(2), 2nd subpara.

230 Under Article 1(21), a "financial holding company" is defined as a financial institution that has subsidiaries that are either exclusively or mainly credit institutions or financial institutions, of which one must be a credit institution. They do not include mixed financial holding companies within the meaning of Article 2(15) of EP/Council Directive 02/87 on the supplementary supervision of credit institutions, insurance undertakings and investment firms in a financial conglomerate (OJ L35/03).

231 Article 2(2), 1st subpara. Under Article 1(22), "a mixed-activity holding company" is defined as an undertaking, other than a financial holding company, a mixed financial holding company or a credit institution that has subsidiaries that include at least one credit institution.

232 A "qualifying holding" is defined in Article 1(10) as a direct or indirect holding in an undertaking that represents 10% or more of its capital or voting rights or which makes it possible to exercise a significant influence over the management of the undertaking.

233 Preamble, 12th recital.

234 Article 4.

235 This is the implication of the Preamble, 9th recital and Article 6(2).

236 Preamble, 9th recital and Article 6(2), 2nd indent.

237 Article 24(2).

238 Article 23(1)(a).

holding company from another Member State, there must be prior consultation between the home Member State and the other Member State concerned.[239]

Financial institutions do not require an authorization to pursue their activities, but their Memorandum and Articles of Association must be verified to see whether they permit the conduct of these activities and certain conditions must be complied with.[240]

In order to obtain an authorization, credit institutions must meet the national requirements of the home Member State as well as the requirements set out by the Directive.

National Requirements

National requirements for granting an authorization must be consistent with the rules of the Directive.[241] For instance, the Directive prohibits a home Member State from making an authorization dependent on the economic needs of the market.[242] Nor may host Member States require branches of credit institutions authorized in other Member States to be authorized anew.[243] On the other hand, the Directive permits home Member States to lay down stricter rules with respect to initial capital and qualifying holdings.[244]

Requirements under the Directive

1. The Directive requires a credit institution to have separate own funds and an initial capital of at least 5 million Euros in order to obtain an authorization.[245] Own funds are defined in Articles 34 to 38 and discussed later. The initial capital of an institution consists of three of the various items that make up own funds, namely the paid-up amounts, regardless of their actual designations, that are regarded under national law as subscribed equity capital plus share premium accounts and all types of reserves.[246] Home Member States may authorize particular categories of credit institutions with an initial capital that is lower than 5 million Euros, but it cannot be less than 1 million Euros and the Member State concerned must notify the Commission of the reason for the exception.[247] Credit institutions that do not meet the requirement of separate own funds but which were in existence on December 15th, 1979 may be allowed by home Member States to continue their ac-

239 Article 12.

240 Article 19. *See infra* in the text.

241 Article 4.

242 Article 9.

243 Article 13.

244 Preamble, 12th recital.

245 Article 5(1).

246 Article 1(11). *See* also Articles 22 and 23 of Council Directive 86/635 on the annual accounts and consolidated accounts of banks and other financial institutions (OJ L372/86).

247 Article. 5(2)(a) and (b).

tivities.[248] Likewise, credit institutions that have own funds below 5 or 1 million Euros, depending on which amount is applicable, may continue their activities if they were in existence on January 1st, 1993.[249] Home Member States are free to impose higher amounts for initial capital than these two amounts if they wish.[250]

The above rules do not apply to electronic money institutions, which are governed in this matter by Directive 00/46. They must have an initial capital of not less than 1 million Euros.[251]

2. The Directive requires a credit institution to have at least two persons that effectively direct its business in order to obtain an authorization.[252] Home Member States may exempt credit institutions that were in existence on December 15th, 1979 from this requirement.[253] The persons concerned must be of sufficiently good repute and possess sufficient experience to perform their duties.[254]

3. Home Member States may not grant an authorization to a credit institution before its competent authorities have been informed of the identities of the shareholders or members, whether direct or indirect, that have qualifying holdings[255] and the amounts of these holdings.[256] The home Member State must refuse authorization if it is not satisfied as to the suitability of these shareholders or members with respect to the need to ensure the sound and prudent management of the credit institution.[257] Member States are free to impose stricter rules regarding qualifying holdings.[258]

4. Where close links[259] exist between a credit institution and other natural or legal persons, authorization can only be accorded if these links do not prevent the proper supervision of the credit institution.[260] This is a particularly important

248 Article 5(1), 2nd sub-para.

249 Article 5(4).

250 Preamble, 12th recital and Article 5(1).

251 Article 4(1).

252 Article 6(1), 1st subpara.

253 Article 5(1), 2nd sub-para.

254 Article 6(1), 2nd subpara.

255 Qualifying holdings are defined in note 232.

256 Article 7(1).

257 Article 7(2).

258 Preamble, 12th recital.

259 Close links" are defined by Article 1(26) as a situation where two or more legal or natural persons are linked by a participation (*see* note 337) or control in the sense of the relationship between a parent undertaking and a subsidiary as defined in Council Directive 83/349 on consolidated accounts (OJ L193/83) or a similar relationship between any natural or legal person and an undertaking.

260 Article 7(3), 1st sub-para.

issue where the close links are with natural or legal persons subject to the laws of a third country.[261]

5. Home Member States must require applications for authorization to be accompanied by a program of operations, setting out *inter alia* the types of business envisaged and the structural organization of the institution.[262]

6. Credit institutions that have a registered office in the home Member State must also have their head office in this Member State.[263] Credit institutions that have only a head office in their home Member State must also carry on business there.[264]

7. An authorization should not be granted to a credit institution where such factors as the content of the activities programs or the geographical distribution of the institution's activities indicate clearly that the institution has opted for authorization in the Member State in question for the purpose of evading the stricter standards in force in the Member State where it intends to carry on the greater part of its activities.[265]

Decisions on the grant of an authorization should be taken within six months of receiving the application.[266] Where an authorization is refused, the home Member State must give precise grounds for doing so and inform the undertaking in question. Member States must ensure that decisions relating to authorizations are subject to a right of appeal to the courts, with respect both to a refusal and a failure to respect the six-month time limit.[267]

Withdrawal of an Authorization

A home Member State may withdraw an authorization from a credit institution in the following circumstances:[268]

- where the authorization is not used within twelve months or is renounced;
- where the credit institution has ceased to engage in business for more than six months;
- where the authorization was obtained by false statements or other irregular means, which would seem to cover the situation where an authorization was obtained for the purpose of evading the stricter standards in force in the

---

261 Article 7(3), 2nd subpara.

262 Article 8.

263 Article 6(2), 1st indent.

264 Article 6(2), 2nd indent.

265 Preamble, 9th recital.

266 Article 10.

267 Article 33.

268 Article 14(1).

Member State where the credit institution carries on the greater part of its activities;[269]

- where the institution no longer fulfills the conditions for authorization, such as where it can no longer be properly supervised because of close links with another natural or legal person;[270]
- where the institution no longer possesses sufficient own funds;
- where the national law provides for withdrawal.

Reasons must be given for a decision to withdraw an authorization, and the credit institution must be able to appeal the decision to the courts.[271]

3. Liberalization

General Provisions

Credit institutions duly authorized in their home Member State are free to carry on any of the activities for which they have been authorized, either through a branch or by way of provision of services, in all Member States of the EU.[272] provided that their authorization covers the activities in question.[273]

Financial institutions other than credit institutions similarly have the right to carry on their activities throughout the EU, either through a branch or by way of provision of services, subject to the following conditions:[274]

- the Memorandum and Articles of Association of the financial institution must permit the carrying on of the activities in question;
- the financial institution must be the subsidiary of one or more credit institutions authorized in the Member State whose law governs the financial institution;
- the activities in question must actually be carried on in this same Member State;
- the parent[275] credit institution or institutions must hold 90% or more of the voting rights in the subsidiary;
- the parent credit institution or institutions must satisfy the competent authorities of the home Member State regarding the prudent management of the financial institution;

269 The ninth recital of the Preamble requires that an authorization be withdrawn in this situation.

270 The tenth recital of the Preamble requires that an authorization be withdrawn in this situation.

271 Articles 14(2) and 33.

272 Article 18.

273 Article 5. *Cf.* Directive 73/239, Article 7.

274 Article 19, 1st para.

275 A "parent undertaking" is one that exercises effective control over another undertaking, its subsidiary—*see* Article 1(12) and Articles 1 and 2 of Directive 83/349.

- the parent credit institution or institutions must have declared, with the consent of the home Member State, that they jointly and severally guarantee the commitments entered into by the financial institution;
- the financial institution must be effectively included in the consolidated supervision by the home Member State of its parent(s), in particular for the calculation of the solvency ratio, the control of large exposures and the limitation of qualifying holdings in non-financial undertakings.

The same right applies *mutatis mutandis* to subsidiaries of financial institutions.[276]

Credit financial institutions may carry on their activities under their own name, supplemented by certain explanatory particulars where there is a danger of confusion in the host Member State,[277] and in the same manner as in the home Member State, subject to any legal provisions protecting the general good in the host Member State.[278] They may also advertise their services in other Member States, subject to any rules adopted by the latter in the interest of the general good.[279]

The EU banking regime only applies to the activities that are listed in Annex I and to qualifying credit institutions and financial institutions. The carrying on of activities beyond those in the Annex and any activity by a non-qualifying institution are not covered by the Directive but by the general provisions of the EC Treaty. These guarantee freedom of establishment and freedom to provide services throughout the EU but not on the basis of a single license, one-state supervision and the other rights granted by the Directive.

Freedom of Establishment

All that a credit institution is required to do in order to carry on its activities under the Directive through a branch in another Member State is to notify its home Member State and provide the following information:[280]

- the Member State where it plans to establish the branch;
- a program of operations setting out *inter alia* the types of business envisaged and the structural organization of the branch;
- the address in the host Member State from which documents may be obtained;
- the names of those responsible for the management of the branch.

Financial institutions must observe the same formality. In addition, compliance with the conditions outlined earlier must be verified by the competent authorities

276 Article 19, 4th para.

277 Article 15.

278 Preamble, 17th recital.

279 Article 22(11).

280 Article 20(1) and (2).

of the home Member States, and the ensuing certificate of compliance must form part of the notification.[281]

It is the responsibility of the home Member State to communicate this information to the host Member State within three months as well as the amount of own funds and the solvency ratio of the credit institution.[282] In the case of financial institutions, the home Member State must communicate the amount of own funds of the institution and the consolidated solvency ratio of the parent credit institution.[283]

It is only if the home Member State has doubts about the adequacy of the administrative structure or the financial situation of the credit or financial institution that it may refuse to communicate the information to the host Member State.[284] It must give reasons for such refusal to the institution within three months.[285] The refusal is subject to a right of appeal to the courts.

The host Member State cannot require an authorization or endowment capital for the branch,[286] and it must within two months of receiving the information from the home Member State indicate to the credit or financial institution the conditions under which, in the interest of the general good, its activities may be carried on.[287] On receipt of such communication from the host Member State or in any event after the expiry of the two month period, the branch may be established and commence its activities.[288]

Branches of credit institutions from another Member State that commenced their activities in a host Member State before January 1st, 1993 are deemed to have met all the above requirements.[289] This provision does not apply to financial institutions[290] or electronic money institutions.[291]

Freedom to Provide Services

A credit or financial institution that wishes to provide services in another Member State for the first time must notify its home Member State of the activities that it intends to carry on in the host Member State.[292] Financial institutions must

281 Article 19, 2nd para.

282 Article 20(3), 1st and 2nd subparas.

283 Article 19, 5th para.

284 Article 20(3), 1st subpara.

285 Article 20(3), 3rd subpara.

286 Article 13.

287 Article 20(4).

288 Article 20(5).

289 Article 20(7).

290 Article 19, 1st para.

291 Article 2(2) of Directive 00/46.

292 Article 21(1).

include in their notification the certificate of compliance supplied by the home Member State that was mentioned earlier.[293] The home Member State must send the notification to the competent authorities of the host Member State within one month.[294]

The procedure is simpler than for the establishment of a branch. In particular, there is no provision for the home Member State to refuse to send the notification to the host Member State, and the provider of the services does not have to wait for any communication from the host Member State before commencing its activities. However, the institution must nevertheless comply with the legal provisions applicable to it in the host Member State to the extent that they do not conflict with the Directive.[295]

Rights acquired by credit institutions that have provided services in another Member State before January 1st, 1993 are not affected by these provisions.[296] This does not include financial institutions.[297]

4. Prudential Supervision

General Provisions

The main responsibility for the prudential supervision of the activities of a credit institution or a subsidiary financial institution, including those that it carries on in other Member States either through a branch or the cross-border provision of services, lies with the home Member State, subject to the rules on consolidated supervision.[298] This supervision involves monitoring and applying the rules on qualifying holdings in the institution, the adequacy of own funds, the solvency ratio, large exposures and the institution's qualifying holdings in the non-financial sector. With respect to a subsidiary financial institution of a credit institution, however, only the adequacy of its own funds and qualifying holdings in the institution are subject to prudential supervision by the home Member State.[299] Home Member States must require credit institutions to have sound administrative and accounting procedures and adequate internal control mechanisms.[300]

The supervisory powers of the host Member State are limited to the liquidity of the branches of credit institutions from other Member States operating in its territory and, to the extent that it retains responsibility for monetary policy, to mea-

293 Article 19, 2nd para.

294 Article 21(2).

295 *See* Article 22(2) and (5).

296 Article 21(3).

297 Article 19, 1st para.

298 Article 26. The rules on consolidated supervision are discussed *infra* in the text.

299 Article 19, 3rd para.

300 Article 17. *See* also Article 7 of Directive 00/46.

sures resulting from the implementation of this policy.[301] For these purposes, it may require these branches to provide the same information as it requires from national credit institutions.[302] Moreover, it may require a credit or financial institution that has a branch or is providing services within its territory to comply with legal provisions relating to its supervisory powers under the Directive.[303] If the institution does not respond, the host Member State informs the competent authorities of the home Member State, which must then take measures to ensure that the institution concerned puts an end to this non-compliance.[304] If these measures are not forthcoming or prove inadequate, the host Member State may itself take appropriate action, which can include preventing the institution from initiating further transactions within its territory.[305] The host Member State can take similar action to prevent or punish infractions of legal rules that it has adopted for the general good.[306] In all these case, the institution concerned must have a right of appeal to the courts.[307] Finally, a host Member State must take appropriate measures to end the activities within its territory of a credit institution or its subsidiary financial institution where the authorization of the credit institution has been withdrawn by its home Member State.[308]

All Member States must provide that their respective competent authorities may, as against credit institutions or those who effectively control them, impose penalties or measures specifically aimed at ending breaches of any laws, regulations or administrative provisions regulating the supervision or pursuit of their activities, including presumably the activities of their subsidiary financial institutions.[309] Home Member States must be empowered by host Member States to carry out on-the-spot verification of branches established in another Member State.[310] The competent authorities of all Member States are under an obligation to collaborate with each other.[311]

Member States must ensure that any decisions taken by them in pursuance of their supervisory duties are subject to a right of appeal to the courts.[312]

301 Article 27. In the cases of Austria, Belgium, Finland, France, Germany, Greece, Ireland, Italy, Luxembourg, Netherlands, Portugal and Spain, monetary policy is decided at EU level.

302 Article 22(1), 2nd subpara.

303 Article 22(2).

304 Article 22(3).

305 Article 22(4).

306 Article 22(5).

307 Article 22(6).

308 Article 22(9).

309 Article 32.

310 Article 29(1).

311 Articles. 12, 28 and 56.

312 Article 33.

Own Funds

A home Member State must monitor the adequacy of a credit institution's own funds, which may not fall below the amount of initial capital required by national law at the time of the institution's authorization.[313] As a general minimum, this amount is not less than 5 million Euros,[314] although home Member States may permit the amount of initial capital for certain categories of credit institutions to be as low as 1 million Euros.[315] Home Member States may also set higher minimum amounts in these two cases.[316]

Credit institutions in existence on January 1st, 1993 whose own funds do not attain the levels prescribed for initial capital but which are nonetheless allowed by the home Member State to carry on their activities, must not let their own funds fall below the highest level reached with effect from December 22nd, 1989.[317] The own funds of electronic money institutions must meet two criteria. Firstly, they must not fall below the initial capital requirement of 1 million Euros, and secondly, they must always be equal to or above 2% of the higher of the current amount or the average of the preceding six months' total amount of their financial liabilities related to outstanding electronic money.[318]

If the own funds of a credit institution fall below the applicable minimum amount, it may, where the circumstances justify it, be allowed a limited period by the home Member State to rectify the situation.[319] Otherwise its authorization is withdrawn and it must cease its activities.[320]

The Member States are obliged to construe the concept of own funds in accordance with the definition contained in the Directive,[321] which does, however, allow them a fairly large measure of discretion.

The following items make up the own funds of credit institutions under the Directive:[322]

1. Paid-up capital[323] plus share premium accounts but excluding cumulative preferential shares;

313 Article 5(3). Somewhat perversely, these rules are contained in the section on authorization.

314 Article 5(1), 1st subpara.

315 Article 5(2)(a).

316 Preamble, 12th recital

317 Article 5(4).

318 Article 4(1) and (2) of Directive 00/46.

319 Article 5(7).

320 Article 14(1)(d).

321 Article 34(1).

322 Article 34(2), pts. 1 to 8.

323 Capital is understood in the sense of Article 22 of Directive 86/635 to mean all amounts that are regarded under the national law of the home Member State as equity capital subscribed by the shareholders or owners.

2. Reserves[324] and profits and losses brought forward as a result of the application of the final profit or loss;

3. Funds for general banking risks;[325]

4. Revaluation reserves;[326]

5. Value adjustments;[327]

6. Additional items included by the home Member State under Article 35 of the Directive;

7. Commitments of members of credit institutions set up as cooperative societies and the joint and several commitments of the borrowers of certain institutions organized as funds;

8. Fixed-term cumulative preferential shares and subordinated loan capital.

The items in this list are subject to certain limitations. Thus, the commitments of the members of credit institutions referred to in point 7 comprise those societies' uncalled capital together with the legal commitments of the members to make additional non-refundable payments where the society incurs a loss.[328] These commitments and those of the borrowers of certain institutions organized as funds may only be included in own funds where national law recognizes them as such.[329]

Fixed-term cumulative preferential shares and subordinated loan capital may only be included in own funds if binding agreements exist under which, in the event of the bankruptcy or liquidation of the credit institution, they rank after the claims of all other creditors.[330] Subordinated loan capital must also fulfill the following criteria:[331]

- the funds must be fully paid up;
- the loans involved must have an original maturity of at least five years or be only repayable subject to five years' notice or to the prior consent of the competent authorities;

---

324 Reserves are understood in the sense of Article 23 of Directive 86/635 to include: a) legal reserves, b) reserves for own share, c) reserves provided for in the Articles of Association and d) other reserves.

325 According to Article 38(1) of Directive 86/635, these funds comprise the amounts that a credit institution decides to put aside to cover such risks where that is required by the particular risks associated with banking.

326 According to Article 33 of Directive 86/635, this item covers sundry items, such as credits from the recovery of written-off loans and advances.

327 Pursuant to Article 37(2) of Directive 86/635, Member States are permitted to show certain assets, such as loans and advances, at a lower than real value. These values may subsequently be adjusted.

328 Article 36(1), 1st subpara.

329 Article 36(1), 3rd subpara.

330 Article 36(3), 1st subpara.

331 Article 36(3), 2nd subpara.

- the extent to which it is included as own funds is reduced during at least the last five years before the repayment date; and
- except in the event of the winding-up of the credit institution, the loan agreement must not provide for the debt to become repayable before maturity.

The total amount of the items in points (4) to (8) may not exceed a maximum of 100% of the items in points (1) plus (2) and (3) minus points (9), (10) and (11) on the list of items to be deducted in calculating own funds.[332] The total amount of the items in points (7) and (8) may not exceed a maximum of 50% of the items in points (1) plus (2) and (3) minus points (9), (10) and (11) on the list of items to be deducted in calculating own funds.[333] The items listed in points (1) to (5) must be available to a credit institution for unrestricted and immediate use to cover risks or losses as soon as they occur.[334]

With respect to items that a Member State may include pursuant to point (6), they must have the following characteristics:[335]

- they are freely available to the credit institution to cover normal banking risks where revenue or capital losses have not yet been identified;
- their existence is disclosed in internal accounting records;
- their amount is determined by the management of the credit institution, verified by independent auditors, made known to competent authorities and placed under the supervision of the latter.

Securities of indeterminate duration and other instruments except the shares referred to in point (8) may be included when they meet the following criteria:[336]

- they may not be reimbursed at the request of the bearer or without the prior approval of the competent authorities;
- the debt agreement must accord the credit institution the option of deferring payment of interest on the debt;
- the instrument is wholly subordinated to the claims of all non-subordinated creditors;
- the issue of the securities must provide for debt and unpaid interest to be such as to absorb losses, whilst leaving the credit institution in a position to continue trading; and
- only fully paid-up amounts are included.

332 Article 38 (1)(a). The items to be deducted are discussed *infra* in the text.

333 Article 38(1)(b).

334 Article 34(4).

335 Article 35(1).

336 Article 35(2).

Member States may not include in the own funds of public credit institutions guarantees that they or their local authorities extend to such entities.[337]

The following items are to be deducted under the Directive when calculating own funds:[338]

9. Own shares at book value held by the credit institution;

10. Intangible assets;[339]

11. Material losses of the current financial year;

12. Holdings in other credit and financial institutions and subordinated claims amounting to more than 10% of their capital;

13. Subordinated claims and the other instruments referred to above that a credit institution holds in respect of credit and financial institutions in which it has holdings exceeding 10% of the capital;

14. Holdings in other credit and financial institutions of up to 10% of their capital, subordinated claims and the other instruments referred to above that a credit institution holds in respect of credit and financial institutions in which it has holdings of up to 10% of their capital and subordinated claims and instruments that exceed 10% of a credit institution's own funds calculated before the deduction of the items in points 12 to 16;

15. Participations[340] that a credit institution holds in an insurance undertaking, re-insurance undertaking or insurance holding company as defined under the relevant EU legislation;

16. Certain instruments[341] that a credit institution holds in respect of the entities defined in point (15).

There is an additional rule that applies to points (12) and (13). The total amount of these items must be deducted from the total of the items.

The list of items to be included in own funds is a maximum number.[342] Member States are free to exclude any items and to fix lower ceilings for those which they include. Conversely, the list of items to be deducted is a minimum list. Member

337 Article 36(2).

338 Article 34(2), points (9) to (16).

339 According to Article 4(9) of Directive 86/635, intangible assets comprise formation expenses, costs of research and development, concessions and intellectual property rights, goodwill and payments on account.

340 A "participation" is defined in Article 1(9) as the ownership, direct or indirect, of 20% or more of the voting rights or capital of an undertaking.

341 *See* Article 16(3) of Council Directive 73/239 on the coordination of laws, regulations and administrative provisions relating to the taking up and pursuit of direct insurance other than life insurance (OJ L228/73) and Article 27(3) of EP/Council Directive 02/83 concerning life assurance (OJ L345/02).

342 Article 34(3), 1st. subpara.

States may deduct items other than those listed.[343] However, Member States are at the same time under an obligation to consider increased convergence with a view to a common definition of own funds.

The provisions on own funds apply to the subsidiary financial institutions of credit institutions operating in another Member State under the terms of the Directive.[344]

Solvency Ratio

It is the responsibility of the home Member State to ensure that the solvency ratio of a credit institution under its supervision does not fall below the minimum solvency ratio as established by the Directive or any higher ratio that the State may prescribe.[345] If this happens, the home Member State must ensure that the credit institution takes appropriate measures to rectify the situation as soon as possible.[346] The Directive does not say what should happen if there is no rectification. This is up to the provisions of the national law of the home Member State and could well include the withdrawal of the institution's authorization.[347]

The solvency ratio of a credit institution is the proportion of the risk-adjusted value of its total assets and off-balance-sheet items that is represented by its own funds.[348] In other words, a credit institution's own funds, as calculated by the home Member State in accordance with the rules of the Directive, are the numerator in a fraction where the denominator is the total of the risk-adjusted values of the credit institution's assets and off-balance-sheet items.[349] Thus, where an institution has 5 million Euros in own funds and risk-adjusted assets and items of 20 million Euros, the solvency ratio is 25%. The minimum solvency ratio that credit institutions must maintain under the Directive is 8%,[350] but the home Member State may prescribe a higher minimum ratio.[351] The solvency ratio must be calculated not less than twice a year, either by the credit institution or by the competent authorities of the home Member State.[352]

A solvency ratio of 8% as set out in the Directive means that, in the scenario given above, the risk-adjusted value of assets and items of the credit institution cannot rise above EUR 62.5 million. Otherwise, with own funds at 5 million Euros, the solvency ratio would fall below 8%. The same would occur, were the amount of the institution's own funds to decline below 1.6 million Euros with assets and

343 *Idem.*

344 *See* Article 19, 3rd para.

345 Article 47(1) and (2).

346 Article 47(3).

347 *See* Article 14(1)(e).

348 Article 40(1).

349 Articles 41 and 42(4).

350 Article 47(1).

351 Article 47(2).

352 Article 40(5).

items remaining at 20 million Euros. However, in this latter situation, the problem would fall under the rules on the maintenance of adequate own funds.[353]

The adjustment for risk of the value of the assets and off-balance-sheet items of a credit institution takes place as follows. In the first place, their value is established in accordance with Section 7 of Directive 86/635.[354] With respect to off-balance-sheet items listed in Annex II, they are then grouped according to their risk grouping.[355] 100% of the value of full-risk items such as forward deposits is taken into account, 50% of the value of medium-risk items such as confirmed documentary credits, 20% of the value of medium/low risk items such as self-liquidating transactions and 0% of the value of low-risk items such as undrawn credit facilities. The value of the off-balance-sheet items listed in Annex IV, which comprise interest rate contracts, foreign-exchange contracts, contracts concerning gold and contracts of a similar nature, are subject to the rather complex rules set out in Annex III.[356]

Once the value of the assets and off-balance-sheet items has been established, a degree of credit risk in the form of a percentage weighting is assigned to each asset and item, and their balance-sheet value is then multiplied by the relevant risk weighting to produce a risk-adjusted value.[357] The higher the risk, the higher the multiplication factor, so that the result is to adjust the value upwards, which in turn requires a greater amount of own funds in order to maintain the solvency ratio at 8% or higher.

The applicable risk weightings are: 0% for low-risk assets such as cash in hand and claims on the EU or Zone A central governments,[358] 20% for medium/low-risk assets such as claims on the European Investment Bank, 50% for medium-risk assets such as mortgages, and 100% for full-risk assets such as claims on Zone B regional governments[359] and unsecured non-bank sector claims.[360] However, in the case of Annex IV off-balance-sheet items, the 100% weighting is replaced by a 50% weighting.[361] Where asset and off-balance-sheet items are given a lower weighting because they are covered by explicit guarantees

353 *See supra* in the text.

354 Article 40(6).

355 Article 43(2).

356 Article 43(3).

357 Article 42(1).

358 Zone A comprises all Member States of the EU, full members of the OECD and countries that have concluded special lending arrangements with the IMF. Any country that reschedules its external sovereign debt, however, is precluded from Zone A for a period of five years.

359 Zone B comprises all countries that are not in Zone A. *See* note 355.

360 The details are set out in Article 43(1). *See also* Article 62 for transitional provisions valid until December 31st, 2006.

361 Article 42(3).

or collateral acceptable to the competent authorities of the home Member State, the lower weighting only applies to the part that is so covered.[362]

Home Member States are permitted to fix higher risk weightings than those set out in the Directive.[363] Conversely, they may fix a weighting of 0% instead of 20% for assets or items involving their own regional governments and local authorities if there is no difference in risk between claims on the latter and claims on the central government.[364]

With respect to subsidiary financial institutions operating in another Member State under the terms of the Directive, they are included in the supervision of their parent credit institution(s) with respect to solvency.[365]

Large Exposures

The rules with respect to large exposures comprise reporting requirements, internal procedural requirements and limits on the value of large exposures that credit institutions may incur. In this context, a credit institution includes branches of EU credit institutions in third countries and credit institutions authorized in a third country that carry on business in the EU.[366] The home Member State is responsible for the supervision and control of large exposures.

Exposures are the assets and off-balance-sheet items that were discussed in the context of own funds. They are normally calculated without applying risk weightings or degrees of risk,[367] but Member States may apply a risk weighting to items constituting claims on Member State regional or local authorities and claims on credit institutions.[368] A large exposure is a claim of any sort on a client or a group of connected clients that constitutes a single risk and the value of which is equal to or exceeds 10% of a credit institution's own funds.[369] However where a claim is entirely covered by own funds that are not included in the calculation of the credit institution's solvency ratio or any other monitoring ratio provided for in the Directive, the home Member State may deem it not to constitute an exposure.[370] Exposures incurred in the ordinary course of settlement of foreign exchange transactions or the purchase or sale of securities are excluded as long as settlement takes place within forty-eight hours or five working days, respectively.

362 Article 43(5).

363 Article 43(1).

364 Article 44(1).

365 Article 19, 3rd para.

366 Article 1(1), 3rd subpara.

367 Article 1(24).

368 Article 49(8), (9) and (10).

369 Article 48(1).

370 Article 1(24).

A credit institution must report every large exposure to the competent authorities of the home Member State.[371] This must be done either at least four times a year or at least once a year combined with ongoing reporting during the year of all new large exposures and increases of 20% or more in the value of reported large exposures. The choice is up to the home Member State. The reporting frequency for certain exposures, such as claims on Member State regional or local authorities, may be reduced to twice a year.[372] Home Member States must require credit institutions to have sound administrative and accounting procedures and adequate internal control mechanisms for the purpose of identifying and recording large exposures.[373]

Credit institutions may not incur an exposure to a client or group of connected clients that has a value which exceeds 25% of an institution's own funds.[374] This limit is reduced to 20% where the exposure is incurred to a parent undertaking or a subsidiary of the credit institution or another subsidiary of the parent.[375] The total of all large exposures of a credit institution must not exceed 800% of its own funds.[376] Member States may impose more stringent limits than those laid down by the Directive.[377]

There are exceptions to these rules. Home Member States may exempt exposures to a parent or subsidiaries of the parent or to subsidiaries of the exposed credit institution from the 20% limit where they provide for specific monitoring of such exposures by other measures or procedures.[378] The following exposures may be exempted, fully or partially, from all the rules on large exposures, including the reporting requirements:[379]

- claims on Zone A central governments or central banks;
- claims on the European Communities;
- claims attributable to or guaranteed by Zone A central governments or central banks or by the EU;
- claims secured, to the satisfaction of the home Member State, by collateral in the form of Zone A central government or central bank securities, or securities issued by the EU or by Member States' regional or local authorities that have a zero risk weighting for solvency purposes;

371 Article 48(2).

372 Article 48(3).

373 Article 48(4), 1st subpara.

374 Article 49(1).

375 Article 49(2).

376 Article 49(3).

377 Article 49(4).

378 Article 49(2).

379 Articles 48(3) and 49(7)(a), (b), (c), (d), (f), (g) and (h).

- claims secured, to the satisfaction of the home Member State, by collateral in the form of cash deposits placed with the credit institution, its parent or its subsidiary;
- claims secured, to the satisfaction of the home Member State, by collateral in the form of certificates of deposit issued by the credit institution, its parent or subsidiary.

Where an exposure to a client is guaranteed by a third party, the home Member States may treat it as having been incurred to that third party.[380]

Credit institutions must at all times comply with the individual and aggregate limits on large exposures and report any non-compliance immediately to the competent authorities of the home Member State.[381] Where the circumstances warrant it, the home Member State may grant time for a credit institution to restore compliance with the limits. Credit institutions that on February 5th, 1993 had already incurred large exposures exceeding the limits set out in the Directive were obliged bring their exposures into conformity by December 31st, 2001.[382] However, exposures with a longer contractual maturity may be continued until their maturity. The Directive does not say what should happen if compliance is not restored. This is up to the provisions of the national law of the home Member State and could include withdrawal of the authorization.[383]

With respect to subsidiary financial institutions operating in another Member State under the terms of the Directive, they are included in the supervision of their parent credit institution(s) with respect to large exposures.[384]

Qualifying Holdings[385]

The home Member State must monitor qualifying holdings in a credit or financial institution under its supervision.[386] It must require natural or legal persons who propose to hold, directly or indirectly, a qualifying holding in an institution or to increase their existing holding so as to obtain or exceed the thresholds of 20%, 33% or 50% of the voting rights or capital in the institution or so as to make it

380 Article 49(11).

381 Article 49(5).

382 Article 64(1), (2) and (4).

383 *See* Article 14(1)(e).

384 Article 19, 3rd para.

385 Qualifying holdings are defined in note 232. Some of the provisions on qualifying holdings have been discussed in connection with authorization, but the following provisions more correctly belong to the area of prudential supervision.

386 Articles 16 and 19, 3rd para. Given that the parent credit institution or institutions must hold at least 90% of the voting rights in the capital of a financial institution that operates in another Member State under the Directive, it is difficult to see that there is much point to monitoring qualifying holdings in the subsidiary. Yet, Article 19, 3rd para. specifically mentions this supervisory activity.

their subsidiary, to inform the home Member State, indicating the size of the intended holding.[387] Persons who fail to comply with the notification requirement may be subject to injunctions or other sanctions.[388] The home Member State has three months from the date of the notification in which to oppose the plan if it is not satisfied as to the suitability of the person concerned from the perspective of sound and prudent management of the institution.[389] If a holding is acquired despite opposition, the home Member State must suspend or provide for the annulment of the voting rights of the holding.[390]

Institutions must inform home Member States, at least once a year, of the names of shareholders and members possessing qualifying holdings and the sizes of such holdings.[391] They must also inform their home Member State as soon as they become aware of any acquisitions that cause holdings to exceed the thresholds mentioned above.[392]

Where a home Member State determines that the influence of any person with a qualifying holding is likely to operate to the detriment of the prudent and sound management of the institution, it shall take measures to deal with the situation, such as injunctions, other sanctions and suspending the voting rights attached to the qualifying holding in question.[393]

Persons wishing to dispose, directly or indirectly, of their qualifying holding in an institution must similarly inform the home Member State of this fact and the size of the holding.[394] Likewise, the home Member State must be informed by persons reducing their qualifying holding so that their share of the voting rights or capital of the institution falls below any one of the thresholds mentioned above or so that the institution ceases to be their subsidiary. The institution itself must also inform the competent authorities once it becomes aware of disposals that cause a holding to fall below these thresholds.[395]

Qualifying Holdings in Non-Financial Undertakings

Additional rules concern qualifying holdings held by a credit institution in an undertaking that is not a credit institution, a financial institution or an undertaking carrying on activities that are a direct extension of banking or ancillary to banking, such as leasing, factoring etc. A credit institution may not have a qualifying hold-

387 Article 16(1), 1st subpara.

388 Article 16(5), 2nd subpara.

389 Article 16(1), 2nd subpara.

390 Article 16(5), 2nd subpara.

391 Article 16(4), 2nd subpara.

392 Article 16(4), 1st subpara.

393 Article 16(5), 1st subpara.

394 Article 16(3).

395 Article 16(4), 1st subpara.

ing in such a non-financial undertaking that exceeds 15% of its own funds,[396] and the total amount of such holdings may not exceed 60% of its own funds.[397] Home Member States are free to apply lower limits.[398] On the other hand, they are also free not to apply these limits to qualifying holdings in insurance companies.[399] Home Member States may choose not to apply the individual or aggregate limits if they provide that 100% of the amounts by which a credit institution's qualifying holdings in non-financial undertakings exceed these limits must be covered by own funds that are not included in the calculation of its solvency ratio.[400] If both the limits are exceeded, the amount to be covered is the greater of the excess amounts.

The Directive requires credit institutions to comply with the limits on qualifying holdings in non-financial undertakings.[401] Home Member States must require credit institutions that exceed these limits to increase their own funds or take other equivalent measures to ensure comply with the Directive. The nature of these other measures is a matter for the national law of the home Member State. Credit institutions that, on January 1st, 1993, exceeded the limits on qualifying holdings had until January 1st, 2003 to comply with them.[402]

With respect to subsidiary financial institutions operating in another Member State under the terms of the Directive, they are included in the supervision of their parent credit institution(s) with respect to qualifying holdings in non-financial undertakings.[403]

The rules on qualifying holdings in non-financial undertakings do not apply to electronic money institutions.[404] They are subject to a different set of rules. They may have investments of an amount of no less than their financial liabilities related to outstanding electronic money in the following assets only:[405]

- cash in hand and equivalent items;
- claims on Zone A central governments or central banks;
- claims on the EU;
- claims carrying the explicit guarantees of Zone A central governments or central banks or the EU;

396 Article 51(1).

397 Article 51(2).

398 Preamble, 12th recital.

399 Article 51(3).

400 Article 51(6).

401 Article 51(5).

402 Article 65.

403 Article 19, 3rd para.

404 Article 2(1) of Directive 00/46.

405 Article 5(1) and (2) of Directive 00/46.

provided they are sufficiently liquid; and

- sight deposits held with Zone A credit institutions;
- debt instruments other than the claims above that are sufficiently liquid, qualify under Directive 93/6[406] and are issued by undertakings other than undertakings having a qualifying holding in the electronic money institution concerned or which must be included in those undertakings' consolidated accounts

up to a limit of twenty times the own funds of the electronic money institution.

If the value of the above assets falls below the amount of the institution's financial liabilities related to outstanding electronic money, the home Member State must ensure that the institution promptly takes appropriate measures to remedy the situation. If necessary, but for a limited time only, the competent authorities may authorize the institution's financial liabilities to be backed by assets other than those set out above. The Directive does not say what should happen if compliance is not restored. This is up to the provisions of the national law of the home Member State and could include withdrawal of the authorization.[407]

Auditors

Home Member States must provide that the authorized auditors of credit institutions, as well as undertakings that have close links resulting from a control relationship with a credit institution, have a duty to report to their competent authorities any fact or decision concerning the institution of which they become aware that is liable to:[408]

- constitute an infringement of the legal rules governing the authorization of or the pursuit of its activities by a credit institution;
- affect the continuous functioning of the credit institution; or
- entail on the part of the auditor a refusal to certify the accounts of the institution or an expression of reservations.

The disclosure by auditors in good faith of such facts or decisions may not be treated as a breach of professional secrecy and may not involve such persons in liability of any kind.[409]

Professional Secrecy

Member States must provide that the confidentiality of information received by persons who are working or have worked for the competent authorities of Member States as well as by auditors or experts acting on behalf of these authorities is re-

---

406 Council Directive 93/6 on the capital adequacy of investment firms and credit institutions (OJ L141/93), Article 2(12).

407 *See* Article 14(1)(e).

408 Article 31(1).

409 Article 31(2).

spected.[410] Confidential information may only be divulged in summary or aggregate form such that individual credit institutions cannot be identified. Exchange of information within and between Member States is also subject to the rules on professional secrecy.[411] Member States receiving confidential information may only use it to carry out their prudential and other duties, impose sanctions and in administrative appeals and court proceedings.

Supervision on a Consolidated Basis

The Directive requires supervision on a consolidated basis in two situations. Firstly, every credit institution that has as a subsidiary or holds a participation in a credit institution, a financial institution or an ancillary banking services undertaking[412] must be supervised on the basis of its consolidated financial situation.[413] Secondly, every credit institution that is the subsidiary of a financial holding company[414] or a mixed-activity holding company[415] that have their head offices in the EU must be supervised on the basis of the consolidated financial situation of the parent holding company.[416] The rules on consolidated supervision apply also to post office giro institutions and certain credit institutions peculiar to particular Member States.[417] They do not apply to the central banks of the Member States.

The Member State responsible for exercising supervision on a consolidated basis must require full consolidation of all the financial subsidiaries of a parent undertaking.[418] However, where the liability of a parent undertaking is limited to its share of the capital in the subsidiary because of the liability of other shareholders whose solvency is satisfactory, the consolidation may be done on a proportional basis.[419]

Member States responsible for exercising the consolidated supervision may exclude from the consolidation a credit institution, financial institution or ancillary

410 Article 30(1), 1st subpara.

411 Article 30 (2) to (10).

412 Such as undertaking is defined in Article 1(23) as one whose principal activities are owning or managing property, managing data-processing services or any other similar activity that is ancillary to the principal activity of one or more credit institutions.

413 Article 52(1). Ancillary banking services undertakings are included by virtue of Article 54(5). *See also* Article 50(2) with respect to large exposures.

414 A financial holding company is defined in note 228.

415 A mixed-activity holding company is defined in note 229.

416 Article 52(2). This provision does not mention mixed-activity holding companies, but it is clear from Articles 2(2), 1st subpara. and 55(1) that they are included. *See also* Article 50(2) with respect to large exposures.

417 Article 2(2), 2nd subpara.

418 Article 54(1), 1st subpara.

419 Article 54(1), 2nd subpara.

banking services undertaking that is a subsidiary or in which a participation is held if:[420]

- the undertaking concerned is situated in a third country where there are legal impediments to obtaining the necessary information;
- the undertaking concerned is considered by the responsible Member State to be of negligible interest, and in all cases where the balance-sheet total of the undertaking is less than the smaller of 10 million Euros or 1% of the balance-sheet total of the parent undertaking or the undertaking that holds the participation;
- inclusion of the undertaking in the consolidation would be inappropriate or misleading.

In the case of credit institutions that have subsidiaries or hold participations in other institutions, the consolidated supervision is exercised by the home Member State of the parent credit institution.[421] Where the parent and any credit institution that is included in its consolidated supervision have the same home Member State, that Member State may decide not to supervise either on an individual or subconsolidated basis for matters covered by the consolidated supervision.[422] Where a subsidiary credit institution included in the consolidated supervision of its parent credit institution is authorized in another Member State, it is subject as well to individual or subconsolidated supervision in its home Member State unless this State delegates its supervisory responsibility for matters covered by the consolidated supervision to the home Member State of the parent institution.[423]

The situation of a credit institution that is the subsidiary of a financial or mixed-activity holding company is more complex. The basic rule is that it is the home Member State of the subsidiary credit institution that exercises the consolidated supervision.[424] However, if the holding company has subsidiary credit institutions in various Member States including the one where the holding company was set up, the rule is that the latter Member State exercises the consolidated supervision.[425] In this case, the Member State may decide not to supervise the parent or the subsidiary on an individual or subconsolidated basis provided that the financial holding company is subject to the same supervision as that exercised over credit institutions.[426] Member States are free to change these two rules by common

420 Article 52(3).

421 Article 53(1). The provision does not mention participations, but this situation must surely be included.

422 Article 52(7). *See also* Article 50(3) with respect to large exposures.

423 Article 52(8) and (9).

424 Article 53(2), 1st subpara.

425 Article 53(2), 2nd subpara.

426 Article 52(7). Such a situation is not possible with a mixed-activity holding company, which is never likely to be supervised as a credit institution.

agreement if they wish.[427] The third rule is that where a holding company has subsidiaries in more than one Member State but not in the Member State of the holding company, the home Member States of the subsidiaries as well as the Member State in which the holding company was set up, should seek to agree on which is to exercise consolidated supervision.[428] If agreement proves impossible, it is the home Member State of the subsidiary credit institution with the greatest balance-sheet total that exercises consolidated supervision. This rule is not subject to modification.

Consolidated supervision includes at least the supervision of the solvency ratio, the adequacy of own funds and large exposures.[429] However, the solvency ratio of credit institutions that are neither parent undertakings nor subsidiaries must be calculated on an individual basis.[430] A Member State that is supervising a parent credit institution on a consolidated basis may also require the calculation on an individual or subconsolidated basis of the solvency ratios of the parent and any of its subsidiaries of which it is the home Member State.[431]

The Directive permits compliance with limits on the qualifying holdings of credit institutions in non-financial undertakings to be supervised on a consolidated or individual basis.[432] The supervision of qualified holdings in a credit institution itself, on the other hand, is always supervised by the home Member State on an individual basis.

5. Relations with Third Countries

Home Member States must inform the Commission where they authorize a credit institution that is the branch or subsidiary of a parent undertaking based in a third country, and where such a parent undertaking acquires a holding that renders an EU credit institution its subsidiary.[433] These provisions are not controversial, but the Directive also contains some reciprocity provisions that have caused some concern outside the EU.

In the first place, the Member States are required to inform the Commission of any difficulties encountered by their credit institutions in establishing themselves or carrying on banking activities in third countries.[434] On the basis of this information and its own research, the Commission is required to draw up periodically a report on the treatment accorded to EU credit institutions in third countries as

---

427 Article 53(3).

428 Article 53(2), 3rd subpara.

429 Article 52(1), (2) and (5), 1st subpara.

430 Article 40(2).

431 Article 40(4).

432 Article 52(5), 2nd subpara.

433 Articles 23(1) and 24(2).

434 Article 23(2).

regards establishment, the carrying-on of banking activities and the acquisition of holdings in third-country credit institutions.[435]

Whenever, on the basis of these reports or other information, it appears to the Commission that a third country is not granting EU credit institutions effective market access comparable to that available in the EU to credit institutions from that third country, the Commission may propose to the Council that it open negotiations to rectify the situation.[436] It is up to the Council to make the final decision. The Directive does not provide for any sanctions in this situation.

The Directive is more radical where it appears to the Commission that, in a third country, EU credit institutions do not receive national treatment offering the same competitive opportunities as for domestic credit institutions and that the conditions of effective market access are also not fulfilled.[437] In this situation, the Commission may start negotiations with the third country on its own initiative. In addition, it may require Member States to limit or suspend the authorization of credit institutions and the acquisition of holdings in EU credit institutions involving undertakings based in the third country in question.[438] The duration of these retaliatory measures may not exceed three months unless the Council, bearing in mind the results of the negotiations initiated by the Commission, decides to continue them.[439] The limitations or suspensions do not apply to the setting-up of subsidiaries or the acquisition of holdings in EU credit institutions by credit institutions already authorized in the EU.[440] Any retaliatory measures must also comply with the EU international obligations.[441]

Member States may not accord to branches of credit institutions having their head office in a non-Member State treatment that is more favorable than that accorded to branches of EU credit institutions.[442] However, the EU may negotiate agreements with third countries which, on the basis of reciprocity, accord to the branches of their credit institutions identical treatment throughout the EU.[443]

The EU may also negotiate agreements with third countries on the means of exercising consolidated supervision over a) credit institutions authorized in the EU that have parent undertakings with their head office in a non-Member State; and b) credit institutions situated in third countries that have parent undertakings

---

435 Article 23(3).

436 Article 23(4).

437 Article 23(5), 1st subpara.

438 Article 23(5), 2nd subpara.

439 Article 23(5), 3rd subpara.

440 Article 23(5), 4th subpara.

441 Article 23(7).

442 Article 24(1).

443 Article 24(3).

with their head office in the EU,[444] including financial and mixed activity holding companies.[445]

The above rules do not apply to subsidiary financial institutions.

C. THE INSURANCE REGIME OF THE EUROPEAN UNION EP/Council Directive 2002/83 concerning life assurance, OJ L345/02[446]

1. Introduction

Overview

There is separate legislation in the EU[447] on life and non-life insurance. However, to avoid unnecessary duplication, Directive 02/83 on life insurance is used as the model as it regulates everything in one directive. Non-life insurance, by contrast, is regulated by a number of directives.[448] References to equivalent provisions in these directives are given in the footnotes.

Directive 02/83 (henceforth referred to as "the Directive") updates and combines into a single text four earlier directives[449] relating to the freedom to pursue the

444 Article 25.

445 Article 2(2), 1st subpara.

446 As amended by Directive 04/66 (OJ L168/04).

447 The insurance directives are all enacted pursuant to the EC Treaty and references in the them are to the "Community" rather than the EU. However, the Community is part of the EU and it seems simpler to refer to it as such. Under the proposed European Constitution, the term "EU" would have supplanted completely the term "Community" or "EC."

448 These are Council Directive 73/239 on the coordination of laws, regulations and administrative provisions relating to the taking-up and pursuit of direct insurance other than life insurance (OJ L228/73), as amended by Directives 76/580 (OJ L189/76), 84/641 (OJ L239/84), 87/343 (OJ L 185/87), 88/857 (OJ L172/88), 90/618 (OJ L330/90), 92/49 (OJ L228/92), 95/26 (OJ L168/95), 00/26 (OJ L181/00), 02/13 (OJ L77/02) and 02/87 (OJ L35/03); Council Directive 73/240 abolishing restrictions on freedom of establishment in the business of direct insurance other than life insurance (OJ L228/73); Council Directive 88/357 on the coordination of laws, regulations and administrative provisions relating to direct insurance other than life insurance and laying down provisions to facilitate the effective exercise of freedom to provide services and amending Directive 73/239 (OJ L172/239), as amended by Directives 90/618 (OJ L330/90), 92/49 (OJ L228/92) and 00/26 (OJ L181/00); and Council Directive 92/49 on the coordination of laws, regulations and administrative provisions relating direct insurance other than life insurance and amending Directives 73/239 and 88/357 (OJ L228/92), as amended by Directives 95/26 (OJ L168/95), 00/64 (OJ L290/00) and 02/87 (OJ L35/03).

449 These are: Council Directive 79/267 on the coordination of laws, regulations and administrative provisions relating to the taking-up and pursuit of the business of direct life insurance (OJ L63/79); Council Directive 90/619 on the coordination of laws, regulations and administrative provisions relating to direct life insurance, laying down provisions to facilitate the effective exercise of freedom to provide services and amending Directive 79/267 (OJ L330/90); Council Directive 92/96 on the coordination of laws, regulations and administrative provisions relating to direct life insurance and amending Directives 79/267 and 90/619 (OJ L360/92);and Directive 02/12 amending Council Directive 79/267 as regards solvency margin requirements for life insurance undertakings (OJ L77/02). All these directives are repealed by the Directive.

business of life insurance[450] and the supervision and financial viability of life insurance undertakings. It does not deal with the matter of consolidated supervision, which continues to be regulated by a separate directive.[451]

The EU life insurance regime resides on the principles of mutual recognition, one-state supervision, cooperation between the competent authorities[452] of the Member States and a common approach to third countries.[453] Life insurance undertakings can obtain a single authorization from the Member State in which they have their head office that enables them to carry on the activities covered by the Directive throughout the EU, either through a branch or by way of provision of services.

The Directive distinguishes between three types of Member States with respect to the conduct of life insurance operations. The Member State that authorizes an undertaking is called the "home Member State,"[454] and it is responsible for the supervision of all the undertaking's activities within the EU. A Member State where a policy holder has his/her habitual residence or, if the policy holder is a legal person, the Member State where the establishment to which the insurance contract relates is situated is called the "Member State of the commitment."[455] The Member State where an insurance undertaking authorized in another Member State has a branch or is providing services is referred to as the "Member State of the branch or of the provision of services," which is a mouthful. I prefer the more usual term "host Member State." Where insurance services are supplied through the provision of services in a host Member State, it will also be the Member State of the commitment. Where the services are provided from a branch, it may or may not also be the Member State of the commitment depending on whether the policy holder resides or has an establishment there. However, this will mostly be the case. Thus, in this monograph, I have used the more convenient term "host Member State" to mean both the Member State of the commitment and the Member State of the branch or the provision of services unless it is indispensable to make the distinction.

---

450 Assurance is a branch of insurance under which a contract of insurance is made to pay a capital sum on a specified date or on the death of the person concerned. Thus, we talk of life "assurance." However, most people do not make the distinction between assurance and insurance in everyday language, and I have used the more usual term "insurance" throughout.

451 Council Directive 91/674 on the annual accounts and consolidated accounts of insurance undertakings (OJ L374/91).

452 "Competent authorities" means, *per* Article (1)(n), the national authorities that are empowered by law or regulation to supervise insurance undertakings. In the text, I often refer simply to the Member States when their competent authorities are meant.

453 A "third country" is a country that is not a Member State of the EU.

454 Article 1(1)(e).

455 Article 1(1)(g).

Scope

The EU life insurance regime applies to all insurance undertakings carrying on direct insurance in the form of the following activities:[456]

- life insurance;
- annuities;
- supplementary insurance connected with a life insurance policy;[457]
- marriage insurance;
- birth insurance;
- permanent health insurance not subject to cancellation;[458]

and the following, where they are on a contractual basis and to the extent that they are subject to supervision by the same authorities as private insurance:

- tontines;
- capital redemption operations;
- management of group pension funds;
- certain other insurance operations such as those set out in Chapter 1 of Title 4 of Book IV of the French *Code des insurances*;

and

- operations relating to the length of human life that are prescribed by or provided for in social insurance legislation, when they are effected or managed at their own risk by insurance undertakings.

These activities, which are referred to generically as "life insurance" in this monograph are further divided by Annex I into nine classes of insurance:

I. Life insurance, annuities and supplementary insurance, subject to class III;

II. Marriage and birth insurance;

III. Life insurance and annuities that are linked to investment funds;

IV. Permanent health insurance;

V. Tontines;

VI. Capital redemption operations;

VII. Management of group pension funds;

VIII. Certain other insurance operations;

456 Article 2.

457 This includes, in particular, insurance against incapacity for employment resulting from personal injury, an accident or sickness and insurance against death resulting from an accident.

458 This type of insurance only exists in Ireland and the United Kingdom.

IX. Operations relating to the length of human life that are prescribed by or provided for in social insurance legislation when they are effected or managed at their own risk by insurance undertakings.

The Directive does not apply to the various classes of direct insurance other than life insurance that are covered by the non-life insurance directives.[459] Similarly excluded are the operations of provident and mutual-benefit institutions and those of organizations other than insurance undertakings that provide benefits for specific groups of employed or self-employed persons in the event of death, survival or discontinuance or curtailment of activity.[460] Certain mutual associations are also excluded,[461] as are insurance that forms part of a statutory system of social security and life insurance benefits that do not exceed the average funeral costs for a single death or where the benefits are provided in kind.[462]

National Law

The EU insurance regime does not entirely replace the national systems. National law may still apply but subject to the EU rules on authorization, prudential supervision and freedom of movement. Where the Directive sets out minimum standards, the Member States have a general right to lay down stricter rules for undertakings authorized by their competent authorities.[463] Stricter national requirements are specifically permitted in the case of solvency margins.[464] In addition, the Directive on occasion leaves the Member States some measure of discretion in the implementation of its rules.

Applicable Law

The law applicable to life insurance contracts is in principle that of the Member State of the commitment.[465] Nevertheless, the parties may choose the law of another country to the extent that such choice is recognized by the Member State of the commitment. However, it seems that, where the policy holder is a natural person and has the nationality of a Member State other than that of the Member State of the commitment, the parties have an absolute right to choose the law of the

---

459 Article 3(1). This includes, *per* the Annex to Directive 73/239: accident insurance, sickness insurance (but *see* note 12), land vehicle insurance, railway insurance, marine insurance, cargo insurance, insurance against fire and natural forces, property insurance, motor vehicle liability insurance, aircraft liability insurance, general liability insurance, credit insurance, suretyship insurance, financial loss insurance, legal expenses insurance and travel insurance.

460 Article 3(2) and (3).

461 Article 3(6). These associations may continue to operate under the Directive for a period of five years from March 20, 2002 *per* Article 71(1), during which time they achieve compliance with the requirements of the Directive.

462 Article 3(5).

463 Preamble, 28th recital.

464 Preamble, 43rd recital.

465 Articles 32(1). *Cf.* Directive 88/357, Article 7(1)(a).

former State.[466] In all cases, the law of the Member State of the commitment may stipulate that its mandatory rules must be applied regardless of the law applicable to the contract.[467] In particular, insurance contracts must not conflict with the legal provisions of the Member State of the commitment aimed at protecting the general good.[468] Moreover, whatever the applicable law, insurance contracts are subject exclusively to the indirect taxes and parafiscal charges on insurance premiums of the Member State of the commitment.[469] In the case of litigation, the mandatory rules of the forum may also apply.[470]

Subject to these specific rules, the Directive requires the Member States to apply to insurance contracts covered by the Directive their general rules of private international law concerning contractual obligations.[471]

2. Authorization of Insurance Undertakings

General Provisions

Before taking up the business of life insurance, an insurance undertaking must obtain an official authorization from its home Member State. According to Article 4(a) and the eighth recital to the Preamble, this is the Member State where it has its head office. This is also implied by the definition of "home Member State" in Article 1(1)(e). However, the waters are muddied by the twelfth recital to the Preamble, which states that an insurance undertaking must be authorized in the Member State in which it has its registered office.

Recourse must be had to the banking and investment services directives[472] to clear up this confusion. What the Directive undoubtedly means is that where an insurance undertaking has a registered office, the home Member State is where this registered office is located. In the case of undertakings that, under their national law, have no registered office, the home Member State is where they have their head office. The reason for the confusion is that the Directive requires that all insurance undertakings have their head office in the same Member State as their registered office.[473] Thus, in practice, the home Member State is where insurance undertakings have their head office.

---

466 Article 32(2). *Cf.* Directive 88/357, Article 7(1)(b), which is, however, worded somewhat differently.

467 Article 32(4), 2nd subpara. *Cf.* Directive 88/357, Article 7(1)(g).

468 Article 33.

469 Article 50(1). *Cf.* Directive 92/49, Article 46(2).

470 Article 32(4), 1st subpara. *Cf.* Directive 88/357, Article 7(2), 1st subpara.

471 Article 32(5). *Cf.* Directive 88/357, Article 7(3).

472 EP/Council Directive 00/12 relating to the taking up and pursuit of the business of credit institutions (OJ L126/00) and EP/Council Directive 04/39 on market in financial instruments (OJ L145/04). *See* in particular, Directive 04/39, Article 4(1)(20)(a).

473 Article 6(3).

The authorization provisions of the Directive also apply to the authorization of the branches of insurance undertakings whose head offices are outside the EU, subject to the provisions on relations with third countries,[474] as well the direct or indirect subsidiaries of parent undertakings from third countries.[475]

Member States may grant an authorization for a particular class of insurance as listed in Annex I or it may, on its own initiative or at the request of the applicant, restrict the authorization to certain operations within a class.[476] It is also up to the home Member State whether or not it grants an authorization for two or more classes of activities.[477] An authorized insurance undertaking that wishes to extend its business to an entire class of activities or to another class or classes requires a fresh authorization.[478]

As a general principle, the Directive forbids a Member State from authorizing an insurance undertaking under both the Directive and Directive 73/239 relating to direct insurance other than life insurance.[479] However, Member States are free to permit undertakings authorized under the Directive to obtain an authorization under Directive 73/239 for risks with respect to accidents, including industrial injury and occupational diseases, and sickness.[480] Conversely, undertakings that have been authorized under Directive 73/239 solely for these risks may be given an authorization under the Directive.[481] In these two instances, home Member States may require insurance undertakings to comply with the accounting rules set down by the Directive for both types of activities.[482]

Undertakings that on March 15, 1979[483] were carrying on simultaneously both the activities covered by the Directive and those covered by Directive 73/239 may continue to do so provided that each activity is managed separately.[484] This must be done in such a way as to ensure that:[485]

- the respective interests of life policy holders and non-life policy holders are not prejudiced;

---

474 Article 51.

475 Article 58(a).

476 Article 5(2), 1st and 2nd indents. *Cf.* Directive 73/239, Article 7(2).

477 Article 5(2), 3rd indent.

478 Article 4(b). *Cf.* Directive 73/239, Article 6(b).

479 Article 18(1).

480 Article 18(2), 1st indent.

481 Article 18(2), 2nd indent.

482 Article 18(4).

483 The date for Greece is January 1, 1981, January 1, 1986 for Spain and Portugal, January 1, 1995 for Austria, Finland and Sweden and May 1, 2004 for Czech Republic, Estonia, Cyprus, Latvia, Lithuania, Hungary, Malta, Poland, Slovenia and Slovakia.

484 Article 18(3).

485 Article 19(1) and (2)(a).

– the minimum financial obligations, in particular solvency margins, in respect of one type of activities are not borne by the other type of activities;

– accounts show the sources of the results for each type of activities.

Home Member States are free to require these undertakings to cease, within a certain time period, the simultaneous pursuit of both types of activities.[486]

In order to obtain an authorization, an insurance undertaking must meet the national requirements of the home Member State as well as those set out in the Directive.

National Requirements

National requirements for granting an authorization must be consistent with the rules of the Directive. This specifically includes the prohibition in the Directive on prior approval or systematic notification of general and special policy conditions, scales of premiums, technical bases and provisions and printed documents that an undertaking intends to use in its dealings with the public.[487] Nor may a Member State make an authorization dependent on the economic needs of the market.[488] A home Member State may, however, require approval of the memorandum and Articles of association of an undertaking,[489] and it has a general right to lay down stricter rules for authorizations than appear in the Directive.[490]

Requirements under the Directive

The basic requirements of the Directive that must be met before a Member State may grant an authorization for an insurance undertaking to carry on the business of life insurance in the EU are as follows:

1. The insurance undertaking must adopt a specified business form depending on the home Member State.[491] In the case of the United Kingdom, for example, this is "an incorporated company limited by shares or by guarantee or unlimited," "a society registered under the *Industrial and Provident Societies Acts*," "a society registered or incorporated under the *Friendly Societies Acts*" or "the association of underwriters knowns as 'Lloyds'."[492] Alternatively, an insurance undertaking may adopt the form of a European company, which is called somewhat grandly

486 Article 18(6).

487 Article 6(5), 1st subpara. *Cf.* Directive 73/239, Article 8(3), 2nd subpara.

488 Article 6(6).

489 Article 6(5), 3rd subpara.

490 Preamble, 28th recital.

491 Article 6(1)(a). *Cf.* Directive 73/239, Article 8(1)(a).

492 Undertakings set up in the United Kingdom by Royal Charter or by an Act of Parliament may continue to carry on their activity in the legal form in which they constituted on March 15, 1979.

Societas Europea, or *SE* in its abbreviated form.[493] Public corporations may also be set up by Member States and authorized under the Directive as long as they carry on their life insurance activities under the same conditions as private undertakings.

2. Subject to the provisions discussed above with respect to insurance activities carried on pursuant to Directive 73/239, the insurance undertaking must limit its objects to life insurance to the exclusion of all other commercial business.[494]

3. The insurance undertaking must submit an acceptable scheme of operations that includes the following:[495]

- the nature of the commitments that it proposes to cover;
- the guiding principles as to re-insurance;
- the items constituting the minimum guarantee fund;
- estimates of the costs of setting up the business and the resources intended to meet these costs.

In addition, for the first three financial years, the scheme must include:

- a plan setting out detailed estimates of income and expenditure in respect of direct business, re-insurance acceptances and re-insurance cessions;
- a forecast balance sheet;
- estimates relating to financial resources intended to cover underwriting liabilities and the solvency margin.

4. The insurance undertaking must possess a minimum guarantee fund of 3 million Euros.[496] A Member State may reduce the minimum guarantee fund for mutual associations and mutual-type associations and tontines to 2, 250,000 Euros.

5. The insurance undertaking must be effectively run by persons of good repute with appropriate professional qualifications or experience.[497] The home Member State must accept as sufficient evidence of good repute in respect of nationals of other Member States the production of an extract from the judicial record or, failing this, an equivalent document issued by the competent authorities of a Member State.[498] Where the Member State concerned does not issue such documents, they may be replaced by a declaration on oath or a solemn declaration.[499]

---

493 *See* Council Regulation 2157/01 on the statute for the European company (SE) (OJ L294/01).

494 Article 6(1)(b). *Cf.* Directive 73/239, Article 8(1)(b).

495 Articles 6(1)(c) and 7. *Cf.* Directive 73/239, Articles 8(1)(c) and 9.

496 Article 6(1)(d) and 29(2). *Cf.* Directive 73/239, Articles 8(1)(d) and 17(2).

497 Article 6(1)(e). *Cf.* Directive 73/239, Article 8(1)(e).

498 Article 61(1). *Cf.* Directive 73/240, Article 3.

499 Article 61(2). *Cf.* Directive 73/240, Article 3.

No document or declaration may be produced more than three months after its date of issue.[500]

6. Insurance undertakings that have a registered office in their home Member State must also have their head office there.[501] By analogy with the banking and investment service directives,[502] an insurance undertaking that has only a head office in its home Member State must actually carry on business there.[503]

7. Home Member States may not grant an authorization to an insurance undertaking before its competent authorities have been informed of the identities of the shareholders or members that have qualifying holdings[504] and the amounts of these holdings.[505] The home Member State must refuse an authorization if, taking into account the need to ensure the sound and prudent management of the insurance undertaking, it is not satisfied as to the qualifications of these shareholders or members.

8. Where close links[506] exist between an insurance undertaking and other natural or legal persons, an authorization can only be accorded if these links do not prevent the proper supervision of the insurance undertaking.[507] In particular, where the other natural or legal persons are governed by the law of a non-Member State, an authorization cannot be granted if the law of this country or difficulties involved in its enforcement prevent effective supervision.

9. An authorization should not be granted to an insurance undertaking where such factors as the content of the schemes of operations or the geographical distribution of the undertaking's activities indicate clearly that the undertaking has opted for authorization in the Member State in question for the purpose of evading the stricter standards in force in the Member State where it intends to carry on the greater part of its activities.[508]

---

500 Article 61(3).

501 Article 6(3).

502 Directive 00/12, Article 6(2), 2nd indent and Directive 04/39, Article 5(4), 2nd indent.

503 Preamble, 12th recital.

504 A "qualifying holding" is defined in Article 1(1)(j) as a direct or indirect holding in an undertaking that represents 10% or more of its capital or voting rights or which makes it possible to exercise a significant influence over the management of the undertaking. *See also* Directive 92/49, Article 1(g).

505 Article 8. *Cf.* Directive 92/49, Article 8.

506 "Close links" are defined in Article 1(1)(r) as a situation where two or more legal or natural persons are linked by a "participation" (i.e. ownership, direct or by way of control, of 20% or more of the voting rights or capital of an undertaking) or control in the sense of the relationship between a parent undertaking and a subsidiary as defined in Council Directive 83/349 on consolidated accounts (OJ L193/83) or a similar relationship between any natural or legal person and an undertaking.

507 Article 6(2). *Cf.* Directive 73/239, Article 8(1), 2nd and 3rd subparas.

508 Preamble, 12th recital.

Where an undertaking is seeking an authorization to extend its business to an entire class or another class or classes of activities, it is required only to submit an acceptable scheme of operations as per point 3 and to show that it possesses the required guarantee fund and solvency margin.[509]

Decisions on the grant of an authorization should be taken within six months of receiving the application.[510] Where an authorization is refused, the home Member State must give precise grounds for doing so and inform the undertaking in question. Member States must ensure that decisions relating to authorizations are subject to a right of appeal to the courts, with respect both to a refusal and a failure to respect the six-month time limit.

Withdrawal of an Authorization

A home Member State may withdraw an authorization from an insurance undertaking in the following circumstances:[511]

- where the authorization is not used within 12 months or is renounced or where the insurance undertaking has ceased to engage in business for more than six months;
- where the insurance undertaking no longer fulfils the conditions for an authorization;
- where the insurance undertaking has been unable to take in time the measures specified in a restoration plan or finance scheme;
- where the insurance undertaking contravenes in serious fashion the national rules to which it is subject, which normally involves the rules of the home Member State.

In addition, the Preamble to the Directive states that an authorization must be withdrawn where the home Member State becomes aware that it was obtained for the purpose of evading the stricter standards in force in the Member State where the insurance undertaking carries on the greater part of its activities,[512] or where it can no longer properly supervise the undertaking because of its close links with another natural or legal person.[513] This latter situation may also be covered by the second ground for withdrawal given above.

In the case of the withdrawal of an authorization, the home Member State must notify the other Member States, which are responsible for ensuring that the under-

509 Article 6(4). *Cf.* Directive 73/239, Article 8(2). The guarantee fund and solvency margin are discussed *infra* in the text.

510 Article 9.

511 Article 39(1), 1st subpara. *Cf.* Directive 73/239, Article 22(1), 1st subpara.

512 Preamble, 12th recital.

513 Preamble, 9th recital.

taking does not commence any new activities within their territories.[514] A decision to withdraw an authorization must be accompanied by precise reasons and notified to the insurance undertaking in question.[515] The decision can be appealed to the courts.[516]

3. Liberalization

General Provisions

Insurance undertakings duly authorized in their home Member State are free to carry on any of the activities for which they have been authorized, either through a branch or by way of the provision of services, in all Member States of the EU.[517] They may also freely advertise their services in their host Member States, albeit subject to any rules adopted by the latter in the interest of the general good.[518]

Host Member States may not require the prior approval or systematic notification of general and special policy conditions, scales of premiums, technical bases and provisions and printed documents that the undertaking intends to use in its business.[519] On the other hand, they may compel insurance undertakings authorized in other Member States to submit any documents that they may require of them under the Directive in the official language(s) of the host State.[520]

If an insurance undertaking is wound up, commitments that arise out of contracts underwritten through a branch or by way of provision of services must be met in the same way as those arising out of the undertaking's insurance contracts concluded in its home Member State, without distinction as to the lives assured and the beneficiaries concerned.[521]

Establishment of a Branch

All that an insurance undertaking is required to do in order to carry on its activities under the Directive through a branch in another Member State is to notify the home Member State and provide it with the following information:[522]

- the Member State where it proposes to set up the branch;
- a scheme of operations setting out, *inter alia*, the types of business envisaged and the structural organization of the branch;
- the address of the branch in the host Member State;

---

514 Article 39(1), 2nd subpara. *Cf.* Directive 73/239, Article 22(1), 2nd subpara.

515 Article 39(2). *Cf.* Directive 73/239, Article 22(2).

516 Article 67.

517 Article 5. *Cf.* Directive 73/239, Article 7.

518 Article 47. *Cf.* Directive 92/49, Article 41.

519 Article 45. *Cf.* Directive 92/49, Article 39(2) and (3).

520 Articles 44 and 46(1). *Cf.* Directive 92/49, Articles 38 and 40(2).

521 Article 48.

522 Article 40(1) and (2). *Cf.* Directive 73/239, Article 10(1) and (2).

– the name of the branch's authorized agent, who must have the authority to bind the insurance undertaking and represent it in its relations with the authorities and courts of the host Member State.[523]

It is the responsibility of the home Member State to communicate this information within three months to the host Member State.[524] It must also attest that the insurance undertaking has the required solvency margin and meets the minimum requirements for the guarantee fund.[525] It cannot give this attestation where an undertaking has been required to follow a financial recovery plan unless the competent authorities consider that the rights of policy-holders are no longer threatened.[526]

It is only if the home Member State, taking into account the proposed activities, has doubts about the adequacy of the administrative structure or the financial situation of the insurance undertaking or the good repute and professional qualifications of its directors, managers or authorized agent that it may refuse to communicate the information to the host Member State.[527] It must give reasons for such refusal to the institution within three months.[528] The refusal is subject to a right of appeal to the courts.

Within two months of receiving the information from the home Member State, the host Member State must indicate any conditions under which, in the interest of the general good, the undertaking may conduct its activities.[529] On receipt of such communication from the host Member State or in any event after the expiry of the two month period, the branch may be established and start business.[530]

Branches of insurance undertakings from another Member State that commenced their activities in a host Member State before July 1, 1994 are deemed to have met all the above requirements.[531]

Provision of Services

An insurance undertaking wishing to carry on its activities in another Member State by way of the provision of services must likewise notify its home Member State, indicating the nature of the commitments it proposes to cover.[532] The home Member State must inform the host Member State within one month of the classes

---

523 The agent authorized by Lloyds must also be able to bind this group.

524 Article 40(3), 1st subpara. *Cf.* Directive 73/239, Article 10(3), 1st subpara.

525 Article 40(3), 2nd subpara. *Cf.* Directive 73/239, Article 10(3), 2nd subpara. The wording mentions only the solvency margin, but it refers also to Article 29, which deals with the guarantee fund.

526 Article 38(5). *Cf.* Directive 73/239, Article 20a(5).

527 Article 40(3), 1st subpara. *Cf.* Directive 73/239, Article 10(3), 1st subpara.

528 Article 40(3), 3rd subpara. *Cf.* Directive 73/239, Article 10(3), 3rd subpara.

529 Article 40(4). *Cf.* Directive 73/239, Article 10(4).

530 Article 40(5). *Cf.* Directive 73/239, Article 10(5).

531 Article 66(1). *Cf.* Directive 92/49, Article 52(1).

532 Article 41. *Cf.* Directive 88/357, Article 14.

of activity that the insurance undertaking is authorized to offer and the nature of the commitments that it proposes to cover in the host Member State.[533] It must also issue a certificate attesting that the insurance undertaking has the required solvency margin and meets the minimum requirements for the guarantee fund.[534] It cannot issue this certificate where an undertaking has been required to follow a financial recovery plan unless the competent authorities consider that the rights of policy-holders are no longer threatened.[535]

If the home Member State refuses to communicate the necessary information to the host State, it must give reasons to the undertaking within the same one-month time period.[536] The refusal is subject to a right of appeal to the courts.

The subsequent procedure is simpler than for the establishment of a branch. Once an undertaking has been informed of the dispatch of the necessary information and certificate to the host State, it may start to provide the insurance services in question.[537] There is no provision for the host Member State to subject this right to any conditions,[538] but an insurance undertaking is always obliged to follow the legal provisions applicable to it in the host Member State to the extent that they do not conflict with the Directive.[539]

The rights of insurance undertakings that provided services in a host Member State before July 1, 1994 are not affected by these provisions, which presumably means that they may carry on as before.[540]

4. Prudential Supervision

General Provisions

The financial supervision of an insurance undertaking, including the activities it carries on through a branch or by way of services in other Member States, is the responsibility of the home Member State.[541] This supervision involves verification of an undertaking's solvency and the establishment of technical provisions and the assets covering them[542] as well as monitoring qualifying holdings, approving transfers of portfolios, setting the duties of auditors, providing for professional secrecy and other miscellaneous prudential matters.

---

533 Article 42(1)(b) and (c). *Cf.* Directive 88/357, Article 16(1)(b) and (c).

534 Article 42(1)(a). *Cf.* Directive 88/357, Article 16(10(a). The wording mentions only the solvency margin, but it refers also to Article 29, which deals with the guarantee fund.

535 Article 38(5). *Cf.* Directive 73/239, Article 20a(5).

536 Article 42(2). *Cf.* Directive 88/357, Article 16(2).

537 Article 42(3). *Cf.* Directive 88/357, Article 16(3).

538 But *see* Directive 88/357, Articles 12a and 16(1), 2nd subpara.

539 *See* Articles 33 and 46(2).

540 Article 66(2). *Cf.* Directive 92/49, Article 52(2).

541 Article 10(1). *Cf.* Directive 73/239, Article 10(1).

542 Article 10(2) *Cf.* Directive 73/239, Article 13(2).

The home Member State must require every insurance undertaking under its supervision to have sound administrative and accounting procedures and adequate internal control mechanisms.[543] It must also require them to produce an annual account, covering all types of operation, of its financial situation and solvency and to render periodically the returns, together with statistical documents, that are necessary for the purposes of supervision.[544]

The home Member State must ensure that its competent authorities have the powers and means necessary to carry out their prudential obligations.[545] This includes gathering necessary information and requiring the submission of necessary documents as well as on-the-spot investigations at insurance undertakings' premises, including branches in other Member States.[546] The host Member State of the branch must be informed prior to the investigation and may participate in it.

Host Member States are obliged to inform the home Member State when they have reason to consider that that activities of an insurance undertaking in their territory might affect its financial soundness.[547] The home Member State must then determine whether the undertaking is complying with the prudential principles laid down in the Directive.

Host Member States may require insurance undertakings from other Member States operating in their territory to comply with its laws that are consistent with the Directive, such as provisions aimed at protecting the general good,[548] and to put an end to any non-compliance.[549] If an undertaking fails to take the necessary action, the host Member State informs the competent authorities of the home Member State, which must take all appropriate measures to ensure that the undertaking concerned remedies the irregular situation.[550] If these measures are not forthcoming or prove inadequate, the host Member State may itself take appropriate action to prevent or punish further violations of its laws.[551] Where it is strictly necessary, this can include preventing the undertaking from concluding new insurance contracts within its territory.

All Member States have the power to deal with emergency situations, including the possibility of preventing insurance undertakings from concluding new

---

543 Article 10(3). *Cf.* Directive 73/239, Article 13(3).

544 Article 13(1), (2).

545 Article 13(3).

546 Articles 11 and 13(3)(a). *Cf.* Directives 73/239, Articles 14 and 19(3)(a) and Directive 88/357, Article 10, 2nd subpara.

547 Article 10(1).

548 *See* Article 33.

549 Article 46(2). *Cf.* Directive 92/49, Article 40(3).

550 Article 46(3). *Cf.* Directive 92/49, Article 40(4).

551 Article 46(4). *Cf.* Directive 92/49, Article 40(5).

contracts.[552] In addition, they may always penalize infringements within their territory.[553] Any measures taken by Member States under these provisions must be properly reasoned and communicated to the insurance undertaking concerned.[554]

All Member States must ensure that any decisions taken in pursuance of their supervisory duties are subject to a right of appeal to the courts.[555]

Technical Provisions

Home Member States must require every insurance undertaking to establish sufficient technical provisions in respect of its entire business.[556] The technical provisions must be calculated separately for each contract, although the use of appropriate approximations or generalizations is allowed where they are likely to give more or less the same result as individual calculations.[557]

The amount of technical life insurance provisions must be calculated by a sufficiently prudent, prospective, actuarial valuation taking account of all future liabilities with respect to the particular contract in question, including:[558]

- all guaranteed benefits, including guaranteed surrender values;
- bonuses to which policy holders are entitled;
- all options available to the policy holder under the contract;
- expenses, including commissions;
- taking credit for future premiums due.

A prudent evaluation is not a "best estimate" valuation but includes an appropriate margin for adverse deviation of the relevant factors.[559] Moreover, the method of valuation for the technical provisions must not only be prudent in itself but must also be so with respect to the method of valuation of the assets covering these provisions.[560] The use of a retrospective method of valuation is allowed if it can be shown that the resulting technical provisions are not lower than would result from the use of a prospective calculation, or if a prospective method cannot be used for the type of contract involved.[561] Where the surrender value of a contract is guaran-

552 Articles 46(5). *Cf.* Directive 92/49, Article 40(6).

553 Article 46(6). *Cf.* Directive 92/49, Article 40(7).

554 Article 46(8).

555 Article 67. *Cf.* Directive 92/49, Article 56.

556 Article 20(1). *Cf.* Directive 73/239, Article 15(1).

557 Article 20(1)(A)(v).

558 Article 20(1)(A)(i).

559 Article 20(1)(A)(iii).

560 Article 20(1)(A)(iv).

561 Article 20(1)(A)(ii).

teed, the amount of the provisions for the contract at any time must be at least as great as the value guaranteed at that time.[562]

The rate of interest used must be chosen prudently and determined in accordance with the rules of the home Member State, applying certain uniform principles.[563] The home Member State must fix for all contracts one or more maximum rates of interest,[564] except that a single interest rate must be fixed for contracts that contain an interest rate guarantee.[565] The home Member State may decide not to apply a maximum rate of interest to unit-linked contracts, single-premium contracts lasting up to eight years, without-profits contracts and annuity contracts with no surrender value.[566] The establishment of a maximum interest rate does mean that insurance undertakings cannot use a lower rate.[567] Indeed, under no circumstances may the rate of interest be higher than the yield on an undertaking's assets less an appropriate deduction.[568] Home Member States must require insurance undertakings to make special provision in their accounts for interest rate commitments where the present or foreseeable yield on their assets is insufficient to cover these commitments.[569]

In the case of participating contracts, the method of calculating technical provisions may take into account future bonuses.[570] Allowance may be made for future expenses, but it must not be less than a prudent estimate of such expenses.[571] Premiums for new business must be sufficient to enable insurance undertakings to establish adequate technical provisions.[572]

Insurance undertakings must be required to make available to the public the bases and methods used in the calculation of its technical provisions.[573] These methods and bases must not be subject to arbitrary changes from year to year.[574] Technical provisions must be calculated in such a way as to render recognizable the distribution of profits over the duration of a policy.

---

562 Article 20(1)(A)(vi).

563 Article 20(1)(B).

564 Article 20(1)(B)(a).

565 Article 20(1)(B)(a)(i).

566 Article 20(1)(B)(c), 1st subpara.

567 Article 20(1)(B)(b).

568 Article 20(1)(B)(c), 3rd subpara.

569 Article 20(1)(B)(d).

570 Article 20(1)(D).

571 Article 20(1)(E).

572 Article 21.

573 Article 20(2).

574 Article 20(1)(F).

Home Member States must require every insurance undertaking to cover its technical provisions by matching assets.[575] In respect of business written in the EU, these assets should normally be localized within the EU, although not necessarily in a particular Member State. An insurer's commitments are considered as a general principle to be payable in the currency of the contract.[576] However, this rule is subject to certain derogations:

- Member States may authorize insurance undertakings not to cover their technical commitments by matching assets where this would oblige them to hold assets in a currency amounting to not more than 7% of their assets in other currencies;[577]
- Member States may authorize insurance undertakings not to cover their technical commitments by matching assets where commitments are payable in a currency that is subject to exchange controls or otherwise unsuitable for covering technical provisions;[578]
- insurance undertakings are allowed not to hold matching assets to cover an amount not exceeding 20% of their commitments in a particular currency as long as their total assets in all currencies are at least equal to their total commitments in all currencies.[579]
- Member States may provide that commitments that have to be covered by assets expressed in the currency of a Member State outside the Eurozone may be covered by assets expressed in Euros.[580]

Home Member States establish which assets may be accepted as cover for technical provisions,[581] but they are limited in their choice to the following categories of assets:[582]

1. Investments:
   - debt securities, bonds and other money and capital market instruments;
   - loans;
   - shares and other variable-yield participations;
   - units in mutual funds[583] and other investment funds;
   - land, buildings and immovable property rights.

575 Article 20(3). *Cf.* Directive 73/239, Article 15(2).

576 Annex II, 1.

577 Annex II, 2.

578 Annex II, 3.

579 Annex II, 4.

580 Annex II, 5.

581 Article 23(3). *Cf.* Directive 92/49, Article 21(1), 3rd subpara.

582 Article 23(1). *Cf.* Directive 92/49, Article 21(1), 1st subpara.

583 These are called "undertakings for collective investment in transferable securities" (UCITS) or "collective investment undertakings" in Europe.

2. Debts and claims:
   - debts owed by re-assurers including re-assurers' shares of technical provisions;[584]
   - deposits with and debts owed by ceding undertakings;
   - debts owed by policy holders and intermediaries arising out of direct and re-insurance operations;
   - advances against policies;
   - tax recoveries;
   - claims against guarantee funds.
3. Other Assets:
   - tangible fixed assets other than land and buildings;
   - cash at bank and in hand, deposits with credit institutions and other bodies;
   - deferred acquisition costs;
   - accrued interest and rent;
   - reversionary interests.

A Member State may, temporarily and under a properly reasoned decision, accept other categories of assets as cover for technical provisions as long as the safety, yield and marketability of the undertaking's investments are secured.[585] Member States may not prescribe any rules as to the choice of assets that need not be used as cover for technical provisions.[586]

In deciding which assets shall be accepted as cover for technical provisions, home Member States must take account of the type of business carried on by the insurance undertaking in question in such a way as to secure the safety, yield and marketability of its investments.[587] They must also follow the following principles:[588]

- assets must be valued on a prudent basis and net of any debts arising out of the acquisition;
- loans may be accepted only if there are sufficient guarantees as to their security;
- derivative instruments may be used only in so far as they contribute to a reduction of investment risks or facilitate efficient portfolio management;

584 *Per* Article 20(4), where the home Member State allows technical provisions to be covered by claims against re-assurers, it must fix the percentage so allowed. Localization of assets representing such claims cannot be required. *Cf.* Directive 73/239, Article 15(3).

585 Article 23(4).

586 Article 31(1). *Cf.* Directive 73/239, Article 18(1).

587 Article 22.

588 Article 23(3). *Cf.* Directive 92/49, Article 21(1), 4th subpara.

- transferable securities that are not negotiated on a regulated market[589] may be accepted only if they can be realized in the short term or represent holdings in credit institutions, authorized insurance undertakings or investment undertakings established in a Member State;
- debts and claims involving third parties may be accepted net of any amounts owed to the third party;
- debts and claims must be calculated with due allowance for the risk of some amounts being unrealizable. Debts owed by policy holders and intermediaries arising out of insurance and re-insurance operations must not have been outstanding for more than three months;
- where assets represent an investment in a subsidiary undertaking that manages an insurance undertaking's investments on its behalf, the home Member State must take into account the underlying assets held by the subsidiary;
- deferred acquisition costs may be accepted as cover for technical provisions only to the extent that this is consistent with the calculation of mathematical provisions.

Although in principle insurance undertakings are made responsible for ensuring that their investments are diversified and adequately spread,[590] they are also subject to a number of mandatory investment diversification rules as regards their assets covering technical provisions.

In the first place, home Member States must require every insurance undertaking to invest no more than:[591]

- 10% of its total gross technical provisions in any one piece of land or building;
- 5%[592] of its total gross technical provisions in shares, other negotiable securities and other money and capital market instruments from the same undertaking, or in loans granted to the same borrower except loans granted to a State, regional or local authority or an international organization of which one or more Member States are members;

589 A "regulated market" is defined in Article 4(1)(14) of Directive 04/39 as a multilateral system operated and/or managed by a market operator, which may be the regulated market itself, that brings together or facilitates the bringing together of multiple third-party buyers and sellers of financial instruments and which is authorized by a Member State pursuant to the Directive. *Cf.* Directive 92/49, Article 1(j).

590 Article 22.

591 Article 24(1). *Cf.* Directive 92/49, Article 22(1).

592 Pursuant to Article 24(1)(b), this limit may be raised to 10% if the total value of separate 5% investments in securities and loans does not exceed 40% of an undertaking's total gross technical provisions. It may be raised *per* Article 24(4) to 40% in the case of certain debt securities issued by a credit institution which has its head office in a Member State and is subject by law to special official supervision designed to protect the holders of those debt securities. *Cf.* Directive 92/49, arts 22(1)(b) and 22(4).

- 5% of its total gross technical provisions in unsecured loans, including 1% for any single unsecured loan, except loans granted to credit institutions, authorized insurance undertakings and investment undertakings established in a Member State;[593]
- 3% of its total gross technical provisions in the form of cash in hand;
- 10% of its total gross technical provisions in shares and other securities that are not negotiated on a regulated market.

Home Member States may, temporarily and by a properly reasoned decision, allow exceptions from the above rules as long as the safety, yield and marketability of the undertaking's investments are secured.[594] Such exceptions are only possible in exceptional circumstances and at an insurance undertaking's request.

The above rules only set down a limit on the percentage of an insurance undertaking's technical funds that an asset may cover; they do not establish any limit on the monetary amount of the investment. This is left by the Directive up to the home Member State, which must, however, act in accordance with the following principles:[595]

- assets covering technical provisions must be diversified in such a way as not to place excessive reliance on a particular category of asset;
- high-risk and non-liquid investments must be restricted to prudent levels;
- where assets represent an investment in a subsidiary undertaking that manages an insurance undertaking's investments on its behalf, the home Member State must take into account the underlying assets held by the subsidiary;
- where assets represent loans to or debt securities issued by EU credit institutions that are publicly owned and whose business is to extend loans to or guaranteed by the state, the home Member State may take into account the underlying assets held by such credit institutions.

Stricter treatment should be accorded to the following assets:[596]

- unsecured loans;
- UCITS[597] that are not coordinated within the meaning of Directive 85/611;[598]
- securities not negotiated on a regulated market;

---

593 The limits may be raised to 8% and 2%, respectively, by the home Member State on case-by-case basis.

594 Article 24(6). *Cf.* Directive 92/49, Articles 20, 21(2) and 22(6).

595 Article 24(2). *Cf.* Directive 92/49, Article 22(9).

596 Article 24(3). *Cf.* Directive 92/49, Article 22(3).

597 *See* note 583.

598 Council Directive 85/611 on the coordination of laws, regulations and administrative provisions relating to undertakings for collective investments in transferable securities (UCITS) (OJ L375/85).

- bonds, debt securities and other money- and capital-market instruments not issued by Zone A[599] entities or international organizations of which at least one Member State is a member.

Neither set of investment diversification rules permits Member States to require insurance undertakings to invest in particular assets.[600] In addition, the rules on acceptable assets and investment diversification do not apply to assets that are held to match liabilities arising from benefits under a contract that are directly linked to the value of units in a mutual fund or assets in an internal fund held by the insurance undertaking or linked to a share index.[601]

Solvency Margin

The solvency margin that is required by the Directive of insurance undertakings differs according to the classes of insurance underwritten.[602] The rules are extremely technical.

1. For all forms of life insurance, marriage insurance, birth insurance and annuities referred to in Article 2(1)(a) and (b), other than when these insurance operations are linked to investment funds or, in the case of operations relating to human life, prescribed by or provided for in social insurance legislation, the required solvency margin must be equal to the sum of the following two calculations:[603]

- a 4% fraction of the mathematical provisions relating to direct business and re-insurance acceptances gross of re-insurance cessions multiplied by the ratio, for the last financial year, of the total mathematical provisions net of re-insurance cessions to the gross total mathematical provisions. This ratio may not be less than 85%; and
- for policies on which the capital at risk is not a negative figure, a 0.3% fraction[604] of such capital multiplied by the ratio, for the last financial year, of the total capital at risk retained as the undertaking's liability after re-insurance cessions and retrocessions to the total capital at risk gross of re-insurance. This ratio may not be less than 50%.

2. For supplementary insurance connected with a life insurance policy referred to in Article 2(1)(c), the required solvency margin is that laid down for non-life insurance in Article 16a of Directive 73/239, excluding the provisions of Article 17

599 Zone A comprises all Member States of the EU, full members of the OECD and countries that have concluded special lending arrangements with the IMF. Any country that reschedules its external sovereign debt, however, is precluded from Zone A for a period of five years.

600 Article 24(5). *Cf.* Directive 92/49, Article 22(5).

601 Article 25(3).

602 Article 28(1). *Cf.* Directive 73/239, Article 16a.

603 Article 28(2).

604 The fraction is 0.1% for temporary insurance on death of a maximum term of three years and 0.15% where the term is more than three but less than five years.

of that Directive.[605] It is the higher of the annual amount of premiums and contributions and the average burden of claims for the five past years, as calculated according to Article 16a(3) and 16a(4), respectively.

4. For permanent health insurance not subject to cancellation referred to in Article 2(1)(d), the required solvency margin is equal to:[606]

- a 4% fraction of the mathematical provisions calculated as in No.1 above, 1st indent; plus
- the required solvency margin laid down in Article 16a of Directive 73/239 calculated as in No.2 above.[607]

5. For capital redemption operations referred to in Article 2(2)(b), the required solvency margin is equal to a 4% fraction of the mathematical provisions calculated as in No. 1 above, 1st indent.[608]

6. For tontines referred to in Article 2(2)(a), the required solvency margin is 1% of their assets.[609]

7. For the insurance operations mentioned in No.1 above when they are linked to investment funds as well as the management of group pension funds and certain specialized operations, as referred to Article 2(2)(c), (d) and (e), the required solvency margin must be equal to the sum of the following calculations in as far as they apply:[610]

- in so far as the undertaking bears an investment risk, a 4% fraction of the technical provisions calculated as in No. 1 above, 1st indent;
- in so far as the undertaking bears no investment risk but the allocation to cover management expenses is fixed for a period exceeding five years, a 1% fraction of the technical reserves calculated as in No. 1 above, 1st indent;
- where neither of the above applies, an amount equivalent to 25% of the last financial year's net administrative expenses pertaining to such business;
- in so far as the undertaking covers a death risk, a 0.3% fraction of the capital at risk calculated as in No. 1 above, 1st indent.

605 Article 28(3).

606 Article 28(4).

607 However, the condition contained in Article 16a(6)(b) that a provision must be set up for increasing age may be replaced by a requirement that the business be conducted on a group basis.

608 Article 28(5).

609 Article 28(6).

610 Article 28(7).

Home Member States[611] must require insurance undertakings that it has authorized to maintain at all times an adequate available solvency margin in respect of its entire business within the EU.[612] This margin must not be lower than the solvency margin required by the Directive as set out above. Home Member States are free, however, to require an available solvency margin that is higher than the required solvency margin.[613]

Member States may allow insurance undertakings that at March 20, 2002 were carrying on in their territory any of the activities covered by the Directive a period of five years to comply with the rules on solvency margins.[614] A further period of two years may be accorded provided that the undertaking submits a plan under Article 37(2) for establishing a sound financial position.[615]

Three types of items may make up the solvency margin of an insurance undertaking; those prescribed by the Directive, those included at the option of the home Member State and those included at the request of the undertaking.

The first type of assets consists of the assets of the insurance undertaking that are free of any liabilities, less any intangible items and the amount of own shares directly held by the undertaking.[616] They include:

- paid -up share capital or, in the case of a mutual insurance undertaking, the effective initial fund plus any members' accounts as long as payment from these accounts is not made where it would cause the solvency margin to fall below the required level and, where payment is required for reasons other than the individual termination of membership, the competent authorities must be notified and can prohibit the payment;
- statutory and free reserves that are not covering underwriting liabilities;
- profit (or loss in a negative way) brought forward after deduction of dividends; and
- where permitted by national law, profit reserves that are available to cover losses and are not available for distribution to policy holders.

---

611 This is the Member State that is meant, although Article 27(1) of the Directive refers, with unnecessary circumlocution, to the Member State in which the insurance undertaking has its head office.

612 Article 27(1). *Cf.* Directive 73/239, Article 16(1).

613 Article 27(1) and Preamble, 43rd recital.

614 Article 71(1).

615 Article 71(2).

616 Article 27(2). *Cf.* Directive 73/239, Article 16(2).

The second type of assets is items that are included entirely at the option of the home Member State.[617] They consist of:

- cumulative preferential share capital and subordinated loan capital up to 50% of the lesser of the available and required solvency margins, no more than 25% of which may consist of subordinated loans with a fixed maturity or fixed-term cumulative preferential share capital;

  In the event of bankruptcy or liquidation of the insurance undertaking, the subordinated loan and preferential share capital must rank after the claims of other creditors and not be repayable until all other outstanding debts have been settled;

  subordinated loan capital must also:

  - be fully paid up;
  - for loans with a fixed maturity, have an original maturity of at least five years and the undertaking must either submit a plan, no later than one year before maturity, showing how the solvency margin will be maintained at maturity or gradually reduce the extent that the loan ranks as a component of the solvency margin during at least the last five years of its life;
  - for loans without a fixed maturity, be repayable either on five years' notice or with the prior consent of the home Member State, which consent shall be given only if the undertaking's solvency margin does not thereby fall below the required level;
  - except in the case of the winding-up of the undertaking, not be subject to any early repayment clause;
  - be subject to amended terms only with the consent of the home Member State.
- securities with no specified maturity date and other similar instruments (except the cumulative preferential shares referred to above) up to 50% of the lesser of the available and required solvency margins for the total of such securities plus any subordinated loan capital;

  The securities must fulfill the following conditions:

  - they may not repayable on the initiative of the bearer or without the prior consent of the home Member State;
  - the contract of issue must allow the insurance undertaking to defer payment of interest;
  - they rank after the claims of all non-subordinated creditors;
  - the issue documents provide for the loss-absorption capacity of the debt and unpaid interest while enabling the undertaking to continue its business;
  - only fully paid-up amounts are taken into account.

617 Article 27(3). *Cf.* Directive 73/239, Article 16(3).

The third type of assets is items that are included upon the application of the undertaking to the home Member State.[618] The application must be accompanied by supporting evidence. It is up to the competent authorities of the home Member State to agree or not to their inclusion. These items consist of:

- until December 31, 2009, an amount equal to 50% of the undertaking's estimated future profits but not exceeding 25% of the lesser of the available and required solvency margins. The estimated annual profits may not exceed the arithmetical average of the profits made over the last five years in life insurance, marriage insurance, birth insurance, annuities, supplementary insurance connected with a life insurance policy and, in Ireland and the United Kingdom, permanent health insurance.

  The home Member State must require as a pre-condition of including the above amount that:

  - an actuarial report is submitted substantiating the likelihood of the realization of these future profits; and
  - future profits emerging from hidden net reserves referred to below have not already been taken into account;

- where Zillmerising is not used or, if used, is less than the loading for acquisition costs included in the premium, the difference between a non-Zillmerized or partially Zillmerized mathematical provision and a mathematical provision Zillmerized at a rate equal to the loading for acquisition costs included in the premium;

  This figure may not exceed 3.5% of the sum of the difference between the relevant capital sums of life insurance activities and the mathematical provisions for all policies for which Zillmerizing is possible. The difference must also be reduced by any undepreciated acquisition costs entered as an asset;

  - hidden net reserves arising out of the valuation of assets as long as these are not of an exceptional nature;
  - one half of the unpaid share capital or initial fund once 25% is paid up, up to 50% of the lesser of the available and required solvency margins.

Guarantee Fund

The home Member State must ensure that an insurance undertaking maintains a guarantee fund of at least 3 million Euros.[619] Home Member States are free to set a higher amount for the guarantee fund.[620] They may also reduce it to 1,250,000 Euros for mutual associations, mutual-type associations and tontines.[621] Starting on September 20, 2003, the minimum amount of the guarantee fund is to be reviewed

618 Article 27(4). *Cf.* Directive 73/239, Article 16(4).

619 Article 29(2), 1st subpara. *Cf.* Directive 73/239, Article 17(2), 1st subpara.

620 *See* Preamble, 28th recital.

621 Article 29(2), 2nd subpara. *Cf.* Directive 73/239, Article 17(2), 2nd subpara.

annually and revised, if necessary, in accordance with changes in the European index of consumer prices.[622] If the annual percentage change in the index is less than 5%, the fund remains unchanged.

Member States may allow insurance undertakings that at March 20, 2002 were carrying on in their territory any of the activities listed in Annex I to the Directive a period of five years to comply with the rules on the guarantee fund.[623]

One third of the required solvency margin constitutes the guarantee fund.[624] The assets making up the solvency margin that may be included in calculating the amount of the fund are the first two types of assets referred to above and, with the agreement of the home Member State, hidden net reserves arising out of the valuation of assets.

Qualifying Holdings

The home Member State must monitor qualifying holdings in an insurance undertaking under its supervision.[625] It must require natural or legal persons who propose to hold, directly or indirectly, a qualifying holding in an insurance undertaking or to increase their existing holding so as to obtain or exceed the thresholds of 20%, 33% or 50% of the voting rights or capital in the undertaking or so as to make it their subsidiary, must inform the home Member State, indicating the size of the intended holding.[626] Persons who fail to comply with the notification requirement may be subject to injunctions or other sanctions.[627] The home Member State has three months from the date of the notification in which to oppose the plan if it is not satisfied as to the qualification of the person concerned from the perspective of sound and prudent management of the undertaking.[628] If a holding is acquired despite this opposition, the home Member State must suspend or provide for the annulment of the voting rights of the holding.[629]

Insurance undertakings must inform home Member States, at least once a year, of the names of shareholders and members possessing qualifying holdings and the sizes of such holdings.[630] They must also inform their home Member State as soon as they become aware of any acquisitions that cause holdings to exceed the thresholds mentioned above.[631]

622 Article 30(1). *Cf.* Directive 73/239, Article 17a(1).b

623 Article 71(1).

624 Article 29(1). *Cf.* Directive 73/239, Article 17(1).

625 Article 15. *Cf.* Directive 92/49, Article 15.

626 Article 15(1), 1st subpara. *Cf.* Directive 92/49, Article 15(1), 1st subpara.

627 Article 15(4), 2nd subpara. *Cf.* Directive 92/49, Article 15(4), 2nd subpara.

628 Article 15(1), 2nd subpara. *Cf.* Directive 92/49, Article 15(1), 2nd subpara.

629 Article 15(4), 2nd subpara. *Cf.* Directive 92/49, Article 15(4), 2nd subpara.

630 Article 15(3), 2nd subpara. *Cf.* Directive 92/49, Article 15(3), 2nd subpara.

631 Article 15(3), 1st subpara. *Cf.* Directive 92/49, Article 15(3), 1st subpara.

Where a home Member State determines that the influence of any person with a qualifying holding is likely to operate to the detriment of the prudent and sound management of an insurance undertaking, it must take measures to deal with the situation, such as injunctions, other sanctions and suspending the voting rights attached to the qualifying holding in question.[632]

Persons wishing to dispose, directly or indirectly, of their qualifying holding in an insurance undertaking must similarly inform the home Member State of this fact and of the size of the holding.[633] Likewise, the home Member State must be informed by persons reducing their qualifying holding so that their share of the voting rights or capital of the undertaking falls below any one of the thresholds mentioned above or so that the undertaking ceases to be their subsidiary. The undertaking itself must also inform the competent authorities once it becomes aware of disposals that cause a holding to fall below these thresholds.[634]

Transfers of Portfolios

The transfer of all or part of the portfolios of contracts concluded by insurance undertakings in other Member States through their branches or by way of the provision of services to an accepting office established within the EU must be authorized by their home Member State subject to the following rules:

- the home Member State of the accepting office must certify that, after taking the transfer into account, the office possesses the necessary solvency margin.[535] This certificate cannot be accorded where an undertaking has been required to follow a financial recovery plan unless the competent authorities consider that the rights of policy-holders are no longer threatened;[636]
- where a branch is proposing the transfer of the portfolio, the host Member State of the branch is consulted;[637]
- the competent authorities of the Member State of the commitment agree to the transfer.[638]

Where Member States are consulted or asked for their consent, they must respond within three months; otherwise they are deemed to have given a favorable opinion or their consent, respectively.[639] In the event of a consultation, a favorable opinion is not, however, necessary.

632 Article 15(4), 1st subpara. *Cf.* Directive 92/49, Article 15(4), 1st subpara.

633 Article 15(2). *Cf.* Directive 92/49, Article 15(2).

634 Article 15(3), 1st subpara. *Cf.* Directive 92/49, Article 15(3), 1st subpara.

635 Article 14(1). *Cf.* Directive 92/49, Article 12(2).

636 Article 38(5). *Cf.* Directive 73/239, Article 20a(5).

637 Article 14(2). *Cf.* Directive 92/49, Article 12(3).

638 Article 14(3). *Cf.* Directive 92/49, Article 12(4).

639 Article 14(4). *Cf.* Directive 92/49, Article 12(5).

Consumer Protection

There are also some common rules in the area of consumer protection that we might as well discuss in the context of prudential supervision. Each Member State must prescribe a period of between fourteen and thirty days in which a policy-holder may cancel the insurance contract.[640] However, the legal effects and the conditions of cancellation are determined by national law.[641] Moreover, Member States need not apply the right of cancellation to contracts of six months duration or less or where the policy-holder does not need this special protection.[642]

Before an insurance contract can be validly concluded under the Directive, the following information must be communicated to the prospective client:[643]

- name of the insurance undertaking, its legal form, its home Member State and, where appropriate, the host Member State of the agency or branch concluding the contract, plus the address of the head office and, where appropriate, the agency or branch;
- definition of each benefit and option;
- terms of the contract;
- means of payment of premiums and duration of payments;
- means of calculation and distribution of bonuses;
- indication of surrender and paid-up values and extent to which they are guaranteed;
- information on premiums for each benefit;
- definition of units to which benefits are linked in unit-linked policies;
- nature of the underlying assets for unit-linked policies;
- applicable tax arrangements;
- complaints procedures.

Auditors

Home Member States must provide that the authorized auditors of insurance undertakings, as well as undertakings that have close links resulting from a control relationship with an insurance undertaking, have a duty to report to their competent authorities any fact or decision concerning the undertaking of which they become aware that is liable to:[644]

- constitute an infringement of the legal rules governing the authorization of or the pursuit of its activities by an insurance undertaking;

---

640 Article 35(1), 1st subpara.

641 Article 35(1), 3rd subpara.

642 Article 35(2).

643 Article 36(1). *Cf.* Directive 92/49, Article 31(1), but the wording is somewhat different.

644 Article 17(1). *Cf.* Directive 92/49, Article 16a(1).

- affect the continuous functioning of the insurance undertaking; or
- entail on the part of the auditor a refusal to certify the accounts of the undertaking or an expression of reservations.

The disclosure by auditors in good faith of such facts or decisions may not be treated as a breach of professional secrecy and may not involve such persons in liability of any kind.[645]

Professional Secrecy

Member States must provide that the confidentiality of information received by persons who are working or have worked for the competent authorities of Member States as well as by auditors or experts acting on behalf of these authorities is respected.[646] Confidential information may only be divulged in summary or aggregate form such that individual insurance undertakings cannot be identified. Exchange of information within and between Member States is also subject to the rules on professional secrecy.[647] Member States receiving confidential information may only use it to carry out their prudential and other duties, impose sanctions and in administrative appeals and court proceedings.

Simultaneous Activities

Where an insurance undertaking carries on simultaneously both the activities covered by the Directive (life insurance) and some or all of those covered by Directive 73/239 (direct insurance other than life insurance), the home Member State must ensure that the two sets of activity are managed separately in accordance with the provisions of the Directive.[648] These provisions call for the separate management to be organized in such a way that:[649]

- the respective interests of life policy holders and non-life policy holders are not prejudiced and, in particular, the profits from life insurance are used exclusively for the benefit of life policy holders;
- the minimum financial obligations, in particular solvency margins, in respect of one set of activities are not borne by the other set of activities. However, as long as the minimum financial obligations are met for each set, those items of the solvency margin that are still available may be used for one or the other set of activities. Also, where one of the solvency margins is deficient, the home Member State may authorize a transfer from one set of activities to another.[650]

The accounts of insurance companies carrying both sets of activities must be drawn up in such a manner as to show the sources of the results for each of the two

645 Article 17(2). *Cf.* Directive 92/49, Article 16a(2).

646 Article 16(1), 1st subpara. *Cf.* Directive 92/49, Article 16(1), 1st subpara.

647 Article 16(2) to (9). *Cf.* Directive 92/49, Article 16(2) to (6).

648 Article 18(3).

649 Article 19(1).

650 Article 19(3).

sets of activities.[651] Items making up the solvency margin of each set of activities must be clearly identified.[652]

5. Undertakings in Difficulty or in an Irregular Situation

Non-Compliance with Technical Provisions

If an insurance undertaking does not maintain sufficient technical provisions, the home Member State may prohibit the free disposal of its assets.[653] It must first communicate its intention to do so to the Member States of the commitment.

Failure to Maintain the Required Solvency Margin

Where the solvency margin of an insurance undertaking falls below the required minimum, the home Member State must require it to submit a plan to restore a sound financial position.[654] If the home Member State believes that the financial position of the undertaking will further deteriorate, it may also restrict or prohibit the free disposal of the undertaking's assets.[655] It must inform the host Member States of this measure and may request them to do the same. Each of the host Member States must take whatever measures are available to them under their national law to restrain the disposal of assets designated by the home Member State.[656]

If an undertaking does not, within the time allowed, take the measures specified in the restoration plan, the home Member State may withdraw its authorization.[657]

Failure to Maintain the Minimum Guarantee Fund

Where the solvency margin of an insurance undertaking falls below the required minimum guarantee fund, the home Member State must require it to submit a short-term finance scheme for its approval.[658] It may also restrict or prohibit the free disposal of the undertaking's assets. It must inform the host Member States of this measure and may request them to do the same. Each of the host Member States must take whatever measures are available to them under their national law to restrain the disposal of assets designated by the home Member State.[659]

---

651 Article 19(2)(a).

652 Article 19(2)(b).

653 Article 37(1). *Cf.* Directive 73/239, Article 20(1).

654 Article 37(2), 1st subpara. *Cf.* Directive 73/239, Article 20(2), 1st subbpara.

655 Article 37(2), 2nd subpara. *Cf.* Directive 73/239, Article 20(2), 2nd subpara.

656 Article 37(5).

657 Article 39(1)(c).

658 Article 37(3). *Cf.* Directive 73/239, Article 20(3).

659 Article 37(5). *Cf.* Directive 73/239, Article 20(5).

If an undertaking does not, within the time allowed, take the measures specified in the finance scheme, the home Member State may withdraw its authorization.[660]

Other Measures

In all three of the above situations, the home Member State may take all further measures that are necessary to safeguard the interests of insured persons.[661]

Financial Recovery Plan

The competent authorities of the home Member State must have the power to require an insurance undertaking to follow a financial recovery plan where they consider that its financial position places policy holders' rights in jeopardy.[662] As a minimum, the plan must include for the next three financial years[663] particulars or proof of the following items:

- estimates of management expenses;
- detailed estimates of income and expenditure in respect of direct business, re-insurance acceptances and re-insurance cessions;
- forecast balance sheet;
- estimates of the financial resources intended to cover underwriting liabilities and the required solvency margin;
- overall re-insurance policy.

Where the financial position of the undertaking is deteriorating, the competent authorities must also have the power to increase the required solvency margin for an undertaking in order to ensure that it is able to fulfill the solvency requirements in the near future.[664] The level of this higher margin is based on the financial recovery plan. In addition, they must have the power to re-value downwards all elements eligible for the available solvency margin and to decrease the reduction, based on re-insurance, to the required solvency margin.[665]

There is no provision under the Directive for the home Member State to withdraw the authorization of an undertaking that fails to follow a financial recovery plan. However, it is free to do so under its own laws pursuant to Article 39(1)(d).

660 Article 39(1)(c).

661 Article 37(4).

662 Article 38(1). *Cf.* Directive 73/239, Article 20a(1).

663 Under Article 71(1), this period may be extended to five years for insurance undertakings that were carrying on business on March 20, 2002.

664 Article 38(2). *Cf.* Directive 73/239, Article 20a(2).

665 Article 38(3) and (4). *Cf.* Directive 73/239, Article 20a(3) and (4).

6. International Aspects

Establishment of Branches or Agencies in the European Union belonging to Undertakings whose Head Offices are outside the EU

A Member State must require any undertaking whose head office is situated outside the EU (a "foreign undertaking") to obtain an authorization before it may carry on in that Member State, through a branch or agency, any of the activities covered by the Directive.[666] The authorization is given for that Member State alone and is subject to the foreign undertaking meeting at least the following conditions:[667]

- it is entitled to carry on these activities under its national law;
- it undertakes to establish at the place of management of the branch or agency accounts specific to the activity that it carries on there and to keep proper records;
- it designates a general representative who is approved by the authorizing Member State;
- it possesses in the authorizing Member State assets of an amount equal in value to at least one half of the minimum amount of the guarantee fund (i.e. 1.5 million Euros) and deposits one quarter of this amount as security;
- it complies with the solvency rules that apply to it;[668]
- it submits a scheme of operations similar to that required for EU undertakings.[669]

In contrast to the rule with respect to EU insurance undertakings, the authorizing Member State may require from foreign undertakings systematic notification of the technical bases used for calculating premiums and technical provisions. However, this requirement may not be used as a prior condition for according an authorization.

Solvency Margins and Guarantee Fund

Foreign undertakings are required to establish a solvency margin consisting of the same items as for EU insurance undertakings.[670] A minimum solvency margin is calculated for them in the same way as the required solvency margin for EU insurance undertakings,[671] but only operations effected by the branch or agency concerned are taken into account. One third of this minimum solvency margin

666 Article 51(1). *Cf.* Directive 73/239, Article 23(1).

667 Article 51(2). *Cf.* Directive 73/239, Article 23(2).

668 *See infra* in the text.

669 *Ibid.*

670 Article 55(1). *Cf.* Directive 73/239, Article 25(1).

671 *See* Article 28 and *supra* in the text.

constitutes the guarantee fund, which may not be less than 1.5 million Euros.[672] However, the initial deposit that must be lodged as security counts towards the guarantee fund. Assets representing one third of the minimum solvency margin must be kept within the authorizing Member State, but the excess may be kept elsewhere in the EU.[673]

Types of Activity

As a general principle, the Directive prohibits foreign undertakings from carrying on simultaneously activities under both the Directive and Directive 73/239 relating to direct insurance other than life insurance.[674] However, the authorizing Member State may permit foreign undertakings that were carrying on these activities simultaneously in a Member State on March 15, 1979[675] to continue to do so provided that each activity is managed separately in accordance with the rules for EU insurance undertakings benefiting from the same exception.[676] Where the authorizing Member State requires EU insurance undertakings to cease, within a certain time period, the simultaneous pursuit of both types of activities, it must apply this requirement to foreign undertakings.[677]

Transfers of Portfolios

The authorizing Member State may authorize, in accordance with its national law, a foreign undertaking to transfer all or part of its portfolio of contracts elsewhere under the following conditions:[678]

- to an accepting office within the authorizing Member State itself provided that its competent authorities, or those of the Member State supervising the foreign undertaking,[679] certify that, after taking the transfer into account, the accepting office possesses the necessary solvency margin;
- to an insurance undertaking with a head office in another Member State if the competent authorities of that Member State certify that, after taking the transfer into account, the accepting office possesses the necessary solvency margin;
- to a foreign undertaking authorized in another Member State provided that the competent authorities of that State, or those of the Member State supervising the foreign undertaking, certify that, after taking the transfer into account, the accepting office possesses the necessary solvency margin, that the law of the

672 Article 55(2). *Cf.* Directive 73/239, Article 25(2).

673 Article 55(3). *Cf.* Directive 73/239, Article 25(3).

674 Article 52(1)(a).

675 The date for Greece is January 1, 1981, January 1, 1986 for Spain and Portugal, January 1, 1995 for Austria, Finland and Sweden and May 1, 2004 for Czech Republic, Estonia, Cyprus, Latvia, Lithuania, Hungary, Malta, Poland, Slovenia and Slovakia.

676 Article 52(1)(b). *See also* Article 19 and *supra* in the text.

677 Article 52(1)(c).

678 Article 53(1) to (3). *Cf.* Directive 73/239, Article 28a(1) to (3).

679 *See* Article 56(2) and *infra* in the text. *Cf.* Directive 73/239, Article 26(2).

Member State of the accepting office permits such a transfer and that it has agreed to the transfer.

In all three situations, the authorizing Member State must first obtain the agreement of the Member State of the commitment where this is different from the authorizing Member State.[680]

Technical Provisions

The rules on technical provisions set out in Article 20 of the Directive apply to foreign undertakings.[681] However, an important difference is that assets covering these provisions must be localized in the authorizing Member State except where technical provisions are allowed to be covered by claims against re-assurers.

Possibility of European-wide Treatment

A foreign undertaking that is authorized in more than one Member State may apply to be treated in a more European-wide way.[682] This entails the following advantages:

- the solvency margin is calculated in relation to the entire business carried on by the undertaking within the EU;
- the deposit of one quarter of the minimum amount of the guarantee fund is lodged in only one authorizing Member State;
- the assets representing the guarantee fund may be localized in any of the Member States in which the undertaking carries on business.

The application is made to each of the authorizing Member States and must include a reasoned choice as to the authorizing Member State that in future will be solely responsible for supervising the solvency of the whole business of the foreign undertaking.[683] All the authorizing Member States must accept the application, and the Member State chosen to supervise the foreign undertaking must agree to do so.[684]

At the request of one or more of the authorizing Member States, European-wide treatment must be withdrawn by all the concerned Member States.[685] Where the supervising Member State withdraws its authorization, it must inform the other Member States where the foreign undertaking does business, and they must take

680 Article 53(4). *Cf.* Directive 73/239, Article 28(4).

681 Article 54. *Cf.* Directive 73/239, Article 24.

682 Article 56(1). *Cf.* Directive 73/239, Article 26(1).

683 Article 56(2). *Cf.* Directive 73/239, Article 26(2).

684 Article 56(3). *Cf.* Directive 73/239, Article 26(3).

685 Article 56(4). *Cf.* Directive 73/239, Article 26(4).

appropriate measures.[686] If the withdrawal results from the inadequacy of the solvency margin, all other Member States must also withdraw their authorizations.

Relations with Foreign Countries

Member States must inform the Commission where they authorize an insurance undertaking that is the subsidiary of a parent undertaking based in a third country, or where such a parent undertaking acquires a holding that renders an EU insurance undertaking its subsidiary.[687] This provision is not controversial, but the Directive also contains some reciprocity provisions that have caused some concern outside the EU.

In the first place, the Member States are required to inform the Commission of any difficulties encountered by their insurance undertakings in establishing themselves or carrying on life insurance activities in third countries.[688] On the basis of this information and its own research, the Commission is required to draw up periodically a report on the treatment accorded to EU insurance undertakings in third countries as regards establishment, the carrying-on of life insurance activities and the acquisition of holdings in third-country insurance undertakings.[689]

Whenever, on the basis of these reports or other information, it appears to the Commission that a third country is not granting EU insurance undertakings effective market access comparable to that available in the EU to insurance undertakings from that third country, the Commission may propose to the Council that it open negotiations to rectify the situation.[690] The Council makes the final decision. The Directive does not provide for any sanctions in this situation.

The Directive is more radical where it appears to the Commission that, in a third country, EU insurance undertakings do not receive national treatment offering the same competitive opportunities as for domestic insurance undertakings and that the conditions of effective market access are also not fulfilled.[691] In this situation, the Commission may start negotiations with the third country on its own initiative. In addition, it may require Member States to limit or suspend the authorization of insurance undertakings and the acquisition of holdings in EU insurance undertakings involving undertakings based in the third country in question. The duration of these retaliatory measures may not exceed three months unless the Council, bearing in mind the results of the negotiations initiated by the Commission, decides to continue them. The limitations or suspensions do not apply to the setting up of subsidiaries or the acquisition of holdings in EU insurance undertakings by for-

686 Article 52(3). *Cf.* Directive 73/239, Article 28.

687 Article 58. *Cf.* Directive 73/239, Article 29a.

688 Article 59(1). *Cf.* Directive 73/239, Article 29b(1).

689 Article 59(2). *Cf.* Directive 73/239, Article 29b(2).

690 Article 59(3). *Cf.* Directive 73/239, Article 29b(3).

691 Article 59(4). *Cf.* Directive 73/239, Article 29b(4).

eign undertakings already authorized in the EU. Any retaliatory measures must also comply with the EU's international obligations.[692]

D. THE INVESTMENT SERVICES REGIME OF THE EUROPEAN UNION EP/Council Directive 2004/39 on markets in financial instruments, OJ L145/04

1. Introduction

Overview

There is separate legislation in the EU on investment services in general and the activities of collective investment undertakings.[693] However, the overall approach is the same for both, and in this monograph we take Directive 04/39 as the model. Citations are given, however, for the equivalent provisions of Directive 85/611, which regulates UCITS.[694] Directive 04/39 also covers regulated markets[695] and multilateral trading facilities,[696] but this monograph is concerned exclusively with the performance of investment services.

The EU[697] investment services regime resides on the principles of mutual recognition, one-state prudential supervision, cooperation between the competent authorities[698] of the Member States and a common approach to third countries.[699] Investment firms authorized in a Member State can obtain a single license that enables them to pursue their activities throughout the EU, either through a branch or by way of provision of services, on the basis of this one authorization. The Mem-

692 Article 59(6). *Cf.* Directive 73/239, Article 29b(6).

693 This the European term for mutual funds. The full name is "undertaking for collective investment in transferable securities" or UCITS.

694 Council Directive 85/611 on the coordination of laws, regulations and administrative provisions relating to undertakings for collective investments in transferable securities, OJ L375/85.

695 A "regulated market" is defined in Article 4(14) as a multilateral system operated and/or managed by a market operator, which may be the regulated market itself, that brings together or facilitates the bringing together of multiple third-party buyers and sellers of financial instruments and which is authorized by a Member State pursuant to the Directive.

696 A "multilateral trading facility" is defined in Article 4(15) as a multilateral system, operated by an investment firm or a market operator, which brings together multiple third-party buying and selling interests in financial instruments in a way that results in a contract under the term of the Directive.

697 Directive 04/39 is enacted pursuant to the European Community Treaty and references in it are to the "Community" rather than the European Union (EU). However, the Community is part of the EU and it seems simpler to refer to it as such. Under the new European Constitution, the term "EU" will supplant completely the term "Community."

698 "Competent authorities" means the public authorities that are designated by a Member State to carry out the duties imposed on Member States by the Directive (Article 48(1)). In the text, I have normally referred simply to the "Member States" when their competent authorities are meant.

699 A "third country" is a country that is not a Member State of the EU.

ber State that authorizes an investment firm is called the "home Member State"[700] and is largely responsible for the prudential supervision of all its activities within the EU. However, host Member States, which is where an investment firm authorized elsewhere in the EU has a branch or provides services,[701] supervise certain matters pertaining to investor protection in the case of branches.[702]

Scope

The EU investment services regime applies primarily to investment firms that are legal persons whose regular business involves the provision of one or more investment services[703] on a professional basis.[704] Unincorporated undertakings may be included by Member States provided that their legal status ensures an equivalent level of protection for third party interests and they are subject to appropriate prudential supervision.[705] However, where natural persons provide services involving the holding of the funds or transferable securities of third parties, they are only covered by the Directive if they comply with the following conditions:[706]

- the ownership rights of third parties in instruments and funds must be safeguarded;
- the firm must be subject to rules designed to monitor the firm's solvency and that of its owners;
- the firm's annual accounts must be audited by qualified auditors;
- where the firm has only one owner, there is provision for the protection of investors in the event of his/her death, incapacity or other similar event.

Certain provisions of the Directive also apply to credit institutions authorized under the EU banking regime pursuant to Directive 00/12[707] when they provide investment services. These are indicated in footnotes.

The Directive does not apply to the following:[708]

- insurance undertakings;
- investment services provided for parent or subsidiary undertakings;

700 Article 5(1). *Cf.* Directive 85/611, Article 5(1).

701 Article 4(21). *Cf.* Directive 85/611, Article 1a(6).

702 Article 32(7).

703 The Directive distinguishes between investment services and investment activities, but as both are included without distinction in Section A of Annex I, I refer throughout just to "investment services."

704 Article 4(1)(1), 1st subpara.

705 Article 4(1)(1), 2nd subpara.

706 Article 4(1)(1), 3rd subpara.

707 EP/Council Directive 00/12 relating to the taking up and pursuit of the business of credit institutions (OJ L126/00).

708 Article 2(1).

- investment services provided as an incidence of a regulated professional activity;
- persons dealing exclusively on own account;
- administration of employee-participation schemes;
- management of the public debt by the European System of Central Banks[709] and other public bodies;
- collective investment undertakings and pension funds;
- investment services in commodity derivatives and certain derivative contracts that are ancillary to the main business of the firm where this business is not the provision of investment or banking services;
- non-remunerated investment advice provided as an incidence of another professional activity;
- certain Danish, Finnish and Italian associations and agents.

In addition, Member States may choose not to apply the Directive to persons that:[710]

- are not allowed to hold clients' funds or securities or place themselves in debit with their clients;
- only receive and transmit orders in transferable securities and mutual fund units and provide investment advice in this context; and
- in providing this service, may only transmit orders to authorized investment firms or credit institutions, branches of investment firms and credit institutions authorized in a third country, collective investment undertakings and investment companies with fixed capital

provided that the activities of such persons are regulated at national level.

Investment services mean any of the following activities:[711]

- reception and transmission of orders in relation to one or more of the financial instruments;
- execution of orders on behalf of clients;
- portfolio management;
- investment advice;
- underwriting of financial instruments and/or the placing of financial instruments on a firm commitment basis;

709 The ECSB is composed of the European Central Bank and the national central banks of the Member States of the EU.

710 Article 3(1).

711 Annex I, Section A.

- placing of financial instruments without a firm commitment basis;
- operation of multilateral trading facilities.

Investment services also include certain other ancillary services, which may, however, not be supplied on their own. These services comprise:[712]

- safekeeping and administration of financial instruments;
- granting credits or loans to investors for transactions in financial instruments in which the firm is involved;
- advice to undertakings on such matters as capital structure and strategy;
- services relating to mergers and the purchase of undertakings;
- foreign exchange services connected with the provision of investment services;
- investment research and financial analysis;
- underwriting services;
- services related to the underlying of certain derivatives.

The financial instruments that may be the subject of the provision of investment services comprise the following:[713]

- transferable securities;
- money-market instruments;
- units in collective investment undertakings;
- certain options, futures, swaps, forward rate agreements and other derivative contracts relating to securities, currencies, interest rates, commodities, climatic variables, freight rates, emission allowances, inflation rates and other official economic statistics;
- derivative instruments for the transfer of credit risk;
- financial contracts for differences.

National Law

The EU investment services regime does not entirely replace the national systems. National law may still apply but is subject to the EU rules on authorization, prudential supervision and freedom of movement. Unlike the banking and insurance directives, Directive 04/39 does not, as a general principle, allow Member States to establish stricter national rules, but on occasion it leaves the Member States some measure of discretion in the implementation of its own rules.

712 Annex I, Section B.

713 Annex I, Section C.

2. Authorization of Investment Firms

General Provisions

Investment firms must obtain an authorization from their home Member State before commencing their activities.[714] In the case of a legal person, this is where the investment firm has its registered office or, if it has no registered office *under the applicabl*e national law, its head office.[715] In the case of investment firms that are natural persons, the home Member State is where they have their head office.[716] Authorized credit institutions do not need an authorization to provide investment services unless this is a new form of activity.[717]

The authorization provisions of the Directive apply to the branches and direct and indirect subsidiaries of investment firms governed by the law of third countries, but the former may only provide services in the Member State that authorizes them.[718]

The authorization specifies the investment services that the investment firm is authorized to provide.[719] It may cover one or more ancillary services, but it may not grant an authorization solely for the purpose of providing such services.[720] An investment firm that wishes to extend it business to additional primary or ancillary services must apply for an extension of its authorization unless the additional service is not performed on a regular basis.[721]

In order to obtain an authorization, credit institutions must meet the national requirements of the home Member State as well as the requirements set out by the Directive.

National Requirements

National requirements for granting an authorization must be consistent with the rules of the Directive. No particular national rules are singled out as incompatible with the Directive. On the other hand, certain national provisions that derogate from the requirements of the Directive are permitted.

Requirements under the Directive

The home Member State may not grant an authorization until it is fully satisfied that the investment firm complies with all the requirements set out in the

---

714 Article 5(1). *Cf.* Directive 85/611, Articles 4(1), 1st subpara., 5(1) and 12(1).

715 Article 4(20)(a)(ii) and (iii). *Cf.* Directive 85/611, Article 1a(5).

716 Article 4(20)(a)(i).

717 Preamble, 18th recital.

718 Preamble, 28th recital. *See* too Article 15.

719 Article 6(1).

720 *Cf.* Directive 85/611, Article 5(3), 2nd subpara.

721 Article 6(2) and Preamble, 19th recital.

Directive.[722] The investment firm must provide a program of operations setting out *inter alia* the types of business envisaged and the organizational structure in order to demonstrate such compliance.[723]

The requirements of the Directive that must be met before an authorization may be granted are the following:

1. The investment firm must be managed by at least two persons who are of sufficiently good repute and possess sufficient experience to ensure the sound and prudent management of the firm.[724] The home Member State must refuse authorization if this is not the case.[725] However, a home Member State may authorize, in accordance with its national law, an investment firm that is a natural person or a legal person managed by a single natural person as long as it has provisions in place to ensure sound and prudent management.[726]

2. Home Member States may not grant an authorization to an investment firm before its competent authorities have been informed of the identities of the shareholders or members, whether direct or indirect, that have qualifying holdings[727] and the amounts of these holdings.[728] The home Member State must refuse authorization if it is not satisfied as to the suitability of these shareholders or members with respect to the need to ensure the sound and prudent management of the investment firm.[729]

3. Where close links[730] exist between an investment firm and other natural or legal persons, authorization can only be accorded if these links do not prevent the proper supervision of the credit institution.[731] This is a particularly important is-

722 Article 7(1).

723 Article 7(2). *Cf.* Directive 85/611, Articles 5a(1)(c) and 13a(1), 2nd subpara., 1st indent.

724 Article 9(1) and(4), 1st subpara. *Cf.* Directive 85/611, Articles 4(3), 2nd subpara., 5a(1)(6) and 13a(1), 2nd subpara., 2nd indent.

725 Article 7(3).

726 Article 9(4), 2nd subpara.

727 A "qualifying holdings" is defined in Article 4(1)(27) as a direct or indirect holding in an undertaking that represents 10% or more of its capital or voting rights or which makes it possible to exercise a significant influence over the management of the undertaking. *Cf.* Directive 85/611, Article 1a(10).

728 Article 10(1), 1st subpara. *Cf.* Directive 85/611, Article 5b(1), 1st subpara.

729 Article 10(1), 2nd subpara. *Cf.* Directive 85/611, Article 5b(1), 2nd subpara.

730 "Close links" are defined by Article 1(1)(26) as a situation where two or more legal or natural persons are linked by a participation (i.e. ownership, direct or by way of control, of 20% or more of the voting rights or capital of an undertaking) or control in the sense of the relationship between a parent undertaking and a subsidiary as defined in Council Directive 83/349 on consolidated accounts (OJ L193/83) or a similar relationship between any natural or legal person and an undertaking. *Cf.* Directive 85/611, Article 1a(9).

731 Article 10(1), 3rd subpara. *Cf.* Directive 85/611, Articles 5a(2), 1st subpara. and 13a(1), 2nd subpara., 3rd indent.

sue where the close links are with natural or legal persons subject to the laws of a third country.[732]

4. The investment firm must be a member of an authorized investor-compensation scheme[733] at the time of authorization.[734]

5. The investment firm must have sufficient initial capital in accordance with Directive 93/6, having regard to the nature of the services that it provides.[735] The minimum amount of initial capital is set as a general rule at 730,000 Euros but, for certain types of firms or investment services, it may be reduced to 125,000 or 50,000 Euros. However, Member States may continue the authorization of investment firms in existence before the application of Directive 93/6 that do not meet these initial capital requirements, but the own funds of these firms must not fall below the average daily level of own funds calculated over a six-month period preceding the date of calculation.[736]

6. Investment firms that have a registered office in the home Member State must also have their head office in this Member State.[737] Investment firms that have only a head office in their home Member State must also carry on business there.[738]

7. An authorization should not be granted to an investment firm where such factors as the content of the programs of operations or the geographical distribution of the firm's activities indicate clearly that the institution has opted for authorization in the Member State in question for the purpose of evading the stricter standards in force in the Member State where it intends to carry on the greater part of its activities.[739]

Decisions on the grant of an authorization should be taken within six months of receiving the application and the applicant informed.[740] A decision to refuse an authorization must be properly reasoned.[741] Member States must ensure that decisions relating to authorizations are subject to a right of appeal to the courts, with respect both to a refusal and a failure to respect the six-month time limit.

Investment firms already authorized in their home Member State before April 30, 2006 are deemed to be authorized under the Directive if the laws of their home

732 Article 10(2). *Cf.* Directive 85/611, Articles 5a(2), 2nd subpara. and 13a(1), 3rd subpara.

733 Pursuant to EP/Council Directive 97/9 on investor-compensation schemes (OJ L84/97).

734 Article 11. This provision also applies to credit institutions.

735 Council Directive 93/6 on the capital adequacy of investment firms and credit institutions (OJ L141/93), as amended by Directives 98/31 (OJ L204/98) and 04/39 (OJ L145/04), Article 3. *Cf.* Directive 85/611, Articles 5(4), 5a(1)(a) and 13a(1), 1st subpara.

736 Directive 93/6, Article 3(5).

737 Article 5(4), 1st indent. *Cf.* Directive 85/611, Articles 3 and 5a(1)(c).

738 Article 5(4), 2nd indent.

739 Preamble, 22nd recital.

740 Article 7(3). *Cf.* Directive 85/611, Articles 5a(3) and 13a(2).

741 Article 52(1).

Member State required them to comply with conditions comparable to those imposed by the Directive.[742]

Withdrawal of an Authorization

A home Member State may withdraw an authorization from an investment firm in the following circumstances:[743]

- where the authorization is not used within 12 months or is renounced or where the investment firm has ceased to engage in business for more than six months;
- where the firm obtained the authorization by fraudulent or other irregular means, which would seem to cover the situation where an authorization was obtained for the purpose of evading the stricter standards in force in the Member State where the investment firm carries on the greater part of its activities;[744]
- where the firm no longer meets the conditions for an authorization, such the initial capital requirements or where close links prevent proper supervision;
- where firm has seriously and systematically infringed national provisions adopted pursuant to this Directive governing its operating conditions;
- where national law provides for withdrawal.

Home Member States are required to monitor the compliance of investment firms with their conditions for initial authorization.[745] Firms must be required to notify the competent authorities of any material changes in this regard. In particular, they are required to notify any changes in their management and to provide information needed to assess whether the new persons are of sufficiently good repute and possess sufficient experience.[746] Where there are objective and demonstrable grounds for believing that these changes pose a threat to the sound and prudent management of the firm, the authorization may be withdrawn.[747]

Reasons must be given for a decision to withdraw an authorization, and the investment firm must be able to appeal the decision to the courts.[748]

3. Liberalization

General Provisions

Investment firms duly authorized in their home Member State are free to carry on any of the activities for they have been authorized, either through a branch or by

742 Article 71(1). This provision also applies to credit institutions.

743 Article 8. *Cf.* Directive 85/611, Articles 5a(5) and 13a(4).

744 The 22nd recital of the Preamble requires that an authorization be withdrawn in this situation.

745 Article 16(1) and (2). This provision applies to credit institutions. *Cf.* Directive 85/611, Article 5d(1).

746 Article 9(2). *Cf.* Directive 85/611, Article 13a(2).

747 This, at least, would seem to be the implication of Article 9(3).

748 Article 52(1). *Cf.* Directive 85/611, Article 51(2).

way of the provision of services, in all Member States of the EU without the imposition of any additional requirements by the host Member State.[749] Ancillary services may only be provided together with an investment service.[750]

Investment firms have a specific right of membership in or access to regulated markets in the host Member State.[751] They must also have the right of access to central counterparty, clearing and settlement systems in host Member States on the basis of non-discriminatory, transparent and objective criteria.[752] Host Member States may not restrict the use of such facilities to the clearing and settlement of transactions in financial instruments undertaken on a regulated market or multilateral trading facility in their territory. However, operators of these facilities may refuse the requested services on legitimate commercial grounds.[753]

Freedom of Establishment

All that an investment firm is required to do in order to carry on its activities under the Directive through a branch in another Member State is to notify its home Member State and provide the following information:[754]

- the Member State where it plans to establish the branch;
- a program of operations setting out *inter alia* the investment services and ancillary services to be offered and the organizational structure of the branch;
- the address in the host Member State from which documents may be obtained,
- the names of those responsible for the management of the branch.

It is the responsibility of the home Member State to communicate this information to the host Member State within three months as well as details of the accredited compensation scheme of which the investment firm is a member.[755] It is only if the home Member State has doubts about the adequacy of the administrative structure or the financial situation of the investment firm that it may refuse to communicate the information to the host Member State. It must give reasons for such refusal to the firm within three months.[756] The refusal is subject to a right of appeal to the courts.[757]

---

749 Articles 6(3), 31(1), and 32(1). Articles 31(1) and 32(1) also apply to credit institutions. *Cf.* Directive 85/611, Articles 4(1), 2nd subpara. and 6.

750 Articles 31(1), 1st indent and 32(1), 1st indent. This provision also applies to credit institutions.

751 Article 33(1). This provision also applies to credit institutions.

752 Article 34(1). This provision also applies to credit institutions.

753 Article 34(3). This provision also applies to credit institutions.

754 Article 32(2). *Cf.* Directive 85/611, Article 6a(1) and (2).

755 Article 32(3). *Cf.* Directive 85/611, Article 6a(3), 1st subpara.

756 Article 32(5). *Cf.* Directive 85/611, Article 6a(3), 2nd subpara.

757 Article 52(1). *Cf.* Directive 85/611, Article 6a(3), 2nd subpara.

The host Member State may not impose any additional requirements on the organization and operation of the branch.[758] It may only acknowledge the communication from the home Member State, whereupon the branch may be established and commence business.[759] Failing a communication from the host Member State within two months, the same may occur.

Freedom to Provide Services

An investment firm wishing to provide services in another Member State for the first time or to change the range of services that it provides there, must inform the home Member State of the identity of the host Member State and provide a program of operations stating in particular the primary and ancillary services that it intends to carry on.[760] The home Member State must send this information to the competent authorities of the host Member State within one month.[761] The firm may then start to provide services.

The procedure is simpler than for the establishment of a branch. In particular, there is no provision for the home Member State to refuse to send the information to the host Member State, and the investment firm does not have to wait for any communication from the host Member State before commencing its activities.

4. Prudential Supervision

General Provisions

The main responsibility for the prudential supervision of the activities of an investment firm within the EU lies with the home Member State.[762] This supervision involves monitoring continuing compliance with the conditions for initial authorization, the rules on qualifying holdings and the operating conditions.[763] In the case of branches operating in another Member State, however, the operating conditions are largely monitored by the host Member State. All the prudential rules discussed below apply as well to credit institutions providing investment services.[764]

The home Member State must require investment firms to establish adequate policies and procedures to ensure compliance with its obligations under the Directive.[765] It must also have them put in place sound administrative and accounting procedures, internal control mechanisms, effective procedures for risk assessment and effective control and safeguard arrangements for information processing sys-

758 Article 32(1), 2nd subpara. *Cf.* Directive 85/611, Article 6(2).

759 Article 32(1), 2nd subpara. and (6). *Cf.* Directive 85/611, Article 6a(4) and (5).

760 Article 31(2). *Cf.* Directive 85/611, Article 6b(1).

761 Article 31(3). *Cf.* Directive 85/611, Article 6b(2).

762 Article 16(1). *Cf.* Directive 85/611, Article 5d(2).

763 Articles 16 and 17. *Cf.* Directive 85/611, Article 5d(1).

764 Article 1(2), 2nd indent.

765 Article 13(2). *Cf.* Directive 85/611, Article 5(4).

tems.[766] Investment firms must be required to keep records of all services and transactions that are sufficient to enable the competent authorities to monitor compliance with the Directive, in particular with respect to its obligations towards clients.[767] Relevant data relating to all transactions in financial instruments have to be kept at the disposal of the authorities for at least five years.[768] In the case of such transactions carried out on behalf of clients, the records must contain information on the identity of the client and the other information required under the Directive on money laundering.[769] It is up to the host Member State to enforce these recording obligations with respect to branches of investment firms from other Member States operating in their territory.[770]

Host Member States may require branches of investment firms from other Member States to provide the information necessary to enable it to carry out its supervisory duties with respect to operating conditions.[771] These requirements may not be more stringent that those applied to domestic investment firms. Host Member States may also require the branches of investment firms from other Member States to comply with the provisions of the Directive with respect to those matters for which it has the prudential responsibility.[772] If an investment firm fails to take the necessary steps, the host Member State make eventually take measures to prevent or penalize further irregularities, including stopping the firm from initiating any further transactions in its territory.

Where, a host Member State is not responsible for prudential supervision of the particular conduct in question but has good reason to believe that an investment firm is acting within its territory in a manner contrary to the provisions of the Directive, it must inform the home Member State, which shall take appropriate action.[773] If, despite the measures taken by the home Member State, the investment firm persists in its illegal activity, the host Member State, after informing the home Member State, may take whatever measures are needed to protect investors and ensure the proper functioning of the market.[774] These include preventing the firm from initiating any further transactions in its territory.

Member States must ensure that their competent authorities are able to monitor the activities of investment firms to make sure that they act honestly, fairly and pro-

---

766 Article 13(5), 2nd subpara. *Cf.* Directive 85/611, Articles 5(4), 5f(1)(a) and 13c, 2nd subpara.

767 Article 13(6). *Cf.* Directive 85/611, Article 5(4).

768 Article 25(2).

769 Council Directive 91/308 on the use of the financial system for the purpose of money laundering (OJ L166/91).

770 Articles 13(9), 25(6) and 32(7). *Cf.* Directive 85/611, Article 5(4).

771 Article 61(2). *Cf.* Directive 85/611, Article 6c(2).

772 Article 62(2). *Cf.* Directive 85/611, Article 6c(3) to (5).

773 Articles 25(4) and 62(1), 1st subpara.

774 Article 62(1), 2nd subpara.

fessionally, and in a manner that promotes the integrity of the market.[775] They must also make it possible for appropriate administrative measures or sanctions to be taken against the persons responsible in cases of non-compliance with the provisions of the Directive.[776] The competent authorities of the Member States must cooperate within the Member States and between them, including with respect to on-the-spot verifications.[777]

Member States must ensure that any decisions taken by them in pursuance of their supervisory duties are properly reasoned and subject to a right of appeal to the courts.[778]

Qualifying Holdings[779]

The home Member State must monitor qualifying holdings in an investment firm.[780] It must require natural or legal persons who propose to hold, directly or indirectly, a qualifying holding in an investment firm or to increase their existing holding so as to obtain or exceed the thresholds of 20%, 33% or 50% of the voting rights or capital in the investment firm or so as to make it their subsidiary, to inform the home Member State, indicating the size of the intended holding.[781] Persons who fail to comply with the notification requirement may be subject to injunctions or other sanctions.[782] The home Member State has three months from the date of the notification in which to oppose the plan if it is not satisfied as to the suitability of the person concerned from the perspective of sound and prudent management of the investment firm.[783] If a holding is acquired despite opposition, the home Member State must suspend or provide for the annulment of the voting rights of the holding.[784]

Investment firms must inform home Member States, at least once a year, of the names of shareholders and members possessing qualifying holdings and the sizes of such holdings.[785] They must also be required to inform their home Member

775 Article 25(1).

776 Article 51(1).

777 Articles 49, 56(1), 57 and 58. *Cf.* Directive 85/611, Article 52a(1).

778 Article 52(1).

779 Some of the provisions on qualifying holdings have been discussed in connection with authorization, but the following provisions more correctly belong to the area of prudential supervision.

780 Article 10(3) to (6). *Cf.* Directive 85/611, Article 5e(1).

781 Article 10(3), 1st subpara.

782 Article 10(6), 3rd subpara.

783 Article 10(3), 2nd subpara.

784 Article 10(6), 3rd subpara.

785 Article 10(5), 2nd subpara.

State as soon as they become aware of any acquisitions that cause holdings to exceed the thresholds mentioned above.[786]

Where a home Member State determines that the influence of any person with a qualifying holding is likely to operate to the detriment of the prudent and sound management of the investment firm, it shall take measures to deal with the situation, such as injunctions, other sanctions and suspending the voting rights attached to the qualifying holding in question.[787]

Persons wishing to dispose, directly or indirectly, of their qualifying holding in an investment firm or to reduce it below any one of the thresholds mentioned above or so that the institution ceases to be their subsidiary, must similarly inform the home Member State of this fact and of the size of the holding.[788] The institution itself must also inform the competent authorities once it becomes aware of disposals that cause a holding to fall below these thresholds.[789]

Operating Conditions

Investor protection

1. Conflicts of interest. The home Member State must require investment firms to take all reasonable steps to identify conflicts of interest between the firm or any person linked to them by control and their clients, and between the clients themselves.[790] Where a firm's arrangements to manage such conflicts are not sufficient to ensure, with reasonable confidence, that risks of damage to client interests will be prevented, the firm must clearly disclose the general nature and/or sources of conflicts of interest to the client before undertaking business on its behalf.[791]

2. Conduct of business. The home Member State or, in the case of branches in another Member State, the host Member State[792] must require an investment firm to act honestly, fairly and professionally in accordance with the best interests of its clients and the following principles:[793]

- information provided to clients must be fair, clear and not misleading;
- information must be provided in a standardized format about the firm, financial instruments and proposed investment strategies, including any associated risks, execution venues and costs;

786 Article 10(5), 1st subpara.

787 Article 10(6), 1st and 2nd subparas. *Cf.* Directive 85/611, Article 51(2).

788 Article 10(3), 1st subpara.

789 Article 10(5), 1st subpara.

790 Article 18(1). *Cf.* Directive 85/611, Article 5f(1)(b).

791 Article 18(2). *See also* Article 13(3).

792 Article 32(7).

793 Article 19. *Cf.* Directive 85/611, Article 5(4).

- when providing investment advice or portfolio management, information must be obtained about the client's knowledge and experience in the investment field, his/her financial situation and investment objectives; or
- in other cases, except some instances where the services consist only of the execution and/or the reception and transmission of client orders, the client must be asked to provide information about his/her knowledge and experience in the investment field;
- where a client elects not to provide the requested information or does not do so fully, he/she must be warned in a standardized format that the firm cannot determine whether a particular service or product is appropriate for him/her;
- clients must be warned in a standardized format where a particular investment product or service is not appropriate for them;
- a record must be kept of client transactions that includes the document setting out the rights and obligations of the client and the firm;
- the client must receive adequate reports from the firm on the service provided.

Where an investment firm provides services by way of instructions from another investment firm, it may rely on client information transmitted by the latter firm and any recommendation that it has made.[794] The firm mediating the instructions is responsible for the accuracy of the information and appropriateness of the recommendation.

3. Execution policy. The home Member State or, in the case of branches in another Member State, the host Member State[795] must require investment firms to take all reasonable steps to obtain the best possible results for their clients when executing their orders, taking into account factors such as price, costs, speed, likelihood of execution and settlement, size and nature.[796] Investment firms must be required to provide information to their clients on their order execution policy and to obtain the clients' consent to it.[797] They must be able to demonstrate to their clients that they have executed their orders in accordance with this policy.[798]

4. Client order handling. The home Member State or, in the case of branches in another Member State, the host Member State[799] must require investment firms to implement procedures and arrangement that provide for the prompt and fair execution of client orders relative to other client orders or the trading interests of the

794 Article 20.

795 Article 32(7).

796 Article 21(1) and (2).

797 Article 21(3), 2nd subpara.

798 Article 21(5).

799 Article 32(7).

firm.[800] Comparable client orders must be executed in accordance with the time of their reception by the investment firm. In the case of a client limit order[801] involving shares admitted to trading on a regulated market that is not immediately executed under prevailing market conditions, investment firms must be required to take measures to facilitate the earliest possible execution of the order unless the client instructs otherwise.[802]

5. Eligible counterparties. The home Member State or, in the case of branches in another Member State, the host Member State[803] must permit investment firms to undertake transactions with eligible counterparties without being obliged to comply with the obligations with respect to conduct of business, execution policy and client handling policy.[804] Member States shall recognize as eligible counterparties investment firms, credit institutions, insurance companies, collective investment undertakings, pension funds, other financial institutions authorized under EU or national legislation, national governments, central banks and supranational organizations.[805] Member States may also recognize certain other undertakings meeting pre-determined proportionate requirements and equivalent third-country entities.[806] Investment firms must obtain, either in the form of a general agreement or in respect of each individual transaction, an express confirmation that the eligible counterpart agrees to be treated as such.[807]

Market transparency

1. Systematic internalizers.[808] The home Member State or, in the case of branches in another Member State, the host Member State[809] must require systematic internalizers in shares to publish a firm quote in those shares admitted to trading on a regulated market for which they are systematic internalizers and for which there is a liquid market.[810]

Where there is no liquid market, quotes should be disclosed to clients at their request. Each quote includes a firm bid and/or offer price or prices for a size or

800 Article 22(1).

801 A "limit order" is defined in Article 4(16) as an order to buy or sell a financial instrument at a specified price limit or better and for a specified size.

802 Article 22(2).

803 Article 32(7).

804 Article 24(1).

805 Article 24(2).

806 Articles 24(3), 1st subpara and 24(4).

807 Article 24(3), 2nd subpara.

808 A "systematic internalizer" is defined in Article 4(7) as an investment firm that, on an organized, frequent and systematic basis, deals on own account by executing client orders outside a regulated market or a multilateral trading facility.

809 Article 32(7).

810 Article 27(1), 1st subpara.

sizes.[811] Systematic internalizers are free to decide the size or sizes at which they will quote and are entitled to update their quotes at any time. The competent authorities must check that investment firms regularly update bid and/or offer prices and maintain prices that reflect the prevailing market conditions.[812]

Systematic internalizers are not subject to these rules where they only deal in sizes above standard market size.[813] The standard market size for a class of shares is a size representative of the arithmetic average value of the orders executed in the market for the shares included in that class.[814] The competent authority of the most relevant market in terms of liquidity determines for each share at least annually, on the basis of the arithmetic average value of orders executed in the market in respect of that share, the class of shares to which it belongs.[815]

2. Post-trade disclosure. The home Member State or, in the case of branches in another Member State, the host Member State[816] must require investment firms that conclude transactions in shares admitted to trading on a regulated market outside a regulated market or multilateral trading facility to make public the volume and price of these transactions and the time at which they were concluded.[817]

Auditors

Home Member States must provide that the authorized auditors of investment firms have a duty to report to their competent authorities any fact or decision concerning the firm of which they become aware that is liable to:[818]

- constitute an infringement of the legal rules governing the authorization of or the pursuit of its activities by an investment firm;
- affect the continuous functioning of the investment firm; or
- entail on the part of the auditor a refusal to certify the accounts of the firm or an expression of reservations.

The disclosure by auditors in good faith of such facts or decisions may not be treated as a breach of professional secrecy and may not involve such persons in liability of any kind.[819]

811 Article 27(1), 3rd subpara.

812 Article 27(4)(a).

813 Article 27(1), 2nd subpara.

814 Article 27(1), 4th subpara.

815 Article 27(2).

816 Article 32(7).

817 Article 28(1).

818 Article 55(1).

819 Article 55(2).

Professional Secrecy

Member States must provide that the confidentiality of information received by their competent authorities, persons who are working or have worked for these competent authorities as well as auditors or experts acting on behalf of these authorities is respected.[820] Confidential information may only be divulged in summary or aggregate form such that individual investment firms cannot be identified. Member States receiving confidential information may only use it to carry out their prudential and other duties, impose sanctions and in administrative appeals and court proceedings.[821]

5. Relations with Third Countries

Member States are required to inform the Commission of any difficulties encountered by their investment firms in establishing themselves or providing investment services in any third country.[822] Whenever, on the basis of these reports, it appears to the Commission that a third country is not granting EU investment firms effective market access comparable to that granted by the EU to investment firms from that third country, the Commission may propose to the Council that it open negotiations to rectify the situation.[823] It is up to the Council to make the final decision. The Directive does not provide for any sanctions in this situation.

The Directive is more radical where it appears to the Commission that, in a third country, EU investment firms do not receive national treatment affording the same competitive opportunities as for domestic investment firms and that the conditions of effective market access are also not fulfilled.[824] In this situation, the Commission may start negotiations with the third country on its own initiative. In addition, it may require Member States to limit or suspend the authorization of investment firms and the acquisition of holdings in EU investment firms involving undertakings based in the third country in question.[825] The duration of these retaliatory measures may not exceed three months unless the Commission, in the light of the results of the negotiations, decides to continue them.[826] The limitations or suspensions do not apply to the setting-up of subsidiaries or the acquisition of holdings in EU investment firms by investment firms already authorized in the EU.[827] Any retaliatory measures must also comply with the EU international obligations.[828]

820 Article 54(1).

821 Article 54(3).

822 Article 15(1). *Cf.* Directive 85/611, Article 5c(2).

823 Article 15(2). *Cf.* Directive 85/611, Article 5c(1).

824 Article 15(3), 1st subpara. *Cf.* Directive 85/611, Article 5c(1).

825 Article 15(3), 2nd subpara. *Cf.* Directive 85/611, Article 5c(1).

826 Article 15(3), 3rd subpara. *Cf.* Directive 85/611, Article 5c(1).

827 Article 15(3), 2nd subpara. *Cf.* Directive 85/611, Article 5c(1).

828 Article 15(5). *Cf.* Directive 85/611, Article 5c(1).

IV. MERCOSUR: PROTOCOL ON TRADE IN SERVICES

The Annex on Financial Services defines the application of the Protocol to financial services. The rules of the Protocol, as clarified by the Annex, apply to all the modes of supply and all measures affecting the supply of financial services,[829] which are described in a very broad way as including all insurance and insurance-related services and all banking and other financial services.[830] The Member States undertake to harmonize the definitions of the various financial services on the basis of the illustrative list in paragraph 5 of the GATS Annex.

Financial services must be supplied by a natural or legal person of a Member State but the supplier may not be a public entity.[831] Public entities are defined as a government, central bank, monetary authority or an entity owned or controlled by a Member State that is principally engaged in carrying out governmental functions or activities for governmental purposes.[832] Private entities that perform functions normally performed by a central bank or monetary authority are also considered public entities when they exercise these functions.[833]

Financial services supplied in the exercise of governmental authority are excluded from liberalization by virtue of Article II:3(b) of the Protocol. Such services are defined by the Annex as meaning the activities of a central bank, monetary authority or any other public entity in pursuit of monetary or exchange rate policies, activities forming part of a statutory system of social security or public retirement plans and other activities conducted by a public entity involving directly or indirectly government funds.[834] However, if a Member State allows any of these last two sets of activities to be conducted by its financial service suppliers in competition with a public entity or a financial service supplier, such activities are not excluded from liberalization.[835]

The Annex adds prudential supervision to the measures that are permitted as domestic regulation under the Protocol (measure (e)[836]).[837] The measures included by the Annex under prudential supervision are those for the protection of investors, depositors, participants in the financial markets, policy holders or persons to whom a fiduciary duty is owed by a financial service supplier, as well as those needed to ensure the solvency and liquidity of the financial system. If a prudential measure does constitute discrimination in fact, it is nevertheless permitted but must not be used as a means of avoiding a Member State's commitments or obli-

829 Annex, para. 1(a).

830 Annex, para 5(a).

831 Annex, para 5(b).

832 Annex, para 5(c)(i).

833 Annex, para. 5(c)(ii).

834 Annex, para. 1(b) and (d).

835 Annex, para. 1(c).

836 The reference is to the illustrative list of measures falling under domestic regulation in List 6.

837 Annex, para. 3(a).

gations under the Protocol. The Member States are committed to advancing the process of the harmonization of their prudential rules and the sharing of information concerning financial services.[838]

The provisions of the Protocol on mutual recognition are extended by the Annex to prudential supervision, albeit in rather opaque fashion. A Member State may recognize the prudential measures of any other Member State by means of harmonization, an agreement or arrangement or unilaterally.[839] Agreements or arrangements must be notified to the Common Market Group and the Trade Commission of Mercosur.[840] Member States must afford adequate opportunity for other interested Member States to demonstrate equivalency in their prudential rules and, if appropriate, in the procedures concerning the sharing of information between Member States.[841] If equivalency is shown by an interested Member State, it must be afforded adequate opportunity to participate in any agreement or arrangement or to negotiate a comparable one.[842] There is no similar provision where recognition is based on harmonization or accorded unilaterally, but the sense of the Annex is surely that recognition should also be extended in these situations to other Member States.

The Annex supplements the transparency and confidentiality provisions of the Protocol by dispensing Member States from any requirement to reveal information pertaining to the affairs and accounts of individual clients or any confidential or proprietary information in the possession of public entities.[843]

V. ASEAN: FRAME ORK AGREEMENT ON SERVICES

The GATS sectoral rules on financial services that are found in the two Annexes, the Decision on Financial Services and the Fifth Protocol are incorporated into the Agreement by virtue of Article XIV:1. These rules are discussed in the first section of this Chapter. However, it should be noted that the Philippines, Brunei, Myanmar, Vietnam, Laos and Cambodia have not subscribed to the Fifth Protocol.

None of the ASEAN countries belong to the OECD, and so none have subscribed to the Understanding on Commitment in Financial Services. Thus, their commitments in the area of financial services are scheduled in accordance with the GATS approach of ad hoc negotiation.

838 Annex, para. 4.

839 Annex, para. 3(b).

840 Annex, para. 3(e).

841 Annex, para. 3(c).

842 Annex, para. 3(d).

843 Annex, para. 2.

CHAPTER SIX

LIBERALIZATION OF TRADE IN TELECOMMUNICATIONS

I. INTRODUCTION

Telecommunications services are supplied by means of a telecommunications infrastructure consisting of equipment, sites, switches, lines, circuits, software and other transmission apparatus that permits these services to be delivered between and among defined network termination points.[1] Networks are public where they are used to provide services that are required by a country, explicitly or in effect, to be offered to the general public. Private networks are those that are used primarily to communicate within an organization,[2] although they and the services that they provide are also capable of being made available to third parties.[3] However, where these third parties are fundamental to the economic activity of the enterprise, have a continuing relationship with it and the communications are effected on a non-commercial basis,[4] the activity may still be considered private use. Thus, we have three possible forms of telecommunications networks and services: public where they involve the general public, non-public where they involve a closed user group and private where they are restricted to intra-corporate communications. Services that must be offered to the public generally are also referred to, rather clumsily, as public telecommunications transport services.[5]

1 *See* GATS Annex on Telecommunications, Point 3(c); NAFTA, Article 1310.

2 *See* NAFTA, Article 1310.

3 *See* NAFTA, Article 1301:3(c).

4 *Ibid.*

5 *See* Annex on Telecommunications, Point 3(b); NAFTA, Article 1310.

There are two types of telecommunications services. Basic telecommunications services involve end-to-end transmission of customer-supplied information between two or more points without any change being added to the information. They may be offered for public, non-public or private use. Here is an illustrative list.

List 8
Examples of Basic Telecommunications Services

a) voice telephony;

b) packet-switched data transmission;

c) circuit-switched data transmission;

d) telex;

e) telegraph;

f) facsimile;

g) private leased circuit services;

h) analog/digital cellular/mobile telephony;

i) mobile date services;

j) paging;

k) personal communication services;

l) satellite-based mobile and fixed satellite services;

m) tele- and videoconferencing;

n) trunked radio system services.

The second category comprises telecommunications services that employ computer processing applications to enhance the form or content of a customer's information or provide for its storage and retrieval. Such services are called "enhanced" or "value-added" telecommunications services. The latter is the better term for, while value is always added, this is not necessarily through enhancement of the information. Here is an illustrative list of value-added telecommunications services. Value-added telecommunications are offered on a non-public and private basis.

List 9
Examples of Value-Added Telecommunications Services

a) on-line data processing;

b) on-line data base storage and retrieval;

c) electronic data interchange;

d) email;

e) voice mail.

Until recently, telecommunications services were provided in most countries by the same persons that owned the networks involved. They are called facilities-based service operators. The problem was compounded by the fact that these operators were usually monopolies owned or controlled by the state. The challenge of liberalizing telecommunications services thus involved not only creating a competitive environment that permitted others to provide services hitherto reserved to the monopoly but also requiring the monopoly to accord access to its public network by its potential competitors. The liberalization of value-added services proved easier to achieve as either the monopoly operator had not offered these services or it preferred to concentrate on its core basic telecommunications activities. The liberalization of basic telecommunications has been much slower in coming and is still far from complete. A provider of telecommunications by way of network capacity leased from a facilities-based carrier is called a resale-based service supplier.

II. GENERAL AGREEMENT ON TRADE IN SERVICES

A. INSTRUMENTS

There are four major instruments that, together, regulate trade in telecommunications services under GATS. The basic framework remains GATS itself, but it is supplemented by the Annex on Telecommunications, the Fourth Protocol to GATS and the Reference Paper. There are also the Decision and the Annex on Negotiations on Basic Telecommunications. All the instruments date from 1994 except the Fourth Protocol and the Reference Paper, which were agreed in 1997.

B. ANNEX ON TELECOMMUNICATIONS

1. Scope

The Annex imposes significant obligations on host Members with respect to access to and use of public telecommunications transport networks and services by service providers from other Members. It also elaborates the transparency rules of GATS. The Annex does not apply to measures affecting the cable or broadcast distribution of radio and television programs.[6] Nor does it require Members to provide comprehensive telecommunications networks and services,[7] which is an important point for developing countries.

The Annex does not confer any right to supply telecommunications networks or services.[8] This right is conferred exclusively by any specific commitments regarding this sector in a Member's Schedule. However, self-use of private networks and services is implicitly permitted as the Annex defines intra-corporate communica-

---

6 Annex, Point 2(b).

7 Annex, Point 2(c)(ii).

8 Annex, Point 2(c)(i).

tions,[9] which are the subject matter of self-use. Its definition limits intra-corporate communications to communications within the company or among its subsidiaries, branches and, subject to a Member's law, affiliates. It does not include any services supplied to third parties, whether this is done on a commercial or non-commercial basis.[10]

2. Access

Members must ensure that service providers from other Members are accorded access to and use of their public telecommunications transport networks and services for the supply of services on reasonable and non-discriminatory terms and conditions.[11] The public telecommunications transport network means the public telecommunications infrastructure that permits telecommunications between defined network termination points.[12] A network termination point means the final demarcation of the public network at a customer's premises.[13] This access obligation applies only to services that are listed in a Member's Schedule, but these need not be a telecommunications service.[14] Thus, persons supplying banking or transport services, for example, also have a right of access. This is so even if a Member has not made any commitments in the telecommunications sector as long as the banking or transport service is the subject of a specific commitment.

As a general rule, Members must ensure that the obligation of access is implemented by whatever measures that are necessary.[15] There are also a number of specific requirements.

Members must provide access to and use of any public network or service offered within or across their borders, including private leased circuits.[16] To this end, they must permit service suppliers from other Members to:

a) purchase or lease and attach terminal or other equipment that interfaces with the network and which is necessary to supply the service;

b) interconnect private leased or owned circuits with public networks and services or with circuits leased or owned by another service supplier;

9 Annex, Point 3(d).

10 *Cf.* the more extended definition in Article 1310 of NAFTA.

11 Annex, Point 5(a).

12 Annex, Point 3(c).

13 *See* NAFTA, Article 1310.

14 Annex, Points 1 and 5(a).

15 Annex, note 14 to Point 2(a).

16 Annex, Point 5(b). "Private leased circuits"—also called "private leased lines"—provide permanent transmission connection between two customer premises for the exclusive use by a customer.

c) use operating protocols of the service supplier's choice. This right is subject to any domestic regulation that is necessary to ensure the availability of networks and services to the public generally ("universal service"[17]).

Service suppliers from other Members must be able to use public networks and services for the movement of information within and across borders, including for intra-corporate communications, and for access to information contained in data-bases or otherwise stored in machine-readable form in the territory of any Member.[18] This right is subject to domestic regulation aimed at ensuring the security and confidentiality of messages, but the domestic measures must not be applied in a manner that would constitute a means of arbitrary or unjustifiable discrimination or a disguised restriction on trade in services.[19]

No conditions may be imposed by Members on access to and use of public networks and services, but domestic measures are permitted that:[20]

a) safeguard the public service responsibilities of suppliers of public networks and services, in particular their universal service obligation;

b) protect the technical integrity of public networks and services;

c) ensure that service suppliers from other Members only use their right of access and use for listed services.

As long as the three criteria set out above are met, the conditions laid down under domestic regulation by a Member may include:[21]

a) restrictions on the resale or shared use of public services;

b) a requirement to use specified technical interfaces and protocols for interconnection to public networks and services;

c) requirements for the inter-operability of public services and to encourage the promotion of international standards;

d) type approval of terminal or other equipment that interfaces with the public network and technical requirements relating to the attachment of such equipment;

d) restrictions on the inter-connection of private leased or owned circuits with public networks or services or with circuits leased or owned by another service supplier;

e) notification, registration and licensing.

---

17 "Universal service" is the right of individuals within a country to have a particular telecommunications service, mainly telephone, available at an affordable place. The extent of the right depends of course on the Member's economic level.

18 Annex, Point 5(c).

19 Annex, Point 3(d). The proviso is worded similarly to that in Article XIV of GATS.

20 Annex, Point 5(e).

21 Annex, Point 5(f).

There is a general derogation from the access obligations imposed by the Annex for developing Members, who may place reasonable conditions on access to and use of their public networks and services where they are necessary to strengthen their domestic telecommunications infrastructure and service capacity and to increase their participation in international trade in telecommunications services.[22] These derogations must be set out as limitations on market access in the developing Member's Schedule.[23]

The Annex attempts to strike a balance between the needs of service suppliers from other Members and those of telecommunications network operators to maintain the system, protect confidentiality and meet their public service obligations. Its provisions cover market access (barrier (f) on List 3), national treatment (measure (b) on List 4) and most-favored-nation treatment while at the same time permitting certain measures of domestic regulation.

The use of the term "non-discriminatory" in the Annex has a wider sense than elsewhere in the Agreement.[24] It refers not only to MFN and national treatment but also has a sector-specific usage, which means "terms and conditions no less favorable than those accorded to any other user of like public telecommunications transport networks or services under like circumstances."[25] The significance of this latter usage is that, whereas MFN and national treatment under Articles II and XVII of GATS, respectively, entitle a foreign service provider only to the same treatment as that afforded to *like* domestic services and service suppliers, the sector-specific usage of the term "non-discriminatory" extends the treatment to that afforded to *any other* services and service suppliers. This is a necessary extension as the access granted by the Annex is to "any service supplier."[26] Thus, a banker from another Member can claim the same right of access and use as that granted to a domestic shipper.

It has also been suggested that the extension of the term "non-discriminatory" to include sector-specific usage also means that the access obligations under the Annex cannot be limited in a Member's Schedule or be the subject of Article II exemptions.[27] This may be so, but a more solid argument is surely that the obligations cannot be curtailed or exempted because they flow from the Annex and not a Member's Schedule or Article II.

---

22 Annex, Point 5(g).

23 They may also constitute limitations on national treatment, but, pursuant to Article XX:2 of GATS, they are listed only in the market access column.

24 E. McGovern at para. 31.342 makes the same point.

25 Annex, note 15 to Point 5(a).

26 Annex, Point 5(a).

27 *See* McGovern at para. 31.342.

3. Transparency

The Annex elaborates on how the transparency obligations of Article III of GATS with respect to domestic regulation (measure (g) on List 6) should be applied with respect to telecommunications. Each Member must ensure that relevant information on the conditions of access to and use of public networks and services is available to the public.[28] This information should cover in particular:

tariffs;

terms and conditions of service;

technical specifications;

bodies responsible for the preparation and adoption of standards affecting access and use;

conditions applying to the attachment of terminal and other equipment;

notifications and registration and licensing requirements.

The transparency obligations of the Annex, like those of Article III of GATS, are subject to the proviso that no Member is required to disclose confidential information where this would impede law enforcement, contravene the public interest or prejudice the legitimate commercial interests of any public or private enterprise.[29]

4. Standards

The Annex contains no obligations with respect to standards, which relate principally to the hardware involved in providing telecommunications services. It requires merely that Members recognize the importance of international standards in facilitating international trade in services and undertake to promote such standards.[30] Members are permitted to introduce domestic regulation that encourages the achievement of these goals.[31]

C. DECISION AND ANNEX ON NEGOTIATIONS ON BASIC TELECOMMUNICATIONS

Upon the conclusion of the Uruguay Round in 1994, most of the commitments in the telecommunications sector concerned value-added services. The commitments on basic telecommunications were so limited that a Decision was appended to the WTO Agreement providing for continued negotiations on basic telecommunications with the aim of achieving a greater degree of liberalization in this sector.[32] The negotiations covered the provision of all types of basic services by facilities-based or resale-based providers A deadline for conclusion of the negotia-

28 Annex, Point 4.

29 GATS, Article IIIbis.

30 Annex, Point 7(a).

31 Annex, Point 5(f)(iii).

32 Decision, Point 1.

tions was set for April 30, 1996,[33] but this was later extended to February 15, 1997. Participation in the negotiations was voluntary. During the period of negotiation, the MFN obligation of Article II of GATS, including the requirement to list any exemption from the MFN rule in a special Annex, did not apply,[34] except in the case of telecommunications services that were the subject of a specific commitment.[35]

The negotiations were ultimately successful and culminated in the Fourth Protocol to GATS. At the same time, the Members negotiated a set of principles on the regulatory framework for basic telecommunications, which are contained in the Reference Paper.

D. THE FOURTH PROTOCOL

The Fourth Protocol was signed on April 15, 1997 and entered into force on February 5, 1998. It contains as an Annex a new set of Schedules of Specific Commitments and MFN exemptions in the basic telecommunications sector. The commitments concern sixty-nine governments and are contained in fifty-five schedules,[36] which accounts for more than 91% of global telecommunications revenues. However, in a number of cases, a Member's commitments are to be phased in. Unless otherwise noted in a national Schedule, a specific commitment on any basic telecommunications service:[37]

- encompasses local, long distance and international services for public and non-public use;
- includes supply by facilities-based or resale-based service suppliers;
- includes the supply through any means of technology (cable, wireless, satellites etc.).

Here is an idea of the scope of the commitments on basic telecommunications services undertaken by the major trading nations.

---

33 Decision, Point 5.

34 Annex on Negotiations on Basic Telecommunications, Point 1.

35 Annex on Negotiations on Basic Telecommunications, Point 2.

36 As of January 1, 2005, the schedules were those of: Antigua and Barbuda, Argentina, Australia, Bangladesh, Belize, Bolivia, Brunei, Bulgaria, Canada, Chile, Colombia, Czech Republic, Dominican Republic, Ecuador, El Salvador, European Union on behalf of fifteen of its Member States (Austria, Belgium, Cyprus, Denmark, Finland, France, Germany, Greece, Ireland, Italy, Luxembourg, Netherlands, Portugal, Spain, Sweden and the United Kingdom.), Ghana, Grenada, Hong Kong (China), Hungary, Iceland, India, Indonesia, Israel, Ivory Coast, Jamaica, Japan, Kenya, South Korea, Malaysia, Mauritius, Mexico, Morocco, New Zealand, Norway, Pakistan, Peru, Poland, Romania, St. Kitts & Nevis, Senegal, Slovakia, Slovenia, South Africa, Sri Lanka, Switzerland, Thailand, Trinidad & Tobago, Tunisia, Turkey, United States and Venezuela.

37 *Notes for Scheduling Basic Telecommunications Services Commitments.*

European Union

Voice telephony, packet and circuit-switched data transmission, telex, telegraph, fax, leased circuit services, mobile and personal communications services and systems.

Japan

Voice telephony, packet and circuit-switched data transmission, telex, fax, private leased lines.

United States

Voice telephony, packet and circuit-switched data transmission, telex, telegraph, fax, leased circuit services, mobile and personal communications services and systems, analogue/digital cellular/mobile telephone services.

China

Paging services, mobile voice and data services, analogue/digital cellular/mobile telephone services, personal communications, voice telephony, packet and circuit-switched date transmission, fax, private leased circuits.

The only one of the above Members to have listed an exemption in the Annex on Article II (MFN) Exemptions is the United States, which lists one-way satellite transmission of DTH and DBS television services and digital audio services. Here, the United States has differential treatment based on reciprocity agreements with certain Members guaranteeing market access and national treatment.

The schedules annexed to the Fourth Protocol also contain additional commitments on domestic regulation pursuant to Article XVIII that arise from the Reference Paper. There are also some uniform additional commitments in the schedules relating to the telecommunications sector as a whole that deal with transparency, reasonable licensing procedures and dispute resolution. These are indeed matters of domestic regulation, but they also include a commitment on non-discriminatory access to public networks, which falls under the rubric of national treatment. These mixed commitments are nevertheless all placed in the additional commitments column, except in the case of the United States, whose Schedule includes them in its national treatment column. Members may not enter any restrictions on their obligations with respect to domestic regulation under GATS. The fourth column is only for additional commitments.

E. THE REFERENCE PAPER

1. Introduction

The existence of former monopolies that in many Members still operate the public network entails a risk that they may use their dominant market position or their control of the infrastructure to prevent or undermine new entrants to the domestic telecommunications market. In order to prevent this, the Members participating in the post-Uruguay negotiations developed a set of regulatory principles. Some

Members, such as the EU, Japan, the United States and China, have incorporated this Paper into their Schedules and are bound by it. Others have incorporated it partially or used it as a basis for making additional commitments in the regulatory area. Commitments arising from the Reference Paper are made pursuant to Article XVIII of GATS and placed in the column for additional commitments on domestic regulation. Nevertheless, some of the commitments also relate to market access and national treatment.

2. Competitive Safeguards

Appropriate measures must be maintained to prevent suppliers that, alone or together, have a dominant market position from engaging in anti-competitive practices in the telecommunications sector. The practices concerned are:

- anti-competitive cross-subsidization;
- using information obtained from competitors to obstruct competition;
- not making available necessary information on a timely basis to competing service providers.

3. Interconnection

Interconnection with a major supplier must be ensured at any technically feasible point in the network:

a) under non-discriminatory terms, conditions and rates and of a quality no less favorable than that available to the major supplier's own or others' like services;

b) in a timely fashion and at cost-oriented rates that are transparent, reasonable and sufficiently unbundled that the supplier need not pay for items that are not required;

c) upon request, at points in addition to the network termination points offered to the majority of users, subject to charges that reflect the cost of constructing necessary additional facilities.

The procedures for interconnecting to a major supplier must be made available to the public. In addition, the interconnection agreements of major suppliers or a reference interconnection offer must also be made public.

A service supplier requesting interconnection with a major supplier must have recourse to an independent domestic body to resolve disputes regarding appropriate terms, conditions and rates for interconnection unless these have already been established.

4. Universal Service

Members have the right to define the kind of universal service obligations that they wish to maintain. Such obligations are not to be regarded as anti-competitive as long as they are administered in a transparent, non-discriminatory and neutral manner and are not more burdensome than necessary for the kind of universal service at issue.

5. Public Availability of Licensing Criteria

All licensing criteria, the period of time required to decide upon an application and the terms and conditions of individual licenses must be made publicly available. The reasons for the denial of a license must be made known to the applicant upon request.

6. Independent Regulators

The regulatory body must be independent and not accountable to any supplier of basic telecommunications services. It must operate with impartiality towards all market participants.

7. Allocation and Use of Scarce Resources

Procedures for the allocation and use of scarce resources, such as frequencies, numbers and rights of way, must operate in an objective, timely, transparent and non-discriminatory manner.

III. THE NORTH AMERICAN FREE TRADE AGREEMENT (AND THE CHILE AGREEMENTS)

A. INTRODUCTION

Telecommunications services are not excluded from the provisions of Chapter 11 on investment or Chapter 12 on cross-border services.[38] Thus, the general NAFTA rules apply to such services, but they are supplemented and delineated by Chapter 13 on Telecommunications.[39] Once again, the provisions of the agreements of the NAFTA Parties with Chile are very similar to those of NAFTA, and they are cited in the footnotes.

B. SCOPE

Chapter 13 imposes significant obligations on host Parties with respect to access to and use of public telecommunications transport networks and services by service providers from other Parties, which are very similar to those contained in the GATS Annex on Telecommunications. It also contains provisions on the supply of value-added services, monopolies, standards and transparency. Like the Annex, Chapter 13 does not apply to measures affecting the cable or broadcast distribution of radio or television programs, except to ensure that persons operating broadcast stations and cable systems have access to and use of public networks

38 NAFTA, Articles 1101 and 1201. *See also* Articles G-01 and H-01 (Canada), 9-02 and 10-02 (Mexico) and 10.1 and 11.1 (USA).

39 Chapters I (Canada), 12 (Mexico) and 13.1 (USA).

and services.[40] The Annex does not have this proviso. Parties are not obliged to provide comprehensive telecommunications networks and services,[41] which is a less important concession than under the Annex, or to compel broadcasters or cable system operators to make available their facilities as a public network.[42]

Chapter 13 does not confer any right to provide telecommunications services. These are supplied pursuant to Chapters 11 and 12, which do not exclude such services. However, Chapter 13 limits the right to supply telecommunications services under these chapters. Parties are not required to authorize the supply of telecommunications networks or services for public use, whether this is done by means of a public and private network.[43]

By contrast, the supply of value-added telecommunications services is not prohibited under Chapter 13. Trebilcock and Howse maintain that the definition of value-added services in Chapter 13 includes as well basic telecommunications services with the exception of local and long-distance voice telephony.[44] This represents a somewhat broad interpretation of the definition,[45] which after all restricts value-added services to those telecommunications services that are subject to computer processing, but it is significant that Chapter 13 only excepts public telecommunications transport services. This would not include basic telecommunications that are offered on a non-public basis.

Telecommunications services, whether value-added or basic, that are offered on a private basis are certainly not excluded by Chapter 13. Indeed, it defines the intra corporate communications that make up self-use more liberally than the GATS Annex.[46] They include not only communications within a company or among its subsidiaries, branches and affiliates but also communications with third parties that are fundamental to the economic activity of the enterprise and have a continuing relationship with it as long as the communications are effected on a non-commercial basis.[47]

---

40 NAFTA, Article 1301:2. *See also* Articles I-01:2 (Canada), 12-02:2 (Mexico) and 13.1:2 (USA).

41 NAFTA, Article 1301:3(b). *See also* Articles I-01:3(b) (Canada), 12-02:3(b) (Mexico) and 13.1:3(a) (USA).

42 NAFTA, Article 1301:3(d). *See also* Articles I-01:3(d) (Canada), 12-02:3(d) (Mexico) and 13.1:3(b) (USA).

43 NAFTA, Article 1301:3(a) and (c). *See also* Articles I-01:3(a) and (c) (Canada), 12-02:3(a) and (c) (Mexico) and 13.1:3(c) (USA).

44 M. Trebilcock and R. Howse at page 245.

45 NAFTA, Article 1310. *See also* Articles I-10 (Canada) and 12-01:1 (Mexico).

46 *Ibid.*

47 NAFTA, Article 1310. *See also* Articles I-10 (Canada) and 12-01 (Mexico). The US-Chile Agreement does not have a definition.

C. ACCESS

The provisions of NAFTA are similar to those of the Annex, but as there are some important differences and so they are discussed here despite the element of duplication.

Parties must ensure that service providers from other Parties are accorded access to and use of their public telecommunications transport networks and services, including private leased circuits, for the conduct of their business on reasonable and non-discriminatory terms and conditions.[48] The conduct of business comprises self-use and the provision of value-added services and any other services that are liberalized under NAFTA.[49] The obligation applies to any network or service offered within or across their borders.

The access obligation means that Parties must permit service suppliers from other Parties to:[50]

a) purchase or lease and attach terminal or other equipment that interfaces with the public network;

b) interconnect private leased or owned circuits with public networks within or across the borders of the host Party or with circuits leased or owned by another person on terms and conditions mutually agreed;

c) perform switching, signaling and processing functions;

d) use operating protocols of their choice.

Parties must also ensure that the pricing of public telecommunications services reflects their economic cost and that private leased circuits are available on a flat-rate pricing basis.[51]

Service suppliers from other Parties must be able to use public networks and services for the movement of information within or across the borders of the host Party, including for intra-corporate communications, and for access to information contained in data-bases or otherwise stored in machine-readable form in the territory of any Party.[52]

---

48 NAFTA, Article 1302:1. *See also* Articles I-02:1 (Canada), 12-03:2 (Mexico) and 13.2:1 (USA).

49 According to Trebilcock and Howse, value-added services may include basic telecommunications services with the exception of voice telephony—*see supra* in the text.

50 NAFTA, Article 1302:2. *See also* Articles I-02:2 (Canada), 12-03:3 (Mexico) and 13.2:2 (USA).

51 NAFTA, Article 1302:3. *See also* Articles I-02:3 (Canada) and 12-03:4 (Mexico). There is no equivalent provision in the US-Chile Agreement.

52 NAFTA, Article 1302:4. *See also* Articles I-02:4 (Canada), 12-03:5 (Mexico) and 13.2:3 (USA).

No conditions may be imposed by Parties on access to and use of public networks and services, but domestic measures are permitted that:[53]

a) safeguard the public service responsibilities of suppliers of public networks and services, in particular their universal service obligation;

b) protect the technical integrity of public networks and services.

As long as the three criteria set out above are met, the conditions laid down under domestic regulation by a Party may include:[54]

a) restrictions on the resale or shared use of public services;

b) a requirement to use specified technical interfaces and protocols for interconnection to public networks and services;

c) a restriction on interconnection of private leased or owned circuits with public networks or services or with circuits leased or owned by another person, where the circuits are used in the provision of public networks or services;

d) a licensing, permit, registration or notification procedure as long as it is transparent and expeditious.

There is a general derogation from the access obligations imposed by Chapter 13 with respect to domestic measures aimed at ensuring the security and confidentiality of messages and protecting the privacy of subscribers to public networks or services.[55]

Like the Annex, Chapter 13 attempts to strike a balance between the needs of service suppliers from other Parties and those of telecommunications network operators to maintain the system, protect confidentiality and meet their public service obligations. Its provisions cover market access (barrier (f) on List 3), national treatment (measure (b) on List 4) and most-favored-nation treatment while at the same time permitting certain measures of domestic regulation.

The use of the term "non-discriminatory" in Chapter 13 has a wider sense than elsewhere in NAFTA. It refers not only to MFN and national treatment but also has a sector-specific usage, which means "terms and conditions no less favorable than those accorded to any other customer or user of like public telecommunications transport networks or services in like circumstances."[56] The significance of this latter usage is that, whereas MFN and national treatment under Articles 1102,

53 NAFTA, Article 1302:6. *See also* Articles I-02:6 (Canada), 12-03:7 (Mexico) and 13.2:5 (USA).

54 NAFTA, Article 1302:7. *See also* Articles I-02:7 (Canada), 12-03:8 (Mexico) and 13.2:6 (USA).

55 NAFTA, Article 1302:5 *See also* Articles I-02:5 (Canada), 12-03:6 (Mexico) and 13.2:4 (USA).

56 NAFTA, Article 1302:8. *See also* Articles I-02:8 (Canada), 12-03:1 (Mexico) and 13.17 (USA).

1103, 1202 and 1203 of NAFTA[57] could be interpreted as entitling a foreign service provider only to the same treatment as that afforded to *similar* domestic service suppliers, the sector-specific usage of the term "non-discriminatory" extends the treatment to that afforded to *any other* user of public networks or services. This is a necessary extension as the access granted by the Chapter is to persons of another Party.[58] Thus, a banker can claim the same right of access and use as that granted to a domestic shipper.

D. PROVISION OF VALUE-ADDED TELECOMMUNICATIONS SERVICES

Market access for the supply of value-added telecommunications services by providers from other Parties is secured under Chapters 11 and 12 of NAFTA. Chapter 13 merely sets down specific certain national treatment and MFN obligations.

The Parties must ensure that licensing, permit, registration or notification procedures are transparent, non-discriminatory and processed expeditiously (measure (d) on List 4).[59] The information required under such procedures must be limited to that which is necessary to demonstrate financial solvency and to assess the conformity of the applicant's terminal and other equipment with the host Party's standards.[60]

No party may require a provider of value-added telecommunications services from another Party to:[61]

- provide those services to the public generally;
- cost-justify its tariffs;
- file a tariff;
- interconnect its networks with any particular customer or network;
- conform with any particular standard other than for interconnection to a public network.

The above deal with measures (b) and (f) on List 4. However, a Party's domestic rules may require the filing of a tariff where this is done to remedy an anti-competitive practice on the part of the provider from another Party or in the unlikely event that this provider constitutes a public telecommunications monopoly.[62]

---

57 *See also* Articles G-02, G-03, H-02 and H-03 (Canada), 9-03, 9-04, 10-03 and 10-04 (Mexico) and 10.2, 10.3, 11.2 and 11.3 (USA).

58 NAFTA, Article 1302:1. *See also* Articles I-02:1 (Canada), 12-03:2 (Mexico) and 13.2:1 (USA).

59 NAFTA, Article 1303:1(a). *See also* Article I-03:1(a) (Canada) and 12-04:1(a) (Mexico). The US-Chile Agreement does not have an equivalent provision.

60 NAFTA, Article 1303:1(b). *See also* Article I-03:1(b) (Canada) and 12-04:1(b) (Mexico). The US-Chile Agreement does not have an equivalent provision.

61 NAFTA, 1303:2. *See also* Articles I-03:2 (Canada), 12-04:2 (Mexico) and 13.6:1 (USA).

62 NAFTA, 1303:3. *See also* Articles I-03:3 (Canada), 12-04:3 (Mexico) and 13.6:2 (USA).

E. MONOPOLIES

Where a Party maintains a monopoly to provide public networks or services and the monopoly competes in the provision of value-added or other telecommunications services, the Party must ensure that the monopoly does not use its position to obstruct competition in a manner that adversely affect a provider from another Party (measure (g) on List 4).[63] Such anti-competitive behavior includes cross-subsidization, predatory conduct and the discriminatory provision of access to public networks and services.

To prevent such anti-competitive behavior, the Parties must have in place:[64]

- accounting requirements;
- requirements for structural separation;
- rules to ensure that the monopoly accords its competitors access to and use of its public networks or services on terms no less favorable than those it accords itself;
- rules to ensure the timely disclosure of technical changes to public networks and their interfaces.

F. STANDARDS

Standards-related measures, which comprise standards, technical regulations and conformity assessment procedures,[65] are relevant to telecommunications services to the extent that they relate to the attachment of terminal or other equipment to public telecommunications transport networks.

Briefly, the general rule in NAFTA on standards-related measures permits the Parties to adopt or maintain them at whatever level of protection it considers appropriate, subject to certain conditions.[66] These are as follows:

a) the measures must be consistent with the principle of national and MFN treatment of telecommunications services providers from other Parties;[67]

b) the measures must not create an unnecessary obstacle to trade; this is presumed where the demonstrable purpose of a standards-related measure is to

63 NAFTA, Article 1305:1. *See also* I-05:1 (Canada) and 12-06:1 (Mexico). The US-Chile Agreement does not have an equivalent provision.

64 NAFTA, Article 1305:2. *See also* I-05:2 (Canada) and 12-06:2 (Mexico). The US-Chile Agreement does not have an equivalent provision.

65 NAFTA Article 915. *See also* Article 8-01 (Mexico). The Canada-Chile Agreement does not have a chapter on standards, and the chapter in the US-Chile Agreement relates only to goods.

66 NAFTA, Article 904:1 and 2. *See also* Article 8-04:1 and 2 (Mexico).

67 NAFTA, Article 904:3. *See also* Article 8-04:3 (Mexico).

achieve a legitimate objective and does not exclude terminal or other equipment of a provider from another Party that meets such objective;[68]

c) the measures are based on the relevant international standards except where this is not feasible or appropriate;[69]

d) the importing Party treats a technical regulation maintained by an exporting Party as equivalent to its own where the exporting Party demonstrates that it adequately fulfills the importing Party's legitimate objectives;[70]

e) the importing Party accepts the results of a conformity assessment procedure conducted in the territory of another Party provided that it is satisfied with the procedure;[71]

f) a Party's conformity assessment procedures must be conducted in a reasonable, transparent and expeditious fashion.[72]

Chapter 13 adds additional conditions that must be met in the case of terminal or other equipment to be attached to public networks. Thus, the Parties must ensure their standards-related measures with respect to such equipment are only adopted or maintained to the extent necessary to:[73]

- prevent technical damage to public networks;
- prevent technical interference with, or degradation of, public telecommunications services;
- prevent electromagnetic interference and ensure compatibility with other users of the electromagnetic spectrum;
- prevent billing equipment malfunction;
- ensure users' safety and access to public networks or services.

G. TRANSPARENCY

Chapter 13 elaborates on how the transparency obligations of Article 1802 of NAFTA with respect to domestic regulation (measure (g) on List 6) should be applied with respect to telecommunications. Each Party must ensure that its measures relating to access to and use of public networks and services are made available to the public.[74] This includes measures relating to:

- tariffs;
- terms and conditions of service;

---

68 NAFTA, Article 904:4. *See also* Article 8-04:4 (Mexico).

69 NAFTA, Article 905:1. There is no equivalent provision in the Mexico-Chile Agreement.

70 NAFTA, Article 906:4. *See also* Article 8-05:4 (Mexico).

71 NAFTA, Article 906:6. There is no equivalent provision in the Mexico-Chile Agreement.

72 NAFTA, Article 908:3 and 1304:5(a). *See also* Articles 8-07 and 12-05:5(a) (Mexico).

73 NAFTA, Article 1304:1. *See also* Articles-04:1 (Canada) and 12-05:1 (Mexico).

74 NAFTA, Article 1306. *See also* Articles I-06 (Canada), 12-07 (Mexico) and 13.13 (USA)

- specifications of technical interfaces with networks or services;
- information on bodies responsible for the preparation and adoption of standards-related measures affecting access and use;
- conditions applying to the attachment of terminal and other equipment to networks;
- notification, permit, registration and licensing requirements.

The transparency obligations of Chapter 13, like those of Article 1802, are subject to the proviso that no Party is required to furnish or allow access to confidential information where this would impede law enforcement or be contrary to a Party's law protecting personal privacy or the financial affairs and accounts of individual customers of financial institutions.[75]

H. FURTHER LIBERALIZATION

The Parties are obliged to consult with a view to determining the feasibility of further liberalizing trade in all telecommunications services, including basic telecommunications networks and services offered on a public basis.[76] No timetable is set down.

IV. THE EUROPEAN UNION (AND THE EEA AGREEMENT)

A. INTRODUCTION

In 2002, the EU adopted six directives establishing a new regime for the provision of telecommunications services in the EU. The centerpiece is the Framework Directive,[77] which acts as an umbrella for the five other directives. The latter comprise the Authorization Directive,[78] the Access Directive,[79] the Universal Service Directive,[80] the Communications Data Protection Directive[81] and the Competition

75 NAFTA, Article 2105. *See* Articles O-05 (Canada), 19-04 (Mexico) and 23.5 (USA).

76 NAFTA, Article 1309:2. *See* Articles I-08:2 (Canada) and 12-10:2 (Mexico). There is no equivalent provision in the US-Chile Agreement.

77 EP/Council Directive 02/21 on a common regulatory framework for electronic communications networks and services (OJ L108/02).

78 EP/Council Directive 02/20 on the authorization of electronic communications networks and services (OJ L108/02).

79 EP/Council Directive 02/19 on access to, and interconnection of, electronic communications networks and associated facilities (OJ L108/02).

80 EP/Council Directive 02/22 on universal service and users' rights relating to electronic communications networks and services (OJ L108/02).

81 EP/Council Directive 02/58 on the processing of personal data and the protection of privacy in the electronic communications sector (OJ L201/02).

Directive.[82] Together, these six directives replace twenty-six directives that made up the prior regulatory framework. The only directive under the old framework that survives is the 1999 "RTTE" Directive[83] on radio and terminal equipment. We shall look at the three that are most relevant to the liberalization of trade in telecommunications services within the EU, namely the Framework, Authorization and Access Directives.

The secondary legislation of the EU on telecommunications services applies to the Contracting Parties to the EEA Agreement (Iceland, Liechtenstein and Norway).[84]

B. THE FRAMEWORK DIRECTIVE[85]

1. The New Concept of "Electronic Communications Networks and Services"

The purpose of the new framework is to adapt the EU regulatory framework to the realities of convergence. The Directive's fifth recital sums it up:

> The convergence of the telecommunications, media and information technology sectors means all transmission networks and services should be covered by a single regulatory framework.[86]

The Framework Directive attempts to draw a line between transmission and content, which is not easy. The new framework applies to the former (transmission), but not to the latter (content). The dividing line between the two is not always clear. We will get into that in more detail below.

2. What Is Included in "Electronic Communications Networks and Services?"

The Directive defines "electronic communications service" as a service:

- normally provided for remuneration;
- which consists wholly or mainly in the conveyance of signals;
- on electronic communications networks.

The Directive defines "electronic communications network" as:

- transmission systems and, where applicable, switching or routing equipment and other resources;

---

82 Commission Directive 02/77 on competition in the markets for electronic communications networks and services (OJ L249/02).

83 EP/Council Directive 99/5 on radio equipment and telecommunications terminal equipment and the mutual recognition of their conformity (OJ L91/99).

84 EEA Agreement, Articles 7 and 36(2); Annex XI.

85 This material was originally published in *Electronic Communications: the New EU Framework* (ed. W. Maxwell, Oceana, New York, 2002).

86 Framework Directive, Preamble, 5th recital.

- that permit the conveyance of signals;
- by wire, radio, optical or other electromagnetic means.

Each definition then comes with a list of examples of services or facilities that are included and excluded from the definition.

Electronic communications *services* include:

- telecommunications services;
- transmission services in networks used for broadcasting.

But they exclude:

- services providing or exercising editorial control over content transmitted using electronic communications networks and services, such as web-based content, financial services and broadcasting content;
- information society services that do not consist wholly or mainly in the conveyance of signals on electronic communications networks.

Electronic communications *networks* include:

- satellite networks;
- fixed (circuit and packet switched, including Internet) and mobile terrestrial networks;
- electricity cable systems, to the extent that they are used for the purpose of transmitting signals;
- networks used for radio and television broadcasting and cable TV networks;

all irrespective of the type of information conveyed. The Competition Directive adds to this list by indicating that "fiber networks which enable third parties, using their own switching or routing equipment, to convey signals" should also be included in the definition of electronic communications network.[87]

The Directive includes within its scope "associated facilities" and "associated services." "Associated facilities" are defined as:

- facilities associated with an electronic communications network and/or an electronic communications service;
- which enable and/or support the provision of services via that network and/or service.

Associated facilities includes conditional access systems and electronic program guides.

Curiously, the Framework Directive does not define "associated services."

87 Competition Directive, Preamble, 7th recital 7.

3. What Is Excluded from the Framework

Information Society Services

Most information society services fall outside the new framework. Article 1 of the Transparency Directive[88] defines "information society services" as follows:

> Any service normally provided for remuneration, at a distance, by electronic means and at the individual request of a recipient of services.
>
> For the purposes of this definition:
>
> – "at a distance": means that the service is provided without the parties being simultaneously present;
>
> – "by electronic means": means that the service is sent initially and received at its destination by means of electronic equipment for the processing (including digital compression) and storage of data, and entirely transmitted, conveyed and received by wire, by radio, by optical means or by other electromagnetic means;
>
> – at the individual request of a recipient of services": means that the service is provided through the transmission of data on individual request.

Radio broadcasting, television broadcasting services (including near-video-on-demand services), and televised teletext services are not "information society services" because they are not supplied "at the individual request of a recipient of services."[89] Voice telephony, telefax and telex services are not considered "Information Society Services" because they are not provided via electronic processing/inventory systems.[90]

The Framework Directive states that most information society services do not qualify as electronic communications services (and therefore fall outside the new framework) because they "do not consist wholly or mainly in the conveyance of signals on electronic communications networks."[91] The Directive then specifies that voice telephony services and e-mail services *are* covered by the Directive (suggesting that such services might also be considered "information society services" in some circumstances). Reference to voice telephony was unnecessary, however, because as we saw above, the Transparency Directive itself excludes voice telephony from the definition of "information society services." The reference here to voice telephony is confusing. The reference to e-mail makes sense, however, because e-mail falls into both categories: it is both an information society service and an electronic communications service.

---

88 EP/Council Directive 98/34 laying down a procedure for the provision of information in the field of technical standards and regulations and of rules of information society services (OJ L204/98) (the "Transparency Directive"), as amended by Directive 98/48/EC (OJ L217/98).

89 Transparency Directive, Annex V.

90 Transparency Directive, Annex V.

91 Framework Directive, Preamble, 10th recital.

The Directive points out that a given bundle of services will in many cases fall both under rules on content (not covered by the framework) and rules on electronic communication services (covered by the framework). The Directive gives the example of an ISP that offers both electronic communications services, such as Internet access, and content services, such as web-based content.[92]

Content of Broadcasting Services

Broadcasting services in the technical sense fall within the new framework. Broadcasting services in the editorial and content sense fall outside the new framework.

Article 1 of the Television Without Frontiers Directive[93] defines television broadcasting as follows:

> (a) "Television broadcasting" means the initial transmission by wire or over the air, including that by satellite, in unencoded or encoded form, of television programs intended for reception by the public. It includes the communication of programs between undertakings with a view to their being relayed to the public. It does not include communication services providing items of information or other messages on individual demand such as telecopying, electronic data banks and other similar services;

This definition of "television broadcasting" includes services consisting mainly or wholly of the conveyance of signals over electronic communications networks (which is also the definition of "electronic communications services"). The Framework Directive and the Television Without Frontiers Directive would thus appear to overlap. The Framework Directive makes clear, however, that it does not mean to exclude "television broadcasting" from its scope of application, only the *content* of television broadcasting:

> This framework does not therefore cover the content of services delivered over electronic communications networks using electronic communications, such as broadcasting content. . . .[94]

Consequently the Directives do not really overlap. Television broadcasting is covered by the Framework Directive as regards the technical aspects of transmission, and by the Television Without Frontiers Directive as regards the editorial content of the program. As we will see later, the distinction between broadcasting content and electronic communications services can nevertheless raise some difficult questions, particularly in connection with the allocation of rights to use frequency. Audiovisual and content policy objectives, including freedom of expression, media pluralism, impartiality, cultural and linguistic diversity, social inclusion,

---

92 Framework Directive, Preamble, 10th recital.

93 Council Directive 89/552 on the coordination of certain provisions laid down by law, regulation or administrative action in Member States concerning the pursuit of television broadcasting activities, OJ L298/89 (the "Television Without Frontiers Directive"), as last amended by Directive 97/36 (OJ L 202/97).

94 Framework Directive, Preamble, 5th recital.

consumer protection and the protection of minors,[95] can influence the rules applicable to licensing frequency.

The most important point that emerges from these definitions is that Europe has abandoned the traditional separation between telecommunications services (one-to-one transmissions) and broadcasting services (one-to-many transmissions). Now all transmission services, whether one-to-one or one-to-many, are treated alike. This is a drastic change from the prior European approach, which expressly excluded radio-broadcasting and television from the definition of "telecommunications services."[96] It also marks a fundamental shift from the approach taken so far in the WTO negotiations on telecommunications services.[97] The new European approach will have far-reaching consequences, extending perhaps beyond Europe itself.

Law Enforcement

The new framework does not affect law enforcement or national defense activities.[98] Rules on wiretaps, interceptions of e-mails, retention of data for law enforcement purposes and encryption will continue to be governed by the national law of each EU Member State. Those rules fall outside the new Directives. The new Communications Data Protection Directive is intended to remind Member States of the proper limits of law enforcement activity in light of the privacy principles enshrined in Article 10 of the European Convention for the Protection of Human Rights and Fundamental Freedoms.[99] But it is that Convention, not the new Directives, that places limits on the ability of Member States to authorize wiretaps and interceptions by law enforcement authorities.

4. Mission Statement for the New Framework

The Framework Directive contains a mission statement that national regulatory authorities must apply when taking any action under the new framework. The principles contained in the mission statement form the touchstone for all regulatory action. Every regulatory decision under the new framework must be justified with the mission statement in mind. Otherwise, the decision could be subject to legal challenge by the Commission or by affected parties. Previously, the regulatory principles to be applied by national regulatory authorities were scattered among several Directives, with slightly different principles and priorities applying in each case. The new framework conveniently puts all the key principles in one place.

---

95 Framework Directive, Preamble, 6th recital.

96 Commission Directive 90/388 on competition in the markets for telecommunications services (OJ L192/90) (the "Services Directive"), Article 1(1).

97 *See* the GATS Annex on Telecommunications.

98 Framework Directive, Preamble, 7th recital.

99 Council of Europe, Convention for the Protection of Human Rights and Fundamental Freedoms, as amended by Protocol 11, Rome, 4 November 1950, European Treaty Series No. 5.

The key principles are divided into four main categories: (i) proportionality and technological neutrality, (ii) promoting competition, (iii) developing the internal market, and (iv) protecting the end-user.

Proportionality and Technological Neutrality

The first category contains the principles of proportionality and technological neutrality.

The proportionality principle is expressed in Article 8(1):

> Member States shall ensure that. . .the national regulatory authorities take all reasonable measures which are aimed at achieving the objectives set out in paragraphs 2, 3 and 4. Such measures shall be *proportionate* to those objectives.[100]

Proportionality already appeared in the prior regulatory framework and is now part of the Treaty itself.[101] It means that regulatory actions must have a reasonable relationship to the objectives to be attained, and must not go beyond what is necessary to attain those objectives. This last principle of "light handed" regulation is embodied more clearly in Article 16 (3) of the Framework Directive, which requires national regulatory authorities to roll-back regulations in any part of the market that is "effectively competitive." The new framework's philosophy is that sector-specific regulation should disappear as soon as a given market is "effectively competitive." From that point on, competition law alone should apply to the sector. The new framework therefore contains sunset clauses requiring national regulators periodically to review the market and remove sector-specific regulation in areas that are "effectively competitive." As we will see in section 7 below, whether a given market is "effectively competitive" will depend on whether any market player has "significant market power" on that market.

The second key principle in this category (technological neutrality) is expressed as follows:

> Member States shall ensure that in carrying out the regulatory tasks specified in this Directive and the specific directives, in particular those designed to ensure effective competition, national regulatory authorities take the utmost account of the desirability of making regulations *technologically neutral.*[102]

Technological neutrality has not before been a key principle in the European telecommunications landscape. The old regime was not technologically neutral because different bodies of rules applied to different kinds of networks. Technological neutrality becomes particularly important in the context of convergence, when

100 Framework Directive, Article 8(1) (emphasis added).

101 EC Treaty, Article 5. *See also Crispoltoni v. Commission*, 133/93, 300/93 and 362/93, 1999 ECR I-4863.

102 Framework Directive, Article 7(1) (emphasis added).

any network can deliver any service. The Commission's public consultation on the new framework showed broad support of this principle:

> There was general agreement that equivalent services should be regulated in an equivalent (although not necessarily identical) manner. Thus communications services using Internet Protocol (IP)-based networks should for example be treated in the same way as the same services carried over cable TV networks. But many commentators (in particular telecoms operators) were concerned that technological neutrality could be used as a tool for increasing regulation, extending regulation from one market into others not previously regulated, with the risk of creating disincentives to invest.[103]

One of the paradoxes of the new framework is that in an effort to simplify—and ultimately eliminate—regulation, the new Directives bring regulation to areas that were previously unregulated, the Internet for example. In reality, the Internet was never "unregulated" in Europe. The telecommunications operators that own and operate the underlying communications infrastructure that make up the Internet in most cases hold public telecommunications operator licenses in each country, and comply with a host of regulatory obligations. Nevertheless the Internet service providers ("ISPs") that provided services on top of that communications infrastructure were in most cases unregulated. And it is true that under the new framework, those ISPs will become regulated insofar as they provide "electronic communications services." So the comment that technological neutrality leads to the regulation of previously unregulated activities carries some truth.

In the case of spectrum licensing, technological neutrality can clash with other key principles, such as pan-European interoperability. If technological neutrality were the cardinal rule, Member States would not impose a given technology for use in a given spectrum band. But this in turn could foster a patchwork of incompatible technologies for mobile telephone networks, which would interfere with other European priorities such as creating a single European market. That is why Member States have typically linked spectrum in a given band to a service and/or technology, such as GSM or UMTS, and will continue to do so. By contrast, the United States' FCC typically licenses spectrum without limitations on the kind of technology and services that may be deployed. The US approach respects the principle of technological neutrality, and favors innovation and flexibility in spectrum use. For example, mobile operators in the United States can freely implement 3G technology on frequencies originally used for 2G services. This flexibility comes at a price: the US approach tends to hinder the emergence of uniform interoperable services throughout the country.

103 Communication from the Commission of 26 April 2000: The results of the public consultation on the *1999 Communications Review and Orientations for the new Regulatory Framework*, COM (2000) 239 final, para. 2.1.1, p. 7.

Promoting Competition

The second category of principles deals with promoting competition:

> 2. The national regulatory authorities shall *promote competition* in the provision of electronic communications networks, electronic communications services and associated facilities and services by *inter alia*:
>
> (a) ensuring that users, including disabled users, derive maximum benefit in terms of choice, price and quality;
>
> (b) ensuring that there is no distortion or restriction of competition in the electronic communications sector;
>
> (c) encouraging efficient investment in infrastructure, and promoting innovation; and
>
> (d) encouraging efficient use and ensuring the effective management of radio frequencies and numbering resources.[104]

Ensuring that competition is not distorted is one of the key principles of the EC Treaty itself.[105] Moreover, the competition rules of the Treaty apply automatically to the activities of national regulators, who technically could not take any action that distorts or restricts competition.[106] Strictly speaking, objective 8(2)(b) is really unnecessary since it exists already under the Treaty rules. Reiterating the competition law principles as part of the Article 8 "mission statement" is useful, however, not only as a reminder that the principles exist, but also as a reminder that the philosophy of the new framework is in large part based on competition law.

The excerpt of Article 8 quoted above reveals an important semantic difference between key principles. National regulators first have a general obligation to promote competition (they "shall promote competition"). That obligation is absolute, as is evidenced by use of the word "shall." A regulatory decision that does not "promote competition" could be held illegal under the Directive. The Directive then goes on to give examples of how authorities are supposed to go about promoting competition. In some cases, the regulator must "encourage" a given situation. In other cases, the regulator must "ensure" a particular outcome.

For example, to promote competition national regulators need only "encourage" efficient investment in infrastructure and efficient use of radio frequencies and numbering resources. On the other hand, national regulators must "ensure" that:

- users derive maximum benefit in terms of choice;
- there is no distortion or restriction of competition;
- radio frequencies and numbering resources are effectively managed.

---

104 Framework Directive, Article 8(2) (emphasis added).

105 EC Treaty, Articles 3(1)(g), 81, 82 and 86.

106 EC Treaty, Articles 3(1)(g) and 10.

The mandate to "promote competition" and "ensure that there is no distortion or restriction thereof" sounds like the mission of a competition authority. Indeed the role of national regulators will increasingly overlap with that of competition authorities. This will become evident later in this chapter in connection with the new standard of "significant market power" ("SMP"), which is now tied to competition law concepts. The Framework Directive expressly vests national regulatory authorities with competition law responsibilities. That responsibility will generally coexist with the responsibility of national competition authorities. The Framework Directive requires close cooperation between these two authorities. As we will see below, nothing in the Framework Directive requires Member States to have separate regulatory and competition authorities. A Member State could theoretically have a single authority for both, or many authorities, dividing up responsibilities among the various authorities. The Directive leaves that choice to Member States.

One of the trickiest objectives to implement is encouraging efficient investment in infrastructure (objective 2(c)). Historically most Member States have put together regulatory schemes that encourage infrastructure investment, on the theory that lasting competition is best achieved by fostering infrastructure-based competition. Promoting infrastructure investment can have adverse effects, however, by discouraging service-based competition, or by creating artificial and/or unjustified investment decisions. In France, the status of "network operator" brought with it a number of advantages, including lower interconnection rates, and a broader range of interconnection services. This difference in treatment had nothing to do with objective differences in costs. It resulted from a deliberate policy decision to encourage investment in infrastructure. Some French policy-makers viewed resale-based competition as unhealthy cream-skimming. This kind of discrimination in favor of infrastructure investment could conflict with other "key principles," such as technological neutrality and non-discrimination. Another example of measures taken to encourage efficient investment in infrastructure would be a decision to limit to four the number of 3G license holders. Clearly an operator will not invest in costly network deployment (let alone high license fees) if the operator knows that an unlimited number of additional 3G operators could be permitted to enter the market. Measures of this kind are commonplace, and in most cases justified, to encourage infrastructure investment.

Development of the Internal Market

The third category of key principles relates to the development of the internal market. Like proportionality and the development of competition, the internal market is another principle enshrined in the EC Treaty.[107] In the Framework Directive, the principle is worded as follows:

> 3. The national regulatory authorities shall contribute to the development of the internal market by *inter alia*:
>
> (a) removing remaining obstacles to the provision of electronic communications networks, associated facilities and services and electronic communications services at European level;
>
> (b) encouraging the establishment and development of trans-European networks and the interoperability of trans-national services and end-to-end connectivity;
>
> (c) ensuring that, in similar circumstances, there is no discrimination in the treatment of undertakings providing electronic communications networks and services;
>
> (d) cooperating with each other and with the Commission in a transparent manner to ensure the consistent application of this Directive and the specific directives.[108]

Once again, we see different levels of obligation flowing from use of the words "encouraging" in some cases and "ensuring" in others. The obligation on national regulatory authorities to ensure that "there is no discrimination" (objective 3(c)) has the greatest importance for new entrants. As pointed out in the Commission's Seventh Implementation Report, the non-discrimination obligation (which already exists under the current regulatory framework) is enforced poorly:

> Most Member States have transposed the concept of non-discrimination (in particular the Interconnection and Leased Lines Directives), but many have failed to ensure implementation of the principle in detail.[109]

In telecommunications, as in so many other things, the devil is in the detail.

The non-discrimination principle naturally applies to actions by governments and regulators themselves (e.g. licensing conditions should not discriminate based on nationality). As we will see in the section on the Access Directive, the principle also applies to the actions of operators holding "significant market power." The reference to non-discrimination in Article 8(3) of the Framework Directive is primarily intended to cover actions by governments and regulators, rather than actions by SMP operators, since SMP operators are covered by one of the specific directives. Nevertheless, the principle is presented in general terms (regulators ensure that "there is no discrimination") indicating that the principle should be taken into account in *all* circumstances. The non-discrimination obligation also flows from the principles of competition law, as embodied in the EC Treaty[110] and the Competition Directive. The Competition Directive provides for

107 EC Treaty, Article (1)(c).

108 Framework Directive, Article 8(3).

109 Communication from the Commission to the Council, the European Parliament, the Economic and Social Committee and the Committee of the Regions: Seventh Report on the Implementation of the Telecommunications Regulatory Package, COM (2001) 706, p. 14.

110 EC Treaty, Articles 3(1)(g), 81, 82 and 86.

non-discrimination in licensing[111] and in granting of rights of way.[112] The reference to trans-European networks (objective 3(b)) also reflects an express Treaty objective, i.e. the "encouragement for the establishment and development of trans-European networks."[113]

End-User Interests

The last category of key principles relates to protection of the end user.

In terms of the EC Treaty, this category of objectives corresponds roughly to the Treaty objectives related to social cohesion[114] and consumer protection.[115]

Article 8(4) of the Framework Directive provides:

> 4. The national regulatory authorities shall promote the interests of the citizens of the EU by *inter alia*:
>
> (a) ensuring all citizens have access to a universal service specified in Directive 2002/22/EC (Universal Service Directive);
>
> (b) ensuring a high level of protection for consumers in their dealings with suppliers, in particular by ensuring the availability of simple and inexpensive dispute resolution procedures carried out by a body that is independent of the parties involved;
>
> (c) contributing to ensuring a high level of protection of personal data and privacy;
>
> (d) promoting the provision of clear information, in particular requiring transparency of tariffs and conditions for using publicly available electronic communications services;
>
> (e) addressing the needs of specific social groups, in particular disabled users; and
>
> (f) ensuring that the integrity and security of public communications networks are maintained.[116]

Conflicting Objectives

A measure aimed at achieving one of the key policy objectives in Article 8 can run afoul of another.

Charging vastly different levels of fees for spectrum used for 3G networks and for spectrum used for digital terrestrial television could be viewed as discriminatory and not technologically neutral. Theoretically spectrum should be licensed under the same rules and for the same fees, regardless of whether the spectrum is used to carry audiovisual content or traditional one-to-one telecommunications signals. That is what technological neutrality is all about. Nevertheless, the Framework Directive permits regulators to compromise certain principles if doing so contrib-

111 Competition Directive, Article 2(4).

112 Competition Directive, Article 8.

113 EC Treaty, Articles 3(1)(o), 154-156.

114 EC Treaty, Articles 3(1)(k), 158-162.

115 EC Treaty, Articles 3(1)(t) and 153.

116 Framework Directive, Article 8(4).

utes to achieving other important objectives. In the case of digital terrestrial television, giving special incentives to existing analog broadcasters to move out of analog bands into digital bands can be justified as necessary to encourage efficient use and effective management of radio frequencies (objective 2(d)). As explained in the 18th Recital of the Framework Directive, the principle of technological neutrality "does not preclude the taking of proportionate steps to promote certain specific services where this is justified, for example digital television as a means for increasing spectrum efficiency." This kind of tension between competing principles requires regulators continually to balance objectives, in some cases giving priorities to some objectives at the expense of others. During the public consultation on the "1999 Review" measures, certain commentators urged the Commission to give express priorities to certain objectives over others.[117]

The drafters of the Framework Directive elected not to rank the policy objectives by level of priority, leaving the problem of resolving competing interests to national regulators, who are best situated to make decisions affecting their local market. Indeed this approach is consistent with an overriding principle of the new framework that is not spelled out in the Article 8 mission statement, but is implicit throughout the Directives: specific decisions that affect the market should be made by national regulatory authorities, not the Commission, because national regulatory authorities are closest to the market.[118]

As we will see below, this implied principle of decentralization of regulatory decisions is tempered by a system of checks and balances that requires national regulators to communicate draft measures in advance to the Commission for comment and, in some cases, a veto. Such controls are necessary to achieve a single internal market (objective 3), as well as another important principle, unwritten in the Directive but present throughout the 1999 Review: "enhancing legal certainty in a dynamic market."[119]

Cultural and Linguistic Diversity, Media Pluralism

The mission statement contains a "soft" principle that has more to do with content than with electronic communications services. The principle states that regulatory authorities "may contribute within their competencies to ensuring the implementation of policies aimed at the promotion of cultural and linguistic diversity, as well as media pluralism."[120] This principle reflects the fact that certain regulatory decisions affecting electronic communications networks and services will inevitably affect content policies. An example is a "must carry" obligation. "Must carry" obligations require a network operator to carry certain obligatory audiovisual ser-

117 Communication from the Commission of April 26, 2000: the results of the public consultation on the *1999 Communications Review and Orientations for the new Regulatory Framework*, COM (2000) 239 final, para. 2.1.1, p. 7.

118 1999 Communications Review, COM (1999) 539, para. 3.2, p. 13.

119 *Id.* para. 3.2, p. 12.

120 Framework Directive, Article 8.

vices. Regulators can impose must carry obligations pursuant to the Universal Service Directive. Yet a "must carry" rule is clearly a content-motivated decision. It is designed to enhance cultural diversity and pluralism. Thus the limit between regulating "pipes" and "content" is not as clear as it might at first seem. The 5th Recital of the Directive recognizes this overlap:

> The separation between the regulation of transmission and the regulation of content does not prejudice the taking into account of the links existing between them, in particular in order to guarantee media pluralism, cultural diversity and consumer protection.[121]

Ranking the Objectives

While the Framework Directive does not explicitly set any priorities among the key regulatory principles, the language used to describe each objective shows that some objectives are more important than others. For example, national regulatory authorities must "ensure" some principles, while only "encouraging" others. As we saw above, one of the objectives (media pluralism, cultural and linguistic diversity) is optional.

5. Coordination between National Regulatory Authorities and the Commission

The mission statement requires that national regulators cooperate with other national regulators and with the Commission in a transparent manner to ensure consistent application of the Directives. Article 7 of the Framework Directive organizes this cooperation. To compensate for the individual freedom given to national regulators under the Framework Directive, the new "package" creates a system of checks and balances in the form of peer review and a veto system. The new framework gives considerable latitude to national regulators to take measures in light of local market conditions. The measures have to take into account the key principles of the Article 8 mission statement, and other provisions contained in the Framework Directive and specific directives. But within those general limits, national regulators have a free hand:

> Primary responsibility for achieving objectives set out in sector-specific Community legislation should rest with independent national regulators, who are best placed to take account of the different levels of competition and market development in the Member States.[122]

The Commission has learned that giving Member States too much individual freedom can be harmful to creation of a single internal market: witness the current licensing framework for telecommunications services and networks. Europe has become a patchwork of different licensing regimes in spite of the now defunct Li-

121 Framework Directive, Preamble, 5th recital.

122 1999 Review, p. 14.

censing Directive,[123] which was supposed to foster the creation of harmonized licensing conditions throughout Europe. Too much freedom at a national level leads to inconsistent results, which in turn are incompatible with the concept of a single market. Too little freedom, on the other hand, leads to inflexible top-down regulation that is unable to adapt to changing local market conditions. To find a happy medium, the drafters of the Framework Directive reached a compromise whereby national regulators are obliged to inform the Commission and other national regulators in advance of certain regulatory actions, and take "utmost account" of the comments received from the Commission and other regulators. This system rubbed a number of Member States the wrong way, since it implied that the Commission would always be looking over the national regulators' shoulder. The system proposed by the Commission flows from the idea, espoused at the Lisbon Ministerial in March 2000, that national regulators, like companies, can benefit from benchmarking and peer review. By comparing one's own actions to others', one can learn from others' mistakes and strive to attain "best practice" levels at a European level. While commonplace in multinational corporations such as General Electric, this kind of transparency and mutual criticism is foreign to most European governments. Civil servants will be unaccustomed to sending draft measures in advance to the European Commission and to other national regulatory authorities for constructive comment and criticism. At first, these measures will not doubt encounter resistance at a national level, being viewed as an unwarranted intrusion into national sovereignty.

Just as civil servants are not accustomed to sending their draft regulations in advance to the Commission, some governments are unaccustomed to seeking public comment before adopting proposed measures, even though in recent years telecommunications regulators have been pretty good at using "public consultation" procedures. However awkward or unnatural it may seem for many national governments and regulators, the Framework Directive will require that national regulatory authorities systematically consult interested persons and share draft measures with the Commission and other regulators in advance, prior to adoption.

The following sections explain how the consultation and peer review system works.

Level 1 Consultation

Articles 6 and 7 of the Framework Directive adopt a two-level consultation procedure. The first level, which requires consultation of interested parties under Article 6, is triggered whenever a draft measure would have a "significant impact on the relevant market." The Directive does not define what "significant impact on the relevant market" means. The "relevant market" presumably includes, but is not necessarily limited to, the markets for electronic communications services or networks that the national regulator must identify pursuant to Article 15(3) of the Framework Directive (examined in section 7 below). Those markets will in most

123 Directive 97/13 (OJ L117/97).

cases be national. Thus to trigger the first level of consultation, the measure need not have effects that could be felt beyond national borders. This interpretation diverges from the language in the 15th recital of the Framework Directive. The 15th Recital suggests that the consultation of interested parties need only occur for "draft measures, which have an effect on trade between Member States." Some Member States may therefore interpret the threshold of Article 6 consultations as requiring some effect on trade between Member States. That would be incorrect, in our view. In Article 7(3)(b) the drafters of the Directive expressly included the language "affect trade between Member States." In Article 6 they chose not to include that language. The drafters used instead the term "relevant market," the same term as they used in Articles 15(3) and 16, which require national regulatory authorities to define and analyze the "relevant markets." Consequently, Article 6 should be read as requiring national regulatory authorities to consult interested parties on any measure having an impact on a relevant market as defined by the regulator in Article 15 and 16. Almost every decision made by a national regulatory authority will have a significant impact on the relevant market, so one can expect that practically every decision will require a consultation of interested parties (a "Level 1 Consultation"). The only two exceptions to the requirement of conducting Level 1 Consultation are decisions made in a dispute resolution proceeding and decisions made to impose urgent provisional remedies.

For Level 1 Consultations, the Directive only requires transparency in the process. The proposed measure must be made accessible and the consultation procedure itself must be published. But unlike Level 2 Consultations (which we will discuss in a moment), the Directive does not require the national regulator to "take utmost account" of the comments received in a Level 1 Consultation. The national regulator can choose to ignore the comments. Its only requirement is to "take utmost account" of the key principles set forth in the Article 8 mission statement.

Another question that arises in connection with Level 1 Consultations is whether seeking the comments of interested parties is necessarily the same as a "public consultation." Existing approaches vary between Member States. OFTEL applies broadly the concept of public consultation, publishing (like the FCC) proposed decisions on its website and seeking comment. The French *Autorité de regulation des telecommunications* ("ART") occasionally uses public consultation, but prefers in many cases to consult a group of licensed operators through fora such as the "Interconnection Committee." In this case, the ART consults only a preselected group of "interested parties."

The requirement to establish a "single information point though which all current consultations can be accessed" suggests that consultations should be posted on the regulators' website, which is what most regulators do now anyway. The requirement to post consultations on a website suggests that the Directive has in mind a public consultation procedure rather than a procedure limited to a few "interested parties" selected by the regulator. Nevertheless, under the new Directive, the practice of Member States may vary. In some cases a national regulator may consult only a few interested parties; in others it may solicit comments from a broader audience. What is important to remember is that almost every regulatory action will require a prior public consultation of some kind.

Level 2 Consultation

Article 7 describes cases where draft decisions already subject to Level 1 Consultation also must be notified to the Commission and to national regulatory authorities in other Member States (a "Level 2 Consultation"). A Level 2 Consultation is triggered if a measure subject to a Level 1 Consultation also satisfies both of the following two criteria:

1. The measure relates to one of the following areas:
   - defining the relevant market (Articles 15 and 16, Framework Directive);
   - identifying SMP operators (Article 16, Framework Directive);
   - imposing access obligations on non-SMP operators (Article 5, Access Directive);
   - imposing access obligations on SMP operators (Article 8, Access Directive); or
   - imposing retail tariff obligations (Article 16, Universal Service Directive).
2. The measure "would affect trade between Member States."

The 38th recital to the Framework Directive explains exactly what the drafters meant by the terms "affect trade between Member States:"

> Measures that could affect trade between Member States are measures that may have an influence, direct or indirect, actual or potential, on the pattern of trade between Member States in a manner which might create a barrier to the single European market. They comprise measures that have a significant impact on operators or users in other Member States, which include, *inter alia*: measures which affect prices for users in other Member States; measures which affect the ability of an undertaking established in another Member State to provide an electronic communications service, and in particular measures which affect the ability to offer services on a transnational basis; and measures which affect market structure or access, leading to repercussions for undertakings in other Member States.[124]

This definition is not unlike the definition used by the European Court of Justice in competition cases involving Article 81(1) of the Treaty, in which there must be an "appreciable effect on trade between Member States" in order for the Treaty provision to apply.[125]

A Level 2 Consultation means that national regulatory authority must make the draft measure available to the Commission and to national regulatory authorities of other Member States, together with the reasoning on which the draft measure is based. The Commission and other national regulators must have an opportunity to

124 Framework Directive, Preamble, 38th recital.

125 EC Treaty, Article 81(1); *Consten and Grundig v. Commission* 56 & 58/64, [1966] ECR 299 at 341ff.

make comments on the proposed measure, and the regulatory authority proposing the measure must "take utmost account" of those comments. The time period for making comments is one month, unless a longer period is provided for in the consultation procedure for interested parties under the Level 1 Consultation procedure.

Level 3 Veto

For certain measures subject to a Level 2 Consultation, the Commission can suspend, and even veto, the proposed measure. Measures that reach this level ("Level 3 Veto Measures") are Level 2 Consultation measures that also satisfy one or both of the following criteria:

1. The proposed measure defines a relevant product or service market that departs from the relevant product and service markets defined by the Commission in its Recommendation;[126] or

2. The proposed measure identifies SMP operators.

If after receiving the proposed Level 3 Veto Measure the Commission indicates that the measure would create a barrier to the single European market, or if the Commission expresses "serious doubts" as the compatibility of the proposed measure with Community law and in particular the objectives of Article 8 mission statement, then the national regulatory authority must suspend adoption of the proposed measure for two months. During this time, the Commission can take action with in the Communications Committee[127] to require the national regulatory authority to withdraw the proposed measure. To do so, the Commission would have to inform the Communications Committee in advance of the Commission's decision to require withdrawal of the proposed national measure. The Communications Committee would be entitled to express an opinion on the proposed withdrawal decision, and the Commission would have to take "utmost account" of the Committee's opinion. The Commission must report back to the Committee to explain how the Committee's opinion was taken into account.[128] The Committee's opinion is not absolutely binding on the Commission. The Committee's role is only advisory.

The veto power of the Commission gave rise to a great deal of debate with Member State governments and the European Parliament. The original Commission proposal of July 2000 gave the Commission a veto right over a large number of decisions taken at a national level. Gradually, the number of decisions subject to veto was reduced to the bare minimum necessary to ensure consistency in applying the "SMP" rules throughout Europe. As we will see in section 7 below, SMP was previously a simple concept (25% market share) imposed in a uniform man-

126 See section 7 for an explanation of the Recommendation.

127 Discussed in section 14 below.

128 Council Decision 99/468 laying down the procedures for the exercise of implementing powers conferred on the Commission (OJ L184/99), Article 3.

ner throughout Europe following a "top down" approach. The new SMP approach will be more flexible, depending on individual market analysis by national regulators in each Member State using the Commission's Recommendation on relevant product and service markets as a starting point. It is understandable that the new framework gives the Commission power to block national decisions that vary too greatly from the Commission's Recommendations and the SMP rules of the Directive. To give one current example, opinions currently differ in Europe as to whether the service of terminating a call on a given mobile telephone network constitutes a separate market within the broader market of call termination on all mobile networks. If call termination on a single mobile network constitutes a separate market, then even small GSM operators would possess significant market power on the market for terminating calls on their network. Each GSM operator would therefore have to comply with asymmetric regulatory obligations, such as cost-oriented tariffs. This is the approach OFTEL used in the UK. If on the other hand termination on a given GSM network does not constitute a separate market from the broader market of call termination on GSM networks generally, then smaller GSM operators would not be deemed to hold SMP and would not be subject to heavy *ex ante* regulation. If national regulators came to different conclusions on this issue, then the regulatory obligations of a mobile operator would be vastly different in each country, even if the operator had the same market share and same kind of network in each territory. In one country the GSM operator would be considered dominant on the call termination market, and highly regulated, and in another, it would be considered non-dominant, and virtually unregulated. This would destroy harmonization, and the goal of creating a single European market for electronic communications.

Urgent Measures

In exceptional circumstances, a national regulatory authority may take urgent provisional measures needed "to safeguard competition and protect the interest of users."[129] In that case, the national regulatory authority does not have to go through either Level 1 or Level 2 Consultation procedures (let alone a Level 3 Veto). Before making the measure permanent, however, the regulatory must go through a full Level 2 Consultation (provided the matter is one that requires a Level 2 Consultation). Note that the urgent measure must be necessary to safeguard competition AND protect the interests of users. The drafters did not use the word "OR," meaning that the threshold for urgent measures is particularly high.

6. New Definition of Significant Market Power

The Framework Directive fundamentally changes the approach to asymmetric regulation in Europe, by changing the definition of "significant market power" ("SMP"). The previous Directives defined significant market power as a market share greater than 25% in a predefined market. The relevant markets were fixed in advance: the national market for interconnection, the national market for leased

129 Framework Directive, Article 7 (b).

lines, the national market for voice telephony on the public switched network and the national market for voice telephony on mobile networks. Once national regulatory authorities identified an operator as holding "significant market power," a host of obligations automatically befell that operator.

The Framework Directive takes a more nuanced approach. First, the Framework Directive discards the 25% market share threshold and imposes a definition identical to that used to define "dominant position" under EU Competition law:

> An undertaking shall be deemed to have significant market power if, either individually or jointly with others, it enjoys a position equivalent to dominance, that is to say a position of economic strength affording it the power to behave to an appreciable extent independently of competitors, customers and ultimately consumers.[130]

Under traditional competition law analysis, market share alone is not the sole criterion to determine "dominance."[131] But market share is nevertheless important. For example, under competition law a 25% market share is generally not sufficient to create a dominant position. A market share of 40% is likely to constitute dominance (depending on the size of other competitors), and a market share of 50% or more is almost always considered as giving rise to dominance.[132] From now on, SMP will be synonymous with "dominant position" as that term is understood by competition lawyers, whereas before the two terms had completely different meanings.

	Before Framework Directive	After Framework Directive
Definition of "significant market power":	25% market share	Synonymous with "dominant position"

As all competition lawyers know, one cannot assess market power unless one first identifies the relevant market. Previously, the Directives established pre-defined markets. Analyzing market share and dominance was straightforward. All the national regulators had to do was to apply the 25% market share test to those predefined markets. Now the national regulator's task is more complex. The national regulator must define the relevant markets almost from scratch. We use the term "almost" because the Commission intends to guide the regulators by issuing a Recommendation defining the relevant product and service markets, and guidelines on assessing significant market power in accordance with the principles of competition law.[133]

130 Framework Directive, Article 14(2).

131 *United Brands v. Commission*, 27/76, [1978] ECR 207.

132 *United Brands v. Commission*; *AKZO v. Commission*, C-62/86 [1991] ECR I-3359, para. 60; *Irish Sugar v. Commission*, T–228/97, [1999] ECR II–2969, para. 70.

133 Framework Directive, Article 15(2).

The national regulatory authority may not depart from the Recommendation without going through a Level 2 Consultation and Level 3 Veto procedure described in section 6 above.

Under the new Framework Directive national regulatory authorities will have to become experts in competition law. Many national regulatory authorities will no doubt choose to work in close cooperation with competition authorities. Indeed the Framework Directive *requires* such cooperation: when analyzing the relevant market, national regulators must work in cooperation with the national competition authorities.[134] The Framework Directive instructs national regulatory authorities to determine whether a relevant market is "effectively competitive." The 27th recital to the Directive defines markets that are *not* effectively competitive as: "markets where there are one or more undertakings with significant market power, and where national and Community competition law remedies are not sufficient to address the problem."[135] If the market is "effectively competitive," the national regulatory authority shall not impose or maintain any *ex ante* obligations regarding interconnection, access, or universal service.[136] If the market is not "effectively competitive," the national regulatory authority shall identify the undertakings with significant market power on the relevant market.[137] National regulatory authorities will be responsible for fixing the geographic limits to relevant markets:

> National regulatory authorities should analyze whether a given product or service market is effectively competitive in a given geographical area, which could be the whole or a part of the territory of the Member State concerned or neighboring parts of territories of Member States considered together.[138]

National regulatory authorities must also determine whether there is any "joint dominance" in a given market. The concept of joint dominance worries mobile operators in particular, because mobile operators frequently have market shares too small to be considered dominant in an individual capacity, but the operators together constitute an oligopoly, sometimes with coordinated behavior. For example, GSM operators have been accused of abusing a joint dominant position by maintaining artificially high roaming charges. Because of the sensitivity of the joint dominance issue, the Framework Directive includes an Annex listing some of the criteria that indicate the presence of a joint dominant position.[139] Under competition law, joint dominance is hard to prove and is therefore used rarely in practice. Thus the likelihood of national regulatory authorities finding a case of joint dominance, even among mobile operators, is small. That national regulators

134 Framework Directive, Article 3(4), 16(1).

135 Framework Directive, Preamble, 27th recital.

136 Framework Directive, Article 16(3).

137 Framework Directive, Article 16(4).

138 Framework Directive, Preamble, 27th recital.

139 Framework Directive, Annex 2.

have the power to find joint dominance may be sufficient to keep GSM operators from engaging in any coördinated anticompetitive practices.

In addition to looking at joint dominance, the national regulatory authorities are supposed to consider whether a dominant position in one market could be leveraged into a closely related market, thereby strengthening the market power of the undertaking.[140] Where this happens, national regulatory authorities may find that the firm has "significant market power" in the closely related market as well.[141]

A national regulatory authority's proposed decision identifying "SMP" operators must be run through the Level 1 and Level 2 Consultation procedures described in section 6 above, during which the Commission, other national regulators and interested parties may comment. If the Commission finds that the proposed decision violates Community law in particular by violating the key principles of Article 8 mission statement, the Commission can ask that the decision be withdrawn. The Commission can also exercise this right if the national regulatory authority adopts a definition of the relevant product or service market that differs from the definition appearing in the Commission's Recommendation. Indeed the national regulatory authorities are required[142] to take "utmost account" of the Commission's Recommendation and of the Commission's guidelines for market analysis when defining relevant markets.

The new definition of "SMP" is unlikely to change the regulatory status of the incumbent fixed-line operators in each country. BT, Deutsche Telekom, France Télécom, Telefonica and Telecom Italia will continue to be deemed SMP operators for most services in their home markets, even under the new definition of SMP. The real change could come for European mobile operators. In most European countries, three or four GSM operators share the market, no single operator controlling more than 50% of the market. In that case, it may be that no single operator would be deemed to possess "significant market power" under the new standard, whereas previously mobile operators holding a 30% market share were deemed to hold "significant market power" on the retail market.

The Framework Directive does not describe the consequences of an operator holding "significant market power." The consequences of being labeled an "SMP" operator appear in the Access Directive and the Universal Service Directive. Suffice it to say that being labeled "SMP" is highly undesirable for an operator, since it carries with it a load of *ex ante* regulatory obligations that benefit non-SMP operators and end-users.

For incumbent operators, it is a forgone conclusion that they will be deemed to possess "SMP" for basic services such as switched voice and leased lines. The real battle for incumbents will be to avoid being classified as holding "SMP" in

140 Framework Directive, Article 14(3).

141 Framework Directive, Article 14(3).

142 Framework Directive, Article 15(3).

newly-emerging broadband markets. For this reason, the definition of the relevant product and service markets will be crucial. To take just one example, if the relevant market is defined as broadband data services for large corporate customers, the incumbent in a given country may not be deemed to possess significant market power because of the presence of large multinational competitors on the same market. What this definition overlooks, however, is that the two or three competitors on the retail market for corporate data services rely on the infrastructure of the incumbent to cover the last mile to the customer premises. Thus while a given retail market might be found to be "effectively competitive," analysis of the upstream wholesale market may reveal the presence of an "SMP" operator that furnishes essential inputs to the downstream competitors (as well as to itself). Getting the right definition of relevant product and service markets both at the retail and wholesale levels will be key to the success of the new regulatory framework. The Commission's Recommendation on the relevant product and service market will avoid lengthy debate at the national level on what markets are relevant for purposes of determining "significant market power."

Annex I to the Framework Directive contains an initial list of markets that will be included the Commission's first Recommendation. These initial markets are divided roughly between retail and wholesale markets. The relevant retail markets are:

- the provision of connection to and use of the public telephone network at fixed locations;
- the provision of leased lines to end users.

The relevant wholesale markets are:

- call origination in the fixed public telephone network;
- call termination in the fixed public telephone network;
- transit services in the fixed public telephone network;
- call origination on public mobile telephone networks;
- call termination on public mobile telephone networks;
- leased line interconnection (interconnections of part circuits);
- access to the fixed public telephone network, including unbundled access to the local loop;
- access to public mobile telephone networks, including carrier selection;
- wholesale provision of leased line capacity to other suppliers of electronic communications networks or services;
- services provided over unbundled (twisted metallic pair) loops;
- national market for international roaming services on public mobile telephone networks.

This list is only a starting point. One of the first tasks of national regulatory authorities is to analyze these product and service markets—some of which are remnants of the old regulatory framework—to determine if any of them is effectively competitive. If so, national regulatory authorities must withdraw existing regulations on those markets.[143] The Commission will refine its definition of relevant product and service markets, after holding a public consultation and consulting national regulatory authorities.[144] As noted above, the most controversial issue right now is whether there exists a separate market for termination of calls on each individual mobile network.

7. The New Role of the National Regulatory Authorities

Under the previous framework, Member States were required to, and did, set up independent regulatory authorities. The requirement of an "independent" and "impartial" regulatory authority flows from the 1990 ONP Framework Directive and from the Reference Paper to the 1997 WTO Agreement on Basic Telecommunications Services. The Reference Paper gives the meaning of "independent regulator:"

> The regulatory body is separate from, and not accountable to, any supplier of basic telecommunications services. The decisions of and the procedures used by regulators shall be impartial with respect to all market participants.

The definition of "independence" is similar under the Framework Directive. As a practical matter, all fifteen Member States have established bodies legally and functionally independent from the governmental ministries that hold ownership of the incumbent telecommunications operator. The first important step of creating an independent regulatory authority is therefore behind us. But the old framework only covered traditional telecommunications. The new framework includes broadcasting networks and services, which are traditionally regulated by bodies separate from the telecommunications authorities. The new framework will require Member States to rethink the roles and structures of their existing regulatory bodies entrusted with the regulation of audiovisual services. In the UK, this "rethink" has already taken place, with the proposed creation of a single regulatory body called OFCOM, which will be responsible for all communications, both traditional telecommunications and audiovisual broadcasting. In France audiovisual broadcasting is under the jurisdiction of a separate regulatory body called the *Conseil Supérieur de l'Audiovisuel* (CSA). The CSA has jurisdiction not just to regulate content, but also the networks and transmission services used to broadcast it. Because anything having to do with audiovisual services is politically sensitive, no one has yet forwarded a proposal to create a single communications authority (as in the UK) or to limit the CSA's authority to govern solely issues of content, to the exclusion of transmission services. On the contrary, the French parliament recently gave the CSA authority over digital television transmission infrastructure and services. This leads to a situation where a dispute regarding access to

143 Framework Directive, Article 16-3.

144 Framework Directive, Article 15-1.

transmission infrastructure must be brought before the CSA if the infrastructure is used to carry a video signal destined for a digital television set, and before the telecommunications regulatory authority (ART) if the infrastructure is used to carry a video signal destined for a 3G mobile handset. This is just the kind of regulatory confusion that the drafters of the Framework Directive hoped to eliminate. But the Framework Directive does not *require* Member States to merge their broadcasting and telecommunications authorities, or even take responsibility for digital "pipes" away from the broadcasting authority. The Directive does not go that far. In fact, it expressly foresees the possibility of having two or more regulatory authorities responsible in parallel for electronic communications networks and services. The Directive defines "national regulatory authority" as:

> The body *or bodies* charged by a Member State with any of the regulatory tasks assigned in this Directive and the specific directives.[145]

Article 3 goes further to state that if a Member State chooses to assign regulatory tasks to more than one entity, the Member State shall:

- publish in easily accessible form the tasks undertaking by the respective authorities;
- ensure consultation and cooperation between those authorities, and between those authorities and national competition authorities and national consumer protection authorities;
- notify the Commission of all national regulatory authorities assigned tasks under the Framework and specific directives, and their respective responsibilities.[146]

This leaves Member States pretty free to organize regulatory functions however they want, including dividing responsibility for communications networks between the existing telecommunications authority and the broadcasting authority. The subsidiary principle[147] limits how far European Directives can go in organizing the internal affairs of a Member State. If a Member State wants to have a separate regulatory authority for each state or region in the country (as in the case in the United States or Germany), or to have two national authorities (broadcasting and telecommunications) that have overlapping roles (as is the case in France), the Member State is entitled to do so.

However many regulatory authorities a Member State chooses to create, the regulatory authorities must comply with the following principles:

---

145 Framework Directive, Article 2(g) (emphasis added).

146 Framework Directive, Article 3(4).

147 EC Treaty, Article 5.

- the regulatory authority (or authorities) must be "competent;"[148]
- they must be independent, i.e. legally distinct from and functionally independent of all organizations providing electronic communications networks, equipment or services. If a Member State also owns or controls an entity providing electronic communications networks and/or services, the Member State must ensure effective structural separation of the regulatory functions from activities associated with ownership or control;[149]
- they must exercise their powers "impartially and transparently;"[150]
- they should have all necessary resources in terms of staffing, expertise and financial means, for the performance of their tasks.[151]

These requirements are not new; they already existed in the WTO Reference Paper and in the 1990 ONP Framework Directive.

8. Right to Appeal

The Framework Directive requires that Member States provide an appeal mechanism against regulatory decisions of all kinds.[152] The appeal must be available to any user or supplier of electronic communications networks or services who is "affected" by the decision.[153] This language would appear to give a right to appeal even to an entity that is not directly involved in the procedure. For example, a decision involving a mobile operator might give rise to an appeal by another mobile operator adversely affected by the decision, even if the other mobile operator is not expressly named in the decision. The 12th recital contains language that is narrower than the language in Article 4(1) of the Directive. The 12th recital says that "any party who *is the subject* of a decision" shall have the right to appeal. A "party who is the subject of a decision" is not the same thing as a "user or provider . . . who is affected" by a decision. The latter category is broader, including entities that are not actually the target of a given decision, but who may be directly of indirectly affected by it. Member Sates will no doubt take advantage of this ambiguity when enacting their national laws implementing the Directive. Some Member States may interpret the words "affected by" in Article 4(1) as being equivalent to the more narrow language appearing in the 12th recital, thereby giving an appeal right only to entities that are the "subject" a regulatory decision. Other Member States may read the language in Article 4(1) more broadly, giving a right to appeal to any entity directly or indirectly "affected by" the regulatory decision. This is an unfortunate inconsistency between the operative text of the

148 Framework Directive, Article 3(1).

149 Framework Directive, Article 3(2).

150 Framework Directive, Article 3(3).

151 Framework Directive, Preamble, 11th recital.

152 Framework Directive, Article 4(1).

153 Framework Directive, Article 4(1).

Directive and the language in the recitals. The inconsistency could give rise to diverging approaches by Member States.

The appeal body may be a court or another independent body.[154] If the appeal body is not a court, a right of appeal must exist in the last instance to a court. The decision of the national regulatory authority must stand pending the appeal, unless the appeal body itself decides to suspend the regulatory authority's decision pending the appeal. This provision is designed to avoid dilatory tactics used by incumbents in many Member States. The Seventh Report on Implementation deplored the fact that regulatory decisions are made ineffective by systematic appeals by the incumbents.[155] The appellate body must take the merits of the case into account. This is to make sure that the appellate bodies do not only look for errors of law or procedure, but review all the underlying facts of the case. The appellate bodies must have appropriate expertise available to carry out their functions.[156] Where an appeal is to a judicial body, appellate judges need to acquire specialized knowledge in the field of electronic communications in order to be in a position to effectively exercise their appellate review of the merits of the case.

9. Scarce Resources

The Framework Directive sets forth basic principles that Member States must apply when allocating scarce resources such as frequencies, blocks of numbers and IP addresses, as well as principles for granting rights of way over public and (sometimes) private property. These principles are closely tied to authorization procedures and will be discussed in the next section.

10. Technical Standards and Interoperability

Terminal Equipment

The Framework Directive does not deal with terminal equipment at all, except for consumer digital television equipment. For traditional radio and telecommunications terminal equipment, the existing terminal equipment Directive[157] remains in effect.

The Framework Directive and the Universal Service Directive do address consumer equipment for digital television. These issues, together with interoperability and conditional access systems for digital television, will be discussed later.

---

154 Currently only Denmark has special appeals boards for regulatory decisions. In most other Member States, regulatory decisions are appealed to the courts, either administrative or civil. For an inventory of appeal mechanisms available, see OECD, *Telecommunications Regulations: Institutional Structures and Responsibilities*, May 26, 2000, DSTI/ICCP/TISP (99) 15/FINAL.

155 European Commission, Seventh Implementation Report, COM (2001) 706, § 4.2.1, p. 15.

156 Framework Directive, Article 4(1).

157 EP/Council Directive 99/5 on radio equipment and telecommunications terminal equipment and the mutual recognition of their conformity (OJ L91/99).

Technical Standards

The existence of a single technical standard throughout Europe was one of the keys to the success of GSM phone technology. In some cases, imposing a uniform standard in Europe can clearly help interoperability and consumer well-being (two key principles in the Article 8 mission statement). The risk of course is that the standard chosen by European bureaucrats will somehow be wrong, thereby foreclosing other more innovative technological solutions. Aware of this risk, the Commission is reluctant to impose mandatory standards, and prefers to let standards emerge by themselves as a result of industry cooperation.[158]

Nevertheless, the Commission cannot allow incompatible technical standards to develop in different parts of the EU, because incompatible standards would undermine the goal of creating a single European market for services and terminal equipment. Consequently, while preferring and encouraging a bottom-up consensual approach to standards, the Commission retains the power to impose top-down solutions when necessary. This approach is reflected in the Framework Directive, which states that the Commission shall draw up and publish a "list of standards and/or specifications to serve as a basis for encouraging the harmonized provision of electronic communications networks, electronic communications services and associated facilities and services."[159] This list is not compulsory. Member States only have to "encourage" use of the standards and specifications published by the Commission. However, if the Commission finds that the standards and/or specifications have not been adequately implemented so that "interoperability of services in one or more Member States cannot be ensured,"[160] the Commission can, after public consultation and after seeking the opinion of the Communications Committee, make the standards mandatory to the extent strictly necessary to ensure such interoperability and to improve freedom of choice of users. (See chart below for an explanation.)

Finally, if a standard published either on the recommended list or on the compulsory list of the Commission "no longer contribute[s] to the provision of harmonized electronic communications services, or . . . no longer meet[s] consumers' needs or [is] hampering technological development," the Commission shall remove the standard from the relevant list.[161]

Interoperability of Digital Interactive Television Services

The original Commission proposal contained no special section dealing with interactive television. The original philosophy was that emerging gateways in digital interactive television would be dealt with under the Access Directive, just like any other new bottleneck facility. There is no reason why interactive television

158 An example of this is the Commission's approach to digital television standards, which have been developed in an industry forum called the DVB Group.

159 Framework Directive, Article 17(1).

160 Framework Directive, Article 17(3).

161 Framework Directive, Article 17(5) and (6).

platforms should be singled out for special treatment as compared to other new platforms (such as 3G mobile platforms).

Nevertheless, the specter of proprietary software platforms for interactive television lead to strong lobbying at the European Parliament to ensure that Europe's interactive television would be built on open standards so as not to endanger media pluralism and cultural diversity. The final wording of the Framework Directive reflects a political compromise. The Directive calls on Member States to "encourage" the use of an open application program interface ("API") in digital interactive television platforms, both at the service provider level and the equipment manufacturer level.[162] The Directive also calls on Member States to "encourage" owners of APIs to make information available to third party service providers on a non-discriminatory basis so that service providers can develop and offer services supported by the API. According to the Directive, "open APIs facilitate interoperability, i.e. the portability of interactive content between delivery mechanisms, and full functionality of this content on enhanced digital television equipment."[163] Owners of the API may require "appropriate remuneration" in exchange for providing this information. If the Commission concludes on July 24, 2004 that "interoperability and freedom of choice for users have not been adequately achieved in one or more Member States,"[164] the Commission may take more drastic action, such as making an open standard compulsory by following the procedure outlined in section 11.2 above. In any event, in making decisions on open APIs, regulators are supposed also to take into account the need to protect receiving equipment from malicious attacks by viruses.[165]

Article 18 of the Framework Directive overlaps with Article 5(1) of the Access Directive, which permits national regulators to force access to APIs and EPGs for digital television services to the extent necessary to ensure accessibility for end-users to certain digital radio and television broadcasting services designated by the Member State on non-discriminatory terms.

11. Accounting Separation and Financial Reports

Entities benefiting from special or exclusive rights in other fields (such as water or electricity distribution) must either (i) maintain separate accounts for their electronic communications activities as if those activities were carried out by a legally independent company, or (ii) implement full structural separation.[166] The choice is left to Member States. Member States also have the option of exempting from this requirement companies that derive less than 50 million Euros in revenues from electronic communications services. The Directive requires providers of electronic communications networks and services who are not already subject to the requirements of

162 Framework Directive, Article 18(1).

163 Framework Directive, Preamble, 31st recital.

164 Framework Directive, Article 18 (3).

165 Framework Directive, Preamble, 31st recital.

166 Framework Directive, Article 13(1).

company law to have their financial statements published and audited. Small and medium-sized businesses are not exempt from this requirement.

12. Exchanges of Information

Supplying Information to National Regulatory Authorities

The Framework Directive requires that entities providing electronic communications networks or services comply with information requests from the national regulatory authority.[167] The national regulatory authority's information requests must be proportionate to the performance of the regulator's tasks under the Directive, and must include reasons for the request.

Supplying Information to the Commission

National regulatory authorities in turn must comply with reasoned information requests from the Commission.[168] Like the national regulatory authorities' requests, the Commission's requests must be proportionate to the performance of the Commission's tasks under the Treaty. The Commission may make the information it receives available to national regulatory authorities in other Member States, unless the regulatory authority furnishing the information makes an explicit and reasoned request to the contrary.

Each national regulatory authority shall also make the information it receives available to other regulatory authorities, either in the same country or in another Member State, after a substantiated request. When information is deemed confidential by the national regulatory authority under applicable national or EU rules on business secrecy, the Commission and national authorities shall ensure such confidentiality is maintained for the information they receive.

Supplying Information to the Communications Committee

The Commission shall provide to the Communications Committee information on the outcome of regular consultations with operators, service providers, users, consumers, manufacturers, trade unions, third countries and international organizations.[169] The Committee shall foster an exchange of information between Member States, and between Member States and the Commission.[170]

Information regarding Application of the Directives

Member States must publish information on the application of the Directives, and make such information available to the Commission (who in turn will make it available to the Communications Committee).[171]

167 Framework Directive, Article 5(1).

168 Framework Directive, Article 5(2).

169 Framework Directive, Article 23(1).

170 Framework Directive, Article 23(2).

171 Framework Directive, Article 24(1).

Finally, national regulatory authorities must publish such information as would contribute to an open and competitive market.[172] National regulatory authorities must publish rules for obtaining access to any such information.[173] The requirement to publish "such information as would contribute to an open and competitive market" is a well-meaning attempt to foster transparency, but the requirement is too vague to have any real teeth. Member States will no doubt enact national laws giving broad discretion to national regulatory authorities to determine what information they want to publish. Of much greater practical effect will be the requirement to consult interested parties prior to adopting a measure that has a "significant impact on the relevant market."[174] That measure leaves little room for interpretation, and will have to be implemented as-is into national law.

13. Communications Committee

The "Communications Committee" consists of representatives of the Member States, and is chaired by the Commission. In practice the Member States will send representatives of their respective Ministries of Telecommunications and/or Broadcasting. The Communications Committee is the place where Member States are able to keep tabs on the Commission in connection with actions taken under the new framework.[175] The Framework Directive requires the Commission to seek the Committee's opinion before vetoing the decision of a national regulatory authority under the Level 3 Veto Procedure outlined in section 6 above.[176] In that case the Committee's role is only advisory.[177] For those matters, the Committee's opinion is also advisory when it comes to recommended technical standards drawn up by the Commission,[178] or recommendations to Members States intended to facilitate harmonized application of the Directives.[179] The Commission is not bound to follow the Committee's decision. For *compulsory* technical standards,[180] pan-European numbering decisions,[181] or decisions identifying transnational markets,[182] the Commission must take account of the Committee's position before implementing the measure. Otherwise the matter has to be referred to the European Council and European Parliament.[183]

---

172 Framework Directive, Article 5(4).

173 Framework Directive, Article 5(5).

174 Framework Directive, Article 6.

175 For a general description of the role of committees in EU procedures, *see* P. Raworth, *Introduction to the Legal System of the European Union* (Oceana, New York, 2001) at pp.177-180.

176 Framework Directive, Article 7(4).

177 Council Decision 99/468, Article 3.

178 Framework Directive, Article 17(1).

179 Framework Directive, Article 19(1).

180 Framework Directive, Article 17(4).

181 Framework Directive, Articles 10(4) and 19(2).

182 Framework Directive, Article 15(4).

183 Comitology Decision, Article 5.

The Communications Committee sets up its own rules of operation, in accordance with the "Comitology Decision."[184] The Communications Committee will assume the role previously filled by the ONP and Licensing Committees established under the old framework. It is not clear from the text of the Framework Directive whether the old ONP and Licensing Committees will actually disappear and be replaced by the Communications Committee, but that outcome appears inevitable. The old ONP and Licensing Committees were established under the previous ONP Directives, all of which are cancelled under the new framework. Logically, therefore, the committees set up under the old ONP Directives would have to disappear once their statutory authority also disappears. The Commission must keep the Communications Committee informed of the outcome of consultations with operators, service providers, consumers, users, manufacturers, trade unions, third countries and international organizations.[185]

14. European Regulators Group

As we saw in section 13 above, the "Communications Committee" consists of representatives of national governments, in practice the Telecommunications Ministry of each government. The Telecommunications Ministry in a given country is generally *not* the "national regulatory authority." To give themselves a forum to examine European telecommunications issues, national regulatory authorities created in 1997 the "Independent Regulators Group" ("IRG"). The IRG has set up a number of working parties on interconnection and pricing issues, unbundling, regulatory accounting, and has contributed valuable analysis to the sector. The work of the IRG has helped each national regulatory authority to learn from the experiences of authorities in other Member States and, if possible, to adopt coherent regulatory decisions.

Pursuant to the new framework, the European Commission created on July 29, 2002 a new forum for national regulatory authorities called the "European Regulators Group" ("ERG").[186] One would have thought that the ERG would simply be the new name for the existing IRG. The IRG recently decided, however, that it would remain alive as an organization separate from the ERG.[187] Perhaps the decision to keep the IRG alive is attributable to some of the uncertainties linked to the future ERG. For one thing, most Member States will have to undertake an overhaul of their existing national regulatory authorities, and try to face the difficult question of how to divide responsibilities between broadcasting and telecommunications authorities (or whether to merge the two authorities). Over time, it may be that the ERG will assume all of the functions of the IRG, and that the IRG will disappear.

184 Council Decision 99/468, Article 7(1).

185 Framework Directive, Article 23(1).

186 Commission Decision 02/627 establishing the European Regulators Group for Electronic Communications Networks and Services (OJ L200/02) (the "ERG Decision").

187 IRG Press Release, September 16, 2002.

It is premature to guess how the ERG will function in practice, but we can say what its official role is. The ERG Decision states that the ERG will provide "an interface for advising and assisting the Commission in the electronic communications field."[188] The ERG will consist of the heads of each "relevant national regulatory authority in each Member State or their representatives."[189] This raises the interesting question of what happens when there are several national regulatory authorities in a given country. This might happen in a country that decides to divide responsibilities for electronic communications between the telecommunications regulator and the broadcasting regulator. The ERG Decision tries to provide an answer to this dilemma, by stating that the "relevant regulatory authority" means "the public authority established in each Member State to oversee the day-to-day interpretation of the provisions of the Directives."[190] Note that this definition says "the public *authority*" established in each Member State, not "the public authority *or authorities*." This language suggests that only one "authority" is permitted from each Member State. In Member States that maintain multiple authorities, those authorities will have to decide among themselves which authority will participate in the ERG. Both authorities (telecommunication and broadcasting) may feel that they "oversee the day-to-day interpretation and application" of the Directives and therefore have a legitimate claim to sit on the ERG. The IRG (which today only includes telecommunications regulators) has already taken the lead, by naming from its members a candidate for the first chairmanship of the ERG.[191]

The ERG must "consult extensively and at an early stage with market participants, consumers and end-users in an open and transparent manner."[192] As we saw in section 6.1 above, national regulators already have an obligation to consult interested parties prior to adopting any decision having a significant impact on the relevant market.[193] Article 6 of the ERG Decision states that the ERG must also "consult extensively and at an early stage."[194] This means that in addition to consultations conducted at a national level, the ERG may launch its own European public consultations on subjects that have a pan-European interest. If nothing else, the new framework will pose a logistical challenge in connection with the numerous public consultations that are required at both the European and national levels. The ERG otherwise is free on its own initiative to advise and assist the Commission on any subject linked to electronic communications services and net-

188 ERG Decision, Preamble, 5th recital and Article 3.

189 ERG Decision, Article 4.

190 ERG Decision, Article 2.

191 IRG Press Release of September 16, 2002.

192 ERG Decision, Article 6.

193 Framework Directive, Article 6.

194 ERG Decision, Article 6.

works.[195] The ERG's input will be particularly important for the Commission in drafting and updating its Recommendation on relevant product and service markets.[196] The ERG must prepare an annual report of its activities and submit it to the Commission.[197] The Commission shares the report with the European Parliament and the Council.[198]

15. Commission's Power to issue Recommendations

The Commission has a general power to issue recommendations to Member States on the harmonized application of the Directives in a manner to achieve the objectives of the Article 8 mission statement.[199] The Commission can adopt the recommendations only after seeking the opinion of the Communications Committee. Member States must ensure that national regulatory authorities take "utmost account" of the various recommendations issued by the Commission. If a national regulatory authority chooses not to follow a recommendation, it must so inform the Commission, and give reasons for its position.

16. Dispute Resolution

Previously, national regulatory authorities had jurisdiction to resolve only disputes relating to interconnection and access. Under the new framework, national regulatory authorities will have jurisdiction to resolve any and all disputes "arising in connection with obligations arising under this Directive or the Specific Directives between undertakings providing electronic communications networks or services in a Member State."[200] The only requirement is that the dispute relate to obligations arising under the new Directives. The time limit for issuing a binding decision is four months. Previously the maximum time period was six months.[201] The Framework Directive gives national regulatory authorities one possible out: Member States may make provisions allowing national regulatory authorities to decline jurisdiction if other mechanisms (such as mediation) are available, that would better contribute to the timely resolution of the dispute in accordance with the key principles of the Article 8 mission statement.[202] If after four months, however, the dispute is still not resolved, and neither party has brought an action before the courts, the national regulatory authority will have to accept jurisdiction

---

195 ERG Decision, Article 5.

196 *See* section 7 above.

197 ERG Decision, Article 8.

198 ERG Decision, Article 8.

199 Framework Directive, Article 19(1).

200 Framework Directive, Article 20(1).

201 EP/Council Directive 97/33 on interconnection in telecommunications with regard to ensuring universal service and interoperability through application of the principles of open network provision (ONP) (OJ L199/97) (the "Interconnection Directive"), Article 9(5).

202 Framework Directive, Article 20(2).

and issue a binding decision within four additional months.[203] The decision of the national regulatory authority in a dispute resolution procedure must aim at achieving the key principles set forth in the Article 8 mission statement. Obligations that a regulator imposes on parties must conform to the provisions of the Directives. The decision must be made publicly available after redaction of confidential information. The national regulatory authority's jurisdiction is not exclusive; the parties can always bring their dispute directly before the courts.[204] The new dispute resolution role of national regulatory authorities goes way beyond their current role, and will probably lead to a flood of new cases, requiring regulatory authorities to build up their case-handling capabilities.[205] Under the new Directives, a communications network or service provider need only allege (a) that the respondent is also an entity providing electronic communications networks or services and (b) that the dispute has arisen "in connection with" one of the obligations arising under one of the new Directives (access, data protection, universal service, authorization). These new disputes may include disputes based almost solely on competition law claims. Under the new framework, many of the obligations arising under the Directives are pure competition-law obligations. National regulatory authorities must be able to handle those claims, with help from the national competition authority. One of the main challenges for national regulators will be to weed out disputes that are purely commercial or contractual, that do not raise any bona fide issues under the Directives. National regulators will no doubt draw up guidelines to assist parties in determining whether their dispute relates to obligations under the Directives and therefore falls within the regulator's jurisdiction.

The Directive provides for a mechanism involving cross border disputes.[206] When a cross-border dispute arises, the national regulators of the relevant countries must resolve the dispute together. In that case, the time limit of four months no longer applies. The Framework Directive does not describe how national regulatory authorities would go about resolving a cross-border dispute jointly. National regulators—perhaps in the context of the European Regulators Group—will have to develop joint dispute resolution procedures to be used in the case of cross-border disputes. Joint procedures could give rise to a number of tricky procedural questions, such as the language of the proceeding, and relevant appeal mechanisms.

---

203 Framework Directive, Article 19(2).

204 Framework Directive, Article 20(5).

205 National regulators already suffer from lack of budgetary and human resources. See, Seventh Implementation Reports, COM (2001)706, & 4.2.1 p. 16.

206 Framework Directive, Article 21(2).

17. Application of the Directive; Three-year Review

Member States had to implement the Directives by July 24, 2003.[207] Three years after the implementation date, the Commission must review the functioning of the Framework Directive and issue a report to the European Parliament and the Council.[208] Two consequences would flow from non-transposition of the Directives:

1) The Commission could initiate infringement proceedings against the guilty Member State;

2) Provisions in the Directives that are sufficiently unambiguous could in certain circumstances be enforced directly by private parties.

C. THE AUTHORIZATION DIRECTIVE[209]

1. Introduction

As is evident from the foregoing discussion, the current licensing framework for telecommunications operators in Europe is far from perfect. The drafters of the original Licensing Directive envisaged a light-handed procedure, expressing a preference for general authorizations in all but "justified cases." Licensing conditions and procedures were supposed to be more or less identical throughout Europe, thereby contributing to the creation of a single market. Yet Member States proceeded to enact their own licensing procedures with their own conditions, requiring operators in most cases to obtain individual licenses. Individual licenses were supposed to be the exception, not the rule. They in fact became the rule. If there is one area in the European telecommunications regime that clearly needed fixing, it was licensing. To reach the twin objectives of harmonization and ease of market entry, the new Authorization Directive does away entirely with individual licenses, relying solely on general authorizations in the future. These general authorizations would require that the operator file a simple declaration. Thereafter the operator would be allowed to provide services, as long as it complied with a list of standard conditions. The conditions are supposed to be pretty much the same in each Member State, thereby contributing to harmonization. After its 1999 Review consultation, the Commission reported that the idea of doing away with individual licenses had received "widespread support." One could have expected support from operators (particularly pan-European operators), who were fed up with individual licensing procedures. Support from Member State governments was less predictable, particularly from Member States with a tradition of strong governmental intervention in the economy. Be that as it may, the directive's principle of abolishing individual licenses is now part of the European Framework, making life for new entrants a whole lot simpler. As we will see below, operators will still need individual permits to obtain critical numbering resources,

207 Framework Directive, Article 28.

208 Framework Directive, Article 25.

209 This material was originally published in *Electronic Communications: the New EU Framework* (ed. W. Maxwell, Oceana, New York, 2002).

frequencies and rights of way. So it may turn out that the directive has merely displaced the regulatory bottleneck, not abolished it entirely.

2. Networks and Services Subject to General Authorizations

The Authorization Directive starts out by announcing that Member States shall guarantee the freedom of supplying electronic communications networks and services, but that they make the exercise of that freedom subject to the conditions set forth in general authorizations.[210] Member States may not prevent an entity (particularly a foreign entity) from offering services or networks except for reasons based on health, national security, or public policy. Member States may not require operators to obtain an individual license as a precondition to providing service.[211] The most that Member States can require is that operators file a declaration before starting service. But the declaration must remain a true declaration. It cannot subtly transform itself into an individual license. For instance, Member States cannot provide that the declaration will only become effective once the relevant authority has acknowledged its receipt. Under the new directive, a declaration is only a declaration. Once the operator sends it in, the declaration becomes effective. The operator need not await a stamp of approval, or even an acknowledgment of receipt from the national regularity authority. The filing is effective immediately.

Form of Declaration

The declaration may only include:

> minimal information which is required to allow the national regulatory authority to keep a register or list of providers of electronic communications networks and services. This information must be limited to what is necessary for the identification of the provider, such as company registration numbers, and the provider's contact persons, the provider's address, a short description of the network or service and an estimated date for starting the activity.[212]

What a change this will make from current licensing procedures. Would-be operators today have to file license applications that include multi-year business plans, cash flow and capital expenditure projections, anticipated headcount, sources of funds, and proof of financing. In many cases the license application is so demanding that operators hire consultants to help prepare it. By contrast, the new directive calls for an ultra-simplified declaration, including the name and address of the provider, a short description of the network and/or service, and the anticipated starting date. This is good news for operators and bad news for consultants. Of course, the directive's use of the words "such as" suggests that Member States might be able to ask for *more* than simply the name and address of the provider and a brief description of the network or service. But the directive does limit the

210 Authorization Directive, Article 3(1).

211 Authorization Directive, Article 3(2).

212 Authorization Directive, Article 3(3).

information to "what is necessary for the identification of the provider." This would prevent Member States from insisting on detailed business plans, for example, as part of the declaration procedure. Based on how certain Member States implemented the 1997 Licensing Directive, some surprises may be in store in connection with implementation of the new directive. Some Member States may require, for example, information going beyond the name and address of the provider and a simple description of the network. In any event, even if some Member States ask for too much information, the result will still be a great improvement over the current regime.

What Networks or Services Require a Declaration?

The prior declaration procedure can apply to *all* electronic communications networks and services, whether public or private. Unlike the old directive, the new directive does not envisage different levels of procedures for public and private networks. All electronic communications networks and services are treated alike, and should be subject to the same light-handed declaration procedure. As we will see below, the rights and obligations that result from the declaration may differ for public and private networks and services. But the declaration should be the same for both. Member States can, if they wish, require that *all* electronic communications networks and services require the filing of a declaration. This maximalist approach would require even Internet access providers ("IAPs") to file a declaration before starting business. IAPs are providers of electronic communications services and as such will be subject to the new Authorization Directive. IAPs will no doubt view a filing requirement as an unwelcome incursion of telecommunications regulations into the free-wheeling world of the Internet. Traditional telecommunications operators, on the other hand, will view this filing requirement as a welcome break from the heavy licensing procedures of the past.

Some new entrants that have already suffered through the heavy licensing procedures in Europe may feel that this new lighter procedure unfairly advantages new rivals that are just now entering the market. New entrants are generally against heavy licensing procedures until they themselves obtain a license. Once in the market, those new entrants will view their hard-earned license as a competitive advantage creating value for the company and its shareholders. Being difficult and costly to obtain, the license became a valuable asset. Looked at in a certain way, the new directive could actually destroy value for existing telecommunications operators (including established new entrants) by removing regulatory barriers to entry for new operators only now making their foray into Europe. Existing operators should take comfort in the fact that licenses are only one of many regulatory barriers to entry. As noted below, obtaining frequencies and rights of way will still present difficulties under the new framework, so market entry will not be so easy. Through frequencies, numbering resources and rights of way existing operators will still have a regulatory advantage over newcomers, in addition to the many other advantages associated with being first to market.

Advantages of Filing a Declaration

Some entities will be tempted not to file a declaration in order to fly below the radar of competitors and regulators. That would be the case, for example, for entities whose status as an operator is not clear. Filing a declaration is an admission that an entity is a provider of electronic communications networks or services, subject to telecommunication-style regulations. In borderline cases, entities will have every reason *not* to file a declaration, unless the entity needs something that only a declaration can provide.

Obviously some important advantages come from filing a declaration, the first being that it allows an entity to ply its trade legally. An entity providing electronic communications networks or services without having filed a declaration would be operating illegally; it could be sanctioned and prevented from conducting business. Sanctions would be a credible threat only to providers who clearly fall within the definition of electronic communications networks or services. For borderline cases where the status of the provider is not clear, the likely result of any enforcement action would be to require the provider to file a declaration. Monetary sanctions would be unlikely. The provider would have lost nothing by adopting a "wait and see" attitude.

In addition to the peace of mind that goes with operating legally, filing a declaration affords several rights that can be of particular value to a network operator or service provider:

- the right to apply for rights of way over public, and in some cases private, property;
- the right to negotiate interconnection with other operators of public electronic communications networks or services;[213]
- the right to request access to network elements of operators holding significant market power;
- the right to be designated as a universal service provider.

Filing a declaration may also help in obtaining frequency usage rights and numbering usage rights (although as we will see below, one doesn't necessarily need to be registered as an operator or service provider to obtain such rights under the new framework). Obtaining rights of way and interconnection rights are extremely important to operators in the traditional telecommunications sense. But Internet access providers, for example, may feel that these rights have little practical use for them, thereby raising the issue of whether IAPs have any interest in filing a declaration under the new regime, other than in an effort to ensure that its operations are conducted legally in a given jurisdiction.

213 Authorization Directive, Article 4(2)(a).

Filing a declaration also can be a source of obligations, such as triggering the obligation to make contributions to a universal fund, or the obligation to provide information to the national regulatory authority.

RIGHTS CONFERRED BY A GENERAL AUTHORIZATION

PUBLIC OR PRIVATE NETWORKS OR SERVICES	ART. 4-1 (a)	Right to provide electronic communications networks and services
	ART. 4-1 (b)	Right to have application for rights of way considered
PUBLIC NETWORKS OR SERVICES	ART. 4-2 (a)	Negotiate interconnection with and where applicable obtain access to the network of other providers of public communications networks anywhere in the Community as provided in the Access Directive
	ART. 4-2 (b)	Be given the opportunity to be designated to provide different elements of a universal service

Let us examine each of these "rights" in more detail.

Right to negotiate interconnection

We will examine interconnection in more detail in the next section. Suffice it to say here that the status of provider of publicly available electronic communications networks or services gives the provider the right "to negotiate" interconnection with other providers of public electronic communications networks or services.[214] In practice, filing a declaration will be the only way to establish one's status as an operator of publicly available electronic communications networks or services. As will be seen below, national regulatory authorities will be required to deliver a status certificate to operators that have filed a declaration so that they can avail themselves of this right to negotiate interconnection. There could be situations where the party requesting interconnection has filed a declaration as a public operator but the requested party has not. The requested party will claim that it is not a provider of a publicly available electronic communications network or service (not having filed a declaration) and that it therefore has no obligation to negotiate with the requesting party. The requesting party will say that filing a declaration is not dispositive of whether the requested party is an operator or not for purposes of negotiating interconnection. That the entity is actually providing publicly available electronic communications networks or services is what counts to trigger the obligation to negotiate interconnection. The language of the Authorization Directive and the language of the Access Directive unfortunately diverge on this issue.

214 Authorization Directive, Article 4(2)(a).

The Access Directive defines "operator" as "an undertaking providing *or authorized to provide* a public communications network or an associated facility."[215] According to this language, the access and interconnection obligations apply to any undertaking providing a public communications network or associated facility, whether or not the undertaking is "authorized." The Authorization Directive on the other hand states that a declaration gives the requesting party the right to negotiate interconnection with "other providers of publicly available communications networks and services *covered by a general authorization. . . .*" This language suggests that if the requested party has not filed a declaration, it is not "covered by a general authorization" and has no duty to negotiate interconnection. This is quite a different outcome from the one reached under the Access Directive. Member States may correct this inconsistency when they draft implementing laws. Member States should use the Access Directive's language as the controlling text, since the Access Directive is the source of the duty to negotiate in the first place, and should take precedence over the language in the Authorization Directive. Moreover, making access obligations dependent on whether an operator files a declaration would encourage operators not to file.

Right to request access to network elements and services from significant market power operators

The second "right" that companies obtain by filing a declaration is the right to obtain access to network elements and services from operators with significant market power. As we will see in the next section, "access" includes such diverse things as standard interconnection, unbundled access to the local loop, access to ducts and masts, wholesale service offerings, and access to technology and key intellectual property rights. Exactly what kinds of access are available in a given situation depends on the national regulatory authority in each country. One thing is clear, however: a new entrant will not even be able to *think* about obtaining access from an SMP operator until the new entrant files a declaration confirming its status as a "provider of electronic communications networks or services to the public." Otherwise the significant market power operator will treat the entity as a retail customer, not as a wholesale customer holding rights under the Access Directive. When approaching an SMP operator to request access or interconnection, the first question the SMP operator will ask is: "Who are you? Show me evidence that you are a provider of electronic communications networks or services to the public. Otherwise you need to go talk to our retail sales division." For this purpose, filing a declaration will be essential.

The declaration need not be filed in the same Member State as the one where the SMP operator is located. For example, a new entrant that has filed a declaration as a provider of electronic communications networks to the public in Belgium would have the right to negotiate interconnection with France Telecom in France, even

215 Access Directive, Article 2(c) (emphasis added).

though the new entrant has not filed a declaration in France.[216] Article 3(1) of the Access Directive provides that: "The undertaking requesting access or interconnection does not need to be authorized to operate in the Member State where access or interconnection is requested, if it is not providing services and does not operate a network in that Member State."[217] Consequently, while filing a declaration is a prerequisite to engaging discussions on interconnection or access, the declaration need not necessarily be filed in the same country as that in which the SMP operator is located.

Right to provide universal service

Another benefit that flows from filing a declaration as a provider of electronic communications networks or services to the public is the possibility of being designated as a universal service provider for certain services in certain parts of the national territory.[218] As a universal service provider, an entity would be eligible to receive subsidies from the national universal service fund (if any). Universal service is limited to connection to the public switched telephone network, either through fixed or wireless means, the provision of basic voice telephone service and the ability to connect to the Internet at narrowband speeds. So there is no room for becoming the universal service provider of broadband to schools, for example.[219] If the last several years are any indication, new entrants will not be lining up to become universal service providers. Most new entrants are content to let the incumbent national operator be the universal service operator and receive the corresponding universal service subsidies. For the vast majority of new entrants, the possibility of being designated as a universal service provider will not weigh in the decision of whether or not to file a declaration as a provider of electronic communications networks and services to the public. On the contrary, the prospect of paying universal service charges may be an incentive *not* to file a declaration.

Right to apply for rights of way and for rights to use frequencies and numbering resources

Filing a declaration gives an operator the right to apply for the right to install facilities on public, and in some cases private, property. Filing a declaration may also give an entity special rights to apply for frequencies and numbering resources. Filing a declaration is not a precondition to obtaining rights to use frequencies or numbers. Depending on national legislation, the right to use frequency and numbering resources can be granted directly to "users." Nevertheless, if an entity is not a user, the only way to obtain usage rights would be to file a declaration as a "provider" of electronic communications networks or services.

---

216 Authorization Directive, Article 4(2)(a).

217 Access Directive, Article 3(1).

218 Authorization Directive, Article 4(2)(b).

219 Broadband for schools may well qualify for government subsidies, but such subsidies would not come from the universal service fund.

Rights of way, frequencies and numbering resources will be examined in sections 5 and 6 below.

Delivery of an Attestation by the National Regulatory Authority

Once an operator files a declaration, the operator will be able immediately to start providing services. The operator does not have to wait for the national regulatory authority to provide a receipt.[220] The directive requires national regulatory authorities to issue, on request, a certificate attesting to the fact that the entity has made a declaration as an operator.[221] The purpose of the certificate is to help the operator prove its status as an operator when it goes to negotiate interconnection (or access) with other operators, or when it seeks rights of way from other governmental authorities. National regulatory authorities must issue the certificate within one week after request. Presumably the certificate will indicate whether the operator has filed a declaration as a provider of "publicly available" electronic communications networks or services.

Providers of "publicly available" electronic communications networks and services have more rights than do providers of non-public networks and services. The certificate must indicate "under what circumstances any undertaking providing electronic communications networks or services under the general authorization has the right to apply for rights to install facilities, negotiate interconnection, and/or obtain access or interconnection in order to facilitate the exercise of those rights for instance at other levels of government or in relation to other undertakings."[222] The attestation will be the only official paper that an entity possesses in order to prove its status as a provider of electronic communications networks or services. The Authorization Directive suggests that the attestations could be generated as an automatic reply to the filing of a declaration.[223]

3. Conditions Attached to General Authorizations

Network or service providers that have filed a declaration will automatically be bound by standard license conditions. The Authorization Directive contains an Annex of the standard license conditions that Member States may impose. Member States cannot go beyond what is contained in the list: "The general authorization . . . may be subject *only* to the conditions listed respectively in parts A, B and C of the Annex."[224] The first Licensing Directive also contained a list of conditions beyond which Member States were not supposed to venture. Some Member States ventured beyond the list anyway. The new list has a number of items in common with the old list.

---

220 Authorization Directive, Article 3(2).

221 Authorization Directive, Article 9.

222 Authorization Directive, Article 9.

223 Authorization Directive, Article 9.

224 Authorization Directive, Article 6(1) (emphasis added).

List of Conditions

(i) *Universal Service*. The provider can be required to contribute to universal service funding (where applicable). This obligation flows from the Universal Service Directive.

(ii) *Administrative charges*. The provider must pay administrative charges associated with the general authorization. Section 4 below will discuss license fees.

(iii) *Interoperability*. The provider must ensure interoperability of its network and/or services to the extent required by the Access Directive; if the provider operates a publicly available network, the provider must negotiate interconnection with other providers of publicly available networks or services. This obligation flows from the Access Directive discussed in the next section.

(iv) *Connectivity*. The provider must ensure access by end-users to numbers from the national numbering plan. This is to ensure universal connectivity, meaning that the operator must interconnect with another operator (such as the incumbent) capable of completing calls to all subscribers in the country, either directly or via other interconnections.

(v) *Local land use restrictions*. The provider must comply with town and country planning requirements "as well as requirements and conditions linked to the granting of access to or use of public or private land and conditions linked to co-location and facility sharing in conformity with [the Framework Directive] and including, where applicable, any financial or technical guarantees necessary to ensure the proper execution of infrastructure works." As we will see in section 7 below, this obligation potentially opens a can of worms, by allowing governmental authorities in charge of rights of way or town planning to impose a broad range of conditions on operators.

(vi) *"Must carry."* Where applicable, the operator can be required to carry certain mandatory audiovisual programs.

(vii) *Data protection*. The provider must apply data protection rules, and ensure security of its public network against unauthorized access, as required by the Communications Data Protection Directive.

(viii) *Consumer protection*. The provider must apply consumer protection rules as required by the Universal Service Directive.

(ix) *Illegal content*. The authorization may include restrictions in relation to the transmission of "illegal content" as permitted under the Electronic Commerce Directive, and "harmful content" as contemplated by the Television Without Frontiers Directive. Here is one of the instances where content regulation flows over into the regulation of electronic communications networks and services. Conceptually it would probably have been unnecessary to include in the general authorization conditions related to the content of the service being transmitted. Restrictions in relation to illegal content refer to measures taken by Member

States to "ensure a high level of protection of objectives of general interest, in particular the protection of minors and human dignity, consumer protection and the protection of public health."[225] Restrictions in relation to harmful content refer to the prohibition of "programmes which might seriously impair the physical, mental or moral development of minors, in particular programmes that involve pornography or gratuitous violence,"[226] or broadcasts that contain "incitement to hatred on grounds of race, sex, religion or nationality."[227] Attempting to include detailed conditions on content in general authorizations would open a host of problems, including issues of liability of transmission intermediaries and freedom of expression issues. On content issues, Member States should simply indicate in general authorizations that the provider shall comply with the provisions of applicable law in connection with the transmission of illegal and harmful content. Any other approach would be unmanageable.

(x) *Providing information*. The authorization may require the operator to provide information to national regulatory authorities to the extent permitted by Article 11 of the Authorization Directive. This is examined in section 8 below.

(xi) *Law enforcement*. The authorization may contain provisions requiring operators to enable law enforcement authorities to intercept communications in conformity with the Communications Data Protection Directive and national rules on criminal investigations. The authorization may impose usage restrictions and priorities during major disasters.

(xii) *Radio interference and health*. The authorization may include provisions on radio interference, and protection of human health against exposure to electromagnetic fields. This provision will permit Member States to implement measures to comply with Council Recommendation 1999/519/EC.[228]

(xiii) *Standards*. The authorization may include provisions to ensure compliance with standards and/or specifications. The section above discussed standards.

(xiv) *Access obligations*. The authorization may include access obligations that apply to non-SMP operators. Those obligations include, for operators of publicly available networks, the obligation to negotiate interconnection with other operators of publicly available networks; for providers of conditional access services, the obligations include the obligation to offer services to all broadcasters

225 EP/Council Directive 00/31 on certain legal aspects of information society services, in particular electronic commerce, in the Internal Market ("Directive on Electronic Commerce") (OJ L178/00), Preamble, 10th recital.

226 Council Directive 89/552 on the coordination of certain provisions laid down by law, regulation or administrative action in Member States concerning the pursuit of television broadcasting activities, OJ L298/89, as amended by Directive 97/36 (OJ L202/97) ("Television Without Frontiers Directive"), Article 22(1).

227 Television Without Frontiers Directive, Article 22a.

228 Council Recommendation 99/519 on the limitation of exposure of the general public to electromagnetic fields (0Hz to 300 GHz) (OJ L199/99).

on a non-discriminatory basis. The next section discusses the kinds of access obligations that can be imposed on non-SMP operators.

(xv) *Maintenance and network integrity.* The authorization may include provisions regarding the maintenance and integrity of the networks.

The obligations of "SMP operators" contained in the Access Directive and the Universal Service Directive must be separate from obligations appearing under the general authorization.[229] The general authorization should not contain the special access obligations that weigh on significant market power operators, for example. Those obligations should appear in separate rulings adopted by the national regulatory authority.

Other conditions can accompany rights to use frequencies and numbering resources. We will examine those conditions below, in the sections dealing with frequencies and numbering resources.

The list of conditions that Member States can include in general authorizations resembles the list annexed to the 1997 Licensing Directive with one big exception. The 1997 Licensing Directive contained a broad clause permitting national regulatory authorities to verify the financial, managerial and technical competence of the applicant and to impose conditions related to the quality, availability and permanence of a service or network. Those provisions are no longer allowed, meaning that in the absence of some violation of consumer protection or security measure, a national regulatory authority would have no business looking into the technical and financial aspects of the operator's business. Unfortunately, this clause has not disappeared entirely. It has moved to a new section dealing with rights of way (discussed in section 7 below). This leaves local authorities with the possibility of imposing measures related to the applicant's "financial or technical guarantees." Moreover, the bankruptcy of several prominent European operators (including the Internet backbone provider Ebone) may prompt national governments to ignore the provisions of the directive, and continue to insert conditions relating to the financial capacity, quality, availability and permanence of service. National governments could perhaps justify such measures as being necessary not only for consumer protection, but also as a matter of national security, on the theory that major communications networks constitute critical national infrastructure.

4. Administrative Charges

Under the old Licensing Directive, administrative charges for licenses were supposed to be based on the costs incurred in issuing and monitoring the relevant license. In practice, administrative charges were all over the map. Member States did pretty much whatever they wanted. Some Member States charged no fees at all, and others charged fees reaching $1 million per year (these fees covered just the license; they did not even include fees for frequency). Member States with ex-

229 Authorization Directive, Article 6(2).

cessively high fees eventually lowered them after operators challenged the fees in court. The old directive evidently was not precise enough. In particular, it gave little guidance to Member States as to what costs could be taken into account when setting the level of fees.

The new directive maintains the principle of "cost-oriented" administrative charges, but attempts to be more precise in hopes of preventing Member States from creating wildly diverging fee structures as they did in the past. First, the directive makes a clear distinction between "administrative charges" and "fees." Member States can impose administrative charges on all entities operating under a general authorization. Administrative charges are solely destined to cover the costs incurred in management, control and enforcement of general authorizations and usage rights. The charges are cost-based. Usage "fees," on the other hand, do not have to be cost-based. Member States can impose fees on operators seeking access to scarce resources. The fees correspond to the price of the scarce resource, *i.e.*, its economic value. This price can be unrelated to costs.

We will discuss "usage fees" in section 5.4 below, in connection with the discussion on usage rights for frequencies.

Second, the new directive changes the manner in which cost orientation is calculated. Previously, there had to be a one-to-one correlation between the amount of administrative charge levied on a given operator and the costs incurred in managing that particular operator's license. That approach proved too difficult to manage, and many Member States ignored the provision altogether. The new directive takes a more global approach. The new directive states that the total aggregate charges collected by a national regulatory authority during a given year should match the total aggregate costs incurred by the national regulatory authority during that year. But what costs? The old directive limited the costs to those involved in the management, control and enforcement of the "applicable individual license" (in the case of an individual license) or the "applicable general authorization scheme" (in the case of general authorizations). Under the old directive, only costs related to the licenses could be recovered via license charges. The new directive takes a broader approach. The relevant costs will include not only costs related to the general authorizations, but also costs related to enforcement of obligations against significant market power operators, "costs for international cooperation, harmonisation and standardization, market analysis, monitoring compliance and other market control, as well as regulatory work involving preparation and enforcement of secondary legislation and administrative decisions, such as decisions on access and interconnection."[230] The notion of costs now covers about all of the national regulatory authority's activity and budget. The basket of costs to be taken into account is much broader than it was before. This is not necessarily a bad thing. Currently national regulatory authorities are often dependent on their government for budget allocations. In France, for example, the national regulatory authority collected in 2000 license fees of 28 million Euros, yet had to operate on a

230 Authorization Directive, Article 12(1)(a).

budget of only 15 million Euros.[231] A large portion of the license fees collected ended up funding other national budget items. This means that operators were not getting value for money. Their high license fee payments were helping the national budget, but not the national regulatory authority do its job. Under the new directives, the roles and responsibilities of national regulatory authorities will increase dramatically. The national regulators will now be responsible for audiovisual infrastructure and will be pretty much alone in defining relevant markets, SMP operators and access conditions. The regulator's dispute resolution function will also expand. All this will require more resources if national regulators are to do their jobs properly. Those resources will come from the communications sector in the form of administrative charges. While in some countries this may lead to an increase in charges, in others it should have no impact. More important, the operators that pay charges will in theory get value for money, since the charges will correspond to the regulator's budget.

True, the new Directive does not say how Member States should finance their national regulatory authority or authorities: doing so would violate the subsidiary principle. But the directive certainly points the way by indicating that incoming administrative charges should match the costs of the national regulatory authority. There should be a one-to-one correlation between overall costs of the national regulatory authority and administrative charges. In the event that national regulatory authority costs exist that do not qualify as costs for purposes of administrative charges, the additional costs can be covered through usage fees charged for spectrum or number resources.[232]

The Directive leaves to each Member State the choice of how to allocate the global costs between the various entities. Should all entities operating under a general authorization pay an equal amount? Should a small ISP pay as much as a large incumbent operator? The Directive says that Member States must divide the burden among those entities in an "objective, transparent and proportionate manner which minimizes additional administrative costs and attendant charges."[233] The Directive's preamble gives some guidance as to what kind of apportionment system would be appropriate:

> An example of a fair, simple and transparent alternative for these charge attribution criteria could be a turnover related distribution key. Where administrative charges are very low, flat rate charges, or charges combining a flat rate basis with a turnover related element could also be appropriate.[234]

Currently Spain links administrative charges to revenues. France does the same, but only for 3G spectrum fees. If charges are linked to revenues, the issue then arises as to what revenues should be included in the base. For example, for every

231 ART, Annual Report for 2000, p. 178.

232 Authorization Directive, Preamble, 32nd recital.

233 Authorization Directive, Article 12(1)(b).

234 Authorization Directive, Preamble, 31st recital.

1.00 € of international voice communications sold at the retail level by Operator A, there may be 0.50 € of revenues invoiced by wholesale Operator B. The question is whether Operator A and Operator B should pay charges on the basis of 1.00 € and 0.50 € respectively, or whether Operator A should declare only 0,50 € to compensate for the fact that the wholesale minute included in Operator A's retail revenues was already declared at the wholesale level by Operator B. We may end up with a system resembling value added tax, in which each operator deducts from its calculation of revenues wholesale "inputs" that the operator purchased upstream, and that were already included in the upstream operator's declared revenues.

However the burden is divided, operators will take comfort in the fact that if the global amount collected by the national regulatory authority exceeds the authority's total costs, the excess will be reimbursed or credited to the following years. The Directive requires that national regulatory authorities publish "a yearly overview of their administrative costs and of the total sum of the charges collected."[235] The national regulatory authority shall then make an "appropriate adjustment" in light of the difference between the total costs and charges collected.

5. Rights to Use Frequencies

A general authorization gives an operator the right to provide electronic communications networks and services; it does not give an operator the right to use radio frequencies. For radio frequencies, the Authorization Directive sets up a system for individual permits (referred to as "grants of individual rights of use") that Member States must use when they allocate spectrum. First, the Directive states that Member States "shall, where possible, in particular where the risk of harmful interference is negligible, not make the use of radio frequencies subject to the grant of individual rights of use."[236] This sounds like the recommendation in the old Licensing Directive to avoid individual licenses wherever possible. Most Member States ignored that recommendation and set up complex individual licensing schemes for many kinds of public networks and services. For frequencies, the new Directive urges Member States to avoid individual grants whenever radio interference is not a significant concern. This should be the case for VSATs operating in the frequency bands reserved for VSATs,[237] and Wi-Fi networks operating within certain power and geographical limits. Yet, if the experience of the old Licensing Directive serves as an example, Member Sates will feel inclined to maintain the requirement for individual permits for most kinds of frequency use, even where the risk of interference is slight.

---

235 Authorization Directive, Article 12(2).

236 Authorization Directive, Article 5(1).

237 See European Radiocommunications Committee Decision of March 28, 2000 on Exemption from Individual Licensing of very Small Apertune Terminals (VSAT) (ERC/DEC/(00)05).

Who May Obtain a Right of Use?

The Directive instructs Member States to grant individual rights of use of frequency to any "provider" or "user" of electronic communications network or services.[238] Member States may decide, for example, to grant frequency usage rights to the provider of the content, *i.e.*, a "user" of electronic communications services. This possibility is particularly significant in television and radio broadcasting, where Member States tend to use frequency as a way to control audiovisual content.

When the grant of frequency is linked to a particular program provider, regulators clearly mix up the rules on "pipes" and the rules on "content." In the ideal world as envisaged by the new Directives, the grant of frequency should be separated from the content provider. The purpose of the EU reform was to separate the regulation of the digital pipes from the regulation of digital content. Yet in a nod to political reality the Authorization Directive steps away from this ideal world, and admits that frequency may in some cases be linked to content. The Directive even permits Member States to deviate from the obligation of applying "open, transparent and non-discriminatory procedures" when granting frequency to providers of radio and television broadcast content services. When granting spectrum to such broadcasters, Member States need only "pursue general interest objectives in conformity with Community law."[239] This means that the allocation of frequencies to broadcasters need not follow objective telecom-style rules, but instead may be based on cultural policy. Member States could not bring themselves to relinquish frequency as a tool for controlling media. For as long as radio has existed, governments have used the licensing of frequencies as a means to control broadcasting content. In today's digital world, this approach seems as archaic as regulating printing presses in order to control the editorial content of newspapers. But the practical reality is that this last tie between the digital pipes and digital content could not be completely severed without jeopardizing the political consensus built around the new regulatory framework.

The Framework Directive confirms that rights to use frequency should be granted according to "objective, transparent and non-discriminatory criteria, taking into account the democratic, social, linguistic and cultural interests related to the use of frequency."[240] That phrase says it all: the terms "objective, transparent and non-discriminatory" come from the world of telecommunications regulation; the terms "democratic, social, linguistic and cultural interest" come from the world of media regulation. The licensing of frequency usage rights will have to marry both worlds of regulation in spite of the Commission's efforts to separate the two.

238 Authorization Directive, Article 5(2).

239 Authorization Directive, Article 5(2).

240 Framework Directive, Preamble, 19th recital.

How are Frequency Rights Granted?

Each Member State is free to set up its own system for allocating rights to use frequency, as long as the system does not violate any of the Directive's principles.

Open, objective, transparent and non-discriminatory procedures and criteria

The first principle is that national procedures be "open, transparent and non-discriminatory."[241] This principle for granting usage rights also appears in the Framework Directive, albeit in slightly different terms:

> [Member Sates] shall ensure that the allocation and assignment of such radio frequencies by national regulatory authorities are based on objective, transparent, non discriminatory and proportionate criteria.[242]

The Framework Directive refers to "criteria" instead of "procedures" and states that such criteria should be "objective," instead of "open." The adjective "open" would make little sense to describe the noun "criteria," particularly since the adjective "transparent" follows shortly thereafter. "Open criteria" and "transparent criteria" would be synonymous. The Framework Directive also uses the word "proportionate" whereas the Authorization Directive does not. Nevertheless, the requirement of proportionality applies to all regulatory actions by virtue of Article 8(1) of the Framework Directive. The Authorization Directive therefore does not need to refer to proportionality because proportionality already exists as an implicit requirement for all regulatory action.

To summarize, therefore, the first principle for granting usage rights for frequency is that procedures be "open, transparent and non-discriminatory," and that the criteria used be "open, transparent, non-discriminatory and proportionate."

The "cultural exception": As noted above, Article 5(2) of the Authorization Directive suggests that Member States may be able to deviate from the "objective transparent and non-discriminatory" principle when allocating spectrum to providers of radio or television broadcast program services. Article 5(2) states that:

> Without prejudice to specific criteria and procedures adapted by Member States to grant rights of use of radio frequencies to providers of radio or television broadcast content services with a view to pursuing general interest objectives in conformity with Community law, such rights of use shall be granted through open, transparent and non-discriminatory procedures.

Curiously, this exception appears in Article 5 of the Authorization Directive, but not in Article 7, which describes specific principles that Member States must apply when limiting the number of grants of spectrum rights. The exception does not appear in Article 9(1) of the Framework Directive either, which requires allocation to be based on "objective, transparent, non-discriminatory and proportionate criteria." It is difficult to gauge just how big an exception the "without prejudice"

241 Authorization Directive, Article 5(2).

242 Framework Directive, Article 9(1).

language in Article 5(2) of the Authorization Directive is meant to be, or even whether it is an exception at all.

Perhaps the answer lies in the language of the 19th recital of the Framework Directive, which indicates that Member States must grant frequency usage rights under objective, transparent and non-discriminatory criteria, "taking into account the democratic, social, linguistic and cultural interests." This language suggests that the "without prejudice" clause is not an exception at all, but rather a clarification that when Member States fix "objective, transparent and non-discriminatory" selection criteria for television or radio content broadcasters, Member States may include cultural interests among those selection criteria. Again, this cultural exception (or cultural "clarification") does not appear in the section of the Authorization Directive dealing with beauty contests and/or auctions, which is strange because in most cases spectrum would be granted to broadcasters through a beauty contest.

Overall, it is a pity that the new directives did not go to greater lengths to explain this "cultural exception" to standard licensing procedures, and how it interacts with the other rules surrounding grants of usage rights for frequency. The possibility given to national regulatory authorities to license spectrum based on linguistic and cultural interests really undermines the central thesis of the new framework, which is that content-based policy measures should no longer influence the regulatory framework applicable to electronic communications networks and services. No doubt required as a political gesture, the cultural exception in the Authorization Directive nonetheless blemished the intellectual purity of the new framework.

Transferability

The second principle is that Member States must specify whether the usage rights are transferable or not. The transferability of spectrum rights will be discussed in section 5.5 below.

Appropriate duration

The third principle is that the duration of the grant must be "appropriate for the service concerned."[243] Though not explained in the Directive, this principle suggests that the grant should not be shorter than the minimum time needed for the provider to recoup its investments, and should also take into account the difficulty of moving the spectrum user to another frequency band if needed. For example, the grant of spectrum for a 3G mobile network might have a longer duration than a grant of spectrum for a point-to-point microwave link both because of the long period needed for the 3G operator to roll out its network and recoup its investment, and because of the high cost of relocating the 3G operator to a different band. By comparison, a point-to-point microwave link could be modified to operate on a different band with relatively little cost.

243 Authorization Directive, Article 5(2).

No limitation to number of grants

The fourth principle is that the number of grants shall not be limited "except where this is necessary to ensure the efficient use of radio frequencies in accordance with Article 7."[244]

When may a Member State limit the number of grants? Of course in many cases national regulatory authorities will want to limit the number of radio licenses granted, both to limit risks of interference and also to encourage operators to invest in areas where they may not otherwise invest. As noted in the previous section, a 3G wireless operator would be reluctant to invest billions of Euros to build a network in hard-to-reach places if it knew that an unlimited number of future competitors would be allowed into the market. Where a Member State wants to limit the number of radio licenses, the Directive imposes a procedure.

First, the Member State must "give due weight to the need to maximize benefits for users and to facilitate the development of competition."[245] Placed here, this principle seems redundant with the Article 8 mission statement of the Framework Directive that we examined in the previous section. National regulatory authorities are supposed to keep end-user benefits and competition at the forefront of their minds *anyway* under Article 8 of the Framework Directive. A more general reference to Article 8 of the Framework Directive would have been sufficient and more appropriate. As the language stands, one wonders whether this partial reference to the principles of the Article 8 mission statement means that the other principles in Article 8 should be ignored or given lower priority. Presumably not.

Second, if a Member State wants to limit the number of grants, it must consult interested parties, including users and consumers, in accordance with Article 6 of the Framework Directive. This is unlikely to pose a problem since most national regulatory authorities conduct public consultations anyway before launching procedures for major radio licenses (such as 3G mobile).

Third, Member States must publish any decision to limit the number of radio licenses, stating the reasons therefore. This step seems redundant as well, since Article 9 of the Framework Directive already requires that allocation of frequency be based on "objective, transparent, non-discriminatory and proportionate criteria." Objectivity and transparency would mandate publication of the regulatory decision limiting the number of players in the market, together with the reasons for such limitation. There is certainly no harm, however, in expressly requiring publication.

Fourth, once the procedure has been set, Member States must invite applications for rights of use.[246] This is a curious requirement, since it is unlikely that a Member State would go to the trouble of setting up a procedure for allocating licenses

244 Authorization Directive, Article 5(5).

245 Authorization Directive, Article 7(1)(a).

246 Authorization Directive, Article 7(1)(d).

unless it had the intention of inviting applicants. The purpose of this requirement is presumably to ensure that Member States do not develop a procedure and then sit on it for an indefinite period, inviting tenders only later, at a time when most potential candidates are caught unawares.

Fifth, the procedures for selecting candidates must be objective, transparent, non-discriminatory and proportionate.[247] This principle overlaps with Article 5(2) of the Authorization Directive,[248] as it does with Article 9 of the Framework Directive.[249] Unlike Article 5(2), Article 7 of the Authorization Directive contains no exception allowing cultural or general interest considerations to be taken into account when granting frequency usage rights to television or radio content providers. The omission is strange, since grants of frequency to television or radio broadcasters would almost certainly occur in the context of a limited number of grants. One would have expected the "cultural exception" language to appear here, yet it doesn't.

Sixth, the selection criteria must give due weight to the achievement of the key principles of the Article 8 mission statement of the Framework Directive.

The Authorization Directive does not go into any detail about what selection criteria a national regulatory authority must use, leaving considerable latitude to each national regulatory authority to organize its own selection and grant procedures. The Authorization Directive does provide, however, that Member States "may verify whether the applicant [for usage rights] will be able to comply with the conditions attached to such rights."[250] The applicant can be asked to submit necessary information to prove that it can comply with license conditions, such as (where applicable) minimum coverage obligations and network build-out commitments. If the applicant does not provide sufficient information, the Member State or national regulatory authority may deny the application.[251] This resembles the licensing procedure under the old Licensing Directive, when national regulatory authorities were able to verify the applicant's "financial, managerial and technical competence."[252]

Beauty contest or auction?

When the number of radio licenses is limited, Member States may organize a competitive or comparative selection procedure. It is not immediately clear from the language of the Directive whether competitive selection procedures could be in the form of a pure auction, since selection criteria must in all cases "give due

247 Authorization Directive, Article 7(3).

248 Article 5(2) of the Authorization Directive requires "open, transparent and non-discriminatory procedures" for all grants of frequency usage rights.

249 Article 9 of the Framework Directive requires "objective, transparent, non-discriminatory and proportionate criteria" for all grants of frequency usage rights.

250 Authorization Directive, Preamble, 13th recital.

251 Authorization Directive, Preamble, 13th recital.

252 Directive 97/13/EC, Annex, Point 4.8.

weight to the achievement of the objectives of Article 8 [of the Framework Directive]."[253] If the only selection criterion is the price candidates are willing to pay for the frequency, the procedure would not give due weight to the achievement of the Article 8 mission statement objectives (which include promoting competition and encouraging infrastructure investment).

Member States that want to go the auction route will no doubt have to implement a hybrid beauty contest/auction procedure where candidates are first screened by qualitative selection criteria (designed to satisfy Article 8 of the Framework Directive) and *then* invited to bid for frequency. National regulatory authorities may, in the interest of promoting competition, set up objective, non-discriminatory and proportionate selection criteria that result in certain entities (such as the incumbent fixed operator) being excluded from the procedure.[254] This might occur, for example, where the national regulatory authority attributes a point system in connection with certain selection criteria, such as (for example) the candidate's contribution to the creation of competition at the local loop. The incumbent fixed operator would receive a low score on this subject and could thereby be eliminated without violating the principle of non-discrimination.[255]

Time periods

The normal time period for allocating rights of use for frequency is six weeks when the frequency use is already foreseen in the national frequency plan.[256] If a Member State uses competitive or comparative selection procedures to choose operators, the Member State can extend the normal period of six weeks "for so long as necessary to ensure that such procedures are fair, reasonable, open and transparent to all interested parties, but by no longer than eight months."[257] This language means that the maximum time period is nine and a half months (*i.e.*, eight months *plus* six weeks; the time period can be extended *"by"* eight months).

Conditions Attached to Rights to Use Radio Frequencies

Part B of the Directive's Annex contains a list of eight conditions that can be imposed on entities benefiting from an individual right to use frequencies (in addition to conditions associated with the general authorizations):

> *Condition 1: Designation of service or type of network or technology for which the rights of use for the frequency has been granted, including, where applicable, the exclusive use of a frequency for the transmission of specific content or specified audiovisual services.*

253 Authorization Directive, Preamble, 23rd recital and Article 7(3).

254 Authorization Directive, Preamble, 23rd recital.

255 A point system such as this was used in the French procedures for award of licenses for fixed wireless local loop.

256 Authorization Directive, Article 5(3).

257 Authorization Directive, Article 7(4).

This condition permits national regulatory authorities to go a long way toward controlling how an operator runs its business. A country adopting a light-handed or minimalist approach to this condition would simply require that the beneficiary of the usage right use the frequency to operate a mobile network, for example. A country adopting a more heavy-handed approach could go into much greater detail, dictating for example:

- the kind of mobile technology used;
- the kind of service provided (voice, data or both);
- whether the operator may provide audiovisual content;
- whether the operator must provide audiovisual services from a particular content provider or portal, or provide certain general interest services (such as weather information).

The list of requirements that a national regulatory authority could impose is potentially quite long. An interventionist national regulatory authority could use this clause to justify imposing a wide range of requirements linked to attaining social objectives and content regulation. Regulations designed to attain social objectives are permitted under the Universal Service Directive and expressly referred to in clauses 1 and 8 of Part A of the Annex to the new Authorization Directive. It seems inappropriate to use clause 1 of the radio license conditions as a means to introduce regulations that would not otherwise be permitted under the Universal Service Directive. Whether national regulatory authorities should specify the particular technology used by the network operator is also open to debate. In the United States, the FCC generally grants frequencies for a given service (such as mobile telephony) but the FCC does not dictate the technology that the operator should use. This has lead to a patchwork of non-compatible standards in the US market for mobile telephony, but some say that the US approach fosters greater innovation. Europe, on the other hand, has generally linked licenses to a particular technology (such as GSM or UMTS). This approach favors pan-European compatibility, but carries with it the risk that the standard chosen may not be the optimal one from a technological standpoint.

Condition 2: Effective and efficient use of frequencies in conformity with the Framework Directive, including, where appropriate, coverage requirements.

This condition will in most cases include network roll-out and coverage obligations permitting the national regulatory authority, if necessary, to take spectrum away from an operator that has not deployed its network within the time stipulated in the grant. For example, the French 3G licenses contain coverage obligations which, if not complied with, would permit the French regulatory authority to revoke the license.[258]

258 *See, e.g.*, Article 1.3(b) of the license conditions attached to the license of SFR (arrêté dated 18 July 2001, OJ of 21 August 2001, p. 13422.)

Condition 3: Technical and operational conditions necessary for the avoidance of harmful interference and for the limitation of exposure of the general public to electromagnetic fields, where such conditions are different from those included in the general authorization.

This condition will include frequency coordination obligations vis à vis other users of the frequency band, obligations relating to regions situated on national borders, as well as health-related obligations. The European Council issued in 1999 a recommendation on the maximum permitted exposure levels to radio emissions.[259] Because it is only a recommendation, the Council decision is not binding on Member States. Nevertheless, as voters have become concerned about the proliferation of radio transmitters, particularly located around schools and hospitals, Member States have begun to enact laws that implement the 1999 Council Recommendation.[260]

Condition 4: Maximum duration in conformity with Article 5 of the Authorization Directive, subject to any changes in the national frequency plan.

We spoke of the duration of radio usage rights in section 5.2.3 above. The phrase "subject to any changes in the national frequency plan" permits national regulatory authorities to relocate users of frequency to other frequency bands when the country modifies its frequency plan. In many countries, usage of frequency is considered a temporary use of public resources that can always be revoked in case of public necessity.

Condition 5: Transfer of rights at the initiative of the right holder and conditions for such transfer in conformity with the Framework Directive.

The transfer of rights to use frequency is discussed in section 5.5 below.

Condition 6: Usage fees in accordance with Article 13 of the Authorization Directive.

Usage fees will be discussed in section 5.4 below.

Condition 7: Any commitments, which the undertaking obtaining the right has made in the course of competitive or comparative selection procedure.

Like the first condition, this condition permits national regulatory authorities to impose numerous public interest obligations under the guise of "voluntary commitments" made by candidates in a beauty contest. We saw this in the French 3G licenses, where candidates received points based *inter alia* on commitments made to maintain an open and non-discriminatory position vis à vis service

259 Council Recommendation 99/519 on the limitation of exposure of the general public to electromagnetic fields (0Hz to 300 GHz) (OJ L199/99).

260 European Commission: *Implementation report on the Council Recommendation limiting the public exposure to electromagnetic fields* (undated).

providers.[261] In the course of organizing a beauty contest, national regulatory authorities could suggest that candidates agree to certain undertakings in order to maximize their chance of success. For example, a candidate may commit to build out its network to cover rural areas at the same time as urban areas, so as to avoid a "digital divide" between the two. Those undertakings would become part of the conditions attached to the usage rights for frequency.

Condition 8: Obligations under relevant international agreements relating to the use of frequencies.

This clause is usually cast in general terms in the relevant license:

> The operator shall comply with the rules defined by the ITU convention, by the radiocommunications rules, by international agreements and the rules of the European Community.[262]

Usage Fees

The Directive permits Member States to impose frequency usage fees in addition to the administrative charges referred to in section 4 above. Unlike administrative charges, frequency usage fees do not have to match costs incurred by the national regulatory authority. Member States can freely set the level of usage fees for frequency, subject to compliance with the following principles:

- the fees must reflect the need to ensure optimal use of the frequency resources;
- the fees must be "objectively justified, transparent, non-discriminatory and proportionate in relation to their intended purpose;"[263]
- in setting the level of fees, Member States must take into account the objectives of Article 8 of the Framework Directive

The first (and obvious) question that emerges from this text is whether fees set through a pure auction process would comply with these requirements. Fees resulting from an auction could be justified as encouraging the optimal use of frequency resources, because the highest bidder would presumably attach the highest value to the frequency and make the most productive use of it. An auction conducted according to objective and published rules would also be transparent and non-discriminatory. More difficult is the question of whether fees set via an auction are "proportionate in relation to their intended purpose" when the fees attain multi-billion dollar levels. The "intended purpose" of fees is to encourage efficient use of spectrum while promoting the objectives of the Article 8 mission statement. Maximizing revenues for the general government budget, though a nice by-product of spectrum fees, is not their "intended purpose." Consequently, a multibillion-dollar fee could well be considered disproportionate to the intended purpose of the fees.

261 Articles 1.2 and 13.3, 3G, license conditions of SFR, OJ of 21 August 2001, p. 13424.

262 3G License Conditions of SFR, Article 1.5, O.J. 21 August 2001, p. 13425.

263 Authorization Directive, Article 13.

The Directive requires that usage fees for frequency be used as an instrument to ensure the optimal use of such resources, and that the level of fees "not hinder the development of innovative services and competition in the market."[264] Moreover, if a competitive or comparative selection process leads to a lump-sum payment, Member States must ensure that the payment arrangement ensures that the fees "do not in practice lead to selection on the basis of criteria unrelated to the objective of ensuring optimal use of radio frequencies."[265] The Commission may publish "best practice" benchmarks for the assignment of radio frequencies. Finally, as discussed above,[266] a pure auction would not further the objectives of the Article 8 mission statement. All this suggests that pure auctions may not be an acceptable means of setting usage fees under the new Authorization Directive.

Transferability of Usage Rights

The Framework Directive requires that the assignment of radio frequencies be managed "as efficiently as possible," and suggests that "the transfer of radio frequencies can be an effective means of increasing efficient use of spectrum."[267] The Framework Directive does not require Member States to make frequency usage rights transferable, but says that Member States "may" foresee that possibility. Whether a Member State can make frequency transferable will depend on its national administrative law provisions. In France, the use of frequency is the equivalent of a lease of public property, and such leases are by nature non-transferable. In countries like France, it may be difficult to make frequency rights transferable. For countries that decide to allow the transfer of frequency usage rights, the Framework Directive requires that the transfer (a) be notified in advance to the relevant national regulatory authority, (b) take place in accordance with the transfer procedures established by the national regulatory authority, and (c) be made public.[268] The Framework Directive instructs national regulatory authorities to ensure that "competition is not distorted" as a result of any such transfer.[269]

One big question left unanswered by the Authorization Directive is whether a change in shareholding can be considered a "transfer" of a usage right. Currently France is the only Member State that has foreign ownership restrictions for licenses to use radio frequency for telecommunications purposes. The French provision mirrors the U.S. law in imposing a 20% foreign ownership limit on licenses that use radio spectrum. The limit does not apply to investors from other European Member States, or to indirect shareholdings held by entities located in countries (such as the U.S.) having made commitments under the GATS Fourth Protocol. The usage rights for frequency used for audiovisual purposes is even more tightly

264 Authorization Directive, Preamble, 32nd recital.

265 Authorization Directive, Preamble, 32nd recital.

266 Section 5.2.5.

267 Framework Directive, Preamble, 19th recital.

268 Framework Directive, Article 8(4).

269 Framework Directive, Article 9(4).

controlled, being closely linked to rules on media concentration. Under the new framework, will Member States continue to be able to control the ownership (and transfers of ownership) in entities using frequency? The conditions listed in the Authorization Directive do not include any condition relating to the share ownership of the entity holding the usage right, which suggests that Member States could not insert foreign ownership restrictions as a condition to frequency usage without violating the Directive. Member States wishing to control the share ownership in entities holding frequency rights might nevertheless be able to do so by framing such a condition in the form of an undertaking in a comparative or competitive selection procedure. Alternatively, a Member State could draft a regulation defining a "transfer" of a usage right as including any significant change in the direct or indirect share capital of the entity holding the usage right. In that way, the Member State could impose any conditions it wanted to (consistent with the EC Treaty and the GATS Fourth Protocol) in connection with changes in shareholdings in the entity holding the usage right.

Harmonized Frequencies

The Authorization Directive provides that in the event frequency usage rights are allocated pursuant to a pan-European selection procedure, Member States shall grant national usage rights strictly in accordance with the pan-European selection procedure.

Member States may not impose any "further conditions, additional criteria or procedures which would restrict, alter or delay the correct implementation of the common assignment of such radio frequencies."[270]

6. Rights to Use Numbering Resources

Many of the comments above relating to the right to use frequencies also apply to the right to use numbering resources. The question of numbering rights is less complex, however, first because numbering resources are not traditionally linked to audiovisual policy, and second because numbering resources do not (for the moment) command the same economic value as frequencies. The question of what body grants the usage rights for numbering resources is the same as for frequency rights. The language of the Directives is inconsistent in defining which body is responsible for granting rights to use numbers. Article 10(1) of the Framework Directive requires that national regulatory authorities control the assignment of all national numbering resources in accordance with objective, transparent and non-discriminatory assigning procedures. Yet Article 5(2) of the Authorization Directive states that the rights are granted by "Member States," which suggests that the assignment could be handled by either the Ministry or the national regulatory authority.

270 Authorization Directive, Article 8.

Beneficiaries of Usage Rights

As for frequencies, usage rights for numbering resources can be granted to any entity *providing* or *using* electronic communications networks or services under a general authorization. The Preamble[271] confirms that "Member States are neither obliged to grant nor prevented from granting rights to use numbers . . . to undertakings other than providers of electronic communications networks or services,"[272] leaving considerable freedom to Member States in deciding what kinds of entities can benefit from the right to use numbering resources.

Procedures

As with the allocation of frequency rights, the allocation of numbering rights is not described in any level of detail. The procedures must be "open, transparent and non-discriminatory."[273] Member States must ensure that enough numbers and numbering ranges are available for all electronic communications services[274] and that "numbering plans and procedures are applied in a manner that gives equal treatment to all providers of publicly available electronic communications services."[275] The decisions granting rights to use numbers must be made by the national regulatory authority within three weeks after receipt of the complete application.

Member States can organize competitive or comparative selection procedures for numbers of "exceptional economic value,"[276] but only after exhausting the public consultation procedure required under Article 6 of the Framework Directive.

Conditions Attached to Usage Rights for Numbers

The Annex to the Authorization Directive contains a list of conditions that can be imposed on beneficiaries of numbering usage rights. These conditions resemble closely those associated with frequency rights, and include in particular:

> *Condition 1: The ability for Member States to link a given numbering resource to a given service*[277]

This condition is necessary in order to ensure that end-users understand which classes of numbers are associated with a given service or tariff scheme (free phone vs. premium services, for example). Member States may also include in this condition "any requirements linked to the provision of that service."[278] This clause would permit Member States to impose tariff obligations. For example, numbers

271 Authorization Directive, Preamble, 14th recital.

272 Authorization Directive, Preamble, 14th recital.

273 Authorization Directive, Article 5(2).

274 Framework Directive, Article 10(1).

275 Framework Directive, Article 10(2).

276 Authorization Directive, Article 5(4).

277 Authorization Directive, Annex Part C (1).

278 Authorization Directive, Annex Part C (1).

in the "0800" range would come with an obligation that services be free for the calling party. Read broadly, the condition could also permit national regulatory authorities to go into great detail as to the kind of services that may be accessed using the particular numbering resource. This would be particularly tempting in connection with numbers associated with premium services often used for adult chat services, to ensure that such services can be accessed only via certain limited kinds of numbers. Such a use of this clause would be unfortunate, however, because it would require the national regulatory authority to delve into content issues, which is not the overall intent of the directives. Access to certain kinds of content must be controlled and in some cases even prohibited. Under the European vision, however, the role of controlling content is best left to authorities and regulatory tools separate from those designed to regulate the digital pipes. To use a simple analogy, traffic regulations contain numerous rules to limit the size of vehicles, their speed, their rights of priority, etc. But traffic regulations are not designed to keep bank robbers from using city streets.[279] Like traffic regulations, rules on the use of numbers should be designed to manage efficiently the number resources, not to keep illegal content providers off the network.

Condition 2: Effective and efficient use of numbering resources in accordance with the Framework Directive[280]

This condition would permit Member States to impose a "use it or lose it" rule to ensure that operators do not sit on numbering resources without exploiting them. Such obligations already exist in most Member States. For certain rare numbering resources, Member States may go so far as imposing infrastructure roll-out obligations.[281] But it is hard to imagine such an infrastructure build-out obligation being imposed in the absence of a comparative bidding procedure, which is authorized under Article 5(4) of the Authorization Directive for numbers of exceptional value. If part of a comparative bidding, infrastructure roll-out commitments would also be covered by condition 4 below (commitments made by the firm in the context of competitive or comparative selection procedures). It is interesting to note that this condition refers to effective and efficient use of numbering resources "in conformity with the Framework Directive." If one examines the Framework Directive, it does not contain provisions regarding the effective and efficient use of numbering resources, as it does for radio frequencies. The Framework Directive says nothing about efficient use of numbering resources. It is difficult to comprehend therefore what the phrase "in conformity with the Framework Directive" means other than reference to the general principles of the Article 8 mission statement.

---

279 Jan Guettler of Cullen International first used this analogy in 1992 in a meeting of the International Chamber of Commerce's EU Committee on telecommunications.

280 Authorization Directive, Annex, Part C (2).

281 Decision No. 97-196 of 16 July 1997 of the Autorité de Régulation des Télécommunications (JO of 2 August 1997).

Condition 3 "Number portability requirements in conformity with the Universal Service Directive[282]

Condition 4: Obligations to provide public directory subscriber information for the purposes of Articles 5 and 25 of the Universal Service Directive[283]

Condition 5: Maximum duration in conformity with Article 5 of the Authorization Directive, subject to any changes in the national numbering scheme[284]

Here the same rules apply as those applicable to rights to use frequency. The duration must be "appropriate for the service concerned."[285]

Condition 6: Transfer of rights at the initiative of the right holder and conditions for such transfer in conformity with the Framework Directive[286]

The reference here to the Framework Directive is curious, since the Framework Directive says nothing about the transfer of usage rights for numbering resources. The Framework Directive speaks only of the transfer of usage rights for frequency. Article 5(2) of the Authorization Directive does stipulate, however, that Member States shall specify whether "those rights" (*i.e.*, usage rights for frequencies or *numbers*) can be transferred at the initiative of the right holder, and under which conditions.[287]

As with frequencies, the transferability of numbering resources will depend on how the use of numbering resources is characterized in Member States. In France, for instance, numbering resources are non-transferable by virtue of an express provision in the Code of Post and Telecommunications.[288] In France, the principle of non-transferability of numbers seems less set in stone than it is for frequencies, since frequencies are clearly part of the public domain, whereas numbering resources are more akin to an intellectual property right. Because the transferability of numbering resources is optional under the new framework, it seems unlikely that countries that currently prohibit the transfer of numbering resources will change their law on this point.

Condition 7: Usage fees in accordance with Article 13 of the Authorization Directive[289]

We will discuss usage fees in section 6.3 below.

---

282 Authorization Directive, Annex, Part C (3).

283 Authorization Directive, Annex, Part C (4).

284 Authorization Directive, Annex, Part C (5).

285 Authorization Directive, Article 5(2).

286 Authorization Directive, Annex, Part C (6).

287 Authorization Directive, Article 5(2).

288 Codes des postes et telecommunications, Article L 34-10.

289 Authorization Directive, Annex, Part C (7).

Condition 8: Any commitments that the undertaking obtaining the usage right has made in the course of a competitive or comparative selection process[290]

As we saw above, Member States can organize competitive or comparative selection procedures only for numbering resources with "exception economic value."[291] The Directive leaves it to national regulatory authorities to determine what numbers have "exceptional economic value," but the Directive requires that national regulatory authorities conduct a public consultation before deciding whether and how to organize the selection procedure. The selection procedure will inevitably be based on promises made by candidates in the selection process. The promises may be to invest in infrastructure or do other things deemed important by the national regulatory authority as a condition to obtaining the number. One good example of this kind of procedure was the French procedure for allocating single-digit carrier selection codes used in 1997.[292] Selected candidates had to agree to have interconnection points in place in each of France's eighteen regions and own at least 60% of their transmission infrastructure. At the time of the selection process, the French national regulatory authority thought that the investment in alternative national backbone infrastructure was an important policy objective, so it linked this policy objective to the allocation of the single-digit carrier selection code. In hindsight, one can question the utility of such a commitment, since there ended up being too much capacity on the long-haul market, and certain operators are now faced with a regulatory commitment to continue building when doing so makes no economic sense, either for the individual operator or for the country. That is always the danger of linking regulatory decisions to certain technological or investment commitments. Such commitments (which typically are implemented over a period of several years) can quickly become pointless and unduly burdensome in light of changes in the market or in technology.

Condition 9: Obligations under relevant international agreements relating to the use of numbers[293]

This condition refers to existing ITU recommendations on numbers as well as to European agreements on things such as the single European emergency number 112 and the European single country code 3883.

Usage Fees

Usage fees for numbering resources are conceptually treated the same way as usage fees for frequency. Until now, numbering resources have not been considered as scarce or as valuable as frequencies. No country has so far felt the need to organize auctions for usage rights to numbering resources. The stakes involved in numbering resources are too low for the moment. As IP addressing eventually

290 Authorization Directive, Annex, Part C (8).

291 Authorization Directive, Article 5(4).

292 Decision no. 97-196 of 16 July 1997 of the Autorité de Régulation des Télécommunications (JO of 2 August 1997).

293 Authorization Directive, Annex, Part C (9).

overtakes traditional telephone numbering as the way people access other network users and services, the economics of numbering resources may evolve. Although the current number of IP addresses is limited, IPv6 will make the number of IP addresses almost limitless, thereby reducing or eliminating any scarcity in numbering resources.

As with frequencies, Member States may charge usage fees (not to be confused with administrative charges) for numbering resources. Member States are free to set the level of fees as long as they comply with the following principles:

A. The fees reflect the need to ensure the optimal use of the numbering resources.

B. The fees are:

i. objectively justified,

ii. transparent,

iii. non-discriminatory,

iv. proportionate in relation to their intended purpose.

C. They take into account the objectives of Article 8 of the Framework Directive, and do not hinder the development of innovative services and competition in the market.[294]

As we saw above in connection with frequencies, raising revenues for the national treasury is not one of the permitted purposes of usage fees. Raising revenues for the treasury can be a helpful by-product,[295] but it cannot be one of the objectives of the fee system.

7. Rights of Way

The ability to lay cable and/or install antennas is an essential requirement for operators, without which they cannot do business. From a regulatory standpoint, rights of way are notoriously difficult to handle because they involve multiple authorities: local and regional authorities, environmental authorities, radio authorities, as well as private landowners. In parts of the United States obtaining rights of way can be a nightmare. The same holds true in many European countries. The Authorization Directive does not attempt to impose a list of hard and fast rules for rights of way, meaning that each Member States will retain considerable freedom to organize the complex relations between the central government, the national regulatory authority, local municipalities, private landowners and communications operators. In sum, the new Directive is not likely to change significantly the way rights of way are granted in Europe.

The principles applicable to the granting and withdrawal of rights of way are contained in Article 11 of the Framework Directive and in Articles 4(1)(b) and 14 of

294 Authorization Directive, Preamble, 32nd recital and Article 13.

295 Authorization Directive, Preamble, 32nd recital.

the Authorization Directive. Rules on fees are contained in Article 13 of the Authorization Directive. Principles on facility sharing are contained in Article 12 of the Framework Directive.

Obligation to Grant Rights of Way

Article 4(1)(b) of the Authorization Directive states that a general authorization gives the holder the right to have its "application for the necessary rights to install facilities considered in accordance with Article 11 of [the Framework Directive]." Article 11 of the Framework Directive provides that when a competent authority considers an application for granting of rights of way:

- it must act on the basis of transparent and publicly available procedures, applied without discrimination and without delay; and
- it must follow the principles of transparency and non-discrimination in attaching conditions to any such rights.

As is evident from the above language, the "competent authority" is not necessarily the national regulatory authority. A "competent authority" could be a national, regional or local authority, a highway or railroad authority, a canal or port authority, the forest service, or even the army. Because of the diversity of bodies that can grant of rights of way, the Directive wisely uses the generic term "competent authorities."

The next point is that the Framework Directive's provisions fall short of an absolute obligation to grant rights of way. The Authorization Directive says that a provider holding a general authorization shall have the right to have its application for rights of way *considered*. The Framework Directive then continues by stating that when a competent authority "considers" an application, it must act "without delay" and apply publicly-available and transparent procedures. But the Directives never state that competent authorities "shall grant" rights of way.

The Framework Directive establishes very few rules governing the granting of rights of way. Competent authorities must have transparent and publicly available procedures for granting rights of way. The term "publicly available" is easy enough to understand. But what about the term "transparent?" "Transparent" procedures suggests that the applicant for the rights of way must have access to the proceedings and know why an application was denied. Every municipality or highway authority that wishes to grant rights of way will have to design and implement a transparent procedure for granting rights of way. But the Directive says nothing about what may or may not be in the procedure. It does not even require that the procedure be proportionate or take into account the all-important objectives of the Article 8 mission statement of the Framework Directive. In fact there appear to be *no* limits on how detailed an application for rights of way needs to be, or how involved the procedure may become. In the United States, certain municipalities have transformed the right of way process into a full-fledged licensing procedure, requiring applicants to file (among other things) business plans, and proof of financial and technical capacity. The Directive imposes no deadlines either, only requiring that the competent authority act on the application "without delay." The term "without delay" could mean almost anything. In certain circumstances a procedure of nine months could be considered to be "without delay," if the local procedure requires (for example) a public consultation and comment period, and consultation with environmental and health authorities (health authorities are becoming involved in antenna siting due to health concerns). Moreover, even once the procedure has been completed, the competent authorities may impose conditions on operators in connection with the rights of way. Once again the Directive offers few guidelines, stipulating only that the conditions must be applied in a transparent and non-discriminatory manner. The Directive fails to provide a list of conditions, so competent authorities are free to impose whatever they want. The Directive does not even impose a proportionality test. In reality, national law will in most cases contain provisions limiting the discretion of local authorities in granting rights of way and the proportionality test will be implied as a matter of law. But operators would have been comforted by certain limits and guidelines in the Directive to prevent abuses (such as linking the granting of the right of way to an obligation to build other facilities for the city).

One of the conditions included in a general authorization is a condition relating to "financial or technical guarantees necessary to ensure the proper execution of infrastructure works," as well as other "requirements and conditions linked to the granting of access to or use of public or private land and conditions linked to co-location and facility sharing."[296] This suggests that national regulatory authorities *may* intervene at a national level to set down, in a uniform and harmonized manner, conditions that might otherwise be imposed at a local level whenever a local authority grants a right of way.

Member States would be well advised to seize this opportunity to set down uniform national rules on how local and regional authorities grant rights of way, including the imposition of time limits and speedy appeal procedures. The Directives leave this field open to Member States and Member States should fill the void through national legislation instead of allowing inconsistent local rules to proliferate. Because national licensing procedures will practically disappear, local authorities will have a tendency to institute more detailed procedures at a local level than they have in the past to ensure that an operator will not pose a security, health or financial risk for the local community. If practically anyone can now call himself an operator under the new authorization regime, mayors will want to make doubly sure that the person installing cables or antennas on or under city property has the paper qualifications to do so. Increased security concerns after the September 11, 2001 terrorist attacks will prompt managers of public infrastructure (sewers, railways, subways, high points) to be extremely careful before allowing a provider of electronic communications networks near critical infrastructure sites. It will be difficult to separate legitimate security measures from anticompetitive stonewalling. For this reason, if there is one area where Member States need to

296 Authorization Directive, Annex, Part A, Point 5.

"fill the gap," it is in fixing uniform national rules governing the granting of rights of way by local authorities.

Fees for Rights of Way

Although the Authorization Directive does not define procedures for how rights of way should by granted, it does set limits on the charging of fees. The fees for rights of way must respect the same principles as the fees for frequency and numbering usage rights, i.e.:

A. The fees must reflect the need to ensure optimal use of the public property.

B. The fees must be:

i. objectively justified;

ii. transparent;

iii. non-discriminatory;

iv. proportionate in relation to their intended purpose;

v. take into account the objectives of Article 8 of the Framework Directive.[297]

Of particular note here is the proportionality condition and the reference to the Article 8 mission statement. Reference to the proportionality principle and to the Article 8 mission statement should be sufficient to contain abusive fee practices by at least *public* landowners. The reference to fees for rights of way over *private* property raises more interesting issues:

> Member States may allow the relevant authority to impose fees for the . . . rights to install facilities on, over or under public *or private* property. . . .[298]

This suggests that fees for rights of way over private property must also be proportionate, non-discriminatory and promote Article 8 objectives. Yet the 22nd recital of the Framework Directive states that its provisions are "without prejudice to national provisions governing the expropriation or use of property, the normal exercise of property rights, the normal use of the public domain, or to the principle of neutrality with regard to the rules in Member States governing the system of property ownership."[299]

The "without prejudice" language quoted above applies by its terms only to the Framework Directive. The rules about fees for rights of way appear in the Authorization Directive, not the Framework Directive. So technically, those rules are not affected by the "without prejudice" language contained in the 22nd recital of the Framework Directive. This leads to the conclusion that for private as well as public property, the fees charged by relevant authorities for rights of way must obey the principles set forth in Article 13 of the Authorization Directive. But what does

297 Authorization Directive, Article 13.

298 Authorization Directive, Article 13 (emphasis added).

299 Framework Directive, Preamble, 22nd recital.

this mean for private property? Do the "relevant authorities" mean private landowners? Surely not. This aspect of the Directive will no doubt give rise to varying interpretations by Member States.

Structural Separation

Another rule relating to rights of way is the requirement that when a public or local authority retains ownership or control of an operator, the branch of the authority responsible for granting rights of way must be structurally separate from the branch in charge of assuring the ownership or control of the relevant operator.[300] This rule is particularly important in countries, such as Sweden and Germany, where cities have the right to operate telecommunications networks. In such a case, conflicts of interest may lead to discriminatory treatment of other operators who are potential competitors of the city's own local operator. The term "public or local authority" covers more than cities, of course, and could apply to port authorities and railways as well. Most European railways have created telecom ventures. As a result of this provision in the Framework Directive, the railways may have to create a separate company[301] in charge of granting rights of way.

The structural separation requirement is triggered whenever the relevant authority owns or controls an entity operating an electronic communications network or service. This raises an important question as to whether structural separation is mandated when the authority controls only passive infrastructure, e.g. dark fiber or masts for antennas. In France, cities have the right to deploy dark fiber but not to "operate" a network. In cities where such dark fiber exists, city officials have every incentive to rent the existing dark fiber to new entrants instead of granting rights of way for laying new fiber. Consequently, conflicts of interest will be a concern even where cities do not provide an electronic communications network or service. New entrants will be more or less forced to rent the dark fiber installed by the city rather than install their own fiber.

The Framework Directive unfortunately will not help new entrants in this situation. Structural separation would not be required because the city does not "operate" a network or service. Dark fiber is an important element of an electronic communications network, but mere ownership of dark fiber will not qualify as "operating" a network. The city would have to comply with non-discrimination and transparency principles, but those principles will not help the new entrant much either. By insisting that *all* operators use the city's existing dark fiber, the city is applying its rule in a non-discriminatory manner. The rule can easily be justified by the city's desire to minimize the disruption of having repeated construction work in the city streets. The transparency requirement would be fulfilled by publishing the decision and the reasons therefore. Member States would be well advised to extend the structural separation rule beyond situations where the rele-

300 Framework Directive, Article 11(2).

301 Structural separation traditionally requires the creation of a separate company.

vant authorities operate a network, to cover situations where the authorities own network elements but do not "operate" the network.

Right to Appeal

The last rule that helps new entrants in connection with rights of way is the right to an appeal.[302] The difficulty in many Member States is that operators have no effective way to appeal an unfavorable decision issued by a local authority on a right of way issue. National regulatory authorities generally lack authority to review local right of way decisions, meaning that the only means of recourse is through traditional administrative appeal mechanisms. Traditional appeal mechanisms for administrative decisions can take months, if not years, and often leave the operator with no choice but to comply with the local authorities' desires, no matter how outrageous or illegal they may seem. The Framework Directive does not dictate how the appeal mechanism should operate. Indeed Member States could probably retain their existing administrative appeal mechanisms without violating the Directive. A far preferable solution, however, would be to give the national regulatory authority jurisdiction to review contested right of way decisions or, at the very least, give the national regulatory authority the ability to issue a non-binding opinion to the administrative court as to how the dispute should be resolved. Member States may be reluctant for political reasons to give their national regulatory authority power directly to overrule a municipal decision. But at a minimum the national regulatory authority should systematically give its opinion in any right of way dispute, and a fast-track appeal procedure should be available before administrative judges where it is not already available.

Public versus Private Land

As noted above, the Directives impose no affirmative obligation to grant rights of way, whether over public or private property. Authorities are in theory free not to grant rights of way to *anyone*. The Framework Directive says that when a competent authority considers an application, the authority must do so without delay in a transparent and non-discriminatory fashion. The Framework Directive describes two kinds of "applications" for rights of way: applications from firms authorized to provide *public* communications networks, and applications from firms authorized to provide electronic communications networks "other than to the public."[303] The former applications are for the "granting of rights to install facilities on, over or under public or private property." The latter applications are for the "granting of rights to install facilities on, over or under *public* property." This suggests that only operators of *public* communications networks shall have the right to apply for rights of way over private property.

The Framework Directive states that the procedures for granting rights of way may vary depending on whether the applicant is a public network operator or not.

302 Framework Directive, Article 11(3).

303 Framework Directive, Article 11(1).

These provisions suggest that Member States should set up procedures whereby public network operators have access to rights of way over both public and private property. Operators of non-public networks, on the other hand, should have access to rights of way over public property only. This approach makes sense, because as a general matter public network operators shoulder more regulatory burdens than do operators of non-public networks. Consequently their entitlements should also be greater. What is a shame, however, is that the Directive does not come out and say that public network operators are entitled to rights of way. The Directive merely says to Member States that in the event they provide for access to rights of way over public and private property for operators of public networks, they should do so in a non-discriminatory basis; in the event Member States provide for access to rights of way over public property for operators of *private* networks, they should do so on a non-discriminatory basis. This language is so loose that Member States will be able to do practically whatever they want.

Modification or Withdrawal of Rights of Way

The Authorization Directive provides that Member States may not modify rights to install facilities, or the procedures for granting rights, without giving interested parties, including users and consumers, an opportunity to comment.[304] The period for comment must not be less than four weeks, except in exceptional cases.

Once an operator has a right of way, Article 14(2) of the Authorization Directive prohibits Member States from restricting or withdrawing the right of way before the end of the period for which the right of way was granted, "except where justified and where applicable in conformity with relevant national provisions regarding compensation for the withdrawal of rights."[305] This highlights one of the problems with rights of way over public property: they are usually revocable as a matter of public policy. If a city, road, or canal authority needs to remove an operator from a site, it can almost invariably do so if the move is required for the public interest. The withdrawal of the right of way may or may not give rise to compensation, and the authority may or may not have an obligation to find another site or route for the operator. Because of the inherent revocability of rights of way under administrative law, Article 14(2) of the Authorization Directive unfortunately does not bring much additional security to operators holding rights of way over public property. This revocability also makes facility sharing a perilous exercise, because not only the main holder of the facility would be affected by a revocation or relocation, but so would all the entities sharing the relevant site.

Co-location and Facility Sharing

We saw above that the Directives fail to be very "directive" when it comes to how Member States grant rights of way. The directives leave tremendous freedom

304 Authorization Directive, Article 14(1).

305 Authorization Directive, Article 14(2).

to Member States. The directives show no more muscle when it comes to facility sharing.

Article 12(2) of the Framework Directive allows (but does not *require*) Member States to impose facility sharing:

> In particular where undertakings are deprived of access to viable alternatives because of the need to protect the environment, public health, public security or to meet town and country planning objectives, Member States may impose the sharing of facilities or property (including physical co-location) on an undertaking operating an electronic communications network or take measures to facilitate the coordination of public works only after an appropriate period of public consultation during which all interested parties must be given an opportunity to express their views.[306]

The word "may" used in the Framework Directive shows that facility sharing, like the granting of rights of way, will be left to the discretion of Member States. The second point that jumps out is the Framework Directive's reference to "an undertaking operating an electronic communications network." This suggests that facility sharing may not be imposed on entities that do not operate an electronic communications network. As we will see in the next section, there are many kinds of entities that do not necessarily operate electronic communications networks but that nevertheless control facilities for which facility sharing would be appropriate, particularly where equivalent rights of way have been denied to the new entrant. Tower companies, or companies owning dark fiber, for instance, technically do not operate electronic communications networks yet they can be powerful actors controlling key resources for other operators. Under the Framework Directive's Article 12(2), they would appear to be immune from facility sharing obligations.

Read in their most unfavorable light, these provisions of the Framework Directive paint a bleak picture for a new entrant. First, Member States have no obligation to grant rights of way at all. That already is surprising. Second, if a Member State denies a right of way, the Member State has no obligation to impose facility sharing under the Framework Directive. Finally, if a Member State imposes facility sharing, the facility sharing obligation would extend to operators but not to pure infrastructure companies. This would motivate large operators benefiting from extensive rights of way to spin off their infrastructure into separate infrastructure companies, which would not be considered "operators of electronic communications networks" so as to avoid facility sharing obligations. Member States could close this loophole by drafting national facility-sharing legislation broadly enough to cover not only operators of electronic communications networks, but also infrastructure companies.

Public Consultation

Article 12(2) of the Framework Directive requires Member States to conduct public consultations before imposing facility sharing. The public consultation would presumably occur at a local level, organized by the competent authority that has

306 Framework Directive, Article 12(2).

authority to grant rights of way in the first place. During the consultation, "all interested parties must be given an opportunity to express their views." This consultation obligation apparently differs from the consultation process imposed by Article 6 of the Framework Directive, which is controlled by the national regulatory authority. Indeed Article 12(2) of the Framework Directive refers to consultation of interested parties without referring either to the national regulatory authority or to Article 6 of the Framework Directive. This makes sense insofar as the consultation will in most cases involve only local issues (digging up streets for example). Conducting a nationwide consultation would be disproportionate.

Sharing Costs

In another characteristically permissive sentence, Article 12(2) of the Framework Directive states that the facility sharing arrangements imposed by Member States "may" include rules for apportioning the costs of facility or property sharing. Figuring out the right cost for facility sharing is no easy task. In setting the rules for sharing costs, Member States should refer to the rules established under Article 13 of the Authorization Directive, which requires that fees be objectively justified, transparent, non-discriminatory, and proportionate. Member States may refer to existing national rules for expropriation to set the price. Otherwise guidelines for setting the cost could be set at a national level, then implemented at a local level. Currently France gives the national regulatory authority power to arbitrate disputes involving facility sharing.[307] That has the advantage of fostering fast dispute resolution, and uniformity in decisions. If cost issues are arbitrated at a local level, decisions could be influenced by local politics, giving a clear advantage to whatever entity employs the most voters in the city. Moreover local decision-making could yield results that vary greatly from region to region: the price of sharing a mast could be ten times higher in one region compared to another even if the price of real estate and costs of construction are identical. For the sake of uniformity, national regulatory authorities should be given the power under national law to set guidelines on costs for facility sharing, and to resolve disputes. Putting dispute resolution with the national regulatory authority will bring one additional benefit: national regulatory authorities will be required to make decisions that promote the objectives of Article 8 of the Framework Directive (the regulator's "mission statement"). Other dispute resolution forums, such as administrative courts, would not necessarily take the interests of competition and end-users into account when arbitrating decisions on facility sharing.

8. Enforcement

Information Gathering

The Authorization Directive and the Framework Directive require that national regulatory authorities have certain information-gathering powers. The information gathering has a dual objective, statistical and enforcement-related.

307 Code of Post and Telecommunications, Article L 47.

Statistical information gathering

National regulatory authorities may require entities holding a general authorization to provide information for "clearly defined statistical purposes,"[308] for the "publication of comparative overview of quality and price of services for the benefit of consumers,"[309] as well as for market analysis purposes.[310] The information requested must be "proportionate and objectively justified."[311]

Verification and enforcement

The second class of information that a national regulatory authority can require is information needed to verify compliance with the conditions in the general authorization or right of usage. Systematic verification is allowed only with regard to: (i) payment of administrative charges or usage fees, and (ii) compliance with access and universal service obligations.[312] For all other matters, the Authorization Directive permits only case-by-case verifications. The national regulatory authority may initiate a verification either based on a complaint by a third party, or at its own initiative.[313] In any case, whether the request for information is for statistical or enforcement purposes, the national regulatory authority must inform the entity of the specific purpose of the request.[314]

Information in connection with granting usage rights

National regulatory authorities may also request information from entities in connection with the granting of rights of use of radio spectrum and numbering resources.[315] For these information requests, and only these, the national regulatory authority may make receipt of the information a condition to market entry.[316] In other words, the national regulatory authority need not grant the right of use until it has received all the information requested. This is similar to the current practice in some countries for the granting of individual licenses to operate a network. The national regulatory authority can continue to ask for further information about a candidate's financial or technical capacity, or about the candidate's future network. The candidate for the individual license must wait until the national regulatory authority has received all the information it wants before the clock starts ticking for the granting of the license.

This practice will fortunately disappear for individual licenses, since individual licenses will themselves disappear under the new framework. A national regulatory

---

308 Authorization Directive, Article 11(1)(e).

309 Authorization Directive, Article 11(1)(d).

310 Authorization Directive, Article 11(1)(f).

311 Authorization Directive, Article 11(1).

312 Authorization Directive, Article 11(1)(a).

313 Authorization Directive, Article 11(1)(b).

314 Authorization Directive, Article 11(2).

315 Authorization Directive, Article 11(1)(c).

316 Authorization Directive, Article 11(1).

authority will no longer be able to prohibit an entity from providing an electronic communications network or service on the ground that the entity has not yet provided the national regulatory authority with sufficient information about its network or financial capacity. Cases may arise where the national regulatory authority feels that the declaration filed by the entity is incomplete. In that case the national regulatory authority may take the position that the declaration is not effective until it has been completed properly. This could lead again to the endless goings back and forth that the drafters of the Authorization Directive wanted to avoid. In theory, the declaration should be so simple as to leave no room for argument. The information in the declaration "must be limited to what is necessary for the identification of the provider, such as company registration numbers, and the provider's contact persons, the provider's address, a short description of the network or service, and an estimated date for starting the activity."[317] The only item that could potentially give rise to controversy is the "short description of the network or service." In drafting their national legislation, certain Member States may be tempted to overlook the word "short," and impose detailed information requirements on entities filing a declaration as a provider of electronic communications networks or services. In theory that should not happen in light of the Directive's unambiguous language. In practice, it very well could happen in at least some Member States.

The Authorization Directive also treats the question of information requests in connection with the granting of rights of use for frequencies and numbering resources. National regulatory authorities can request information in connection with applications for rights of use, but the requests must be "proportionate and objectively justified."[318] Neither the Authorization Directive nor the Framework Directive deals with information requests made in connection with the granting of rights to install facilities on public or private property. Such information requests, presumably made by local or regional authorities, are not limited at all by the directives, except insofar as the directives require local procedures to be transparent and non-discriminatory. We can anticipate therefore that the various "competent authorities" granting rights of way will be tempted to request vast quantities of information from network providers as a condition to granting rights of way. It will be for national legislation to limit how far local authorities can go in their information requests.

Enforcement Procedures

The Authorization Directive sets down procedures for national regulatory authorities to follow when they take enforcement actions against network operators, service providers or beneficiaries of rights of use. If the national regulatory authority detects (or is notified of) a breach of one of the conditions attached to the general authorization or right of use, the national regulatory authority must first send a notice to the allegedly breaching entity giving the entity a reasonable opportunity to

---

317 Authorization Directive, Article 3(3).

318 Authorization Directive, Article 11(1).

state its views or remedy the breaches.[319] The entity must respond within one month, or such longer period as may be stipulated by the national regulatory authority. In case of repeated breaches, or if agreed to by the entity, the national regulatory authority may set a period less than one month. As we will see below, the national regulatory authority may in some cases shorten the notice period or even eliminate it entirely to treat immediate and serious problems. But under the normal procedure, the entity must generally be given one month to answer the national regulatory authority's notice of breach. If the entity does not remedy the breach within the thirty-day period, then the national regulatory authority may apply "appropriate and proportionate measures" to ensure compliance, including if appropriate financial penalties.[320] In the event of "serious and repeated breaches," and provided the "appropriate and proportionate measures" referred to above have failed, then the national regulatory authority may revoke the entity's general authorization or right of use.[321]

Interim Measures

The national regulatory authority can bypass the normal procedure outlined above and take urgent interim measures if a breach is such that it "represents an immediate and serious threat to public safety, public security or public health or will create serious economic or operational problems for other providers or users of electronic communications networks or services."[322] The entity targeted by an interim measure must have a reasonable opportunity to state its views and propose any remedies after the interim measure has been adopted. Providing for a right to be heard after-the-fact is highly unusual, and could in some circumstances violate due process rights guaranteed by Article 6 of the *European Convention for the Protection of Human Rights and Fundamental Freedoms*.[323] Indeed, unless an element of surprise is required (as when attaching an asset of a recalcitrant debtor) interim measures generally require a hearing prior to the decision, at which the person or entity has the right to present its defense. In extremely urgent cases, the hearing may be held on 24 hours' notice, but there is still a prior hearing. To satisfy basic due process, Member States will probably adopt national laws providing that the national regulatory authority must give the breaching entity an opportunity to be heard *before* the interim measure is adopted, except in the most extreme circumstances.

Right of Appeal

As noted in the previous section on the Framework Directive, entities affected by a decision of the national regulatory authority must always benefit from a right to

319 Authorization Directive, Article 10(2).

320 Authorization Directive, Article 10(3).

321 Authorization Directive, Article 10(5).

322 Authorization Directive, Article 10(6).

323 *Convention for the Protection of Human Rights and Fundamental Freedoms*, as amended by Protocol No. 11, Rome, November 4, 1950, Article 6.

appeal.[324] The appeal must relate not only to legal and procedural aspects of the case issues, but also to the underlying factual issues.[325]

9. Existing Authorizations

Member States must modify existing authorizations so that they comply with the new conditions in the Authorization Directive no later than July 25, 2003.[326] Where the modification would result in a decrease of an entity's rights or in an increase of its obligations, the Member State may allow the preexisting rights or obligations to survive for an additional period of up to nine months, provided that the rights of other entities under Community law are not affected thereby.[327] Finally, Member States may ask the Commission for permission to extend certain access obligations if the Member State can show that the removal of the condition would create "excessive difficulties" for other entities that have benefited from the mandatory access provisions in the past.[328] It is hard to imagine situations in which this provision would be applied. As explained in the next section, all existing access obligations on SMP operators under the old Interconnection Directive and ONP Voice Telephony Directive will survive until such time as the relevant national regulatory authority conducts a market analysis and replaces the old obligations with new ones under the Access Directive.[329] When the national regulatory authority decides that a particular product or service market is "effectively competitive," the national regulatory authority must withdraw access obligations.[330] Under this scheme, none of the important access obligations will disappear on July 23, 2003. It is difficult to understand therefore why the drafters of the Authorization Directive felt it necessary to give Member States a special procedure to request a prolongation of certain access conditions.

There will no doubt be some resistance to modifying all existing licenses on July 23, 2003 as required by Article 17(1) of the Authorization Directive. Having worked hard and invested significant money to obtain an individual license, existing operators will in some respects feel cheated by the new regime. By waving a magic wand Member States will transform the operator's precious individual license into a general authorization that anyone can obtain simply by filing a short declaration. One can imagine that Member States will come under pressure to maintain some special grandfather privileges for new entrants that obtained individual licenses the hard way, under the old regime.

324 Authorization Directive, Article 10(7).

325 Framework Directive, Article 4.

326 Authorization Directive, Article 17(1).

327 Authorization Directive, Article 17(2).

328 Authorization Directive, Article 17(3).

329 Framework Directive, Article 27.

330 Framework Directive, Article 16(3).

10. Three-year review

Like all the directives in the new framework, the Authorization Directive calls for a review after three years.[331] The Commission must report to the Council and the European Parliament no later than July 23, 2006 on the functioning of the new authorization scheme in Member States.

D. THE ACCESS DIRECTIVE[332]

1. Introduction

Like its predecessor, the Interconnection Directive,[333] the Access Directive gives new entrants the ability to use parts of a competitor's network or services under conditions that the competitor would never have otherwise accepted. The Access Directive is the regulatory crowbar that permits new entrants to pry open networks operated by former monopolies, and sometimes (though more rarely) networks operated by other new entrants.

The old Interconnection Directive established an identical set of obligations that applied to all operators holding "significant market power" in each Member State. National regulatory authorities simply had to apply the rules laid down by the Directive. It was a one-size-fits-all approach. The Access Directive, on the other hand, gives national regulatory authorities broad discretion to choose from a toolbox of regulatory access measures. The tools in the toolbox are predetermined, but the national regulatory authorities are free to choose which tool(s) to use in a given situation. This will put much more responsibility on the shoulders of the national regulators than previously was the case. The other big difference is of course the kind of networks and services that can be subject to access obligations. Previously limited to the traditional public switched telephone network ("PSTN"), the access measures under the new Directive apply in theory to any electronic communications network or associated facility, including television and radio transmission facilities, IP backbones, cable TV and satellite networks. As we will see below, even software could be subject to forced access in certain conditions.

2. Definition of "Access"

Previously EU law differentiated between "interconnection," defined under the Interconnection Directive, and "special access," defined under the ONP Voice Telephony Directive. Differentiating between the two concepts was not always easy, particularly outside the domain of traditional voice telephony. The new approach is

331 Authorization Directive, Article 16.

332 This material was originally published in *Electronic Communications: the New EU Framework* (ed. W. Maxwell, Oceana, New York, 2002).

333 EP/Council Directive 97/33 on interconnection in telecommunications with regard to ensuring universal service and interoperability through application of the principles of open network provision (ONP), OJ L199/97.

conceptually simpler. Access is defined broadly. Interconnection is a smaller subset of "access." The Access Directive defines "access" as follows:

> "access" means the making available of facilities and/or services, to another undertaking, under defined conditions, on either an exclusive or non-exclusive basis, for the purpose of providing electronic communications services. It covers *inter alia*: access to network elements and associated facilities, which may involve the connection of equipment, by fixed or non-fixed means (in particular this includes access to the local loop and to facilities and services necessary to provide services over the local loop); access to physical infrastructure including buildings, ducts and masts; access to relevant software systems including operational support systems; access to number translation or systems offering equivalent functionality; access to fixed and mobile networks, in particular for roaming; access to conditional access systems for digital television services; access to virtual network services.[334]

The first thing that jumps out under the new definition is the number of elements to which one can gain access: the local loop, buildings, ducts, masts, software systems, intelligent network systems, fixed and mobile networks, conditional access systems, virtual network services. This list is not exhaustive. Basically anything that a new entrant needs to provide electronic communications services could be considered "access." This at least will end the theoretical debate of whether a given service requested by a new entrant is special access, interconnection, or neither. In almost every case in which this author has been involved, the incumbent has tried to argue that the service requested by the new entrant is technically not "interconnection" and therefore does not fall within the regulatory framework for interconnection services. This required then a relatively deep theoretical analysis of the nature of interconnection as compared to the nature of the service being requested by the new entrant. In later booklets, we will look at some practical aspects of access. Suffice it to say for the moment that the question of whether a given service is access will be easier to resolve under the new Directive.

The Access Directive defines "interconnection" as follows:

> 'interconnection' means the physical and logical linking of public communications networks used by the same or a different undertaking in order to allow the users of one undertaking to communicate with users of the same or another undertaking, or to access services provided by another undertaking. Services may be provided by the parties involved or other parties who have access to the network. Interconnection is a specific type of access implemented between public network operators.[335]

This definition copies almost verbatim the pre-existing definition of interconnection under the Interconnection Directive. Except that at the end, the new Access Directive explains that interconnection is a subset (a "specific type") of "access."

334 Access Directive, Article 2(a).

335 Access Directive, Article 2(b).

3. What Entities are Subject to Access Obligations?

From the outset, the Directive states that its obligations apply only to networks used for the provision of publicly available electronic communications services. As pointed out in the Preamble:

> Non-public networks do not have obligations under this Directive except where, in benefiting from access to public networks, they may be subject to conditions laid down by Member States.[336]

The exception contained in this clause refers to obligations such as interoperability and respect of essential requirements designed to protect public networks from damages and interference. Private networks have to comply with such requirements. But private networks are excluded from the scope of the Access Directive, as are providers of content, such as entities that offer packages of television or radio content and entities that provide Internet portals.[337]

4. What is a Network?

As noted above, access obligations only apply to operators of communications networks used for publicly available communications services. The Directive does not define "network operator," but does point out that an operator need not own facilities in order to be considered an operator.[338] In some Member States (such as France), the concept of network operator is closely tied to ownership or control of underlying network infrastructure: in order to be considered a network operator in France one has to own or control transmission facilities. Renting network capacity in the form of leased lines is not sufficient to qualify as an "operator" under French regulations. The reason why being a network operator is important is that in some Member States operators benefited from better regulatory treatment (notably in relation to interconnection) than did service providers. This was done on purpose in order to encourage entities to invest in alternative transmission infrastructure. But under the new Access Directive, this sort of preferential treatment is prohibited:

> National legal or administrative measures that link the terms and conditions for access or interconnection to the activities of the party seeking interconnection, and specifically to the degree of its investment in network infrastructure, and not to the interconnection or access services provided, may cause market distortion and may therefore not be compatible with competition rules.[339]

The definition of "network operator" will still remain important under the new regime, however, because only providers of public electronic communications *networks* have access obligations. Providers of electronic communications *services*

336 Access Directive, Preamble, 1st recital.

337 Access Directive, Preamble, 2nd recital; Universal Service Directive, Preamble, 45th recital.

338 Access Directive, Preamble, 3rd recital.

339 Access Directive, Preamble, 7th recital; *see also* Article 3(2).

have no such obligations. The Access Directive therefore ensures that the definition of network (and network operator) does not depend on ownership of facilities.

5. General Framework for Access

Commercial Negotiation

Like the prior regime, the new regime puts emphasis on commercial negotiations for entering into access agreements, and prohibits Member States from imposing restrictions that would prevent such negotiation, either between undertakings in the same Member State or between undertakings in different Member States.[340]

The best way to understand the Access Directive is to look at each kind of operator and determine what kinds of access obligations apply to that operator. Some operators will have no obligations at all, and some will be hit by the set of "hard core" access obligations reserved for operators holding significant market power.

Entities that do not Operate Public Networks

Subject to two exceptions,[341] only operators of public communications networks have obligations under the Directive. Operators of private networks will have no obligations at all under the Directive, other than technical obligations that might flow from being connected to a public network (technical obligations to ensure that there is no interference with the public network).[342] The question of what is a public—as opposed to a non-public—communications network will in most cases be easy to answer, because operators of public networks will in most cases have registered themselves as such with the national regulatory authority.[343] The operator's status as an operator of a public communications network will be public knowledge in most cases.

Difficult cases could arise where an entity requests access from an operator of a communications network that has not registered itself as a public operator under the Authorization Directive, but that the requesting entity believes should nevertheless be treated as a public communications operator. This situation might occur when an operator requests access (for example) from an electric utility that operates a communications network for its own internal purposes. If the electric utility has operations as a public communications operator, chances are that the communications activity is conducted through a separate subsidiary. Chances are also that the separate subsidiary operating the network will own no fiber or ducts of its own, leasing what it needs from the parent company (the electric utility). The parent company itself (the electric utility) will not have declared itself as an operator.

---

340 Access Directive, Article 3(1); Preamble, 5th recital.

341 The two exceptions relate to providers of conditional access systems, which we will examine below.

342 Access Directive, Preamble, 1st recital.

343 The Authorization Directive permits Member States to put into place a prior declaration procedure for operators.

The access obligation (if any) will weigh only on the subsidiary, and the subsidiary may have very little infrastructure of its own available to share or to which to provide access. The Access Directive defines "operator" as an entity *providing* or *authorized to provide* a public communications network or associated facility. The fact that an entity (in this case the electric utility) has not filed for an authorization to provide a public communications network would not in itself pose a problem, provided that it can be shown that the entity *in fact provides* a public communications network or associated facility. Under the definition in the Framework Directive, ducts can be an "associated facility." The question then is whether by offering some ducts for rental to its subsidiary, the utility is providing ducts "to the public," thereby becoming de facto an "operator" providing a public communications network or associated facility. In our hypothetical, the electric utility would in all likelihood *not* be deemed to be providing fiber and ducts to the public, since its only customer (other than itself) would be its communications subsidiary. The same analysis would apply to a tower company. Towers and high points do not constitute themselves an electronic communications network. But they do constitute "associated facilities." If a tower company is in the business of leasing space or facilities on its towers to third parties, then it would be deemed, for purposes of the Access Directive, to be providing an associated facility to the public, even if the tower company has not registered itself as a public operator.[344]

Operators of Public Networks and Associated Facilities that do not have Significant Market Power

Even if an entity is found to be an operator of a public communications network or associated facility, that does not mean much, unless the operator is found to hold "significant market power".(a situation we'll look at in detail below). If the operator is simply a public operator without significant market power, then its only obligation under the Access Directive is to negotiate interconnection with other public network operators. The Directive does not require that the negotiations succeed, but it requires operators to try in good faith to negotiate with other public operators.[345] The negotiations need only relate to interconnection, i.e. a service permitting the customer of one operator to send communications to and receive communications from customers of the other operator or to access services provided by the other operator. There is no obligation on non-SMP operators to negotiate any other form of "access." To use the previous example, the provisions of the Access Directive would not help a new entrant gain access to ducts or towers owned by the electric utility or the tower company even if those entities were deemed "operators of public communications networks." Obtaining access to a duct or tower is not "interconnection." It is only in the case where the relevant operator is also deemed to hold "significant market power" that a new entrant could have any hope of forcing access to ducts or towers.

---

344 Registering as an operator would make no sense for a tower company unless the company also provided transmission services.

345 Access Directive, Preamble, 5th recital.

The obligation to negotiate would only cover situations where one operator wants to be able to send messages to and receive messages from the customers of another operator, or otherwise ensure that users of one operator can communicate with users of the other operator. In voice telephony, the concept of interconnection is well understood. For data, the concept is less clear-cut. We will examine the interconnection concept as applied to the Internet in a subsequent booklet.

Where negotiations fail, either party can bring the dispute before the national regulatory authority. The regulatory authority's power to force interconnection will depend in part on whether the public operator being asked to interconnect also controls access to end-users. If the operator does not control access to end-users, then the regulatory authority does not necessarily have to possess the power to force that operator to interconnect. The national regulatory authority *may* have this ability under national law, but the Directive does not require it. If the public operator only works in the wholesale market (as an Internet backbone provider, for example), then a regulatory authority will probably *not* force interconnection if commercial negotiations fail. This makes sense because on the wholesale or transit markets other alternatives for reaching the end-user generally exist. If one operator on the wholesale market refuses to interconnect, the requesting operator will generally be able to negotiate with other operators in order to reach the end-user. We're speaking of course about wholesale operators that do not hold "significant market power." If a wholesale operator were to hold "significant market power," a whole set of access obligations could befall it.

Now let us look at operators who do not hold "significant market power," but who do control access to end-users. For this category of operators, regulatory authorities will have enhanced powers. The Access Directive states that operators may control access to end-users through:

> ownership or control of the physical link to the end-user (either fixed or mobile), and/or the ability to change or withdraw the national number or numbers needed to access an end-user's network termination point. This could be the case for example if network operators were to restrict unreasonably end-user choice for access to Internet portals and services.[346]

When a non-SMP operator controls access to an end-user, the Access Directive requires that national regulatory authorities have the power to impose objective, transparent and non-discriminatory obligations, including in justified cases the obligation to interconnect where necessary to ensure end-to-end connectivity.[347] National regulatory authorities may impose interconnection in justified cases where necessary to ensure end-to-end connectivity, while taking into account the objectives of the Article 8 mission statement. The Access Directive leaves some ambiguity as to whether a national regulatory authority can impose only *interconnection* on non-SMP operators, or whether it can impose other access measures as well.

---

346 Access Directive, Preamble, 6th recital.

347 Access Directive, Article 5(1)(a).

Article 4(1) indicates that public network operators have an obligation to negotiate "interconnection." The 5th recital refers to both interconnection and access:

> undertakings which receive requests for access or interconnection should in principle conclude such agreements on a commercial basis, and negotiate in good faith.

Article 5(1) also refers to access and interconnection, whereas Article 5(1)(a) refers only to interconnection:

> national regulatory authorities shall be able to impose:
>
> (a) to the extent that is necessary to ensure end-to-end connectivity, obligations on undertakings that control access to end-users, including in justified cases the obligation to interconnect their networks where this is not already the case.

This ambiguity is maintained in the sixth and eighth recitals. The sixth recital refers to regulators having the power to secure "adequate access and interconnection," whereas the eighth recital refers to the need for operators to deliver traffic to the customers controlled by the other operator and to "interconnect directly or indirectly" with the other operator.

In our view, the Directive requires that regulators have power to force non-SMP operators to interconnect where one of the operators controls access to end-users. Regulators may also impose other access measures (such as carrier selection services) necessary to accompany successful interconnection. But the intent of the Directive is not to permit national regulators to impose full-fledged access measures on non-SMP operators, such as an obligation to share ducts or make dark fiber available. Those access measures are reserved for SMP operators only.

Operators already Subject to Obligations under the Interconnection Directive, ONP Voice Telephony Directive or the ONP Leased Lines Directive

The Framework and Access Directives foresee a new approach to market analysis and the designation of so-called "SMP" operators. Each national regulatory authority will have responsibility for conducting this new market analysis as soon as possible after the Directives come into force.[348] Nevertheless, to avoid a situation where existing SMP operators are temporarily released from their obligations[349] while the regulator is figuring out the new rules, the Access Directive requires that all obligations under the former directives remain in effect until such time as the national regulatory authority has made its new determination of SMP under Article 16 of the Framework Directive.[350]

Operators Designated as Possessing Significant Market Power under the New Directives

As we saw in the section on the Framework Directive, national regulatory authorities must undertake a review of relevant product and service markets (as defined

348 Access Directive, Article 7(3).

349 Access Directive, recital 12.

350 Access Directive, Article 7(1).

in the Commission's Recommendation) to determine whether they are "effectively competitive." The Commission defines the relevant product and service markets and lists them in a recommendation that the Commission updates from time to time. If a national regulatory authority deviates from the Recommendation, the Commission can veto the national regulatory authority's decision. The purpose of conducting the market analysis is to determine which operators will fall under the "hard core" access obligations defined in the Access Directive. As noted above, the Framework Directive fundamentally changed the method for determining significant market power by making "significant market power" ("SMP") synonymous with "dominant position" under competition law. The national regulatory authorities have a lot of discretion, but the Commission can keep tabs on the regulatory authorities' activities through the consultation and veto process set forth in Articles 6 and 7 of the Framework Directive.

Once a national regulatory authority determines that an operator holds significant market power on a given product or service market, then the Access Directive provides a list of hard-core obligations that the national regulatory authority *can* decide to apply. The national regulatory authority can apply some or all of the hard-core obligations, but unlike the situation under the old Interconnection Directive, the national regulator does not have to apply them all. The national regulatory authority has considerable discretion to pick and choose among the obligations contained in the Access Directive's toolbox. This "pick and choose" approach differs from that of the Interconnection and ONP Voice Telephony Directives, both of which gave Member States a comprehensive list of obligations that they had to apply to every SMP operator. The old approach was binary, all-or-nothing. All national regulators had to do under the old directives was identify which operators possessed SMP. The rest followed automatically.

Under the new approach, regulators have (as before) the responsibility for identifying SMP operators. They now also have the responsibility for choosing which of the "hard-core" obligations will apply to each SMP operator. This added responsibility will increase significantly the national regulator's discretion and power compared to the old regime.

In section 6, we will look at how national regulations go about choosing the right tools.

The Directive says that regulatory authorities shall not impose any hard-core obligations on non-SMP operators, except as required by Article 5(1) (operators that control access to end-users, operators distributing digital radio or television), Article 5(2) (standards) and Article 6 (conditional access service providers) of the Access Directive. The message is clear: hard-core obligations are for SMP operators only. The only obligations that may be imposed on non-SMP operators are those reviewed above in section 5.3.

Operators that Distribute Digital Television Services

All operators (SMP or non-SMP) that distribute digital television services must be capable of distributing wide-screen television services and programs.[351] Operators that redistribute wide screen programs and services must maintain the wide screen format.

Providers of Conditional Access Services and Systems

This category of operator is in fact a special subset of operators that control access to end-users. For historic reasons linked to the Digital Television Standards Directive,[352] operators of conditional access services and systems are subject to a special set of obligations. Operators of conditional access systems generally control access to the end-user's terminal through management of entitlement messages that permit the viewer to unscramble an encrypted television or radio signal. The conditional access operator is a gateway through which a broadcaster must pass in order to be able to deliver its program to an end-user. The Access Directive requires that operators of conditional access systems offer to all radio or television broadcasters, on a "fair, reasonable and non-discriminatory basis" technical services enabling the broadcasters' digitally-transmitted services to be received by viewers or listeners authorized by means of decoders administered by the service operators.[353] The Access Directive justifies this measure as being necessary to ensure "cultural diversity and media pluralism."[354]

Operators of conditional access systems must also keep separate accounts regarding their activity as conditional access providers.[355] Finally, the conditional access systems must permit "cost-effective transcontrol" allowing the possibility for full control by network operators at a local or regional level of services using such conditional access systems.[356]

Although a host of obligations apply from day one to providers of conditional access services, the Access Directive allows national regulatory authorities to undertake a review of the applicable market as provided in Article 16 of the Framework Directive, in order to determine whether the access conditions imposed on conditional access providers are justified.[357] If the national regulatory authority finds that the provider does not hold significant market power on the relevant market, then the national regulatory authority may remove some or all of the access obli-

351 Access Directive, Article 4(2).

352 EP/Council Directive 95/47 on the use of standards for the transmission of television signals (OJL281/95).

353 Access Directive, Annex I, Part 1 (b).

354 Access Directive, Preamble, 10th recital.

355 Access Directive, Annex I, Part 1 (b).

356 Access Directive, Annex I, Part 1 (a).

357 Access Directive, Article 6(3)(a).

gations, but only to the extent withdrawal of the obligations would not harm end-user access to designated public service channels,[358] nor the prospects for effective competition on the retail broadcasting market and wholesale conditional access services market.[359]

The Directive mentions here that its provisions are "without prejudice" to Member States' ability to enact measures regarding "presentational aspects of electronic programme guides and similar listing and navigation facilities."[360] This confirms that the manner in which content is presented on a screen goes to Member States' content regulation and competition law, and does not fall under the "access" rules imposed under the Access Directive.

Holders of Industrial Property Rights to Conditional Access Products or Systems

This class of entities is not made up of operators at all, but of holders of intellectual property rights. This is one of the cases where the Access Directive's provisions apply to entities that are neither operators of communications networks nor even providers of electronic communications services. The Access Directive requires that when granting intellectual property licenses to manufacturers of consumer equipment, holders of intellectual property rights for conditional access products and systems grant such licenses on fair, reasonable and non-discriminatory terms.[361] They may not make the granting of the license conditional on the licensee agreeing not to include in the product a common interface, or technology for another conditional access system. This obligation is a hold-over from the Digital Television Standards Directive.[362]

Operators Involved in the Distribution of Digital Television or Radio

This category is similar to the category mentioned above regarding wide screen television, except that the category also includes distributors of digital radio. For this class of operators, national regulatory authorities are supposed to be alert to the emergence of new gateways such as electronic program guides (EPGs) and application program interfaces (APIs).[363] If the national regulatory authority deems necessary to ensure accessibility to digital radio and television broadcasting services "specified by the Member State," then the national regulatory authority may require operators to grant access to EPGs and APIs on fair, reasonable and

---

358 Access Directive, Article 6(3)(a).

359 Access Directive, Article 6(3)(b).

360 Access Directive, Article 6(4).

361 Access Directive, Annex I, Part 1 (c).

362 EP/Council Directive 95/47 on the use of standards for the transmission of television signals (OJ L281/95).

363 Access Directive, Preamble, 9th recital.

non-discriminatory terms.[364] The Access Directive provides no guidance as to what broadcasting services are covered by this special accessibility measure, other than to state that they must be "digital," and that Member States may specify them by any legislative, regulatory or administrative means.[365] It is also unclear whether the digital broadcasting services designated by Member States for purposes of this section of the Access Directive are the same as the services designated by Member States for purposes of the "must carry" obligations referred to in Article 31 of the Universal Service Directive. One difference is that the television and radio broadcasting services referred to in Article 5(1) of the Access Directive are limited to digital services, whereas services covered by must carry rules can be either analog or digital. The power of national regulators under the Access Directive to force access to APIs under fair, reasonable and non-discriminatory terms dovetails with Member States' obligations under the Framework Directive to encourage the use of open APIs for digital interactive television platforms.[366]

International Exception

The other case where obligations could be imposed on non-SMP operators is the case where such obligations may be necessary to comply with international commitments. This is to cover the hypothetical situation in which an operator may not be deemed to hold SMP under the new European directives, but may nevertheless be considered a "major supplier" under the GATS Fourth Protocol. The WTO Reference Paper defines "major supplier" as:

> a supplier which has the ability to materially affect the terms of participation (having regard to price and supply) in the relevant market for basic telecommunications services a result of:
>
> a) control over essential facilities; or
>
> b) use of its positions on the market.[367]

The Reference Paper requires that "major suppliers" be subject to various interconnection conditions similar to those imposed on SMP operators under the new Directives. A subsequent booklet will look in detail at the similarities and differences between the WTO approach and the new European regime.

---

364 Access Directive, Article 5(1)(b). Article 31 of the Universal Service Directive also requires that Member States "specify" certain radio and television broadcast channels and services for purposes of applying "must carry" rules.

365 Access Directive, Preamble, 10th recital.

366 Framework Directive, Article 18.

367 Council Decision 97/838 concerning the conclusion on behalf of the European Community, as regards matters within its competence, of the results of the WTO negotiations on basic telecommunications services (OJ L347/97).

OPERATORS SUBJECT TO ACCESS OBLIGATIONS

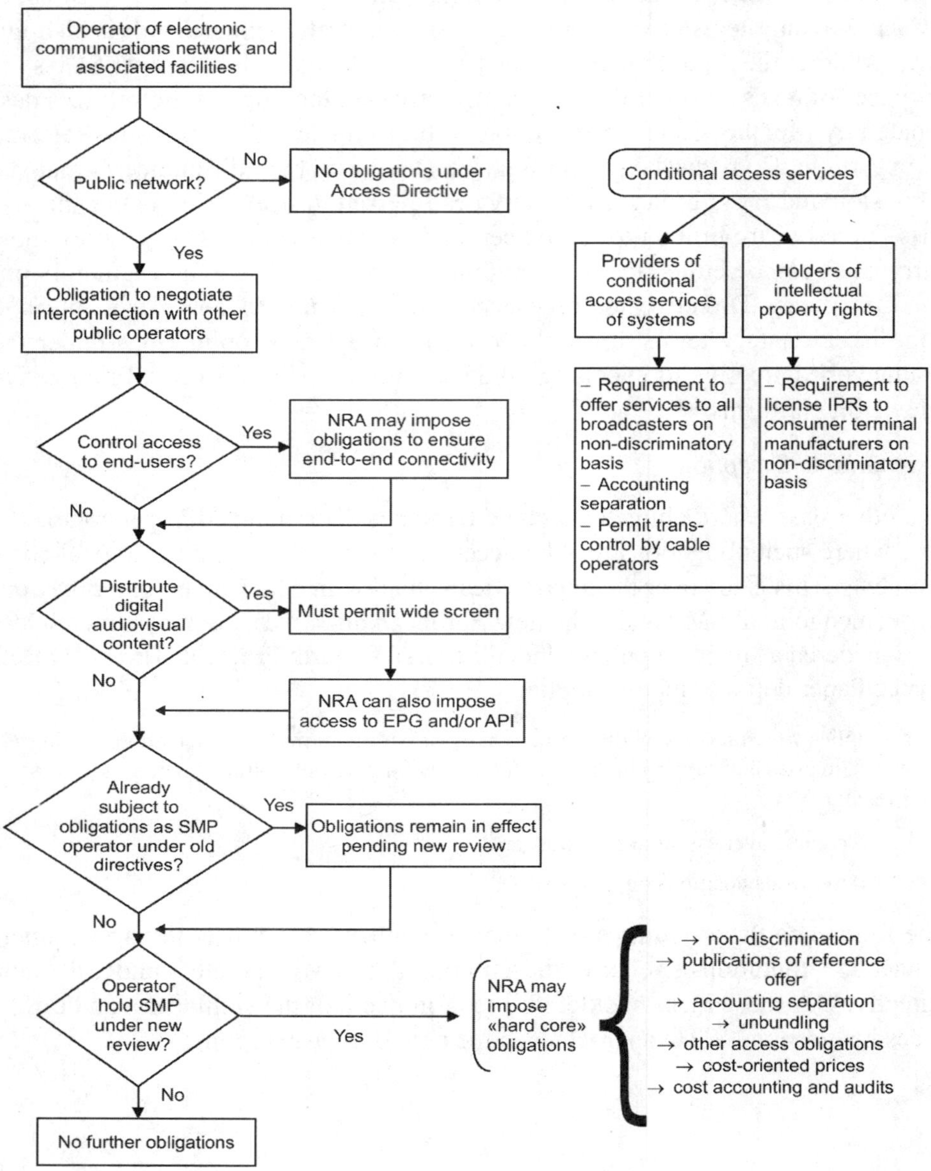

6. Choice of Tools

The national regulatory authorities are supposed to choose from among the tools in the Access Directive's toolbox. Before looking at each of the tools in the regulatory toolbox, let us look at the method that national regulator's must use when selecting the appropriate tools. The Access Directive starts by stating that national regulatory authorities "shall impose" on operators designated as having SMP on a specific market the hard-core access obligations listed in the Access Directive, "as appropriate." The term "as appropriate" softens the more direct phrase: "shall impose." The Access Directive says that the regulatory authorities "shall impose" the hard-core obligations on SMP operators, implying that the national regulatory authorities have no discretion in whether or not to impose them. But the Access Directive then indicates that regulatory authorities shall impose only those hard-core obligations that they judge "appropriate," implying that the regulatory authorities have discretion in deciding which obligations in the package to impose.

If the national regulator wants to use a tool not included in the toolbox, it may do so only in "exceptional circumstances"[368] and after giving the Commission an opportunity to comment on or veto the proposal. Regulatory authorities should make their choice from the Access Directive's list "based on the nature of the problem identified."[369] The choice should be "proportionate and justified"[370] in the light of the objectives described in the Article 8 mission statement in the Framework Directive. Section IV:B of this Chapter above discusses the Article 8 mission statement in more detail, but the main themes are promoting competition, technological neutrality, development of the internal market for communications networks and services, and consumer protection. Every time a regulatory authority wants to impose one or more of the hard-core obligations on an SMP operator, the regulatory authority must go through the consultation procedures set forth in Articles 6 and 7 of the Framework Directive.[371]

7. Specific "Hard-core" Access Obligations

Let us examine below the various access obligations in the regulatory toolbox.

Non-discrimination

The first obligation in the regulatory toolbox is the obligation of non-discrimination. For new entrants, this is one of the most important obligations of SMP operators. The non-discrimination obligation means "in particular, that the operator applies equivalent conditions in equivalent circumstances to other undertakings providing equivalent services, and provides services and information to others under the same conditions and of the same quality as it provides for its own services, or those of its subsidiaries or partners."[372] This definition refers to the all-important problem of vertical integration, announcing the rule that

368 Access Directive, Article 8(3).

369 Access Directive, Article 8(4).

370 Access Directive, Article 8(4).

371 *See* Section IV.B.5 of this Chapter.

372 Access Directive, Article 10(2).

upstream operators holding SMP may not treat their downstream retail arm any more favorably than they treat third party operators. Regrettably the Directive's definition of non-discrimination omits to mention pricing as part of the non-discrimination obligation. But pricing undoubtedly forms an integral part of it. The previous interconnection directive required that SMP operators charge other operators the same prices as what the SMP operators charge their own retail branches for interconnection services. The new Directive is different in that it does not require that SMP operators automatically apply the non-discrimination rule. Each regulatory authority is free to decide whether to impose the non-discrimination obligation on a given SMP operator. One can anticipate that regulatory authorities will almost always impose the non-discrimination obligation on SMP operators, because non-discrimination goes hand-in-hand with the competition law concept of dominant position.[373] Paragraph (c) of Article 82 of the Treaty indicates that one example of abuse of a dominant position is: "applying dissimilar conditions to equivalent transactions with other trading parties, thereby placing them at a competitive disadvantage."[374] Moreover, the case law of the Court of Justice requires that an entity controlling "essential facilities" must apply the same conditions to its downstream retail arm as it applies to third party competitors.[375] These obligations are summarized in the Commission's guidelines on the application of competition law to access agreements.[376] The new consolidated Competition Directive mentions non-discrimination (though limited to vertically integrated public undertakings),[377] as does Article 2.2(a) of the WTO Reference Paper.[378] All this is to say that it would be extremely unusual and surprising for a national regulatory authority to designate an operator as holding SMP (synonym of "dominant position"), and then elect *not* to impose a non-discrimination obligation on that operator. The non-discrimination obligation would exist anyway under applicable competition law, including Article 82(c) of the EC Treaty.

That price terms are not expressly mentioned in the non-discrimination section of the Access Directive is not problematic. In the section of the Access Directive

373 EC Treaty, Article 82(c).

374 EC Treaty, Article 82(c).

375 For an excellent analysis of the essential facilities doctrine as applied to telecommunications, *see* P. Larouche, *Competition Law and Regulation in European Telecommunications* (Oxford: Hart Publishing, 2000).

376 Notice on the application of the competition rules to access agreements in the telecommunications sector: framework, relevant markets and principles (98/C 265/02), OJ C 233/02. para. 85.

377 Competition Directive, Article 3.

378 Council Decision 97/838 concerning the conclusion on behalf of the European Community, as regards matters within its competence, of the results of the WTO negotiations on basic telecommunications services, OJ L347/97.

on accounting separation it becomes clear that non-discrimination applies to pricing terms:

> A national regulatory authority may require a vertically integrated company to make transparent its wholesale prices and its internal transfer prices *inter alia* to ensure compliance where there is a requirement for non-discrimination. . . .[379]

Non-discrimination is so important that certain Member States imposed non-discrimination obligations on all operators, whether or not they held SMP.[380] Under the new Access Directive's language in Article 8(3), Member States would not be able to impose non-discrimination obligations on non-SMP operators. Any Member States that impose across-the-board non-discrimination obligations, even on non-SMP operators, would have to change their legislation to ensure that such obligations apply only to SMP operators, and then only when the national regulatory authority decides to impose such an obligation.

Transparency

The second major access obligation is the obligation of transparency. Transparency is necessary to ensure that an SMP operator complies with its non-discrimination obligations. Under the heading of transparency lie a number of specific obligations such as the following:

The obligation to publish a reference offer

Under the previous Interconnection Directive operators possessing SMP on the interconnection market for fixed voice had to publish a reference interconnection offer (sometimes called a "RIO"). Under the new Directive, this obligation could spread to other SMP operators, including mobile, voice, data and operators of broadcasting transmission facilities. The Access Directive leaves it to the national regulator to decide which operators should have to publish a reference offer, and for what services. The Access Directive indicates that only operators having a "non-discrimination" obligation should be required to publish a reference offer. The offer must be:

> sufficiently unbundled to ensure that undertakings are not required to pay for facilities which are not necessary for the service requested, giving a description of the relevant offerings broken down into components according to market needs, and the associated terms and conditions including prices.[381]

National regulatory authorities shall have discretion to define what information should be included in the reference offer, and force changes in the reference offer if needed.

---

379 Access Directive, Article 11(1).

380 This was the case in France until France modified Article 34-8 of the Code of Post and Communications in July 2001.

381 Access Directive, Article 9(2).

Reference offer for unbundled access to the local loop

The one area where the Directive leaves no discretion to the national regulator is in a reference offer for unbundled access to the twisted metal pair of the incumbent's local loop. If a regulator decides to impose unbundling obligations on an SMP operator as is permitted by Article 12 of the Access Directive, then the operator must publish a reference offer covering predefined items such as collocation, line sharing, ordering and provisioning procedures, etc. These elements of the reference offer are defined in detail in an annex to the Access Directive.[382] Because unbundling gave rise to such difficult debates in 2000 and 2001,[383] the Access Directive elected to keep these detailed obligations intact, instead of letting national regulators define them from scratch.

Other publication requirements

The Access Directive provides that national regulatory authorities may require operators to make public other information such as accounting information, technical specifications, network characteristics, terms and conditions for supply and use, and prices.[384] Curiously the Access Directive does not expressly require the publication of interconnection agreements entered into by SMP operators. A national regulator *could* impose such an obligations under the general terms of Article 9(1), but it is unfortunate that the Directive makes no express reference to the public availability of interconnection agreements. Under the previous directive, filing interconnection agreements was obligatory for all SMP operators, and was an important tool to ensure compliance with the non-discrimination obligation.

Accounting Separation

Like publication of a reference offer, accounting separation is a mechanism designed to make sure that an SMP operator complies with its non-discrimination obligation. The Access Directive provides that a national regulatory authority may "impose obligations for accounting separation in relation to specified activities related to interconnection and/or access."[385] As noted above, obligations for accounting separation may include the obligation to make public internal transfer prices of a vertically integrated company so as to ensure compliance with the non-discrimination obligation or "where necessary, to prevent unfair cross-subsidy."[386] National regulators shall have power to require the filing of accounting information, and the publication of "such information as would contribute to an open and competitive market, while respecting national and Community rules on

382 Access Directive, Annex II.

383 EP/Council Regulation 2887/00 on unbundled access to the local loop (OJ L366/00).

384 Access Directive, Article 9(1).

385 Access Directive, Article 11(1).

386 Access Directive, Article 11(1).

commercial confidentiality."[387] This wording is exceptionally loose, leaving national regulators with broad discretion to decide what accounting information should be filed, and what information is protected by rules on commercial confidentiality. Countries (such as the United Kingdom) that traditionally require transparency from operators will likely require the publication of significant information whereas other countries (such as France) are likely to withhold publication of most information on the grounds of commercial confidentiality. This difference is already visible in connection with the obligations under the Interconnection Directive to make interconnection agreements available to third parties. The terms of the obligation are quite clear: under the Interconnection Directive, the only parts of the agreements that may be protected from disclosure are passages that relate to the "commercial strategy" of the parties. Yet France, for example, permits the redaction of all passages that contain "business secrets," a term considerably broader than the term "commercial strategy." This can lead to the redaction of any provision in the agreement that relates to non-standard or customized interconnection services. Unfortunately, those kinds of non-standard services are the most interesting for competitors from a non-discrimination point of view. The purpose of the publication measure in the Interconnection Directive was largely defeated in practice by a broad reading of the Interconnection Directive's confidentiality exception. The Interconnection Directive's language on this issue ("commercial strategy") left little room for interpretation, yet several Member States liberally interpreted the language. The Access Directive's language "commercial confidentiality" leaves even more room for loose interpretation by Member States.

Accounting separation is not the same as cost accounting systems that national regulatory authorities may impose under Article 13 of the Access Directive. As we will see in section 12 below, cost accounting measures are destined to ensure that the tariffs of the SMP operator are "cost oriented," whereas accounting separation is designed to ensure that the SMP operator's upstream network operations do not discriminate in favor of the operator's downstream retail arm. Cost accounting guarantees cost-oriented tariffs whereas accounting separation guarantees non-discrimination. As noted above, national regulators will almost always impose a non-discrimination obligation on SMP operators. Accounting separation necessarily follows. Cost orientation measures may be more limited, applying to only certain upstream (wholesale) or downstream (retail) services of the SMP operator. Being originally based on the competition law doctrine of "essential facilities," cost-orientation may be used more sparingly than non-discrimination, which under competition law applies to all entities holding a dominant position, not just entities controlling essential facilities. To the extent cost-orientation measures apply to upstream services and facilities, cost accounting and accounting separation complement one another: cost accounting systems would justify the "cost oriented" price charged by the SMP operator's upstream network arm for access to the network, while accounting separation would ensure that the SMP operator's

387 Access Directive, Article 11(2).

upstream arm charges that price not only to third parties but also to the SMP operator's own retail operation in the form of an internal transfer price.

8. Specific Access Obligations

Article 12 of the Access Directive contains the most interesting access tools in the regulator's toolbox. As with the tools in the preceding sections, national regulators may use the tools in Article 12 against SMP operators only. Non-SMP operators are immune from Article 12 access obligations. Article 12 begins with the general statement that national regulators may require SMP operators to meet reasonable requests for access to and use of specific network elements and associated facilities, *inter alia* in situations where the regulator considers that "denial of access or unreasonable terms and conditions having a similar effect would hinder the emergence of a sustainable competitive market at a retail level, or would not be in the end-user's interest."[388]

We see here the emphasis on the retail market. Regulators should impose specific access obligations not for the sake of protecting competitors *per se*, but only as a means to improve conditions on the retail market for end-users. This is consistent with the competition law philosophy that underpins the new framework.

List of Measures

Article 12 then goes on to list nine specific access obligations that regulators can impose on SMP operators:

1. The obligation to give third parties access to specified network elements and/or facilities, including unbundled access to the local loop.
2. The obligation to negotiate in good faith with undertakings requesting access.
3. The obligation not to withdraw access to facilities already granted.
4. The obligation to provide specified services on a wholesale basis for resale by third parties.
5. The obligation to grant open access to technical interfaces, protocols or other key technologies that are indispensable for the interoperability of services or virtual network services.
6. The obligation to provide collocation or other forms of facility sharing, including duct, building or mast sharing.
7. The obligation to provide specified services needed to ensure interoperability of end-to-end services to users, including facilities for intelligent network services or roaming on mobile networks.
8. The obligation to provide access to operational support systems or similar software systems necessary to ensure fair competition in the provision of services.
9. The obligation to interconnect networks or network facilities.

388 Access Directive, Article 12(1).

The list is preceded by the introductory sentence: "Operators may be required *inter alia*:." This suggests that the nine items are non-exhaustive, and that national regulators may impose other obligations where appropriate. As we saw above, Article 8(3) of the Access Directive permits the national regulatory authorities to go outside the listed items in the toolbox only in "exceptional circumstances." The national regulators must notify the Commission of the measure envisaged and the Commission has the power to veto it. Because of this extra constraint, national regulatory authorities will probably venture only rarely beyond the approved list of access measures.

Article 12's list of nine access measures illustrates how broad and all-encompassing the term "access" is under the new Directive. The term includes: "access to specified network elements and/or facilities, including unbundled access to the local loop."[389] Operators in Europe are already familiar with unbundled access to the twisted metallic pair required under the Regulation 2887/2000. But this provision would permit the national regulatory authorities to go much farther, including requiring access to the incumbent's dark fiber and ducts, for example.

Obligation number two (negotiate interconnection) already exists, even for operators that do not possess SMP.

Obligation number three (obligation not to withdraw access) is a natural extension of obligation number one (obligation to grant access).

Obligation number four states that national regulators may require the SMP operator "to provide specified services on a wholesale basis for resale by third parties."[390] This measure could include an obligation on the incumbent to provide voice telephony, including local service and the basic subscription, on a wholesale basis to switchless resellers, to provide wholesale ADSL or leased line services to other operators, or to provide directory assistance services on a wholesale basis (which could be resold by a competitor under its own brand). Under the new framework, a request for a wholesale service would conceptually be deemed a request for "access" when the requesting party is a provider of electronic communications networks or services to the public.

Intellectual Property Rights

Measure number five includes access to "technical interfaces, protocols or other key technologies that are indispensable for the interoperability of services or virtual network services."[391] This means that national regulatory authorities would have the power to order an SMP operator to grant software licenses to a competitor if the SMP operator's software becomes a bottleneck for the provision of inter-

389 Access Directive, Article 12(1)(a).

390 Access Directive, Article 11(1)(d).

391 Access Directive, Article 12(1)(e).

operable services. The Digital Television Standards Directive required holders of intellectual property rights to conditional access systems to license technology on a non-discriminatory basis. This obligation is repeated in Annex I of the Access Directive. But directives have never before given national regulators a broad power to force licensing of intellectual property rights. Previously, the only cases of mandatory licensing resulted from the application of competition law. Handing this power to national regulators represents an enormous increase in their powers, that could extend to navigational software and APIs. (APIs and EPGs are also covered by Annex I, part 2 of the Directive.) This new regulatory power could worry owners of instant messaging platforms or any other proprietary communication software. The application of this access measure to software would really depend on whether the holder of the relevant intellectual property rights could be deemed an "operator" of a "communications network" or an "associated facility." In most cases the "operator" itself will not control the intellectual property rights; it will only hold a non-transferable license to use the software. The holder of the intellectual property rights themselves would probably be a software publisher. It is doubtful that national regulator's jurisdiction could extend so far as to oblige software publishers to grant licenses to their code. As we saw in section 5 above, access obligations can be imposed on "operators" and holders of intellectual property to conditional access systems. In this section we are dealing only with access obligations that can be imposed on *operators* holding *significant market power.*

Could Microsoft be considered an SMP operator in connection with instant messaging software? The first question is whether Microsoft can be considered an "operator." We saw above that the term covers any entity that provides or is authorized to provide a public electronic communications network or associated facility. Instant messaging software could be deemed an "associated facility," because it is a facility associated with an electronic communications service, which enables and/or supports the provision of services via that network and/or service.[392] By providing this associated facility to the public, Microsoft could be deemed an "operator." But being an operator of an associated facility is not enough. It does not trigger any significant access obligations unless the operator is also found to hold significant market power. To be found to hold significant market power, Microsoft would have to hold a dominant position on the market for instant messaging software. This means that a national regulator would first have to identify instant messaging software as a relevant product or service market, by showing that there is no demand or supply-side substitutability. The national regulators would have to consult the Commission and other national regulators, and if instant messaging software is not already on the Commission's list of relevant product and service markets, then the Commission would have a veto right over the national regulator's decision to define this separate market. The regulator would

392 Framework Directive, Article 2(e).

then apply the Commission's guidelines[393] to determine whether Microsoft holds significant market power on that market. Once Microsoft has been identified as an SMP operator, a national regulator could force Microsoft to grant "open access to technical interfaces, protocols or other key technologies that are indispensable for the interoperability of services or virtual network services."[394] That is a long list of requirements, and it appears unlikely that a national regulatory authority could get so far as to impose *ex ante* access obligations on a software publisher. It is much more likely that aggrieved parties would look to more traditional competition law remedies.

Facility Sharing

Access measure number six covers "co-location and other forms of facility sharing, including duct, building or mast sharing."[395] For new entrants, one of the big advances brought about by the new directives is that interconnection and access questions are no longer limited to the traditional public switched telephone network. Networks and facilities are defined in their broad sense, without regard to technology. It will now be possible to ask national regulatory authorities for access to high points used by television broadcasters, entities previously excluded from the scope of the interconnection directive. Similarly, ducts owned by the incumbent telephone operator, or by cable TV companies, may now be fair game, provided the relevant operator has been identified as holding significant market power. Again, the challenge under the new framework will be qualifying an owner of ducts or towers as an "operator" with significant market power. In many cases, traditional operators will be tempted under the new framework to transfer ownership of key facilities to separate companies in hopes of avoiding the qualification as "operator." For example, a mobile network operator might sell its portfolio of masts and towers to a tower company, which then might lease back antenna space to the mobile operator. Requesting facility sharing from a tower company would require showing *first* that the tower company is an "operator" of a "communications network" or an "associated facility," and *second* that the operator holds significant market power. This in turn requires a showing that the facility in question constitutes a separate product or service market, and that the tower company holds a dominant position on that market.

Overcoming all these hurdles could well discourage new entrants and regulators. Consequently one unintended result of the Directive may be to encourage incumbent operators to spin-off their key infrastructure into separate companies. Regulators do not necessarily have to go this route in order to impose facility sharing. Another option is to include a facility sharing obligation in the operator's license terms. By placing the obligation in the license terms, regulators would not have to

393 *Commission Guidelines on market analysis and the assessment of significant market power under the Community regulatory framework for electronic communications networks and services*, published July 7, 2002.

394 Access Directive, Article 12(1)(e).

395 Access Directive, Article 12(1)(f).

make a showing that the operator holds significant market power. As mentioned in the previous section, the Authorization Directive permits Member States to impose conditions linked to the protection of the environment or town planning. Facility sharing is just such a measure, in that it avoids the construction of multiple masts and radio towers, and the digging of multiple trenches. Regulators may prefer, therefore, to make facility sharing a license condition rather than to rely solely on the specific access measure available in the Access Directive's toolbox.

Some Member States already have provisions that encourage or require infrastructure sharing for environmental and/or town planning reasons. This is true for example in France, where Article L 47 of the Code of Post and Telecommunications permits local authorities to encourage facility sharing by operators as a condition to granting rights of way. Similarly the license conditions applicable to 3G mobile operators require a certain level of site or antenna sharing.[396]

Intelligent Network

Access measure number seven permits national regulators to impose access to facilities for intelligent network services or roaming for mobile services.[397] In traditional fixed-line networks, "intelligent networks" are computers within the network that translate one number into another. For example, a call to a toll-free number beginning with "0800" would first go to the intelligent network computer to be translated into a number that corresponds to the geographic number of the called party. In mobile network infrastructure, the intelligent network functions involve advanced services such as location of the user's terminal, billing, security and authentication, the sending of SMS messages, etc. Access to mobile operator's intelligent network functions will be critical for entities wishing to offer "m-commerce" or other value-added services to mobile subscribers. Mobile operators will have a natural tendency to limit such access to service and content providers that are the mobile operators' "partners" or subsidiaries. The mobile operator derives value from its gatekeeper function, and its ability to control revenues for value added services. Mobile operators view intelligent network functions as strategic assets. Competitors see these network elements as anti-competitive bottlenecks. Regulators will have to strike a fair balance.

Roaming

Roaming refers to reciprocal agreements between mobile network operators whereby each operator agrees to accept the other operator's subscribers on the first operator's network. A subscriber to France's OrangeFrance GSM network can travel to the Netherlands, and his terminal will be recognized by the KPN Mobile network, which will in turn allow the subscriber to make calls. KPN Mobile bills its services to OrangeFrance, which then bills the subscriber. Currently, inter-

---

396 See, e.g., Chapter V of the license conditions attached to the license of SFR (arête dated 18 July 2001, OJ of 21 August 2001, p. 13422.

397 Access Directive, Article 12(1)(g).

national roaming agreements are entered into in the context of the GSM Association, the club of European GSM operators.[398] Because of the limited number of GSM operators, and because roaming is so lucrative for GSM operators, problems of access have not yet emerged in the context of *international* roaming. *National* roaming is an entirely different matter. National roaming amounts to allowing the customer of an operator with no infrastructure in a given area to make calls using another (competing) operator's infrastructure. This will become a significant issue in 3G mobile network rollout. Imagine two 3G operators in a given country: operator A and operator B. Operator A has built out, at great expense, 3G infrastructure so that its customers can use Operator A's 3G service anywhere, even in rural areas. Operator B, on the other hand, has only built out in lucrative urban areas. Operator B would naturally like to enter into a national roaming agreement with Operator A, in order to obtain coverage in rural areas as well. Operator A will resist on the ground that Operator B is a direct competitor, and should have invested in its own network build-out if it wanted ubiquitous coverage. Operator B may ask the regulator to order Operator A to provide national roaming services access under Article 12 of the Access Directive. As we will see in section 11, regulators will have to resolve this kind of dispute taking into account (among other things) Operator A's initial investment and the risks associated therewith. National roaming could be an attractive solution if Operator A and B were to agree in advance which parts of the country to cover: "You build in the north, I'll build in the south, and together we'll cover the country." But this obviously raises other competition law concerns, namely a horizontal agreement to divide geographic markets.

OSS

Access measure number eight permits regulators to force access to operational support systems ("OSS") or "similar software systems necessary to ensure fair competition in the provision of services."[399] From the outset, US regulations recognized the importance of access to the incumbents' operational support systems in connection with introducing local competition. Operational support systems are defined as: "methods and procedures (mechanized or not) which directly support the daily operation of the telecommunications infrastructure."[400] In simple terms, the OSS is the incumbent's back office for order processing. Competitors require access to the incumbent's OSS in order to ensure that the incumbent's back office handles orders for local service relating to the competitor's customers in the same way as the back office handles orders for the incumbent's own retail branch. As a practical matter, new entrants need access to a real-time, web-based interface to send requests for unbundling the local loop, number portability or pre-selection to

---

398 European Commission, DG Competition, *Working Document on the Initial Findings of the Sector Inquiry Into Mobile Roaming Changes*, December 13, 2000.

399 Access Directive, Article 12(1)(h).

400 *Newton's Telecom Dictionary* 16th edition, p. 619.

the incumbent's order processing department, as well as to verify whether a given loop is eligible for ADSL.[401] OSS might also include access to systems showing in real time the status of leased line provisioning or repairs.

Basic Interconnection

Last but not least, access measure number nine allows national regulators to require "interconnection" of networks or network facilities.[402] Interconnection is a now-familiar notion to national regulators, who have had four years of experience arbitrating interconnection disputes and approving reference interconnection offers ("RIOs") of the incumbent. In its most basic form, interconnection permits the customers of two different networks to communicate with one another. Under the Interconnection Directive and the ONP Voice Telephony Directive the interconnection concept has been extended to cover other activities such as the provision of partial leased lines to competitive carriers. Suffice it to say that the concept of interconnection as mentioned in this section of the Access Directive will not create any surprises for national regulatory authorities. Moreover, because Article 12(1) of the Access Directive contains so many kinds of access measures other than interconnection, it will be less critical for a national regulatory authority to make the determination whether the service requested from the incumbent operator is "interconnection" or not. Previously, these definitional issues were important and could trip up new entrants in disputes with the incumbent operator. The new regime will be simpler, by grouping all measures under the generic term "access."

Fairness Conditions

Article 12(1) of the Access Directive closes by indicating that national regulatory authorities may impose conditions of "fairness, reasonableness and timeliness" to any of the access obligations listed.

9. Choosing the Right Tool

Article 12(2) gives the national regulators guidelines to use when imposing access obligations, in addition to the objectives contained in the Article 8 mission statement of the Framework Directive. These guidelines are supposed to help national regulators determine whether granting a particular access request would serve, and be proportionate to, the "big picture" objectives set forth in the Article 8 mission statement of the Framework Directive. (Readers will recall that Article 8 of the Framework Directive contains a list of overriding principles that govern all regulatory decisions under the new regime.) The guidelines in Article 12(2) of the Access Directive are worthy policy considerations, but are so general as to be of little practical use. When deciding whether to impose access obligations on SMP

---

401 *See, e.g.*, French Competition Council, Decision no. 02-MC-03 of 27 February 2002, ordering France Télécom to make an Extranet available to independent Internet access providers to verify eligibility of local loops for ADSL.

402 Access Directive, Article 12(1)(i).

operators national regulators are supposed to balance the legitimate interests of the SMP operator against the legitimate interests of new entrants and of long-term competition. This difficult balancing act was previously done by the drafters of the Interconnection and ONP Voice Telephony Directives. The solutions were found in the text of the directives themselves. Now the difficult choices have been pushed down to the individual regulatory authorities. The choice was relatively easy in connection with legacy network infrastructure of the former PTTs, since that infrastructure was financed by public funds thanks to the operator's former monopoly status. It was therefore legitimate that this infrastructure, funded by a state-sponsored monopoly situation, be opened to competitors as part of liberalization. In a way, the telephone network built out by the incumbent during its monopoly years can be thought of as quasi-public property.

More difficult is the decision to open infrastructure financed by new entrants, or new broadband infrastructure financed by the now-privatized incumbent. This was the crux of the "open access" debate in relation to U.S. cable networks. Policy makers are sharply divided on the issue. On the one hand, an upgraded bi-directional broadband cable network can be seen as a new broadband bottleneck that should be opened in order to enhance end-user choice and retail competition. On the other hand, the large investments made to upgrade the network resulted from private shareholders putting their money at risk with the expectation that the fruit of their investment would not be shared with rivals. The same considerations apply to new fiber or wireless access networks, including those built by the incumbent operator. Several European incumbent operators have already indicated that they would slow or stop investment in new broadband infrastructure if the infrastructure will have to be shared with rivals. This tough policy choice will now fall on national regulatory authorities, whereas before the choices were made in the directives themselves. It could be argued that such important policy decisions should be left to the legislature, not to regulators. The new Directives may be asking too much from national regulatory authorities.

Article 12(2) of the Access Directive expresses the policy tension surrounding access as follows:

> [National regulatory authorities] shall take into account in particular the following factors:
>
> (a) the technical and economic viability of using or installing competing facilities, in the light of the rate of market development, taking into account the nature and type of interconnection and access involved;
>
> (b) the feasibility of providing the access proposed, in relation to the capacity available;
>
> (c) the initial investment by the facility owner, bearing in mind the risks involved in making the investment;
>
> (d) the need to safeguard competition in the long term;
>
> (e) where appropriate, any relevant intellectual property rights;
>
> (f) the provision of pan-European services.

It is no easy task to balance so many competing interests. Courts in the United States apply balancing-of-interests tests routinely on many constitutional issues. Balancing-of-interests tests are important if the objective is to reach the "correct" substantive outcome in each factual situation. But this search for accuracy in individual cases comes with a price: it diminishes speed and predictability, which are among the principal objectives of *ex ante* regulation in the first place. Just as in US case law applying the First Amendment of the US Constitution, European regulatory decisions on access will depend on a case-by-case balancing-of-interests approach, leading no doubt to inconsistent results in various Member States, even in seemingly similar fact situations. Not only will this put a strain on regulators (who are not, after all, lawmakers), it could result in different outcomes in seemingly similar fact situations. The work of the European Regulators Group will be essential to bring some consistency to these difficult access decisions.

10. Price Controls

Article 13 of the Access Directive defines what price obligations national regulators can impose on SMP operators in connection with "access." The traditional approach under the prior directives was simple: any interconnection service provided by an SMP operator had to be provided to other operators at cost-oriented prices. Predictably, the new Directive sets no hard-and-fast rules on pricing, and leaves it (again) to the national regulatory authority to do the right thing. National regulators "may" require an SMP operator to charge cost-oriented prices for certain kinds of access, but regulators are not required to do so. Once again, national regulators must balance interests.

Before imposing price controls on access, the national regulatory authority must find that:

> a lack of effective competition means that the operator concerned might sustain prices at an excessively high level, or apply a price squeeze, to the detriment of end-users.[403]

This language is confusing, since to get to Article 13 of the Access Directive in the first place the national regulator must have already determined that the operator possesses "significant market power." Under the new framework, significant market power is synonymous with "dominant position" and dominant position is synonymous with the ability to sustain prices at an excessively high level. Article 13(1) suggests that the national regulatory authority needs to ask itself the question whether an operator that has been found to hold SMP might sustain prices at excessively high levels. The question seems superfluous since an operator holding SMP (*i.e.*, a dominant position) by definition is likely to sustain prices at an excessively high level. Otherwise the operator would not be classified as SMP in the first place.

403 Access Directive, Article 13(1).

In fact, under Article 13(1) of the Access Directive, a national regulatory authority must satisfy two cumulative steps before imposing an obligation of cost-oriented prices on an operator:

– first the regulator must determine that the relevant operator holds SMP (that is the test that permits us to get us to Article 13 of the Access Directive in the first place);

– second the regulator must find that the SMP operator might (a) sustain prices at an excessively high level, or (b) apply a price squeeze, to the detriment of end-users.

As we saw above, the first branch ("a") of the second test seems redundant, because an SMP operator under the new framework by definition will be likely to maintain prices at an artificially high level. That is what "dominant position" is all about. Thus the first branch of the second test will always be satisfied. And because the two branches in the second test are separated by the disjunctive "or," if one branch of the test is satisfied, the whole test is satisfied. One does not even have to get to the second branch "b."

Even after running through these two tests, the national regulator is still not supposed to impose cost-orientation unless the regulator first does some more balancing. Before deciding to impose cost-oriented access tariffs, the national regulator:

> shall take into account the investment made by the operator and allow him a reasonable rate of return on adequate capital employed, taking into account the risks involved.[404]

This goes back to the policy tension described above in connection with forcing an SMP operator to grant access: how to strike the right balance between ensuring access to bottlenecks and protecting legitimate investment expectations. Though not a factor for the legacy telephone network, the tension between open access and fair return on investment will be particularly acute in connection with new investments in broadband technology such as fiber, or 3G radio networks.

When imposing price controls or cost recovery rules for access services, national regulatory authorities must ensure those rules "promote efficiency and sustainable competition and maximize consumer benefits."[405] Here is yet another difficult policy balancing act. The Directive allows regulators to "take account of prices available in comparable competitive markets."[406] This is a reference to international benchmarking, which has proven the most practical way of making pricing decisions under the old interconnection framework. European benchmarking and best practices will continue to be the principal tool used by regulators to set access prices. The Access Directive naturally allows regulators

404 Access Directive, Article 13(1).

405 Access Directive, Article 13(2).

406 Access Directive, Article 13(2).

to continue use of cost models, including "cost accounting methods independent of those used by the [SMP operator]."[407] As a general matter, SMP operators subject to cost-orientation measures have the burden of proving that their tariffs are derived from costs including a reasonable rate of return on investment.[408] The old Interconnection Directive had a similar provision, which placed on SMP operators the burden of proving that their tariffs are cost-based. This provision of the 1997 Interconnection Directive was of little help to new entrants, however, in the context of interconnection disputes. In practice, the new entrant generally had to bring proof (through cost studies and benchmarking) that the incumbent's tariffs were not cost-based. Whatever its practical drawbacks, the rule that SMP operators must prove that their tariffs are derived from relevant costs is a good rule, and it is reiterated in Article 13(3) of the new Access Directive. In order to prove that its tariffs are cost-based, SMP operators must implement cost accounting measures. The Access Directive requires that the SMP operator publish a description of its cost accounting system showing at a minimum the main categories under which costs are grouped and the rules for allocation of costs. An independent entity must audit the SMP operator's compliance with its cost accounting system. The audit may be conducted by the national regulatory authority itself or by an independent auditor.[409] "A statement concerning compliance shall be published annually."[410] From this language it is not clear whether the "statement" of compliance should come from the independent auditor or from the SMP operator itself.

11. Publication of, and Access to, Information

The Access Directive requires that access-related obligations imposed at a national level be published together with the identification of the relevant product/service and geographical markets.[411] Member States must send the same information to the Commission and to the Communications Committee.[412] National regulatory authorities must also inform the Commission of the names of the SMP operators identified in the national market and the obligations imposed on those operators.[413]

---

407 Access Directive, Article 13(3).

408 Access Directive, Article 13(3).

409 Access Directive, Preamble, 21st recital.

410 Access Directive, Article 13(4).

411 Access Directive, Article 15(1).

412 Access Directive, Article 15(2).

413 Access Directive, Article 16(2).

12. Review Procedures

As with the other directives, the Commission must review the functioning of the Access Directive no later than July 24, 2006, and prepare a report to the Council and European Parliament.[414]

V. MERCOSUR MONTEVIDEO PROTOCOL ON TRADE IN SERVICES

Telecommunications services are not excluded as such by the Protocol, but, as with GATS, any right to supply such services flow from specific commitments in the Schedules of Member States attached to the Protocol. The Protocol has no special provisions on telecommunications such as those found in the GATS Annex on Telecommunications.

Member States are supposed to liberalize trade in services generally by 2008. This includes telecommunications services. In its Schedule, Paraguay has committed itself on interconnection to the public telecommunications network and to the publication of general conditions for such interconnection. It has also a commitment on the removal of the state monopoly in telephone, telex, telegraph and fax services. Beyond this, little has been achieved that goes beyond the Member States' obligations under GATS. Only Argentina has subscribed to the GATS Fourth Protocol.

VI. ASEAN FRAMEWORK AGREEMENT ON SERVICES

The GATS rules on telecommunications services, as set out in the main Agreement, the Annex on Telecommunications and the Fourth Protocol, are incorporated into the Agreement by virtue of Article XIV:1.[415] In addition, the Fourth Protocol to the Framework Agreement, which was concluded in 2004, includes a significant liberalization of the telecommunications sector. The *e-ASEAN Framework Agreement*, which was signed on November 24, 2000, also obliges the Member States to achieve higher levels of liberalization of trade in telecommunications services through successive rounds of negotiations.[416]

414 Access Directive, Article 17.

415 These rules are discussed in Section II of this Chapter. However, only Brunei and Thailand have subscribed to the Fourth Protocol.

416 Article 6:3.

CHAPTER SEVEN

LIBERALIZATION OF TRADE IN TRANSPORT SERVICES

I. THE GENERAL AGREEMENT ON TRADE IN SERVICES

A. INTRODUCTION

Transport services are *a priori* covered by GATS, and some commitments in this area are contained in the Members' Schedules. Air transport services are also subject to the Annex on Air Transport Services, which limits GATS coverage. By contrast, the Decision and Annex on Negotiations on Maritime Transport Services do not modify in any way the application of the GATS rules.

B. ANNEX ON AIR TRANSPORT SERVICES

Air transport services are covered by GATS subject to the limitations set out in the Annex on Air Transport Services. There are three limitations.

In the first place, the Annex provides that GATS, including its dispute settlement procedures, does not apply to measures affecting:[1]

- traffic rights, however granted; and
- services directly related to the exercise of traffic rights.

Traffic rights are defined as the right of scheduled and non-scheduled air transport services to operate and/or to carry passengers, cargo and mail from, to, within or over the territory of a Member, including points to be served, routes to be oper-

1 Annex on Air Transport Services, Point 2.

ated, types of traffic to be carried, capacity to be provided, tariffs to be charged and their conditions, and criteria for designation of airlines.[2]

Services directly related to the exercise of traffic rights do not include:

- aircraft repair and maintenance as long as such activities are undertaken on an aircraft that is withdrawn from service; it does not include line maintenance;[3]
- selling and marketing air transport services, not including the pricing of air transport services nor the applicable conditions;[4]
- computer reservation system services.[5]

The second limitation contained in the Annex is that any specific commitment with respect to air transport and ancillary services that is assumed under GATS may not reduce or affect a Member's obligations under any bilateral or multilateral agreements that were in effect on the date of entry into force of the WTO Agreement.[6]

Finally, the dispute settlement procedures of GATS may only be invoked with respect to specific commitments and where the dispute settlement procedures in bilateral or multilateral agreements have been exhausted.[7]

C. DECISION AND ANNEX ON NEGOTIATIONS ON MARITIME TRANSPORT SERVICES

The level of commitments in the maritime transport area was so low at the end of the Uruguay Round that a Decision was appended to the WTO Agreement providing for continued negotiations on maritime transport services with the aim of achieving a greater degree of liberalization in this sector.[8] The negotiations covered international shipping, auxiliary services and access to and use of port facilities. A deadline for concluding the negotiations was set for June 1996, but the participants failed to agree on a package of commitments. The talks have resumed with the new services round that started in 2000. During the period of negotiation, the MFN obligation of Article II of GATS, including the requirement to

2 Annex on Air Transport Services, Point 6(d).

3 Annex on Air Transport Services, Points 3(a) and 6(a).

4 Annex on Air Transport Services, Points 3(b) and 5(b).

5 Annex on Air Transport Services, Point 3(c).

6 Annex on Air Transport Services, Point 1.

7 Annex on Air Transport Services, Point 4.

8 Decision, Point 1.

list any exemption from the MFN rule in a special Annex, did not apply,[9] except in the case of maritime transport services that were the subject of a specific commitment.[10]

D. SERVICES AUXILIARY TO ALL MODES OF TRANSPORT

This sector includes cargo handling services, storage and warehouse services, freight transport agency services, freight brokerage services, bill auditing and freight rate information services, transportation document preparation services, packing and unpacking services, freight inspection, weighing and sampling services and freight receiving and acceptance services. It is included in the present round of negotiations.

II. THE NORTH AMERICAN FREE TRADE AGREEMENT (AND THE CHILE AGREEMENTS)

Both Chapter 11 on investment and Chapter 12 on cross-border services apply generally to transportation services, but, in the case of cross-border services, this does not include air services, including domestic and international air transportation services, whether scheduled or non-scheduled.[11] Auxiliary air services are also excluded except in the case of aircraft repair and maintenance services on aircraft that are withdrawn from service—thus no line maintenance—and specialty air services. The latter are defined as aerial mapping, aerial surveying, aerial photography, forest fire management, fire-fighting, aerial advertising, glider towing, parachute jumping, aerial construction, heli-logging, aerial sightseeing, flight training, aerial inspection and surveillance and aerial spraying services.[12] The Chile Agreements broadly take the same approach.[13] In all cases, the Parties have entered significant reservations on air, land and water transportation services that apply to both Chapters.

The Annex on Land Transportation appended to NAFTA requires the Free Trade Commission to oversee the effective liberalization of bus and truck transportation in accordance with each Party's liberalization commitments as set out in Annex I.[14] The Parties are also obliged to consult with a view to further liberalization of this sector.

---

9 Annex, Point 1.

10 Decision, Point 5; Annex, Point 2.

11 NAFTA, Article 1201:2(b).

12 NAFTA, Article 1213.

13 Articles H-01:2(b) and H.12 (Canada), 10-01 and 10-02:3(b) (Mexico) and 11.1:4(b) and 11.12 (USA). The Mexico-Chile Agreement also covers computer reservation systems. It should also be noted that air transport services are regulated between Chile and Mexico by the *Convention on Air Transport* that they signed on January 14, 1997.

14 Annex 1212, Point 2. The Chile Agreements do not contain this Annex.

III. THE EUROPEAN UNION (AND THE EEA AGREEMENT)

A. INTRODUCTION

The liberalization of transport services within the EU is pursued within the framework of the common transport policy.[15] The secondary legislation that is adopted by the Council and the European Parliament lays down, *inter alia,* common rules applicable to international transport to and from the Member States or passing through the territory of one or more Member States as well as the conditions under which non-resident carriers may operate transport services within a host Member State ("cabotage").[16] This secondary legislation applies to the Contracting Parties to the EEA Agreement (Iceland, Liechtenstein and Norway).[17]

B. MARITIME TRANSPORT SERVICES

1. Liberalization of International Maritime Transport Services

Council Regulation 4055/86[18] establishes the freedom to provide maritime transport services between Member States and between Member States and third countries by EU citizens[19] established in a Member State other than that of the person for whom the services are intended.[20] The right is also enjoyed by EU citizens established outside the EU and by shipping companies established outside the EU that are controlled by EU citizens as long as the vessels concerned are registered in the Member State of the EU citizen.[21]

Maritime transport services are defined by the Regulation as intra-EU and third-country traffic involving the carriage of passengers or goods by sea.[22] The right to provide such services includes the right temporarily to pursue the activity in the host Member State where the service is provided under the same conditions as nationals of that Member State.[23]

If a Member State's nationals or shipping companies experience or are threatened by a situation where they do not have an effective opportunity to ply for trade to and from a particular third country, the Member State concerned must inform the

15 EC Treaty, Article 70.

16 EC Treaty, Article 71(1)(a) and (b).

17 EEA Agreement, Articles 7 and 36(2); Annex XIII.

18 Council Regulation 4055/86 applying the principle of freedom to provide services to maritime transport between Member States and between Member States and third countries (OJ L378/86), as amended by Regulation 3573/90 (OJ L353/90).

19 Every citizen of a Member State of the EU is a EU citizen—*see* EC Treaty, Article 17.

20 Council Regulation 4055/86, Article 1(1).

21 EC Treaty, Article 1(2).

22 Council Regulation 4055/86, Article 1(4).

23 Council Regulation 4055/86, Article 8.

other Member States and the Commission.[24] The Council then decides on the action to be taken, which may include the negotiation of cargo-sharing arrangements.[25] If the Council fails to decide on the necessary action within six months, the Member State may take whatever action may be necessary to remedy the situation.[26]

2. Liberalization of Maritime Cabotage

The freedom to provide maritime transport services within a Member State is granted by Council Regulation 3577/92[27] to EU shipowners who have their ships registered in and flying the flag of a Member State.[28] An "EU shipowner" means:[29]

- an EU citizen established in a Member State and pursuing shipping activities there;
- a shipping company established under the legislation of a Member State and whose principal place of business is situated and effective control is exercised in a Member State; or
- an EU citizen established outside the EU or a shipping company established outside the EU but controlled by EU citizens as long as the ships are registered in and fly the flag of a Member State.

Maritime cabotage comprises the carriage of passengers or goods by sea:[30]

- between ports situated on the mainland or the main territory of a Member State without calls at islands ("mainland cabotage");
- between any port in a Member State and installations or structures situated on that Member State's continental shelf ("offshore supply services");
- between ports situated on the mainland and on one or more of the islands of a Member State or between ports situated on the islands of a Member State ("island cabotage").

In the case of mainland cabotage, all matters related to manning are the responsibility of the Member State in which the vessel is registered (the flag state), except for ships smaller than 650 gt where host State conditions may be applied.[31] In the case of island cabotage, the host Member State has responsibility for manning, ex-

24 Council Regulation 4055/86, Article 6(1).

25 Council Regulation 4055/86, Article 6(2).

26 Council Regulation 4055/86, Article 6(3).

27 Council Regulation 3577/92 applying the principle of freedom to provide services to maritime transport within Member States (maritime cabotage) (OJ L364/92).

28 Council Regulation 3577/92, Article 1(1).

29 Council Regulation 3577/92, Article 2(2).

30 Council Regulation 3577/92, Article 2(1).

31 Council Regulation 3577/92, Article 3(1).

cept for vessels over 650 gt where the voyage follows or precedes a voyage to or from another State. In the latter situation, the flag State has responsibility.[32]

The host Member State may impose public service obligations on shipping companies providing regular services to, from and between islands as a condition for the provision of cabotage services.[33] In imposing these public service obligations, Member States must act in a non-discriminatory way and limit their requirements to ports to be served, regularity, continuity, frequency, capacity to provide service, rates to be charged and manning of the vessel.[34] Compensation for public service obligations must be available to all EU shipowners.

In the event of a serious disturbance of the internal transport market due to the liberalization of cabotage, a Member State may request the Commission to adopt safeguard measures.[35] Such measures may include the temporary exclusion, not exceeding twelve months, of the area concerned from liberalization. If the Commission takes no decision within thirty days of the request, or in the event of an emergency, the Member State concerned may act unilaterally. The Commission may also adopt safeguard measures on its own initiative.[36]

C. AIR TRANSPORT SERVICES

1. The Licensing of Air Carriers

No undertaking established in the EU is permitted within the territory of the EU to carry by air passengers, mail and/or cargo unless it has a valid operating license issued by a Member State.[37] Such a license may only be issued to an undertaking that meets the requirements of Regulation 2407/92[38] and of the national law of the Member State granting the license to the extent that the latter is compatible with EU law.[39]

No undertaking may obtain an operating license from a Member State unless its principal place of business and its registered office, if it has one, are located in that Member State and its main occupation is air transport.[40] Subject to any agreements to which the EU is a party, the undertaking must in addition be owned directly or through majority ownership by a Member State and/or EU citizens.[41] It must at all times be effectively controlled by the Member State or EU citizens. An air carrier must be able, on request, to demonstrate at any time that it meets these

32 Council Regulation 3577/92, Article 3(2) and (3).

33 Council Regulation 3577/92, Article 4(1).

34 Council Regulation 3577/92, Article 4(1) and (2).

35 Council Regulation 3577/92, Article 5(1).

36 Council Regulation 3577/92, Article 5(2).

37 Council Regulation 2407/92, Article 3(3).

38 Council Regulation 2407/92 on licensing of air carriers (OJ L240/92).

39 Council Regulation 2407/92, Article 15.

40 Council Regulation 2407/92, Article 4(1).

41 Council Regulation 2407/92, Article 4(2).

requirements.[42] However, air carriers controlled by a third country or nationals of a third country retain any rights that they possessed prior to the entry into force of Regulation 2407/92.[43]

An undertaking to which an operating license is granted for the first time must demonstrate that:[44]

- it can meet at any time its actual and potential obligations for a period of twenty-four months from the start of operations; and
- it can meet its fixed and operational costs incurred from its operations for a period of three months from the start of operations, without taking into account any income from its operations.

An air carrier must be insured to cover liability in case of accidents.[45] The ownership of aircraft is not a condition for the granting of a license, but a Member State must require that an undertaking licensed by it have one or more aircraft at its disposal through ownership or lease.[46]

Where an undertaking meets the requirements of Regulation 2407/92—and any national requirements—it is entitled to receive an operating license.[47] However, the license does not confer in itself any rights of access to specific routes or markets. Moreover, the granting and validity of an operating license is dependent upon the possession of a valid air operator's certificate,[48] which is a document issued by a Member State affirming that the operator has the professional ability and organization to secure the safe operation of aircraft for the aviation activities specified in the certificate.[49]

The procedures for granting operating licenses must be made public by the Member States.[50] Decisions on application must be taken not later than three months after all the necessary information has been submitted and communicated to the applicant air transport undertaking.[51] A refusal must be accompanied by reasons and can be referred to the Commission to see whether it is consistent with Regulation 2407/92.[52]

---

42 Council Regulation 2407/92, Article 4(5).

43 Council Regulation 2407/92, Article 4(3)(a).

44 Council Regulation 2407/92, Article 5(1).

45 Council Regulation 2407/92, Article 7.

46 Council Regulation 2407/92, Article 8(1).

47 Council Regulation 2407/92, Article 3(2).

48 Council Regulation 2407/92, Article 9(1).

49 Council Regulation 2407/92, Article 2(d).

50 Council Regulation 2407/92, Article 13(1).

51 Council Regulation 2407/92, Article 13(2).

52 Council Regulation 2407/92, Article 13(2) and (3).

An operating license is valid as long as the air carrier meets the requirements set out in Regulation 2407/92 and any applicable national requirements.[53] Member States may make provision for a review one year after a new operating license has been issued and every five years thereafter. An air carrier against which insolvency or similar proceedings are opened must not be permitted to retain its operating license if the Member State that issued the license is convinced that there is no realistic prospect of a satisfactory financial reconstruction within a reasonable time.[54] A Member State may also suspend or revoke an operating license if it is no longer satisfied that an air carrier can meet its actual and potential obligations for a twelve-month period.[55] Alternatively, it may issue a temporary license pending financial reorganization as long as safety is not at risk.

2. Access to Intra-EU Air Routes

Air carriers with a valid operating license issued by a Member State pursuant to Regulation 2407/92 are permitted to carry passengers, cargo and/or mail by scheduled or non-scheduled air services ("air traffic rights") on routes within the EU in accordance with Council Regulation 2408/92.[56] As from April 1, 1997, this includes cabotage air services.[57] These rights are subject to certain conditions and limitations.

A Member State may impose a public service obligation in respect of scheduled air services to an airport serving a peripheral or development region in its territory or on a thin route to any regional airport in its territory so as to ensure on that route the adequate provision of air services that satisfy standards of continuity, regularity, capacity and pricing that an air carrier would not assume if it were solely considering its commercial interest.[58] In a situation where other forms of transport cannot ensure adequate and uninterrupted service, a Member State may require air carriers to guarantee that they will operate the route for a certain period.[59] If no air carrier has commenced scheduled air services on a route in accordance with the public service obligation that has been imposed on the route, a Member State may limit access to that route to only one air carrier for an initial period of up to three years.[60] The right to operate the route must be offered by pub-

---

53 Council Regulation 2407/92, Article 11(1).

54 Council Regulation 2407/92, Article 12.

55 Council Regulation 2407/92, Article 5(5).

56 Council Regulation 2408/92 on access for Community air carriers to intra-Community air routes (OJ L240/92), as amended by Regulation 1882/03 (OJ L284/03), Articles 1(1), 2 and 3(1).

57 Council Regulation 2408/92, Article 3(2).

58 Council Regulation 2408/92, Article 4(1)(a).

59 Council Regulation 2408/92, Article 4(1)(c).

60 Council Regulation 2408/92, Article 4(1)(d).

lic tender. The Member States must ensure that any decision taken can be reviewed effectively.[61]

Member States are free to regulate the distribution of traffic between their airports as long as this is done without discrimination on grounds of nationality.[62] Moreover, air traffic rights are subject to EU and national rules relating to safety, the protection of the environment and the allocation of slots.[63] Measures applied by Member States pursuant to these provisions may be referred by another Member State to the Commission, which decides whether the Member State may continue to apply the measures.[64] Any Member State may refer the Commission's decision to the Council, which may take a different decision.[65]

Where serious congestion or environmental problems exist, a Member State may impose conditions on, limit or refuse the exercise of air traffic rights as long as the action taken:[66]

- is non-discriminatory on grounds of nationality or identity of air carriers;
- has a limited initial period of validity not exceeding three years;
- does not unduly affect the objectives of Regulation 2408/92;
- does not unduly distort competition between air carriers;
- is not more restrictive than necessary to resolve the problem.

Measures applied by Member States pursuant to this provision may be referred by another Member State to the Commission, which decides whether the action is appropriate and in conformity with EU law.[67] Any Member State may refer the Commission's decision to the Council, which may take a different decision.[68]

Apart from the limitations permitted under the above provisions, no capacity limitations may be applied to air services covered by Regulation 2408/92.[69] However, where the operation of air services leads to serious financial damage to the scheduled air carriers licensed by a particular Member State, the Commission must carry out a review at the request of that Member State with a view to determining whether the capacity for scheduled air services to and from that State should be

---

61 Council Regulation 2408/92, Article 4(1)(i).

62 Council Regulation 2408/92, Article 8(1).

63 Council Regulation 2408/92, Article 8(2).

64 Council Regulation 2408/92, Article 8(3).

65 Council Regulation 2408/92, Article 8(4).

66 Council Regulation 2408/92, Article 9(1) and (2).

67 Council Regulation 2408/92, Article 9(4).

68 Council Regulation 2408/92, Article 9(6).

69 Council Regulation 2408/92, Article 10(1).

stabilized for a limited period.[70] Any Member State may refer the Commission's decision to the Council, which may take a different decision.[71]

3. Allocation of Slots at EU Airports

Council Regulation 95/93[72] regulates the allocation of airport slots at EU airports to air transport undertakings holding a valid operating license under Regulation 2407/92 or its equivalent in the case of third country air carriers. An airport slot is a permission given by the coordinator at a coordinated airport to use the full range of airport infrastructure necessary to operate an air service on a specific date and time for the purpose of landing or taking off.[73] A coordinated airport is an airport where, in order to land or take off, it is necessary for an air carrier to have been allocated a slot.[74]

The determination of the parameters for slot allocation must be done twice yearly at coordinated airports.[75] They are communicated to the airport coordinator before the initial slot allocation. Series of slots are allocated from the slot pool to applicant air carriers for the scheduling period for which they are requested, at the expiry of which they are returned to the slot pool.[76] However, an air carrier is entitled to the same series of slots in the next scheduling period where it meets the following two conditions:[77]

- it has used the series of slots for the operation of scheduled and programmed non-scheduled air services; and
- it can demonstrate that the series of slots in question has been operated for at least eighty percent of the time during the scheduling period for which it was allocated.

Where it is not possible to accommodate all the requests for slots, preference must be given to commercial air services, in particular scheduled and programmed non-scheduled services. In the case of competing requests, priority is given to year-round operations.[78] If a requested slot cannot be accommodated, the coordinator must inform the air carrier of the reasons therefore and indicate the nearest

70 Council Regulation 2408/92, Article 10(2).

71 Council Regulation 2408/92, Article10(3).

72 Council Regulation 95/93 on common rules for the allocation of slots at Community airports (OJ L14/93), as amended by Regulations 894/02 (OJ L142/02), 1554/03 (OJ L221/03) and 793/04 (OJ L138/04).

73 Council Regulation 95/93, Article 2(a).

74 Council Regulation 95/93, Article 2(g).

75 Council Regulation 95/93, Article 6(1).

76 Council Regulation 95/93, Article 8(1).

77 Council Regulation 95/93, Article 8(2).

78 Council Regulation 95/93, Article 8(3).

available alternative slot.[79] Where a public service obligation has been imposed on a route pursuant to Regulation 2408/92, a Member State may reserve at a coordinated airport the slots required for the operations envisaged on that route.[80]

Slots may be transferred by an air carrier between routes or types of service and between parents and subsidiaries or as part of an acquisition or takeover of an air carrier.[81] They may also be exchanged between air carriers. These transfers or exchanges do not take effect until they have been confirmed by the coordinator.[82]

Any complaints regarding slot allocation are submitted to a coordination committee,[83] which is composed of the air carriers that use the airport in question regularly, their representative organizations, the managing body of the airport, the air traffic control authorities and representatives of general aviation using the airport regularly.[84] If the complaint cannot be settled, the Member State responsible may provide for mediation.

Whenever it appears that a third country does not grant EU air carriers treatment with respect to the allocation and use of airport slots that is comparable to that granted by Regulation 95/93 to air carriers from that country, or where it does not grant EU air carriers national treatment, or where it grants air carriers from other third countries more favorable treatment than EU air carriers, the Commission may decide that the Member States should take retaliatory measures.[85] These may include the suspension, in whole or in part, of the application of Regulation 95/93 to air carriers from that third country.

D. ROAD PASSENGER TRANSPORT SERVICES

1. Liberalization of International Road Passenger Transport Services

Council Regulation 684/92[86] regulates the international carriage of passengers by coach and bus within the EU.[87] It provides that any carrier for hire or reward established in a Member State may provide road passenger transport services between the Member States without discrimination as to nationality if it:[88]

- is authorized in the Member State of establishment to provide these services;

79 Council Regulation 95/93, Article 8(6).

80 Council Regulation 95/93, Article 9(1).

81 Council Regulation 95/93, Article 8a(1).

82 Council Regulation 95/93, Article 8a(2).

83 Council Regulation 95/93, Article 11(1).

84 Council Regulation 95/93, Article 5(1).

85 Council Regulation 95/93, Article 12(1).

86 Council Regulation 684/92 on common rules for the international carriage of passengers by coach and bus (OJ L74/92), as amended by Regulation 11/98 (OJ L4/98).

87 Council Regulation 684/92, Article 1(1).

88 Council Regulation 684/92, Article 3(1).

- complies with the EU rules on admission to the occupation of road passenger transport operator in national and international transport operations;[89]
- meets legal requirements on road safety as far as the standards for drivers and vehicles are concerned.

The carrier must also hold an EU license for the international carriage of passengers by coach and bus issued by the Member State of establishment.[90] This license is issued for a period of five years.[91] It may not be issued or renewed if the carrier does not meet the three conditions outlined above.[92] Moreover, it must be withdrawn where the holder no longer meets these conditions or if it has supplied inaccurate information in its application for a license.[93] In the case of a serious breach or repeated minor breaches of road safety regulations, the Member State of establishment may withdraw the license.[94]

There are three types of road passenger transport services. "Regular services" provide for the carriage of passengers at specified intervals along specified routes, passengers being taken up and set down at predetermined stopping points.[95] "Special regular services" provide for the carriage of specified categories of passengers on a regular basis, such the carriage of workers to and from work, school pupils to and from school and soldiers to and from their barracks.[96] All other road passenger transport services are categorized as "occasional services;" they are characterized above all by the fact that they concern the carriage of groups of passengers assembled on their own initiative or that of the carrier.[97]

Regular services and special regular services that are not covered by a contract between the organizer and the carrier require an authorization from the Member State in whose territory the place of departure is situated.[98] The authorization is valid for a maximum period of five years and entitles the holder to operate the ser-

---

89 *See* Council Directive 96/26 on admission to the occupation of road haulage operator and road passenger transport operator and mutual recognition of diplomas, certificates and other evidence of formal qualifications intended to facilitate for these operators the right to freedom of establishment in national and international transport operations, (OJ L124/96).

90 Council Regulation 684/92, Article 3a(1).

91 Council Regulation 684/92, Article 3a(4).

92 Council Regulation 684/92, Article 3a(7).

93 Council Regulation 684/92, Article 16(1).

94 Council Regulation 684/92, Article 16(3).

95 Council Regulation 684/92, Article 2(1.1).

96 Council Regulation 684/92, Article 2(1.2).

97 Council Regulation 684/92, Article 2(3.1).

98 Council Regulation 684/92, Articles 4(2) and (4) and 6(1).

vice in all the Member States over which the routes of the service pass.[99] It specifies the following:[100]

- the type of service;
- the route of the service, giving in particular the points of departure and destination;
- the period of validity of the authorization;
- the stops and the timetable.

Authorizations are issued in agreement with all the Member States in whose territories passengers are picked up or set down.[101] These Member States must notify the Member State issuing the authorization of their decision on the application within two months. If no reply is received within this time, the issuing Member State may deem agreement to have been given.[102] If the issuing Member States feels incapable of deciding upon the application, the matter may be referred to the Commission, which, after consulting the Member States concerned, takes a decision that applies until such time as agreement is reached between the Member States.[103]

Member States are obliged to grant an authorization unless:[104]

a) the applicant is unable to provide the service;

b) in the past, the applicant has not complied with national or international legislation on road transport or has committed serious breaches of road safety legislation;

c) in the case of an application for renewal of the authorization, the conditions of the authorization have not been complied with;

d) it is shown that the service in question would directly compromise the existence of regular services already authorized;

e) it appears that the operation of services covered by the application is aimed only at the most lucrative services existing on the links concerned;

f) a Member State decides that the service would seriously affect the viability of a comparable rail service on the direct sections concerned.

With respect to (f) above, as from January 1, 2000 a Member State may, with the agreement of the Commission, suspend or withdraw an authorization to run an ex-

99 Council Regulation 684/92, Article 5(2) and (5).

100 Council Regulation 684/92, Article 5(3).

101 Council Regulation 684/92, Article 7(1).

102 Council Regulation 684/92, Article 7(2).

103 Council Regulation 684/92, Article 7(6), (7) and (8).

104 Council Regulation 684/92, Article 7(4).

isting international bus service where the service seriously affects the viability of a comparable rail service.

The fact that a carrier offers lower prices than other road carriers or, without prejudice to (d) above, the fact that the link in question is already operated by other road carriers does not in itself justify a rejection of the application for an authorization.

A decision to refuse an application for an authorization must state the reasons on which it is based.[105] The transport undertakings involved must be given the opportunity to make representations in this event.

Where an authorization is granted, the operator of the regular or special regular service must, except in the case of *force majeure*, take all measures to guarantee a transport service that fulfills the standards of continuity, regularity and capacity and complies with the other conditions laid down in the authorization.[106]

Occasional services, which do not require an authorization, must be carried out under cover of a journey form, which contains at least information concerning the type of service, the main itinerary and the carrier(s) involved.[107] A carrier operating occasional services must fill out a journey form before each journey.[108]

2. Liberalization of Cabotage Road Passenger Transport Operations

Cabotage road passenger transport is regulated by Council Regulation 12/98.[109] Any carrier established in a Member State who operates road passenger transport services and who holds the EU license referred to in Article 3a of Council Regulation 684/92 may, without discrimination on the grounds of nationality or Member State of establishment, temporarily operate these transport services in another Member State (cabotage).[110] The carrier is not obliged to have a registered office or other establishment in the host Member State.

Cabotage transport operations are to be permitted for special regular services covered by a contract between the organizer and the carrier, occasional services and regular services performed by the non-resident carrier in the course of a regular international service authorized under Council Regulation 684/92.[111] Urban and suburban services, which involve transportation meeting the needs of an urban center or conurbation and those between it and the surrounding areas, are excluded.

---

105 Council Regulation 684/92, Article 8(2).

106 Council Regulation 684/92, Article 10(1).

107 Council Regulation 684/92, Article 11(1) and (3).

108 Council Regulation 684/92, Article 11(2).

109 Council Regulation 12/98 laying down the conditions under which non-resident carriers may operate national road passenger transport services within a Member State, OJ L4/98.

110 Council Regulation 12/98, Article 1.

111 Council Regulation 12/98, Article 3.

The performance of the cabotage operations covered by Council Regulation 12/98 are subject to the law of the host Member State with respect to:[112]

- rates and conditions governing the transport contract;
- weights and dimensions of road vehicles;
- requirements relating to the carriage of certain categories of passengers, such as children and handicapped persons;
- driving and rest time;
- VAT (value-added tax) on transport services in accordance with Council Directive 77/388.[113]

In the case of regular services, the cabotage operations are also subject to the law of the host Member State with respect to authorizations, tendering procedures, the routes to be operated and the regularity, continuity and frequency of the services as well as the itineraries.[114] All national provisions must be applied in such a way as effectively to prevent any open or hidden discrimination.[115]

A host Member State may require cabotage operations involving regular services to be authorized.[116] Cabotage operations in the form of occasional services must be carried out under cover of a journey form, which sets out the points of departure and destination and the relevant dates.[117] In the case of special regular services, the contract between the carrier and the organizer serves as the control document.[118]

In the event of a serious disturbance of the internal transport market in a given geographical area caused or aggravated by cabotage, a Member State may refer the matter to the Commission with a view to the adoption of safeguard measures.[119] The Commission makes its decision within one month. This decision may be referred by any Member State to the Council, which may take a different decision.[120] If the Council fails to act within thirty days, the Commission decision stands.[121]

112 Council Regulation 12/98, Article 4(1).

113 Council Directive 77/388 on the harmonization of the laws of the Member States relating to turnover taxes (OJ L145/77), as amended.

114 Council Regulation 12/98, Article 4(2).

115 Council Regulation 12/98, Article 4(4).

116 This is not explicitly stated in Regulation 12/98, but it is implicit in Articles 4(2) and 6.

117 Council Regulation 12/98, Article 6(1) and (2).

118 Council Regulation 12/98, Article 6(4).

119 Council Regulation 12/98, Article 9(1).

120 Council Regulation 12/98, Article 9(3) and (5).

121 Council Regulation 12/98, Article 9(5).

E. CARRIAGE OF GOODS BY ROAD

1. Liberalization of International Carriage of Goods by Road

Council Regulation 881/92[122] regulates the international carriage of goods for journeys carried out within the EU.[123] In order to come within the meaning of "international carriage," the journey must:[124]

- start and end in two different Member States;
- be undertaken by a vehicle from a Member State to a third country; or
- be undertaken between third countries with transit through one or more Member States.

International carriage in the sense set out above requires an EU authorization and, if the driver is a national of a third country, a driver attestation.[125] Any haulier carrying goods by road for hire is entitled to a Community authorization if it:[126]

- is established in a Member State,
- is entitled in the Member State of establishment, in accordance with national and EU provisions concerning admission to the occupation of road haulage operator, to carry out the international carriage of goods by road.[127]

The EU authorization is issued by the Member State of establishment. It is valid for a renewable period of five years and is non-transferable.[128]

A driver attestation is issued by the Member State of establishment at the request of any haulier who holds an EU authorization and who lawfully employs or uses in that Member State drivers who are nationals of third countries.[129] A driver attestation is issued for a maximum renewable period of five years.[130]

---

122 Council Regulation 881/92 on access to the market in the carriage of goods by road within the Community to or from the territory of a Member State or passing across the territory of one or more Member States (OJ L95/92), as amended by Regulation 484/02 (OJ L76/02).

123 Council Regulation 881/92, Article 1(1).

124 Council Regulation 881/92, Article 2, 2nd indent.

125 Council Regulation 881/92, Article 3(1).

126 Council Regulation 881/92, Article 3(2).

127 *See* Council Directive 96/26 on admission to the occupation of road haulage operator and road passenger transport operator and mutual recognition of diplomas, certificates and other evidence of formal qualifications intended to facilitate for these operators the right to freedom of establishment in national and international transport operations, (OJ L124/96).

128 Council Regulation 881/92, Article 5(4) and (5).

129 Council Regulation 881/92, Articles 3(3) and 6(1) and (2).

130 Council Regulation 881/92, Article 6(5).

It belongs to the haulier and is put at the disposal of the driver when he/she undertakes a journey.[131]

If the conditions set out above for the issue or renewal of an EU authorization or driver attestation are not met, the Member State of establishment must reject an application to issue or renew.[132] Furthermore, it must withdraw an EU authorization or driver attestation in these circumstances or where the haulier has supplied incorrect information for the issue of the documents.[133] It may also do so in the event of serious infringements or repeated minor infringements of carriage regulations.[134] Member States must provide for appeals against any decision to refuse or withdraw an EU authorization or driver attestation.[135]

2. Liberalization of Cabotage Carriage of Goods by Road

Cabotage carriage of goods by road is regulated by Council Regulation 3118/93.[136] Any haulier established in a Member State who carries goods for hire and who holds an EU authorization under Council Regulation 881/92 is entitled temporarily to operate national road haulage services for hire in another Member State (cabotage) without having a registered office or other establishment therein.[137]

Cabotage operations are subject to authorization by the host Member State.[138] A cabotage authorization is valid for one or two months and is not transferable.[139] It can be used by only one vehicle at a time.[140]

The performance of the cabotage operations covered by Council Regulation 3118/93 are subject to the law of the host Member State with respect to:[141]

- rates and conditions governing the transport contract;
- weights and dimensions of road vehicles;
- requirements relating to the carriage of certain categories of goods, such as dangerous goods, perishable foodstuffs and live animals;

131 Council Regulation 881/92, Article 6(4).

132 Council Regulation 881/92, Article 8(1).

133 Council Regulation 881/92, Article 8(2).

134 Council Regulation 881/92, Article 8(3).

135 Council Regulation 881/92, Article 9.

136 Council Regulation 3118/93 laying down the conditions under which non-resident carriers may operate national road haulage services within a Member State (OJ L279/93), as amended by Regulation 3315/94, OJ L350/94

137 Council Regulation 3118/93, Article 1(1).

138 Council Regulation 3118/93, Article 2(1).

139 Council Regulation 3118/93, Articles 2(1) and (2) and 3(3).

140 Council Regulation 3118/93, Article 3(3).

141 Council Regulation 3118/93, Article 6(1).

- driving and rest time;
- VAT (value-added tax) on transport services in accordance with Council Directive 77/388.[142]

These national provisions must be applied in such a way as to prevent any open or hidden discrimination on grounds of nationality or place of establishment.[143]

In the event of a serious disturbance of the internal transport market in a given geographical area caused or aggravated by cabotage, a Member State may refer the matter to the Commission with a view to the adoption of safeguard measures.[144] The Commission makes its decision within one month.[145] This decision may be referred by any Member State to the Council, which may take a different decision.[146] If the Council fails to act within thirty days, the Commission decision stands.

F. INLAND WATERWAY TRANSPORT SERVICES

1. Liberalization of International Inland Waterway Transport Services

Council Regulation 1356/96 regulates the international carriage of goods or passenger by inland waterway.[147] An operator who transports goods or passengers by inland waterway is allowed to transport them between and through Member States without discrimination on grounds of nationality or place of establishment, provided that it:[148]

- is established in a Member State;
- is entitled in the Member State of establishment to carry out the international transport of goods or passengers by inland waterway;
- uses vessels that are registered in a Member State;
- satisfies the conditions laid down by Council Regulation 3921/91 laying down the conditions under which non-resident carriers may transport goods or passengers by inland waterway within a Member State (cabotage).[149]

---

142 Council Directive 77/388 on the harmonization of the laws of the Member States relating to turnover taxes (OJ L145/77), as amended.

143 Council Regulation 3118/93, Article 6(3).

144 Council Regulation 3118/93, Article 7(1).

145 Council Regulation 3118/93, Article 7(2).

146 Council Regulation 3118/93, Article 7(5).

147 Council Regulation 1356/96 on common rules applicable to the transport of goods or passengers by inland waterway between Member States with a view to establishing freedom to provide transport services, OJ L175/96.

148 Council Regulation 1356/96, Articles 1 and 2.

149 OJ L373/91.

2. Liberalization of Cabotage Inland Waterway Transport Services

Cabotage inland waterway transport services are regulated by Council Regulation 3921/91. Any carrier who carries goods or passengers by inland waterway for hire may temporarily operate such services in a Member State without having to set up a registered office or other establishment there, provided that it:[150]

- is established in a Member State;
- is entitled in the Member State of establishment to carry out the international transport of goods or passengers by inland waterway;
- uses for this purpose vessels owned by EU citizens domiciled in a Member State or legal persons whose registered place of business is in a Member State and that is majority-owned by EU citizens.

The carrier must produce a certificate to prove that it complies with the third condition above.[151]

The performance of the cabotage operations covered by Council Regulation 3921/91 are subject to the law of the host Member State with respect to:[152]

- rate and conditions governing the transport contract, and chartering and operating procedures;
- technical specifications for vessels;
- navigation and police regulations;
- navigation time and rest periods;
- VAT (value-added tax) on transport services.

These national provisions must be applied in such a way as effectively to prevent any discrimination on grounds of nationality or place of establishment.[153]

G. RAILWAY TRANSPORT SERVICES

Council Directive 91/440[154] establishes access and transit rights for international groupings in the Member States of establishment of their constituent railway undertakings, as well as transit rights in other Member States, for international

150 Council Regulation 3921/91, Articles 1 and 2(1).

151 Council Regulation 3921/91, Article 2(3).

152 Council Regulation 3921/91, Article 3(1).

153 Council Regulation 3921/91, Article 3(2).

154 Council Directive 91/440 on the development of the Community's railways (OJ L237/91), as amended by Directives 01/12 (OJ L75/01) and 04/51 (OJ L164/04).

services between the Member States where the undertakings constituting the said groupings are established.[155] This includes:[156]

- access on equitable conditions to the infrastructure in other Member States for the purpose of operating international combined transport goods services;
- access on equitable conditions to the Trans-European Rail Freight Network and, at the latest by January 1, 2006, the entire rail network for the purpose of operating international freight services;
- access on equitable conditions, at the latest by January 1, 2007, to the infrastructure in all Member States for the purpose of operating all types of rail freight services;
- non-discriminatory track access to, and supply of services in, the terminals and ports linked to the rail activities referred to above.

Any railway undertaking engaged in rail transport services is obliged to conclude the necessary agreements with the infrastructure managers of the railway infrastructure used.[157] The conditions governing such agreements must be non-discriminatory and transparent and conform to the provisions of Directive 01/14.[158]

In order to operate rail transport services in the EU, railway undertakings must obtain a license pursuant to Council Directive 95/18.[159] The license is valid throughout the EU[160] but does not in itself entitle the holder to access the railway infrastructure.[161] The following railway undertakings may be excluded from the scope of the Directive by Member States:[162]

- those which only operate rail passenger services on local and regional standalone railway infrastructure;
- those which operate only urban or suburban railway passenger services;
- those whose activity is limited to the provision of regional rail freight services not covered by Directive 91/440;

155 Council Directive 91/440, Article 10(1).

156 Council Directive 91/440, Article 10(2), (3) and (6).

157 Council Directive 91/440, Article 10(5).

158 EP/Council Directive 01/14 on the allocation of railway infrastructure capacity and the levying of charges for the use of railway infrastructure and safety certification (OJ L75/01), as amended.

159 Council Directive 95/18 on the licensing of railway undertakings (OJ L143/95), as amended by Directives 01/13 (OJ L75/01) and 04/49 (OJ L164/04), Articles 4(4).

160 Directive 95/18, Article 1(5).

161 Directive 95/18, Article 4(4).

162 Directive 95/18, Article 1(2).

- those which only carry out freight operations on a privately-owned railway infrastructure that exists solely for use by the infrastructure owner for its own freight operations;

Undertakings whose business is limited to providing shuttle services for road vehicles through the Channel Tunnel are obligatorily excluded.[163]

A railway undertaking applies for a license in the Member State where it is established and is entitled to receive the license if it meets the requirement imposed by Directive 95/18.[164] Member States must not issue or renew licenses unless the railway undertaking:[165]

- demonstrates that it will at any time be able to meet the requirements relating to good repute, financial fitness, professional competence and coverage for its civil liability;
- is adequately insured, in accordance with national and international law, in the event of accidents.

Member States must make public their procedures for granting licenses.[166] They must make a decision within three months and any refusal must state the grounds therefore.[167] The decisions of a Member State's licensing authority must be subject to judicial review.[168]

A license is valid as long as the railway undertaking meets the requirements laid down in Directive 95/18.[169] Where a Member State is satisfied that a railway undertaking no longer meets these requirements, it must suspend or revoke the license.[170]

In addition to the requirements of Directive 95/18, a railway undertaking must also comply with non-discriminatory national laws that are compatible with EU law and relate to:[171]

- specific technical and operational requirements for rail services;
- safety requirements applying to staff, rolling stock and the internal organization of the undertaking;
- provisions on health, safety, social conditions and the rights of workers and consumers.

---

163 Directive 95/18, Article 1(3).

164 Directive 95/18, Article 4(1) and (3).

165 Directive 95/18, Articles 4(2), 5(1) and 9.

166 Directive 95/18, Article 15(1).

167 Directive 95/18, Article 15(2).

168 Directive 95/18, Article 15(3).

169 Directive 95/18, Article 10(1).

170 Directive 95/18, Article 11(1).

171 Directive 95/18, Article 12.

IV. MERCOSUR: MONTEVIDEO PROTOCOL ON TRADE IN SERVICES

A. INTRODUCTION

Transportation services are covered by the Protocol and specific commitments have been made in this sector during the five rounds of negotiations. However, two Annexes are appended to the Protocol that deal with the relationship between the Protocol and international agreements concluded by the Member States before the entry into force of the Protocol.

B. ANNEX ON LAND AND WATER TRANSPORT SERVICES

Any bilateral or multilateral agreements concluded between the Member States in this sector before the entry into force of the Protocol continue in effect, as supplemented by any specific commitments undertaken under the Protocol.[172] However, whereas the Protocol does not apply at all to bilateral agreements, except with respect to specific commitments,[173] it does not affect the rights and obligations flowing from any multilateral agreement only to the extent that such agreements concern the harmonization and supervision of the conditions of competition between transport undertakings.[174] These arrangements were supposed to be temporary until the agreements could be brought into conformity with the objectives and principles of the Protocol,[175] but this has not yet happened.

C. ANNEX ON AIR TRANSPORT SERVICES

With respect to scheduled or non-scheduled air transport services and those ancillary services that are covered by GATS, the application of the Protocol does not affect the rights and obligations of the Member States flowing from bilateral, plurilateral or multilateral agreements signed by them that were in effect at the moment of the entry into force of the Protocol.[176] Moreover the Protocol does not apply to measures that affect rights established for commercial air traffic on routes granted under bilateral agreements between the Member States, and the exclusion of cabotage traffic is maintained.[177] As for sub-regional scheduled or exploratory air services on different routes from those actually operated under the terms of the aforementioned bilateral agreements, the 1996 *Agreement on Subregional Air Services* applies in addition to any specific commitments in the Member States' Schedules to the Protocol.[178]

---

172 Annex on Land and Water Transport Services, Point 4.

173 Annex on Land and Water Transport Services, Point 3.

174 Annex on Land and Water Transport Services, Point 2.

175 Annex on Land and Water Transport Services, Point 5.

176 Annex on Air Transport Services, Points 1 and 2.

177 Annex on Air Transport Services, Point 3.

178 Annex on Air Transport Services, Point 4.

The Mercosur dispute settlement procedures apply to the air transport services covered by the Annex unless another specific dispute settlement procedure is contemplated between the Member States involved.[179]

The Common Market Group was supposed to revise this Annex within three years on the basis of proposals from specialists on air transport from the four Member States.[180] No amendments have yet been made to the Annex.

V. ASEAN FRAMEWORK AGREEMENT ON SERVICES

The GATS rules on transport services, including the provisions of the Annex on Air Transport Services, are incorporated into the Agreement by virtue of Article XIV:1. The Fourth Protocol (2004), which ended the most recent round of negotiations between the ASEAN Members, led to a significant liberalization of the air and maritime transport sectors.

VI. OTHER INTERNATIONAL AGREEMENTS

This monograph is concerned with trade liberalization. Thus, the various international agreements that deal with the harmonization of rules, contract standardization, carrier liability and other aspects of the regulation of transportation services or administrative and customs formalities in the field of international transportation are beyond the scope of the monograph. However, to enable readers to obtain a general idea of the background against which GATS and the other international agreements attempt to liberalize this sector, here is a brief overview of the more important of these other international agreements. Two of these agreements are, in fact, liberalizing agreements, but with a limited number of participants. Agreements that deal with specific problems such as accidents and pollution are not included.

A. ROAD TRANSPORT

1. Convention on the Contract for the International Carriage of Goods by Road (CMR) (1956, amended by Geneva Protocol, 1978) and the Convention on the Contract for the International Carriage of Passengers and Luggage by Road (CVR) (1973, amended by Geneva Protocol, 1978)

These Conventions standardize the conditions governing the contract for international carriage by road, including liability for loss.

179 Annex on Air Transport Services, Point 5.

180 Annex on Air Transport Services, Point 6.

2. Convention of the International Carriage of Goods under Cover of TIR Carnets (TIR Convention) (1975, as amended)

This Convention deals with the simplification and harmonization of administrative and customs formalities.

B. RAIL TRANSPORT

Convention concerning International Carriage by Rail (COTIF) (1980, as amended)

This Convention contains as Appendix A the *Uniform Rules concerning the Contract for International Carriage of Passengers and Luggage by Rail (CIV)* and the *Uniform Rules concerning the Contract for International Carriage of Goods by Rail (CIM)*. They both establish a uniform system of law applicable to carriage by rail and a standardization of the contracts involved.

C. AIR TRANSPORT

1. Convention for the Unification of Certain Rules relating to International Carriage by Air (Warsaw Convention) (1929, amended by the Hague Protocol (1955), Guadalajara Convention (1961), Guatemala City Protocol (1971) (not yet in force) and the three Montreal Protocols (1975)[181])

The Warsaw Convention creates uniform rules for the liability of international air transport operators and standardizes air tickets and consignment notes.

2. Chicago Convention on International Civil Aviation (1944, amended by the Montreal Protocols (1977), (1980) and (1984))

This Convention regulates many aspects of civil aviation and establishes the International Civil Aviation Organization (ICAO). Among the issues it deals with are overflights for non-scheduled international air services, customs procedures and licenses. It specifically does not confer a right of cabotage (i.e. the right to carry passengers, mail or cargo between points within a country).

3. International Air Services Transit Agreement (1944)

This Agreement provides for overflights and technical landings (e.g. for refueling) for scheduled international air services.

4. International Air Transport Agreement (1944)

This Agreement represents a failed attempt to liberalize commercial air transport. Only eleven nations have accepted it, not including the United States and most of the European nations.

181 The 3rd Montreal Protocol is not yet in effect.

5. Montreal Convention for the Unification of Certain Rules for International Carriage by Air (1999)

This Convention replaces the Warsaw Convention for the signatory states that have ratified the Montreal Convention, which include the United States, the EU, Canada and a number of other nations.

6. Multilateral Agreement on the Liberalization of International Air Transportation (2001)

This Agreement aims to liberalize air transport services between the members of the Asia Pacific Economic Cooperation Forum.[182] At present, it has been accepted by Brunei, Chile, New Zealand, Peru, Samoa, Singapore, Tonga and the United States.

Under the Agreement, each Party gives the other Parties the right for the conduct of international air transportation by their airlines:[183]

a) to fly across its territory without landing;

b) to make stops in its territory for non-traffic purposes;

c) to perform scheduled and charter international air transportation between points on the following routes;

i) from points behind the Party designating the airline via the territory of that Party and intermediate points to any point or points in the territory of the Party granting the right and beyond;

ii) for all-cargo services, between the territory of the Party granting the right and any point or points.

Each designated airline may at its option:[184]

a) operate flights in either or both directions;

b) combine different flight numbers within one aircraft operation;

c) serve behind, intermediate, and beyond points and points in the territories of the Parties on the routes in any combination and in any order;

d) omit stops at any point or points;

e) transfer traffic from any of its aircraft to any of its other aircraft at any point on the routes;

---

182 The members are: Australia, Brunei, Canada, Chile, China, Hong Kong, Indonesia, Japan, Korea, Malaysia, Mexico, New Zealand. Papua New Guinea, Peru, Philippines, Russia, Singapore, Taipei, Thailand, United States and Vietnam.

183 Article 2(1).

184 Article 2(2).

f) serve points behind any point in its territory with or without change of aircraft or flight number and hold out and advertise such services to the public as through services;

g) make stopovers at any points whether within or outside the territory of any Party;

h) carry transit traffic through any other Party's territory;

i) combine traffic on the same aircraft.

However, the above rights apply subject to the requirement that, with the exception of all-cargo services, the service serves a point in the territory of the Party designating the airline.[185] The Agreement does not confer any rights of cabotage.[186]

The Parties have the right to designate as many airlines as they wish to conduct international air transportation in accordance with the Agreement.[187] International air transportation is defined as air transportation that passes through the airspace of more than one State or APEC member.[188] On receipt of a designation and an application from the designated airline, each Party shall grant the necessary authorizations and permissions.[189]

The airlines of each Party have the right to:[190]

a) establish offices in the territory of the other Parties for the promotion and sale of air transportation:

b) engage in the sale of air transportation in the territory of the other Parties;

c) convert and remit to the territory of its incorporation local revenues in excess of sums locally disbursed;

d) pay for local expenses, including purchases of fuel, in the territories of the other Parties in local currency.

The designated airlines of each Party shall further have the right to:[191]

a) bring in and maintain in the territories of the other Parties managerial, sales, technical, operational and other specialist staff required for the provision of air transportation in accordance with the laws of the other Parties relating to entry, residence and employment;

b) perform their own ground-handling in the territory of the other Parties;

185 Article 2(3).

186 Article 2(5).

187 Article 3(1).

188 Article 1(6).

189 Article 3(2).

190 Article 8(1).

191 Article 3(2).

c) enter into cooperative marketing arrangements such as blocked-space, code-sharing or leasing arrangements with approved airlines.

The Parties must also obey certain rules of fair competition to allow the designated airlines of all Parties an equal opportunity to compete in providing international air transportation services under the Agreement.[192] To this end, Parties must:[193]

a) allow each designated airline to determine the frequency and capacity of the international air transportation that it offers based upon commercial considerations;

b) not impose on another Party's designated airlines a first-refusal requirement, uplift ratio, no-objection fee or any other requirement with respect to capacity, frequency or traffic;

c) not require the filing of schedules, programs for charter flights or operational plans by airlines of the other Parties for approval, except as may be required on a non-discriminatory basis to enforce certain uniform conditions;

d) not apply their laws, regulations and rules to restrict the operation or sale of the charter international air transportation provided for in this Agreement, except with respect to requirements relating to the protection of charter passenger funds and charter passenger cancellation and refund rights;

e) permit the airlines of each Party to market their services on a fair and non-discriminatory basis through computer reservation systems used by travel agencies or travel companies in the territories of the Parties.

Prices for international air transportation operated pursuant to this Agreement must not be made subject to the approval of any Party.[194]

D. MARITIME TRANSPORT

1. International Convention for the Unification of Certain Rules of Law relating to Bills of Lading ("Hague Rules") (1924, amended by the Hague-Visby Rules (1968) and the Brussels Protocol (1979))

These instruments set out uniform rules of law relating to carrier liability and bills of lading.

2. International Convention relating to the Limitation of the Liability of Owners of Sea-going Ships (1957, amended by the Brussels Protocol (1979))

These instruments set out uniform rules with respect to the limitation of the liability of owners of seagoing ships for loss of life or personal injury, loss of or damage

192 Article 11(1).

193 Article 11(2) to (6).

194 Article 12.

to property and for wreck and damage to harbor works, basins and navigable waterways.

3. Athens Convention relating to the Carriage of Passengers and their Luggage by Sea (1974, amended by the 1976 Protocol[195])

The Convention establishes uniform rules for liability for damage suffered by passengers carried on a seagoing vessel. A carrier is liable for damage or loss suffered by a passenger personally or to his/her luggage if the incident causing the damage occurred in the course of the carriage and was due to the fault or neglect of the carrier.

4. London Convention on the Limitation of Liability for Maritime Claims (1976, amended by the 1996 Protocol)

This Convention sets out certain uniform rules relating to the limitation of liability for maritime claims.

5. United Nations Convention on the Carriage of Goods by Sea ("Hamburg Rules") (1978)

The Hamburg Rules cover the liability of carriers and transportation documents and were intended to replace the Hague-Visby Rules. However, none of the world's major trading nations have acceded to them, and its provisions have not been widely incorporated into national legislation. The Rules probably govern around only five per cent of world maritime trade.

195 The 1990 and 2002 Protocols are not yet in force. This Convention largely replaces two earlier Brussels Conventions, which were not widely accepted. These were the *International Convention for the Unification of Certain Rules relating to the Carriage of Passengers by Sea* (1961) and the *International Convention for the Unification of Certain Rules relating to Carriage of Passenger Luggage by Sea* (1967).

CHAPTER EIGHT

LIBERALIZATION OF THE GOVERNMENT PROCUREMENT SECTOR

I. INTRODUCTION

Procurement of products and services by government agencies for their own purposes represents an important share of total government expenditure and thus has a significant role in domestic economies. Although best value for money is best secured through an open and non-discriminatory procurement regime, governments sometimes seek to achieve certain other domestic policy goals through their purchasing decisions, such as the promotion of local industrial sectors or business groups. Measures to this effect may be either explicitly prescribed in national legislation—for example prohibitions against the purchase of foreign goods or services or purchases from foreign suppliers, preference margins, set-asides and offsets—or take the form of less overt measures or practices that have the effect of denying foreign products, services and suppliers the opportunity to compete in domestic government procurement markets. These include excessive use of selective tendering, non-open technical specification requirements and, in particular, lack of transparency in tendering procedures including contract awards. Such discriminatory government procurement procedures and practices represent a significant restriction on the global trade in services.

Because of the importance of the government procurement sector to national economies, government procurement is generally excluded from the liberalization of trade in services carried out by international agreements. Instead it is subject to a more limited liberalization and special rules to deal with the particular forms of restriction inherent in the sector. We shall now look at these specific sectoral rules.

II. THE WTO AGREEMENT ON GOVERNMENT PROCUREMENT

A. INTRODUCTION

A growing awareness of the trade-restrictive effects of discriminatory procurement policies and of the desirability of filling these gaps in the trading system resulted in a first effort to bring government procurement under internationally agreed trade rules in the Tokyo Round of Trade Negotiations. As a result, the first Agreement on Government Procurement was signed in 1979 and entered into force in 1981. It was amended in 1987, with this amended version entering into force in 1988. It only covered procurement of goods.

Government procurement was not included in the revamped GATT or GATS,[1] but, in parallel with the Uruguay Round, negotiations were held to extend the scope and coverage of the 1979 Agreement. The Agreement on Government Procurement (GPA) was signed in Marrakesh on April 15, 1994 at the same time as the Agreement Establishing the WTO and extended to the procurement of services. The new Agreement entered into force on January 1, 1996. The GPA is one of the "plurilateral" Agreements included in Annex 4 to the WTO Agreement, signifying that only subscribing WTO Members are bound by it.[2]

The GPA establishes an agreed framework of rights and obligations among the subscribing Parties with respect to their national laws, regulations, procedures and practices in the area of government procurement. The cornerstone of the rules in the Agreement is non-discrimination. In order to ensure that this basic principle of non-discrimination is followed and that access to procurement is available to foreign services and service suppliers, the Agreement lays heavy emphasis on procedures for providing transparency of laws, regulations, procedures and practices regarding government procurement.

According to the statistics collected under the Tokyo Round Agreement, the 1979 Agreement applied annually to a total value of contracts of around US$30 billion during the period 1990 to 1994. Under the new 1994 Agreement, the value of procurement that is opened up to international competition is estimated to have increased by ten times, given the extension of the rules to cover procurement of services as well as sub-central entities and public utilities.

B. SCOPE OF THE AGREEMENT

The GPA applies to any law, regulation, procedure or practice regarding procurement by the entities listed in Annexes 1 to 3 of services listed in Annexes 4 and 5

1 GATS, Article XIII:1 excludes government procurement from the Agreement's provisions on MFN treatment as well as market access and national treatment commitments.

2 The Members who have subscribed to the GPA are: Canada, the EU and its twenty-five Member States, Hong Kong China, Iceland, Israel, Japan, Korea, Liechtenstein, Netherlands with respect to Aruba, Norway, Singapore, Switzerland and the United States.

under contracts of a value of not less than the relevant threshold specified in each Party's Annexes.[3] The Agreement requires that notices of invitation to participate in an intended procurement make it clear, either in the notice itself or in the publication in which it appears, whether the procurement in question is covered by the Agreement.[4]

The entities included in Annexes 1 to 3 comprise central and sub-central government entities and all other public entities that procure in accordance with the provisions of the GPA.[5] It is up to the Parties to list which of these entities are to appear in the Annexes. The GPA allows withdrawal of entities on the ground that government control or influence has been effectively eliminated.[6] Other signatories may seek compensation, taking into account market-opening effects.

The services to which the GPA applies also depends on the Parties. The EU, for instance, includes in its Annex 4 maintenance and repair services, land transport services, air transport services except transport of mail, transport of mail by land, telecommunications services, financial services, computer and related services, accounting, auditing and bookkeeping services, market research and public opinion polling services, management consulting and related services, architectural services, engineering services, advertising services, building-cleaning and property management services, publishing and printing services and sewage, refuse disposal and sanitation services. Annex 5 sets out which construction services a Party is making subject to the GPA.

The thresholds for procurement contracts are not uniform because some variances exist between the Parties. The thresholds for services are expressed in national currencies, but the norms for most countries are 130,000SDR[7] for central government entities, 200,000SDR and for all other public entities, 355,000SDR. The normal threshold for construction services is a uniform 5,000,000SDR. The valuation of contracts must take account of all forms of remuneration, including any premiums, fees, commissions and interest receivable.[8] The selection of the valuation method must not be used, nor may any procurement requirement be divided, with the intention of avoiding the application of the GPA.[9]

The GPA authorizes Parties to modify the mutually agreed coverage of Appendices I to IV,[10] subject to the procedures for rectification and modification set out in Article XXIV:6. Since its signature in April 1994, the Agreement's scope has been expanded through its incorporation of the results of a series of bilateral agreements

3 GPA, Article I:1, 2 and 4.

4 GPA, Article IX:11.

5 GPA, note 1 to Article I:1.

6 GPA, Article XXIV:6(b).

7 On March 14, 2005, the special drawing right was worth US$1.54.

8 GPA, Article II:2.

9 GPA, Article II:3.

10 Appendix I contains a Party's five Annexes while Appendices II to IV contain the publications utilized by a Party to make known the information required by the GPA.

between individual Parties. A loose-leaf system for Appendices to the GPA is designed to reflect the up-to-date status of the Appendices as such changes occur.

When reading the annexes in Appendix I to ascertain whether a particular procurement contract is covered by the GPA, it is important to check not only whether the procuring entity is covered, the threshold level and whether the service in question is covered, but also the General Notes at the end of most Parties' Appendix, which provide for a number of exceptions. Many Parties have made explicit derogations to the commitments that are contained in their Annexes, either on a general basis or with respect to certain other Parties. Often Parties specify that they will only extend non-discriminatory treatment, with respect to the procurement of entities listed in their Annexes, to undertakings from Parties that give comparable access. Many, the EU for example, specify that the services listed by them are covered only to the extent that other Parties provide reciprocal access to that service.

It should be noted that exceptions from the obligations of the Agreement are also allowed for developing countries in certain situations,[11] for security reasons[12] and for measures to protect public morals, order or safety, human, animal or plant life or health or intellectual property, etc. as long the measures are not applied in a manner that constitutes a means of arbitrary or unjustifiable discrimination.[13] The GPA does not apply as between any two Parties if either of them, at the time either accepts or accedes to the Agreement, does not consent to such application.[14]

C. NON-DISCRIMINATION

In respect of a procurement covered by the GPA, Parties to the Agreement are required to give the services and service suppliers of any other Party to the Agreement treatment no less favorable than that which they give to their domestic services and service suppliers and not to discriminate among services and service suppliers of other Parties.[15] Furthermore, each Party is required to ensure that its entities do not treat a locally-established supplier less favorably than another locally-established supplier on the basis of the degree of foreign affiliation or ownership and do not discriminate against a locally-established supplier on the basis of the country of production of the service being supplied, provided that the country of production is a Party to the GPA.[16]

11 GPA, Article V.

12 GPA, Article XXIII:1.

13 GPA, Article XXIII:2.

14 GPA, Article XXIV:11.

15 GPA, Article III:1.

16 GPA, Article III:2.

D. TENDERING PROCEDURES

1. Introduction

The GPA contains a number of detailed procedural obligations that procuring entities have to fulfill to ensure the effective application of its basic principles.[17] The purpose of these procedural requirements is to guarantee that access to covered procurement is effectively open and that an equal opportunity is given to foreign services and suppliers in competing for government contracts.

The GPA allows the use of open, selective and limited tendering procedures, provided they are applied in a non-discriminatory manner and consistently with the provisions of the Agreement.[18] Open procedures are where all interested suppliers may submit a tender.[19]

2. Selective Tendering

Selective tendering procedures are where only those suppliers invited to do so by the entity may submit a tender.[20] To ensure optimum effective international competition, purchasing entities are required to invite tenders from the maximum number of foreign suppliers.[21] Safeguards to ensure that the procedures and conditions for qualification of suppliers do not discriminate against suppliers of other Parties include the following:[22]

- any conditions for participation in tendering procedures must be published in adequate time to enable interested suppliers to complete the qualification procedures;
- any conditions for participation in tendering procedures by suppliers are limited to those which are essential to ensure the firm's capability to fulfill the contract and which do not infringe the national treatment or MFN principles;
- the process of, and the time required for, qualifying suppliers must not be used in order to keep suppliers of other Parties off a suppliers' list or from being considered for a particular intended procurement;
- entities maintaining permanent lists of qualified suppliers must ensure that suppliers may apply for qualification at any time and can be included in the list within a reasonable time;
- suppliers of another Party that are not yet qualified but which request to participate in the procurement must be considered provided there is sufficient time for them to complete the qualification procedure;

17 GPA, Articles VII to XVI.

18 GPA. Article VII:1.

19 GPA. Article VII:3(a).

20 GPA, Article VII:3(b).

21 GPA, Article X:1.

22 GPA, Article VIII.

- any supplier having requested to become a qualified supplier is advised by the entities concerned of their decision in this regard;
- each Party must ensure that each entity follows a single qualification procedure, where possible, and that efforts are made to minimize differences in qualification procedures between entities.

Once a year the entities using the selective tendering method are required to publish, in a publication indicated in a Party's Appendix III, their lists of qualified suppliers, and to specify the period of validity of those lists and the conditions that need to be met for inclusion of interested suppliers in the lists.[23]

3. Limited Tendering

Limited tendering procedures are where the entity contacts the potential suppliers individually.[24] The Agreement restricts the situations in which this method can be used in the case of services to the following:[25]

- absence of valid tenders in response to an open or selective tender;
- where, for reasons connected with the protection of exclusive rights, or in the absence of competition for technical reasons, the services can only be supplied by a particular supplier;
- for reasons of extreme urgency brought about by events unforeseeable by the entity;
- for additional services by the original supplier;
- where an entity procures a first service that is developed at its request;
- in the case of contracts awarded to the winner of an architectural design contest;
- where an entity needs to procure consulting services regarding matters of a confidential nature.

Limited tendering may not in any situation be used to avoid maximum possible competition or in a manner that infringes the national treatment or MFN principles.[26]

Entities may hold negotiations with suppliers making tenders, provided this is indicated in the initial tender notice or if it appears from the tender evaluation that no one tender is obviously the most advantageous.[27] The negotiations must be used primarily to identify the strengths and weaknesses in tenders[28] and are sub-

23 GPA, Article IX:9.

24 NAFTA, Article 1025.

25 NAFTA, Article 1016:2. *See also* Article 9.9:2 (USA).

26 NAFTA, Article 1016:1.

27 GPA, Article XIV:1.

28 GPA, Article XIV:2.

ject to the following safeguards to ensure that such negotiations do not discriminate between suppliers:[29]

- any elimination of participants is carried out in accordance with the criteria set forth in the notices and tender documents;
- all modifications to the criteria and technical requirements are transmitted in writing to all remaining participants;
- all remaining participants are afforded an opportunity to submit new or amended submissions;
- all remaining participants are permitted to submit final tenders in accordance with a common deadline.

4. Deadlines

The GPA prescribes certain minimum deadlines for the preparation, submission and receipt of tenders.[30] These deadlines must provide adequate time to allow all suppliers, domestic and those of other Parties, to prepare and submit tenders before the closing of the tendering procedures.[31] In general, the minimum time limit for receipt of tenders is forty days from the date of publication of an invitation to tender.[32] The minimum time-limit may be reduced to twenty-four or even ten days in certain well-defined circumstances.[33]

5. Tender Documentation

In the tender documentation, the purchasing entity is required to give all necessary information related to the procurement in question to enable potential suppliers to submit responsive tenders. This includes the information required to be published in tender notices[34] as well as the following:

- the address of the entity to which tenders should be sent;
- the address from which supplementary information should be sent;
- the language or languages in which the tender should be submitted;
- the closing date and time for receipt of tenders;
- the persons authorized to be present at the opening of tenders, as well as the date, time and place of the opening;
- any economic and technical requirements, financial guarantees and information and documents required from the suppliers;

---

29 GPA, Article XIV:4.

30 GPA, Article XI.

31 GPA, Article XI:1(a).

32 GPA, Article XI:2.

33 GPA, Article XI:3.

34 *See infra* in the text.

- a complete description of the services required as well as any requirements to be fulfilled;
- the criteria for awarding the contract;
- the terms of payment;
- other terms and conditions.

6. Award of Contracts

The objective of the procedural rules for submission, receipt and opening of tenders is to ensure fairness, equity and transparency in the procurement process.[35] All tenders solicited under open and selective procedures by entities must be received and opened under procedures and conditions guaranteeing the regularity of the openings.

Only tenders that conform to the essential requirements of the tender notice or documentation and are from a supplier who complies with the conditions for participation can be considered for an award.[36] Unless the entity decides in the public interest not to award the contract, it must award the contract to the tenderer who has been determined to be fully capable of undertaking the contract and whose tender is either the lowest tender or the tender which is determined to be the most advantageous in terms of the specific evaluation criteria set forth in the notices or tender documentation.[37] An entity that has received a tender abnormally lower than other tenders may enquire with the tenderer to ensure that it can comply with the conditions of participation and is capable of fulfilling the terms of the contract.[38] Awards must be made in accordance with the criteria and essential requirements specified in the tender documentation.[39] Tenders must normally be submitted in writing directly or by mail, but the use of telex, telegram or facsimile may be permitted.[40]

E. OTHER PROVISIONS FOR OPEN PROCUREMENT

1. Offsets

The use of offsets—measures to encourage local development or improve the balance-of-payments accounts by means of domestic content, licensing of technology, investment requirements, counter-trade or similar requirements—are explicitly prohibited by the GPA.[41] Notwithstanding this, developing countries may negotiate, at the time of their accession, conditions for the use of offsets provided

---

35 GPA, Article XIII:1 to 3.

36 GPA, Article XIII:4(a).

37 GPA, Article XIII:4(b).

38 GPA, Article XIII:4(a).

39 GPA, Article XIII:4(c).

40 GPA, Article XIII:1(a).

41 GPA, Article XVI:1.

these are used only for the qualification to participate in the procurement process and not as criteria for awarding contracts.[42]

2. Technical Specifications

Technical specifications must not be prepared, adopted or applied with a view to, or with the effect of, creating unnecessary obstacles to trade.[43] They must be stated, where appropriate, in terms of performance and be based on international standards, where they exist, or otherwise on national technical regulations, recognized national standards or building codes.[44]

3. Rules of Origin

Parties must apply the same rules of origin to services supplied for the purposes of government procurement under the GPA as those applied in the normal course of trade and at the time of the transaction in question to supplies of services from the same Parties.[45]

4. Transparency

Prior Information

Except in the case of limited tendering, Parties are required to publish an invitation to participate for all intended procurements in the appropriate publication indicated in their Appendix II.[46] The purpose is to inform all interested suppliers about the procurement opportunity and the relevant aspects of the procurement in question. Entities at the central government level in Annex 1 are required to use a notice of proposed procurement, whereas the other entities in Annexes 2 and 3 may use a notice of planned procurement.[47]

Each notice of proposed procurement must contain the following information with respect to services:[48]

- the nature and quantity of the services, including any options for further procurement;
- whether the procedure is open or selective or will involve negotiation;
- the date for starting delivery or completion of the supply of the services;

42 GPA, Article XVI:2.

43 GPA. Article VI:1.

44 GPA, Article VI:2.

45 GPA, Article IV:1.

46 GPA, Article IX:1.

47 GPA, Article IX:2 and 3.

48 GPA, Article IX:6.

- the address and final date for submitting an application to be invited to tender or for qualifying for the suppliers' lists or for receiving tenders, as well as the language or languages in which it must be submitted;
- the address of the entity concerned;
- any economic and technical requirements, financial guarantees and information;
- the amount or terms of payment of any sum payable for the tender documentation;

Each notice of planned procurement must contain as much of the above information as possible and must in any case contain the following:[49]

- a statement that interested suppliers should express their interest in the procurement to the entity;
- a contact point with the entity from which to obtain further information;
- the subject matter of the contract;
- the time-limits for submission of tenders or applications to be invited to tender;
- the addresses from which documents may be requested.

Post-award Information and Publication

No later than seventy-two days after the award of the contract, the awarding entity must publish a notice in the appropriate publication listed in Appendix II containing the following information:[50]

- the nature and quantity of the services included in the contract;
- the name and address of the awarding entity;
- the date of the award;
- the name and address of the winning supplier;
- the value of the contract; and
- the tendering procedure used.

Moreover, in response to a request from a supplier from a Party to the GPA, the procuring entity must provide the following:[51]

- an explanation of its procurement practices and procedures
- pertinent information concerning the reasons why the supplier's application to qualify was rejected, why its existing qualification to tender was brought to an end or why it was not selected; and

49 GPA, Article IX:7 and 8.

50 GPA, Article XVIII:1.

51 GPA, Article XVIII:2.

- to an unsuccessful tenderer, pertinent information concerning the reasons why its tender was not selected and the characteristics and relative advantages of the tender selected as well as the name of the winning tenderer.

However, entities are entitled to withhold certain information where its release would impede law enforcement or otherwise be contrary to the public interest or would prejudice the legitimate commercial interest of particular enterprises, or might prejudice fair competition between suppliers.[52]

The GPA permits the government of an unsuccessful tenderer that is Party to the Agreement to seek such additional information on the contract award as is necessary to ensure that the procurement was made fairly and impartially.[53]

Publication

There is a general requirement to publish laws, regulations, judicial decisions, administrative rulings of general application and any procedures regarding government procurement covered by the GPA in the appropriate publications listed in Appendix IV.[54] As a further element of transparency under the Agreement, each government must collect and provide to the other Parties on an annual basis statistics on its government procurements.[55]

F. SPECIAL RULES FOR DEVELOPING COUNTRIES

The GPA recognizes the development, financial and trade needs of developing countries, in particular least-developed countries, and allows special and differential treatment in order to meet their specific development objectives.[56] Development objectives of developing countries should be taken into account in the negotiation of coverage of procurement by entities in developed and developing countries.[57] There are also provisions on technical assistance,[58] establishment of information centers giving information on procurement practices and procedures in developed countries[59] and special treatment for least-developed countries.[60]

52 GPA, Article XVIII:4.

53 GPA, Article XIX:2.

54 GPA, Article XIX:1.

55 GPA, Article XIX:5.

56 GPA, Article V:1.

57 GPA, Article V:3, 5 and 6.

58 GPA, Article V:8 to 10.

59 GPA, Article V:11.

60 GPA, Article V:12 and 13.

G. ENFORCEMENT

Disputes between Parties under the GPA are subject to the procedures of the regular WTO dispute settlement procedure.[61] However, there are some special rules. The suspension of concessions or other obligations under the GPA as a result of disputes arising under the other WTO Agreements as well as the suspension of concessions or other obligations under any other WTO Agreement because of any dispute arising under the GPA (so-called "cross-retaliation") is prohibited.[62] Under the GPA, the DSB has the authority to authorize consultations among parties to the dispute regarding remedies when withdrawal of the violating measures is not possible.[63]

A new and unique feature of the enforcement procedures under the GPA is the mandatory requirements for the establishment of a domestic bid challenge system.[64] Suppliers who believe that a procurement has been handled inconsistently with the requirements of the GPA have a right of recourse to an independent domestic tribunal. Parties may confer the authority to hear challenges by suppliers on national courts or on an impartial and independent review body. In the event that a bid challenge is heard by a review body that does not have the status of a court of law, either its decisions must be subject to judicial review or it must follow the following procedures and criteria:[65]

- participants are heard before an opinion is given or a decision is made;
- participants may be represented and accompanied;
- participants have access to all proceedings;
- opinions or decisions are given in writing with a statement describing the basis for them;
- witness may be presented;
- documents are disclosed to the review body.

The challenge body must have the authority to order the correction of a breach of the GPA or compensation for any loss suffered by a supplier, but these may be limited to costs for tender preparation or protest. Pending the outcome of the challenge, the body must be able to order rapid interim measures, including the suspension of the procurement process, to correct breaches of the Agreement and to preserve commercial opportunities.[66]

61 GPA, Article XXII:1.

62 GPA, Article XXII:7.

63 GPA, Article XXII:3.

64 GPA, Article XX.

65 GPA, Article XX:6.

66 GPA, Article XX:7.

H. FURTHER NEGOTIATIONS

Further negotiations on the liberalization of the government procurement sector are taking place in the Working Party on Transparency in Government Procurement and the Working Party on GATS Rules. Ongoing discussions also take place within the plurilateral Committee on Government Procurement.

III. THE NORTH AMERICAN FREE TRADE AGREEMENT (AND THE US-CHILE AGREEMENT)

A. SCOPE OF THE AGREEMENT

Government procurement is regulated in NAFTA by Chapter 10.[67] It applies to all measures adopted by a Party relating to procurement:[68]

- by a federal government entity listed in Annex 1001.1a-1 or government enterprise listed in Annex 1001.1a-2;
- of all services and construction services except those excluded in Annexes 1001.1b-2 and 1001.1b-3, respectively;
- where the value of the contract is of a value not less than the specified threshold amount.

Chapter 10 requires that notices of invitation to participate in an intended procurement indicate whether the procurement in question is covered by NAFTA.[69]

It is up to the Parties to list which federal government entities and enterprises are to appear in the Annexes. Chapter 10 allows withdrawal of government enterprises on the ground that the entity is no longer subject to federal government control.[70] Any Party that objects to the withdrawal may have recourse to the NAFTA dispute settlement procedure.[71] Provincial and state government entities are not covered by Chapter 10, but it provides for future negotiations to include them in an Annex 1001.1a-3.[72]

The services to which Chapter 10 applies also depends on the Parties, who are free to exclude service sectors. For example, Canada excludes *inter alia* health and social services, financial services and dredging; the United States excludes *inter alia* utilities, transportation services and dredging; and Mexico excludes *inter alia* util-

67 Chapter 9 in the US-Chile Agreement, but there are quite significant differences between the two chapters. Neither Canada-Chile nor Mexico-Chile Agreements cover government procurement. Chile and Mexico have not subscribed to the GPA either.

68 NAFTA, Article 1001:1. *See also* Article 9.1:1 (USA).

69 NAFTA, Article 1010:8.

70 NAFTA, Article 1023:2. *See also* Article 9.14:3 (USA).

71 NAFTA, Article 1023:3. This procedure is described in Chapter Four, Section I.G.1.

72 NAFTA, Article 1024:2(b)(ii).

ities and financial services. Further restrictions are set out by the Parties in their General Notes in Annex 1001.2b.[73]

The thresholds for procurement contracts involving services generally are US$50,000 for federal government entities and US$250,000 for government enterprises.[74] For construction services, the thresholds are US$6.5 million for federal government entities and US$8 million for government enterprises. The valuation of contracts must take account of all forms of remuneration, including any premiums, fees, commissions and interest receivable.[75] The selection of the valuation method must not be used, nor may any procurement requirement be divided, with the intention of avoiding the application of Chapter 10.[76]

Chapter 10 authorizes the Parties to modify their coverage under Chapter 10 in exceptional circumstances.[77] Unless the changes are minor or of a purely formal nature, the modifying Party must propose appropriate compensatory adjustments to its coverage.[78] In the case of a dispute over these provisions, a Party may have recourse to the NAFTA dispute settlement procedure.[79]

Exceptions from the obligations of Chapter 10 exist for security reasons[80] and for measures to protect public morals, order or safety, human, animal or plant life or health or intellectual property, as long the measures are not applied in a manner that constitutes a means of arbitrary or unjustifiable discrimination.[81]

A Party may deny the benefits of Chapter 10 to a service supplier of another Party where the Party establishes that the service is being provided by an enterprise that is owned or controlled by persons of a non-Party and which has no substantial business activities in any Party.[82] It may also may deny the benefits of Chapter 10 to an enterprise controlled or owned by nationals of a non-Party if:[83]

- the denying Party does not maintain diplomatic relations with the non-Party; or
- the denying Party adopts or maintains measures with respect to the non-Party that prohibit transactions with the enterprise or that would be violated or circumvented if benefits under the Chapter were accorded to the enterprise.

73 NAFTA, Article 1001:2(b).

74 NAFTA, Article 1001:1(c). *See also* Annex 9.1 (USA).

75 NAFTA, Article 1002:3.

76 NAFTA, Articles 1001:4 and 1002:4. *See also* Article 9.1:5 (USA).

77 NAFTA, Article 1022:1. *See also* 9.14:1 (USA).

78 NAFTA, Article 1022:2(c) and 3. *See also* Article 9.14:1 and 2 (USA).

79 NAFTA, Article 1022:5.

80 NAFTA, Article 1018:1.

81 NAFTA, Article 1018:2. *See also* Article 9.16 (USA).

82 NAFTA, Article 1005:1.

83 NAFTA, Article 1005:2.

B. NON-DISCRIMINATION

In respect of a procurement covered by Chapter 10, the Parties are required to accord the service suppliers of another Party treatment no less favorable than that they accord to their own service suppliers or to the service suppliers of another Party.[84] Furthermore, no Party may treat a locally-established supplier less favorably than another locally-established supplier on the basis of the degree of foreign affiliation or ownership.[85] Nor may a Party discriminate against a locally-established supplier on the basis that the services supplied for a particular procurement are the services of another Party.[86]

C. TENDERING PROCEDURES

1. Introduction

Chapter 10 contains a number of detailed procedural obligations that procuring entities have to fulfill to ensure the effective application of the basic principle of non-discrimination.[87] It envisages the use of open, selective and limited tendering procedures, provided they are applied in a non-discriminatory manner and consistently with the provisions of the Agreement.[88] Open procedures are where all interested suppliers may submit a tender.[89]

2. Selective Tendering

Selective tendering procedures are where only those suppliers invited to do so by the entity may submit a tender.[90] To ensure optimum effective international competition, purchasing entities are required to invite tenders from the maximum number of domestic suppliers and suppliers of other Parties.[91] The process for qualifying suppliers must not discriminate between suppliers of the other Parties or between domestic suppliers and the suppliers of other Parties.[92] It must observe the following safeguards:[93]

- conditions for participation in tendering procedures must be published in adequate time to enable interested suppliers to complete the qualification procedures;

---

84 NAFTA, Article 1003:1. *See also* Article 9.2:1 (USA).

85 NAFTA, Article 1003:2(a). *See also* Article 9.2:2(a) (USA).

86 NAFTA, Article 1003:2(b). *See also* Article 9.2:2(c) (USA).

87 NAFTA, Articles 1008-1016.

88 NAFTA, Article 1008:1. *See also* Article 9.9:1 (USA).

89 NAFTA, Article 1025.

90 *Ibid.*

91 NAFTA, Article 1011:1.

92 NAFTA, Article 1009:1.

93 NAFTA, Article 1009:2 and 3.

- conditions for participation in tendering procedures by suppliers are limited to those which are essential to ensure the supplier's capability to fulfill the contract;
- the process of, and the time required for, qualifying suppliers must not be used in order to keep suppliers of other Parties off a suppliers' list or from being considered for a particular intended procurement;
- an entity shall recognize as qualified suppliers those of another Party that meet the conditions for participation in a particular procurement;
- suppliers of another Party that are not yet qualified but which request to participate in the procurement must be considered provided there is sufficient time for them to complete the qualification procedure;
- entities maintaining permanent lists of qualified suppliers must ensure that suppliers may apply for qualification at any time and can be included in the list within a reasonable time;
- any supplier having requested to become a qualified supplier is advised by the entities concerned of their decision in this regard;
- each Party must ensure that each entity follows a single qualification procedure, where possible, and that efforts are made to minimize differences in qualification procedures between entities.

Once a year the entities using the selective tendering method are required to publish, in a publication indicated in Annex 1010.1, their lists of qualified suppliers, and to specify the period of validity of those lists and the conditions that need to be met for the inclusion of interested suppliers in the lists.[94]

3. Limited Tendering

Limited tendering procedures are where the entity contacts the potential suppliers individually.[95] The Agreement restricts the situations in which this method can be used in the case of services to the following:[96]

- absence of valid tenders in response to an open or selective tender;
- where, for reasons connected with the protection of exclusive rights, or in the absence of competition for technical reasons, the services can only be supplied by a particular supplier;
- for reasons of extreme urgency brought about by events unforeseeable by the entity;
- for additional services by the original supplier
- where an entity procures a first service that is developed at its request;

94 NAFTA, Article 1010:6.

95 NAFTA, Article 1025.

96 NAFTA, Article 1016:2. *See also* Article 9.9:2 (USA).

- in the case of contracts awarded to the winner of an architectural design contest;
- where an entity needs to procure consulting services regarding matters of a confidential nature.

Limited tendering may not in any situation be used to avoid maximum possible competition or in a manner that infringes the national treatment or MFN principles.[97]

Entities may hold negotiations with suppliers making tenders, provided this is indicated in the initial tender notice or if it appears from the tender evaluation that no one tender is obviously the most advantageous.[98] The negotiations must be used primarily to identify the strengths and weaknesses in tenders[99] and are subject to the following safeguards to ensure that such negotiations do not discriminate between suppliers:[100]

- any elimination of participants is carried out in accordance with the criteria set out in the notices and tender documents;
- all modifications to the criteria and technical requirements are transmitted in writing to all remaining participants;
- all remaining participants are afforded an opportunity to submit new or amended submissions;
- all remaining participants are permitted to submit final tenders in accordance with a common deadline.

4. Deadlines

Chapter 10 prescribes certain minimum deadlines for the preparation, submission and receipt of tenders.[101] These deadlines must provide adequate time to allow suppliers of another Party to prepare and submit tenders before the closing of the tendering procedures.[102] In general, the minimum time limit for receipt of tenders is forty days from the date of publication of an invitation to tender.[103] The minimum time-limit may be reduced to twenty-four or even ten days in certain well-defined circumstances.[104]

97 NAFTA, Article 1016:1.

98 NAFTA, Article 1014:1.

99 NAFTA, Article 1014:2.

100 NAFTA, Article 1014:4.

101 NAFTA, Article 1012. *See also* Article 9.5:1 (USA).

102 NAFTA, Article 1012:1(a). *See also* Article 9.5:1(a) (USA).

103 NAFTA, Article 1012:2. *See also* Article 9.5:2 (USA).

104 NAFTA, Article 1012:3. *See also* Article 9.5:3 (USA).

5. Tender Documentation

In the tender documentation, the purchasing entity is required to give all necessary information related to the procurement in question to enable potential suppliers to submit responsive tenders. This includes the information required to be published in tender notices[105] as well as the following:

- the address of the entity to which tenders should be sent;
- the address to which supplementary information should be sent;
- the language or languages in which the tender should be submitted;
- the closing date and time for receipt of tenders;
- the persons authorized to be present at the opening of tenders, as well as the date, time and place of the opening;
- any economic and technical requirements, financial guarantees and information and documents required from the suppliers;
- a complete description of the services required as well as any requirements to be fulfilled;
- the criteria for awarding the contract;
- the terms of payment;
- other terms and conditions.

6. Award of Contracts

The objective of the procedural rules for submission, receipt and opening of tenders is to ensure fairness, equity and transparency in the procurement process.[106] All tenders solicited under open and selective procedures by entities must be received and opened under procedures and conditions guaranteeing the regularity of the openings.

Only tenders that conform to the essential requirements of the tender notice or documentation and are from a supplier who complies with the conditions for participation can be considered for an award.[107] Unless the entity decides in the public interest not to award the contract, it must award the contract to the tenderer who has been determined to be fully capable of undertaking the contract and whose tender is either the lowest tender or the tender that is determined to be the most advantageous in terms of the specific evaluation criteria set forth in the notices or tender documentation.[108] An entity that has received a tender abnormally lower than other tenders may enquire with the tenderer to ensure that it

105 *See infra* in the text.

106 NAFTA, Article 1015:1 to 3.

107 NAFTA, Article 1015:4(a).

108 NAFTA, Article 1015:4(c): *See also* Article 9.10:2 (USA).

can comply with the conditions of participation and is capable of fulfilling the terms of the contract.[109] Awards must be made in accordance with the criteria and essential requirements specified in the tender documentation.[110] No entity of a Party may condition the award of a contract on the fact that the supplier has previously been awarded a contract by an entity of the Party or has previous work experience in the territory of that Party.[111] Tenders must normally be submitted in writing directly or by mail,[112] but the use of telex, telegram or facsimile may be permitted.[113]

D. OTHER PROVISIONS FOR OPEN PROCUREMENT

1. Offsets

The use of offsets—measures to encourage local development or improve the balance-of-payments accounts by means of domestic content, licensing of technology, investment requirements, counter-trade or similar requirements—are explicitly prohibited by NAFTA.[114]

2. Technical Specifications

Technical specifications must not be prepared, adopted or applied with a view to, or with the effect of, creating unnecessary obstacles to trade.[115] They must be stated, where appropriate, in terms of performance and be based on international standards, where they exist, or otherwise on national technical regulations, recognized national standards or building codes.[116]

3. Transparency

Prior Information

Except in the case of limited tendering, Parties are required to publish an invitation to participate for all intended procurements in the appropriate publication indicated in Annex 1010.1 to Chapter 10.[117] The purpose is to inform all interested suppliers about the procurement opportunity and the relevant aspects of the procurement in question. The invitation takes the form of a notice of

---

109 NAFTA, Article 1015:4(b).

110 NAFTA, Article 1015(4)(d).

111 NAFTA, Article 1015:5.

112 NAFTA, Article 1015:1(a).

113 NAFTA 1015:1(b).

114 NAFTA, Article 1006. *See also* Article 9.2:4 (USA).

115 NAFTA, Article 1007:1. *See also* Article 9.7:1 (USA).

116 NAFTA, Article 1007:2. *See also* Article 9.7:2 (USA).

117 NAFTA, Article 1010:1. *See also* Article 9.4:1 (USA).

proposed procurement and must contain the following information with respect to services:[118]

- the nature and quantity of the services, including any options for further procurement;
- whether the procedure is open or selective or will involve negotiation;
- the date for starting delivery or completion of the supply of the services;
- the address and final date for submitting an application to be invited to tender or for qualifying for the suppliers' lists, as well as the language or languages in which it must be submitted;
- the address and final date for submitting tenders as well as the language or languages in which they must be submitted;
- the address of the entity concerned;
- any economic and technical requirements, financial guarantees and information and documents required from the suppliers;
- the amount or terms of payment of any sum payable for the tender documentation;

Government enterprises may use as an invitation to participate a notice of planned procurement that must contain as much of the above information as possible and must in any case contain the following:[119]

- a statement that interested suppliers should express their interest in the procurement to the entity;
- a contact point within the entity from which to obtain further information;
- the subject matter of the procurement;
- the time-limits for the receipt of tenders or applications to be invited to tender;
- the address from which documents may be requested.

Post-award Information and Publication

No later than seventy-two days after the award of the contract, the awarding entity must publish a notice in the appropriate publication listed in Annex 1010.1 to Chapter 10 containing the following information:[120]

- the nature and quantity of the services included in the contract;
- the name and address of the awarding entity;
- the date of the award;

118 NAFTA, Article 1010:2. *See also* Article 9.4:2 (USA).

119 NAFTA, Article 1010:3.

120 NAFTA, Article 1015:7. *See also* Article 9.11:2 (USA).

- the name and address of the winning supplier;
- the value of the contract; and
- the tendering procedure used.

Moreover, in response to a request from suppliers participating in the tendering procedure, an entity must inform them of decisions on contract awards and, in the case of an unsuccessful tenderer, provide pertinent information concerning the reasons why its tender was not selected and the relevant characteristics and advantages of the tender selected as well as the name of the winning tenderer.[121]

However, entities are entitled to withhold certain information where its release would impede law enforcement or otherwise be contrary to the public interest or would prejudice the legitimate commercial interest of a particular person or might prejudice fair competition between suppliers.[122]

Chapter 10 permits a Party to seek such additional information on the award of a contract as may be necessary to determine whether the procurement was made fairly and impartially.[123]

Publication

There is a general requirement to publish laws, regulations, judicial decisions, administrative rulings of general application and any procedures regarding government procurement covered by Chapter 10 in the appropriate publications listed in Annex 1010.1.[124] As a further element of transparency, each Party must collect and provide to the other Parties on an annual basis statistics on its government procurements.[125]

E. ENFORCEMENT

Disputes between Parties with respect to the government procurement rules in Chapter 10 are subject to the general dispute settlement procedures of NAFTA.[126] However, Chapter 10 also contains bid challenge procedures for procurements covered by the Chapter. The rules are as follows:[127]

- suppliers must be allowed to submit bid challenges concerning any aspect of the procurement process;

121 NAFTA, Article 1015:6.

122 NAFTA, Article 1015:8.

123 NAFTA, Article 1019:3.

124 NAFTA, Article 1019:1.

125 NAFTA, Article 1019:7.

126 These are discussed in Chapter Four, Section I.G.1.

127 NAFTA, Article 1017:1. *See also* Article 9.13 (USA).

- entities must accord fair and timely consideration of any complaint concerning procurements covered by Chapter 10;
- whatever the outcome of the complaint procedure, the supplier must be allowed to initiate a bid challenge or seek any other relief;
- a Party may limit the period within which a bid challenge may be initiated, but this period may not be less than ten working days from the time when the basis of the complaint became known or should have become known to the supplier;
- a reviewing authority must be established with no substantial interest in the matter to deal with bid challenges expeditiously;
- in investigating the challenge, the reviewing authority must be able to delay the award pending resolution of the challenge, except in cases of urgency or where the delay would be contrary to the public interest;
- the reviewing authority must be able to issue a recommendation to resolve the challenge, which may include a directive to re-evaluate offers or terminate or re-compete the contract;
- entities must normally follow the recommendation of the reviewing authority;
- the reviewing authority must provide its findings and recommendations with respect to bid challenges in writing and in a timely manner.

The Parties also have certain rights regarding bid challenges. They may encourage a supplier to seek a resolution of any complaint before initiating a bid challenge;[128] they may require a supplier to notify the entity upon initiating the bid challenge;[129] and they may require their reviewing authorities to limit their considerations to the challenge itself.[130]

F. FURTHER NEGOTIATIONS

Chapter 10 provides for negotiations to take place on the further liberalization of government procurement, in particular with respect to adding government enterprises to those already listed in Annex 1001.1a-2, thus making the Chapter applicable to provincial and state governments, and reviewing thresholds.[131]

128 NAFTA, Article 1017:1(b).

129 NAFTA, Article 1017:1(e).

130 NAFTA, Article 1017:1(i).

131 NAFTA, Article 1024:1 and 2. *See also* Article 9.19 (USA).

IV. THE EUROPEAN UNION (AND THE EEA AGREEMENT)[132]

A. THE DEVELOPMENT OF THE GOVERNMENT PROCUREMENT REGIME OF THE EUROPEAN UNION

The EC and EEA Treaties do not contain special provisions on government procurement of services, but this sector falls within the general provisions of the Treaties on the freedom to provide services.[133] These provisions prohibit, *inter alia*, discrimination by governments against services and service providers from other Member States.

However, as they do not explicitly regulate government procurement of services, the EU has adopted a number of specific directives on this matter. These apply as well to the Contracting Parties to the EEA Agreement (Iceland, Liechtenstein and Norway).[134]

Council Directive 71/304[135] was the first of these directives. It prohibits discriminatory practices in public works contracts with respect to a certain number of construction-type services, which are listed in an Annex. However, prohibiting discriminatory conduct does not effectively remove trade barriers in government procurement. This is not only because of the difficulties of proving discriminatory treatment, but also for structural reasons, such as inefficient sourcing practices or the use of different standards for products and services in different Member States. Hence, there is also a need for specific directives on the coordination of government procurement.

Thus, Council Directive 71/304 was accompanied by Council Directive 71/305,[136] which embodies two main principles reflecting the two problems mentioned above: the difficulties of proving discrimination, and the absence of concrete opportunities for non-domestic providers. First, it seeks to ensure that no discrimination occurs in award procedures by regulating the award procedure so that it is more difficult to hide discrimination. Secondly, the Directive requires certain positive steps that improve access to public contracts for providers from outside the awarding Member State, such as the obligation to advertise contracts in the *Official Journal of the European Union* (OJ). Unfortunately, it had a marginal impact, if any at all, in opening up the European government procurement market to ser-

---

132 This material is based on material provided by Matthias Öhler Friedens, Tassul and Partners (Vienna, Austria) and originally published in *International Public Procurement* (ed. D. and C. Campbell).

133 EC Treaty, Articles 49-55. *See* also EEA Agreement, Articles 36 to 41.

134 EEA Agreement, Article 7 and Annex XVI.

135 Council Directive 71/304 concerning the abolition of restrictions on freedom to provide services in respect of public works contracts and on the award of public works contracts to contractors acting through agencies or branches (OJ L185/71).

136 Council Directive 71/305 concerning coordination of procedures for the award of public works contracts ("Public Works Directive") (OJ L185/71). This Directive is no longer in force.

vices. As a consequence, the 1985 White Paper on the single market highlighted government procurement as one of the key areas for action and prompted major legislative initiatives.

First, Directive 71/305 on public works was amended and strengthened.[137] Secondly, Council Directive 90/531[138] extended the government procurement rules to four important industrial sectors—water, transport, energy and telecommunications—that had been excluded from the scope of the EU's government procurement rules, but this did not include services. Finally, Council Directive 92/50[139] extended the rules of government procurement to services in general. In addition to the regulation of the award procedures, specific directives were also adopted to deal with enforcement of the rules. These were Council Directive 89/665,[140] which deals with the public works sector and services generally, and Council Directive 92/13, which deals with the utilities sector.

In 1993, Council Directive 93/37[141] was adopted on public works contracts that consolidated all existing rules into a single text. At the same time, Council Directive 90/531 was replaced by Council Directive 93/38,[142] which brought services within the utilities regime. This completed the EU rules on the public procurement of services. However, on January 31, 2006, Directives 93/37 on public works contracts and 92/50 on public service contracts will be replaced by EP/Council Directive 04/18[143] and Directive 93/38 on the utilities sector by EP/Council Directive 04/17.[144] These new directives are not confined to amendments that are essential to harmonize the EU rules with the GPA regime but go further, in particular by applying the more stringent obligations that are imposed on some entities under the GPA to all entities covered by the EU regime.

---

137 Council Directive 89/440 amending Directive 71/305 concerning coordination of procedures for the award of public works contracts (OJ L210/89). This Directive is no longer in force.

138 Council Directive 90/531 on the procurement procedures of entities operating in the water, energy, transport and telecommunications sectors, OJ L297/90.

139 Council Directive 92/50 relating to the coordination of procedures for the award of public service contracts ("Services Directive") (OJ L209/92).

140 Council Directive 89/665 on the coordination of the laws, regulations and administrative provisions relating to the application of review procedures to the award of public supply and public works contracts (OJ L396/89), as amended by Directive 92/50 (OJ L209/92).

141 Council Directive 93/37 concerning the coordination of procedures for the award of public works contracts (OJ L199/93), as amended by Directive 97/52 (OJ L328/97).

142 Council Directive 93/38 coordinating the procurement procedures of entities operating in the water, energy, transport and telecommunications sectors (OJ L199/93), as amended by Directives 98/4 (OJ L101/98) and 01/78 (OJ L285/01).

143 EP/Council Directive 04/18 on the coordination of procedures for the award of public works contracts, public supply contracts and public service contracts (OJ L134/04), as amended by Regulation 1874/04 (OJ L326/04).

144 EP/Council Directive 04/17 coordinating the procurement procedures of entities operating in the water, energy, transport and postal services sectors (OJ L134/04), as amended by Regulation 1874/04 (OJ L326/04).

B. THE EC Treaty

Certain general principles embodied in the EC Treaty are of significance for procurement. These supplement the rules in the directives and also apply to contracts outside the scope of directives, such as those falling under the thresholds. The most significant provisions are found in Articles 43 and 49.[145]

Article 43 of the EC Treaty guarantees the right of EU nationals and firms to set up a business in other Member States. Article 49 of the EC Treaty is concerned with the right to provide services in other Member States without necessarily setting up a business there. Similar rules apply to the two provisions. These rules apply to individuals who are nationals of Member States and also to EU companies, i.e. companies that are set up under the law of a Member State and which have their registered office, central administration or principal place of business in the EU.[146] Article 43 of the EC Treaty forbids government measures that hinder these individuals and companies from establishing themselves in other Member States, or which hinder their activities once they are established.

Article 49 of the EC Treaty is concerned with the freedom to provide services. It seeks to open up markets for individuals established in one Member State who seek to provide services in another Member State on a temporary basis. It covers measures that limit contracts to providers who are nationals of, or are established in, that Member State or which give such persons any form of preference, such as price preferences or preferential treatment in deciding whom to invite to tender. In *Commission v. Italy,*[147] the Court of Justice held contrary to Article 49 of the EC Treaty Italian legislation requiring contractors for certain public works to reserve a proportion of the works for subcontractors who had their registered office in the region of the works. Also forbidden are measures that are indistinctly applicable but have the effect of favoring national firms. This is illustrated by *Re Data Processing.*[148] It concerned Italian legislation limiting participation in contracts for certain data processing systems to firms whose shares are held in Italian public ownership. Although, in theory, the Italian government might own non-Italian firms, in practice all data processing firms in Italian public ownership at that time were Italian.

Finally, Article 12 of the EC Treaty[149] provides that within the scope of application of the EC Treaty, any discrimination on grounds of nationality is prohibited.

145 Arrowsmith, "The Application of the European Community Treaty Rules to Public and Utilities Procurement," [1995] 6 *Public Procurement Law Review,* at p. 225.

146 EC Treaty, Article 58, 1st para.

147 360/89, [1992] ECR I-3401.

148 C-3/88, [1989] ECR 4035.

149 EEA Agreement, Article 4.

However, discriminatory procurement of services is generally covered by Articles 43 and 49 of the EC Treaty, so that Article 12 will not be invoked.[150]

C. EU SECONDARY LEGISLATION

1. Government Procurement Contracts Award Procedure: the Works and Services Directives

Scope of the Public Sector Procurement Directives

Directive 93/37 on public works ("Works Directive") and Directive 92/50 on public services ("Services Directive") apply to the procurement of contracting authorities. The Directives define contracting authorities as the state, regional or local authorities and bodies governed by public law, as well as associations formed by one or several of such authorities or bodies governed by public law.[151]

A "body governed by public law" means any body:

- established for the specific purpose of meeting needs in the general interest, not having an industrial or commercial character;
- having legal personality; and
- financed, for the most part, by the state or regional or local authorities or other bodies governed by public law or subject to management supervision by those bodies, or having an administrative, managerial or supervisory board, more than half of whose members are appointed by the state, regional or local authorities or by other bodies governed by public law.

Bodies considered to fall within this category are listed in Annex I to the Works Directive, and the Services Directive refers to this Annex. The list in this Annex is not exhaustive for it merely serves as an interpretation guideline.

Thus, the government procurement rules apply not merely to traditional forms of government, but to the whole variety of bodies set up in modern states to assist in the work of government. In *Beentjes*[152] the Court of Justice held that a local committee for land consolidation fell within the definition of the term "state." This committee was a body with no legal personality of its own whose functions and composition were governed by legislation and its members appointed by the provincial administration. It was bound to apply rules laid down by a central committee established by a royal decree whose members were appointed by the Crown.

The Court held that the term "state" must be interpreted in functional terms since the aim of the Works Directive would be jeopardized if it were held to be inapplicable solely because the entity concerned is not formally a part of the state administration.

---

150 In government procurement cases, the Court of Justice only once referred to this provision in *Beentjes,* 31/87, [1988] ECR 4635 at para. 30.

151 Directives 93/37, 92/50 and 93/36, Articles 1(b). *See* Directive 04/18, Article 1.

152 31/87, [1988] ECR 4635; confirmed in C-247/89, *Commission v. Portugal* [1991] ECR I-3659.

As well as applying to contracting authorities, the Works and Services Directives regulate certain contracts that are subsidized by more than 50% by contracting authorities, even though the purchaser is a private entity.[153] In addition, this applies to certain service contracts in connection with a works contract.[154]

Contracts Covered

Works contracts are contracts for pecuniary interest concluded in writing between a contractor and a contracting authority that have as their object:[155]

- either the execution, or both the execution and design, of works related to one of the activities referred to in Annex II of the Works Directive;
- a work defined as the outcome of building or civil engineering that, taken as a whole, is sufficient in itself to fulfill an economic and technical function; or
- the execution, by whatever means, of the work corresponding to the requirements specified by the contracting authority.

A service contract is a contract for non-construction services. The Services Directive does not define service contracts in a positive way but covers all contracts that are not works or supply contracts and are not explicitly excluded, such as contracts for the acquisition of land and certain telecommunications and financial services.[156] Services are divided into "priority" services, which are subject to the full rules under the Directive, and "non-priority" services, which are subject only to the rules on technical specifications, post-award notices and certain obligations on the provision of statistics ("two-tier-application").[157]

Priority services are *inter alia* consulting services, advertising services, transport services, maintenance and repair services, engineering services, financial services and computer services. They are listed in Annex 1A of the Directive. All other services are "non-priority" services.[158] They have been selected on the basis of the potential scope for cross-border trade, the potential savings, and the availability of information on the service.

The Directives state that a contract for both products and services is a supply contract if the value of the consideration attributable to the supplies is greater than that for the services; otherwise it is a service contract.[159] There are no express provisions on the boundary between works/service and works/supply contracts. This

153 Works Directive, Article 2.

154 Services Directive, Article 3. *See* Directive 04/18, Article 2.

155 Works Directive, Article 1(a) and (c). *See* Directive 04/18, Article 1.

156 Services Directive, *see* Article 1(a). *See* Directive 04/18, Article 1.

157 Council Directive 93/38, Article 8.

158 Annex 1B.

159 Services Directive, Article 2; Council Directive 93/36 coordinating procedures for the award of public supply contracts (OJ L199/93), as amended by Directives 97/52 (OJ L328/97) and 01/78 (OJ L285/01), Article 1(a). *See* Directive 04/18, Article 1.

is an important issue since the threshold for the Works Directive is much higher than that for the Services Directive.

As regards the works/services boundary, the Court of Justice has ruled that a contract involving both works and services is not a works contract where the works are incidental to the services.[160] However, it did not define the term "incidental." This could look either to the main purpose of the contract or at whether the works or services are of greater value. The Court has not considered the works/supply division yet; again, either the "main purpose" or the "greater value test" could be applied.

Concession Contracts

A concession is a contract of the same type as the public contracts defined in the Directives except that the consideration for the works to be carried out consists either solely in the right to exploit the construction or this right together with a payment.[161] The concessionaire accepts the financial risk of providing a public service, in the broadest sense, in return for the chance of making a profit through the exploitation of that service.

The award of works concessions by a contracting authority is not subject to the same rules as the award of a works contract, but only to an obligation to advertise the concession in the *Official Journal* and to give at least fifty-two days for firms to respond.[162] In addition, the Works Directive places obligations on a party holding a works concession when awarding its own works contracts (sub-contracts) for the purpose of the concession, even though the concessionaire is not itself a contracting authority.

In contrast to the Works Directive, concessions are not explicitly mentioned in the Services Directive. A provision on services concessions was originally included in the proposed Directive but was later removed.[163] Hence, it is generally assumed that service concessions are not covered.[164]

Design Contests

The Services Directive contains special rules on design contests.[165] Design contests are procedures that provide the contracting entity with a plan or design that is selected by a jury on the basis of a competition, with or without the award of prizes. Such contests are held mainly in the fields of area or town planning, architecture and civil engineering or data processing. These contests may be part of a

---

160 *Gestión Hotelera Internacional*, C-331/92, [1994] ECR I-1929.

161 Works Directive, Article 1(d). *See* Directive 04/18, Article 1.

162 Works Directive, Article 3. *See* Directive 04/18, Articles 60, 62 and 63.

163 COM (90) 372 of September 6, 1990, at note 69.

164 Trepte, *Government Procurement in the European Community* (1993), at p. 92.

165 Services Directive, Article 13. *See* Directive 04/18, Articles 66. 67 and 72 to 74.

procedure that leads to the award of a service contract or may be held independently under a separate procedure.

Thresholds

The Works and Services Directives only apply to contracts above certain thresholds, but it should be borne in mind that contracts below the thresholds are still subject to the provisions of the EC Treaty. The threshold values have been set at levels that are intended to reflect those contracts which are likely to attract bidders from far afield. Contracts falling below these thresholds are considered to attract local competition only so that it is inappropriate to apply the procurement rules. The Directives generally apply only to contracts with an estimated value greater than, or equal to, the following amounts net of value-added tax:

- public works contracts—5,923,000 Euros;[166]
- public service contracts 154,000 Euros or 236,000 Euros.[167]

The Directives expressly prohibit authorities from splitting up purchases to bring the value of the contracts below the threshold, and prohibit them from using to the same end special methods of calculating the value of the contracts. They further contain rules requiring aggregation of certain contracts.

Excluded Contracts

The Works and Services Directives do not cover contracts connected with utilities activities; Council Directive 93/38 (the "Utilities Directive") exclusively covers such contracts.[168]

The Directives also contain certain exemptions on grounds of secrecy and security, either military or non-military. There are further exemptions under certain conditions for contracts connected with joint projects with certain non-Member States, *i.e.*, those by international organizations made pursuant to the procedures of that organization, such as the United Nations, and those made pursuant to international agreements on the stationing of troops.[169]

According to Article 6[170] of the Utilities Directive, service contracts are exempt where services are provided by another contracting authority with an exclusive right to provide them or an exclusive right necessary for their provision.

166 This is the new figure in Directive 04/18, Article 7(c).

167 This is the new figure in Directive 04/18, Article 7(a) and (b).

168 On the scope of the Utilities Directive, *see infra* in the text.

169 Works Directive, Article 5; Services Directive, Article 12. *See* Directive 04/18, Articles 15 and 41.

170 *See* Directive 04/17, Article 20(1).

Non-Discrimination and Equality of Treatment

Article 12 of the EC Treaty sets out one of the fundamental principles of the EU by providing for the prohibition of any discrimination on grounds of nationality.

Only the Services Directive contains in Article 3(2)[171] a general provision that there shall be no discrimination between providers. However, the Court of Justice has ruled in *Storebaelt*[172] that a general principle of equality of treatment is implied into the Works Directive as well.

Types of Procedures

Contracts that come within the Works and Services Directives must generally be awarded in accordance with one of the three procedures:

- open procedure, whereby all interested contractors or service providers may submit tenders;
- restricted procedure, whereby only those contractors or service providers invited by the contracting authority may submit tenders; and
- negotiated procedure, whereby contracting authorities consult contractors or service providers of their choice and negotiate the terms of the contract with one or more of them.

The procedures to be followed in each case are set out in the Directives and must be strictly followed. According to the Works and Services Directives, the contracting authority is free to choose between the open or restricted procedure.[173] Only in the exceptional cases listed in the Directives may an authority award a contract by the negotiated procedure. While the negotiated procedure still requires the contract award to be made on the basis of objective commercial criteria, it does not provide the same guarantees for monitoring objectivity as formal tendering and is hence confined to a few cases. The grounds for its use are narrowly construed,[174] and the burden is on the contracting authority to show that these grounds are met.[175]

Two different versions of the negotiated procedure exist: the negotiated procedure without advertisements and the negotiated procedure with advertisements. The ne-

---

171 *See* Directive 04/18, Article 3.

172 C 243/89, [1993] ECR I-3353.

173 Works Directive, Article 7; Services Directive, Article 11. *See* Directive 04/18, Article 28.

174 *Commission v. Italy*, 199/85, [1987] ECR 1039; *Commission v. Spain*, C-71/92 [1993] ECR I-5329; *Commission v. Spain*, C-328/92 [1994] ECR I-1569; *Commission v. Italy*, C-57/94, [1995] ECR I-1249.

175 *Commission v. Spain*, C-328/92, [1994] ECR I-1569; *Commission v. Italy*, C-57/94 [1995] ECR I-1249.

gotiated procedure without advertisements may be used under both Directives only where:[176]

- the works or services can be provided only by one particular provider for technical or artistic reasons, or reasons connected with exclusive rights (such as intellectual property rights);
- it is strictly necessary for reasons of extreme urgency that were unforeseeable and cannot be attributed to the contracting authority;
- an open or restricted procedure has failed to produce a satisfactory result; or
- in certain cases where extra work is awarded to an existing contracting partner.

Notices

Under both Directives, the contracting authorities must publish indicative notices in the *Official Journal* giving information on the contracts to be awarded to make award procedures more transparent. Prior to the award of the contract, two forms of indicative notices exist.

Prior Information on Procurement Programs

These are additional to the contract notices published at the start of each award procedure. They give advance warning of award procedures, so that firms can prepare to participate. Under the Works Directive, a notice must be published in the *Official Journal* as soon as possible after the decision approving the planning of any proposed works contract.[177] Under the Services Directive, a notice must be published at the beginning of each budgetary year on the services expected to be purchased in the next twelve months whenever the total estimated value of procurement in one of the categories of priority services listed in the Annex of the Services Directive is equal to or greater than 750,000 Euros.[178]

Publication of Tender Notices

Contracting authorities that wish to award a public works or service contract must make known their intention by means of a notice in the *Official Journal* drawn up in accordance with the models annexed to the Directives, thus ensuring that information is available throughout Europe. Notices may not be published in the national press prior to their dispatch to the *Official Journal,* nor may national notices contain additional information.

176 Works Directive, Article 7, Services Directive, Article 11. *See* Directive 04/18, Article 28.

177 Works Directive, Article 11. *See* Directive 04/18, Article 35.

178 Services Directive, Article 15 *See* Directive 04/18, Article 35.

Time Limits

Under the open procedure any interested firm may bid. The contract documents must be sent to firms requesting them within six days of receipt of the request.[179] Firms must generally be given fifty-two days to bid, calculated from the date of dispatch of the contract notice, although for works and services it may be reduced to thirty-six days when an indicative notice referring to the contract has been published. The notice must be published by the Office of Official Publications of the European Union within twelve days of dispatch.

Under the restricted procedure,[180] firms must contact the purchaser to express interest. Generally, firms must be given thirty-seven days to respond after dispatch of the notice, which again must generally be published within twelve days. When these time limits are impracticable for reasons of urgency, purchasers may invoke an accelerated version of the procedure under which the thirty-seven-day period becomes a period of not less than fifteen days.[181] Following the dispatch of invitations, firms must be given forty days to bid; under the accelerated procedure, this may not be less than ten days.

As to the negotiated procedure with advertisement, firms must contact the purchaser to express interest and must be given thirty-seven days to respond or not less than fifteen days when the thirty-seven-day-period is impracticable for reasons of urgency. Once invitations have been issued, the authority will simply negotiate with the invitees that it chooses. This may, or may not, involve some form of tendering.

Qualification of Tenderers

The term "qualification" is used here to refer to the process of deciding which firms are eligible to participate in a bidding competition. The Directives permit contracting authorities to exclude firms only on certain grounds set out in the Directives and also control the process of exclusion. They significantly limit an authority's discretion in this area.

Financial and Economic Standing

Firms may be excluded because they lack financial and economic standing, which refers broadly to whether firms have adequate resources to perform the contract alongside their other commitments. The Directives list certain evidence that

179 Works Directive, Article 12, Services Directive, Article 18. *See* Directive 04/18, Article 38.

180 Works Directive, Article 13, Services Directive, Article 19. *See* Directive 04/18, Articles 39, 40 and 42.

181 Works Directive, Article 14, Services Directive, Article 20. In cases of extreme urgency purchasers may, under certain conditions, use the negotiated procedure as explained above. *See* Directive 04/18, Articles 38 to 40.

authorities may demand, such as banker's statements or statements of turnover in the previous three financial years.[182]

However, for matters relevant to financial and economic standing that cannot be deduced from this evidence, contracting authorities may call upon other evidence.[183] If firms cannot produce the particular evidence specified by the authority, whether or not it is listed in the Directives, they may always offer other appropriate evidence instead.

It is for the contracting authority to determine the standards that firms must meet; they must be set out in the contract notice of the tender invitation.

Technical Capacity and Capability

Firms may further be excluded when they lack the technical capacity to perform. The Directives list certain evidence that authorities may demand as means of proof of standing, such as a statement of the tools, plants and technical equipment available and the list of works carried out over the last five years.[184] In contrast with the position for financial standing, contracting authorities may not demand evidence other than that listed in the Directives.[185] Only those criteria that can be deduced from the listed evidence may be taken into account.

As with financial and economic standing, the standards for qualification, such as the amount and type of equipment needed, are for the contracting authority to decide.

Enrolment in Trade and Professional Registers and Possession of Licenses

Contracting authorities may require firms to be registered in certain trade or professional registers in the Member State of establishment.[186]

Other Grounds for Exclusion

The Directives provide for other grounds for exclusion of firms, such as bankruptcy or being subject to a winding up order.[187] For some cases, there are rules on the evidence that must be accepted as proof that these grounds are not met.

Technical Specifications

The Directives contain detailed rules on the use of technical specifications.[188] Generally, contracting authorities are required to use relevant European standards, i.e. national standards implementing European standards such as the standards

182 Works Directive, Article 26, Services Directive, Article 31. *See* Directive 04/18, Article 47.

183 27-29/86, *CEI and Bellini* [1987] ECR 3347.

184 Works Directive, Article 27, Services Directive, Article 32. *See* Directive 04/18, Article 48.

185 Case 76/81 *Transporoute* [1982] ECR 417; C-71/92, *Commission v. Spain* [1993] ECR I-5923.

186 Works Directive, Article 25, Services Directive, Article 30. *See* Directive 04/18, Article 46.

187 Works Directive, Article 24, Services Directive, Article 29. *See* Directive 04/18, Article 45.

188 Works Directive, Article 10, Services Directive, Article 14. *See* Directive 04/18, Article 23.

drawn up by CEN, CENELEC and ETSI. However, the obligation to use European standards is subject to certain exemptions. The most significant is where their use would involve incompatibility with existing equipment or disproportionate cost. Where no European standards exist, authorities are obliged to make reference to any relevant national specifications complying with the basic requirements of any applicable harmonizing directive.[189]

In all other cases, the Directives state that authorities may use certain other standards, namely national technical specifications relating to design and method of calculation and execution of works, national standards implementing international standards (such as those of the ESO) and any other standards, which could include those of third country institutions such as ANSI in the United States.

The Directives explicitly prohibit the use of technical specifications that refer to inputs of a specific make or origin or to a particular process where this has the effect of favoring or eliminating particular firms.

In addition to the Directives, the basic rules underlying the EC Treaty have an important impact in ensuring that the way in which contract specifications are drafted does not restrict competition. These rules apply to contracts both above and below the thresholds.[190]

Terms and Conditions by Authority and Tenderer

The Directives only govern the procedure for the award of public contracts; they do not, however, contain any rules on how to implement a public contract once it has been awarded. However, they state that authorities may give information in the contract documents on where providers may obtain information on the relevant employment protection provisions and working conditions that are applicable to the contract. They may indeed be required by the Member State to do so. In this case, authorities must request participants to indicate that these have been taken into account in drawing up bids.

Evaluation of Bids and Award of the Contract

Once bids have been received, the contract must be awarded either to the lowest bidder or the bidder whose tender is the most advantageous.[191] In the case where a contracting entity chooses the economically most advantageous tender, the Directives list certain factors that may be taken into account by the contracting authority (*e.g.*, price, quality, delivery dates and technical merit), but these factors are non-exhaustive. However, it seems that the factors considered must, like the illustrations in the Directive, relate to the performance of the specific contract.

---

189 Such as the Council Directive 89/106 on the approximation of the laws, regulations and administrative provisions of the Member States relating to construction products (OJ L40/89).

190 *See supra* in the text and 45/87 *Dundalk* [1988] ECR 4929, and C-359/93 *UNIX* [1995] ECR 1-157.

191 Works Directive, Article 30, Services Directive, Article 36. *See* Directive 04/18, Article 53.

However, in *Beentjes,*[192] the Court of Justice considered a clause in the tender documents that stated that the workforce must be made up of at least seventy per cent of long-term unemployed persons to be employed through the regional employment office as neither being a qualification criteria nor an award criteria but an "additional specific condition." The court held such an additional specific condition was compatible with the Directives if the condition:

> . . . complies with all relevant provisions of Community law, in particular the prohibitions flowing from the principles laid down in the Treaty in regard to the right of establishment and the freedom to provide services.[193]

The authority must state in advance—in the contract notice or documents—precisely which factors it intends to consider, where possible in order of priority.

Where a bid is very low, a purchaser may wish to reject it because of the risk of default. The Directives provide that where a bid appears abnormally low, a purchaser must seek a written explanation before rejecting it.[194] This provision was introduced to prevent rejection of bids that appear low but which reflect the cost advantages of the provider's home Member State.

The Directives state that the purchaser may take into account explanations that are justified on objective grounds, such as the technical solutions suggested and the exceptionally favorable conditions available. However, the Directives are not entirely clear on the extent of discretion of the contracting authority to accept such an explanation. It appears that, where consideration of the reasons for the low bid leads to the conclusion that there is a risk of bad performance, the contracting authority has the right to reject the bid. In all cases where the authority rejects a bid in an award procedure based on the lowest price criterion, it is required to provide a report to the European Commission.

Post-Award Notices

For each contract that has been awarded, the contracting authorities must publish in the *Official Journal* certain details, such as date of award, award criteria, number of offers received and the name and address of the successful tenders. The notice must be sent not later than forty-eight days after the contract in question has been awarded.

The Directives further require contracting authorities to inform, within fifteen days of the date on which the request is received, any eliminated candidate or tenderer who so requests the reasons for rejection of its application or tender and, in the case of a tender, the name of the successful tenderer.[195]

---

192 31/87, [1988] ECR 4635.

193 31/87, [1988] ECR 4635 at para. 29.

194 Works Directive, Article 30, Services Directive, Article 37. *See* Directive 04/18, Article 55.

195 Works Directive, Article 8, Services Directive, Article 12. *See* Directive 04/18, Articles 41 and 43.

2. Utilities Public Contracts Award Procedure: the Utilities Directive

Entities Operating in the Utilities Sector

Council Directive 93/38 on the procurement of entities operating in the utilities sector (the "Utilities Directive") regulates the procurement of bodies engaged in certain activities in the sectors of water, transport, energy and telecommunications (utility services). Bodies whose procurement of services is, in general, covered by the Works and Services Directives are covered by the Utilities Directive where they engage in utility services.

However, in contrast to the other two Directives, the Utilities Directive is not confined to the public sector. It also applies to a number of other bodies engaged in utility activities, including many in the private sector. Contracts that relate to non-utility services are either covered by the Works or Services Directives, in the case of contracting authorities covered by these Directives, or are unregulated, in the case of bodies not covered by the Directives. Utility services are defined in Article 2(2) of the Utilities Directive.[196]

The Water Sector

In the water sector, the Utilities Directive covers the provision or operation of a fixed network intended to provide a service to the public in connection with the production, transport or distribution of drinking water or the supply of drinking water to such networks.[197] Contracts connected with hydraulic engineering, land drainage and irrigation are also covered where they are carried out by bodies engaged in supplying drinking water through such a network, and where more than twenty per cent of the volume of water made available by these activities is drinking water.[198]

The Directive also applies to contracts made by these entities relating to the disposal or treatment of sewage. Entities in this sector are not covered where they make contracts to purchase water.[199] At the time the Directive was adopted, it was felt that water needs to be procured from close to its source, and there would be no competition for its supply in such a case.

The Energy Sector

The Directive covers, first, the provision or operation of a fixed network intended to provide a service to the public in connection with the production, transport or distribution of electricity, gas or heat to the public and, secondly, the supply to such networks.[200]

---

196 *See* Directive 04/17, Articles 3 to 7.

197 Utilities Directive, Article 2(2)(a)(i). *See* Directive 04/17, Article 4(1).

198 Utilities Directive, Article 6. *See* Directive 04/17, Articles 4(2), 20 and 62(1).

199 Utilities Directive, Article 9. *See* Directive 04/17, Article 26.

200 Utilities Directive, Article 2(2)(a)(ii) and (iii). *See* Directive 04/17, Article 3(1) and (3).

In the energy sector, the Directive also covers exploitation of a geographical area for the purpose of exploration for, or extraction of, oil, gas and solid fuels.[201] In respect of these activities, however, the Member States may apply to the Commission for an exemption under Article 3 of the Directive.[202] This was originally intended for entities that had to compete against each other for licenses to operate under national law. The Commission may have then given an exemption if there were fair procedures for the award of these licenses.

However, the exemption under Article 3 of the Utilities Directive is not a complete one. Entities taking advantage of the exemption are still required to show that they adhere to certain minimum standards of non-discriminatory and competitive procurement.

For all activities in the energy sector, there is an exemption for the purchase of energy and fuel for the production of energy;[203] It was considered that the absence of competition for cross-border supplies would make the Directive's application pointless.

The Transport Sector

In the transport sector, the Directive covers, first, the exploitation of a geographical area for the purpose of the provision of airports, maritime or inland ports or other terminal facilities to carriers by air, sea or inland waterway.[204] The actual activity of transportation is not included (*e.g.*, the actual operation of air or sea transport by airlines or ferry companies) but merely the provision of facilities. Secondly, the Utilities Directive covers the operation of networks providing a service to the public in the field of transport by railway, automatic systems, tramway, trolley bus, bus or cable.[205]

The term "network" is defined as existing where services are provided under operating conditions laid down by a competent authority of a Member State relating to matters such as routes to be served, the capacity to be made available or the frequency of the service. There is, however, an exemption for bus transport services where other entities are free to provide the service under the same conditions.

The Telecommunications Sector

In the telecommunications sector, the Directive covers the provision or operation of public telecommunications networks or the provision of one or more public telecommunications services as defined in Article 1 of the Utilities Directive.

201 Utilities Directive, Article 2(2) (b) (i). *See* Directive 04/17, Article 7.

202 *See* Directive 04/17, Article 27.

203 Utilities Directive, Article 9. *See* Directive 04/17, Article 26.

204 Utilities Directive, Article 2(2)(b)(ii).

205 Utilities Directive, Article 2(2)(c). *See* Directive 04/17, Article 5(1).

However, these activities are not covered where others are free to offer the same services in the same geographical area under substantially the same conditions.[206] This exemption was included because it was thought commercial purchasing would occur anyway in competitive markets to which entry is not restricted following the liberalization of the EU telecommunications market.

The telecommunications sector is not included in Directive 04/17, which will replace the Utilities Directive. The sector is now regulated by the various telecommunications directives that were referred to in Chapter Six, Section IV. Instead, Directive 04/17 will include postal services.

Scope of the Utilities Directive

The Utilities Directive covers three groups of entities as follows:[207]

- entities that are contracting authorities within the meaning of the Works and Services Directives;[208]
- entities that are public undertakings; and
- other entities that engage in utility activities and which operate on the basis of special or exclusive rights granted by a competent authority of a Member State.

Entities in the first group are referred to in the Utilities Directive as "public authorities." The Works and Services Directives govern the contracts of most of these entities, but their contracts in relation to utility activities are, in general, excluded from those Directives and governed instead by the Utilities Directive.

A public undertaking is defined as an undertaking over which public authorities may exercise, directly or indirectly, a dominant influence by virtue of their ownership, financial participation in the entity or the rules that govern it.[209] This category overlaps with the first but includes many entities that are not within the first category, such as those which are mainly controlled or financed by public authorities but which are not within the definition of public authorities because they are of a commercial or industrial nature.

With respect to the third group, according to the Utilities Directive, special or exclusive rights mean rights deriving from authorizations granted by a competent authority of the Member State concerned by law, regulation or administrative action that result in the reservation for one or more entities of the exploitation of a utilities activity.[210] This provision brings within the EU government procurement

206 Utilities Directive, Article 8.

207 Utilities Directive, Article 2(1). *See* Directive 04/17, Article 2(2).

208 *See supra* in the text. The definition of bodies governed by public law is slightly different—*cf.* Utilities Directive, Article 1(1) and Directive 04/17, Article 2(1)(a).

209 Utilities Directive, Article 1(2). *See* Directive 04/17, Article 2(1)(b).

210 Utilities Directive, Article 2(3). *See* Directive 04/17, Article 2(3).

regime many privately owned entities. It should be noted, however, that the term "special or exclusive rights" still remains unclear.[211]

These rules cover all entities that might be influenced by government pressure to buy nationally, either because of the influence of the government over the entity itself or because of its dependence on the state for its privileges. Such pressures are particularly effective where the entity does not operate in a competitive environment because of the legal or physical barriers to market entry.

Contracts Covered

The Utilities Directive, like the Works and Services Directives, applies to works and service contracts in writing for consideration. The same issues arise here as in the public sector.[212]

Thresholds

According to its Article 14, the Utilities Directive, like the Works and Services Directives, applies only to contracts exceeding an estimated threshold value net of value-added tax. The thresholds are:

- for works contracts, 5,923,000 Euros;[213]
- for service contracts, 473,000 Euros;[214]
- for telecommunications contracts, 600,000 Euros.[215]

The Utilities Directive contains special methods of calculating the value of the contracts as well as rules requiring aggregation of certain contracts that are similar to those in the Works and Services Directives.

Excluded Contracts

The Utilities Directive contains exemptions that parallel those in the public sector for secrecy and security. These apply to contracts:

- connected with joint projects with certain non-EU states or those awarded by international bodies;[216]
- made pursuant to international agreements on the stationing of troops;[217] and

211 *See* Arrowsmith, "Interpretation of the Concept of 'Special or Exclusive Rights' under the Utilities Directive: The Leased Lines Decision," [1997] 4 *Government Procurement Law Review,* CS 122.

212 *See supra* in the text.

213 This is the new figure contained in Directive 04/17, Article 16(b).

214 This is the new figure contained in Directive 04/17, Article 16(a).

215 Telecommunications is not included in Directive 04/17.

216 Utilities Directive Article 10. *See* Directive 04/17, Article 21.

217 Utilities Directive Article 12. *See* Directive 04/17, Articles 22 and 62(1).

- for services provided by a public authority that has an exclusive right to provide them or an exclusive right that is necessary for their provision.[218]

As with the Works and Services Directives, certain explicitly listed service contracts are excluded.[219] There are also additional general exemptions for:

- activities involving the physical use of a network or geographic area outside the EU;[220]
- certain contracts made for the purpose of acquiring work or services to resell them, or to hire or provide them to another;[221] and
- service contracts with companies in the same group as the purchaser[222] ("affiliated undertakings").

The affiliated undertakings exemption is designed to deal with the situation where the affiliated company is created mainly for the purpose of allowing that other entity to provide a certain type of services to the group. Thus, the exemption applies only where 80% of the provider's EU turnover from providing services within the previous three years comes from providing services to the group.

Non-Discrimination and Equality of Treatment

The Utilities Directive stipulates in Article 4(2)[223] that there may be no discrimination between providers. In any case, as already explained, the Court of Justice has ruled that a general principle of equality of treatment is implied into all the procurement directives.

The Three Award Procedures

As under the Works and Services Directives, entities must use one of these three procedures: the open procedure, the restricted procedure or the negotiated procedure.[224] However, the utilities regime is much less rigid than that for the public sector since it allows purchasers a free choice among the three procedures. Thus, the Utilities Directive permits the use of the negotiated procedure in all cases.

218 Utilities Directive Article 11. *See* Directive 04/17, Article 25.

219 Utilities Directive Article 1(4) (c). *See* Directive 04/17, Article 1(2)(d).

220 Utilities Directive Article 6(1). *See* Directive 04/17, Articles 20 and 62(1).

221 Utilities Directive Article 7. *See* Directive 04/17, Article 19.

222 Utilities Directive Article 13. *See* Directive 04/17, Article 23.

223 *See* Directive 04/17, Article 10.

224 Utilities Directive Article 20. *See* Directive 04/17, Article 40.

Notices

Article 22 of the Utilities Directive[225] requires contracting entities to make known their planned contracts by means of periodic indicative notices (PIN). Such a notice must be published every twelve months.

In addition, each contract must be published in the form of a call for competition.[226] However, the requirements are less onerous than the notice requirements for public works or service contracts; it is not necessary to publish a notice for each separate contract. There are, in fact, three methods of making a call for competition:

- by an individual contract notice in the *Official Journal;*
- through a PIN; or
- by advertising the existence of a qualification system in the *Official Journal.*

Individual contract notice is the only method available for the open procedure but may also be chosen for contracts awarded by the restricted or negotiated procedures. A PIN may be used as a means of satisfying the call for competition requirements as well as for giving the market advance notice of the purchaser's general requirements, provided that the notice refers specifically to the services that are the subject of the specific contract and meets certain other conditions.

A qualification system is a system under which firms interested in supplying future needs of a particular entity may apply to be registered on a list of approved firms. This list is then used to select firms to participate in future (restricted or negotiated) award procedures. It must be advertised when first established and, if it has operated or is expected to operate for more than three years, must be re-advertised annually.

In a number of specified circumstances, a utility is exempt from making a call for competition. These circumstances are almost the same as those allowing the use of a negotiated procedure without advertisement in the public sector.[227]

Time Limits

The process of obtaining tenders under the open procedure in the utilities sector and for submitting bids (generally fifty-two days) is the same as under the public sector rules. The procedure must be advertised by a contract notice.

With the restricted procedure, tenders are invited from those responding to a contract notice or PIN or those registered on a qualification list, according to which of the three methods is chosen for the call for competition. Where a contract notice is used, five weeks must be given for firms to respond to the notice as a general rule, and at least twenty-two days in all cases. Specific justification will be needed for a

---

225 *See* Directive 04/17, Article 41.

226 Utilities Directive Article 21. *See* Directive 04/17, Article 42.

227 Utilities Directive Article 20(2). *See* Directive 04/17, Article 40.

period shorter than five weeks, such as urgency or the simple nature of the procurement. Where a PIN is used, the purchaser must ask firms who earlier responded to the notice to confirm their interest, and the same time periods must be allowed for a response. Where participants are selected from qualification lists, the entity simply invites firms from its list; it is not necessary to ask them to confirm their interest.

The Utilities Directive provides that the bid deadline is to be fixed by agreement between the purchaser and participants; if no agreement is reached, the deadline must, as a general rule, be at least three weeks from the issue of invitations, and at least ten days in all cases.

In the negotiated procedure, the same rules apply as with the restricted procedure.

Qualification of Tenderers

Article 31 of the Utilities Directive[228] states that objective criteria and rules must be applied. Clearly, this allows exclusion of firms that do not meet the financial and technical requirements. In addition, however, the Directive expressly states that firms may be excluded on miscellaneous grounds as in the Works and Services Directives, such as conviction of an offense. In addition, the rules on evidence that purchasers may demand as proof of qualification are also less restrictive than in the public sector, especially in relation to technical capacity.

Where qualification systems are used, certain additional rules apply to the operation of the system.[229] The criteria and rules for qualification must be made available to providers and their updating communicated to them. Applicants must be informed of the qualification decision within a reasonable period. If the decision will take longer than six months from the date of application, the applicant must be informed within two months of the application of the reason for this, and when the decision will be given.

Technical Specifications

Rules requiring the use of European standards and other European specifications apply to utilities as well as the public sector.[230]

Evaluation of Bids and Award of the Contract

The same rules apply as in the public sector. However, Article 36 of the Utilities Directive[231] stipulates that:

- contracting entities may reject third country offers (*i.e.*, offers containing products that originate more than fifty per cent in countries with which the EU has not concluded an agreement ensuring comparable access to their markets); and

---

228 *See* Directive 04/17, Article 54.

229 Utilities Directive Article 30. *See* Directive 04/17, Articles 49, 52 and 53.

230 Utilities Directive Article 18. *See* Directive 04/17, Article 34.

231 *See* Directive 04/17, Article 58.

– contracting entities must reject such offers where the price advantage of this offer over the next best offer is less than three per cent.

Post-Award Notices

Entities must send to the *Official Journal* a notice giving details of contracts awarded not later than two months after the award.

D. REMEDIES

1. Introduction

There are two main ways in which the government procurement rules are enforced.[232] One is through the European Commission and the Court of Justice, the other is through actions by aggrieved parties—mainly firms that have failed to win contracts—in the national courts of the respective Member States.

2. Enforcement by the Commission

General

The Commission both monitors procurement on its own initiative, for example by analyzing *Official Journal* notices, and investigates complaints by firms. If it considers that a breach of the rules has occurred, it may—after intervening with the competent authorities in the Member States to correct these infringements—as a last resort initiate proceedings under Article 226 of the EC Treaty before the Court of Justice.

Proceedings under Article 226 are taken against the Member State, not against the purchaser as such. The Member States are responsible for the actions of all their public authorities and are probably accountable for all purchasers who are contracting authorities under the Works and Services Directives or public undertakings under the Utilities Directive.[233] However, there is some uncertainty over the accountability of private undertakings operating on the basis of special or exclusive rights under the Utilities Directive.

If the Court of Justice finds a breach of the rules, it declares the Member State in breach of the EC Treaty and/or the government procurement directives. No immediate sanctions can be applied, but the Member State is obliged under Article 228 of the EC Treaty to take the necessary measures to comply with the judgment. If the Member State does not, the Commission may initiate a second infringement procedure before the Court for failure to comply with its judgment.

Penalty payments could then be imposed under Article 228(2) of the EC Treaty. Where an award procedure has not yet resulted in a contract, Article 228 probably

232 *See* Arrowsmith (ed.), *The Remedies for Enforcing the Works and Supplies Directives in the 12 Member States* (1992); Arrowsmith, *The Law of Public and Utilities Procurement* (1996), at p. 897; Trepte, *Government procurement in the European Community* (1993), at p. 188.

233 C-243/89, *Storebaelt* [1993] ECR I-3353; C-87/94, *Wallonia Buses,* [1994] ECR I-2043.

requires in general that any defect in the procedure be corrected. It is not clear, however, whether Article 228 requires Member States to set aside concluded contracts.[234]

As the average length of an infringement proceeding under Article 226 of the EC Treaty is over twenty months, the contract will often have been completed before the Court hears the case. The Court may, however, order suspension of the procedure under its power to award interim measures under Article 243 of the EC Treaty. Interim measures may only be obtained once proceedings have been instituted. To obtain such measures, the Commission must show a *prima facie* case and urgency, a condition that is satisfied where the refusal of interim measures would mean that the contract would be performed before the judgment.

The Court must then consider the balance of interest. In *Wallonia Buses,*[235] the Court refused interim measures in relation to a contract for the purchase of buses because of the danger to the public in keeping the existing fleet in service, even though the problem had been caused by the delay of the purchaser in replacing the fleet. This appears to indicate a reluctance to award such measures where delay would cause inconvenience.

In *Lottomatica*[236] and *Wallonia Buses,*[237] the Court held that interim measures could, in principle, be awarded even after the contract in question had already been concluded, provided that the Commission quickly and unequivocally informs the Member State concerned of its intention to seek a suspension.

The Corrective Mechanism

Both Council Directive 89/665 on remedies in the public sector[238] and Council Directive 92/13 on remedies in the utilities sector[239] (the "Remedies Directives") empower the Commission to intervene directly in procedures covered by the Directives before the contract in question has been concluded if it believes that there is a clear and manifest breach of the law. It can notify the relevant Member State as well as the contracting entity of its reasons and request a correction. The Member State (not the contracting entity) is obliged to reply within twenty-one days and either confirm that the infringement has been corrected or explain why not, unless the procedure has been suspended, in which case it simply notifies the Commission of this.

---

234 *See* Arrowsmith, *The Law of Public and Utilities Procurement* (1996), at p. 932.

235 C-87/94, [1994] ECR 1395.

236 C-272/91, [1992] ECR I-457.

237 C-87/94, [1994] ECR I-1395.

238 Directive 89/665, Article 3.

239 Council Directive 92/13 coordinating the laws, regulations and administrative provisions relating to the application of Community rules on the procurement procedures of entities operating the water, energy, transport and telecommunications sectors, Article 8.

Failure to respond does not, however, attract any sanctions. The Commission is given no special enforcement powers except to address directly the contracting entity. However, the rules do not restrict or replace its powers under Article 226 of the EC Treaty. Thus, if a satisfactory reply is not received, the Commission will simply institute proceedings under this Article.

3. Remedies in the National Courts

General Principles

The second main method of enforcement is by legal action in the national courts. Under general EU law principles, remedies and procedures are, in principle, a matter for national law.[240] However, as with all actions to enforce EU law, this is subject to two important principles:

- the principle of effectiveness, which means that remedies must be effective; and
- the principle of non-discrimination, which means that remedies must be as favorable as those for enforcing comparable rules of domestic law.

EU law further requires the Member States to provide aggrieved firms with certain specific forms of relief, such as the right to damages and interim relief.[241]

The Remedies Directives

In addition to these principles, the Remedies Directives lay down specific minimum standards for national remedies systems in the field of government procurement. These Directives apply to any breaches of EU law or national implementing rules that occur in procedures covered by the Directives. This covers both breaches of the Directives themselves and breaches of other EU rules, such as those in the EC Treaty. The Remedies Directives do not, however, apply to breaches of EU law in awarding contracts that are excluded from the government procurement directives, such as those below the thresholds.

The Remedies Directives harmonize the remedies available in Member States for the purpose of ensuring the correct application of the government procurement directives. They require Member States to introduce procedures for reviewing, effectively and as swiftly as possible, decisions on the part of the contracting entities that infringe EU rules on government procurement or national rules implementing those rules.[242]

As regards the forum for review, the Remedies Directives are concerned to respect the traditional approaches in different Member States, while imposing certain

240 *See* for rights flowing from the EC, C-312, *Peterbroeck* [1995] ECR I-4599; for rights flowing from EU secondary legislation. C-433/93, *Commission v. Germany* [1995] ECR I-2303.

241 C-5/94, *Hedley Lomas* [1996] ECR I-2553; 213/89; *Factortame I* [1990] ECR 2433.

242 Directives 89/665/EEC, Article 1(1) and 92/13/EEC, Article 1(1).

minimum safeguards.[243] Essentially, the forum is left to each Member State, and the Directives make it clear that it is acceptable to confer review powers on a body that is not of a judicial character. However, certain safeguards must be respected in this case.

First, the non-judicial authority must give reasons for its decisions. Secondly, its decisions must be subject to binding review by another body. This second body must itself be a judicial body. Alternatively, the second body must be a body that is a court or tribunal capable of making a reference for a preliminary ruling to the Court of Justice and which is independent of the contracting authority and the review body. Its members are subject to certain conditions stated in the Directives, which are designed to ensure that its members are independent and that its president is suitably qualified.

The Remedies Directives also require that certain specific forms of relief be available:[244] First, the review body must have the power to award interim relief to suspend the award procedure or the implementation of any decision. In principle, the criteria for the award of interim relief are for the national courts to decide, and the Directives expressly provide that Member States may refuse relief if the adverse consequences from holding up the procurement exceed the benefits.

Secondly, review bodies must also have the power to set aside unlawful decisions such as awards based on unlawful criteria. This must include a power to remove unlawful provisions (*e.g.*, discriminatory specifications) from tender documents. The Remedies Directives expressly state that the effect of a remedy on a contract that has already been concluded is for national law to decide, which may limit remedies following conclusion of a contract to damages only. Thus, national law may preclude the remedies of setting aside or suspension in such a case. This protects the interests of legal certainty.

Thirdly, there must be a power to award damages to affected firms. There is nothing in Council Directive 89/665 with respect to the public sector on the principles for calculating damages. Thus, this remains in principle a matter for national law. However, discretion may again be limited by the effectiveness requirements. Council Directive 92/13 with respect to the utilities sector provides expressly that a claim for damages for the costs of preparing a bid or participating in a procedure must be available on proof only that a party would have had a real chance of winning a contract awarded in breach of the rules.[245]

All this ensures a minimum degree of effectiveness in the damages remedy and introduces some certainty. However, if the aggrieved firm can prove that it would have won the contract had the breach not occurred, it will still be entitled to the full amount of damages, which is the lost profit.

---

243 Directives 89/665/EEC, Article 2(8) and 92/13/EEC, Article 2(9).

244 Directives 89/665/EEC, Article 2(1) and 92/13/EEC, Article 2(1).

245 Directive 92/13/EEC, Article 2(7).

Utilities Sector Alternative System of Financial Penalties

According to Article 2(1) of the Council Directive 92/13,[246] the Member States may decline to provide interim measures and set aside remedies as explained above. Instead, they may provide for other measures to correct infringements and prevent injury to affected interests. In particular, it is envisaged that this alternative system may involve orders for payment of a financial sum where the breach is not corrected or avoided.

Such measures must always be made available on interlocutory proceedings and also in final proceedings where appropriate. This option was created because of the sensitivity of this sector and the constitutional difficulties faced by some Member States in providing for direct challenges to decisions of entities in this sector, especially those operating in the private sector. The requirement to provide damages for affected persons, as outlined above, still applies.

Conciliation Procedure in the Utilities Sector

Council Directive 92/13 also provides for a special procedure for resolving disputes on EU law, referred to as "conciliation."[247] Essentially, it involves a decision on the dispute by independent third parties. The procedure may be invoked by any party with an interest in a contract covered by the Utilities Directive. It can proceed only with the consent of the purchaser, and either party may withdraw at any time.

The conciliation panel consists of three persons; one appointed by the Commission (subject to the agreement of the parties) and one by each party. The panel may also appoint experts to assist it, subject to the veto of either party or the Commission. The conciliators' duty is to endeavor as quickly as possible to reach an agreement between the parties that is in accordance with EU law, after giving an opportunity to the parties and any other provider participating in the award procedure to make representations.

Attestation Mechanism in the Utilities Sector

Council Directive 92/13 provides for entities to have access to a system of attestation, whereby they may voluntarily submit their procurement to independent scrutiny for compliance with EU rules.[248] This enables an entity to demonstrate its compliance and may also provide a method for entities to check that their procedures are lawful.

The responsibility for providing an attestation system lies with the Member States. The European Committee for Standardization (CEN) developed a European Standard 45503, which involves a periodical review of both the procedures and practices of the entity. This means any relevant procurement rules or guidelines and

246 *See* Directive 04/17, Article 2(2).

247 Directive 92/13/EEC, Article 9.

248 Directive 92/13/EEC, Article 3.

what is done in practice, including whether purchasers follow their guidelines. The attestors must be independent of purchasers and completely objective in carrying out their duties, and they must possess relevant professional qualifications and experience. They must report in writing on their examination to the purchaser.

V. MERCOSUR: PROTOCOL ON GOVERNMENT PROCUREMENT

A. INTRODUCTION

Neither the Treaty of Asunción setting up Mercosur nor the Montevideo Protocol on Trade in Services apply to government procurement,[249] but the Protocol envisages the establishment of common disciplines in this sector within Mercosur.[250] A set of rules was elaborated in 2003,[251] but these were revised and updated in December 2004 by the Protocol on Government Protocol.[252] The Protocol applies to services and public works as well as goods.[253]

B. SCOPE OF THE PROTOCOL

The Protocol applies in principle to procurement:[254]

- by entities at all levels of federal and sub-federal government listed in Annex I, subject to any reservations of the Member States set out in Annex A;
- of those services and public works listed in Annexes III and IV, respectively;
- where the value of the contract is of a value not less than the specified threshold amount in Annex V;
- by any contractual method.

The Protocol requires tender documentation to indicate whether the procurement in question is covered by the Protocol.[255]

It is up to the Member States to list the federal and sub-federal entities that appear in Annex I. In addition, they are free to enter reservations in Annex A. Argentina and Brazil do not apply the Protocol to sub-federal entities, and in turn, Paraguay will not apply the Protocol to these two Member States until government procurement is liberalized in the states and provinces that border Paraguay. The Protocol allows the withdrawal of entities that are no longer subject to effective govern-

249 *See* Montevideo Protocol, Article XV:1.

250 Montevideo Protocol, Article XV:2.

251 Decision 40/03 of the Common Market Council.

252 Decision 27/04 of the Common Market Council.

253 Protocol, Article 1:1.

254 Protocol, Article 2:1 and 2.

255 Protocol, Article 23:1((n).

ment control.[256] Any Member State that objects to the withdrawal may have recourse to the Mercosur dispute settlement procedure.[257]

The services and public works to which the Protocol applies also depends on the Member States, which are free to list whatever services and works they choose in Annexes III and IV. With respect to public works, only Brazil has any listed.

The thresholds for procurement contracts are set out in Annex V. For contracts involving services, they vary between the Member States. For Paraguay and Uruguay, the threshold is US$200,000, for Argentina US$150,000 and for Brazil US$75,000. The threshold for public works contracts for Brazil is set at US$3,000,000. The valuation of contracts must take into account any expense that affects the final value of the contract.[258] The selection of the valuation method must not be used, nor may any procurement requirement be divided, with the intention of avoiding the application of the Protocol.[259]

Services and public works covered by the Protocol are subject to the rules of the Montevideo Protocol, and limitations on market access and national treatment affecting them are set out in a Member State's Schedule of Specific Commitments.[260]

The Protocol authorizes the Member States to modify their coverage.[261] However, unless the changes are of a purely formal nature, the modifying Party may have to agree to appropriate compensatory adjustments to its coverage.[262] In the case of a dispute over these provisions, a Member State may have recourse to the Mercosur dispute settlement procedure.[263]

Exceptions from the obligations of the Protocol exist for security reasons[264] and for measures to protect public morals, order or safety, human, animal or plant life or health or intellectual property, as long the measures are not applied in manner that constitutes a means of arbitrary or unjustifiable discrimination.[265]

A Member State may deny the benefits of the Protocol to a service supplier of another Member State where it establishes that the service or public work is being

256 Protocol, Article 13:1.

257 Protocol, Article 29. This procedure is described in Chapter Four, Section III.G.2.

258 Protocol, Article 3:1.

259 Protocol, Articles 2:8 and 3:2.

260 Protocol, Article 2:5.

261 Protocol, Article 13:4.

262 Protocol, Article 13:4 and 5.

263 Protocol, Article 29.

264 Protocol, Article 12:1.

265 Protocol, Article 12:2.

provided by a person from a country that is not a Member State or by an enterprise that has no substantial business activities in any Member State.[266]

C. MOST-FAVORED NATION TREATMENT

In respect of a procurement covered by the Protocol, the Member States are required to accord to the listed services and public works and the suppliers of such services and public works from another Member State treatment no less favorable than that which they accord to listed services and public works or suppliers of such services or public works from any other Member State or non-Member State.[267]

D. NATIONAL TREATMENT

In respect of a procurement covered by the Protocol, the Member States are required to accord the services and public works and the suppliers of such services and public works from another Member State treatment no less favorable than that which they accord to their own services and public works and the suppliers of such services or public works.[268] However, Member States are permitted to maintain limited exceptions, which are listed in Annex VI to the Protocol.

Furthermore, no Member State may discriminate against a supplier established in a Member State on the basis of the degree of foreign affiliation or ownership.[269] Nor may a Member State discriminate against a locally-established supplier on the basis that the services or public works supplied for a particular procurement originate in another Member State.[270]

E. DOMESTIC REGULATION

The Protocol is applied in conformity with the domestic rules of each Member State,[271] but each Member State must take steps to see that its laws, regulations and administrative procedures involving the entities it has listed in Annex I conform to the provisions of the Protocol.[272] Member States must publish their rules on government procurement and any amendments to them[273] and administer them in a reasonable, objective and impartial manner.[274] They must institute courts or judicial, arbitral or administrative procedures to deal with any disputes

266 Protocol, Article 7.

267 Protocol, Article 4.

268 Protocol, Article 5:1.

269 Protocol, Article 5:2(a).

270 Protocol, Article 5:2(b).

271 Protocol, Article 10:1.

272 Protocol, Article 10:2.

273 Protocol, Article 10:3.

274 Protocol, Article 10:4.

that may arise in connection with the government procurement of services and public works.[275]

F. TENDERING PROCEDURES

1. Introduction

Procurements covered by the Protocol may be effected by means of limited or selective tendering procedures.[276] The general rules applicable to all procedures are:[277]

- they must be applied in a non-discriminatory manner in conformity with the principles of equality, competition and transparency;
- entities must not set down specifications or terms that favor particular persons or entities;
- all suppliers must have equal access to the information regarding a procurement.

2. Limited Tendering

Limited tendering is allowed provided that that it is not used to avoid the maximum possible competition or to discriminate among or against suppliers from other Member States.[278] It may be used in the following situations:[279]

- absence of valid tenders in response to an open or selective tender;
- where, for reasons connected with the protection of exclusive rights, or in the absence of competition for technical reasons, the services can only be supplied by a particular supplier;
- for reasons of extreme urgency brought about by events unforeseeable by the entity;
- for additional services by the original supplier
- where an entity procures a first service that is developed at its request;
- in the case of contracts awarded to professionals or entities that are considered in their field of activity to be the most able to fulfill the contract;
- where an entity needs to procure consulting services regarding matters of a confidential nature;
- where the legislation of the Member State provides for limited tendering by entities that are part of or controlled by the State for scientific and technological research purposes.

---

275 Protocol, Article 10:5.

276 Protocol, Article 16.

277 Protocol, Article 17.

278 Protocol, Article 18:1.

279 Protocol, Article 18:2.

3. Selective Tendering

The process for qualifying suppliers for selective tendering must not discriminate between domestic suppliers and those of other Member States.[280] The tendering entities must recognize as qualified suppliers those which meet the conditions set down.[281] These must only involve legal, fiscal, economic, financial or technical requirements. The qualifying procedure must observe the following safeguards:[282]

- conditions for participation in tendering procedures must be made known as far in advance as will allow the participation of the greatest number of suppliers from the Member States;
- in evaluating the economic, financial and technical capacity of the supplier, any activity exercised in another Member State or other states must be equally recognized;
- the participation of a supplier may not be conditioned on its having obtained one or more contracts with the awarding Member State or having previous work experience there;
- Member States must ensure that each of their entities follows a single qualification procedure, where possible, and that efforts are made to minimize differences in qualification procedures between entities;
- each Member State must ensure that when the qualification of a supplier is refused, it is informed of the reasons for this decision.

In addition, Member States must ensure that, in the case of their entities that use permanent lists or registers of suppliers of services or public works:[283]

- suppliers can request their inclusion at any time;
- all suppliers that request it, are included in such lists or registers as expeditiously as possible;
- all suppliers included in such lists or registers are notified of the temporary suspension and cancellation of these lists or registers or their removal from them.

4. Deadlines

All deadlines set down with respect to the tendering procedure must provide adequate time to allow suppliers to prepare and submit tenders.[284] In general, the minimum time-limit for receipt of tenders is forty days from the date of publication of

280 Protocol, Article 19:1.

281 Protocol, Article 19:2.

282 Protocol, Article 19:5 and 6.

283 Protocol, Article 20:1.

284 Protocol, Article 22:8.

the tender notice. However, in the case of electronic tenders, the time-limit may be reduced to fifteen days for the supply of services.[285]

5. Tender Documentation

Tender documentation must be publicly available after notice has been given of the procurement and contain all necessary information to enable potential suppliers to submit responsive tenders.[286] It must include the following:

- name and address of the entity to which tenders should be sent;
- tendering procedure;
- subject matter of the procurement, including the nature and quantity of the services or works, including the technical specifications;
- conditions for participating in the tendering procedure, such as financial guarantees, juridical and fiscal suitability, technical and economic-financial qualifications;
- place for delivery of the services or works;
- form and language for presenting the tenders;
- currency for the presentation of the tenders and payment;
- penalties for breaches of the contract;
- place, date and time for receiving the tenders;
- criteria for evaluating the tenders, including any factors other than price;
- place, day and time for the opening and evaluation of tenders;
- an indication that the procurement in question is covered by the Protocol;
- the terms of payment;
- other terms and conditions.

6. Award of Contracts

The opening of tenders is done in public at a place and time set out in the tender documentation.[287] Tenders must be submitted in writing unless the tender documentation provides for a non-written submission, such as one by telex, telegram or facsimile.[288] Only those persons that are not legally disqualified may submit tenders.[289]

285 Protocol, Article 22:9.

286 Protocol, Article 23:1.

287 Protocol, Article 24:5.

288 Protocol, Article 24:1.

289 Protocol, Article 24:2.

Only tenders that conform to the requirements of the tender documentation and are from a supplier that complies with the conditions for participation can be considered for an award.[290] Unless the entity decides in the public interest not to award the contract, it must award the contract to the tenderer that it considers capable of carrying it out and whose tender is the most advantageous in terms of the specific evaluation criteria set forth in the tender documentation.[291] Tenders from suppliers of a Member State enjoy a preference over tenders of suppliers from a non-Member State. If the tender is equal to the non-Member State tender in other aspects, its price may be up to three percent higher.[292] An entity that has received a tender abnormally lower than other tenders may enquire with the tenderer if it is capable of fulfilling the terms of the contract.[293] No entity of a Member State may condition the award of a contract on the fact that the supplier has previously been awarded a contract by it or has previous work experience in the territory of that Member State.[294]

G. TECHNICAL SPECIFICATIONS

Technical specifications must not be prepared, adopted or applied with a view to, or with the effect of, creating unnecessary obstacles to trade and discriminating against suppliers.[295] They must be stated in terms of performance and serve objectives that are essential to the fulfillment of the contract.[296] Technical specifications should be based on the standards of the Mercosur Standards Association, international standards or national standards.[297]

H. RULES OF ORIGIN

The normal rules of origin applicable in Mercosur apply to government procurement.[298]

I. TRANSPARENCY

1. Prior Information

Each Member State must ensure that its entities effectively make known their procurement opportunities in such a way that interested suppliers from the other Member States have all the information necessary to take part in the procurement

290 Protocol, Article 25:2.

291 Protocol, Article 25:1 and 12.

292 Protocol, Article 25:6.

293 Protocol, Article 25:4.

294 Protocol, Article 25:3.

295 Protocol, Article 9:1.

296 Protocol, Article 9:2.

297 Protocol, Article 9:3.

298 Protocol, Article 6.

process.[299] Tender notices must be published at least once and should include the following information:[300]

- name and address of the awarding entity;
- tendering procedure;
- nature and quantity of the services or works and place where they are to be supplied;
- whether the procurement is covered by the Protocol;
- terms, place, date and time how suppliers can have access to the full tender documentation as well as additional information on the procedure;
- cost of the documentation and terms of payment;
- place, date and time of the submission, opening and evaluation of the tenders.

2. Post-Award Information

The Member States must make sure that their entities make public the results of selective tendering procedures.[301] They must provide suppliers with all the information bearing on the procedure and, in particular, the bases of the award and the characteristics of the winning tender. In all cases, once the contract has been signed, an entity must publish, *inter alia,* the name of the winning tenderer, the value of the contract, the subject matter of the contract, the name and address of the awarding entity and the tendering procedure used.[302]

However, entities are entitled to withhold certain information where its release would be contrary to a Member State's essential security interests, impede law enforcement or otherwise be contrary to the public interest or would prejudice the commercial interests of public or private undertakings.[303]

The Protocol permits a Member State to seek additional information on the award of a contract, particularly with respect to tenders that have not been accepted, in order to determine whether the procurement was made in accordance with the provisions of the Protocol.[304]

---

299 Protocol, Article 23:1.

300. Protocol, Article 23:2.

301 Protocol, Article 26:1.

302 Protocol, Article 26:3.

303 Protocol, Article 11.

304 Protocol, Article 25:9.

J. ENFORCEMENT

Disputes between Member States with respect to the government procurement rules in the Protocol are subject to the general dispute settlement procedures of Mercosur.[305] In addition, the Protocol requires the Member States to make procedures available to interested parties to enable them to defend their interests.[306] These procedures must conform to the following rules:

- interested parties must be able to present challenges at any stage in the procurement process;
- the entities of the Member States must consider in an opportune and impartial manner any challenge with respect to procurements covered by the Protocol;
- entities may not make a decision on a challenge without giving the interested party the opportunity to make its case;
- once the administrative procedures have been exhausted, no interested party may be prevented from applying to the courts.

K. FURTHER NEGOTIATIONS

The Member States are committed to future negotiations with a view to completing the liberalization of the government procurement sector within Mercosur.[307] The first round of these negotiations is supposed to start at the latest in early 2007.[308] Subsequent negotiations are to take place every two years.[309]

The negotiations are aimed at evaluating the application of the Protocol, attempting to increase its scope and revising the threshold amounts.[310] However, even before negotiations start, the Member States must consult with a view to extending the Protocol to the sub-federal government level, which has been largely exempted from coverage.[311]

VI. ASEAN: FRAMEWORK AGREEMENT ON SERVICES

Government procurement is excluded from the application of the Framework Agreement by virtue of the incorporation of Article XIII:1 of GATS. Only Singapore among the Member States of ASEAN is a signatory to the GPA.

---

305 Protocol, Article 29.

306 Protocol, Article 27:1.

307 Protocol, Article 14:1.

308 Protocol, Article 14:2.

309 Protocol, Article 14:3.

310 Protocol, Article 14:4.

311 Protocol, Article 14:5.

INDEX

G